CCNP
Support
Study Guide

"Concise . . . to the point . . . got me my CCNA! . . . It provides good practical exercises and the practice tests are great!"

"Great reading for a tough exam. [Lammle's *CCNA: Cisco Certified Network Associate Study Guide*] is an excellent introduction to the world of Cisco routers. . . . The author's writing style is approachable and light, making the often-tough topic easy to learn. . . . The plethora of network-activity traces really elucidates certain concepts, especially for those who've dealt with trace analysis before. The questions included at the end of each chapter were very helpful in studying and reviewing the material just read."

"Todd Lammle has done it again! Lammle's [*CCNP: Advanced Cisco Router Configuration Study Guide*] is unquestionably better [than other ACRC study guides] for ACRC test preparation. . . . Compared to a 5-day ACRC course which costs $1900 in my area (and likely requires another week or more of study before testing), this book for less than a 50 spot is a staggering bargain. Buy it and spend ample time with it. . . . Todd, my pocketbook thanks you."

"[The *CCNA: Cisco Certified Network Associate Study Guide* is] a must for professionals wanting to learn about Cisco routers. I have gone through Todd Lammle's book a couple of times before certifying, and countless times afterwards to review and pick up additional detail. It is fantastic. He has put together excellent sections discussing the theory and then shows you how to actually do the work. . . . He not only knows the information, but knows how to present it for ease of learning. I have never had information given to me in such a smooth manner and retained it so well."

"Like talking to a buddy. [*CCNA: Cisco Certified Network Associate Study Guide*] was a very good book and very easy to read. . . . [It] gives very good information, and isn't as dry as those 'other' books. Todd Lammle knows exactly when to throw in little analogies and jokes that help the learning process along."

"[*CCNP: Advanced Cisco Router Configuration Study Guide* is] clear and concise, with great detail. . . . This ACRC Study Guide, is a great study tool for the exam, and explains in great detail the harder, advanced Cisco routing concepts."

CCNP™
Support
Study Guide

Todd Lammle

Kevin Hales

San Francisco • Paris • Düsseldorf • Soest • London

Associate Publisher: Neil Edde
Contracts and Licensing Manager: Kristine O'Callaghan
Acquisitions & Developmental Editor: Linda Lee
Editors: Suzanne Goraj, Colleen Wheeler Strand, Rebecca Rider
Production Editor: Judith Hibbard
Technical Editors: John Chong, Kevin Mahler
Book Designer: Bill Gibson
Graphic Illustrator: Tony Jonick
Electronic Publishing Specialists: Susie Hendrickson, Judy Fung
Proofreaders: Dave Nash, Word/one, Edith Kaneshiro
Indexer: Ted Laux
CD Coordinator: Kara Schwartz
CD Technician: Ginger Warner
Cover Designer: Archer Design
Cover Photographer: Tony Stone Images

Library of Congress Card Number: 00-105116

ISBN: 0-7821-2713-4

To the Cisco Academy instructors, the unsung heros of the networking industry. —TL

For my loving and beautiful wife, Claudia, my energetic and curious son, Christopher, and also the newest precious addition to our family. —KH

Acknowledgments

I would like to acknowledge Kevin Hales for his hard work and dedication. He is a great team member and can always be counted on. Also, thanks to the great team at Sybex for always supporting me and believing in me. —T.L.

I would like to thank, first and foremost, my wife for her patience and support as always. Thanks need to go to my cohorts and friends Mike Cleary, Ross Nakamura, John Storm, and Tim Keanini. Also, thanks go to all of the staff at Sybex who facilitated this project, Linda Lee, Suzanne Goraj, Judith Hibbard, Colleen Wheeler Strand, and the technical editors, John Chong and Kevin Mahler.—K.H.

Contents at a Glance

Contents

Introduction

This book is intended to help you continue on your exciting new path toward obtaining your CCNP and CCIE certification. Before reading this book, it is important to have at least read the Sybex CCNA: Cisco Certified Network Associate Study Guide. You can take the tests in any order, but the CCNA exam should probably be your first test. Many questions in the Support exam are built upon the CCNA material. However, we have done everything possible to make sure that you can pass the Support exam by reading this book and practicing with Cisco routers.

The new Cisco certifications reach beyond the popular certifications, such as the MCSE and CNE, to provide you with an indispensable factor in understanding today's network—insight into the Cisco world of internetworking.

Cisco—A Brief History

A lot of readers may already be familiar with Cisco and what they do. However, those of you who are new to the field just coming in fresh from your MCSE, or maybe even with 10 or more years in the field but wishing to brush up on the new technology, may appreciate a little background on Cisco.

In the early 1980s, a married couple who worked in different computer departments at Stanford University started up cisco Systems (notice the small c). Their names are Len and Sandy Bosack. They were having trouble getting their individual systems to communicate (like many married people), so in their living room they created a gateway server to make it easier for their disparate computers in two different departments to communicate using the IP protocol.

In 1984, Cisco Systems was founded with a small commercial gateway server product that changed networking forever. Some people think the name was intended to be San Francisco Systems, but the paper got ripped on the way to the incorporation lawyers—who knows? But in 1992, the company name was changed to Cisco Systems, Inc.

The first product it marketed was called the Advanced Gateway Server (AGS). Then came the Mid-Range Gateway Server (MGS), the Compact Gateway Server (CGS), the Integrated Gateway Server (IGS), and the AGS+. Cisco calls these "the old alphabet soup products."

In 1993, Cisco came out with the amazing 4000 router, and then created the even more amazing 7000, 2000, and 3000 series routers. These are still around and evolving (almost daily, it seems).

Cisco Systems has since become an unrivaled worldwide leader in networking for the Internet. Its networking solutions can easily connect users who work from diverse devices on disparate networks. Cisco products make it simple for people to access and transfer information without regard to differences in time, place, or platform.

Cisco Systems' big picture is that it provides end-to-end networking solutions that customers can use to build an efficient, unified information infrastructure of their own or to connect to someone else's. This is an important piece in the Internet/networking-industry puzzle because a common architecture that delivers consistent network services to all users is now a functional imperative. Because Cisco Systems offers such a broad range of networking and Internet services and capabilities, users needing regular access to their local network or the Internet can do so unhindered, making Cisco's wares indispensable.

Cisco answers this need with a wide range of hardware products that are used to form information networks using the Cisco Internetworking Operating System (IOS) software. This software provides network services, paving the way for networked technical support and professional services to maintain and optimize all network operations.

Along with the Cisco IOS, one of the services Cisco created to help support the vast amount of hardware it has engineered is the Cisco Certified Internetworking Expert (CCIE) program, which was designed specifically to equip people to effectively manage the vast quantity of installed Cisco networks. The business plan is simple: If you want to sell more Cisco equipment and have more Cisco networks installed, ensure that the networks you installed run properly.

However, having a fabulous product line isn't all it takes to guarantee the huge success that Cisco enjoys—lots of companies with great products are now defunct. If you have complicated products designed to solve complicated problems, you need knowledgeable people who are fully capable of installing, managing, and troubleshooting them. That part isn't easy, so Cisco began the CCIE program to equip people to support these complicated networks. This program, known colloquially as the Doctorate of Networking, has also been very successful, primarily due to its extreme difficulty. Cisco continuously monitors the program, changing it as it sees fit, to make sure that it remains pertinent and accurately reflects the demands of today's internetworking business environments.

Building upon the highly successful CCIE program, Cisco Career Certifications permit you to become certified at various levels of technical proficiency, spanning the disciplines of network design and support. So, whether you're beginning a career, changing careers, securing your present position, or seeking to refine and promote your position, this is the book for you!

Cisco's Network Support Certifications

Cisco has created new certifications that will help you get the coveted CCIE, as well as aid prospective employers in measuring skill levels. Before these new certifications, you took only one test and were then faced with the lab, which made it difficult to succeed. With these new certifications that add a better approach to preparing for that almighty lab, Cisco has opened doors that few were allowed through before. So, what are these new certifications, and how do they help you get your CCIE?

Cisco Certified Network Associate (CCNA) 2.0

The CCNA certification is the first certification in the new line of Cisco certifications and it is a precursor to all current Cisco certifications. With the new certification programs, Cisco has created a type of stepping-stone approach to CCIE certification. Now, you can become a Cisco Certified Network Associate for the meager cost of the Sybex CCNA *Study Guide* book, plus $100 for the test. And you don't have to stop there—you can choose to continue with your studies and achieve a higher certification called the Cisco Certified Network Professional (CCNP). Someone with a CCNP has all the skills and knowledge they need to attempt the CCIE lab. However, because no textbook can take the place of practical experience, we'll discuss what else you need to be ready for the CCIE lab shortly.

Cisco Certified Network Professional (CCNP) 2.0

This new Cisco certification has opened up many opportunities for the individual wishing to become Cisco-certified but who is lacking the training, the expertise, or the bucks to pass the notorious and often failed two-day Cisco-torture lab. The new Cisco certifications will truly provide exciting new opportunities for the CNE and MCSE who just don't know how to advance to a higher level.

So, you're thinking, "Great, what do I do after I pass the CCNA exam?" Well, if you want to become a CCIE in Routing and Switching (the most popular certification), understand that there's more than one path to that much-coveted CCIE certification. The first way is to continue studying and become a Cisco Certified Network Professional (CCNP). That means four more tests, and the CCNA certification, to you.

The CCNP program will prepare you to understand and comprehensively tackle the internetworking issues of today and beyond—not limited to the Cisco world. You will undergo an immense metamorphosis, vastly increasing your knowledge and skills through the process of obtaining these certifications.

Remember that you don't need to be a CCNP or even a CCNA to take the CCIE lab, but to accomplish that, it's extremely helpful if you already have these certifications.

What Are the CCNP Certification Skills?

Cisco is demanding a certain level of proficiency for its CCNP certification. In addition to those required for the CCNA, these skills include the following:

- Installing, configuring, operating, and troubleshooting complex routed LAN, routed WAN, and switched LAN networks, and Dial Access Services.

- Understanding complex networks, such as IP, IGRP, IPX, Async Routing, AppleTalk, extended access-lists, IP RIP, route redistribution, IPX RIP, route summarization, OSPF, VLSM, BGP, Serial, IGRP, Frame Relay, ISDN, ISL, X.25, DDR, PSTN, PPP, VLANs, Ethernet, ATM LAN-emulation, access-lists, 802.10, FDDI, and transparent and translational bridging.

To meet the Cisco Certified Network Professional requirements, you must be able to perform the following:

- Install and/or configure a network to increase bandwidth, quicken network response times, and improve reliability and quality of service.

- Maximize performance through campus LANs, routed WANs, and remote access.

- Improve network security.

- Create a global intranet.

- Provide access security to campus switches and routers.

- Provide increased switching and routing bandwidth—end-to-end resiliency services.

- Provide custom queuing and routed priority services.

How Do You Become a CCNP?

After becoming a CCNA, the four exams you must take to get your CCNP are as follows:

Exam 640-503: Routing This exam continues to build on the fundamentals learned in the CCNA course. It focuses on large multiprotocol internetworks and how to manage them with access-lists, queuing, tunneling, route distribution, router maps, BGP, OSPF, and route summarization.

Exam 640-504: Switching   This exam tests your knowledge of the 1900 and 5000 series of Catalyst switches. The Sybex *CCNP: Switching Study Guide* covers all the objectives you need to understand for passing the Switching exam.

Exam 640-506: Support   This tests you on the troubleshooting information you will learn about in this book. You must be able to troubleshoot Ethernet and Token Ring LANS, IP, IPX, and AppleTalk networks, as well as ISDN, PPP, and Frame Relay networks.

Exam 640-505: Remote Access   This exam tests your knowledge of installing, configuring, monitoring, and troubleshooting Cisco ISDN and dial-up access products. You must understand PPP, ISDN, Frame Relay, and authentication. The Sybex *CCNP: Remote Access Study Guide* covers all the exam objectives.

If you hate tests, you can take fewer of them by signing up for the CCNA exam and the Support exam, and then take just one more long exam called the Foundation R/S exam (640-509). Doing this also gives you your CCNP—but beware, it's a really long test that fuses all the material listed previously into one exam. Good luck! However, by taking this exam, you get three tests for the price of two, which saves you $100 (if you pass). Some people think it's easier to take the Foundation R/S exam because you can leverage the areas that you would score higher in against the areas in which you wouldn't.

Remember that test objectives and tests can change at any time without notice. Always check the Cisco Web site for the most up-to-date information (www.cisco.com).

Cisco Certified Internetworking Expert (CCIE)

You've become a CCNP, and now you fix your sights on getting your CCIE in Routing and Switching—what do you do next? Cisco recommends that before you take the lab, you take test 640-025: Cisco Internetwork Design (CID) and the Cisco authorized course called Installing and Maintaining Cisco Routers (IMCR). By the way, no Prometric test for IMCR exists at the time of this writing, and Cisco recommends a *minimum* of two years of on-the-job experience before taking the CCIE lab. After jumping those hurdles, you then have to pass the CCIE-R/S Exam Qualification (exam 350-001) before taking the actual lab.

To become a CCIE, Cisco recommends the following:

1. Attend all the recommended courses at an authorized Cisco training center and pony up around $15,000–$20,000, depending on your corporate discount.

2. Pass the Drake/Prometric exam ($200 per exam—so hopefully you'll pass it the first time).

3. Pass the two-day, hands-on lab at Cisco. This costs $1,000 per lab, which many people fail two or more times. (Some never make it through!) Also, because you can take the exam only in San Jose, California; Research Triangle Park, North Carolina; Sydney, Australia; Halifax, Nova Scotia; Tokyo, Japan; or Brussels, Belgium, you might just need to add travel costs to that $1,000. Cisco has added new sites lately for the CCIE lab; it is best to check the Cisco web site for the most current information.

The CCIE Skills

The CCIE Router and Switching exam includes the advanced technical skills that are required to maintain optimum network performance and reliability, as well as advanced skills in supporting diverse networks that use disparate technologies. CCIEs just don't have problems getting a job. These experts are basically inundated with offers to work for six-figure salaries! But that's because it isn't easy to attain the level of capability that is mandatory for Cisco's CCIE. For example, a CCIE will have the following skills down pat:

- Installing, configuring, operating, and troubleshooting complex routed LAN, routed WAN, switched LAN, and ATM LANE networks, and Dial-Access Services.

- Diagnosing and resolving network faults.

- Using packet/frame analysis and Cisco debugging tools.

- Documenting and reporting the problem-solving processes used.

- Having general LAN/WAN knowledge, including data encapsulation and layering; windowing and flow control, and their relation to delay; error detection and recovery; link-state, distance vector, and switching algorithms; management, monitoring, and fault isolation.

- Having knowledge of a variety of corporate technologies—including major services provided by Desktop, WAN, and Internet groups—as well as the functions, addressing structures, and routing, switching, and bridging implications of each of their protocols.

- Having knowledge of Cisco-specific technologies, including router/ switch platforms, architectures, and applications; communication servers; protocol translation and applications; configuration commands and system/network impact; and LAN/WAN interfaces, capabilities, and applications.

- Designing, configuring, installing and verifying voice over IP and voice over ATM networks.

Cisco's Network Design Certifications

In addition to the Network Support certifications, Cisco has created another certification track for network designers. The two certifications within this track are the Cisco Certified Design Associate and Cisco Certified Design Professional certifications. If you're reaching for the CCIE stars, we highly recommend the CCNP and CCDP certifications before attempting the lab (or attempting to advance your career).

This certification will give you the knowledge to design routed LAN, routed WAN, and switched LAN and ATM LANE networks.

Cisco Certified Design Associate (CCDA)

To become a CCDA, you must pass the DCN (Designing Cisco Networks) test (640-441). To pass this test, you must understand how to do the following:

- Design simple routed LAN, routed WAN, and switched LAN and ATM LANE networks.

- Use Network-layer addressing.

- Filter with access lists.

- Use and propagate VLAN.

- Size networks.

The Sybex *CCDA: Cisco Certified Design Associate Study Guide* is the most cost-effective way to study for and pass your CCDA exam.

Cisco Certified Design Professional (CCDP) 2.0

If you're already a CCNP and want to get your CCDP, you can simply take the CID 640-025 test. If you're not yet a CCNP, however, you must take the CCDA, CCNA, Routing, Switching, Remote Access and CID exams.

CCDP certification skills include the following:

- Designing complex routed LAN, routed WAN, and switched LAN and ATM LANE networks

- Building upon the base level of the CCDA technical knowledge

  CCDPs must also demonstrate proficiency in the following:

- Network-layer addressing in a hierarchical environment

- Traffic management with access-lists

- Hierarchical network design

- VLAN use and propagation

- Performance considerations: required hardware and software; switching engines; memory, cost, and minimization

What Does This Book Cover?

This book covers everything you need to pass the CCNP: Support exam. It teaches you how to troubleshoot processes on Cisco Routers and Catalyst Switches. Each chapter begins with a list of the topics covered related to the CCNP Support test, so make sure to read them over before working through the chapter.

Chapter 1 starts with learning about the troubleshooting methodology that should be followed to successfully resolve network problems. Different troubleshooting approaches will be discussed.

These different troubleshooting approaches are the foundation of the application of knowledge that will be gained throughout the book. Chapter 2 discusses Layer 2 and Layer 3 technologies and protocols. An overview is provided for all major LAN and WAN protocols.

Chapter 3 gives you an introduction to generic troubleshooting tools. This chapter is dedicated to making you familiar with all of the different troubleshooting tools that are available to effectively troubleshoot network problems. You move on from there to Chapter 4, in which you learn about Cisco's diagnostic commands. The infrastructure of high- and low-end routers is discussed in detail, as well as the switching paths used by each. Some global Cisco commands are also covered. Chapter 5 teaches you how to apply the commands and tools that are learned in previous chapters.

Chapter 6 is dedicated exclusively to TCP/IP troubleshooting. Commands and techniques are discussed in detail. A summary sheet is provided at the end of the chapter that is a great quick reference guide.

Chapter 7 covers serial line and Frame Relay troubleshooting. The show and debug commands that are specific to these technologies are introduced.

Chapter 8 is dedicated to ISDN connectivity issues. Chapters 9 and 10 deal with LAN protocols, such as Novell and AppleTalk. Both debug and show commands relating to these protocols are discussed thoroughly.

Chapter 11 covers the Cisco Catalyst 5000 switch and switched Ethernet networks. SPAN and other troubleshooting targets are also addressed. Chapter 12 provides information about Cisco Systems and the information that it provides.

Each chapter ends with review questions that are specifically designed to help you retain the knowledge presented. To really nail down your skills, read each question carefully, and, if possible, work through the hands-on labs in some of the chapters.

Where Do You Take the Exam?

You may take the exams at any of the more than 800 Sylvan Prometric Authorized Testing Centers around the world. For the location of a testing center near you, call (800)755-3926. Outside of the United States and Canada, contact your local Sylvan Prometric Registration Center.

To register for a Cisco Certified Network Professional exam:

1. Determine the number of the exam you want to take. (The Support exam number is 640-506.)

2. Register with the nearest Sylvan Prometric Registration Center. At this point, you will be asked to pay in advance for the exam. At the time of this writing, the exams are $100 each and must be taken within one year of payment. You can schedule exams up to six weeks in advance or as soon as one working day prior to the day you wish to take it. If something comes up and you need to cancel or reschedule your exam appointment, contact Sylvan Prometric at least 24 hours in advance. Same-day registration isn't available for the Cisco tests.

3. When you schedule the exam, you'll get instructions regarding all appointment and cancellation procedures, the ID requirements, and information about the testing-center location.

Tips for Taking Your CCNP Exam

The CCNP: Support test contains about 70 questions to be completed in 90 minutes. You must schedule a test at least 24 hours in advance (unlike the Novell or Microsoft exams), and you aren't allowed to take more than one Cisco exam per day.

Many questions on the exam have answer choices that at first glance look identical—especially the syntax questions! Remember to read through the choices carefully because "close doesn't cut it." If you get commands in the wrong order or forget one measly character, you'll get the question wrong. So, to practice, do the hands-on exercises at the end of the chapters over and over again until they feel natural to you.

Unlike Microsoft or Novell tests, the exam has answer choices that are really similar in syntax—although some syntax is dead wrong, it is usually just *subtly* wrong. Some other syntax choices may be right, but they're shown in the wrong order. Cisco does split hairs, and they're not at all averse to giving you classic trick questions. Here's an example:

`access-list 101 deny ip any eq 23` denies Telnet access to all systems.

This question looks correct because most people refer to the port number (23) and think, "Yes, that's the port used for Telnet." The catch is that you can't filter IP on port numbers (only TCP and UDP).

Also, never forget that the right answer is the Cisco answer. In many cases, more than one appropriate answer is presented, but the *correct* answer is the one that Cisco recommends.

Here are some general tips for exam success:

- Arrive early at the exam center, so you can relax and review your study materials.

- Read the questions *carefully*. Don't just jump to conclusions. Make sure that you're clear about *exactly* what each question asks.

- Don't leave any questions unanswered. They count against you.

- When answering multiple-choice questions that you're not sure about, use a process of elimination to get rid of the obviously incorrect answers first. Doing this greatly improves your odds if you need to make an educated guess.

- You can no longer move forward and backward through the Cisco exams except the CCIE written and the CCDA exam.

After you complete an exam, you'll get immediate, online notification of your pass or fail status, a printed Examination Score Report that indicates your pass or fail status, and your exam results by section. (The test administrator will give you the printed score report.) Test scores are automatically forwarded to Cisco within five working days after you take the test, so you don't need to send your score to them. If you pass the exam, you'll receive confirmation from Cisco, typically within two to four weeks.

How to Use This Book

This book can provide a solid foundation for the serious effort of preparing for the Cisco Certified Network Professional Support (Cisco Internetworking Troubleshooting) exam. To best benefit from this book, use the following study method:

1. Take the Assessment Test immediately following this Introduction. (The answers are at the end of the test.) Carefully read over the explanations for any question you get wrong, and note which chapters the material comes from. This information should help you plan your study strategy.

2. Study each chapter carefully, making sure that you fully understand the information and the test objectives listed at the beginning of each chapter. Pay extra close attention to any chapter where you missed questions in the Assessment Test.

3. Complete all hands-on exercises in the chapter, referring to the chapter so that you understand the reason for each step you take. If you do not have Cisco equipment available, make sure to study the examples carefully. Also, check www.routersim.com for a router simulator. Answer the review questions related to that chapter. (The answers appear at the end of the chapter, after the review questions.)

4. Note the questions that confuse you, and study those sections of the book again.

5. Take the Practice Exam in this book. You'll find it in Appendix A. The answers appear at the end of the exam.

6. Before taking the exam, try your hand at the bonus practice exam that is included on the CD that comes with this book. The questions in this exam appear only on the CD. This will give you a complete overview of what you can expect to see on the real thing.

7. Remember to use the products on the CD that is included with this book. The electronic flashcards, the Boson Software utilities, and the EdgeTest exam preparation software have all been specifically picked to help you study for and pass your exam. Study on the road with the *CCNP: Support Study Guide* eBook in PDF, and be sure to test yourself with the electronic flashcards.

The electronic flashcards can be used on your Windows computer or on your Palm device.

8. Make sure and read the Key Terms list and the Commands in this Chapter list at the end of each chapter. Appendix B includes all the commands used in the book, including explanations for each command.

To learn all the material covered in this book, you'll have to apply yourself regularly and with discipline. Try to set aside the same time period every day to study, and select a comfortable and quiet place to do so. If you work hard, you will be surprised at how quickly you learn this material. All the best!

What's on the CD?

We worked hard to provide some really great tools to help you with your certification process. All of the following tools should be loaded on your workstation when studying for the test.

The EdgeTest for Cisco Support Test Preparation Software

Provided by EdgeTek Learning Systems, this test preparation software prepares you to successfully pass the Support exam. In this test engine you will find all of the questions from the book, plus an additional bonus Practice Exam that appears exclusively on the CD. You can take the Assessment Test, test yourself by chapter, take the Practice Exam that appears in the book or on the CD, or take an exam randomly generated from any of the questions.

To find more test-simulation software for all Cisco and NT exams, look for the exam link on www.lammle.com and www.boson.com.

Electronic Flashcards for PC and Palm Devices

After you read the *CCNP: Support Study Guide*, read the review questions at the end of each chapter and study the practice exams included in the book and on the CD. But wait, there's more! Test yourself with the flashcards included on the CD. If you can get through these difficult questions, and understand the answers, you'll know you'll be ready for the CCNP: Support exam.

The flashcards include more than 150 questions specifically written to hit you hard and make sure you are ready for the exam. Between the review questions, practice exam, and flashcards, you'll be more than prepared for the exam.

CCNP: Support Study Guide in PDF

Sybex is now offering the Cisco Certification books on CD so you can read the book on your PC or laptop. The *Dictionary of Networking* and the *CCNP: Support Study Guide* are in Adobe Acrobat format. Acrobat Reader 4 with Search is also included on the CD.

This will be extremely helpful to readers who travel and don't want to carry a book, as well as to readers who find it more comfortable reading from their computer.

Boson Software Utilities

Boson Software is an impressive company. They provide many services for free to help you, the student. Boson has the best Cisco exam preparation questions on the market, and at a very nice price. On the CD of this book, they have provided for you the following:

- IP Subnetter
- Superping
- System-Logging
- Wildcard Mask Checker and Decimal-to-IP Calculator
- Router GetPass

CCNA Virtual Lab AVI Demo Files

The *CCNA Virtual Lab e-trainer* provides a router and switch simulator to help you gain hands-on experience without having to buy expensive Cisco gear. The demos are .avi files that you can play in RealPlayer, which is included.The AVI demo files on the CD will help you gain an understanding of the product features and the labs that the routers and switches can perform. Read more about the CCNA Virtual Lab e-trainer at `http://www.sybex.com/cgi-bin/rd_bookpg.pl?2728back.html`. You can upgrade this product at `www.routersim.com`.

How to Contact the Authors

You can reach Todd Lammle through Globalnet System Solutions, Inc. (`www.lammle.com`)—his Training and Systems Integration Company in Colorado—or e-mail him at `todd@lammle.com`.

To contact Kevin Hales, you can e-mail him at `hales@eng.utah.edu`.

Assessment Test

1. Which of the following are possible causes for zones not appearing in a user's Chooser? (Choose all that apply.)

   A. Phase one/phase two addressing mismatch

   B. Duplicate network numbers

   C. ZIP storm

   D. Local configuration set to LocalTalk instead of EtherTalk

2. Which are reasons for using a troubleshooting method? (Choose all that apply.)

   A. Problem isolation and resolution will occur more quickly.

   B. No documentation needs to be done when following a method.

   C. Due to complex topologies and technologies, a systematic method is the most efficient way to resolve network problems.

   D. All of the above.

3. Which devices may be considered physical media test equipment? (Choose all that apply.)

   A. Time Domain Reflector

   B. Multimeter

   C. Optical Time Domain Reflector

   D. Breakout box

4. Which channel do q.931 and q.921 use for communication?

   A. A channel

   B. B channel

   C. D channel

   D. Both B and D

5. Which functions can be performed via the CCO Case Management Toolkit? (Choose all that apply.)

   A. Case priority escalation

   B. Open a case

   C. Close a case

   D. Update a case

6. Which protocol attributes are associated with the Internet Protocol (IP)? (Choose all that apply.)

   A. Connection-oriented

   B. Connectionless

   C. Layer 2

   D. Layer 3

7. Which LMI type is on by default on a Cisco router?

   A. LMI

   B. Cisco

   C. ANSI

   D. ITU-T

   E. IETF

8. Which commands should be used in conjunction for thorough problem isolation? (Choose two.)

   A. `ping`

   B. `Show ip interface`

   C. `traceroute`

   D. `ARP`

9. What do the following lines of router output indicate? (Choose all that apply.)

```
Router_C#show int ethernet 0/1
Ethernet0/1 is up, line protocol is up
  Hardware is Lance, address is 0000.0c47.abea (bia
  0000.0c47.abea)
  Internet address is 172.16.60.1/24
  MTU 1500 bytes, BW 10000 Kbit, DLY 1000 usec, rely
  255/255,    load 46/255
  Encapsulation ARPA, loopback not set, keepalive set
  (10 sec)
  ARP type: ARPA, ARP Timeout 04:00:00
```

A. The interface is up and appears to be functioning properly.

B. This interface is in loopback.

C. The encapsulation type for this interface is ARPA.

D. The bandwidth metric for this interface is 100Mbps.

10. What is/are the benefit(s) of gathering additional facts for trouble-shooting? (Choose all that apply.)

A. Possible causes may be identified.

B. A specific problem definition may be created.

C. Information is provided for a baseline.

D. All of the above.

11. Which ISDN protocol is used for Layer 3 connection setup?

A. CHAP

B. PPP

C. q.921

D. q.931

12. Which command should be used to display the connection setup for Layer 3?

   A. `show interface bri` *n*

   B. `debug isdn q931`

   C. `debug interface bri`

   D. `debug isdn q921`

13. What command(s) may be issued on a Windows 98 system to provide interface IP information? (Choose all that apply.) See Chapter 6.

   A. `show ip interface`

   B. `ipconfig /all`

   C. `winipcfg`

   D. `ipcfg`

14. Which of the following are possible actions for resolving phase one/phase two incompatibility? (Choose all that apply.)

   A. Use unary cable ranges

   B. Use one zone per network

   C. show appletalk neighbors

   D. show appletalk globals

15. Which configuration register setting will cause the router to boot the IOS image from the boot ROM?

   A. 0x2000

   B. 0x2101

   C. 0x1002

   D. 0x2102

16. Which protocols are used for dynamic IP address assignment? (Choose two.)

    A. AutoIP

    B. AutoARP/IP

    C. BootP

    D. DHCP

17. What are the three major roles of a router when configured with VLANs? (Choose three.)

    A. Define the collision domain.

    B. Provide Layer 2 VLAN switching.

    C. Provide Layer 2 VLAN translation.

    D. Provide Layer 3 VLAN routing.

18. Which of the following are key components of creating an action plan?

    A. Multiple changes as long as they are documented

    B. Changes that do not compromise security

    C. Changes that have only brief network impact

    D. Back-out plans

19. Which of the following VLAN encapsulation types do Cisco router's support? (Choose all that apply.)

    A. Interswitch Link (ISL)

    B. IEEE Ethernet 802.3

    C. IEEE 802.1Q

    D. IEEE 802.1Z

20. Which ISDN protocol is used for Layer 2 connection setup?

    A. CHAP

    B. PPP

    C. q.921

    D. q.931

21. What are the valid LMI types? (Choose all that apply.)

A. LMI

B. Cisco

C. ITU-T

D. ANSI

22. When is a "default gateway" used on the router? See Chapter 6.

A. When a packet leaves the router

B. When no route exists in the route table

C. When a static route has been set

D. Only when the router is in boot mode

23. What are the valid Frame Relay encapsulation types? (Choose all that apply)

A. IETF

B. ITU-T

C. Cisco

D. ANSI

24. What do the following lines of router output indicate? (Choose all that apply.)

```
Router_A#show interface to0
... some output deleted ...
  MTU 4464 bytes, BW 16000 Kbit, DLY 630 usec, rely
  255/255,    load 1/255
  Encapsulation SNAP, loopback not set, keepalive set
  (10 sec)
  ARP type: SNAP, ARP Timeout 04:00:00
  Ring speed: 16 Mbps
... output removed ...
  Last clearing of "show interface" counters never
```

A. The ring speed is 4Mbps.

B. The ring speed is 16Mbps.

C. The interface counters have never been cleared.

D. Encapsulation is SNMP.

25. What are the five attributes of network management software? (Choose five.)

   A. Connectivity

   B. Network Availability Monitoring

   C. Reachability

   D. Graphical User Interface

   E. Network Modeling and Simulation

   F. Security

   G. Quality of Service

   H. Traffic Monitoring and Analysis

26. Which of the following are characteristic of extended IPX access lists? (Choose all that apply.)

   A. Numbered between 100 and 199

   B. Numbered between 800 and 899

   C. Numbered between 900 and 999

   D. Filters on Novell Service

27. When using a router, which of the following scenarios will not work?

   A. VLAN 10 uses ISL while VLAN 20 uses 802.1q.

   B. The switch is configured to use ISL and the router uses 802.1q.

   C. VLAN 10 uses 802.1q, then tries to communicate with a remote host, not on a VLAN.

   D. Both VLAN 10 and VLAN 20 use 802.1q.

28. Choose the troubleshooting tool that is used to test for reachability and connectivity.

    A. traceroute

    B. Debug

    C. Show interface

    D. Ping

29. What is SNMP used for?

    A. Creating network maps

    B. Traffic Analysis

    C. Statistical/Environmental data collection

    D. All of the above

30. In the following line, what is the zone name?

    ```
    (43199n,145a,244s)[0]:    'clientzone:AFPServer@Piper'
    ```

    A. clientzone

    B. piper

    C. AFPServer@Piper

    D. Piper

    E. 43199

31. Which of the following protocols can be used with IPX? (Choose all that apply.)

    A. IGRP

    B. BGP

    C. EIGRP

    D. NLSP

    E. RIP

32. Which of the following Cisco resources was established to aid in preventing problems? (Choose all that apply.)

A. Software Center

B. Cisco Connection Documentation CD-ROM

C. Cisco TAC

D. Bug Navigator

33. Which Cisco NMS packages are included in CiscoWorks 2000? (Choose all that apply.)

A. CiscoWorks 4.0

B. Cisco Works for Switched Internetworks

C. Threshold Manager

D. NetSys

E. NetFlow Collector and Analyzer

F. Resource Manager Essentials

G. CiscoView

H. ATM Director

34. Which of the following is a troubleshooting target for AppleTalk? (Choose all that apply.)

A. Local host configuration

B. Routers connected to AppleTalk networks

C. Remote host configuration

D. ARP protocol

35. Which of the following are information items that will be requested upon opening a TAC case? (Choose all that apply.)

A. Output from a show tech-support

B. Support contract number

C. Mailing address

D. Specify priority

36. Which of the following are possible actions for resolving a configuration mismatch? (Choose all that apply.)

   A. `debug NBP events`

   B. `show running-configuration`

   C. `show appletalk interface`

   D. `debug appletalk gns`

37. Which of the following are valid switching types for Cisco routers? (Choose all that apply.)

   A. Cisco Express Forwarding

   B. Buffer switching

   C. Netflow switching

   D. Process switching

   E. Silicon switching

   F. Fast switching

   G. Optimum switching

   H. VIP switching

38. How many methods of problem isolation exist?

   A. 2

   B. 3

   C. 4

   D. 6

39. Choose the best definition of packet flow as it relates to a Cisco router.

   A. The flow of packets from the source to a destination

   B. The flow of packets from one router to another

   C. The path a packet takes inside the router's architecture

   D. The path that packets take to get from one place to another

40. How many levels of `ping` and `traceroute` are there on Cisco routers?

   A. One

   B. Two

   C. Three

   D. Four

41. Which of the following are valid troubleshooting targets when trouble-shooting Novell NetWare (IPX) networks? (Choose all that apply.)

   A. ARP

   B. GNS

   C. Encapsulation type

   D. SAP

42. Which encapsulation is used by default on Cisco Serial interfaces?

   A. SDLC

   B. PPP

   C. HDLC

   D. X.25

43. Which of the following are main categories of troubleshooting targets for Novell NetWare networks? (Choose all that apply.)

   A. Novell client configuration

   B. Novell server configuration

   C. Cisco router configuration

   D. IP connectivity

44. Look at the outputs from two different interfaces connected to each other. Why aren't the interfaces functioning properly?

```
Router_A#show interface to0
TokenRing0 is up, line protocol is down
  Hardware is TMS380, address is 0007.787c.e14b (bia
  0007.787c.e14b)
  Internet address is 172.16.30.1, subnet mask is
```

255.255.255.0

MTU 4464 bytes, BW 16000 Kbit, DLY 630 usec, rely 255/255,   load 1/255

Encapsulation SNAP, loopback not set, keepalive set (10 sec)

ARP type: SNAP, ARP Timeout 04:00:00

Ring speed: 16 Mbps

Single ring node, Source Route Transparent Bridge capable

Ethernet Transit OUI: 0x000000

Last input never, output never, output hang never

Last clearing of "show interface" counters never

Queueing strategy: fifo

Output queue 0/40, 0 drops; input queue 0/75, 0 drops

5 minute input rate 0 bits/sec, 0 packets/sec

5 minute output rate 0 bits/sec, 0 packets/sec

  0 packets input, 0 bytes, 0 no buffer

  Received 0 broadcasts, 0 runts, 0 giants

  0 input errors, 0 CRC, 0 frame, 0 overrun, 0 ignored,   0 abort

  0 packets output, 0 bytes, 0 underruns

  0 output errors, 0 collisions, 0 interface resets

  0 output buffer failures, 0 output buffers swapped out

  5 transitions

Router_B#**show interface to1**

TokenRing0 is up, line protocol is down

  Hardware is TMS380, address is 0007.787c.e14b (bia 0007.787c.e14b)

  Internet address is 172.16.30.2, subnet mask is 255.255.255.0

  MTU 4464 bytes, BW 4000 Kbit, DLY 630 usec, rely 255/255,   load 1/255

  Encapsulation SNAP, loopback not set, keepalive set (10 sec)

  ARP type: SNAP, ARP Timeout 04:00:00

  Ring speed: 4 Mbps

  Single ring node, Source Route Transparent Bridge

```
capable
Ethernet Transit OUI: 0x000000
Last input never, output never, output hang never
Last clearing of "show interface" counters never
Queueing strategy: fifo
Output queue 0/40, 0 drops; input queue 0/75, 0 drops
5 minute input rate 0 bits/sec, 0 packets/sec
5 minute output rate 0 bits/sec, 0 packets/sec
   0 packets input, 0 bytes, 0 no buffer
   Received 0 broadcasts, 0 runts, 0 giants
   0 input errors, 0 CRC, 0 frame, 0 overrun, 0
   ignored,         0 abort
   0 packets output, 0 bytes, 0 underruns
   0 output errors, 0 collisions, 0 interface resets
   0 output buffer failures, 0 output buffers swapped
   out
   5 transitions
```

A. Duplicate IP addresses

B. Lobe wire fault

C. Ring speed mismatch

D. Five carrier transitions

45. Select the attributes of a connectionless protocol. (Choose all that apply.)

A. Broadcast control

B. Sequenced PDUs

C. Broadcast transmissions

D. Wireless connectivity

46. Which is the primary function of a protocol analyzer?

A. Collect and analyze frames or packets from the network.

B. Analyze protocol distributions only.

C. Monitor the network for security holes.

D. Provide a real-time baseline.

47. Which of the following were established to correct problems? (Choose all that apply.)

   A. Software Center

   B. Bug Navigator

   C. Open Forum

   D. Troubleshooting Engine

48. Which of the following are valid hardware components of the Catalyst switch? (Choose all that apply.)

   A. EARL

   B. DUKE

   C. SAINT

   D. SAGE

49. Which of the following commands are troubleshooting commands specific to IPX troubleshooting? (Choose all that apply.)

   A. show ipx servers

   B. ping <network.node>

   C. ping ipx *<network.node>*

   D. debug ipx servers

50. What does the term "blocking" mean with regard to a Catalyst 5000 port?

   A. An access list has been applied to the port.

   B. Packets are not allowed out of the port.

   C. Spanning tree has blocked the port to prevent a loop.

   D. The port has been shut down.

51. Which channel does PPP use when negotiating the connection?

   A. A channel

   B. B channel

   C. D channel

   D. Both B and D

52. Choose all protocols that operate on Layer 3 from the following list.

    A. PPP

    B. IP

    C. EIGRP

    D. SDLC

    E. NetWare

    F. X.25

    G. BGP

53. What type of tests are useful in testing for end-to-end serial link integrity?

    A. Ping

    B. traceroute

    C. Loopback

    D. Loopup

54. Choose all Layer 2 protocols listed below.

    A. TCP

    B. Ethernet

    C. UDP

    D. IP

    E. Token Ring

    F. FDDI

    G. EIGRP

55. Which of the following steps are part of the troubleshooting method? (Choose all that apply.)

　A. Observation of results

　B. Observation of changes

　C. Iteration

　D. Documentation

　E. Problem definition

　F. Problem resolution

　G. Troubleshooting

56. Why is a default metric setting necessary for route redistribution?

　A. It isn't necessary.

　B. The routes being injected need to be assigned metrics that the parent protocol understands.

　C. It provides better metrics when performing route redistribution.

　D. It converts the parent protocol's metric to match the protocol being redistributed.

57. Choose the troubleshooting tool that is used for testing the path from a source host to a destination host.

　A. traceroute

　B. Debug

　C. Show interface

　D. Ping

58. Choose two attributes that a connection-oriented protocol possesses.

　A. Flow control

　B. Error control

　C. Broadcast control

　D. Collision detection

59. Which of the following factors may contribute to excessive collisions on an Ethernet interface? (Choose all that apply.)

A. Ethernet interface

B. Transceiver

C. Cable

D. Encapsulation

60. How does the Troubleshooting Assistant work?

A. Access is given to Cisco Systems; they in turn evaluate the router and suggest any necessary changes.

B. An interactive dialog intended to resolve common networking/ configuration problems is used.

C. Questions can be posted, and CCIEs will respond.

D. It is a Voice Response Unit that guides you through trouble-shooting steps.

Answers to Assessment Test Questions

1. C, D. Both ZIP (Zone Information Protocol) storms and incorrect local configuration can cause this symptom. See Chapter 10 for more information.

2. C. Quick problem resolution is not guaranteed by using a model, and documentation should always be performed. For further explanation of the reasons for using a troubleshooting method, see Chapter 1.

3. A, B, C, and D. All of these devices are used to test physical media. For additional information on physical media test equipment, see Chapter 3.

4. C. These protocols use the D channel for information signaling. See Chapter 8 for more information.

5. B, C, D. Users are not allowed to escalate a case priority via the Web; TAC must be contacted via phone or e-mail. See Chapter 12 for more information.

6. B, D. IP is a connectionless protocol and is a Layer 3 protocol. For further information about IP, see Chapter 2.

7. B. Cisco LMI is on by default. See Chapter 7 for more information.

8. A, C. Using both of these tools in conjunction greatly aids problem isolation. See Chapter 6 for more information.

9. A, C. The interface is not in loopback and the bandwidth metric is only 10Mbps. See Chapter 5 for more information.

10. A, B. Option C is incorrect because a baseline contains information taken from a normally functioning network. For further explanation of gathering facts for troubleshooting, see Chapter 1.

11. D. CHAP and PPP are not specific to ISDN and q.921 is used for Layer 2 setup. See Chapter 8 for more information.

12. B. This **debug** command displays all steps of the connection sequence. See Chapter 8 for more information.

13. B, C. Both commands are recognized in Windows 98. A is for use on a router, and D is incorrect syntax. See Chapter 6 for more information.

14. A, B, C, D. All of these are valid actions that will lead to the resolution of phase one/phase two incompatibility. See Chapter 10 for more information.

15. B. 0x2101 is the correct configuration register setting for a router to enter boot mode. See Chapter 5 for more details about configuration register settings.

16. C, D. These two protocols are used for IP address assignment. (The other two don't exist.) See Chapter 6 for more information.

17. B, C, D. A router provides other roles in a switched network as well, but the collision domain is defined by the switch port, not the router. See Chapter 11 for more information on this subject.

18. B, D. Making multiple changes creates more difficulty when trying to back out of changes as well as not allowing for good observation results. Changes should not create any adverse network impact. For further explanation of creating an action plan, see Chapter 1.

19. A, C. Cisco routers support both ISL and 802.1Q. See Chapter 11 for more information.

20. C. CHAP and PPP are not specific to ISDN and q.931 is used for Layer 3 setup. See Chapter 8 for more information.

21. B, C, D. LMI is the Local Management Interface. See Chapter 7 for more information.

22. B. The term "default" indicates that no other route has been specified. So instead of dropping the packet, the router forwards it out the default gateway. See Chapter 6 for more information.

23. A, C. There are only two valid encapsulation types for Frame Relay. See Chapter 7 for more information.

24. B, C. The encapsulation is SNAP. See Chapter 5 for more information.

25. B, E, F, G, H. Connectivity and Reachability belong to the Network Availability Monitoring attribute. For additional information on Network Management Software, see Chapter 3.

26. C. Novell services are filtered using SAP filters, which are different from IPX filters. See Chapter 9 for more details about IPX access lists.

27. B. The router and switch must use the same encapsulation across the connection. Other interfaces do not matter. See Chapter 11 for more information.

28. D. Ping uses ICMP to test for connectivity of remote hosts. See Chapter 4 for more details.

29. C. Simple Network Management Protocol is used to collect statistical/environmental data from network devices. For additional information on SNMP, see Chapter 3.

30. D. Note that resource names are case-insensitive, but zone names are not. See Chapter 10 for more information.

31. C, D, E. These protocols are known as IPX-EIGRP, NLSP, and IPX-RIP. These protocols can all be used in conjunction with IPX. See Chapter 9 for more information about IPX settings.

32. A, B. The TAC is primarily for problem support and to provide information that a user may not have access to. See Chapter 12 for more information.

33. B, C, F, G, H. These are all individual components of CiscoWorks 2000. NetSys is an analysis package that is a stand-alone from CiscoWorks 2000; NetFlow Collector is also a stand-alone. For additional information about Cisco's NMS packages, see Chapter 3.

34. A, B, C. All of these items are major troubleshooting targets for AppleTalk. Of course, each major target will have subsequent targets. See Chapter 10 for more information.

35. A, B, D. In addition, you may be asked to provide the serial number of the device you are calling about. See Chapter 12 for more information.

36. B, C. Both of these commands will allow you to see how the interface and router are configured for AppleTalk. See Chapter 10 for more information.

37. A, C, D, E, F, G. Buffer switching is not a valid term and VIP switching is known as Distributed switching. See Chapter 4 for more details about switching types.

38. B. There are three methods for isolating the source of a network problem: outside-in, inside-out, and divide-by-half. For further explanation of methods of problem isolation, see Chapter 1.

39. C. The packet flow as it relates to the router is the path that it takes inside the router to get from one interface to another, otherwise through the router's architecture. See Chapter 4 for more information about packet flow.

40. B. There are two levels, user and privileged. See Chapter 4 for more details.

41. B, C, D. ARP is associated with IP lookup; it is not related to the IPX protocol. See Chapter 9 for more detail about troubleshooting NetWare networks.

42. C. HDLC is an enhancement over SDLC, and PPP is a protocol, not an encapsulation. X.25 is not configured by default. See Chapter 7 for more information.

43. A, B, C, D. All of these are main troubleshooting targets when working on Novell networks. The reason IP connectivity is a target is to provide isolation. If IP connectivity is malfunctioning, you can determine that it may not be solely an IPX issue. See Chapter 9 for more information about troubleshooting NetWare networks.

44. C. The carrier transitions could be caused by the ring speed mismatch. See Chapter 5 for more information.

45. C. Connectionless protocols do not use any type of control. B is a type of control. Physical connectivity does not determine the protocol properties. For further information about connectionless protocols, see Chapter 2.

46. A. Several different analyses may be executed once the frames or packets have been captured to a buffer. A protocol distribution can be performed, but it is a report or a specific type of analysis. An analyzer cannot monitor your network efficiently. It can be used to get an idea of real-time activity, but that is not its primary function. For additional information on protocol analyzers, see Chapter 3.

47. B, C, D. These services all provide solutions to known problems. See Chapter 12 for more information.

48. A, C, D. These are all valid components of the Catalyst 5000 series switches. You should be familiar with the role of each. See Chapter 11 for more information.

49. A, C. In order to use the `<network.node>` address, you must specify the IPX Ping. See Chapter 9 for more information about IPX troubleshooting.

50. C. Blocking is a step or state in the spanning tree protocol that prevents loops. See Chapter 11 for more information.

51. B. Since data (payload) is going to be from point to point, the PPP link must be set up between the local and remote TE on the B channel. See Chapter 8 for more information.

52. B, C, G. NetWare covers the top five layers of the OSI model and is not isolated to Layer 3. The remaining protocols are all Layer 2. See Chapter 2 for further information.

53. C. Loopback tests can test for link integrity without any additional protocols such as PPP, IP, or others. See Chapter 7 for more details.

54. B, E, F. These are all Layer 2 technologies with their accompanying protocols. For further information, see Chapter 2.

55. A, C, D, E. There are additional steps in the method, but they are not included here. For further explanation of Cisco's troubleshooting method, see Chapter 1.

56. B. Routes from the incoming protocol must be assigned new metrics so they can be redistributed. See Chapter 6 for more information.

57. A. traceroute tests the route or path from a source to a destination. See Chapter 4 for more details.

58. A, B. These two attributes allow for complete connection and data transfer control. For further information about connection-oriented protocols, see Chapter 2.

59. A, B, C. Collisions can be caused by any piece of hardware involved in an Ethernet connection. See Chapter 5 for more information about collisions.

60. B. Initial questions are posed and a response received; based on the response, additional questions are posed, and this process continues until the problem is resolved. See Chapter 12 for additional information.

Chapter

1

Troubleshooting Methodology

TOPICS COVERED IN THIS CHAPTER INCLUDE:

✓ Using a problem-solving method when troubleshooting internetwork problems.

✓ Learning the importance of documenting the actions taken to resolve network problems.

roubleshooting is a skill that takes time and experience to fully develop. To be successful when trying to diagnose and repair network failures, a good set of troubleshooting tools and skills is essential.

This chapter emphasizes the importance of following a specific set of troubleshooting steps when you try to diagnose and solve network problems. An effective troubleshooting methodology is needed because of the complexity of today's network environments. As a Cisco Certified Network Professional, you need to understand and be able to apply an efficient and systematic troubleshooting methodology. Otherwise, you would be required to have a very intimate understanding of the network you are troubleshooting. The ability to learn troubleshooting skills and understand the information available to you while solving network problems is imperative.

The Complexity of Internetworks

When a network failure occurs, time is of the essence. When a production network goes down, several things are affected. The most important of these is the bottom line—network failures cost money. A good example is a call-center network. The company relies on the network to be available for its employees so that they may take phone orders, answer inquiries, or perform other business transactions that generate income. A failure in this environment needs to be diagnosed and repaired in a timely manner. The longer the network is down, the more money the company loses.

To minimize monetary and productivity losses, network failures must be resolved quickly. Troubleshooting is an integral part of getting the problem solved quickly. Intimate knowledge of a network also facilitates rapid resolution. However, armed with a few troubleshooting skills and intimate knowledge of the network, you can solve most problems rather quickly, thus saving money.

Hold on a minute. What if you're new on the job and you don't have an intimate knowledge of the network? You can probably get up to speed quickly enough, right? Although that may have been the case in the past, getting up to speed becomes overwhelming with today's complex networks. These networks consist of routing, dial-up, switching, video, WAN (ISDN, Frame Relay, ATM, and others), LAN, and VLAN technologies. Refer to Figure 1.1 to get an idea of how these technologies intertwine. Notice that ATM, Frame Relay, Token Ring, Ethernet, and FDDI all are present. Each technology has different properties and different commands to allow for troubleshooting. Different protocols are used for each of these technologies. In addition, different applications require specific network resources. (At least the seven-layer OSI model, which you will review in Chapter 2, is used to maintain a common template when designing new technologies and protocols.) It would take you a long time to master all of the technologies implemented in the network and to be able to solve network problems, based on your knowledge of the network alone. All of these factors contribute to today's complex network environments.

There must be an easier, more logical way to efficiently and successfully troubleshoot without having to become intimately familiar with every network environment. Well, you'll be happy to know that there is an easier option—following a troubleshooting model—and it is discussed in detail in this chapter. By following a troubleshooting model, the need for intimate knowledge of the network is minimized.

A troubleshooting model should be adopted to help resolve network malfunctions and reduce downtime. Now, let's move on to discuss Cisco's model in detail.

FIGURE 1.1   Today's complex enterprise network

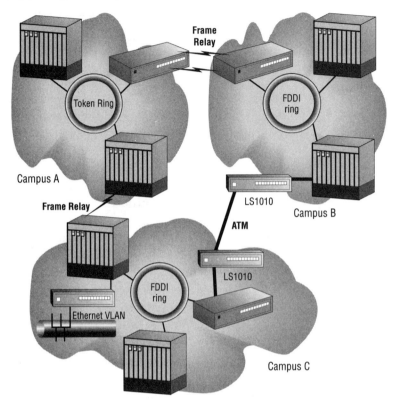

The Problem-Solving Model

Imagine trying to solve a network failure by using a different approach every time. With such complex networks, the possible scenarios would be innumerable. Because so many different things can go wrong within a network, it would be possible to start from many different points. Not only is this an ineffective method of troubleshooting, but it is also time-consuming, and time is very valuable in a "network-down" situation.

Cisco has designed an effective *troubleshooting model* that contains seven steps. A troubleshooting model is a list of troubleshooting steps or processes that can be followed to provide an efficient manner of resolving network problems. The headings below contain information specific to each step of the troubleshooting model. (Two of the steps are combined into one section of the chapter—creating and implementing the action plan.) After the seven steps are completed and the problem is resolved, a few more steps follow, such as documentation.

To be effective when troubleshooting and to achieve faster resolution times, follow the model outlined in Figure 1.2. This flow chart shows the eight steps.

The process begins when a network failure is reported to you. The steps to take are as follows:

1. Define the problem.

2. Gather detailed information.

3. Consider possible scenarios (brainstorm and come up with several possible or probable causes of the failure).

4. Devise a plan to solve the problem.

5. Implement the plan.

6. Observe the results of the implementation.

7. Repeat the process if the plan doesn't fix the problem.

8. Document changes after the problem is solved.

FIGURE 1.2 Cisco's troubleshooting model

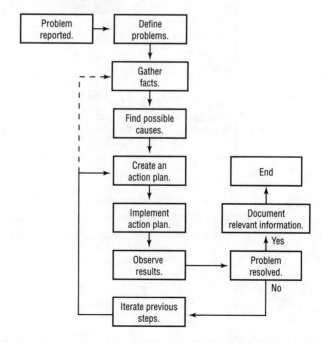

Following an example is the best way to understand how Cisco's model works and how you should use it. The example that you will follow here is the network pictured in Figure 1.3. There are two campus networks, connected via a Frame Relay cloud. Within each network, VLANs are connected to a Catalyst 5500 switch and then to a core router that has a connection to the Frame Relay cloud in one way or another.

FIGURE 1.3 Example campus network

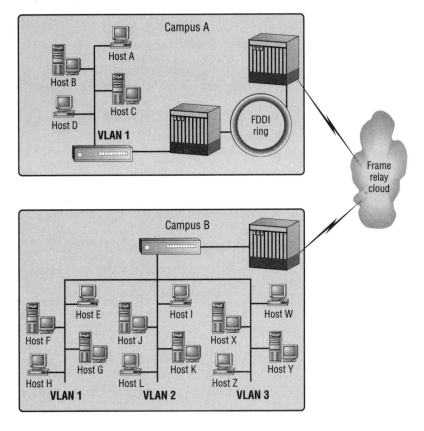

The fun begins when you get a call from a user who can't get to Host Z. Armed with that information, you are supposed to make it all better. Let's use the model to make our customer happy and fix the network.

Step 1: Define the Problem

As you can see, the user's problem is really vague; you need more information if you are to solve the problem any time soon. This is where *problem definition* comes in. Problem definition is the step in the troubleshooting model when details are used to define what the most likely cause of a problem is. Now, while you still have the user on the line, the first step is to ask him what he means when he says he can't "get" to Host Z. The user then defines the situation by telling you that he can't FTP to Host Z. Ask the user if he experiences any other problems or if this is the only one. After these preliminary questions, you have a basic idea of what is and isn't working. Unfortunately, you can't simply assume that the FTP is broken because there are many other pieces of the network that can contribute to the problem.

It is also important to realize that you may want or need to gather facts before you actually form your problem statement. By gathering facts to help define the problem, the diagnosis of the problem or problems will be more accurate and will help you solve the problem more quickly in the end. Problem definition and fact gathering should be used in tandem for a quick and accurate resolution.

Once you have enough information to define the problem, you should create a problem statement that is specific, concise, and an accurate description of the problem that needs to be solved. In this case, you can have a statement that says: *User A from Campus A cannot FTP to Host Z on Campus B.* With a good problem statement, it is easier to focus on the problem and not try to troubleshoot problems that do not fall within the problem definition.

Step back for a moment before you actually form your final problem statement. You need to gather more information before you can form an accurate problem statement. Now, you move on to the fact-gathering step. Keep in mind, however, that after you gather all the information, you have to come back and create your problem statement.

Step 2: Gather Facts

At this point, the problem is still pretty vague and needs more definition. This is where the fact-gathering step of the troubleshooting model is employed. *Fact gathering* is the process of using diagnostic tools to collect information specific to the network and network devices that are involved in a problem. Additional information should include data that excludes other possibilities and helps pinpoint the actual problem. An example is to verify that you can ping, Traceroute, or Telnet to Host Z, thus reducing the number of possible causes.

Depending on the user, you may or may not be able to get more detailed information. It is up to you as a network engineer or administrator to solve the problem, which means that you may have to get the information yourself.

To be more specific, it is important that you gain as much information as possible to actually define the problem while in the problem-definition phase of the troubleshooting model. Without a proper and specific definition of what the problem is, it will be much harder to isolate and resolve. Information that is useful for defining a problem is listed in Table 1.1.

TABLE 1.1   Useful Information for Defining a Problem

Information	Example
Symptoms	Can't Telnet, FTP, or get to the WWW.
Reproducibility	Is this a one-time occurrence, or does it always happen?
Timeline	When did it start? How long did it last? How often does it occur?
Scope	What are you able to Telnet or FTP to? Which WWW sites can you reach, if any? Who else does this affect?
Baseline Info	Were any recent changes made to the network configurations?

All of this information can be used to guide you to the actual problem and to create the problem statement. Use your network diagram and go through the checklist.

Identify Symptoms

First, you need to define what is working and what isn't. You can do this by identifying the symptom and defining the scope. Figure 1.4 is a picture of your network. Although the large X on the Frame Relay cloud represents that there is an FTP connectivity issue, it does not indicate the location of the failure. Right now, all you know is that a single user could not FTP to Host Z.

Reproduce the Problem

Before spending time and effort trying to solve this problem, verify that it is still a problem. Troubleshooting is a waste of time and resources if the problem can't be reproduced. It's just like a dog chasing his tail.

Understand the Timeline

In addition to verifying whether the problem is reproducible, it is important to investigate the frequency of the problem. For instance, maybe it happens only once or twice a day. By establishing a timeframe you can more readily identify any possible causes.

FIGURE 1.4 Host A can't FTP to Host Z

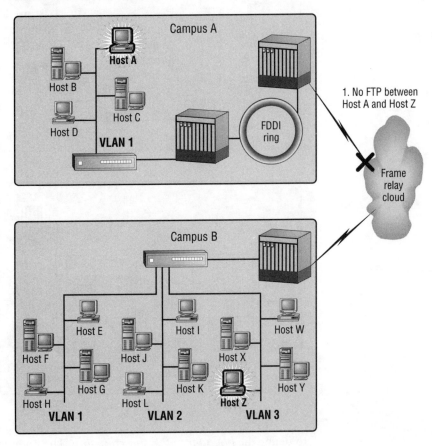

Determine the Scope of a Problem

Next, you need to find out whether anyone else is unable to FTP to Host Z. If others can FTP to Host Z (for the sake of this example, assume that they can), you can be pretty sure that the problem is specific to the user, either on their station or on the destination box. This step is determining the scope of the problem and helps to differentiate between a user-specific problem and a more widely spread problem. Figure 1.5 shows that other hosts can FTP to Host Z without any problems.

FIGURE 1.5 Other hosts can FTP to Host Z

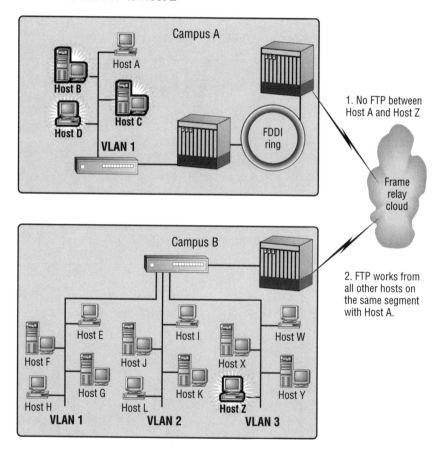

Now that you have the problem narrowed down to a single user, you need to define the *boundary of dysfunctionality*. The boundary of dysfunctionality is the limit or scope of the network problem. A distinction can be made between where nodes are functioning properly and where they are not. To define this boundary in this example, you need to know whether the user can successfully FTP anywhere.

Outside-in Troubleshooting

There are three methods of establishing the boundary of dysfunctionality. The first method consists of choosing the opposite end of the connection, known as *outside-in troubleshooting.* In this case, we would start at Campus B, VLAN 3, and work back toward the user's machine. This method is depicted in Figure 1.6. The corresponding test would be for the user to try to FTP to another machine on the same VLAN as Host Z, indicated by the X (2) on the diagram. If the result of that test is negative, then we need to come back one step. By coming back one step, we would try to FTP to a machine on a different VLAN, indicated by the X (3) on the diagram. If that test failed, the only thing left to try would be to FTP to another machine on the user's segment. In our example, we assume that the user can FTP to other hosts that are directly connected to the same Ethernet segment.

FIGURE 1.6   Starting from the outside and working in

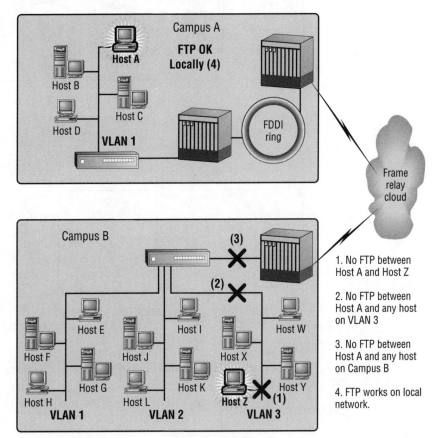

Inside-out Troubleshooting

The second method is to start near the user and work your way toward Host Z, otherwise known as the *inside-out troubleshooting* method. Figure 1.7 contains a diagram that describes this testing method. You see that the user can FTP to machines within the same network, but can't FTP to any machine on the Campus B network. The steps are marked by the Xs, with the step number in parentheses.

FIGURE 1.7 Starting from the inside and working out

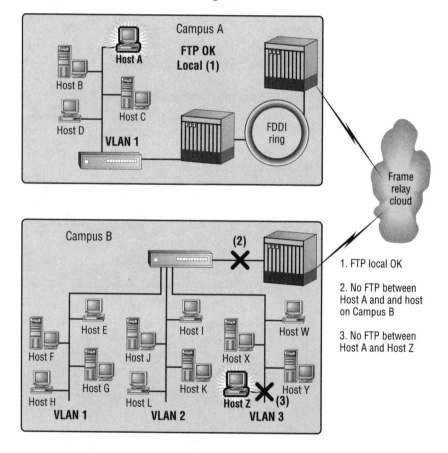

1. FTP local OK

2. No FTP between Host A and and host on Campus B

3. No FTP between Host A and Host Z

Using the second method saved you one step—three instead of four. Statistically, however, you isolate the boundary with fewer steps by using the first method. The important thing is that the boundary be established.

Divide-by-Half Troubleshooting

The third and final method is the *divide-by-half troubleshooting* method, which is depicted in Figure 1.8. Divide-by-half indicates that a point between two ends of a network problem is used as a troubleshooting reference point. Either half may be investigated first. In this example, you start by trying to FTP to any machine within Campus B. Depending on the results, you can divide in half again and test. If the test results in a successful FTP to any machine on the Campus B network, then the new point to test is another machine on VLAN 3. If the test fails, the new testing point is to try to FTP to a local machine. In this case, the divide-by-half method takes three steps, just as the inside-out method does.

FIGURE 1.8   Divide-by-half method

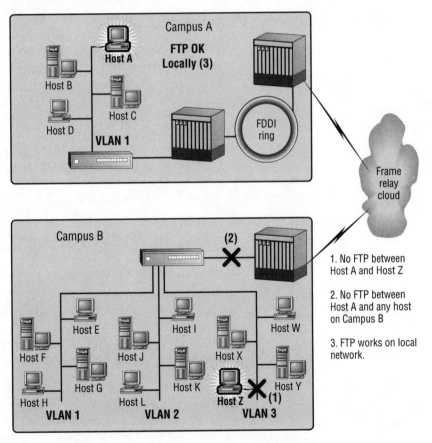

You now have isolated the problem to anything outside the immediate network. Upon further inspection and fact gathering, you find that the user can't ping external hosts, either. With all of this information, you can now start to contemplate possible causes of this failure and move on to the following Consider Possibilities section.

Using Baseline Information

Baseline information can be a great asset to troubleshooting network problems. Baseline information includes historical data about the network and routine utilization information. This information can be used to determine whether there were recent changes made to the network that may contribute to the problem at hand.

Step 3: Consider Possibilities

This step within the troubleshooting model is used to contemplate the possible causes of the failure. Obviously, it is quite easy to create a very long list of possible causes. That is why it is so important to gather as much relevant information as you can and to create an accurate problem statement. By defining the problem and assigning the corresponding boundaries, the resulting list of possible causes diminishes because the entries in the list will be focused on the actual problem and not on "possible" problems.

First, review what you know about your sample problem:

- Host A can't FTP to Host Z.

- Host A can't FTP to any host on Campus B.

- Host A can FTP to any host on its own network.

- All other hosts on Host A's network can FTP to Host Z, as well as to other hosts.

- Host A can't ping to anywhere outside its own network.

Based on what you know, you now need to list possible causes. These possible causes are:

- No default gateway is configured on Host A.

- There is a duplicate IP address.

- The wrong subnet mask is configured.

- There is an inbound access list on the router connected to the switch on Campus A.

If you had not gathered such specific information, the list could have included all of the possible problems with any piece of equipment between Host A and Host Z. That would have been a long list, and it would take a lot of time to eliminate all of the possible causes.

Remember that because these are only possible causes, you still have to create an action plan, implement it, and observe to see whether the changes made were effective. When the list of possible problems is long, it may require more iterations to actually solve the problem. In this example, you have only four possible causes, so this is a much more manageable list. Although there may be other possible causes that you can think of (that's great), for this example and in the interest of simplicity, only these four are listed.

Here's when the fun starts. You now have to check each of these possibilities and fix them if they are the cause of our problem. To do this, move on to the next step, which is to create an action plan.

Steps 4 and 5: Create and Implement the Action Plan

Creating an *action plan* is actually very easy. It entails the documentation of steps that will be taken to remedy the cause of the network problem. Most of the hard work was done while gathering information about the problem. The investigation gave you four leads about the source of the problem. Now, it is simply a matter of checking out each possibility.

The majority of the possibilities point directly at the host machine, so start there first. The first three causes are configuration issues of the host. Now, assume that after checking the TCP/IP configuration on the host, everything is configured properly, and you can eliminate the host machine as the culprit.

You then move on to the last possible cause, which is an access list on the router. While looking at the configuration on the router, you see that an access list is applied to the Ethernet 0 interface. After reviewing the syntax of the access list, you determine that it is the cause of the failure.

Great—you've found the problem. Now what? Once you find the problem, you must decide what is needed to fix it. In this case, it is an access list problem, so it will take some special considerations about how to restore functionality. You must be careful because that list may have other entries that provide security or other network administrative functionality. You can't just remove it—you could cause new problems as you fix the original one.

The best thing to do in this situation is to make a copy of the access list in a text editor, and then make changes that are specific to your problem. When editing the access list, change the number of the access list. After all of the changes are made, you can paste the access list back into the router. Finally, go to the interface and apply the new access list. By following this procedure, the access list is never removed from the interface.

When you create and implement action plans, it is important that you don't fix one problem and cause another. Before implementing an action plan, think it through or discuss it with coworkers to pick it apart, and make sure that your solution will fix the problem without doing anything to create adverse side effects.

Another good practice, when creating and implementing action plans, is to change only one thing at a time, if possible. If multiple changes must be made, it is best to make the changes in small sets. This way it is easier to keep track of what was done, what worked, and what didn't. The observation step becomes much more effective if only a few changes are made at one time; ideally, make only one change at a time.

To summarize, follow these practices and guidelines to create a good action plan:

- Make one change or a set of related changes at a time, and then observe the results.

- Make non-impacting changes. This means trying not to cause other problems while implementing the changes. The more transparent the change, the better.

- Do not create security holes when changing access lists, TACACS+, RADIUS, or other security-oriented configurations.

- Most important, be able to revert to the original configuration if unforseen problems occur as a result of the change. Always have a backup or copy of the configuration.

Now that we have discussed creating and implementing changes, you need to be able to monitor the network and interpret the information to verify whether the changes implemented were effective.

Step 6: Observe Results

Observing results consists of using the exact same methods and commands that were used to obtain information to define the problem—to see whether the changes implemented were effective. By making a change and then testing it to see whether the change was effective, you move toward the correct solution.

It may take one or more changes to fix the problem, but you should observe each change separately to monitor progress and to make sure that the change doesn't create any adverse effects. After the first change is made, you should be able to gather enough information to inform you whether or not the change was effective, even though it doesn't entirely solve the problem.

Once all of the changes from the action plan are implemented and the results are observed, you can verify whether the action plan solved the problem. If the problem is solved, move on and document the changes made to the network.

If the changes did not work, you need to go back and either gather more information or create a new action plan. While working through the action-plan process, you might get more ideas of possible causes. Write them down; if the current action plan doesn't work, you have notes about some other possibilities.

If you feel that you exhausted all of the possible causes, you should probably go back and gather more information. You will probably find additional information that can give you insights into more possible causes. These steps are covered in the iteration process.

Step 7: Iterate as Needed

Iterations, or repetitions of certain steps within the troubleshooting model, are simply ways of whittling away at a larger problem. By implementing action plans and monitoring the results, you can move toward solving the overall problem.

Iterations of the troubleshooting process allow you to focus, with more and more detail, on the possible causes of the failure. The result of focusing on the problem is the ability to identify specific possible causes for the failure.

This is also the time to undo any changes that had adverse effects or that did not fix the problem. Make sure to document what was done, so it will be easier to undo the changes made to any configurations.

When the Problem Is Resolved

The problem is resolved after you implement a change, observe that the symptoms of the problem have disappeared, and you can successfully execute the tests that were used to aid in gathering information about the problem.

In this example, the way to verify that the problem is solved is for Host A to try to FTP to Host Z. If this test is successful, then the problem is resolved.

Step 8: Document the Changes

Documentation is an integral part of troubleshooting. When you keep track of the changes that were made; which routers, switches, or hosts were changed; and when the changes occurred, you have valuable information for future reference. There is always the possibility that something you changed affected something else, and you didn't notice it. If this happens, you have documentation to refer to, so you can undo the changes. If a similar problem occurs, you can refer to these documents to resolve the current problem, based on what was done the last time.

Historical information is very useful in the case of a network failure. It provides a reference for the network engineer to use to see what changes were most recently made to the network.

The Problem-Solving Checklist

The easiest way to solve network problems is to be able to compare current configurations against previous configurations. This sounds easy, but it requires a lot of effort to get a system established to keep an historical baseline of your network. A historical *baseline* is simply a collection of network settings and configurations kept over time. This baseline makes it easy to locate changes or differences between a current configuration and a previous one.

Baselines provide the following types of information:

- Network topology

- Router configurations

- Network and routing protocols

- Traffic levels and network events

- Applications

- Changes made to network configurations

- Historical information that documents previous troubleshooting sessions

In addition to having all of this data available to you, it is helpful to have a checklist that you can refer to when you troubleshoot. A list may be created from baseline information if desired. Each individual knows their network and the types of changes that are made on it; each network's checklist would look different. For me to create a model checklist here and say that this is the checklist that everyone should use when resolving network problems would be pointless.

Summary

In this chapter, you learned about the complexity of today's networks and the importance of adhering to a troubleshooting model to aid in efficiently and effectively isolating and resolving network problems.

Different methods of problem isolation were discussed as well as the troubleshooting method itself. Along with the discussion were examples of what should be done in each step.

Here are some highlights of this chapter:

- Troubleshooting skills are gained through experience. It is unreasonable to expect that you can jump in on your first network failure and be able to solve it quickly. Experience is the best teacher.

- Following a problem-solving model helps you to reach a timely solution to network failures. Knowing your network helps, but the "shooting-from-the-hip" style of troubleshooting is nowhere near as effective as a methodical and logical process.

- Three methods of problem isolation were discussed in this chapter, but it is up to each individual to use a method they are comfortable with.

- Having a network baseline is an invaluable troubleshooting tool. The information contained in a network baseline can be used for reference and comparison to aid in quick problem resolution.

- It is important to document changes so you have a "trail" of what was done on the network. It also aids in reversing any changes that were made that adversely affected the network.

Key Terms

Before you take the exam, be sure you are familiar with the following key terms:

action plan

baseline

boundary of dysfunctionality

divide-by-half troubleshooting

fact gathering

inside-out troubleshooting

iterations

observing results

outside-in troubleshooting

problem definition

troubleshooting model

Review Questions

1. What are valid reasons for using a troubleshooting model? (Choose all that apply.)

   A. Networks are complex and require thorough troubleshooting.

   B. Difficult problems require a systematic and logical method.

   C. Problems are always resolved more quickly by using a systematic model.

   D. Cisco equipment requires diagnostic commands to be entered in a systematic manner.

2. What are the eight steps of the Cisco troubleshooting model? (Choose all that apply.)

   A. Document the changes.

   B. Create a baseline.

   C. Create an action plan.

   D. Undo the wrong changes.

   E. Define the problem.

   F. Observe changes.

   G. Observe results.

   H. Implement an action plan.

   I. Gather facts.

   J. Consider solutions.

   K. Consider possibilities.

   L. Define the problem boundary.

   M. Iterate the process.

3. Place the eight steps of the troubleshooting model in the correct order.

   A. Define Problem, Gather Facts, Consider Possibilities, Create and Implement Action Plan, Observe Results, Iterate Process, Document Changes

   B. Define Problem, Gather Facts, Create and Implement Action Plan, Observe Results, Iterate Process, Document Changes, Consider Possibilities

   C. Consider Possibilities, Gather Facts, Define Problem, Create and Implement Action Plan, Observe Results, Document Changes, Iterate Process

   D. Define Problem, Create and Implement Action Plan, Document Changes, Gather Facts, Consider Possibilities, Observe Results, Iterate Process

4. What is the main purpose of the Define Problem step in the problem-solving model?

   A. To consider the possible causes of the problem

   B. To establish the correct troubleshooting method to be used

   C. To form a specific and concise problem statement that directs the focus of the troubleshooting effort

   D. To exactly diagnose the problem

5. What are the two major reasons for gathering facts when troubleshooting? (Choose two answers.)

   A. To isolate the possible causes of the failure.

   B. To isolate the boundary of the problem.

   C. To use as a substitute for the `debug` command.

   D. It is required as part of the troubleshooting model.

6. Which of the following types of information are relevant while gathering facts for troubleshooting? (Choose all that apply.)

   A. Network baseline info

   B. The scope of the failure

   C. Whether the trouble is reproducible

   D. The timeline of the failure

   E. Symptoms of the failure

7. What are efficient methods of troubleshooting a network failure? (Choose all that apply.)

   A. "Shooting-from-the-hip" method

   B. Inside-out method (starting on the far end and working back)

   C. Outside-in method

   D. Partitioning or dividing-by-half method (dividing the path by half and isolating the problem that way)

8. Why is establishing the failure boundary important? (Choose all that apply.)

   A. It focuses on the portion of the network or application that is failing.

   B. You know whether you can assign the task to someone else.

   C. It focuses on the relevant information.

   D. It narrows the possibilities for causes of the failure.

9. Why should you gather specific information before considering the possible causes of the failure?

   A. It is part of the process.

   B. It shortens the list of possible causes of failure.

   C. It provides sufficient documentation.

   D. All of the above.

10. A good action plan should follow which of the following guidelines? (Choose all that apply.)

   A. Make one change at a time.

   B. Make any changes necessary to fix the problem.

   C. Make non-service-impacting changes.

   D. Do not create security holes while implementing changes.

   E. Leave an avenue available, in case you need to back out of the changes you made.

11. Which other step of the troubleshooting model is most similar to the Implement Action Plan step?

   A. Defining the Problem

   B. Gathering Facts

   C. Considering Possibilities

   D. Observing Results

   E. Iteration Process

12. What are the benefits of the iteration process? (Choose all that apply.)

   A. It allows small steps to be made to resolve a larger network failure.

   B. It takes longer to solve the problem, but it is effective.

   C. It allows the troubleshooting process to focus on a problem with more and more detail.

   D. It allows for ineffective changes to be removed.

13. What important information can be found in a network baseline? (Choose all that apply.)

   A. Router configurations

   B. Software versions

   C. Applications that run on the network

   D. Recent changes made to the network

   E. Network topology

   F. Inventory of network equipment

14. What should you do after implementing the action plan? (Choose all that apply.)

   A. Call the user and tell them the problem is solved.

   B. Document the changes.

   C. Verify that the changes worked without causing additional problems.

   D. Iterate the process.

15. Why should you document changes? (Choose all that apply.)

   A. It is part of the Cisco Troubleshooting Model.

   B. It is important to keep an historical record of changes made to the network.

   C. It is important to show the user what was done to fix the problem.

   D. It can facilitate backing out of ineffective or damaging configuration changes.

16. Which of the following is the correct method of isolating the boundary of dysfunctionality? (Choose all that apply.)

   A. Divide-by-half

   B. Outside-in

   C. Inside-out

   D. Step-by-step

17. Why should you make only one change at a time? (Choose all that apply.)

   A. It further isolates the problem.

   B. It makes it easier to back out if the change was ineffective.

   C. It eliminates one possible cause at a time.

   D. All of the above.

18. What is an important part of the iteration process? (Choose all that apply.)

    A. Creating more possible causes

    B. Gathering more information

    C. Homing in on the cause of the failure

    D. Creating a new action plan

19. How should you verify that changes made to the network were effective?

    A. Use `show ip route`.

    B. Use `show tech`.

    C. Perform all tests that were used to gather information about the problem.

    D. Ask the user if they are still experiencing the problem.

20. Which of the following attributes is necessary to troubleshoot network problems successfully?

    A. An intimate knowledge of the network

    B. A good troubleshooting method

    C. Expensive troubleshooting equipment

    D. A good understanding of the problem

(The answers to the questions begin on the next page.)

Answers to Review Questions

1. A, B. Problems may not always be resolved more quickly with a troubleshooting model, but they are still very efficient. Cisco equipment has no requirement for troubleshooting.

2. A, C, E, G, H, I, K, M. Creating a baseline is a good method for identifying problems when they occur, but this is not part of the troubleshooting method. Undoing wrong changes is part of the iteration process—reversing changes is done when a new action plan is created. You can't observe changes, just the results of changes. Solutions also belong to the action plan step of the troubleshooting method. Defining the problem boundary is part of the fact-gathering process.

3. A. You must create an action plan before its implementation. You cannot consider possibilities if you do not know what the problem is. You cannot create an action plan without knowing the details of the problem.

4. C. Without forming a specific problem statement, it is more difficult to identify possible solutions.

5. A, B. By isolating the possible causes and the boundary of the problem, the possible solutions can be more accurately drawn.

6. A, B, C, D, E. All of these items are very helpful when gathering information about network problems.

7. B, C, D. Shooting from the hip is not efficient because it is the same as guessing at what the problem may be and is not founded on research into what the possible causes could be.

8. A, C, D. In the case of B, instead of assigning the task to someone else, if the failure is outside of your jurisdiction, you should coordinate efforts to solve the problem.

9. B. To consider possible causes of failure without having specific information regarding the problem would lead to a very long list.

10. A, C, D, E. Any changes made should be included in the action plan and documentation. By doing that, you can make sure you hold to the requirements listed in the other answers.

11. B. The methods used to gather facts can also be used to plan how the changes will be implemented. You can implement changes on the far end first and work back, or you can start on your side and work your way out—implementing necessary changes as you go.

12. A, C, D. The iteration process actually allows you to shorten the time it would normally take to fix a problem if you were "shooting from the hip."

13. A, B, C, D, E, F. All answers depict valuable information that can or should be found in a network baseline.

14. B, C. The customer should not be told a solution has been implemented until it has been verified. Iteration is useless as well without observing the results of the changes first.

15. B, D. These are the best answers because they deal directly with aiding you in efficiently solving the problem.

16. A, B, C. All three of these methods require step-by-step execution.

17. D. These are all correct answers. When multiple changes are made, you can't be sure whether you caused any observed results or which of the changes solved the problem.

18. B, C, D. If you use A as part of the iteration process, you are doing something wrong and you need to go back to the very beginning and gather facts regarding the problem.

19. C. The most effective method of observing to see if anything changes after the action plan is implemented is to use the exact same tests that were used to gather facts and define the action plan.

20. B. A good troubleshooting method allows even people unfamiliar with the network architecture to efficiently troubleshoot network problems.

Protocol Attributes

TOPICS COVERED IN THIS CHAPTER INCLUDE:

✓ Becoming familiar with frame types and names of Layer 2, Layer 3, and Layer 4 protocols.

✓ Distinguishing between connectionless and connection-oriented protocols and what each type is.

✓ Learning troubleshooting methods and skills for Layer 2, Layer 3, and Layer 4 protocols.

✓ Learning separate troubleshooting methods and skills for connectionless protocols and for connection-oriented protocols.

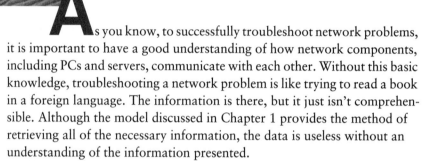

As you know, to successfully troubleshoot network problems, it is important to have a good understanding of how network components, including PCs and servers, communicate with each other. Without this basic knowledge, troubleshooting a network problem is like trying to read a book in a foreign language. The information is there, but it just isn't comprehensible. Although the model discussed in Chapter 1 provides the method of retrieving all of the necessary information, the data is useless without an understanding of the information presented.

This chapter is a review of the protocols that are used by Layers 2, 3, and 4 of the OSI model. We briefly review the seven layers of the OSI model, and then discuss how they communicate with one another. We then discuss Layer 2 and Layer 3 protocols.

The OSI Reference Model

This section is a review of the OSI model, which was originally discussed in *CCNA: Cisco Certified Network Associate Study Guide,* 2nd ed., by Todd Lammle (ISBN 0-7821-2647-2, Sybex, 2000). The OSI model (or the Open Systems Interconnection reference model) is the template used to design applications or protocols that allow non-homogenous computers or networks to communicate with one another. The ISO (International Organization for Standardization) developed the OSI model.

The OSI model consists of seven layers. Each layer communicates directly with its adjacent layers, as well as with the corresponding layer of the destination system (depicted in Figure 2.1). Communication between layers facilitates the transfer of data up and down the OSI model. Communication between the corresponding layers of the source system and the destination system enables two heterogeneous networks or computers to understand each other.

FIGURE 2.1 OSI layer communication scheme

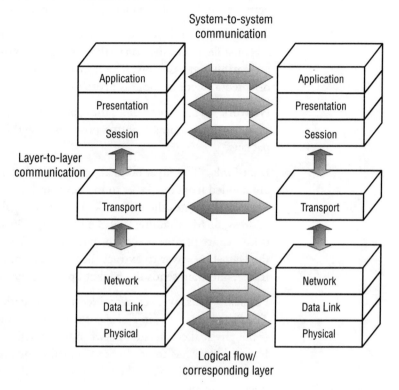

The OSI template defines the services and roles that each layer is to provide. Because each layer provides different services and functions, the layers need to communicate so that the data can be transmitted up and down the seven layers and onto the destination system. The following list summarizes the responsibility of each of the seven layers, starting from the Application layer and working down to the Physical layer:

Application   This is the user and application interface. The Application layer is responsible for data exchange and job management. It also handles file, print, message, database, and application services.

Presentation   This layer negotiates syntax, so it is responsible for the proper method of presenting the data to the Application layer. Some of the functions are compression and decompression, and encryption and decryption of data.

Session   This layer is responsible for coordinating communication between applications, which it does through dialog-control methods.

Transport   This layer takes care of end-to-end communications. It is responsible for connection to the destination system, as well as packet segmentation and assembly. The transport layer includes both connection-oriented and connectioness protocols (for example, TCP and UDP).

Network   This layer defines the topology of the network through the use of logical addressing. Routing protocols use this information to route packets.

Data-Link   This layer takes all of the data that is accumulated as packets are handed from one layer to the next, and then packages it into frames. This layer equates the Network layer address (IP address) to a data-link address, or MAC address, of the next hop. Once the physical address is known, the frame is sent to that address. The receiving interface uses the Data-Link layer to extract the packet from the frame, discards the frame, and then sends the packet up to the Network layer.

Physical   This layer sends and receives bits with values of ones or zeroes. The Physical layer is in charge of determining how it sends these values. If the physical connection between two machines is fiber optic, then the Physical layer has to use light to transmit the ones and zeroes. If the connection is electrical, then electrical signals are sent to represent the ones and zeros.

You saw how the logical data flow of the OSI model works, but look at Figure 2.2, in which you can see the actual data flow. The figure depicts data that is handed from the Application layer all the way down to the Physical layer. At that point, the data is transmitted across any variety of physical media to the next hop, or destination system. Once the ones and zeroes arrive at the Physical layer of the destination system, the information is sent to Layer 2. This layer discards the frame, and then the extracted packet is handed up to the Network layer. The network packet header is stripped off, and the resulting packet is handed up to the Transport layer. This process is repeated for each layer until it arrives at the Application layer.

FIGURE 2.2 Data flow through the OSI model

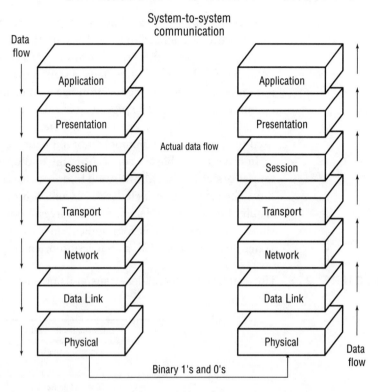

Now that each layer of the OSI reference model has been explained briefly, you need to focus on the functions of each layer in detail. This detail provides the necessary background and information to effectively troubleshoot network problems that occur within specific layers of the OSI model.

Global Protocol Classifications

As mentioned before, each level of the OSI model utilizes specific protocols that enable the layer to perform the necessary functions and communicate with each adjacent layer. Each protocol has different properties, based on the functions that it needs to accomplish. Throughout all seven layers, there are two major protocol classifications: connection-oriented and connectionless.

Connection-Oriented Protocols

Connection-oriented protocols are protocols that contain inherent functions that control the connection as well as data transfer. These functions are very detailed in the procedures that are followed to enable reliable and error-free data transfer. When a source open system needs to transfer data to a destination open system, the connection-oriented protocols actually establish a communication pipe. The *pipe*, as it is called here, is nothing more than a logical connection between two open systems. A great deal of information is used to establish this communication pipe, however.

In order to establish a connection, the two open systems must share certain information that allows them to negotiate terms and finally establish a link. The information includes the common protocol that will be used, required resources, and available resources. Look at Figure 2.3. This figure shows the steps taken as communication is established between two open systems when using TCP, a connection-oriented protocol.

FIGURE 2.3 Link establishment and data transfer using a connection-oriented protocol

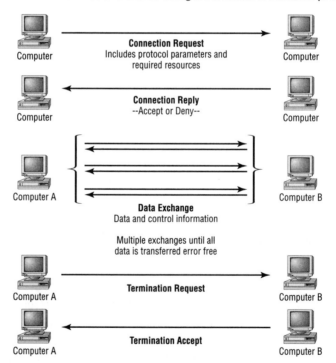

The originating system first sends a connection request to the destination system. This request contains information that the two systems need to agree upon before the connection can be established. Some of the information includes the common protocol, protocol parameters, and required resources. *Protocol parameters* are the window sizes and other possible parameters. The *window size* is the amount of data that a station can transmit before needing an acknowledgment from the destination system that all the data was received without error, or that errors existed and part of the data will need to be retransmitted. *Required resources* can include necessary bandwidth, specific port numbers, or other network resources.

The destination system receives this request; if it can accommodate the common protocol, protocol attributes, and required resources, it replies with a connection accept. If, for some reason, the destination system cannot accommodate any of the requirements sent by the originating system, it responds with a connection deny. A denied connection may result from a blocked port on the destination system, insufficient bandwidth between the systems, or other unavailable requested resources.

Assuming that a connection is established between the two systems, data and control information are exchanged during the life of the connection. This data exchange can be considered as a dialogue. First, the originating system sends data until the window size is reached. It then waits for a response from the destination system. The destination system sends control information that informs the originating system what needs to happen next. The transmission can be an acknowledgment that all data in the transmission was received without error and that the originating system can send the next batch of data. In addition, the destination system can also send a message informing the originating system that some of the data was missing, corrupted, or had other errors that require the data to be retransmitted.

This procedure can be summarized with the description of three processes:

Sequenced data transfer   Each packet of a session is assigned a sequence number

Flow control   Acknowledgments are required after a specified amount of data has been sent.

Error control   Verification of contiguous and non-erroneous packets.

You will learn more about each of these three processes in the following sections.

Sequenced Data Transfer

Systems send protocol data units (PDUs) to one another, and each level of the OSI model has its own type of PDU. Figure 2.4 shows the PDU names for all seven OSI layers. For example, the Application layer's PDU name is a Layer 7 PDU. Although this convention can be used for all layers, some layers use other names as well. For instance, a Layer 3 PDU can be called a *packet* and a Layer 2 PDU is called a *frame*. When a system sends data to another system, the data has to be segmented so that it fits the MTU (maximum transmission unit). Therefore, several frames may be needed to transfer the original data. Connection-oriented protocols assign a sequence number to each outgoing and incoming PDU.

FIGURE 2.4 OSI layer PDU names

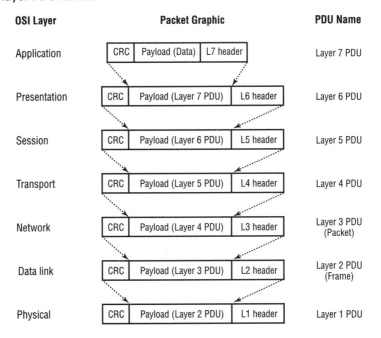

OSI Layer	Packet Graphic	PDU Name
Application	CRC | Payload (Data) | L7 header	Layer 7 PDU
Presentation	CRC | Payload (Layer 7 PDU) | L6 header	Layer 6 PDU
Session	CRC | Payload (Layer 6 PDU) | L5 header	Layer 5 PDU
Transport	CRC | Payload (Layer 5 PDU) | L4 header	Layer 4 PDU
Network	CRC | Payload (Layer 4 PDU) | L3 header	Layer 3 PDU (Packet)
Data link	CRC | Payload (Layer 3 PDU) | L2 header	Layer 2 PDU (Frame)
Physical	CRC | Payload (Layer 2 PDU) | L1 header	Layer 1 PDU

Figure 2.5 shows you how sequencing works. There is a possibility that the destination system will receive the PDUs out of order. If this happens, the protocol on the destination system uses the sequence numbers to put the PDUs back into the correct order so the original data is obtained.

FIGURE 2.5 Connection-oriented PDU sequencing

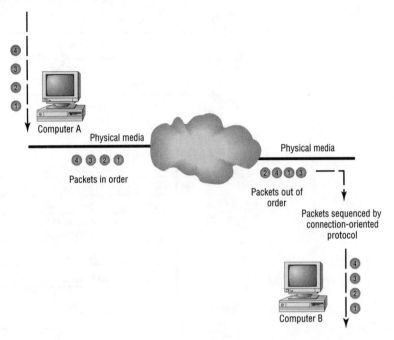

Flow Control

Although flow control was briefly described previously, this section contains more detail. Flow control is responsible for assuring that the transmitting station does not send data faster than the receiving station can process it. This is done by establishing a window size for the transportation.

Look at Figure 2.6 to see how windowing works. Notice that the originating system sends out a specified number of PDUs. Once that number is reached, the originating system waits for a response from the destination system. After the response is received, the system continues to transmit data.

FIGURE 2.6 Flow and error control

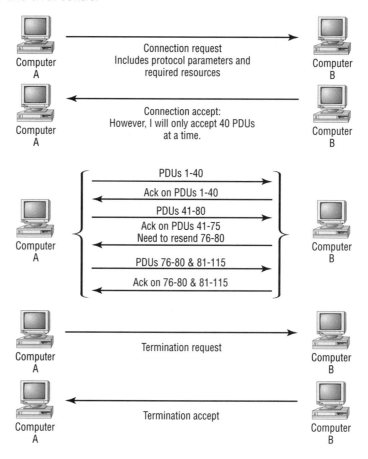

Error Control

Error control is responsible for checking each transmission and verifying that all of the PDUs are contiguous and not erroneous. If there are missing or damaged PDUs, the destination will not send an ACK packet for the previous transmission. (Refer to Figure 2.6).

Once all of the data is transferred without errors, the originating system sends a termination request, which tells the destination system that no more data needs to be transmitted. The destination system then responds with a termination acknowledgment.

As you can see, both systems do a lot of communicating, aside from the exchange of data. From the connection request to the termination acknowledgment, every exchange is accompanied with control information that keeps the data transfer reliable and error-free. Table 2.1 gives examples of several connection-oriented protocols.

TABLE 2.1 Connection-Oriented Protocols

Protocol Name	Protocol Description
ATM	ATM (Asynchronous Transfer Mode) uses virtual circuits from one node to another. The permanent virtual circuits, or PVCs, are established by using connection-oriented procedures.
TCP	TCP (Transmission Control Protocol) was developed to overcome reliability problems. It uses flow and error control extensively.
Novell SPX	Novell SPX (Sequenced Packet Exchange) is Novell's implementation of a network protocol that provides error-free and reliable data transport.
AppleTalk ATP	Apple uses ATP (AppleTalk Transaction Protocol) to provide connectivity between two socket clients. It is based on the request/response interaction of the two clients.

Connectionless Protocols

Now that connection-oriented protocols have been discussed, we'll move on to connectionless protocols. *Connectionless protocols* differ from connection-oriented protocols because they do not provide for flow control.

Figure 2.7 shows you how connectionless protocols work. This figure looks somewhat like Figure 2.3, except that there are no steps that involve a connection setup or termination. It is also missing the flow and error control information sent by the receiving system.

FIGURE 2.7 Connectionless data transfer

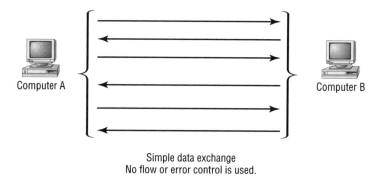

Simple data exchange
No flow or error control is used.

Connectionless protocols do not send data relative to any other data units. The data included in the PDU must contain enough information for the PDU to get to its destination and for the receiving system to properly process it. Because there is no established connection, flow and error control cannot be implemented. Without flow and error control, the originating system has no way of knowing whether all of the transmitted data was received by the destination system without errors. Table 2.2 shows examples of connectionless protocols.

TABLE 2.2 Connectionless Protocols

Protocol Name	Protocol Description
UDP	UDP (User Datagram Protocol) is a connectionless protocol used by IP.
AppleTalk DDP	DDP (Datagram Delivery Protocol) is a connectionless network protocol used for service between two network sockets.
Novell IPX	Novell IPX (Internetwork Packet Exchange) is Novell's Layer 3 protocol.

In this section, you learned the difference between connection-oriented and connectionless protocols. These protocol characteristics may be found at any level of the OSI model. The Transport layer, or Layer 4, of the OSI model is most notably known for the functions it provides by using connection-oriented or connectionless protocols. Some of the Transport layer's responsibilities are session establishment, flow and error control, and session teardown. The following sections begin discussions of protocols that are specific to the Network and Data-Link layers, respectively.

OSI Layer 3: Routed and Routing Protocols

The Network layer is used by the Transport layer to provide the best end-to-end services and path for PDU delivery. This means that the Network layer also uses protocols to accomplish this task. This section discusses seven different protocols that are used within Layer 3 of the OSI model. Some of these protocols use protocols within them for finer granularity of certain functions.

There are also some other differences between these seven protocols. Some are routing protocols and others are protocols that are routed by the routing protocols. Routing protocols are used to exchange route information and to create a network topology, thus enabling routing decisions to be made. The routed protocols are protocols that contain information regarding the end systems, how communication is established, and other information relevant to the transfer of data.

Internet Protocol (IP)

It is important to distinguish between the Internet Protocol suite and the actual Internet Protocol that is used in the Network layer of the OSI model. The IP suite consists of several different protocols that are implemented at different levels of the OSI model.

The Internet Protocol (IP) is a Network-layer protocol of the Internet Protocol suite. It is used to allow routing among internetworks and heterogeneous systems. IP is a connectionless protocol, even though it can provide error reporting, and performs the segmentation and reassembly of PDUs.

IP Packet Structure

Now that you know what IP is, look at the actual packet structure in more detail. Following is an IP packet that was broken down by EtherPeek. The entire header has six layers, and each layer consists of 32 bits. Look at each section of the header and get an explanation for each.

```
IP Header - Internet Protocol Datagram
    Version:                4
    Header Length:          5
    Precedence:             0
    Type of Service:        %000
    Unused:                 %00
    Total Length:           60
    Identifier:             0
    Fragmentation Flags:    %000
    Fragment Offset:        0
    Time To Live:           2
    IP Type:                0x58   IGRP
    Header Checksum:        0x10dc
    Source IP Address:      205.124.250.7
    Dest. IP Address:       224.0.0.10
No Internet Datagram Options
```

At this point, we will define each of the key fields that appear above. As you can see, the packet IP header starts out with the Version field. Right now, the standard is IPv4. The version parameter uses four bits of the 32 bits available.

The next field is the IP Header Length, or IHL. This field also uses another four bits and it specifies the datagram header length in 32-bit words.

The Type of Service (TOS) follows the IHL. This field uses eight bits and indicates datagram priority and how other OSI layers are to handle the datagram once they receive it.

Following the TOS is the Total Length parameter. This field indicates how long the packet is, including header and payload or data. The length is in units of bytes. The field itself uses 16 bits, which brings the total for the first layer to 32 bits. Because 32 bits have been used, move on to the next layer.

The second layer begins with the Identifier or identification field. The Identifier is a 16-bit field that contains an integer value that identifies the packet. It is like a sequencing number that is used when reassembling datagram fragments.

The `Flags` field follows, using only three bits. This field is used to control fragmentation of a datagram. If the datagram may be fragmented, the first bit has a value of 0. A value of 1 is assigned to the first bit if the datagram is not to be fragmented. The second bit is used to indicate the last fragment of a fragmented datagram. The third bit is an undefined bit and is set to 0.

`Fragment Offset` follows the `Flags` field. This value uses 13 bits and specifies the fragments position in the original datagram. The position is measured from the beginning of the datagram and marked off in 64-bit increments. This again brings you to 32 bits, so you must move down to the next layer in the IP packet.

The third layer begins with the `Time-to-Live` (TTL) field. This field is a counter whose units are measured in hops. A starting value is given and it counts decrements by one as it passes through each hop or router. Once the value of this field is 0, the packet is discarded. This field uses eight bits.

The `protocol` field (IP Type) follows the TTL parameter. This field tells Layer 3 which upper-layer protocol is supposed to receive the packet. It uses a decimal value to specify the protocol. This field uses eight bits.

The `Header Checksum` field finishes the third layer. The checksum is used to help verify the integrity of the IP header. This field uses 16 bits.

Layers 4 and 5 are 32 bits long, Because IP addresses use four octets— eight bits each—the IP address occupies the entire level. Layer 4 is reserved for the source address, and the fifth layer is reserved for the destination address.

An `Options` field occupies the sixth and final layer of the header. The field needs to be 32 bits long so that any additional empty bits are padded.

Figure 2.8 gives a good visual representation of the IP packet structure.

FIGURE 2.8 The IP packet structure

0	4	8	16	19	31
Version	IHL	Type of service	Total length		
Identification			Flags	Fragment offset	
TTL		Protocol	Header checksum		
Source IP address					
Destination IP address					
Options				Padding	

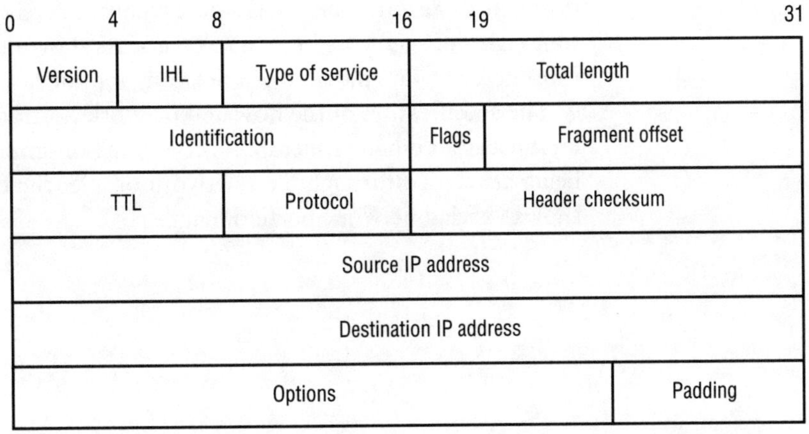

IP Addressing Review

IP addresses are composed of a network portion and a host portion. They can be compared to a two-part ZIP code, having a five-digit prefix and a four-digit suffix. The prefix directs the post office to a general destination—the city and state—and the suffix resolves to a street address or P.O. box. An IP address, with its network and node portions, works much the same way, as shown in Figure 2.9.

FIGURE 2.9 The makeup of an IP address

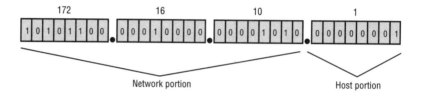

This section is intended as a review of IP addressing. If you need a more detailed explanation, see *CCNA: Cisco Certified Network Associate Study Guide*, 2nd ed., by Todd Lammle (ISBN 0-7821-2647-2, Sybex, 2000).

The network portion works just like the five-digit prefix of a ZIP code; the node, or host portion, is the unique identifier, which is similar to the four-digit suffix of a ZIP code. An IP address consists of 32 bits, broken down into four eight-bit segments known as *octets*. As shown in Figure 2.9, the first three octets define the network portion, and the last octet defines the host.

The specification of the host and network portions within an IP address establishes an inherent hierarchy, consisting of different network lengths being advertised throughout a network or over the Internet. Figure 2.10 shows varying network portion length.

FIGURE 2.10   Hierarchical IP address structure

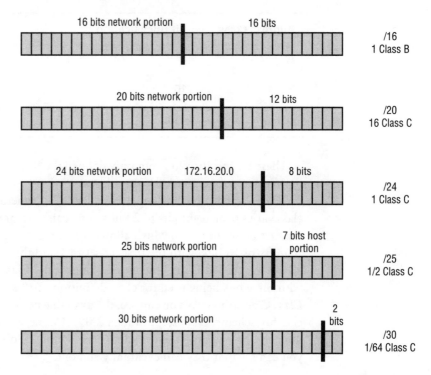

Longer network prefixes reside near the bottom of the network tree. The network length is depicted by a /24 or /25 suffixed to an IP address, which specifies the number of bits (beginning from the left) that define the network portion. In this figure, the address 172.16.20.0/24 is equivalent to a Class C address, however it is a Class B address with a /24 mask. You can tell that because the first 24 bits are used to define the network portion, leaving 256 host addresses available. The first 24 binary bits are equal to the first three octets in the dotted decimal format of an IP address.

In the beginning (referencing RFC 760), IP addresses weren't assigned classes. Instead, the network portion of the address was assigned to the first octet. This allowed for only 254 IP networks. To resolve this dilemma, RFC 791 was defined and written. This RFC converted a previously classless IP address structure into specific classes—five classes, to be exact. The three most common ones are Classes A, B, and C. Prefix lengths were defined as eight bits, 16 bits, and 24 bits, corresponding to Classes A, B, and C, respectively. The first three bits in the first octet were used to determine the IP address class. Table 2.3 shows how the classes were defined.

TABLE 2.3 RFC 791 IP Class Assignments

Address Class	Bit Specification
A	0
B	10
C	110

These bit specifications not only defined the IP class, but also predefined the shortest subnet mask for the address.

The assigned masks are depicted in Table 2.4, wherein the prefix for each class varies from eight bits to 24 bits. You can see a prefix of eight bits with the first bit set to 0 (2^7), which allows for 128 Class A networks. The Class B prefix of 16 bits, with the first bit set to 1 and the second set to 0 (2^{14}), allows for 16,384 Class B networks. Finally, the Class C prefix of 24 bits, with three bits being used for class definition (2^{21}), allows for 2,097,152 Class C networks. As you can see, the available network numbers, using the classfull scheme, is finite. Although 2,097,152 networks seems like a great number of networks, when you look at it within a global frame of reference, you can see that they can eventually run out.

TABLE 2.4 Classfull IP Subnet Mask Assignments

Address Class	Subnet Mask
A	255.0.0.0
B	255.255.0.0
C	255.255.255.0

Because this is just a review, we leave IP addressing at this point and move on to some of the other protocols that are used within the IP suite.

Internet Control Message Protocol (ICMP)

The *Internet Control Message Protocol (ICMP)* is used throughout IP networks. ICMP was designed to provide routing failure information to the source system. This protocol provides four different types of feedback that are used to make the IP routing environment more efficient. These feedback types are as follows:

Reachability   This is determined by using ICMP echo and reply messages.

Redirects   These messages tell hosts to redirect traffic or choose alternative routes.

Timeouts   These messages indicate that a packet's designated TTL is expired.

Router Discovery   These messages discover directly connected routers' IP addresses. Router discovery actually uses ICMP Router Discovery Protocol to do this. This passive method gathers directly connected IP addresses without having to understand specific routing protocols.

Here is a look at a couple of ICMP packets (echo request and reply):

```
ICMP - Internet Control Messages Protocol
  ICMP Type:              8  Echo Request
  Code:                   0
  Checksum:               0x495c
  Identifier:             0x0200
  Sequence Number:        512
  ICMP Data Area:
    abcdefghijklmnop      61 62 63 64 65 66 67 68 69 6a 6b 6c
6d 6e 6f 70
    qrstuvwabcdefghi      71 72 73 74 75 76 77 61 62 63 64 65
66 67 68 69
Frame Check Sequence:  0x342e3235
ICMP - Internet Control Messages Protocol
  ICMP Type:              0  Echo Reply
  Code:                   0
  Checksum:               0x515c
  Identifier:             0x0200
```

```
Sequence Number:        512
ICMP Data Area:
abcdefghijklmnop    61 62 63 64 65 66 67 68 69 6a 6b 6c
6d 6e 6f 70
qrstuvwabcdefghi    71 72 73 74 75 76 77 61 62 63 64 65
66 67 68 69
Frame Check Sequence:  0x342e3235
```

As with the IP packet structure, the ICMP structure is similar in that it has a type, checksum, identifier, and sequence number. The names differ a little, but have the same functionality.

Transport Control Protocol (TCP)

The *Transport Control Protocol (TCP),* a connection-oriented protocol on the Transport layer that provides a reliable delivery of data, is an integral part of the IP suite. Look at the structure of the TCP packet. The following EtherPeek frame was taken during a POP3 transaction:

```
TCP - Transport Control Protocol
  Source Port:        110   POP3
  Destination Port: 1097
  Sequence Number:  997270908
  Ack Number:       7149472
  Offset:           5
  Reserved:         %000000
  Code:             %010000
            Ack is valid
  Window:           8760
  Checksum:         0x8064
  Urgent Pointer:   0
  No TCP Options
  No More POP Command or Reply Data
Extra bytes (Padding):
  UUUUUU            55 55 55 55 55 55
  Frame Check Sequence:  0x04020000
```

This structure is similar to the IP packet structure. The TCP header is 32 bits long and has a minimum length of five layers, but can be six layers deep when options are specified. The first layer starts with `Source` and `Destination Port` fields. Each of these fields is 16 bits long.

A `Sequence Number` field occupies all of the second layer, meaning that it is 32 bits long. TCP is a connection-oriented protocol and this field is used to keep track of the different requests that have been sent.

The third layer is a 32-bit length field that contains the acknowledgment sequence number that is used to track responses.

The fourth layer begins with the `Offset` field, which is four bits and specifies the number of 32-bit words present in the header. Six bits are reserved for future use (this is called the `Reserved` field). This field follows the `Offset` field.

The next field, called the `Flag` or `Code` field, is also a six-bit field, and it contains control information. Look at Table 2.5 for an explanation of the six bits within the Flag field.

The `Window` field specifies the buffer size for incoming data. Once the buffer is filled, the sending system must wait for a response from the receiving system. This field is 16 bits long.

Layer five of the TCP header begins with the `Checksum` Parameter, which also occupies 16 bits. It is used to verify the integrity of the transmitted data.

The `Urgent Pointer` field references the last byte of data, so the receiver knows how much urgent data it will receive. This is also a 16-bit field.

Finally, there is the `Option` field, which must also be 32 bits long. If the options do not occupy 32 bits, padding is added to reach the correct length.

TABLE 2.5 Flag Bit Assignments

Bit number (right to left)	Control Information	Definition
1	URG	Urgent pointer is significant
2	ACK	Acknowledgment pointer is significant
3	PSH	Push function
4	RST	Reset connection
5	SYN	Synchronize sequence numbers
6	FIN	No more data to transfer

This finishes our discussion on some of the protocols present in the IP suite. We now move on to the routing protocol RIP.

Routing Information Protocol (RIP)

The Routing Information Protocol (RIP) is a distance-vector routing protocol. The metrics used by RIP is the *hop count*, which specifies the number of steps or nodes that a packet must transit in order to reach the destination host.

The major problem with RIP is that it has a hop-count limit. The maximum hop limit that the packet can travel is 15 hops. If the destination exceeds 15 hops, the destination is tagged as unreachable. This is good for small networks because it also helps prevent the count-to-infinity in a routing loop, but it is inefficient for today's Internet.

Now that you know a little about how RIP works, look at the packet structure in Figure 2.11. The packet is 24 bytes long. RIP uses five parameters to define packet information. The packet is divided into nine fields, and zeroes are used to pad the packet to the full 24 bytes.

FIGURE 2.11 RIP packet structure

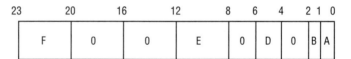

Table 2.6 shows a legend of the five different parameters used within the RIP packet. As you can see from the figure, some of the fields are empty. They are just padded with zeroes.

TABLE 2.6 RIP Parameters

Parameter Key	Description
A	Command: Identifies the packet as a request (value=1) or a response (value=2). Requests tell the receiving router to send its route table information. Response packets include the route table information.

TABLE 2.6 RIP Parameters *(continued)*

Parameter Key	Description
B	`Version number`: Specifies the version of RIP being used.
D	`Address family identifier`: Address family type. This means which protocol is carrying the RIP packet.
E	`Address`: The 32-bit IP address.
F	`Metric`: The hop count to the destination system.

Interior Gateway Routing Protocol (IGRP)

The *Interior Gateway Routing Protocol (IGRP)* is a Cisco proprietary routing protocol that uses a distance-vector algorithm because it uses a vector (a one-dimensional array) of information to calculate the best path. This vector consists of four elements:

- Bandwidth
- Delay
- Load
- Reliability

MTU, or maximum transmission unit, information is included in the final route information, but it is not used as part of the vector of values when calculating the metric. IGRP is intended to replace RIP and create a stable, quickly converging protocol that will scale with increased network growth.

IGRP Features and Operation

IGRP has several features included in the algorithm—these features and brief descriptions can be found in Table 2.7. The features were added to make IGRP more stable, and a few were created to deal with routing updates and make network convergence happen faster.

TABLE 2.7 IGRP Features

Feature	Description
Configurable metrics	Metrics involved in the algorithm responsible for calculating route information. They may be configured by the user.
Flash update	Updates are sent out prior to the default time setting. This occurs when the metrics for a route change.
Poison reverse updates	Implemented to prevent routing loops. These updates place a route in *holddown.* Holddown means that the router won't accept any new route information on a given route for a certain period.
Unequal-cost load balancing	Allows packets to be shared/distributed across multiple paths.

IGRP is a classfull protocol, which means it doesn't include any subnet information about the network with route information. Three types of routes are recognized by IGRP:

Interior   Networks directly connected to a router interface.

System   Routes advertised by other IGRP neighbors within the same AS (autonomous system). The AS number identifies the IGRP session because it's possible for a router to have multiple IGRP sessions.

Exterior   Routes learned via IGRP from a different AS number, which provide information used by the router to set the *gateway of last resort.* The gateway of last resort is the path that a packet takes if a specific route isn't found on the router.

Figure 2.12 gives an example of the different route types used by IGRP. In addition to route types, IGRP can store multiple routes to the same destination by using the topology table.

FIGURE 2.12   Route types recognized by IGRP

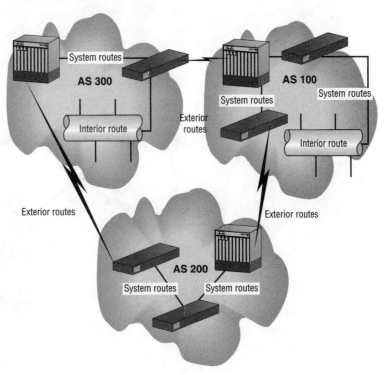

Routing Stability

Three methods are used to help stabilize the routing environment:

- Holddown timers
- Split horizon
- Poison reverse updates

Holddown timers prevent an invalid route from being injected back into the route table. The timers allow routing updates to be communicated throughout the network, thus avoiding advertisement of the invalid route while the new valid route is being propagated.

With *split horizon*, route information learned from a given interface isn't sent back out the same interface. Using Figure 2.13 as a reference, we'll explain split horizon updates.

FIGURE 2.13   Poison reverse and holddown

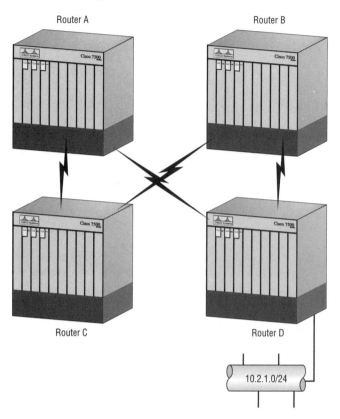

Router D advertises network 10.2.1.0/24 to Routers A and B. After Router B receives the update and recalculates its own route table, a broadcast update is sent. Specific route information learned from Router D isn't advertised back to Router D, however.

Poison reverse updates use the holddown function within IGRP, which stops the router from being confused about multiple routes to a given network. When a route's associated metric increases by a factor of 1.1, IGRP sends out a poison reverse update that removes the affected route from a router's route table and places it in holddown.

Enhanced IGRP (EIGRP)

Enhanced IGRP (EIGRP) is a hybrid link-state and distance-vector routing protocol that was created to resolve some of the problems with IGRP. Problems include the fact that the entire route table is sent when changes are made in the network and that there is a lack of formal neighbor relationships with connected routers. EIGRP is a hybrid of both link-state and distance-vector routing algorithms, which brings the best of both worlds together.

EIGRP allows for equal-cost load balancing, incremental routing updates, and formal neighbor relationships, all of which overcome the limitations of IGRP. This enhanced version uses the same distance-vector information as IGRP, yet with a different algorithm. EIGRP uses DUAL (Diffusing-Update Algorithm) for metric calculation.

EIGRP's specific features are detailed in Table 2.8. The features offered by EIGRP make it a stable and scalable protocol. Just as IGRP is a Cisco proprietary protocol, so is EIGRP.

TABLE 2.8 EIGRP Features

Feature	Description
Route tagging	Distinguishes routes learned via different EIGRP sessions.
Formal neighbor relationships	Uses the Hello protocol to establish peering.
Incremental routing updates	Only changes are advertised, instead of the entire route table.
Classless routing	EIGRP supports subnet and VLSM information.
Configurable metrics	Metric information can be set through configuration commands.
Equal-cost load balancing	Allows traffic to be sent equally across multiple connections.

To aid in calculating the best route and load sharing, EIGRP utilizes several databases of information. These databases are as follows:

- The route database, where the best routes are stored

- The topology database, where all route information resides

- A neighbor table, which is used to house information concerning other EIGRP neighbors

Each of these databases exists for IP-EIGRP, IPX-EIGRP, and AT-EIGRP or AppleTalk-EIGRP. Therefore, it is possible for EIGRP to have nine active databases when all three protocols are configured on the router.

Route Tagging

EIGRP functions within defined autonomous systems on a router. It is possible for multiple sessions of EIGRP to run on a single router. Each session is distinguished by the AS number assigned to it. Routers that have Enhanced IGRP sessions running under the same AS number speak to and share their routing information with the other routers in the same AS. Routes learned via other routers within the AS are considered to be internal EIGRP routes. It is also possible for one AS session to learn routes from a different EIGRP AS session through redistribution (redistribution is covered later in this section). When this occurs, the routes are tagged as being learned from an external EIGRP session. Each type of route is assigned its own administrative distance value.

Neighbor Relationships

The manner in which EIGRP establishes and maintains neighbor relationships is derived through its link-state properties. EIGRP uses the Hello protocol (similar to OSPF) to establish and maintain peering relationships with directly connected routers. Hello packets are sent between EIGRP routers to determine the state of the connection between them. Once the neighbor relation is established via the Hello protocol, the routers can exchange route information.

Each router establishes a neighbor table, in which it stores important information regarding the neighbors that are directly connected to it. The information consists of the neighbor's IP address, hold time interval, smooth round trip timer (SRTT), and queue information. These data are used to help determine when the link state changes.

When two routers initialize communication, their entire route tables are shared. Thereafter, only changes to the route table are propagated. These changes are shared with all directly connected EIGRP-speaking routers. The steps are summarized as follows:

1. Hello packets are multicast out of all of the router's interfaces.

2. Replies to the Hello packets include all routes in the neighbor router's topology database, including the metrics. Routes that are learned from the originating router are not included in the reply.

3. The originating router acknowledges the update to each neighbor via an ACK packet.

4. The topology database is then updated with the newly received information.

5. Once the topology database is updated, the originating router then advertises its entire table to all the new neighbors.

6. Neighbor routers acknowledge the receipt of the route information from the originating router by sending back an ACK packet.

These steps are used in the initialization of EIGRP neighbors; they change somewhat when only updates are sent to existing neighbors.

Route Calculation and Updates

Because EIGRP uses distance-vector and link-state information when calculating routes by using the DUAL algorithm, convergence is much faster than with IGRP. The trick behind the convergence speed is that EIGRP calculates new routes only when a change in the network directly affects the routes contained in its route table. To make that a little clearer, look at Figure 2.14, in which you see three routers meshed, and each has an Ethernet segment connected as well.

It is important to understand the difference between accepting a routing update and calculating a new route. If a change occurs to a network that is directly connected to a router, all of the relevant information is used to *calculate* a new metric and route entry for it. After the router calculates the new route, it is advertised to the neighbors.

Using Figure 2.14 as the example, assume that Ethernet 0 on Router C is very congested because of high traffic volumes. Router C then uses the distance and link information to calculate a new metric for network 172.16.30.0. With the new metric in place, the change is propagated to Routers A and B. To understand completely, you need to recognize that the other routers don't do any calculation—they just receive the update. Routers A and B don't need to calculate a new route for network 172.16.30.0 because they learn it from Router C.

FIGURE 2.14 Route updates vs. calculation

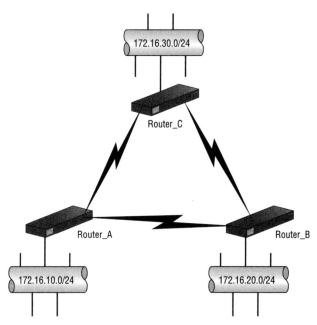

On the other hand, if the link between Router A and Router C becomes congested, both routers have to calculate a new route metric. The change is then advertised to Router B by both Routers A and C.

Topology and Route State Information

The topology database stores all routes and metrics known via adjacent routers. Six routes can be stored for each destination network. From these six routes, the router must select a primary and backup route; the primary route will be added to the route table. While the best route is being chosen for a destination, the route is considered to be in an *active* state. After the route is chosen, the route status changes to *passive*.

Information given in Table 2.9 closely, though not exactly, represents what is contained in an actual topology table. The Status field shows whether a new route is being calculated or whether a primary route has been selected. In our example, the route is in passive state because it has already selected the primary route.

TABLE 2.9 Topology Table Information

Status	Route—Adjacent Router's Address (Metrics)	Number of Successors	Feasible Distance
P	10.10.10.0/24via 10.1.2.6 (*3611648*/3609600)via 10.5.6.6 (4121600/3609600)via 10.6.7.6 (5031234/3609600)	1 (Router C)	3611648

The route with the best metric (lower is better) is chosen as the primary route. The backup route is chosen by selecting the route with the second-lowest metric. Primary routes are moved to the route table after selection. It is possible to have more than one primary route.

 EIGRP uses the same vector information as IGRP: bandwidth, delay, reliability, load, and MTU. Bandwidth and delay are the two metrics used by default; the others can be configured manually. Configuring reliability, load, and MTU can cause the topology table to be calculated more often.

Updates and Changes

EIGRP also has link-state properties. One of these properties is that it propagates only changes in the route table instead of sending an entire new route table to its neighbors. When changes occur in the network, a regular distance-vector protocol sends the entire route table to neighbors. By avoiding sending the entire route table, less bandwidth is consumed. Neighboring routers don't have to reinitialize the entire route table, which would cause convergence issues. They just have to insert the new route changes. This is one of the big enhancements over IGRP.

Updates can follow two paths. If a route update contains a better metric or a new route, the routers simply exchange the information. If the update contains information that a network is unavailable or the metric is worse than before, an alternate path must be found. The flow chart in Figure 2.15 describes the steps that must be taken to choose a new route.

FIGURE 2.15 Handling route changes

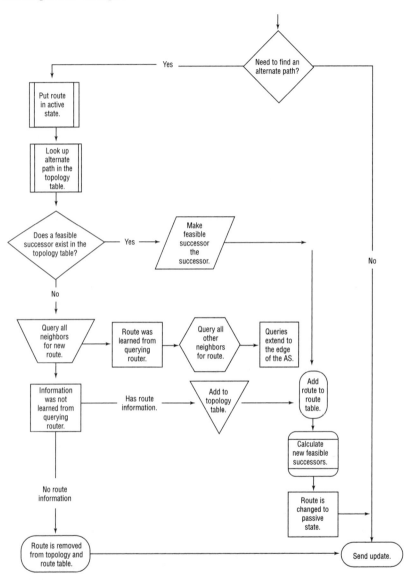

The router first searches the topology database for feasible successors. If no feasible successors are found, a multicast request is sent to all adjacent routers. Each router then responds to the query. Depending on how the router answers, different paths are taken. After the intermediate steps are taken, two final actions can occur. If route information is eventually found, the route is added to the route table and an update is sent. If the responses from the adjacent routers do not contain any route information, the route is removed from the topology and route tables. After the route table is updated, the new information is sent to all adjacent routers via a multicast.

Open Shortest Path First (OSPF)

Open Shortest Path First (OSPF) is a link-state routing protocol. OSPF differs from IGRP and Enhanced IGRP because it is a pure link-state routing technology. It is an open standard routing protocol, which means that it was not developed solely by Cisco. OSPF was designed and developed by the Internet Engineering Task Force (IETF) to provide a scalable, quickly converging, and efficient routing protocol that could be used by all routing equipment. Complete details for OSPF are found in RFC2328.

OSPF is an enhancement over RIP that provides a scalable routing solution. It supports several features that RIP does not—for example, VLSM and route summarization are supported.

The hop count was eliminated with OSPF, thus giving it limitless reachability. RIP was limited to 16 hops. Because of the algorithm used to calculate and advertise routes, network convergence is fast with OSPF. OSPF is like EIGRP because it sends route updates only when changes occur in the network. A formal neighbor relationship is established with all adjacent OSPF routers.

Areas are used within OSPF to define a group of routers and networks belonging to the same OSPF session. Links connect routers, and the information about each link is defined by its link state. On each broadcast or multi-access network segment, two routers must be assigned the responsibilities of designated router (DR) and backup designated router (BDR).

Like EIGRP, OSPF maintains three databases: adjacency, topology, and route. The adjacency database is similar to the neighbor database used by EIGRP. It contains all information about OSPF neighbors and the links connecting them. The topology database maintains all route information. The best routes from the topology database are placed in the route database or route table.

Initializing OSPF

The Hello protocol is used to establish peering sessions between routers. Hello packets are multicast out every interface. The information that is multicast includes the router ID, timing intervals, existing neighbors, area identification, router priority, designated and backup router information, authentication password, and stub area information. All this information is used when establishing new peers. Descriptions of each element can be found in Table 2.10.

TABLE 2.10 OSPF Multicast Information

Information	Description
Router ID	This is the highest active IP address on the router.
Time intervals	Contains intervals between Hello packets and the dead time interval.
Existing neighbors	Contains addresses for any existing OSPF neighbors.
Area identification	OSPF area number and link information must be the same for a peering session to be established.
Router priority	This value is used when choosing the DR and BDR.
DR and BDR	If they have already been chosen, their information is contained in the Hello packet.
Authentication password	All peers within the same area must have the same authentication password if authentication is enabled.
Stub area flag	This is a special area—two routers must share the same stub information. This is not necessary to initiate a regular peering session with another OSPF router.

Figure 2.16 displays a flow chart that depicts each step of the initialization process. The process starts by sending out Hello packets. Every listening router then adds the originating router to the adjacency database. The responding routers reply with all of their Hello information so that the originating router can add them to its adjacency table.

Once adjacencies are established, the DR and BDR need to be chosen before route information and link-state information can be exchanged. After the DR and BDR are chosen, route information is exchanged, and the OSPF peers continue to multicast Hello packets every 10 seconds to determine whether neighbors are still reachable.

FIGURE 2.16   OSPF peer initialization

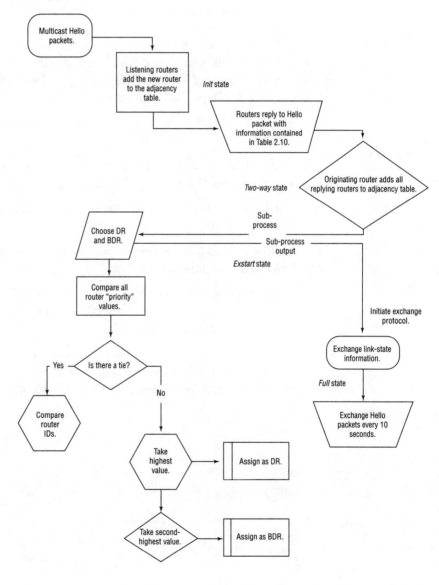

Before we go any further with peer initialization, we need to discuss several terms that are specific to OSPF. These terms are key to understanding OSPF and how it functions.

The easiest way to understand OSPF is to build from what you already know about EIGRP. You learned that EIGRP uses autonomous system numbers to specify routing processes and the routing process that individual routers belong to. OSPF uses areas in place of an autonomous system. An OSPF area consists of a group of routers or interfaces on a router that is assigned to a common area.

OSPF also allows and uses different area types. When deploying OSPF, there must be a backbone area. Standard and stub areas connect to the backbone area. Following is a list of each area type, followed by a short description of that area type:

Backbone This area accepts all link-state advertisements (LSAs) and is used to connect multiple areas.

Stub This area does not accept any external routing update, but it will accept summary LSAs.

Totally Stub These areas are closed off from accepting external or summary advertisements.

Standard This is the normal area that accepts internal and external LSAs, and summary information.

Not So Stubby This type of area is similar to Stub areas except that Type 5 LSAs are not flooded into the area from the core. It can import external AS routes into the area.

Move on now to learn the different types of link-state advertisements. LSAs are the heart of OSPF's information exchange. Different types of LSAs represent different types of route information. All of the defined and used LSA types are summarized in Table 2.11.

TABLE 2.11   OSPF LSA Types

LSA Type	Description of LSA
(1) Router link entry	This LSA is broadcast only within its defined area. The LSA contains all of the default link-state information.
(2) Network entry	This LSA is multicast to all area routers by the DR. This update contains network-specific information.
(3/4) Summary entry	Type 3 LSAs contain route information for internal networks and are sent to backbone routers. Type 4 LSAs contain information about Autonomous System Border Routers (ASBRs). Summary information is multicast by the Area Border Router (ABR) and the information reaches all backbone routers.
(5) Autonomous System entry	As the name indicates, these advertisements originate from the ASBR. These packets contain information about external networks.
(7) Not So Stubby Area	Not So Stubby Area (NSSA) permits Type 7 AS external routes to be imported inside the NSSA area by redistribution.

Different LSA types represent the type of route that is being advertised, and assist in restricting the number and type of routes that are accepted by a given area. As is shown in the table, an LSA of Type 5 is sent only by the Autonomous System Border Router. This brings you to the point where you need to define the different router types that belong to OSPF areas.

Multiple router types can exist within an OSPF area. Table 2.12 lists all of the OSPF router types and the role that each plays within the area.

TABLE 2.12 OSPF Router Types

Router Type	Description of Responsibility
Internal	All interfaces are defined on the same area. All internal routers have an identical link-state database.
Backbone	This type of router has at least one interface assigned to area 0.
Area Border Router (ABR)	Interfaces are connected to multiple OSPF areas. Information specific to each area is stored on this type of router.
Autonomous System Border Router (ASBR)	This type of router has an interface connected to an external network or a different AS.

In addition to the above-listed responsibilities, a router can also be assigned additional responsibilities. These additions are assumed when a router is assigned the role of DR or BDR.

OSPF Packet Structure

Finally, look at the packet structure. It is important to realize that all OSPF packets begin with the same 24-byte header. Different information can be appended, depending on the type of OSPF packet, but all share the same first 24 bytes. Figure 2.17 gives a visual of the OSPF packet header.

FIGURE 2.17 OSPF packet header structure

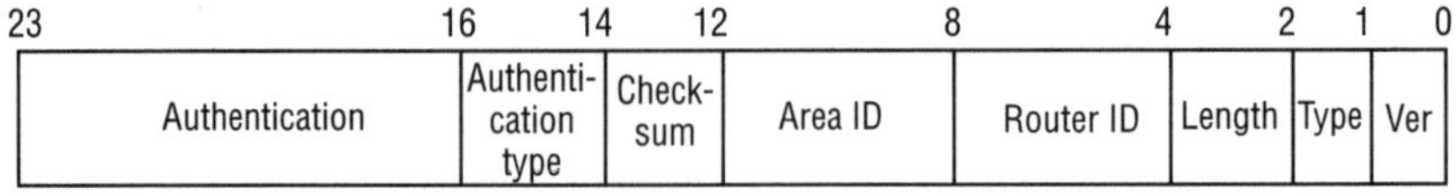

23	16	14	12	8	4	2	1	0
Authentication		Authentication type	Checksum	Area ID	Router ID	Length	Type	Ver

As you can see, the 24-byte header was divided into eight segments. Each field contains specific information. Starting from the right and working left, you see that the first field is for the version number. This field is one byte long and contains the OSPF version number.

Moving on, you see that the second field is also one byte long and contains the packet type. There are five values that can be used in this field: hello, database description, link-state request, link-state update (LSU), and link-state advertisement (LSA).

The next field is the packet length. This field is two bytes long and includes the packet length in bytes.

The next two fields, `Router ID` and `Area ID`, are a little longer. Each field is four bytes long. The router ID is the source ID for the packet. Each router in an OSPF area has a unique ID. Each AS also has an ID that is included in the packet, so not only the packet's source router is identified, but the AS is as well.

The remaining fields consist of the remaining space of the 24 bytes. The fields are `Checksum`, `Authentication type`, and `Authentication`, respectively. The `checksum` field, two bytes long, is used to calculate CRC information. The `authentication type` field, two bytes, contains OSPF password information or other `authentication` types. Finally, the authentication field contains authentication information.

BGP (Border Gateway Protocol)

The Internet consists of a number of commercial networks that connect to each other via tier-one providers such as Sprint, WorldCom/MCI/UUNet, and others. Each enterprise network or ISP must be identified by an autonomous system number. This number allows a hierarchy to be maintained when sharing route information.

We are now familiar with several IGPs (Interior Gateway Protocols), such as IGRP, EIGRP, and OSPF. For enterprise networks to communicate with other autonomous systems or ISPs, the IGP information has to be injected into BGP, which is used by all network entities that compose the Internet.

BGP (Border Gateway Protocol) is an open standard protocol that was developed and defined in several RFCs: 1163, 1267, 1654, and 1655. Complete technical details can be found in these articles. One of the requirements of BGP was that it needed to be a loop-free protocol.

The two types of BGP are iBGP and eBGP. There are several differences between the two. Primarily, iBGP (internal BGP) is used to share BGP information with routers within the same AS, whereas eBGP (external BGP) is used to share route information between two different autonomous systems. More details will be given as we discuss each type separately.

iBGP (Internal Border Gateway Protocol)

Internal BGP is used by routers that belong to the same autonomous system. iBGP may use loopback interfaces to provide greater reachability. This is possible because the IGP can provide multiple routes to any given destination address if the network has redundant or multiple links to each router. If one interface on a router goes down, the TCP connection to the loopback address can be maintained by using redundant interfaces.

It is important to understand that before any BGP route information can be exchanged between two routers, a TCP connection has to be established. The TCP connection is made by a three-way handshake using a SYN-ACK-SYN sequence. Once a TCP connection has been established, route information can be exchanged.

An important feature of iBGP is that route information from one peer is not advertised to another iBGP peer. This avoids inconsistent route information and routing loops. To share route information between all iBGP routers, establish a logical mesh. (Figure 2.18 shows a picture of what is meant by this.) Route information is exchanged only between routers. Router B can learn BGP networks only from Router A. When Router C sends its BGP information, only its information is sent. Routes learned from Router A are not included.

FIGURE 2.18 iBGP information exchange

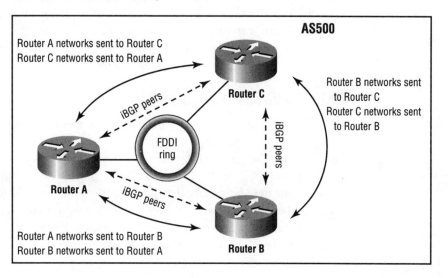

eBGP (External Border Gateway Protocol)

External BGP is used to exchange route information between two different autonomous systems. When only one link connects two autonomous systems, the IP address of the connected interface is used to establish the BGP session. It is also possible to use other IP addresses, but the address must be reachable without using an IGP. This is accomplished by using static routes or additional BGP commands when configuring eBGP. If multiple links are used to connect to the other AS, using loopback addresses is the best option.

The purpose of eBGP is to inject routes owned by the enterprise network into another AS. Two prerequisites need to be met for internal routes to be propagated via BGP:

- The route to be advertised must be present in the router's IGP route table.

- BGP must learn the route.

You can fulfill the first condition by using one of three methods: inject the routes into a router's route table via an IGP, a static route, or directly connected networks. BGP has a synchronization option that requires BGP and the IGP routes to synchronize before BGP will advertise IGP learned networks. The no synchronization command indicates that BGP and the IGP do not have to synchronize before BGP advertises the routes.

You can also accomplish the second prerequisite in one of three ways: BGP learns of networks that it needs to advertise through other BGP advertisements, network statements, and redistribution of an IGP into BGP. The last option is not recommended because of the instability incurred—redistribution can cause routing loops and route flapping.

BGP Packet Structure

The BGP header is only 20 bytes long and contains three fields. The first field is 16 bytes long and is called the *marker field*. This field contains a value that can be predicted by the receiving system. It is used for authentication purposes.

The next field is the *length field* and it is two bytes long. The length field contains the size of the entire message, in bytes. Finally, the *type field* is the last field, and it is two bytes in length. It is used to indicate the message type. Figure 2.19 gives a graphical representation of a BGP packet header.

FIGURE 2.19 BGP packet header

Now that we have mentioned message types, we need to explain them. BGP uses four different message types: open, update, notification, and keepalives.

Open messages are sent to each other after the TCP connection is established. The open messages must be accepted by the peer; otherwise, the remaining messages, update, notification, and keepalives are not sent.

Update messages are the actual routing updates exchanged among BGP peers. Other BGP-specific information is also included in these messages: origin, AS path, next hop, unreachable, and Inter-AS-metric.

Notification messages are used when errors are detected. Information includes an explanation about why the connection was closed. Each reason has a code. Notification updates use the following codes: message-header error, open-message error, update-message error, and hold time expired.

Keepalive messages are sent to make peers aware that the connection can be kept active. This is accomplished by updating the holddown timers.

Novell NetWare Protocols

NetWare differs from the previous protocols because it is a network operating system and not a routing protocol. The basis of a network operating system is a hierarchy of clients and servers: clients request services and information from servers.

NetWare uses the top five layers of the OSI model to run the network operating system. It uses proprietary protocols that fulfill the respective OSI layer requirements. Figure 2.20 shows the relationship between the OSI layers and Novell NetWare's use of the upper five layers.

FIGURE 2.20   OSI to NetWare comparison

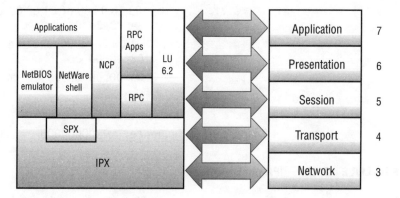

Because the upper five layers are proprietary to Novell, they must use special mappings to use the lower layers of the OSI model. To gain access to Layer 2, NetWare uses Ethernet/IEEE 802.3 or Token Ring/IEEE 802.5, FDDI, ARCnet, and PPP over WAN links.

IPX Packet Structure

Internetwork Packet Exchange (IPX) is Novell's equivalent for Layers 3 and 4 of the OSI model. Look at Figure 2.21 to get a picture of the IPX packet structure. Following is an EtherPeek analysis of an IPX packet, which gives you the information you need to define the packet structure:

```
IPX - NetWare Protocol
    Checksum:            0xffff
    Length:             73
```

```
Transport Control:
  Reserved:              %0000
  Hop Count:             %0000
Packet Type:           0  Novell
Destination Network:   0x00000000
Destination Node:      ff:ff:ff:ff:ff:ff Ethernet Brdcast
Destination Socket:    0x9001  IPX Static
Source Network:        0x00000010
Source Node:           00:00:0c:3e:82:2a
Source Socket:         0x9001  IPX Static
IPX Data Area:
............>.*.  83 1b 02 00 0f 01 00 00 11 00 00 0c
                 3e 82 2a 00
..+@...>.*. ....  01 00 2b 40 00 00 0c 3e 82 2a 01 c0
                 08 00 00 00
..... ...         00 00 00 00 00 c5 04 00 00
Extra bytes (Padding):
  . .                    05 dc 06
Frame Check Sequence:  0x00000000
```

FIGURE 2.21 IPX packet structure

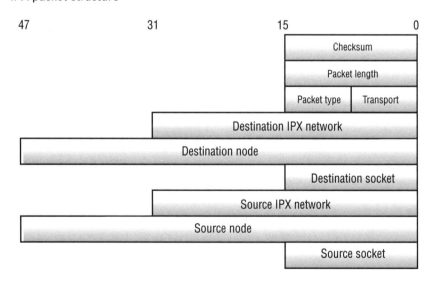

We start out with the 16-bit `Checksum` field with a default setting of 0xFFFF. This field is followed by the 16-bit `Packet length` field. The length field indicates the complete length, in bytes, of the IPX packet, header, and payload.

The next two fields (`Transport control` and `Packet type`) are eight bits each. `Transport control` is a counter that counts the number of routers a packet has transited. `Packet type` indicates which of the upper-layer protocols are to receive the PDU after Layer 4 is through processing it.

The fourth layer contains the `Destination IPX network` field, a 32-bit field that contains the IPX network for the destination host. The fifth layer is the `Destination node`. This field is 48 bits long and contains the MAC address of the destination host. The `Destination socket` is a 16-bit field on the sixth layer of the IPX header. This identifies the socket number for the upper layers.

Following the destination information, three more layers contain the same type of information for the source host. The seventh layer is the `Source IPX Network`, another 32-bit field containing the source network. This is followed by the `Source node`, a 48-bit field containing the MAC address of the source host. Finally, the last field of the header contains source host socket information, the `Source socket` field, which is 16 bits in length.

Certain codes are used to specify which socket numbers are assigned to which protocols. The codes used are shown in Table 2.13.

TABLE 2.13 IPX Socket Number Assignments

Socket Number	Upper-Layer Protocol
0451	NetWare Core Protocol
0452	SAP (Service Advertising Protocol)
0453	RIP
0455	NetBIOS
0456	Diagnostics
4000-6000	Temporary file server and network communications

NetWare has to use special formats to connect to the Data-Link layer. It uses encapsulation to do this. This encapsulation takes all of the upper-layer data and frames it in preparation for transport. NetWare originally used 802.3 raw. Now, NetWare uses several encapsulation types for Ethernet/ IEEE 802.3.

When you talk about frame types, you need to be careful to understand whose definition or name you are using. Table 2.14 summarizes the names and equivalencies for the Layer 2 frame types. Figure 2.22 gives a graphical description of the following encapsulations.

TABLE 2.14 Names for Layer 2 Ethernet Frame Types

Standard Name	Novell Equivalent	Cisco Equivalent	Characteristics
Ethernet V. 2	Ethernet_II	ARPA	Ethertype
IEEE 802.3	Ethernet_802.2	SAP	Length and SAPs
Novell 802.3 raw	Ethernet_802.3	NOVELL-ETHER	Length but no SAPs
SNAP	Ethernet_SNAP	SNAP	SAP and SNAP headers

FIGURE 2.22 Encapsulation types

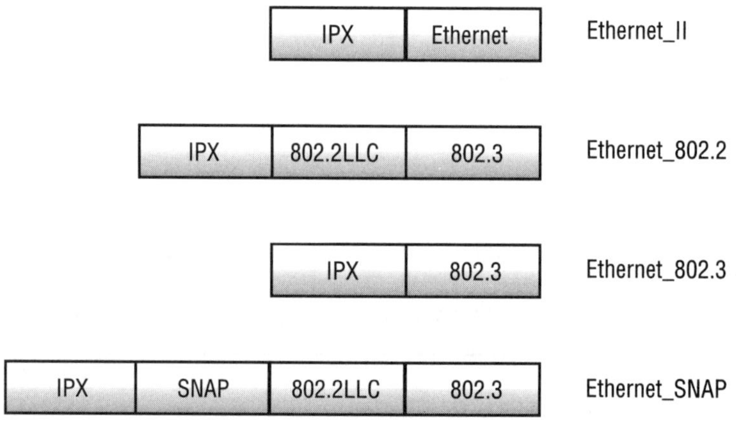

| IPX | Ethernet | Ethernet_II |

| IPX | 802.2LLC | 802.3 | Ethernet_802.2 |

| IPX | 802.3 | Ethernet_802.3 |

| IPX | SNAP | 802.2LLC | 802.3 | Ethernet_SNAP |

NLSP

NetWare Link Services Protocol (NLSP) is based on ISO's IS-IS routing protocol. It is a link-state routing protocol, not a distance-vector protocol such as RIP. Most of the problems with RIP that were listed previously are common to all distance-vector routing protocols. NLSP is not subject to these problems.

The current version of NLSP, version 1.1, supports a multitude of advanced routing features:

- Multiple areas
- Route aggregation
- Hierarchical addressing
- Network summarization

NLSP is similar to IS-IS because it defines areas. It offers solutions to many of the problems that we discussed with RIP and SAP, and can actually work as a replacement for all RIP and SAP communication between servers (or routers).

Every NLSP router (remember that NLSP-enabled NetWare servers are NLSP routers) builds and maintains three databases:

- Adjacency
- Link state
- Forwarding

These three databases are listed in the order in which they are built. The adjacency database can be unique on every router. On each of its NLSP-enabled interfaces, each router meets every other NLSP router on that network segment. On an Ethernet interface, for example, there can be several other NLSP-enabled devices (other routers, servers, and so on). On a point-to-point WAN interface, there is only one other device. All of this information goes into the adjacency database; once it is built, each router knows all of its NLSP neighbors on all connected networks.

AppleTalk Protocols

Just as IP and IPX had their own rules, AppleTalk has its own way of doing things. Addressing, location of services, and communication are a bit different than with other protocols. There are also several concepts that just don't have parallels elsewhere.

AppleTalk is similar to NetWare because it is a client/server-based technology. Mac users launch an application called Chooser to locate resources on the internetwork. Once users launch the Chooser application, they select an AppleTalk zone and type of resource (file server, printer, and so on). Chooser then builds a dynamic list of workstation names that offers the requested service in the selected zone. The user selects one of the names and then proceeds with their work. The following steps give a more detailed explanation of the procedure:

1. The user launches the Chooser application.

2. The Chooser queries the router for available zones and presents the list of available zones to the user.

3. The user selects a zone and the type of resource requested.

4. The user's Mac issues an NBP request, identifying the requested type of resource and zone.

5. The routers ensure that the NBP broadcast is forwarded to all specified network segments for that zone.

6. All nodes in the requested zone receive the NBP broadcast, and the nodes that provide the requested service reply to the requesting workstation.

7. Routers forward the responses to the requesting workstation's segment.

8. The Chooser builds a list of available services.

9. The user selects a service and proceeds with their work.

With this arrangement, it's obvious that the proper forwarding of broadcasts is crucial to locating resources on the internetwork. From the users' perspective, they can just use the dynamic Chooser to find out which resources are available on the internetwork. If you get a new laser printer, you simply plug it in and tell it which zone it's in, and Chooser automatically lets users looking for that type of printer know that it's available. Figure 2.23 depicts the location of AppleTalk services in relation to the OSI model.

FIGURE 2.23 AppleTalk's relation to the OSI model

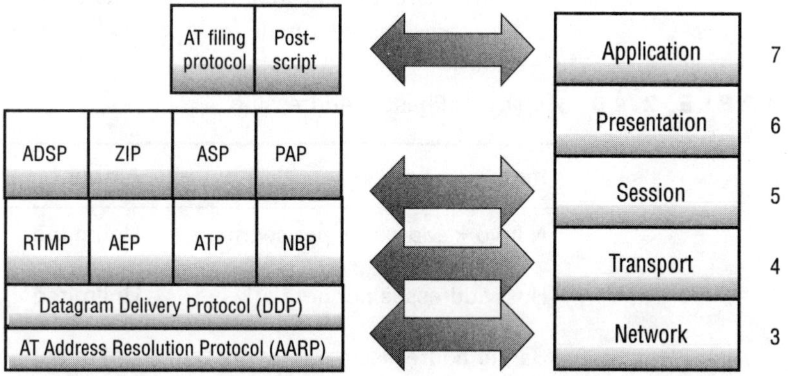

AppleTalk Addressing

AppleTalk uses a 24-bit address written in dotted decimal format—*network.node*. The network portion is always 16 bits long; the node portion is always eight bits long. Therefore, as with IPX, there's no subnetting and no classes. There are two versions of AppleTalk—Phase 1 and Phase 2. In Phase 1, there were certain limitations in addressing. Table 2.15 shows these limitations.

TABLE 2.15 AppleTalk Phase 1 Addressing

Item	Amount
Network addresses per segment	1
Host addresses per network	127
Server addresses per network	127
Zones per network	1

Because you can have only one network address per segment, the number of nodes per segment is also limited. If that isn't enough, there's also an imposed limitation of one zone per network, which obliterates an administrator's ability to create multiple logical networks within the same segment. There must be a better way! Thankfully, Apple thought so, too. Look at some changes made for AppleTalk Phase 2 (see Table 2.16).

TABLE 2.16 AppleTalk Phase 2 Addressing

Item	Amount
Network addresses per segment	Unlimited
Host addresses per network	Unlimited
Server addresses per network	Unlimited
Zones per network	255

With Phase 2, there can be an unlimited number of network addresses per segment. In addition, there are ample node addresses available, despite the fact that network addresses are still only eight bits long.

There really isn't an unlimited number of networks available per segment—you're still limited by the 16-bit network portion of the address, giving you approximately 65,000 potential networks. It's highly unlikely that you'd ever need anywhere near 65,000 network addresses for a single network, however.

In addition, you can now have multiple zones per network, allowing you to create multiple logical networks (zones) within a single network segment.

As is the case with IP, there are a few reserved network and node addresses. Network address 0 (zero) is reserved for use by nodes that haven't yet learned their segment's address, so it can't be assigned. Node addresses 254 and 255 are also reserved and can't be assigned to nodes.

The technique used by AppleTalk Phase 2 to assign multiple network addresses to a single segment is called *extended addressing*. Instead of having a single network address on a segment, you can assign a range—an extension—of addresses to a segment. Here's an example: A non-extended address for a segment can be network 100, and an extended address for the same segment can be network 100–110—a range of 11 network addresses. What if you need even more node addresses, however? Well, how about network 100–1000 (901 network addresses)? Need fewer node addresses? Try network 100–100 (one network address). All you have to do is specify a range of network addresses that you want included on the segment in the extended address.

AppleTalk nodes dynamically obtain node addresses upon startup. When a new machine starts up, it sends out a ZIP to find the network address or the address range, if extended addressing is being used. The machine then selects a random node address and issues an AARP (AppleTalk Address Resolution Protocol) to see if anyone is using that particular network node address. If there's no response, the machine continues using that address. Node addressing is completely dynamic and requires no administration.

When an AppleTalk node starts up, it sets up a provisional address. If the node is being started for the very first time, it chooses a network number between 65,280 and 65,534 at random. This range is referred to as the *startup range*. The node number is also chosen at random. If the node was started before, it uses its previous address as a *hint*. In either case, the node uses AARP to check whether the selected provisional address is in use. If the address is in use, it selects another node number and checks again. If the node is using a hint and subsequently exhausts all available node numbers without finding an unused address, it chooses a new network address from the startup range and a new node number, and then repeats the check for an unused address.

Once the node has selected an unused provisional address, it can send a ZIP `GetNetInfo` request to a router to determine the actual segment's cable range. If the network number for the provisional address falls between the segment's cable range, the address is kept. Otherwise, a new network number is chosen from this cable range, and the resulting node address is checked by using AARP. If the address is in use, the node selects another node number. If it runs out of node numbers, it chooses another network number from within the segment's cable range and repeats the node-address check process. Once the node finds an unused network number and node number combination, it becomes its final node address. The address is saved and used as a future hint.

Datagram Delivery Protocol (DDP)

Datagram Delivery Protocol (DDP), in conjunction with *AppleTalk Address Resolution Protocol (AARP)*, makes up the OSI Layer 3 equivalent. DDP is responsible for connectivity to the upper-layer protocols, whereas AARP is charged with connectivity to the lower layers.

Look at a DDP packet. The following EtherPeek trace analysis gives you what you need to know about the packet. It is important to realize that there is a Layer 2 heading that is prepended to the DDP header. We start from the beginning of the DDP header in this discussion.

```
Long DDP Header - Datagram Delivery Protocol
  Unused:           %00
  Hop Count:        %0000
  Datagram Length:  21
  DDP Checksum:     0x0000
  Dest. Network:    107
  Source Network:   101
  Dest Node:        1
  Source Node:      217
  Dest. Socket:     6   Zone Information
  Source Socket:    245
  DDP Type:         3   ATP
```

As you can see, the DDP header starts with an unused field. The next field is four bits and is used for the hop count. The count is incremented as the packet transits additional routers.

Following the hop count, you see the Datagram Length field. This field is 10 bits long and it measures the length of the datagram in bytes. After the datagram length field, we move onto the DDP Checksum field. The DDP checksum field is a full 16 bits, and is used to aid in CRC calculation.

The next four fields are used only in the long (extended) DDP header. They represent destination and source information, each according to the description. Following the extended information, you see the DSN and SSN. These fields are used to define destination and source socket numbers. The allowable socket numbers are RTMP (value = 1), names information (value = 2), echoer (value = 4), and zone information (value = 6).

There are seven different DDP types that can be specified by the DDP Type field using eight bits. These types include: RTMP response or data (value = 1), NBP (value = 2), ATP (value = 3), AEP (value = 4), RTMP requests (value = 5), ZIP (value = 6), and ADSP (value = 7). The actual DDP datagram follows the DDP type.

Routing Table Maintenance Protocol

Routing Table Maintenance Protocol (RTMP) is responsible for AppleTalk routing tables and their information. This is AppleTalk's proprietary method of maintaining route tables on AppleTalk–enabled machines. Look at the RTMP packets, which are different from other packet structures. They contain *x* number of fields called *routing tuples*. Depending on the type of network, non-extended or extended, the tuple structure changes.

The example below is a sample from an extended network. The packet structure is 16 bits long. The packet starts with the router's network number, which occupies the full 16 bits. Following the network number, the ID Length field occupies eight bits. This field specifies the length of the sender's node address. The next field is used for specifying the actual router's node address.

After 16 bits of padding, the routing tuples 1 through *x* follow. Each tuple contains the same field, as long as it is of the same tuple type. Non-extended tuples actually follow 16 bits of padding with eight bits of version number identification. They begin with the network number field, followed by some padding and a distance field. Extended tuples follow 16 bits of padding, and then begin with a 16-bit start range. After the start range, there are three more fields: Distance, Range End, and Version. The version number becomes part of an extended tuple. It has a default value of 0×82.

```
RTMP - Routing Table Maintenance Protocol
    Router's Net:        106
    ID Length:           8
    Router's Node ID:    74
RTMP Tuple # 1
    Range Start:         100
    Range Flag:          %100    Extended
    Distance:            0
    Range End:           110
    Version:             0x82
RTMP Tuple # 2
    Range Start:         300
    Range Flag:          %100    Extended
    Distance:            1
    Range End:           210
    Version:             0x82
RTMP Tuple # 3
    Range Start:         500
    Range Flag:          %100    Extended
    Distance:            2
```

Range End:	310	
Version:	0x82	
RTMP Tuple # 4		
Range Start:	200	
Range Flag:	%100	*Extended*
Distance:	0	
Range End:	1000	
Version:	0x82	
RTMP Tuple # 5		
Range Start:	400	
Range Flag:	%100	*Extended*
Distance:	1	
Range End:	1001	
Version:	0x82	
Frame Check Sequence:	0x00000000	

OSI Layer 2: Data-Link Layer Protocols and Applications

This section is dedicated to Layer 2 protocols and applications. It is a very important section because it provides specific information on how the Layer 2 protocols work. What better way to be able to troubleshoot a problem than by understanding the intricacies of the protocol in question?

This section covers the following Layer 2 protocols:

- Ethernet/IEEE 802.3

- Token Ring/IEEE 802.5

- FDDI

- PPP

- SDLC

- X.25

- Frame Relay

- ISDN

As you can see, there are quite a few technologies to understand, and this is where we will start.

Ethernet/IEEE 802.3

These two terms actually refer to different things. *Ethernet* is a communication technology and *IEEE 802.3* is a variety of Ethernet. Ethernet, in the more specific sense, is a *carrier sense, multiple access/collision detection (CSMA/CD)* local area network. This means that the network uses these attributes—carrier sense, multiple access, and collision detection—to enhance communication. This definitely does *not* mean that Ethernet is the only technology that uses these attributes. In today's technical jargon, however, Ethernet is getting closer to meaning all CSMA/CD technologies.

Both Ethernet and IEEE 802.3 are broadcast networks. All frames that cross a given segment can be heard by all machines populating that segment. Because all machines on the segment have equal access to the physical media, each station tries to wait for a quiet spot before it transmits its data. If two machines talk at the same time, a collision occurs.

Ethernet services both the Physical and Data-Link layers, whereas IEEE 802.3 is more concerned with the Physical layer and how it talks to the Data-Link layer. Several IEEE 802.3 protocols exist; each one has a distinct name that describes how it is different from other IEEE 802.3 protocols. Table 2.17 summarizes the differences between the different IEEE 802.3 versions.

TABLE 2.17 IEEE 802.3 Characteristics

	802.3 Values 10Base5	10Base2	1Base5	10BaseT	100BaseT	10Broad36
Data rate (Mbps)	10	10	1	10	100	10
Signaling Method	Baseband	Baseband	Baseband	Baseband	Baseband	Broadband
Maximum Segment Length (m)	500	500	185	250	100	1800
Media	50 Ohm coax	50 Ohm coax	Unshielded twisted pair	Unshielded twisted pair	Unshielded twisted pair	75 Ohm coax
Topology	Bus	Bus	Star	Star	Star	Bus

This is an excerpt from Cisco; for the full document, please see `http://www.cisco.com/univercd/cc/td/doc/ciscintwk/ito_doc/ethernet.htm`.

Frame Structures

Frame formats are similar between Ethernet and IEEE 802.3. Figure 2.24 depicts the similarities and differences between the two frames. The frame structures are read right to left. Starting at the right, you see that both frames begin with a preamble. The `Preamble` is a seven-byte field. Notice that you have moved from bits to bytes to specify field lengths. This value consists of alternating 1s and 0s.

FIGURE 2.24 Ethernet vs. IEEE 802.3 frames

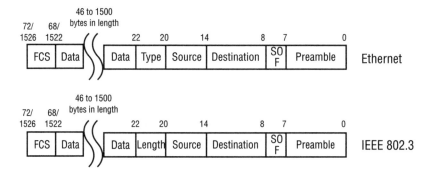

The next field is the SOF, or start-of-frame delimiter. It is used to synchronize the frame reception portions of all of the machines on the segment. This field is only one byte long.

The two fields following the SOF are six bytes each; they are the `Destination` and `Source` MAC addresses of the receiving and sending stations. Each MAC address is unique.

Up to this point, the frames were exactly the same. Now, the differences start. The following field is a two-byte field in both frame structures. Ethernet defines the field as a `Type` field, whereas IEEE 802.3 defines it as a `Length` field. Ethernet uses the field to specify which upper-layer protocol will receive the packet. IEEE 802.3 uses the field to define how many bytes the payload (802.2 header and data) field is.

The following field in both formats is the Data field. The only difference is that Ethernet uses a variable byte size between 46 and 1500 for data. This data is what will be handed to the upper-layer protocols. IEEE 802.3 uses a variable byte size between 46 and 1500 as well, but the information here contains the 802.2 header and the encapsulated data that will eventually be passed to an upper-layer protocol that is defined within the Data field.

Finally, you have the last field, which is the Frame Check Sequence (FCS) field. It is a four-byte long field that is used to store information that will be used for calculating the CRC after the data has been sent or received.

Token Ring/IEEE 802.5

Token Ring and IEEE 802.5 have the same relationship as Ethernet and IEEE 802.3. However, in this case, the IEEE 802.5 specification follows IBM's Token Ring much more closely. Both implementations specify baseband signaling, token passing, and data rates. Token Ring is IBM's token-passing LAN technology. It has bandwidth capabilities of either 4Mbps or 16Mbps in a ring topology.

Token Ring/IEEE 802.5 differ greatly from Ethernet/IEEE 802.3. Ethernet/IEEE 802.3 are CSMA/CD LANs, whereas Token Ring/IEEE 802.5 are apportioned networks. *Apportioned* means that equal time is allotted to every station on a ring. This is achieved by passing a token around the ring. The next section explains in a little more detail.

Tokens

The physical design of Token Ring/IEEE 802.5 is just as the name indicates—a ring. Multiple stations connect to the same ring, just as Ethernet/IEEE 802.3 stations connect to the same segment.

The main idea behind Token Ring/IEEE 802.5 was that a station may not transmit data onto the ring without first possessing the *token*. The token is just a small frame containing control information. Use Figure 2.25 as a visual reference for the following example. The frame or token is sent around the ring. Each station on the ring waits its turn to receive the token. If a station receives the token but doesn't have anything to transmit, it simply passes the token on to the next station in line. However, if the station does have information to send, it alters the frame, changing it into a start-of-frame identifier, and then appends the data to the frame. While the token frame has been changed into a start-of-frame identifier, no other station on the ring can use the token to transmit data, thus eliminating collisions.

The altered frame leaves the source station and circles the ring in search of the destination station. Each station looks at the frame and determines whether it is the destination host. If a station is the destination, it copies the frame and then processes it, as necessary. The frame continues to travel around the ring until it reaches the source host. Once reaching the source, the frame is removed and a new token is generated and sent out onto the ring. This way, each station has an equal opportunity to transmit data.

FIGURE 2.25 Token passing

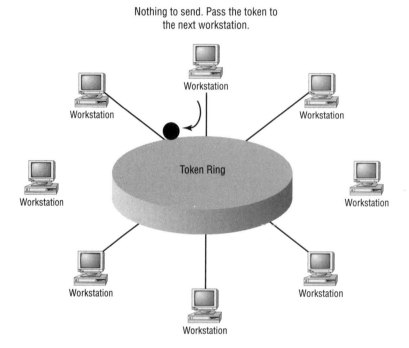

Fault Recovery

Token Ring/IEEE 802.5 uses several methods to help prevent and heal network failures quickly and efficiently. An *Active Monitor* is designated by the workstations on the ring. The Active Monitor is responsible for token monitoring, token generation when the token seems to have disappeared, purging recycling frames, and other ring maintenance.

The physical connectivity of Token Ring/IEEE 802.5 is also fault-tolerant. If a machine on a ring becomes unreachable, the machine is electrically disconnected from the ring. The MAU in which the Token Ring/IEEE 802.5 cabling is located shuts down the port that is unreachable, thus healing the ring. Physical connectivity is tested by using *beaconing*, which locates the fault and reports back with the nearest active upstream neighbor, or NAUN. This information helps to isolate network failures and shortens troubleshooting time.

Token Frame Format

We now look at the two frame types used by Token Ring/IEEE 802.5. Remember that while referencing ., we will move from right to left. The two principal frame types used in Token Ring and IEEE 802.5 are the token frame and the data, or command, frame formats.

FIGURE 2.26   Token and data/command frames

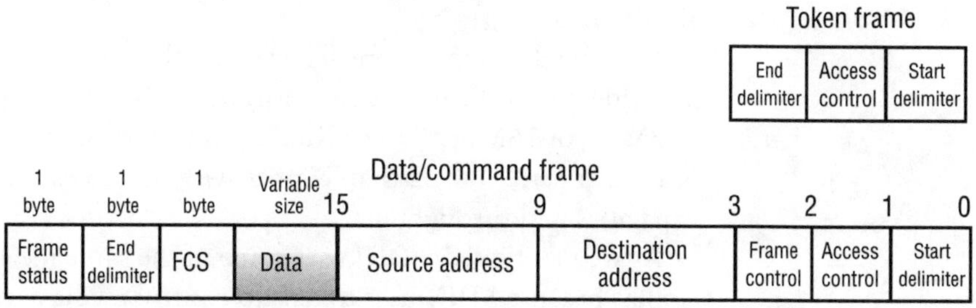

Figure 2.26 shows that both frames start with a `start delimiter` and `access control`. These two fields are each only one byte long. `Start delimiter` alerts each station on the ring that the frame is a data or command frame, not a simple token frame. The `Access control` field is used to assign priority to the frame and to help distinguish what frame type it is. Possible frame types are token, data/command, and a monitor frame.

Here is where the difference starts. The data frame contains additional fields that the token frame does not have. All of the station's data is inserted into the frame following the access control field. The data segment commences with a one-byte field that holds information regarding frame control. This is an indicator of whether the frame contains data or command information.

The next two fields are six bytes long and contain the packet's destination and source addresses. The `Data` field, of variable length, carries all of the data that is to be encapsulated. The length is determined by how long the sending station can hold a token.

Error-checking information follows the header and data fields. It is used in CRC calculation.

Now you are at the end of the frame and it is again the same as a token frame. Both data/command and token frames have end delimiters. The only difference is that end delimiters end a token frame, but a data/command frame has one more field.

The End delimiter field is only one byte long. It is used to indicate the end of a data/command frame. The last field, the Frame status, or FS, has two values that it can relay: frame-copied or address-recognized.

Fiber Distributed Data Interface (FDDI)

Fiber Distributed Data Interface (FDDI) is a LAN technology that has bandwidth capabilities up to 100Mbps per ring. This along with other changes makes it an improvement over Token Ring and Ethernet. FDDI uses some of the same ideas as Token Ring. It uses fiber optics as its physical media, but the topology is a dual ring instead of just a single ring as used by Token Ring/IEEE 802.5.

Several advantages were achieved by the improvements made by FDDI. The ring has 100Mbps bandwidth, which is much more than 10Mbps 10BaseT, or 16Mbps Token Ring. Another advantage was the fact that fiber is a much better media than copper wire. It allows for higher bandwidth capacities and throughput.

As we mentioned, FDDI uses some of the same ideas as Token Ring. It is similar because FDDI uses tokens to control media access, uses a ring topology, and has some of the same fault-tolerant features as Token Ring. Look at Figure 2.27. You can see the back of three routers, each of which has a FDDI processor board in it. Notice how the routers are connected. Port A on Router A is connected to port B on Router B. Port A on Router B is connected to port B on Router C. Port A on Router C is connected to port B on Router A.

Each of the ports has two fiber optic connections. One fiber is considered the primary ring and the other is considered to be the secondary ring. Data flows in opposite directions on these two rings. Figure 2.28 shows that the data on the primary ring flows clockwise, whereas the data on the secondary ring flows counterclockwise.

FIGURE 2.27 FDDI interfaces

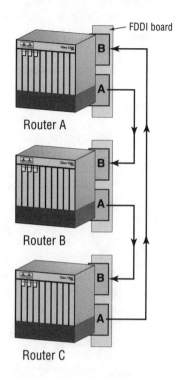

FIGURE 2.28 Counter data flows on dual rings.

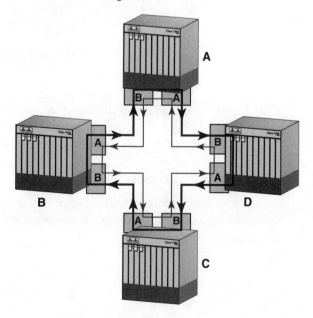

Fault tolerance is another of FDDI's big improvements. Because FDDI utilizes dual rings, the ring goes into a wrapped state and dynamically isolates the failed section any time a failure occurs. When the ring wraps, the adjacent FDDI interfaces loop the ring. Thus, instead of transmitting data out the primary ring on the outgoing port, it transmits the data out the outbound port on the secondary ring. Figure 2.29 gives a better picture of what actually happens.

FIGURE 2.29 FDDI's self-healing ring

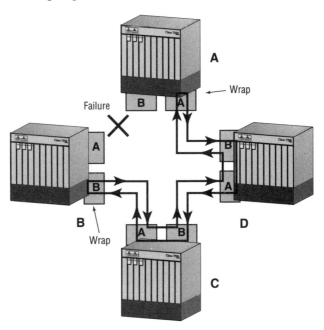

There are many different fiber/equipment failure scenarios, but FDDI's fault-tolerant technology can resolve most of them. In addition to having the dual ring, FDDI also uses beaconing to help isolate ring problems.

FDDI Specifications

Now that we have discussed what FDDI is and some of the features it has, we need to understand how it is implemented with respect to the OSI model and the frame type it uses.

Most of FDDI's specifications lie within Layer 1, but there are specifications that merge it with the MAC portion of Layer 2. Here is a summary of the four specifications used by FDDI:

- Physical Layer Medium Dependant (PMD)
- Physical Layer Protocol (PHY)
- Media Access Control (MAC)
- Station Management (SMT)

The first standard defines physical transmission characteristics. This deals with the light levels within the fiber optics, the allowable bit errors, decibel loss, and actual physical equipment.

The second standard is just what it says. The protocol encodes and decodes the data, before and after transmission over the physical media.

The third standard bridges FDDI with Layer 2 of the OSI model. This specification is charged with the way FDDI runs as a Layer 2 technology, the physical addresses, and the way the data is presented to the Physical layer.

Finally, there is station management. This specification is responsible for station and ring configuration, fault recovery, and other management duties.

Frame Structure

Figure 2.30 gives a picture of FDDI data and token frames. They are very similar to those used by Token Ring/IEEE 802.5. We begin at the right and work our way to the left.

FIGURE 2.30   FDDI token and data frame structures

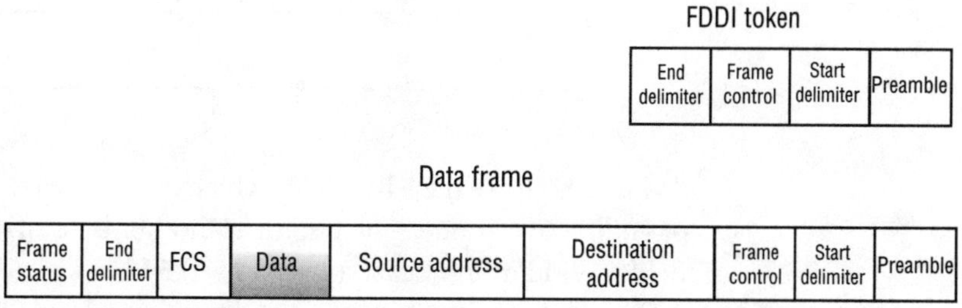

FDDI token

End delimiter	Frame control	Start delimiter	Preamble

Data frame

Frame status	End delimiter	FCS	Data	Source address	Destination address	Frame control	Start delimiter	Preamble

Both frames begin with the `preamble` field, which tells the stations that they should get ready to process a frame. Following the preamble, both frames have the `Start delimiter` field, which specifies the actual beginning of the frame.

Unlike Token Ring/IEEE 802.5, both frames also have `Frame control` fields. The `Frame control` field tells the station the size of the address field and the type of data that is being carried by the frame.

In data frames, the `Frame control` field is followed by the `destination` field and `source address` field, which are six bytes long. Continuing with the data frame, the actual `Data` field follows. This is the information that will be processed by upper-layer protocols. The `Data` field is followed by the `Frame check sequence`, which calculates the CRC for the received frame.

Again, both frame types contain an `End delimiter` field. For data frames, this field is followed by the `Frame status` field. Token frames end with the end delimiter. As with Token Ring/IEEE 802.5, the frame status indicates whether the frame was copied or stored by any stations on the ring.

Point-to-Point Protocol (PPP)

Point-to-point Protocol (PPP) is used to transfer data over serial point-to-point links. It accomplishes this by using a Layer 2 serial encapsulation called *High-level Data Link Control (HDLC)*. HDLC is used for frame encapsulation on synchronous serial lines. It uses a Link Control Protocol (LCP) to manage the serial connection. Network Control Protocols (NCPs) are used to allow PPP to use other protocols from Layer 3, thus enabling PPP to assign IP addresses dynamically.

PPP uses the same frame structure as HDLC. Figure 2.31 gives you a picture of what the frame looks like. As always, we move from right to left.

FIGURE 2.31 PPP packet structure

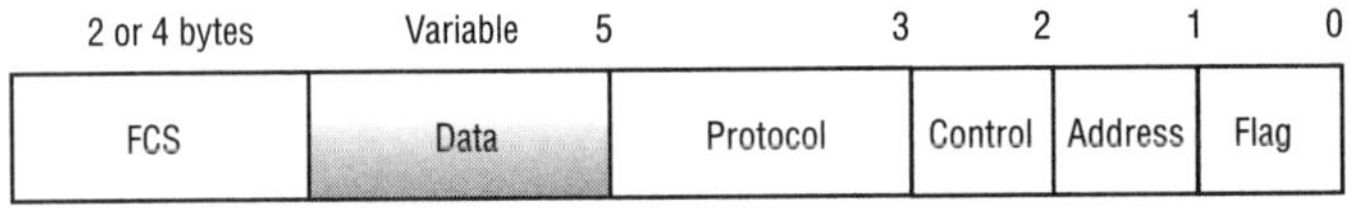

2 or 4 bytes	Variable	5	3	2	1	0
FCS	Data	Protocol	Control	Address	Flag	

First, we have the `Flag` field, which uses one byte to specify the beginning or ending of a frame. Then there is another byte that is used in the `Address` field to hold a broadcast address of 11111111.

The `Address` field is followed by the one-byte `Control` field. The `Control` field requests a transmission of user data. The two-byte `Protocol` field follows the `Control` field. This field indicates the encapsulated data's protocol.

The Data field contains the information that will be handed to the upper-layer protocols. It is a variable-length field. Following the data field is the FCS. Like the other protocols, it is used for CRC calculation.

Synchronous Data Link Control (SDLC)

Synchronous Data Link Control (SDLC) is based on a synchronous, more efficient, faster, and flexible bit-oriented format. SDLC has several derivatives that perform similar functions with some enhancements: HDLC, LAPB (Link Access Procedure, Balanced), and IEEE 802.2, just to name a few.

SDLC is used for many link types. Two node types exist within SDLC: *primary nodes* and *secondary nodes*. Primary nodes are responsible for the control of secondary stations and for link management, such as link setup and teardown. Secondary nodes talk only to the primary node when they fulfill two requirements. First, they have permission from the primary node; second, they have data to transmit. Even if a secondary node has data to send, it cannot send the data if it does not have permission from the primary node.

Both stations can be configured together in four different topologies:

Point-to-point   This topology requires only two nodes—a primary and a secondary.

Multipoint   This configuration uses one primary station and multiple secondary stations.

Loop   This configuration uses one primary and multiple secondary stations. The difference between loop and multipoint setups is that here the primary station is connected between two secondary stations, which makes two directly connected secondary stations. When more secondary stations are added, they must connect to the other secondary stations that are currently in the loop. When one of these stations wants to send information to the primary node, it must transit the other secondary stations before it reaches the primary.

Hub go-ahead   This configuration is different. It also uses one primary and multiple secondary stations, but it uses a different communication topology. The primary station has an outbound channel. This channel is used to communicate with each of the secondary stations. An inbound channel is shared among the secondary stations and has a single connection into the primary station.

Frame Structure

SDLC uses three different frame structures: information, supervisory, and unnumbered. The overall structure of the frames is similar, except for the control frame. The control frame is varied to distinguish the type of SDLC frame that is being used. Figure 2.32 gives the structure for the different SDLC frames. Pay close attention to the bit values next to the send sequence number within the control frame.

FIGURE 2.32 SDLC frame structures

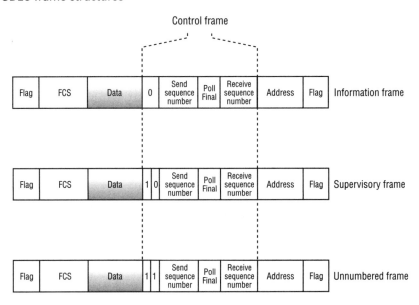

First, let's talk about the frame fields that are common among all three frame types. As you can see, all three frames depicted in Figure 2.32 start with a `Flag` field that is followed by an `Address` field. The `Address` field of SDLC frames is different from other frame structures because only the address of the secondary node is used instead of a destination and source address. The secondary address is used because all communication is either originated or received by the primary node; thus, it is not necessary to specify its address within the frame.

The control frame follows the `Address` field. Information contained within the control frame defines the SDLC frame type. The control frame begins with a receive sequence number. This sequence number is used to tell the protocol the number of the next frame to be received.

The P/F or Poll Final number, following the receive sequence number, is used differently by primary and secondary nodes. Primary nodes use the information to communicate to the secondary node that it requires an immediate response. The secondary node uses the information to tell the primary node that the frame is the last one in the current dialogue.

After the P/F bit, the send sequence number is used to identify the current frame's sequence number. Following the send sequence number, one or two bits are used to define the frame type. Table 2.18 specifies the bit values and the corresponding frame type.

TABLE 2.18 SDLC Frame Types

Bit Value	Frame Type
0	Information
0 1	Supervisory
1 1	Unnumbered

The Data field follows the control field. As with other frame types, the FCS field follows and is used to calculate the CRC. SDLC frames differ again with the last field. As with the beginning of the frame, the frame ends with another Flag field.

Now that we have discussed the frame structure, we need to discuss the three different frame types. We will begin with Information frames. Information frames carry exactly that—information destined for the upper-layer protocols. Supervisory frames control SDLC communications; they are responsible for flow-and-error control for I-frame (information). Unnumbered frames provide the initialization of secondary nodes, as well as other managerial functions.

SDLC Derivatives

Other protocols, such as HDLC, Link Access Procedure, Balance (LAPB), IEEE 802.2, and Qualified Logical Link Control (QLLC), are derivatives of SDLC.

HDLC

High-level Data Link Control (HDLC) is used in the same manner as SDLC—for serial connections and for synchronous operations. This protocol is an enhancement over SDLC because it provides a 32-bit checksum and three different transfer modes: normal, asynchronous response, and asynchronous balanced.

These modes allow secondary nodes to communicate with primary nodes by using different methods. The normal modes are the same as SDLC uses; the secondary nodes can talk only to the primary node when they have permission. The other two methods are unique to HDLC.

Asynchronous response allows the secondary node to communicate with the primary node without first having to obtain permission from the primary node.

The final method, asynchronous balanced, creates a third type of node, known as a combination node. As you can imagine, this node combines the roles of a primary and secondary node.

IEEE 802.2

This protocol uses three different frame types to provide different services to IEEE 802.3, IEEE 802.5, and IEEE 802.4. The nomenclature for the different types is simply Type 1, Type 2, and Type 3:

Type 1 Unacknowledged connectionless service, which does not provide for any flow or error-control information.

Type 2 Connection-oriented service. Connections are established and flow-and-error control is inherent.

Type 3 Acknowledged connectionless service. Connections are not established, yet flow-and-error control is inherent.

LAPB

This protocol uses the ABM (asynchronous balanced method) transfer mode. All nodes are combination modes. Hierarchy is established by the node initiating the communication. The frame for LAPB is similar to that of SDLC and HDLC.

This ends our discussion of SDLC and its derivative protocols. As you have seen, they all have many similarities to SDLC. Enhancements were made to create more effective and efficient protocols.

X.25

Layers 1, 2, and 3 of the OSI model coincide with the *X.25 protocol*. Layer 3 X.25 is responsible for upper-layer protocol agreement and data exchange. Layer 2 X.25 uses LAPB as its protocol. Layer 1 X.25 maps to Layer 1 of the OSI model, which is in charge of data transmission across the physical medium.

X.25 uses virtual circuits to communicate with end systems. These circuits can be permanent (PVC) or switched (SVC) once they are inside of the carrier's switching network. The upper layers of X.25 are concerned only that communication is established with the destination system. Once a virtual circuit is created, it has unique numerical identifiers assigned to it, which distinguish it from other connections.

Figure 2.33 shows how PVCs or SVCs are used to connect two end systems. You can see four routers sitting outside of a switching cloud. Router A has a virtual circuit to Router B, and Router C has a virtual circuit to Router D. Within the switching cloud, Switches X and Y have two circuits running on them. In order for these switches to keep data flowing to the right destinations, they assign circuit identifiers to each virtual circuit. When a packet is sent, it is told which virtual circuit it belongs to.

FIGURE 2.33 Example of virtual circuits

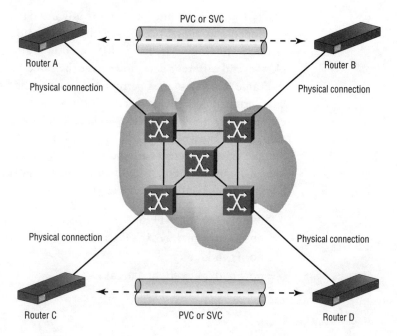

Frame Structure

Now that you understand how the two end systems communicate, move a little deeper into X.25 by looking at the frame structure. Refer to Figure 2.34 for the graphical representation of the X.25 frame. X.25 frames are very similar to SDLC frames. Each end is bounded with a `Flag` field. Starting from the right and moving to the left, we start with a `Flag` segment. After the `Flag` field, the frame contains the `frame field control and address` field.

FIGURE 2.34 X.25 frame structure

Flag	FCS	Data	Frame control and address	Flag

Next is the `Data` field that contains the Layer 3 X.25 packet, which in turn holds the Layer 3 packet header and upper-layer data. Finally, the frame ends with the `FCS` and `Flag` fields. The Layer 2 frame is simply a LAPB frame.

Frame Relay

The *Frame Relay* technology is more advanced than X.25. Frame Relay was developed as a digital packet-switching technology, whereas X.25 was an analog technology. The technology used in Frame Relay allows it to multiplex several different data flows over the same physical media.

Frame Relay also uses permanent and switched virtual circuits between data terminal equipment (DTE). These virtual circuits have unique identifiers that allow the Frame Relay to keep track of each logical data flow. The identifier is known as a DLCI (data link connection identifier). The DLCI number is used to create a logical circuit within a physical circuit. Multiple logical circuits can be created within one physical circuit. Look at the following router-configuration excerpt:

```
interface Serial1/5
 description Physical Circuit
 no ip address
 no ip directed-broadcast
 encapsulation frame-relay
 !
```

```
interface Serial1/5.1 point-to-point
 description To Building A
 ip address 172.16.1.17 255.255.255.252
 no ip directed-broadcast
 frame-relay interface-dlci 17 IETF
!
interface Serial1/5.2 point-to-point
 description To Building B
 ip address 172.16.1.25 255.255.255.252
 no ip directed-broadcast
 frame-relay interface-dlci 22 IETF
!
interface Serial1/5.3 point-to-point
 description To Building C
 ip address 172.16.1.29 255.255.255.252
 no ip directed-broadcast
 frame-relay interface-dlci 18 IETF
!
interface Serial1/5.4 point-to-point
 description To Building D
 ip address 172.16.1.33 255.255.255.252
 no ip directed-broadcast
 frame-relay interface-dlci 21 IETF
!
```

From this configuration, you can see that four logical circuits have been defined to communicate over one physical circuit. Notice that each sub-interface or logical circuit has a unique DLCI. Each DLCI maps to another DLCI within the Frame Relay cloud. This mapping continues throughout the Frame Relay cloud until it maps to another DTE on the destination side of the virtual circuit.

Frame Structure

The frame used in Frame Relay is similar to the frame used in X.25, except for two major differences. The first difference is that Frame Relay leaves flow-and-error control to the upper-layer protocols. Frame Relay does provide congestion detection and can notify the upper layers of possible problems, but it is only concerned primarily with the transmission and reception of data. Because Frame Relay does not worry about flow-and-error control, it does not reserve any space within the frame for this information.

The second difference is the DLCI number. Ten bits of the two-byte `Address` field are used to define the DLCI. To a Frame Relay frame, the DLCI is the most significant address in the header. Figure 2.35 depicts a Frame Relay frame. As you can see it is very similar to the X.25 frame, except for the flow/error control field.

FIGURE 2.35 Frame Relay frame structure

Flag	FCS	Data	Address	Flag

Integrated Services Digital Network (ISDN)

Integrated Services Digital Network (ISDN) is a service that allows telephone networks to carry data, voice, and other digital traffic. There are two types of ISDN interfaces: *Basic Rate Interface (BRI)* and *Primary Rate Interface (PRI)*. BRI uses two B channels and one D channel. Each of the two B channels operates at 64Kbps bidirectionally; the D channel operates at 16Kbps. The B channels are used for transmitting and receiving data. The D channel is used for protocol communications and signaling.

In contrast, PRI uses 23 B channels and one D channel. All 23 B channels are added to a rotary group, as well. The D channel runs at the same line speed as the B channels—64Kbps. Because of the D channel's additional line speed, PRI has the equivalent line speed of a T1 circuit (1.5Mbps). In Europe, PRI offers 30 B channels and 1 D channel, making it the equivalent of an E1 circuit.

Just as there are two types of ISDN interfaces, there are two terminal equipment types. Type 1 (TE1) is equipment that was built specifically for use on ISDN. Type 2 (TE2) is equipment that was made before the ISDN specifications, and it requires a terminal adapter to actually interface with ISDN. Terminal equipment is comparable to DTE, mentioned in the Frame Relay section. It is equipment such as computers or routers.

In order for terminal equipment to work, there must be a network termination to connect to. Three types of ISDN network terminations exist. These devices are known as NT devices. Type 1 (NT1) devices are treated as customer premises equipment. Type 2 (NT2) devices perform Layer 2 and Layer 3 functions. The last type is a combination of the previous two types. It is known as a Type 1/2 or NT1/2.

Frame Structure

Look at Figure 2.36 to get a picture of the ISDN frame. As you can see, this frame is similar to the HDLC frame that you saw earlier. ISDN uses LAP on the D channel for Layer 2 functions. Just like X.25, the ISDN frame is bounded by Flag fields.

FIGURE 2.36   ISDN frame format

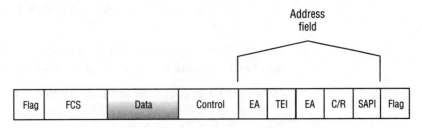

Starting from the right and working to the left, we see the Address field. The Address field contains several bits of key information:

SAPI   This field is the service access point identifier. It defines which services are provided to Layer 3.

C/R   This field designates the frame as a command or a response.

EA   This is the last bit of the first byte of the Address field. This bit defines the Address field as one or two bytes. If it is set to one byte, this is the last field within the Address field. If it is set to two, then one more field follows ending with another EA bit.

TEI   Terminal endpoint identifier. This is used to define a single terminal or multiple terminals.

Summary

A great deal of information was covered in this chapter. The focus of the chapter has been on Network and Data-Link Layer protocols. It is important to understand this information to facilitate troubleshooting. If you do not sufficiently understand the protocols present in Layers 2 and 3 of the OSI model, you should study them in depth. The majority of networking problems occur in these two layers.

Let's review what was covered:

Connectionless vs. Connection-Oriented Protocols   You learned that connection-oriented protocols use flow and error control information to ensure error-free data transfer. Connectionless protocols do not provide such features.

Network Layer Protocols   We discussed IP and other members of the IP suite, such as ICMP and TCP. Routing protocols were also discussed.

Data-Link Layer protocols and technologies   This section included information on all major Layer 2 technologies, such as Ethernet, Frame Relay, FDDI, X.25, ISDN, and SDLC.

Key Terms

Before you take the exam, be certain you are familiar with the following terms:

Active Monitor

AppleTalk Address Resolution Protocol (AARP)

Basic Rate Interface (BRI)

Border Gateway Protocol (BGP)

carrier sense, multiple access/collision detection (CSMA/CD)

connectionless protocols

connection-oriented protocols

Datagram Delivery Protocol (DDP)

Enhanced IGRP

error control

Ethernet

extended addressing

Fiber Distributed Data Interface (FDDI

flow control

Frame Relay

High-level Data Link Control (HDLC)

IEEE 802.3

Integrated Services Digital Network (ISDN)

Interior Gateway Routing Protocol (IGRP)

Internet Control Message Protocol (ICMP)

Internet Protocol (IP)

Internetwork Packet Exchange (IPX)

NetWare Link Services Protocol (NLSP)

Open Shortest Path First (OSPF)

Point-to-point Protocol (PPP)

primary nodes

Primary Rate Interface (PRI)

protocol parameters

required resources

Routing Information Protocol (RIP)

Routing Table Maintenance Protocol (RTMP)

secondary nodes

sequenced data transfer

Synchronous Data Link Control (SDLC)

token

Token Ring

Transmission Control Protocol (TCP)

window size

X.25

Review Questions

1. Which global protocol type provides error and flow control?

   A. Connectionless

   B. Connection-oriented

   C. IP

   D. UDP

2. Which of the following protocols are considered connection-oriented protocols? (Choose all that apply.)

   A. ATM

   B. UDP

   C. TCP

   D. IP

   E. Novell SPX

   F. AppleTalk ATP

3. Which of the following protocols are considered connectionless protocols? (Choose all that apply.)

   A. Frame Relay

   B. UDP

   C. PPP

   D. Novell IPX

   E. SDLC

   F. AppleTalk DDP

   G. IP

4. Which protocol of the IP protocol suite provides environmental information regarding IP networks, such as congestion and reachability?

   A. ICMP

   B. UDP

   C. TCP

   D. SMTP

5. What are window sizes used for in TCP data transfers?

   A. They define the size of the packet, otherwise known as MTU.

   B. They define how long the TCP transfer can last.

   C. They define how many bytes are sent before an ACK is received.

   D. They define the port the transfer will use.

6. What advantage do connectionless data transfers have over connection-oriented transfers?

   A. Flow-and-error control

   B. Guarantee of data integrity

   C. A more secure transfer

   D. Less overhead and network traffic

7. What is RIP's major weakness?

   A. Hop count

   B. Distance-vector protocol

   C. Link-state protocol

   D. Inaccurate metric values

8. What are the three types of routes recognized by IGRP? (Choose three.)

   A. Default

   B. Interior

   C. Internal

   D. Redistributed

   E. System

   F. External

   G. Exterior

   H. Static

9. What three routing features help stabilize IGRP and Enhanced IGRP? (Choose three.)

   A. Holddown timers

   B. Incremental updates

   C. Split horizon suppression

   D. Poison reverse updates

   E. Distance-vector metric calculation

   F. Passive interfaces

10. What four attributes were added to IGRP to create Enhanced IGRP? (Choose four.)

    A. Poison reverse updates

    B. Incremental updates

    C. Classless routing

    D. Distance-vector metric calculation

    E. Formal peer relationships

    F. Configurable metric values

    G. Equal-cost load balancing

11. How does OSPF differ from EIGRP? (Choose two.)

    A. It is a pure link-state routing protocol.

    B. All OSPF areas should be connected to Area 0.

    C. It has incremental updates.

    D. It maintains a topology database.

12. What exchange must first occur before a BGP peering session can be established?

    A. There is a multicast request.

    B. The router must broadcast for all other BGP speakers.

    C. A SYN-ACK-SYN TCP handshake establishes a TCP connection.

    D. All of the above.

13. To which OSI layers does Novell NetWare specifically map?

    A. All layers

    B. Layers 3 through 7

    C. Layers 2 through 7

    D. Layers 4 through 7

14. What is the term that Cisco uses to refer to the special frame format that Novell uses?

    A. ARPA

    B. SAP

    C. Novell-Ether

    D. SNAP

15. Which Ethernet IP encapsulation is the default for Cisco routers? Use Cisco terminology.

   A. ARPA

   B. SAP

   C. Novell-Ether

   D. SNAP

16. What features does Token Ring possess that Ethernet does not? (Choose two.)

   A. Faster speeds

   B. Token passing

   C. Fault isolation

   D. MAC addresses

17. What are the enhancements that FDDI provides over Token Ring? (Choose three.)

   A. Faster speeds

   B. Fault isolation

   C. Dual rings

   D. Self-healing ring

18. Which interface type was PPP designed to use?

   A. Ethernet

   B. Token Ring

   C. FDDI

   D. Serial

19. Which node types exist within SDLC and its derivatives? (Choose two.)

    A. Master

    B. Slave

    C. Server

    D. Client

    E. Primary

    F. Secondary

20. Which layer(s) of the OSI model coincide with the X.25 protocol?

    A. All layers

    B. Layer 2

    C. Layers 1 and 2

    D. Layers 1 through 3

(The answers to the questions begin on the next page.)

Answers to Review Questions

1. B. Connection-oriented is a protocol type, in addition, it provides error and flow control. Connectionless protocols, such as IP and UDP, do not.

2. A, C, E, F. UDP and IP are both connectionless protocols.

3. B, D, F, G. Frame Relay, PPP, and SDLC are all connection-oriented protocols.

4. A. ICMP provides environmental statistics for IP networks. The other protocols do not.

5. C. Window sizes are transmission sizes. Once the window size is reached, the sending computer awaits an ACK packet, informing the sending computer that the receiving computer received the entire transmission.

6. D. Due to the simplicity of connectionless protocols, they create less overhead and also use less bandwidth.

7. A. The hop count indicates limitations on how far a packet could go.

8. B, E, G. IGRP classifies the different routes that it can learn into the categories of Interior, System, and Exterior.

9. A, C, D. These features help maintain stable routes within IGRP and EIGRP.

10. B, C, E, G. These items were added to EIGRP to allow it to scale better as well as respond more quickly.

11. A, B. EIGRP is a hybrid protocol that does not use areas. Both OSPF and EIGRP maintain topology databases and use incremental updates.

12. C. A peer cannot connect if there is not a TCP connection first.

13. **B.** NetWare protocols map to these layers and a special frame format is used to "access" the Data-Link layer.

14. **C.** Novell uses the term Ethernet_802.3, Cisco uses Novell-Ether. See Table 2.14.

15. **A.** Cisco uses ARPA as its default Ethernet encapsulation. The other encapsulation types can be set via the command line, but are not on by default.

16. **B, C.** Ethernet does not use a token, nor does it provide fault isolation. It is possible that Ethernet can be faster than Token Ring, and Ethernet also uses MAC addresses.

17. **A, C, D.** Token Ring has fault isolation.

18. **D.** PPP uses serial connections.

19. **E, F.** Primary and secondary are the correct terms for the node types within SDLC.

20. **D.** X.25 covers layers 1 through 3 of the OSI model.

Chapter

3

Generic Troubleshooting Tools

TOPICS COVERED IN THIS CHAPTER INCLUDE:

✓ Becoming familiar with the wide variety of troubleshooting tools and the uses of each.

✓ Learning how to operate a protocol analyzer and use the information to troubleshoot network problems.

✓ Learning to use the LANWatch protocol analyzer.

Many different tools exist for network troubleshooting. Although a majority of them are not Cisco-specific or proprietary, many of these tools can help to troubleshoot problems with Cisco equipment as well as with networks in general.

Troubleshooting tools can be used to analyze several aspects of a network, such as the physical connectivity and the protocols, as well as the applications running on the network. Each area requires a different set of tools and procedures. Often, troubleshooting tools and test equipment are used only when there is a network failure or problem. It is important to recognize that many tools can be used in a proactive method, such as monitoring. Certainly, some tools are not able or not designed to provide monitoring functions. Many are capable of this task, however.

We begin this chapter by discussing the tools designed for physical media troubleshooting, and then move on to protocol analyzers. After a thorough discussion of these two types of instruments, we will discuss using some of these tools in monitoring applications. Cisco has several software packages that provide excellent network monitoring using SNMP (Simple Network Management Protocol) and TCP/IP protocol debugging tools.

Some tools are part of the TCP/IP protocol stack, others are systems that capture frames and decode them using software, and yet others are used to test physical media. The use of all these types of tools provides coverage for many of the seven layers of the OSI model.

Physical Media Test Equipment

Starting at the bottom and working up, we begin with Layer 1 connectivity testing. It is amazing how many network problems can actually be solved by testing and then resolving wiring problems.

In this section you will learn about several different types of physical media testing equipment. These include:

- Multimeters
- Cable testers
- Time domain reflectors and optical TDRs
- Digital interface testing tools

Multimeters and Cable Testers

There is a large variety of physical media testing equipment. The most basic tools are multimeters and cable testers.

Multimeters measure voltage, resistance, and current. They work with electrical-based cabling and can be used to test for physical connectivity.

Cable testers can be very general or they can be made for a specific type of cable. Some cable testers have adapters that allow them to test a wide range of cables. Cable testers are made for electrical and optical cable.

Different from multimeters, cable testers can give the user much more information regarding the cable being tested. Here are some examples of the attributes that are reported by a cable tester:

- Electrical connectivity
- Open pairs
- Crossed pairs
- Out of distance specification
- Out of decibel specification (for optical cable), meaning signal/noise is out of acceptable specifications
- Cross talk
- Attenuation

- Noise/interference

- Wiring maps

- MAC information

- Line utilization

- Time domain reflector (TDR)

 It is important to realize that not all cable testers provide all of this information. A given tester may provide only some of these attributes.

Time Domain Reflectors (TDRs) and Optical TDRs (OTDRs)

Time domain reflectors (TDRs) are complex cable testers. They are used to locate physical problems in a cable. They can detect where an open circuit, short circuit, crimped wire, or other abnormality is located in a cable.

TDRs and Optical TDRs (OTDRs) work on the same principle: a signal is sent down the cable and the unit waits for the reflected signal to come back. Different abnormalities in cabling cause this signal to be reflected at different amplitudes. Based on the signal strength, or amplitude, the meter distinguishes between opens, shorts, crimps, or other failures in the cable. These meters measure the time between the sending of the signal and the arrival of the reflected signal at the unit. This time interval is used to calculate where the failure is occurring in the cable. Optical TDRs can also provide information, such as signal attenuation, fiber breaks, and losses through connectors.

Digital Interface Testing Tools

Digital Interface Testing tools consist of several different tools, such as *breakout boxes,* used to verify pin-outs (e.g., TD—transmit data, RD—receive data, CTS—clear to send) for all types of serial and parallel interfaces, and *bit/block error rate testers,* used for testing the quality of a communication link based on deviance from a known bit pattern. These tools are used to measure signals sent from computer and communication equipment. They are also able to test connections and communication between data terminal equipment and data communications equipment.

Although monitoring line conditions is an option with these types of tools, they are not capable of analyzing protocol information on a line. Their primary use is to verify that digital communication is sent and received by the two devices that are connected to the ends of the cable. A few examples: testing between a PC and a printer, a router and CSU/DSU, or even a modem and a PC.

Software Test Equipment

There are many programs available that help to troubleshoot network problems. We begin by talking about generic programs that can provide troubleshooting capabilities, and then we will move on to Cisco-specific solutions. There are basically two types of software used for aiding network troubleshooting: network monitoring and network analyzing.

Network Monitors

As the word *monitor* describes, this software-based tool simply monitors the network. It can do this in several ways, including the Simple Network Management Protocol (SNMP) and the Internet Control Message Protocol (ICMP).

The *Simple Network Management Protocol (SNMP)* is the most widely used method of gathering network statistics. Once a machine has sufficient information about a network, it continually monitors the availability and connectivity of each device that is specified in its configuration.

No packet analysis is performed by network monitors. It is simply used to gather and keep statistical information about the network. The historical data that monitoring provides can be used to create a network *baseline*.

A baseline is a very important tool. How can you effectively troubleshoot a new problem on a network if you don't know what the network used to be like or how it was configured? By keeping a baseline, you can compare previous performance and traffic levels to what you are currently seeing. Perhaps your problem is a new application that was introduced into your network.

SNMP is not the only method of monitoring a network, however. There are tools that use protocol tools to isolate network problems. For instance, the *Internet Control Message Protocol (ICMP)* can be used to ping a list of hosts. If a host does not respond, the program adds the host to a list and displays it to a monitor.

Network Analyzers

Network analyzers are also known as *protocol analyzers*. Examples of protocol analyzers are EtherPeek (used in the *CCNA: Cisco Certified Network Associate Study Guide, CCNP: Advanced Cisco Router Configuration Study Guide,* and in this book), Network Associate's Sniffer, and RADCOM's PrismLite.

These tools must be connected to the network or broadcast domain that you are interested in troubleshooting. Figure 3.1 depicts a subnetwork. If there is a fault within the 172.16.1.0 subnetwork, the protocol analyzer must be placed on that segment of the subnetwork. Otherwise, you will not see the packets transiting the subnetwork. As you can see in Figure 3.1, the protocol analyzer is connected to the 172.16.1.0 subnetwork. Some analyzers can monitor in-line, but most just act as an additional node on the subnetwork.

FIGURE 3.1 Placement of a protocol analyzer

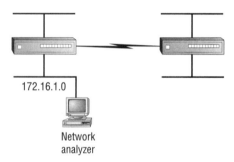

172.16.1.0

Network
analyzer

To better handle the data that is captured by an analyzer, different filters may be used. Most programs allow filters to be placed before or after the packet is copied. After a full capture, display filters may be used to help narrow the field of troubleshooting. If you are trying to troubleshoot an Ethernet problem, you probably don't want to look at all of the routing packets that were also captured. To save memory, filters can be applied before the packet is captured into memory. The analyzer looks at each packet and compares it to user-defined filters. If the necessary criteria are met, the packet is then copied to memory; otherwise, it is dropped.

EtherPeek

Take a look at the front screen of EtherPeek, shown in Figure 3.2. You see the way capture filters work. The graphic in the figure shows five rows of text information. The first row, "Packets Received," indicates the number of packets that the protocol analyzer has seen. The following field, "Packets Filtered," indicates the number of packets that were subjected to and matched the input filter criteria. "Packets Processed" signifies the number of packets that were actually copied into memory for analysis. The byte information deals with the analyzer's buffer size; it varies, depending on the analyzer being used.

FIGURE 3.2   EtherPeek front screen

Different capture filters may be used. EtherPeek has predefined capture filters, such as those seen in Figure 3.3. Filters can be used, based on protocol, protocol offset, or other information. The filters shown in Figure 3.3 are for protocols and well-known port numbers.

FIGURE 3.3   Predefined capture filters

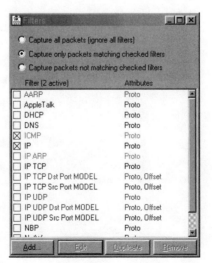

If the filters that are ready-made do not meet the specifications needed, EtherPeek and other protocol analyzers allow custom filters to be created. This is done by using the screen shown in Figure 3.4. The options available for custom filters are similar to those for the predefined filters. You may specify source and destination addresses, protocol, or offset when defining custom filters.

FIGURE 3.4 Custom capture filters

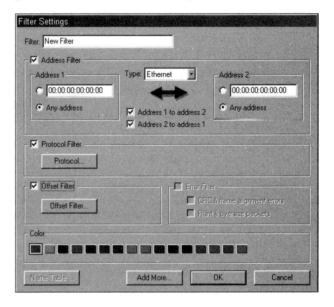

If you are not sure what packets or problems you are looking for, you can turn off the capture filter, and subsequently capture all packets transiting the network. Once you decide what you want to see, you can use display filters. EtherPeek's display filters are depicted in Figure 3.5.

FIGURE 3.5 EtherPeek's display filter options

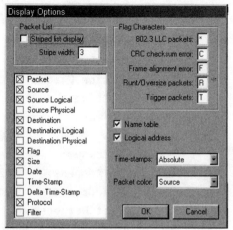

Many software programs can take the data that was captured, analyze it, and then produce reports that detail the probable causes, along with possible solutions. Analyzers can vary greatly in the functions that the software provides.

EtherPeek Sample: Multicast Packet

Now look at some samples from EtherPeek. The first packet is actually a multicast packet. As you see, the packet is broken down by protocol. The first section is the Ethernet header, which contains Layer 2 address information.

Layer 3 follows Layer 2, so you see the IP header. The IP header contains all pertinent information for IP, including the IP source and destination addresses. It also defines the protocol riding above IP, Internet Group Management Protocol (IGMP), which is used for multicast communications. Further down the packet decode, you see the actual IGMP header.

```
Flags:         0x00
  Status:      0x00
  Packet Length:64
  Timestamp:   12:12:58.349000 03/22/1999
Ethernet Header
  Destination: 01:00:5f:00:00:04
  Source:      08:00:20:7e:55:5f
  Protocol Type:08-00  IP
IP Header - Internet Protocol Datagram
  Version:             4
  Header Length:       5
```

```
    Precedence:              0
    Type of Service:         %000
    Unused:                  %00
    Total Length:            32
    Identifier:              10603
    Fragmentation Flags:     %000
    Fragment Offset:         0
    Time To Live:            1
    IP Type:                 0x02   IGMP
    Header Checksum:         0xe6e5
    Source IP Address:       172.16.10.10
    Dest. IP Address:        224.0.0.4
    No Internet Datagram Options
IGMP - Internet Group Management Protocol
    Version:         1
    Type:            3   STR# IP Protocols
    Unused:          1
    Checksum:        56080
    Group Address:1.14.8.3
Extra bytes (Padding):
    6... F..P_.  %m.   36 ee d1 ee ae 46 08 00 50 9e e4 e8
20 25 6d 00
    ..                       00 00
Frame Check Sequence:   0x00000000
```

EtherPeek Sample: Cisco Proprietary Packet

Now, look at a Cisco proprietary packet. The following is a decode for a Cisco Discovery Protocol (CDP) packet. As you can see, this is a Layer 2 packet. You can tell it is a Layer 2 packet because there is no IP or other Layer 3 header decode. The first header section is the Ethernet 802.3 Header, followed by the Logical Link Control (LLC) header. This header contains the Cisco Discovery Protocol data.

```
    Flags:        0x80   802.3
      Status:       0x00
      Packet Length:200
      Timestamp:    14:49:03.211000 03/22/1999
    802.3 Header
      Destination:  01:00:0c:dd:cc:6f   [0-5]
      Source:       00:10:7c:75:8d:cf   [6-13]
```

```
       LLC Length:    182
802.2 Logical Link Control (LLC) Header
   Dest. SAP:       0xaa  SNAP  [14]
   Source SAP:      0xaa  SNAP  Null LSAP  [15]
   Command:         0x03  Unnumbered Information  [16]
   Protocol:        00-00-0c-20-00  Cisco DP  [17-21]
   Packet Data:
   . . ....06902459    01 b4 d7 af 00 01 00 19 30 36 39 30
   32    34 35 39    [22-37]
   9(hostname  )...    39 28 73 77 2d 75 65 6e 2e 6f 72 67
   29    00 02 00    [38-53]
   .......... |....    11 00 00 00 01 01 01 cc 00 04 cd 7c
   fa    f8 00 03    [54-69]
   ..5/19..........    00 08 35 2f 31 39 00 04 00 08 00 00
   00    0e 00 05    [70-85]
   .dWS-C5500 Softw    00 00 00 00 00 00 00 00 00 30 20 53
   6f    66 74 77    [86-101]
   are, Version Mcp    61 72 65 2c 20 56 2d 00 00 00 00 00
   20    4d 63 70    [102-117]
   SW: 4.4(1) NmpSW    53 57 3a 20 34 2e 34 28 31 29 20 4e
   6d    70 53 57    [118-133]
   : 4.4(1).Copyrig    3a 20 34 00 00 00 00 00 00 00 00 00
   00    72 69 67    [134-149]
   ht (c) 1995-1999    68 74 20 28 63 29 20 31 39 39 35 2d
   31    39 39 39    [150-165]
   by Cisco System    20 62 79 20 43 69 73 63 6f 20 53 79 73
   74 65 6d    [166-181]
   s.....WS-C5500      73 0a 00 06 00 0c 57 53 2d 43 35 35
   30    30    [182-195]
   Frame Check Sequence:  0xffff00cd
```

EtherPeek Sample: POP3 Packet

The following example is of a POP3 packet. POP3 is the Post Office Protocol that is used to transfer e-mail from a server to a remote client. The packet decode gives you a great amount of information. It starts out with a Layer 2 header, and then moves on to Layer 3 with the IP header. After Layer 3, you see TCP, which is a Layer 4 protocol. You can see all of the flow control information as part of the TCP packet. POP3 is part of the TCP suite, and is the final decode portion of this packet. The POP3 header shows the mail server as well as other POP3 data.

```
Flags:         0x00
  Status:        0x00
  Packet Length:99
  Timestamp:     14:48:51.539000 03/22/1999
Ethernet Header
```

Destination: 01:a1:32:5a:a6:f1   [0-5]
Source: 08:00:02:32:1f:f2   [6-11]
Protocol Type:08-00   IP   [12-13]

IP Header - Internet Protocol Datagram

Version: 4   [14 Mask 0xf0]
Header Length: 5   [14 Mask 0xf]
Precedence: 0   [15 Mask 0xe0]
Type of Service: %000   [15 Mask 0x1c]
Unused: %00   [15 Mask 0x3]
Total Length: 81   [16-17]
Identifier: 6039   [18-19]
Fragmentation Flags: %010   *Do Not Fragment*   [20 Mask 0xe0]
Fragment Offset: 0   [20-22 Mask 0x1fffff]
Time To Live: 255
IP Type: 0x06   *TCP*   [23]
Header Checksum: 0xd488   [24-25]
Source IP Address: 172.16.12.10   [26-29]
Dest. IP Address: 172.16.12.130   [30-33]
No Internet Datagram Options

TCP - Transport Control Protocol

Source Port: 110 *POP3* [34-35]
Destination Port: 1324 [36-37]
Sequence Number: 3712383331 [38-41]
Ack Number: 31151113 [42-45]
Offset: 5 [46 Mask 0xf0]
Reserved: %000000 [46 Mask 0xfc0]
Code: %011000 [47 Mask 0x3f]

```
                Ack is valid
                Push Request
```

Window: 8760 [48-49]

    Checksum: 0x2d24 [50-51]
    Urgent Pointer: 0 [52-53]
    No TCP Options
POP - Post Office Protocol
    POP Reply: +OK *Positive Reply* [54-56]
    Comment: [57]
    POP3 mail.somewhere.com 50 45 50 33 21 68 61 6d 2f 75
    65   6e 2d 6e 72 67 [58-73]
    v6.50 server re   21 76 36 2a 35 30 21 73 65 72 77 65
    78   20 72 65 [74-89]
    ady   61 46 80   [90-92]
    Newline Sequence: 0x0d0a [93-94]
Frame Check Sequence: 0xffff00cd

EtherPeek Sample: IPX Packet

This last example shows an IPX packet. This is an IPX broadcast packet, as indicated by the destination MAC address within the 802.3 header. The LLC header has the source and destination SAP information. The IPX NetWare packet is a NetWare Core Protocol packet. The destination socket for every machine on a broadcast domain is the same. The IPX broadcast is done by using the Service Advertising Protocol. The decode for that header is located at the bottom of the example. The packet tells you that a machine is using NSQ to find the nearest file server.

    Flags: 0x80 *802.3*
      Status: 0x00
      Packet Length:64
      Timestamp: 14:47:09.831000 03/22/1999
    802.3 Header
      Destination: ff:ff:ff:ff:ff:ff Ethernet Brdcast [0-5]
      Source: 00:00:1d:04:51:43 [6-13]
      LLC Length: 37
    802.2 Logical Link Control (LLC) Header
      Dest. SAP: 0xe0 NetWare [14]
      Source SAP: 0xe0 NetWare Null LSAP [15]
      Command: 0x03 Unnumbered Information [16]
    IPX - NetWare Protocol

```
Checksum:                 0xffff  [17-18]
Length:                   34  [19-20]
Transport Control:
  Reserved:               %0000  [21 Mask 0xf0]
  Hop Count:              %0000  [21-22 Mask 0xfff]
Packet Type:              17  NCP - Netware Core Protocol
Destination Network:  0x00000000  [23-26]
Destination Node:     ff:ff:ff:ff:ff:ff Ethernet Brdcast
[27-32]
Destination Socket:   0x0452  Service Advertising
Protocol      [33-34]
Source Network:       0x00000010  [35-38]
Source Node:          00:00:1e:04:52:43  [39-44]
Source Socket:        0x4010  IPX Ephemeral  [45-46]
SAP - Service Advertising Protocol
  Operation:          3  NetWare Nearest Service Query
[47-48]
  Service Type:       4  File Server  [49-50]
Extra bytes (Padding):
  . ....NBU           03 c1 00 00 00 00 4e 42 55   [51-59]
Frame Check Sequence:  0x01000000
```

As you see from the previous packet decodes, there is a lot of information that can be found out about a given network. The key is to know what you are searching for when looking through the results of a protocol analyzer. By looking at decodes and seeing where problems might be occurring, you can resolve network failures more quickly.

Now, let's look at the way LANWatch works.

LANWatch

LANWatch is a software protocol analyzer made by Precision Guesswork, Inc. It is similar to EtherPeek because it can be installed on machines that have Ethernet connections to the network. The interface watches all of the traffic on the broadcast domain. Here is a screen shot of LANWatch.

Take a look at the front screen of LANWatch, shown in Figure 3.6. The graphic in the figure shows the normal set of menus: File, Edit, View, Filter, Options, Window, and Help.

FIGURE 3.6   Front screen for LANWatch32

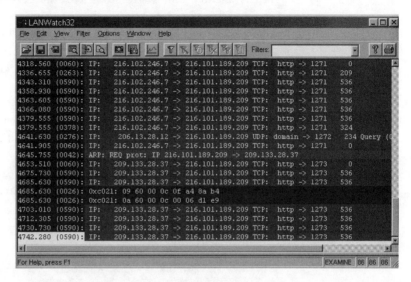

The File menu provides options for loading, saving, and capturing packets, as well as printing options. The menu is shown in Figure 3.7.

FIGURE 3.7   File menu for LANWatch32

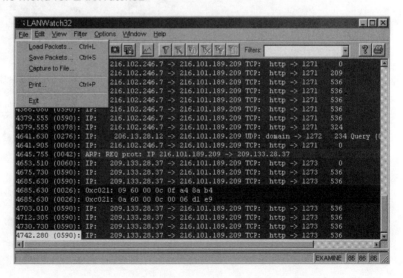

The Edit menu list allows you to delete a single packet, delete all packets, and move within the capture buffer by specifying the line number. You can also insert a comment into the packet buffer, by highlighting where you want the comment to go and then selecting the Insert Comment option.

To aid in troubleshooting, you can tag certain packets by using the Toggle Marker option in the Edit menu. This option is helpful for selecting packets that belong to a single session or machine. It lets you move between marked packets to see the sequence of events relating to the tagged packets. The toggle marker highlights the timestamp of the specified packet. You can move between marked packets by using the toggle options available from the Edit menu.

Finally, the Edit menu allows you to perform searches within the packet buffer. A screen shot of the Edit menu is shown in Figure 3.8.

FIGURE 3.8 Edit menu for LANWatch32

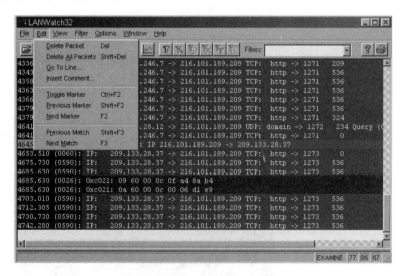

Three views are available with LANWatch: Examine, Summary, and Detail. The different views are used to show all packets, an individual packet summary, and individual packet details, respectively. Figures 3.9, 3.10, and 3.11 show the differences between the three views. Each subsequent view is similar to "drilling down" into the packet's content.

FIGURE 3.9   Examine view for LANWatch32

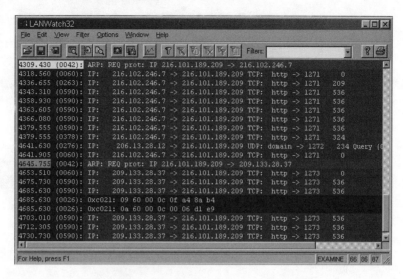

FIGURE 3.10   Summary view for LANWatch32

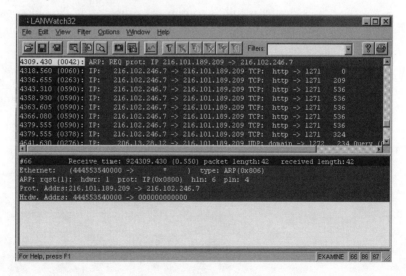

FIGURE 3.11 Detail view for LANWatch32

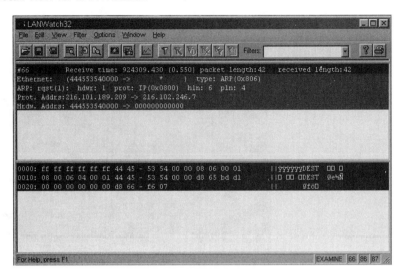

The View menu also provides the options for packet capture. You can initiate a normal capture that will continue to accept packets, even after the buffer is full. It continues by discarding the oldest packets captured and allowing new packets to be stored in the buffer. You also have the option to start a capture that stops once the buffer is filled.

The View menu contains access to statistical and throughput information. Statistical information consists of detailed and summary protocol counts, detailed and summary packet size, and hardware and error counts. Figure 3.12 is a screen shot of the statistical window.

FIGURE 3.12 Statistical window

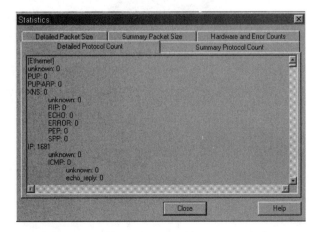

The throughput can be graphed as the packets are captured. Figure 3.13 displays the throughput window.

FIGURE 3.13 Throughput window

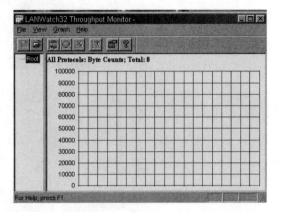

The Filter menu allows you to create, modify, delete, copy, and list current packet filters.

When creating filters, many different criteria can be specified. Figures 3.14 through 3.17 show the filter-creation process using the Filter Wizard. If additional criteria need to be specified, you can add multiple conditions. This is done by selecting the Next button, shown in Figure 3.17.

The filters created are input filters and not display filters. This means that only packets meeting the specified criteria will be copied into the buffer; others are discarded.

FIGURE 3.14 Step 1 in filter creation

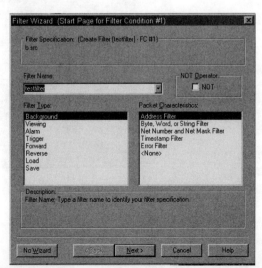

FIGURE 3.15 Step 2 in filter creation

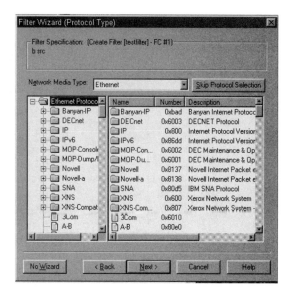

FIGURE 3.16 Step 3 in filter creation

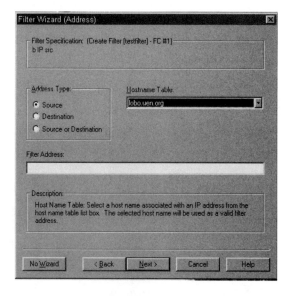

FIGURE 3.17   Final step for first filter condition—additional conditions may be specified

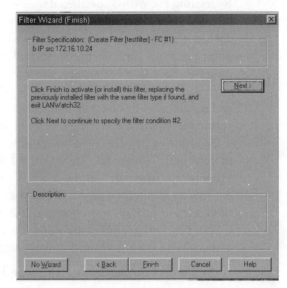

You can see the active filter displayed in the Filters window on the LANWatch front screen. If multiple filters have been created, you can use the scroll button to select the filter you wish to apply.

There are several shortcut buttons displayed underneath the main menu buttons that have just been described. If you leave the cursor on top of a button for a few seconds, the function of the button will be displayed.

Finally, the information provided by the captured frame is the same as can be found in EtherPeek. Once you select the frame by clicking it with the mouse, you can select different details by pressing Enter.

Network Management Systems (NMSs)

*N*etwork management systems (NMSs) are somewhat more complex than simple network monitoring systems. NMSs are more robust because they not only provide monitoring functions for network devices, they also allow for user interaction. Some examples of third-party NMSs are HP OpenView and Sun Net Manager management packages.

The basics behind these systems are that, with some configuration and guidance, they use different methods of *discovering* a network. This is done by starting out with a specified device—a *seed device*. The seed device polls all of its interfaces and comes back with the necessary information that enables the program to move on to the directly connected neighbors. The polling goes on until an edge is reached and there are no more neighbors to discover. Both of these systems draw logical topological network maps.

In addition to network discovery, the NMS monitors for device availability and reachability. If something does affect the connectivity, an alarm is tripped within the software, and it logs the event and displays an alarm.

Monitoring can also be done on a more detailed level (such as threshold monitoring). Thresholds can be defined within the software. They tell the program to trigger an alarm if a specified variable for a given machine exceeds a maximum or descends below a minimal value. These alarms can be dealt with in various ways (for example, e-mail or pages may be sent).

The previous examples are just a few examples of what NMS packages can do. Here is a list of what most management systems try to do:

Availability management   This was described previously as network monitoring.

Network performance management   This is done by measuring traffic loads and other bandwidth-oriented data that can be used to calculate the network's overall performance.

Network security management   This is done by making the NMS the means by which changes are made to network devices. Because the software requires the user to log in, it can also track changes made by the user. Security management can also be done via having a user database within the NMS. When a network device is accessed or a change is attempted, the user is authenticated from the user profiles located within the NMS.

Network service simulation   In today's networks, it becomes very risky to test out configuration changes on a live production network. Simulation software that enables changes to be made off-line and tested before being implemented is a big part of network management. It gives the administrator the ability to see whether the changes will cause any side effects, without endangering the applications on the production network.

Policy-based management   This has to do with QoS, or Quality of Service. When an administrator knows that certain applications require more network resources, he or she can allocate resources accordingly. With policy-based management, the administrator can see where the most resources are needed and make it a higher priority that those resources are available when needed.

As was mentioned before, NMSs are third-party systems. Due to the complexity and diversity of network hardware, most vendors have their own management information base, or MIB, in addition to the standard ones. It doesn't stop there—Cisco has also created its own line of NMSs, which you will learn about in the next section.

Cisco Network Management Software

In order to achieve the five previously mentioned purposes of network management software, Cisco uses three software packages: CiscoWorks 2000, NetSys, and CiscoSecure. By using a combination of these packages, all five NMS purposes are fulfilled.

CiscoWorks 2000

CiscoWorks 2000 is the latest release of CiscoWorks. Cisco united several different network management packages into one centralized package. The primary components of CiscoWorks 2000 are Resource Manager Essentials and CiscoWorks for Switched Internetworks (CWSI). Within CWSI, you find further subcomponents: CWSI Campus, CiscoView, Threshold Manager, Traffic Director, VLAN Director, ATM Director, and UserTracking.

Each of these components fulfills an important role in the overall effectiveness of CiscoWorks 2000. We will now cover the role and basic functionality of each component.

Resource Manager Essentials

This component has taken the place of the original CiscoWorks. This portion of CiscoWorks 2000 is responsible for device inventory, configuration storage and changes, IOS upgrades and inventory, and some low-level security. It also provides monitoring functions, such as syslog monitoring.

This application, along with the other elements of CiscoWorks 2000, uses the *Simple Network Management Protocol (SNMP)* to manage the network. SNMP provides a way to retrieve device information and system information. Each device contains several *management information base* objects, otherwise known as *MIB* objects. These objects are simply variables that are assigned values. When an SNMP agent queries a device, it asks for specified MIB object values. The device then responds with the corresponding values. Look at the following example to see what we mean.

The first line of the debug shows an SNMP request from an SNMP agent (server). In this request, you see the MIB objects that the SNMP agent wants to get values for. The following lines show all MIB objects and their corresponding values. In this case, some of the MIB objects are the System Uptime and IP Address Entries. You can see that each MIB has a value assigned to it. We finish by looking at the line that confirms that the MIB object values were sent to the requesting machine.

Here is the debug:

```
debug snmp packets
SNMP packet debugging is on
Router_A#
Mar 23 22:05:49.751: SNMP: Packet received via UDP from
172.16.2.2 on ATM1/0.2
Mar 23 22:05:49.755: SNMP: Get request, reqid 271128,
errstat 0, erridx 0
sysUpTime.0 = 27315180
 lsystem.57.0 = 11
 lsystem.58.0 = 10
 ipAddrEntry.2.172.16.10.254 = 28
 ipAddrEntry.2.172.16.10.10 = 1
 ipAddrEntry.2.172.16.10.18 = 1
 ipAddrEntry.2.172.16.33.1 = 14
 ipAddrEntry.2.172.16.10.1 = 25
 ipAddrEntry.2.172.16.10.1 - 10
 ipAddrEntry.2.172.16.10.1 = 15
 ipAddrEntry.2.172.16.231.1 = 10
 ipAddrEntry.2.172.16.235.65 = 29
 ipAddrEntry.2.172.16.236.17 = 10
 ipAddrEntry.2.172.16.238.1 = 27
 ipAddrEntry.2.172.16.10.5 = 45
 ipAddrEntry.2.172.16.240.1 = 13
 ipAddrEntry.2.172.16.246.1 = 12
 ipAddrEntry.2.172.16.10.9 = 75
 ipAddrEntry.2.172.16.10.21 = 58
 ipAddrEntry.2.172.16.10.25 = 65
 ipAddrEntry.2.172.16.10.29 = 60
```

```
ipAddrEntry.2.172.16.10.33 = 61
ipAddrEntry.2.172.16.10.37 = 76
ipAddrEntry.2.172.16.10.45 = 59
ipAddrEntry.2.172.16.10.49 = 67
ipAddrEntry.2.172.16.10.53 = 72
ipAddrEntry.2.172.16.10.57 = 73
ipAddrEntry.2.172.16.10.61 = 74
ipAddrEntry.2.172.16.10.65 = 56
ipAddrEntry.2.172.16.10.69 = 57
ipAddrEntry.2.172.16.10.81 = 55
ipAddrEntry.2.172.16.10.85 = 66
ipAddrEntry.2.172.16.10.89 = 68
ipAddrEntry.2.172.16.10.101 = 69
ipAddrEntry.2.172.16.10.105 = 70
ipAddrEntry.2.172.16.10.109 = 71
ipAddrEntry.2.172.16.10.121 = 62
ipAddrEntry.2.172.16.10.249 = 43
 ipAddrEntry.2.172.16.10.9 = 47
Mar 23 22:05:49.815: SNMP: Packet sent via UDP to
172.16.2.2
Router_A#un all
All possible debugging has been turned off
```

SNMP is a very rich protocol, and it is capable of providing detailed information. Because SNMP is not the focus of this book, we don't spend much time explaining its intricacies.

In summary, Resource Manager Essentials provides the following functions. It does all of this via SNMP, with some help from other protocols, such as TFTP for file transfer, even though the command is issued via SNMP.

- Availability/Reachability Monitoring

- Change Reports

- Configuration Management

- Device Inventory

- IOS Management

- Syslog Analysis

- System Administration

- CCO Access and related tools

- Connection Management

- Troubleshooting information

CWSI

CiscoWorks for Switched Internetworks (CWSI) is a composite of several applications. The majority of the applications in CiscoWorks 2000 are applications of the CWSI element. The following lists a brief description of what each application is and what it is used for:

CWSI Campus   This application is responsible for network discovery. It creates a logical topology map of the network and also provides views for VLANs.

VLAN Director   This tool is used to configure, manage, and create reports for VLANs. It provides detailed information regarding physical devices, spanning tree configurations, and ATM-VLANs. It can also be used to provide Quality of Service by providing different resources, based on VLAN assignment.

CiscoView   This application is used to display an image that physically represents the device. Within this program, you can monitor individual ports, the chassis, and interfaces. Some hardware platforms allow environmental information such as temperature and CPU utilization to be monitored.

Threshold Manager   This tool is actually part of CiscoView. It is used to configure the RMON (Remote Monitoring) threshold on network devices. Users can select default or custom MIB objects that are to be monitored. For a given MIB object, the user can then define thresholds that trigger alarms if the values of the MIB object do not fall within the specified criteria.

Traffic Director   This application complements the Threshold Manager. Because Threshold Manager is only a GUI to configure a device with thresholds, the Traffic Director uses RMON to gather the threshold information from the device. In addition to RMON information, Traffic Director provides protocol analysis, traffic monitoring and analysis, and application utilization.

ATM Director   This tool is used to discover ATM devices. It can provide information based on VPI/VCI pairs; it interfaces with switches to provide ATM-VLAN information; and it provides statistical information for PVCs, SVCs, and other ATM information.

UserTracking   Because VLANs are simply logical associations, UserTracking is used to aid in moving user information from one VLAN to another or to provide consistent VLAN assignment if the physical cable is moved from one port to another on the switch.

Cisco provides a very thorough set of network management applications. These programs were developed specifically for Cisco equipment. For example, CWSI uses Cisco Discovery Protocol (CDP) to discover the network. Only Cisco devices respond to CDP packets. Because these tools were developed for Cisco devices, the MIB objects that are needed to manage the devices are preprogrammed into the software. With the CiscoWorks 2000 package, three of the five goals for NMS are fulfilled.

NetSys

NetSys is an off-line tool. It is a complex program that inputs and parses Cisco device configurations, and then creates a model based on the configurations. The program is used to model changes to a network before they are actually implemented. The original configurations can be used to establish a baseline.

The engine used within NetSys can decipher the configurations and pinpoint any problems that might occur with the implementation of the configuration. NetSys creates topological maps, and then enables the user to make changes on the map, thus affecting configurations. There is a connectivity tool that allows the user to test connectivity between any two specified devices.

NetSys also has a performance tool. It can be configured to poll information from the network, download it, and then analyze it. The information copied from the network is used to show protocol distribution, link distribution, and application utilization. Using this tool, the user can create models that enable the network to scale and grow, according to the demands placed on it.

NetSys fulfills the role of an NMS because it allows changes to be modeled off-line, tested, and then implemented into the production network. NetSys is a very powerful tool, and has been called a "CCIE in a can."

CiscoSecure

The CiscoSecure access control server (ACS) application is used to define access levels to individual users. CiscoSecure maintains a user profile for each user. This profile contains authorization and authentication information that is unique to each user.

It functions like AAA (Authentication, Authorization, and Accounting), which provides security for the routers via the IOS on the router or switch. Authentication is used to verify that the user is who they say they are and that they are allowed to log in to a device. Once the user is verified, the authorization information specifies what level of access the user has.

CiscoSecure is flexible and scalable because it is capable of providing services to several devices simultaneously. Multiple servers can be deployed to allow for scalability. This management software completes the five requirements for a network management system by fulfilling the role of security.

Summary

This chapter was concerned with different types and applications of network testing equipment. We discussed physical media testers, as well as software methods for troubleshooting network problems. Let's recap the major points of this chapter:

Physical test equipment   Includes multimeters, cable testers, TDRs, and OTDRs. These methods are good for testing cable integrity and end-to-end physical connectivity.

Software test equipment   Can be used in different ways. Simple software methods may be used to test for device availability. These are known as network monitors.

Protocol analyzers   These devices actually copy and analyze packets on a network. The information provided by protocol analyzers can be invaluable when troubleshooting network problems.

Network management systems (NMSs)   These programs are very robust and provide great manageability for small and large networks. An NMS should have five attributes:

- Network Availability Monitoring
- Network Modeling and Simulation
- Network Security
- Quality of Service Management
- Traffic Monitoring and Analysis

Cisco provides software packages that fulfill all of these requirements; collectively, they possess all five of the above attributes.

Commands Used in This Chapter

The following list contains a summary of all the commands used in this chapter.

Command	Meaning
`debug snmp packets`	Provides detail for SNMP packets destined for the router.

Key Terms

Before you take the exam, be certain you are familiar with the following terms:

baseline

bit/block error rate testers

cable testers

management information base objects

MIB objects

monitor

multimeters

network analyzers

network management systems (NMSs)

physical test equipment

protocol analyzers

seed device

Simple Network Management Protocol (SNMP)

software test equipment

time domain reflectors (TDRs)

Review Questions

1. Of the physical media testing tools below, which one is most appropriate to use when testing signals between a PC and its modem?

A. TDR

B. OTDR

C. Multimeter

D. Breakout box

2. Which tool do you use if you have to test a cabling infrastructure and functionality of your LAN?

A. TDR

B. Cable tester

C. Network analyzer

D. Breakout box

3. What tools can be used to verify fiber optic cable length, cable attenuation, or the approximate location of a fault with the cable? (Choose two.)

A. Optical time domain reflector (OTDR)

B. Cable tester

C. Multimeter

D. Time domain reflector (TDR)

4. Which device do you use to test for physical (electrical) connectivity?

A. OTDR

B. Cable tester

C. Multimeter

D. TDR

5. Which tool do you use if you want to test fiber optic cable?

   A. OTDR

   B. TDR

   C. A flashlight

   D. Cable tester

6. Which protocol is used to collect device and statistical information?

   A. SNA

   B. SAP

   C. SMTP

   D. SNMP

7. On what basis do protocol or network analyzers work?

   A. All packets are analyzed as they pass through the analyzer.

   B. All packets are copied into a buffer if they meet specified criteria.

   C. Random packets are selected, based on the line speed of the media.

   D. Random packets are selected if they meet the specified criteria.

8. What types of filters do most network analyzers use? (Choose all that apply.)

   A. Access lists

   B. Capture

   C. Display

   D. Size

9. While looking at the capture screen of the network analyzer, you see the following information. Explain what it means.

224 Total Frames

128 Frames Accepted

A. The processor on the analyzer is not fast enough to keep up with the line speed, so some packets were missed.

B. Only 128 frames were sent to the analyzer.

C. There is a serious problem on the network: many packets are corrupted or dropped before they make it to the analyzer.

D. A capture filter was applied, and only 128 of the 224 packets match the capture filter's criteria.

10. Imagine that you finish filling the capture buffer of a network analyzer without using a capture filter. How do you display packets only from a specific server?

A. Configure and use a display filter.

B. Cut and paste relevant packets into a text file.

C. Start the capture over, but this time use a capture filter.

D. There is no way to accomplish this task.

11. Use the following decode information to determine what type of packet you are looking at. (Choose all that apply.)

```
Flags:              0x80      802.3
    Status:             0x00
    Packet Length:64
    Timestamp:          10:19:42.712000 12/04/1998
802.3 Header
    Destination:    09:00:07:ff:ff:ff
[0-5]
    Source:         00:10:7b:a4:4a:a1
[6-13]
    LLC Length:        37
802.2 Logical Link Control (LLC) Header
    Dest. SAP:          0xaa      SNAP       [14]
    Source SAP:    0xaa      SNAP      Null LSAP   [15]
    Command:                      0x03
```

Unnumbered Information   [16]
    Protocol: 08-00-07-80-9b   ETalkPh2
[17-21]
Long DDP Header - Datagram Delivery Protocol
    Unused:
%00   [22 Mask 0xc0]
    Hop Count:
%0000   [22 Mask 0x3c]
    Datagram Length: 29   [22-23 Mask 0x3ff]
    DDP Checksum: 0x8a38   [24-25]
    Dest. Network: 0   [26-27]
    Source Network: 1105   [28-29]
    Dest Node: 255
[30]
    Source Node: 179
[31-32]
    Dest. Socket: 1   RTMP
[33]
    Source Socket: 1   RTMP
[34]
    DDP Type: 1
RTMP Response or Data
RTMP - Routing Table Maintenance Protocol
    Router's Net: 1105   [35-37]
ID Length: 8
[38]
Router's Node ID: 179

RTMP Tuple # 1
    Range Start: 1100   [39-40]
    Range Flag: %100   Extended
[47 Mask 0xe0]
    Distance: 0   [41 Mask 0x1f]
    Range End: 1109   [42-43]
    Version: 0x82   [44]
RTMP Tuple # 2
    Range Start: 1000   [45-46]
    Range Flag: %100   Extended

```
[47 Mask 0xe0]
      Distance:              0           [47 Mask
0x1f]
      Range End:                          1005
[48-49]
      Version:                            0x82
[50]
Extra bytes (Padding):
      ........               00 00 00 00 00 00 00
00 00                  [51-59]
Frame Check Sequence:        0xfff0000a
```

A. AppleTalk

B. IPX

C. RTMP

D. Tuple

12. You look at a protocol distribution report from a network analyzer, and it says that there is a large amount of SNMP traffic. What does it mean?

   A. SNMP is using a high percentage of the total available bandwidth.

   B. SNMP is the most important protocol listed, which is why it has the highest percentage.

   C. SNMP needs to be turned off because the link can't handle that much SNMP traffic.

   D. SNMP uses the largest packet size relative to other protocols.

13. What *simple* software tools are used to test for device availability/ reachability?

   A. Cable tester

   B. Network monitors

   C. Network analyzers

   D. NMS

14. Name the five attributes needed by network management systems.

   A. Network Availability Monitoring, Network Modeling and Simulation, Network Security, Quality of Service Management, and Traffic Monitoring and Analysis

   B. SNMP Collection, Change Auditing, Configuration Inventory, IOS Inventory, Quality of Service

   C. SNA, SNMP, PING, TRACEROUTE, DNS

   D. Configurable, manageable, effective, robust, detailed

15. The original CiscoWorks ran in conjunction with which third-party NMSs? (Choose two.)

   A. Solaris

   B. Windows NT

   C. HP OpenView

   D. Sun Net Manager

16. Which attribute or type of NMS do you use if you need to test a new configuration?

   A. NetSys

   B. simulation/modeling tools

   C. VLAN Director

   D. performance monitoring

17. Which Cisco product provides the security NMS attribute?

   A. TACACS+

   B. Radius

   C. CiscoWorks

   D. CiscoSecure ACS

18. How does CiscoWorks (CWSI, specifically) discover the network? (Choose all that apply.)

A. CDP

B. ping

C. Telnet

D. SNMP

19. Which Cisco product uses RMON to manage threshold events once they occur?

A. Threshold Manager

B. CiscoView

C. Traffic Director

D. VLAN Director

20. Which NMS attributes does CiscoWorks 2000 possess? (Choose all that apply.)

A. Availability Monitoring

B. Modeling and Simulation

C. Network Security

D. Quality of Service Management

E. Traffic Monitoring and Analysis

Answers to Review Questions

1. D. A breakout box is the best choice for this application. A multimeter could be used to check for electrical signaling, but you would have to manually test for the proper pin-out.

2. B. A TDR could be used, but a quick test can be accomplished with a cable tester.

3. A, D. Such detailed information can only be supplied by a TDR or an Optical TDR.

4. C. A multimeter is the best tool for this job because it provides information regarding electrical properties such as resistance, voltage, and current.

5. A. An OTDR is the right tool for this task because it is designed for fiber optic Time Domain testing.

6. D. Simple Network Management Protocol collects several types of statistical and environmental information from routers, switches, and computers.

7. B. B is the best answer because it allows for the possibility of filters. If no filter were applied, all packets would be copied into the buffer.

8. B, C. Capture filters define what will be captured and display filters allow frames matching the criteria to be displayed.

9. D. "Total Frames" means that there were 224 frames seen by the analyzer; however, only 128 of them met the filter criteria and were kept in the capture buffer.

10. A. Display filters allow the user to view only frames that meet certain criteria.

11. A, C. RTMP is an AppleTalk protocol, thus the packet is both an RTMP and an AppleTalk packet.

12. A. Protocol distributions analyze all protocol types on a segment and supply a percentage distribution.

13. B. Monitors are simple because they are not intrusive and don't require much configuration or interaction.

14. A.

15. C, D. CiscoWorks worked from within HPOV and SNM as well as a stand-alone tool.

16. B. The question asks for the NMS attribute, not the software package.

17. D. This question asks for the NMS software that corresponds to the attribute. TACACS+ and Radius provide security, but they are not NMS packages.

18. A, D. CDP is used for Cisco proprietary neighbors and then SNMP is used to gather further information about the connected devices.

19. C. Traffic Director uses the information provided by RMON and RMON probes to retrieve threshold information.

20. A, D, E. CiscoWorks 2000 is a combined product of several different NMS programs that allow it to cover a wide range of NMS attributes.

Cisco's Diagnostic Commands

TOPICS COVERED IN THIS CHAPTER INCLUDE:

✓ Learning to use the troubleshooting tools available to you, including learning to use them in a manner that will not negatively impact the network.

✓ Learning to use generic troubleshooting tools as well as Cisco-specific tools on Cisco routers and switches.

✓ Learning and using the Cisco IOS show and debug commands.

✓ Learning how to perform core dumps from the routers.

Cisco equipment functions in accordance with the OSI model. Routers are known as Layer 3—Network devices. Cisco has developed many ways to efficiently and effectively move incoming data to the correct outbound interface. These methods are described in detail in this chapter.

Because different applications use different packet sizes, it is important to gain an understanding of the buffers implemented by Cisco and how they can be configured to provide more efficient use of memory buffers. Buffer configuration is also addressed in this chapter.

Armed with the general information regarding protocols and troubleshooting tools, you're ready to cover Cisco-specific material. This chapter discusses the output of Cisco diagnostic commands, and Cisco-specific routing and switching procedures.

Understanding the Output from Diagnostic Commands

Before an engineer can effectively and successfully troubleshoot network problems, they need to understand the processes being analyzed. If this understanding is not present, then information provided by troubleshooting tools is useless. Troubleshooting is like learning another language—if you don't have a basic vocabulary and knowledge of the jargon, you can't pick up a book written in a foreign language and understand it. Troubleshooting is similar—if you don't understand the technology and processes present in the problems you troubleshoot, diagnostic information is of little use. This section is dedicated to a discussion of the processes that occur on Cisco routers.

Several processes exist simultaneously on a router, and it is important to single out which processes are of interest. Sometimes diagnostic tools can affect available resources on the router. Not only can resources be used, but the efficiency with which routers handle packets may also be affected.

We begin by discussing the routing process that occurs on a router; then we move on to switching paths that routers implement to facilitate and accelerate packet forwarding. Don't confuse switching paths with Layer 2 switching, which does not occur on a router. As we discuss these processes and tools, we will also emphasize proper utilization to avoid excessive intrusion while troubleshooting.

The Routing Process

Routers are Layer 3 devices that are used to forward incoming packets to their destination by using logical addressing. IP addresses are logical addresses. Routers share information about these logical addresses with each other, and this information is stored in route tables. The router uses the route table to map the path through the router to the destination IP address.

Two *processes* must be present for routing to work properly. The first is *path determination*, which means that the router is aware of a route that leads to the desired destination address. The second is the actual moving of the packet from the inbound interface to the proper outbound interface. Look at Figure 4.1 to get a visual idea of this process.

FIGURE 4.1   Routing components

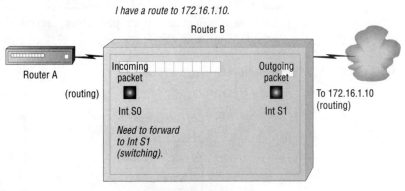

As you can see, a packet is forwarded to Router B via the routing process. Router B told Router A that it knew a route to the destination address. Once Router B has the packet, it must find the outgoing port associated with the destination address of 172.16.1.10. Once the route has been found, the router must move the packet to the outgoing interface Serial 1. After the packet reaches interface Serial 1, it is routed toward the destination of 172.16.1.10.

This is the basic routing process. For routes to be shared among adjacent routers, a *routing protocol* must be used. Routing protocols are used so that routers can calculate, learn, and advertise route table information.

Metrics are associated with each route that is present in the route table. Metrics are calculated by the routing protocol to define a cost of getting to the destination address. Some algorithms use hop count (the number of routers between it and the destination address), whereas others use a vector of values.

Once a metric is assigned to a route, a router advertises this information to all adjacent routers. Thus, each router maintains a topology and map of how to get to connected networks. By *connected*, I do not mean directly connected, simply that there exists some type of network connection between the destination address and the router.

The Switching Process

We now have an overview of how routing works. It is also important to understand the intricate flow of a packet through routers in general. This packet flow is considered to be switching. The description that follows is meant to associate the routing process with the OSI model.

A router leads a pretty boring life (see Figure 4.2 for an example). When a router receives a frame on any of its interfaces, it asks the question "Is this packet for me?" After looking at the Layer 3 header, it sees the destination address and answers its own question. At this point, there are only two possibilities: the packet is intended for the router, or it is not.

FIGURE 4.2 Packet flow through a router

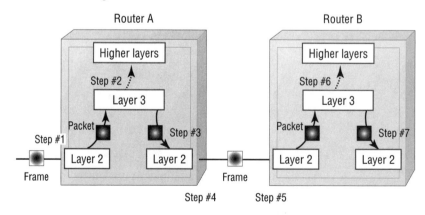

Let's back up a little here. You just read that the router receives a frame. Right now we are going to be very specific with our nomenclature. As you learned in Chapter 2, a frame is a Layer 2 PDU and a packet is a Layer 3 PDU. The router receives a frame because the Layer 3 PDU from the adjacent router had to be encapsulated in order to be sent.

Start with Step 1, pictured in Figure 4.2. Step 1 consists of Layer 2 receiving an incoming frame. Because these are routers, the packet (Layer 3 PDU) must be extracted from the frame, the frame discarded, and the packet passed up to Layer 3.

Layer 3 then performs Step 2. It looks at the packet and says, "Is this for me?" The router then identifies the destination address within the Layer 3 header. If the packet is destined for the router, Layer 3 strips off the Layer 3 header and passes the PDU up to the higher layers. If the packet is not destined for the router, it follows the remaining steps outlined in Figure 4.2.

Assuming that the packet is not intended for the router, it is sent back down to Layer 2 to be encapsulated (Step 3). At this point, the router has done a route table look-up and knows which interface it must send the packet to, but it needs to know the Layer 2 address (MAC address if Ethernet, FDDI, or Token Ring—LAN Media) of the adjacent interface. In the case of Ethernet, if the MAC address does not exist in the ARP table, the router will issue an ARP request for the MAC address for the interface on Router B. Once the MAC address is known, the frame header can be created. With the frame header created, the packet is encapsulated and sent to the next hop (Step 4).

The process is repeated at Router B. The router receives a frame, and then gets the packet and asks, "Is this for me?" Depending on the answer, the packet is forwarded to the upper layers or to an exiting interface. This same procedure is followed along every hop en route to the destination router. Remember that the logical address specified in the packet does not change—only the MAC address changes. The logical address allows the packet to be routed to its destination, whereas the MAC address allows the frame to be forwarded to each next-hop. It seems monotonous, but it is necessary.

We have now discussed generalities concerning packet flow through a router. You may notice that no reference was made about which paths were taken inside the router. The switching path taken by a PDU depends implicitly on the type of router on which it is implemented. Because Cisco makes such a wide variety of routers, we will look at each type individually. By covering the different architectures, you can then better understand the switching types that are described later in this section.

Cisco 7000 Series Router Architecture

The Cisco 7000 router is a high-end router, and the 7000 model is the top end of the series. The key feature of this router is the chassis architecture. The backplane of this router is designed to accommodate a wide variety of interface processors, which can be paralleled to a network interface card (NIC). The Cisco 7000 series routers can support the following network technologies/interface processors:

- AIP (ATM Interface Processor)
- HIP (HSSI Interface Processor)
- EIP (Ethernet Interface Processor)
- FSIP (Fast Serial Interface Processor)
- FEIP (Fast Ethernet Interface Processor)
- FIP (FDDI Interface Processor)
- TRIP (Token Ring Interface Processor)

In addition to these network interfaces, the router uses these other processors:

- CIP (Channel Interface Processor)
- MIP (Multi-channel Interface Processor)
- SP (Switch Processor)
- SSP (Silicon Switch Processor)
- RP (Route Processor)
- RSP7000 (Route Switch Processor 7000 series)

Let's talk about the network interface processors first. Each board that is inserted into the router connects to the CxBus backplane of the router. This backplane serves as the link between all other boards installed in the router. Bandwidth capacity for the backplane is 533Mbps.

Interface processors, which interface with the backplane and allow data transfer, exist on each board. It is possible to oversubscribe the backplane. For example, if you install five Fast Ethernet boards with two interfaces per board, you have a total of 10 interfaces. The aggregate bandwidth is one Gbps, which is almost double what the CxBus can handle.

Interface processors allow network connections, but the RP, RSP7000, SP, and SSP are the heart of the 7000 series router. Look at Figure 4.3 to see how all of these processors relate to one another. You can see that the RP sits at the top of the diagram. The route processor does Layer 3 processing. It maintains the route table, ARP table, system cache, and memory. It also contains the main system IOS and configuration.

FIGURE 4.3   Cisco 7000 processor architecture

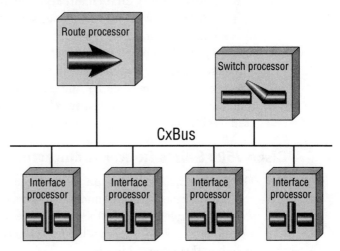

The SP and SSP are responsible for packet switching. This switching process uses both Layer 3 and Layer 2 information. From there, these system processors (RP and SP/SSP) connect to the backplane in order to interface with the individual interface processors.

In Figure 4.4, you see an alternative diagram, in which an RSP 7000 is used in place of the two separate processor boards depicted in Figure 4.3. The switch processor is integrated into the same board with the route processor. The connection to the backplane does not change.

FIGURE 4.4   RSP 7000 processor architecture

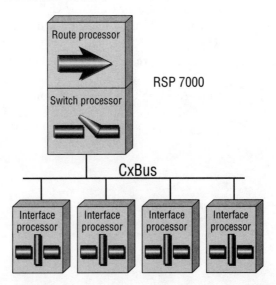

Because of the way different processor boards are used in the 7000 series routers, different switching technologies can be used. At this point in the discussion, we mention the types of switching possible on the 7000 series; a detailed explanation will follow.

The simplest way to define which switching paths are supported is to use a basic configuration of an RP and an SP. Under this configuration, the router may process switch, fast switch, and autonomous switch. If an SSP is used in place of the SP, silicon switching is supported.

Cisco 7500 Series Router Architecture

The 7500 series routers are an enhancement over the 7000 series routers because additional features and network technology support have been included. Simply put, a 7500 series does everything that a 7000 series does—and more. The 7500 supports the same interface processors as the 7000, including these new additions:

- POSIP (Packet Over Sonet Interface Processor)
- VIP2 (Second Generation Versatile Interface Processor)

The big change with the 7500 series routers is the route and switch processors, as well as enhanced backplane architectures. The new backplanes is called a CyBus—Cisco Extended Bus—with a 1.067Gbps capacity. The 7505 has one CyBus, whereas the 7507 and 7513 have two CyBuses. The dual backplanes in the higher-end 7500 series routers allow dual/redundant processors to be inserted simultaneously in the chassis. Not only are redundant processors possible, but if one of the backplanes fails, you can simply move the interface processor from one CyBus to the other (vacancy permitting).

The 7500 series supports four different Route Switch Processors: RSP1, RSP2, RSP4, and RSP8 (the difference is additional processing power). Figure 4.5 depicts the relation between the RSP and IP slots on a dual CyBus. It is important to realize that only one RSP is active at a time. Although one RSP can control both CyBuses, traffic generated on one CyBus does not affect the other. This means that the 7507 and 7513 series routers have a combined backplane speed of 2.134Gbps.

FIGURE 4.5 Dual CyBus architecture

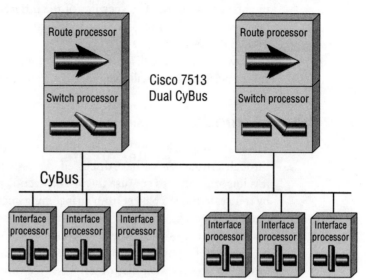

Just like the 7000 series router, the supported switching types for the 7500 series routers depend on the configuration and the IOS that is running on the router. The basic switching paths that are supported by a 7500 series router with the proper IOS are process switching, fast switching, and optimum switching (optimum switching normally replaces fast switching).

When VIP2 boards are added, distributed switching is also supported. Netflow and CEF (Cisco Express Forwarding) can also be implemented if the proper IOS is used. These switching paths are discussed in detail in the switching methods section.

Cisco 4000/2500 Series Architecture

These routers are not nearly as robust as the 7000 series, nor were they intended to be. The 2500 series routers offer many interface configurations, but these configurations are not modular, except the 2524 and 2525. The model used depends on the network interfaces needed. The Cisco 4000 series is a modular system, thus providing for more flexibility with network interfaces.

The key to these routers is that the interfaces do not have independent processors like those in the 70xx/75xx series routers. This greatly restricts the possible switching paths. The router's CPU must handle all of the interfaces for the router.

Fast switching is possible on these routers due to the shared memory on the processor board. The specifics of the different switching paths will be discussed next; for now, we'll just say that fast switching is used on the 4000/2500 series routers.

Now that we have discussed the switching types supported by various router platforms, we will explain the different switching methods in detail.

Switching Methods

The *switching path* is the logical path that a packet follows when it's switched through a router. As we have discussed, there are many types of switching and it is important not to confuse them. This section explains methods used by routers to move a packet from an incoming interface to the correct outgoing interface. By using switching paths, extra lookups in route tables are eliminated, and processing overhead is reduced.

The router's physical design and its interfaces allow for a variety of switching processes on the router. This frees up the processor to focus on other tasks, instead of looking up the source and destination information for every packet that enters the router.

We have already discussed router architecture, so we will focus directly on the details of each switching type. The most processor-intensive method is discussed first; we end with the most efficient method of switching.

Process Switching

Process switching is the action of the processor having to determine the exiting interface for every packet. As a packet arrives on an interface to be forwarded, eventually it is copied to the router's process buffer, and the router performs a lookup on the Layer 3 address (*eventually* means that there are a few steps before the packet is copied to the route processor buffer). Using the route table, an exit interface is associated with the destination address. The processor encapsulates and forwards the packet with the added new information to the exit interface while the router initializes the fast-switching cache. Subsequent packets that require process switching and are bound for the same destination address follow the same path as the first packet.

Overhead ensues because the processor is occupied with Layer 3 lookups—determining which interface the packet should exit from and calculating the CRC for the packets. If every packet required all of that to be routed, the processor could get really bogged down. The answer is to use other types of switching whenever and wherever possible.

Fast Switching

Fast switching is an enhancement from process switching because it uses a fast switching cache that resides on the route processor board. The first packet of a new session is copied to the interface processor buffer. The packet is then copied to the CxBus and sent to the switch processor. A check is made against other switching caches (for example, silicon or autonomous) for an existing entry. Fast switching is then used because no entries exist within the more efficient caches. The packet header is copied and sent to the route processor, where the fast switching cache resides. Assuming that an entry exists in the cache, the packet is encapsulated for fast switching and sent back to the switch processor. Finally, the packet is copied to the buffer on the outgoing interface processor. From there, it is sent out the interface.

Fast switching is on by default for lower-end routers like the 4000/2500 series. Sometimes it's necessary to turn fast switching off when troubleshooting network problems. Because packets don't move across the route processor after the first packet is process-switched, you can't see them with packet-level tracing. It's also helpful to turn off fast switching if the interface card's memory is limited or consumed, or to alleviate congestion when low-speed interfaces become flooded with information from high-speed interfaces.

Autonomous Switching

Autonomous switching works by comparing packets against the autonomous switching cache. You probably recognize a pattern by now. When a packet arrives on the interface processor, it checks the switching cache closest to it. So far, all of these caches reside on other processor boards. The same is found with autonomous switching. The silicon-switching cache is checked first; the autonomous cache is then checked. The packet is encapsulated for autonomous switching and sent back to the interface processor. Notice that this time, the packet header was not sent to the route processor.

Autonomous switching is available only on AGS+ and Cisco 7000 series routers that have high-speed controller interface cards.

Silicon Switching

Silicon switching is available only on the Cisco 7000 with an SSP (Silicon Switch Processor). Silicon-switched packets are compared to the silicon-switching cache on the SSE (Silicon Switching Engine). The SSP is a dedicated switch processor that offloads the switching process from the route processor, which provides a fast-switching solution. Packets must still traverse the backplane of the router to get to the SSP and then back to the exit interface, however.

Optimum Switching

Optimum switching follows the same procedure as the other switching algorithms. When a new packet enters the interface, it is compared to the optimum switching cache, rewritten, and sent to the chosen exit interface. Other packets associated with the same session then follow the same path. All processing is carried out on the interface processor, including the CRC. Optimum switching is faster than both fast switching and Netflow switching, unless you have implemented several access-lists.

Optimum switching replaces fast switching on the high-end routers. As with fast switching, optimum switching also needs to be turned off to view packets while troubleshooting a network problem.

Distributed Switching

Distributed switching happens on the VIP (Versatile Interface Processor) cards (which have a switching processor onboard), so it's very efficient. All required processing is done right on the VIP processor, which maintains a copy of the router's routing cache. With this arrangement, even the first packet doesn't need to be sent to the route processor to initialize the switching path, as it does with the other switching algorithms. Router efficiency increases as more VIP cards are added.

Netflow Switching

Netflow switching is really more of an administrative tool than a performance-enhancement tool. It collects detailed data for use with circuit accounting and application-utilization information. Because of all the additional data that Netflow collects (and may export), expect an increase in router overhead—possibly as much as a five-percent increase in CPU utilization.

Netflow switching can be configured on most interface types and can be used in a switched environment. ATM, LAN, and VLAN technologies all support Netflow switching, and the Cisco 3600, 7200 and 7500 series routers provide its implementation.

As we discussed, Netflow switching does much more than just switching—it also gathers statistical data, including protocol, port, and user information. All of this is stored in the Netflow switching cache, according to the individual flow that's defined by the packet information (destination address, source address, protocol, source and destination port, and the incoming interface). The data can be sent to a network management station to be stored and processed there.

The Netflow switching process is very efficient: an incoming packet is processed by the fast or optimum switching process, and then all path and packet information is copied to the Netflow cache. The remaining packets that belong to the flow are compared to the Netflow cache and forwarded accordingly.

The first packet that is copied to the Netflow cache contains all security and routing information, and if an access-list is applied to an interface, the first packet is matched against it. If it matches the access-list criteria, the cache is flagged so that the remaining packets in the flow can be switched without being compared to the list (this is very effective when a large amount of access-list processing is required).

Do you remember reading that distributed switching on VIP cards is really efficient because it lessens the load to the RSP? Well, Netflow switching can also be configured on VIP interfaces.

Netflow gives you amenities, such as the security flag in the cache that allows subsequent packets of an established flow to avoid access-list processing. It's comparable to optimum and distributed switching, and it is actually superior to them if access-lists (especially long ones) are placed in the switching path. The detailed information Netflow gathers and exports does load down the system, however, so plan carefully before implementing Netflow switching on a router.

Cisco Express Forwarding

Cisco Express Forwarding (CEF) is a switching function, designed for high-end backbone routers. It functions on Layer 3 of the OSI model, and its biggest asset is the capability to remain stable in a large network. However, it's also more efficient than both the fast and optimum default switching paths.

CEF is wonderfully stable in large environments because it doesn't rely on cached information. Instead of using a CEF cache, it refers to two alternate resources. The *Forwarding Information Base (FIB)* consists of information duplicated from the IP route table. Every time the routing information changes, the changes are propagated to the FIB. Thus, instead of comparing old cache information, a packet looks to the FIB for its forwarding information. CEF stores the Layer 2 MAC addresses of connected routers (or next-hop) in the *adjacency table*.

Even though CEF features advanced capabilities, you should consider several restrictions before implementing CEF on a router. According to the document "Cisco Express Forwarding," available from the Cisco Web page Cisco Connection Online (CCO) at `www.cisco.com`, system requirements are quite high. The processor should have at least 128MB of RAM, and the line cards should have 32MB each. dCEF, distributed CEF, takes the place of

VIP distributed switching on VIP interfaces. The following features aren't supported by CEF:

- ATM dixie
- Token Ring
- Multipoint PPP
- access-lists on the GSR
- Policy routing
- NAT
- SMDS

Nevertheless, CEF does many things—even load balancing is possible through FIB. If there are multiple paths to the same destination, the IP route table knows about them all. This information is also copied to the FIB, which CEF consults for its switching decisions.

Load balancing can be configured in two different modes. The first mode is load balancing based on the destination (called *per-destination load balancing*); the second mode is based on the packet (called *per-packet load balancing*). Per-destination load balancing is on by default, and must be turned off to enable per-packet load balancing.

Accounting may also be configured for CEF, thus furnishing you with detailed statistics about CEF traffic. Two specifications can be made when collecting CEF statistics:

- To collect information on traffic that's forwarded to a specific destination
- To collect statistics for traffic that's forwarded through a specific destination

CEF was designed for large networks—if reliable and redundant switching paths are necessary, CEF is the way to go. Keep in mind that its hardware requirements are significant, however, and it lacks support for many Cisco IOS features.

Packet Flow—High-End Routers

You now have all of the pieces of the puzzle, and you understand the router architectures and the switching methods. With this knowledge, you can easily follow a packet as it transits a router. Don't confuse this packet flow with the OSI comparison given earlier in the chapter.

To emphasize, the switching type depends on two factors: which encapsulation is configured on the interface and whether a cache entry exists for the configured method. Look at Figure 4.6 to see a flow chart that describes the process for each packet entering a router.

FIGURE 4.6   Switching method and packet flow

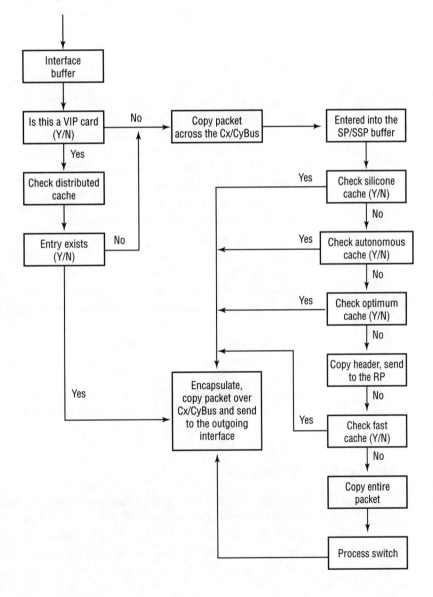

Let's work through the flow chart in Figure 4.6. You can see that the incoming packet is immediately copied to the interface processor buffer. If the card is a VIP/VIP2 card, then the packet will use distributed switching if there is an entry; if not, it is processed like other packets.

The next step in the process is to copy the packet to the SP/SSP/RSP across the CxBus/CyBus. Once the packet reaches the buffers on the SP/SSP/RSP, it is compared to the silicon-switching cache. Two paths can be followed from here. If an entry exists in the silicon-switching cache, the packet is encapsulated and copied to the outgoing interface processor across the CxBus/CyBus. The interface processor then sends out the packet. If an entry is not found in the silicon-switching cache, the autonomous cache is checked.

If an entry exists in the autonomous cache, the packet is encapsulated by the switch processor, copied across the CxBus/CyBus to the outgoing interface processor, and sent. Again, if an entry does not exist, the next step is taken and the optimum cache is compared.

Optimum switching follows the same exit route as autonomous switching: the packet is encapsulated by the switch processor, copied to the outgoing interface, and sent. With each additional step, the packet gets closer and closer to being process-switched.

At this point, if there is no entry in the optimum cache, the Layer 3 header is copied, sent to the RP and then compared against the fast cache. Fast cache can reside in two different places, depending on the router's hardware configuration. If an RSP is used, the fast cache is on the same board as the optimum cache. If an SP/SSP and an RP are used, the silicon and autonomous caches reside on the switch processor, and the fast cache resides on the RP.

If the Layer 3 header does not match any entry in the fast cache, the entire packet is copied and sent to the processor, where the processor does a lookup in the route table. If a route exists, the packet is encapsulated and copied back to the exiting interface. If no route exists, the packet is dropped.

The first packet of each data flow requires process switching. Once the route lookup and proper encapsulation are made, the header is copied into the corresponding switch-type cache. Subsequent packets find the entry in the correct cache and are forwarded along the same outgoing path as the first packet.

The Route Processor

Although you don't like sending packets to the route processor, sometimes it is unavoidable. Packets that are destined or intended for the router require processing. Broadcasts, SNMP requests, access-list processing (in some cases), debugging, protocol updates, error logging, and queuing all require processor time.

This is just another reason why switching is such a good practice. Why burden the route processor with every packet if it's not necessary? By using switching methods, the route processor is free to use valuable CPU time on more important things than doing route lookups for every packet that comes into the router.

There are times when a packet must be processed or process-switched, however. For this reason, the router is engineered so that it can handle the processing and process switching of numerous packets. A system of buffers and queues exists on the route processor, switch processor, and interface processor that allows packets to be held, processed, and forwarded with few packet drops. Different router types have different buffer architecture, so we'll discuss each type in detail.

Buffers and Queues in the Cisco 7000 Series

For the 7000 series routers, the system buffers reside on the RP, with the memory being allocated from the system memory. The buffers on the RP are used to store packets that are waiting to be processed by the CPU.

The buffers come configured with default settings. They can be modified, if necessary, but it is usually a good idea to have a Cisco TAC engineer look at the memory allocation and suggest the new buffer settings. Following is an example of the buffer settings:

```
Buffer elements:
     499 in free list (500 max allowed)
     32642751 hits, 0 misses, 0 created
Public buffer pools:
Small buffers, 104 bytes (total 120, permanent 120):
     110 in free list (20 min, 250 max allowed)
     15486216 hits, 322 misses, 364 trims, 364 created
     26 failures (0 no memory)
Middle buffers, 600 bytes (total 90, permanent 90):
     87 in free list (10 min, 200 max allowed)
     3984956 hits, 113 misses, 105 trims, 105 created
     36 failures (0 no memory)
Big buffers, 1524 bytes (total 90, permanent 90):
     88 in free list (5 min, 300 max allowed)
     471484 hits, 24 misses, 6 trims, 6 created
```

```
        20 failures (0 no memory)
VeryBig buffers, 4520 bytes (total 10, permanent 10):
        10 in free list (0 min, 300 max allowed)
        177588 hits, 10 misses, 1 trims, 1 created
        10 failures (0 no memory)
Large buffers, 5024 bytes (total 10, permanent 10):
        10 in free list (0 min, 30 max allowed)
        10 hits, 0 misses, 0 trims, 0 created
        0 failures (0 no memory)
Huge buffers, 18024 bytes (total 0, permanent 0):
        0 in free list (0 min, 13 max allowed)
        0 hits, 0 misses, 0 trims, 0 created
        0 failures (0 no memory)
Header pools:
```

You can view six buffer distinctions in this output: small, middle, big, very big, large, and huge; and each division is allocated a different amount of buffer space. The output details the buffer name and its size, with the buffer size following immediately after its name. The (total 120, permanent 120) for the small pool specifies that there are a total of 120 spaces allocated to the small pool. The permanent means that the 120 buffer spaces are permanently assigned to the small buffer pool. When a buffer's space is permanent, it cannot be de-allocated and given back to the system memory for other uses.

In the next field, you can see the number of free buffer spaces that are open to accepting a packet. Each pool maintains a minimum and maximum threshold, which it uses to decide whether more buffer space needs to be allocated to the pool. This is seen in the min and max allowed.

The last two lines of information given for each pool describe the activity happening there. This information, which includes all hits, misses, trims, created, and failures, is described in the following list:

Hits   Represents how many times the pool was used successfully.

Misses   Represents the number of times a packet tried to find a space within a pool, but found no available spaces.

Trims   Represents the number of spaces removed from the pool because the amount exceeded the number of *allowed* buffer spaces.

Created   Represents the number of spaces created to accommodate requests for space when there wasn't enough at the time the request was made.

Failures   Represents how many times a buffer pool tried to create space, but was unsuccessful. When a failure occurs, the requesting packet is dropped.

The last field is the `no memory` field, which records the number of failures that occurred due to the lack of sufficient system memory required to create additional buffer space.

If you observe a significant increase in the number of misses while monitoring buffers with the `show buffers` command, the pool can be tuned by assigning different values to the `max-free`, `min-free`, and `permanent` parameters. Increasing the values for these parameters overrides the system defaults—instead of having to create additional spaces on demand within a pool, the spaces can be statically allocated and assigned. This helps you avoid racking up missed and failed packet statuses.

You can adjust these parameters with the following command:

```
buffers {small | middle | big | verybig | large | huge |
type number} {permanent | max-free | min-free | initial}
number
```

The *type* represents interface type, and *number* is the number to be assigned to the specified parameter.

Table 4.1 depicts the sizes of the buffer space within a pool. When a packet needs to be stored in a buffer, it requests space from the pool in proportion to its size requirement. For example, a full-size Ethernet packet at a 1500MTU requires one buffer space from the Big buffer pool.

TABLE 4.1   Sizes of the Buffer within a Pool

Pool Name	Buffer Size (in Bytes)
Small	104
Middle	600
Big	1524
Very Big	4520
Large	5024
Huge	18,024

Buffer and Queue Architecture in a Cisco 7000

Now that you understand the buffer's global setup, let's discuss the buffer architecture and queuing process within a 7000 series router. The architecture is similar to the cache buffers that were explained with the switching methods.

Hardware Buffers

Each interface (not interface processor) has a hardware buffer, which is used as a first line of defense for bursty traffic. If the hardware buffer on certain interfaces fills up, the Layer 2 protocol will signal the sending interface to slow down. This behavior is dependent on the Layer 2 protocol and whether or not it supports congestion control.

Three conditions can exist at the interface level: *ignore*, *overrun*, and *underrun*. An *ignore* can be caused in three ways. We already discussed the first—the hardware buffer fills up and it signals to the transmitting interface to throttle down. The second occurs when the interface is receiving frames faster than the SP can pull them off. The third occurs when the CxBus is so busy that the interface processor is unable to copy the packet from the hardware buffer to the SP buffers. Figure 4.7 depicts all three of these scenarios.

FIGURE 4.7 Ignore scenarios for hardware buffers

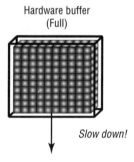

Hardware buffer
(Full)

Slow down!

FIGURE 4.7 continued

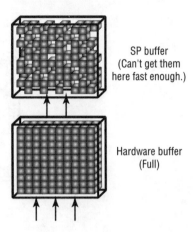

SP buffer
(Can't get them
here fast enough.)

Hardware buffer
(Full)

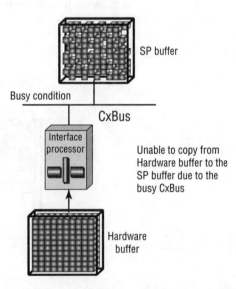

SP buffer

Busy condition

CxBus

Interface
processor

Unable to copy from
Hardware buffer to the
SP buffer due to the
busy CxBus

Hardware
buffer

Overruns occur on the physical interface. Think of the physical interface as consisting of three parts: the buffer, the receiver, and the transmitter. An *overrun* occurs when the receiver receives packets faster than it can transfer them to the hardware buffer. Figure 4.8 gives a graphical description of the process.

FIGURE 4.8 Overruns

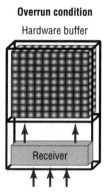

An *underrun* is just the opposite of an overrun. When the transmitter runs at a higher rate than the packets sent from the hardware buffer, an underrun occurs. Look at Figure 4.9.

FIGURE 4.9 Underruns

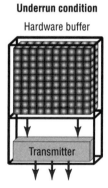

Interface Buffers

Interface buffers are intermediate storage. Packets from all of the hardware buffers are copied to the interface buffers. The switch processor houses the intermediate buffers by using 512KB for the SP board memory. This memory is also shared with the autonomous switching cache. Other boards can have up to 2MB of memory.

Let's get a better understanding of the interface buffers. To see what the router is doing, issue the show controllers cbus command. Here is the output from a 7507 router with one EIP board in it:

```
Router_A# show controllers cbus
MEMD at 40000000, 2097152 bytes (unused 128, recarves 1,
lost 0)
  RawQ 48000100, ReturnQ 48000108, EventQ 48000110
  BufhdrQ 48000120 (2353 items)
  IpcbufQ_classic 48000140 (8 items, 4096 bytes)
  3570 buffer headers (48002000 - 4800FF10)
  pool0: 9 buffers, 256 bytes, queue 48000128
  pool1: 1196 buffers, 1536 bytes, queue 48000130
  pool2: 4 buffers, 1568 bytes, queue 48000138
  slot5: EIP, hw 1.5, sw 20.06, ccb 5800FF70, cmdq
480000A8,    vps 4096
    software loaded from system
    Ethernet5/0, addr 0010.29d1.68a0 (bia 0010.29d1.68a0)
      gfreeq 48000130, lfreeq 48000148 (1536 bytes),
      throttled 0
      rxlo 4, rxhi 598, rxcurr 1, maxrxcurr 1
      txq 48000150, txacc 48000082 (value 341), txlimit
      341
    Ethernet5/1, addr 0010.29d1.68a1 (bia 0010.29d1.68a1)
      gfreeq 48000130, lfreeq 48000158 (1536 bytes),
      throttled 0
      rxlo 4, rxhi 598, rxcurr 0, maxrxcurr 0
      txq 48000160, txacc 4800008A (value 0), txlimit 341
    Ethernet5/2, addr 0010.29d1.68a2 (bia 0010.29d1.68a2)
      gfreeq 48000130, lfreeq 48000168 (1536 bytes),
      throttled 0
      rxlo 4, rxhi 598, rxcurr 0, maxrxcurr 0
      txq 48000170, txacc 48000092 (value 0), txlimit 341
    Ethernet5/3, addr 0010.29d1.68a3 (bia 0010.29d1.68a3)
      gfreeq 48000130, lfreeq 48000178 (1536 bytes),
      throttled 0
      rxlo 4, rxhi 598, rxcurr 0, maxrxcurr 0
```

```
     txq 48000180, txacc 4800009A (value 0), txlimit 341
Ethernet5/4, addr 0010.29d1.68a4 (bia 0010.29d1.68a4)
   gfreeq 48000130, lfreeq 48000188 (1536 bytes),
   throttled 0
   rxlo 4, rxhi 598, rxcurr 0, maxrxcurr 0
   txq 48000190, txacc 480000A2 (value 0), txlimit 341
Ethernet5/5, addr 0010.29d1.68a5 (bia 0010.29d1.68a5)
   gfreeq 48000130, lfreeq 48000198 (1536 bytes),
   throttled 0
   rxlo 4, rxhi 598, rxcurr 0, maxrxcurr 0
   txq 480001A0, txacc 480000AA (value 0), txlimit 341
```

At the top of the output, you can see three pools allocated: pool0, pool1, and pool2. Each interface processor is allocated a certain share of the buffer pool. By default, EIPs are allocated 1524 bytes of the 512KB. Other default settings are listed in Table 4.2.

TABLE 4.2 Interface Processor Buffer Size Allocation

Board Type	Buffer Size (bytes)
FIP	4470
FSIP	4470
AIP	4470
HSSI	4470
TRIP	4470
EIP	1524

Input and Output Queues

Input queues reside on the RP, and they are used to link the SP buffers to the RP buffers. The queue reserves RP buffer space for a packet that was forwarded from the SP/SSP. If the Router Processor doesn't process the queued packets at the same rate, the queue fills up and the incoming packets are dropped.

The *output queue* works in the same manner. Output queues reside on the RP as well, and once a packet is processed, it must be sent to the exiting interface. The *output queue* is used to hold the packet until the packet can be copied to the buffers on the SP/SSP; from there, it is forwarded to the specified interface processor. The interface processor then sends the packet to the interface queue/buffer from which the packet will be sent to the destination.

Packets can be dropped from the output queue, as well. If the other processes on the router are so busy that they can't accept the outgoing packet, they are dropped. These drops are considered normal because the Layer 3 protocol is in the process of slowing down to avoid any further drops.

Buffers and Queues in Low-End Routers

As with switching caches, all buffers are located in shared memory (with the exception of the hardware buffer). The hardware buffer resides on the physical interface.

The difference between the 4000/2500 series routers and the 7000/7500 series routers is that there are no intermediate buffers. A packet is copied directly from the hardware buffer to the system buffers in shared memory.

Let's look at the show buffers results from a 2514 router. You should be able to see the difference between it and the buffer output from the Cisco 7507:

```
Router_A#show buffers
Buffer elements:
    499 in free list (500 max allowed)
    28753345 hits, 0 misses, 0 created
Public buffer pools:
Small buffers, 104 bytes (total 90, permanent 50):
    50 in free list (20 min, 150 max allowed)
    8454394 hits, 0 misses, 0 trims, 0 created
    0 failures (0 no memory)
Middle buffers, 600 bytes (total 25, permanent 25):
    23 in free list (10 min, 150 max allowed)
    1676303 hits, 51 misses, 153 trims, 153 created
    0 failures (0 no memory)
Big buffers, 1524 bytes (total 50, permanent 50):
    50 in free list (5 min, 150 max allowed)
    1255286 hits, 0 misses, 0 trims, 0 created
```

```
                    0 failures (0 no memory)
        VeryBig buffers, 4520 bytes (total 10, permanent 10):
            10 in free list (0 min, 100 max allowed)
            34842 hits, 0 misses, 0 trims, 0 created
            0 failures (0 no memory)
        Large buffers, 5024 bytes (total 0, permanent 0):
            0 in free list (0 min, 10 max allowed)
            0 hits, 0 misses, 0 trims, 0 created
            0 failures (0 no memory)
        Huge buffers, 18024 bytes (total 0, permanent 0):
            0 in free list (0 min, 4 max allowed)
            0 hits, 0 misses, 0 trims, 0 created
            0 failures (0 no memory)
        Interface buffer pools:
        Ethernet0 buffers, 1524 bytes (total 96, permanent 96):
            29 in free list (0 min, 96 max allowed)
            5474 hits, 1998 fallbacks
            32 max cache size, 29 in cache
        Ethernet1 buffers, 1524 bytes (total 96, permanent 96):
            24 in free list (0 min, 96 max allowed)
            154 hits, 265 fallbacks
            32 max cache size, 32 in cache
```

Almost everything looks exactly the same, doesn't it? The only real difference is at the end of the output. The Cisco 2514 displays the interface buffer pools; the Cisco 7507 did not have that information. The Ethernet buffer pool size is consistent with the values in Table 4.2. It is the same size used by the SP/SSP on the Cisco 7000 series.

Troubleshooting Commands

Now we get into the heart of things. You might wonder, "Why did I need to know all the previous information to pass the test?" The answer is that you need to know how packets move across the router to be able to decipher the information provided by the troubleshooting commands that are explained in this section.

We spoke a little about the effect of process-switching every packet. The same goes for troubleshooting commands. Because these tools use the Route Processor, they too can cause high CPU utilization and have adverse effects on ordinary data that tries to transverse the router.

You will learn how to use several troubleshooting tools. Every one of these tools is part of the Cisco IOS. There are many show commands that are supported by the router. In addition to show commands, there is a tool, called *debug,* that is used to see specific information regarding packet transfer and exchange.

Part of effectively using these tools is to learn how to use them without adversely affecting the router or its other processes. You will learn the specifics of several troubleshooting commands, along with the information needed in order to use them without causing additional problems on your network.

We start with nonintrusive, Cisco-specific show commands. After discussing the show commands, we move on to the debug tool. To finalize, we discuss some non-Cisco-specific troubleshooting tools: ping and traceroute.

show Commands

There are a large number of show commands supported by Cisco IOS. It is unrealistic to explain each and every one of them in this book. The most effective and useful show commands are described in the following paragraphs. To get a rough idea of all of the show commands, execute the show ? command from the router prompt. Some useful show commands are listed in Table 4.3.

TABLE 4.3 Frequently Used show Commands

show Command	Description
access-lists	List access-lists
accounting	Accounting data for active sessions
adjacency	Adjacent nodes
appletalk	AppleTalk information
buffers	Buffer pool statistics

TABLE 4.3 Frequently Used show Commands *(continued)*

show Command	Description
cdp	Cisco Discovery Protocol (CDP) information
cef	Cisco Express Forwarding
configuration	Contents of the NVRAM
controllers	Interface controller status
debugging	State of each debugging option
environment	Environmental monitor statistics
extended	Extended interface information
frame-relay	Frame Relay information
interfaces	Interface status and configuration
ip	IP information
ipx	Novell IPX information
line	TTY line information
logging	Show the contents of logging buffers
memory	Memory statistics
ppp	PPP parameters and statistics
processes	Active process statistics
protocols	Active network routing protocols
queue	Show queue contents
queueing	Show queuing configuration
running-config	Current operating configuration

TABLE 4.3 Frequently Used show Commands *(continued)*

show Command	Description
stacks	Process stack utilization
startup-config	Contents of start-up configuration
tcp	Status of TCP connections
tech-support	Show system information for Tech Support
version	System hardware and software version and status

From the information provided in Table 4.3, you can categorize the show commands into four types: global, interface, process, and protocol-related. Depending on the problem you are troubleshooting, you can focus on the problem by using appropriate commands. For example, if you are troubleshooting a protocol-related problem, then you will probably use the protocol family of show commands. If you notice problems on a circuit, you can use the interface family of show commands to give you detailed information about the interface.

Global Commands

Global commands deal with global router settings. This means that information that does not relate to interfaces or protocols, yet has overall router information, is considered to be a global show command. Table 4.4 shows useful global show commands.

TABLE 4.4 Global show Commands

Global show Command	Description
version	System hardware and software status
running-config	Current operating configuration
startup-config	Contents of start-up configuration

TABLE 4.4 Global show Commands *(continued)*

Global show Command	Description
logging	Show the contents of logging buffers
buffers	Buffer pool statistics
stacks	Process stack utilization
tech-support	Show system information for Tech Support
access-lists	List access-lists
memory	Memory statistics

show version

This command is used to display the system hardware and software versions. It also includes information about how long the router was running and the reason it was last restarted. Let's look at the output of the show version command.

```
Router_B>show version
Cisco Internetwork Operating System Software
IOS (tm) GS Software (RSP-JV-M), Version 11.1(25)CC, EARLY
DEPLOYMENT RELEASE SOFTWARE (fc1)
V111_25_CC_THROTTLE_BRANCH Synced to mainline version:
11.1(25)CA
Copyright (c) 1986-1998 by cisco Systems, Inc.
Compiled Mon 11-May-98 19:42 by richardd
Image text-base: 0x60010910, data-base: 0x60A64000

ROM: System Bootstrap, Version 11.1(8)CA1, EARLY
DEPLOYMENT RELEASE SOFTWARE (fc1)
ROM: GS Software (RSP-BOOT-M), Version 11.1(8)CA1, EARLY
DEPLOYMENT RELEASE SOFTWARE (fc1)

Router_B uptime is 14 hours, 43 minutes
System restarted by reload at 05:13:16 MST Sat April 10
1999
```

System image file is "slot0:rsp-jv-mz.111-25.CC.bin", booted via slot0

cisco RSP4 (R5000) processor with 65536K/2072K bytes of memory.

R5000 processor, Implementation 35, Revision 2.1 (512KB Level 2 Cache)

Last reset from power-on

G.703/E1 software, Version 1.0.

G.703/JT2 software, Version 1.0.

SuperLAT software copyright 1990 by Meridian Technology Corp).

Bridging software.

X.25 software, Version 2.0, NET2, BFE and GOSIP compliant.

TN3270 Emulation software (copyright 1994 by TGV Inc).

Chassis Interface.

2 EIP controllers (12 Ethernet).

3 FSIP controllers (24 Serial).

2 AIP controllers (2 ATM).

12 Ethernet/IEEE 802.3 interfaces.

24 Serial network interfaces.

2 ATM network interfaces.

123K bytes of non-volatile configuration memory.

20480K bytes of Flash PCMCIA card at slot 0 (Sector size 128K).

8192K bytes of Flash internal SIMM (Sector size 256K).

Slave in slot 7 is running Cisco Internetwork Operating System Software

IOS (tm) GS Software (RSP-DW-M), Version 11.1(25)CC, EARLY DEPLOYMENT RELEASE SOFTWARE (fc1)

V111_25_CC_THROTTLE_BRANCH Synced to mainline version: 11.1(25)CA

Copyright (c) 1986-1998 by cisco Systems, Inc.

Compiled Mon 11-May-98 19:44 by richardd

Slave: Loaded from system

Slave: cisco RSP4 (R5000) processor with 65536K bytes of memory.

Configuration register is 0x102

Router_B>

As you can see, the output contains a great deal of information. Let's move through it field by field. The first field indicates the revision of software that is actively running on the router. In this case, it is Cisco IOS11.1(25)CC.

The next field is the bootstrap version, which indicates the Cisco IOS that is used in case the IOS isn't found. This IOS is stored on the PROMS or FLASH memory of the router. The router boots by using 11.1(8)CA. This allows the router to actually boot so that you may fix software problems.

Current router status information is located in the field following the bootstrap information. This output tells you the length of time the router has been up and the last date it was reloaded. If an error caused the router to reload, the error message is included in this field. Finally, the file that was used while booting is listed.

The final field describes the route processor and amount of RAM. At the end of the field, all interface processors are listed, followed by the number of interfaces. The last three lines indicate the different amounts and types of memory.

Because this output is from a Cisco 7513 that contains two RSP4 processor boards, the show version command also lists information about the slave board. (In routers with two RSP boards, one board takes the role of the master, and the other becomes the slave.)

startup-config and *running-config*

These two commands are used to view the syntax of the router's configuration. The show startup-config command displays the contents of the configuration that was written to NVRAM. The show running-config, show config, and write term commands are all equivalent commands. The results of these commands display the configuration that was loaded into memory and is running on the router.

Although you should already be familiar with these commands, it is a very good troubleshooting tip to compare the two configurations when working on network problems. It is always possible that configuration changes were made to the running configuration and were not copied to the start-up configuration. There may be extra or missing commands in the different configuration versions. You may be able to solve the problem of missing commands in the running configuration quickly by copying the startup-config to the running-config.

These commands provide you with global, protocol, and interface information. You can analyze them for proper configuration and make changes, if needed. Many problems can be isolated by viewing the configuration. Most of the time you will see something that wasn't there before, see something that shouldn't be there, or notice that something is missing that needs to be in the configuration. For this technique to work, you must be familiar with the router and its configuration. If backups are made of the configurations, you may compare them to the running-config to look for differences.

show logging

The logs kept by the router can be very useful because they can be the first indication of a network problem. The router itself logs errors and details regarding the error. Seven different levels of warning messages exist. The scale is from one to seven—one is the lowest priority and seven is a critical warning.

There are six types of logging: syslog, console, monitor, trap, buffer, and SNMP. Each may be logged to the console, or to a syslog or SNMP server. Following is the output from the show logging command:

```
Router_B>show logging
Syslog logging: enabled(0 messages dropped, 202 flushes, 0
overruns)
    Console logging: level debugging, 9199 messages logged
    Monitor logging: level debugging, 1517 messages logged
    Trap logging:level informational,5 message lines
    logged
        Logging to 172.16.1.1, 2288 message lines logged
        Logging to 272.16.2.4, 2288 message lines logged
    Buffer logging: level debugging, 5688 messages logged
SNMP logging: enabled, retransmission after 60 seconds
    741 messages logged
    Logging to 172.16.34.2, 0/10
Log Buffer (16000 bytes):
```

The output simply tells us that syslog, console, monitor, trap, buffer, and SNMP are all enabled. If they are not enabled, the output indicates the status. It gives some statistical information about the number of messages logged and to where they are logged.

show buffers

The show buffers command was described in detail in the earlier "Buffer and Queue Architecture in a Cisco 7000" section. Please refer to that section if you need to review the output of the show buffers command.

show stacks

The show stacks command is not very useful to you, but it is invaluable information for the Cisco TAC. The output from the command appears below. As you can see, it doesn't make a lot of sense to the user. The information is sent to Cisco; Cisco runs it through a stack decode that provides the information relevant to system problems.

Stacks are used to provide information on the router's processes and processor utilization. The output displayed is from a healthy router. If the router were to crash, the latest stack information is saved so it can be captured once the router comes back up. The data contains information regarding the reason for the reload and any errors that are attributed to the crash.

```
Router_A#show stack
Minimum process stacks:
  Free/Size   Name
10288/12000   Init
 5196/6000    Router Init
 9672/12000   Virtual Exec

Interrupt level stacks:
 Level      Called Unused/Size  Name
   1         49917   8200/9000  Network Interrupt
   2             2   8372/9000  Network Status Interrupt
   3             0   9000/9000  OIR interrupt
   4             0   9000/9000  PCMCIA Interrupt
   5          2561   8652/9000  Console Uart
   6             0   9000/9000  Error Interrupt
   7      27140712   8608/9000  NMI Interrupt Handler
Router_A#
```

show tech-support

The tech-support command is a compilation of several show commands (version, running-config, controllers, stacks, interfaces, diagbus, buffers, process memory, process cpu, context, boot, flash bootflash, ip traffic, and controllers cbus). You can get most of the information you need by issuing the show tech-support command, instead of issuing all of the commands separately.

The `tech-support` command does not allow you to scroll through it on the router because of the enormous amount of information that is displayed. To capture the output, you need a terminal with a large line buffer setting, or you can log the output directly to a terminal.

show access-lists

The `show access-lists` command is useful to view the access-list configuration without sorting through the running or start-up configuration. In addition to displaying the line entries of the access-list, the command uses the access-list number to define what type of access-list is being displayed. The output from the `show access-lists` command follows:

```
Router_B#show access-lists
Extended IP access-list 105
    permit ip 172.16.0.0 0.0.255.255 any (97160 matches)
    permit ip 10.0.0.0 0.255.255.255 any
    deny   ip any any (102463 matches)
Novell access-list 801
    permit 606E3000 (3245 matches)
    permit 506E3074
    permit B06F2E00 (655 matches)
    permit D06F2EFE
    permit 717B012C
    permit E06F2E67
    permit F9BE0714 (5038 matches)
    permit A054AB00
    permit 617B07C4
    permit 017B1900
```

This information gives you a summary of each access-list on the router. The access-list type is defined and the number assigned to it is shown. Each line of the list is displayed individually. The list also specifies which network is matched by using which wildcard mask.

show memory

This command is helpful for diagnosing memory problems such as allocation failures, free memory, and so on. From the following output, you can see that the first field has the memory divided between processor memory and fast memory. The fields are self-explanatory because they describe the total, used, and free amounts of memory.

The second field gives detailed information concerning the memory allocation and utilization. The most relevant information is contained in the first field.

```
Router_C>show memory
        Head        Total(b)    Used(b)    Free(b)    Lowest(b)   Largest(b)
Proc   60DC38E0    52676384    34896328   17780056   15823612    14764584
Fast   60DA38E0    131072      128344     2728       27282684
Processor memory
Address   Bytes  Prev.     Next      Ref  PrevF  NextF  Alloc PC   What
60DC38E0  1056   0         60DC3D2C  1                  601342A4   List Elements
60DC3D2C  2656   60DC38E0  60DC47B8  1                  601342A4   List Headers
60DC47B8  9000   60DC3D2C  60DC6B0C  1                  60135498   Interrupt Stack
60DC6B0C  9000   60DC47B8  60DC8E60  1                  60135498   Interrupt Stack
```

Interface Commands

Interface commands deal with detailed interface settings and configurations. Because each type of interface uses different protocols and technologies, the show interface command is capable of displaying all data related to the specified interface. Table 4.5 shows useful interface-related show commands.

TABLE 4.5 show interface Commands

show interface Command	Description
Queuing/Queue	Show queuing configuration and contents
Interface <interface-type> <interface-number>	Interface status and configuration
Controllers	Interface controller status

show queueing and *show queue*

To verify the configuration and operation of the queuing system, you can issue the following two commands:

```
show queueing [fair | priority | custom]
show queue [interface-type interface-number]
```

Results from these commands on Router C can be seen as follows. Because weighted fair queuing is the only type of queuing that has been enabled on this router, it wasn't necessary to issue the optional command of fair, custom, or priority.

```
Router_C#show queueing
Current fair queue configuration:
Interface  Discard      Dynamic       Reserved
           threshold    queue count   queue count
 Serial0     96           256            0
 Serial1     64           256            0
Current priority queue configuration:
Current custom queue configuration:
Current RED queue configuration:
Router_C#
```

This command shows that weighted fair queuing is enabled on both serial interfaces, and that the discard threshold for Serial 0 was changed from 64 to 96. There's a maximum of 256 dynamic queues for both interfaces—the default value. The lines following the interface information are empty because their corresponding queuing algorithms aren't configured yet.

The next command displays more detailed information pertaining to the specified interface:

```
Router_C#show queue serial0
 Input queue: 0/75/0 (size/max/drops); Total output drops:
0
 Queueing strategy: weighted fair
 Output queue: 0/1000/96/0 (size/max total/threshold/
drops)
    Conversations 0/1/256 (active/max active/max total)
    Reserved Conversations 0/0 (allocated/max allocated)
Router_C#
```

show interface

The show interface command has many derivatives. A simple show interface command can be issued, and you will get the detailed status and configuration of every interface on the router. That can be overwhelming— so many options exist for the command. These options allow you, the engineer, to focus the area of your troubleshooting. If you know that you need to solve a problem on the network that is connected to interface Ethernet 5/0, you don't want to waste your time looking at the status of every interface on the router. Table 4.6 lists many of the options that are available with the show interface command. It is important to recognize that the interface processors listed are there because they are present on the router. For example, you won't see a Token Ring interface listed unless there is a Token Ring interface on the router.

TABLE 4.6 show interface Command Options

show interface Command Option	Description
ATM (interface type)	ATM interface
Ethernet (interface type)	IEEE 802.3
Serial (interface type)	Serial
HSSI (interface type)	HSSI interface
accounting	Show interface accounting
fair-queue	Show interface Weighted Fair Queueing (WFQ) info
rate-limit	Show interface rate-limit info
mac-accounting	Show interface MAC accounting info

Let's look at sample outputs from an Ethernet and Serial interface. After each sample, we will go through a detailed explanation.

```
Router_A#show interface Ethernet 5/4
Ethernet5/4 is up, line protocol is up
  Hardware is cxBus Ethernet, address is 009a.822e.51b6
  (bia 90.323f.acdb)
  Description: Connection to Router_B
  Internet address is 172.16.1.1/24
  MTU 1500 bytes, BW 10000 Kbit, DLY 1000 usec, rely 255/
  255, load 33/255
  Encapsulation ARPA, loopback not set, keepalive set (10
  sec)
  ARP type: ARPA, ARP Timeout 04:00:00
  Last input 00:00:00, output 00:00:00, output hang never
  Last clearing of "show interface" counters never
  Queueing strategy: fifo
  Output queue 0/40, 101553 drops; input queue 0/75, 1327
  drops
  5 minute input rate 247000 bits/sec, 196 packets/sec
  5 minute output rate 1329000 bits/sec, 333 packets/sec
     421895792 packets input, 2524672293 bytes, 1 no
     buffer
     Received 453382 broadcasts, 0 runts, 0 giants
     6 input errors, 1 CRC, 5 frame, 0 overrun, 494
     ignored,        0 abort
     0 input packets with dribble condition detected
     618578101 packets output, 977287695 bytes, 0
     underruns
  0 output errors, 30979588 collisions, 1 interface
  resets
     0 babbles, 0 late collision, 0 deferred
     0 lost carrier, 0 no carrier
     0 output buffers copied, 0 interrupts, 0 failures
Router_A#
```

The output starts with the most pertinent information—the physical interface and line protocol status. In this case, both are up. There is much argument as to what constitutes an "up" interface. It is very simple—the controller sends a signal that there are electrons flowing through the physical interface. So, just doing a "no shut" on an interface brings it into an "up" status, even if nothing is plugged into the interface. Line protocol "up" means that the interface is able to send itself a frame and receive it back.

The next fields contain the Layer 2 MAC address, the interface description, and the Layer 3 IP address. Below the interface address information, you'll find the line settings for the interface. An MTU, bandwidth, delay, reliability, and load are listed. These values are used to calculate a distance-vector protocol route metric.

Default Ethernet encapsulation for Cisco is ARPA. You can see that this is true and that the keepalive is the default at 10 seconds. This line is a very important line when troubleshooting Ethernet problems. If the encapsulation type is not compatible with other machines on the network, you will have communication problems. Let's look at an example.

When the router broadcasts from an interface, it uses the encapsulation that is configured. Look at Figure 4.10. In this case, an ARPA frame (#1) is sent. If the machines on the network do not understand ARPA, they do not respond to the broadcast. On the other hand, if a machine broadcast uses a SNAP frame (#2), the router is designed to understand any incoming frame encapsulation and can respond to the broadcast. Another bit of useful information that the router adds to the ARP table is the encapsulation type of that machine. Then, the next time that the router wants to speak with the given machine, it uses the documented frame type instead of the type configured on the interface. Here's a look at the ARP table (notice that the Type field is SNAP):

```
Router_C>show arp
Protocol  Address       Age (min)  Hardware Addr   Type  Interface
Internet  172.16.1.1    -          0010.296a.a820  ARPA  Ethernet5/0
Internet  172.16.1.22   62         0010.29d1.68a0  SNAP  Ethernet5/0
Router_C>
```

FIGURE 4.10 Ethernet frame encapsulation compatibility

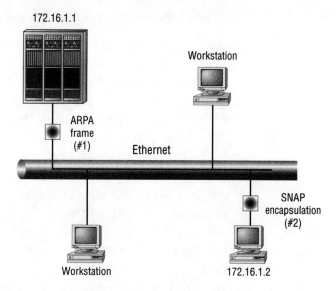

Continuing on—from the output from the show interface command, you can see a great deal of statistical information. You can see that the counters for the interface have not been cleared since the router booted. Queuing type for the interface is first-in-first-out (FIFO). You should be familiar with the next few fields. The input and output queue were discussed in detail previously. Here, you have statistical information that displays the number of drops. The interface traffic statistics follow.

Statistical information describes the number of packets that travel across the interface and the bandwidth utilization. The following fields are dedicated to Ethernet troubleshooting. The cyclic redundancy check fields counts the number of frames that were received that do not pass the CRC test. Next are frame errors and overruns. We discussed overruns previously (they occur when the receiver on the interface receives frames faster than it can move them to the hardware buffer on the interface). The ignore signal is sent if there are buffer problems.

Output errors consist of underruns and collisions. The other fields are counters for the physical interface: resets, lost carrier, and no carrier. These are followed by more buffer error counters.

Now let's look at the output from a Serial interface:

```
Router_D#sho int s1/0
Serial1/0 is up, line protocol is up
  Hardware is cxBus Serial
  Description: Connection to frame-relay cloud
  MTU 1500 bytes, BW 1544 Kbit, DLY 20000 usec, rely 255/
  255, load 1/255
  Encapsulation FRAME-RELAY, loopback not set, keepalive
  set     (10 sec)
  LMI enq sent  195167, LMI stat recvd 195165, LMI upd
  recvd     10, DTE LMI up
  LMI enq recvd 0, LMI stat sent  0, LMI upd sent  0
  LMI DLCI 1023  LMI type is CISCO  frame relay DTE
  Broadcast queue 0/64, broadcasts sent/dropped 0/0,
  interface broadcasts 908350
  Last input 00:00:00, output 00:00:00, output hang never
  Last clearing of "show interface" counters never
  Input queue: 0/75/4 (size/max/drops); Total output
  drops:     22795
  Queueing strategy: weighted fair
  Output queue: 0/64/22795 (size/threshold/drops)
     Conversations  0/59 (active/max active)
     Reserved Conversations 0/0 (allocated/max allocated)
  5 minute input rate 7000 bits/sec, 9 packets/sec
  5 minute output rate 9000 bits/sec, 8 packets/sec
     55695166 packets input, 3680326698 bytes, 1 no buffer
     Received 0 broadcasts, 0 runts, 0 giants
     1 input errors, 0 CRC, 0 frame, 0 overrun, 0 ignored,
     1 abort
     56424159 packets output, 569801054 bytes, 0 underruns
     0 output errors, 0 collisions, 2 interface resets
     8656902 output buffers copied, 0 interrupts, 0
     failures
     3 carrier transitions
     RTS up, CTS up, DTR up, DCD up, DSR up
Router_D#
```

This output has a lot of Frame Relay information that we will discuss in a later chapter. For now, we'll just review the fields of information that are available by using this command.

You can see that the first line is the interface status line. The metric values are also listed. Following the Frame Relay information, you see the interface traffic statistics. At the bottom of the output are the buffer error fields, as well as the physical interface counters. A carrier transition is counted any time that the carrier status change occurs. (We will cover this output in greater detail in Chapter 7.)

show interface accounting

This command simply tracks the protocol traffic on an interface. It counts the number of packets in and out, as well as the number of characters. Here is a sample output:

```
Router_D>show interface accounting
Ethernet5/0 connection to Router_A
Protocol     Pkts In    Chars In    Pkts Out    Chars Out
     IP        30347     2325063       44937      3514333  DEC MOP    0    0
    315    24255
    ARP            9         540          12          720
    CDP         2009      797573        3153      1261200
```

Process Commands

There are two very important process commands that can be executed. Process commands deal directly with the process running on the router. If the standard show processes command is issued, you get a result similar to a ps -ef executed on a Unix box. The output details each process, process ID number (PID), time running, and stack information. The output is too general to be used effectively while troubleshooting.

The two options available with the show processes command are cpu and memory. Each of these options refines the processes output, and makes it more useful and user-friendly.

Start with the cpu command. The output from this command is shown below. This output relates the router's processes and CPU utilization. The first line of the output displays the router's CPU utilization over three time frames.

Underneath the CPU utilization line, you can see the processes running on the router. Starting from the left, you can see the PID, followed by the runtime and other data. The three columns that deal with CPU utilization detail the percentage of CPU cycles that the specified process uses. The process description is found in the far-right column.

```
Router_C>show processes cpu
CPU utilization for five seconds: 15%/6%; one minute: 7%;
five minutes: 7%
PID  Runtime(ms)  Invoked  uSecs    5Sec    1Min    5Min
TTY  Process
  1          272     7306     37   0.00%   0.00%   0.00%
  0  SSCOP Input
  2      8489700   105027  80834   4.50%   0.56%   0.39%
  0  Check heaps

. . . [some output removed] . . .

 23            0        1      0   0.00%   0.00%   0.00%
  0      ATM ARP Input
 24           12      376     31   0.00%   0.00%   0.00%
  0      ATMSIG Timer
 25            0        1      0   0.00%   0.00%   0.00%
  0      Probe Input
 26            0        1      0   0.00%   0.00%   0.00%
  0      RARP Input
 27      7795088 49277831    158   1.96%   0.83%   0.76%
  0      IP Input
 28        19608  1368738     14   0.00%   0.00%   0.00%
  0  TCP Timer
 29           72      272    264   0.00%   0.00%   0.00%
  0  TCP Protocols
 30       265248  1271647    208   0.00%   0.01%   0.00%
  0  CDP Protocol
 31          936     5138    182   0.00%   0.00%   0.00%
  0  BOOTP Server
 32           12     3252      3   0.00%   0.00%   0.00%
  0  MOP Protocols
 33      1835404  1987135    923   0.08%   0.08%   0.06%
  0      IP Background
 34      3486340    32867 106074   0.00%   0.10%   0.15%
  0      IP Cache Ager
 35           48    33410      1   0.00%   0.00%   0.00%
  0      NBF Input
```

36	0	2	0	0.00%	0.00%	0.00%
0	SPX Input					
37	0	2	0	0.00%	0.00%	0.00%
0	SYSMGT Events					
38	0	1	0	0.00%	0.00%	0.00%
0	SNMP ConfCopyProc					
39	948	3899452	0	0.00%	0.00%	0.00%
0	cbus utilization					
40	4	10	400	0.00%	0.00%	0.00%
0	Critical Bkgnd					
41	308	4170	73	0.00%	0.00%	0.00%
0	Net Background					
42	184	1648	111	0.00%	0.00%	0.00%
0	Logger					
43	2992	1950119	1	0.00%	0.00%	0.00%
0	TTY Background					

. . . [some output removed] . . .

48	54040	1083266	49	0.00%	0.00%	0.00%
0	IPX Input					
49	21620	282612	76	0.00%	0.00%	0.00%
0	IPX RIP					
50	63728	843497	75	0.00%	0.00%	0.00%
0	IPX SAP					
51	1160	72474	16	0.00%	0.00%	0.00%
0	IPX RSUpdate					
52	0	2	0	0.00%	0.00%	0.00%
0	IPX GNS					
53	0	2	0	0.00%	0.00%	0.00%
0	IPX Forwarder					
54	68876	546353	126	0.00%	0.00%	0.00%
0	IPX OutputFork					
55	0	2	0	0.00%	0.00%	0.00%
0	IPXWAN Input					
56	0	2	0	0.00%	0.00%	0.00%
0	IPXWAN Timer					
57	4340	2080986	2	0.00%	0.00%	0.00%
0	IGMP Input					
58	3228	2018536	1	0.00%	0.00%	0.00%
0	PIM Process					

```
59            0           1        0    0.00%   0.00%   0.00%
0         FR ARP Input
60       179596     4286958       41    0.00%   0.00%   0.00%
0         FR LMI Input
61            0           1        0    0.00%   0.00%   0.00%
0         FR IP Rcv
62         5404     4277369        1    0.00%   0.00%   0.00%
0         FR LMI Tx
63         1824      975229        1    0.00%   0.00%   0.00%
0         LANE Client
64       793064    34582517       22    0.16%   0.02%   0.01%
0         IP-EIGRP Hello
65            0         114        0    0.00%   0.00%   0.00%
0         Exec
66            8          21      380    0.00%   0.00%   0.00%
0         TCP Listener
67       854728      968616      882    0.00%   0.01%   0.05%
0         IP SNMP
68            0           2        0    0.00%   0.00%   0.00%
0         IPX SNMP
69           84           6    14000    0.00%   0.00%   0.00%
0         SNMP Traps
70         5256     1989681        2    0.00%   0.00%   0.00%
0         NTP
71      2048596    15254055      134    0.00%   0.02%   0.04%
0         IP-EIGRP Router

 . . . [some output removed] . . .

77       860512     6411841      134    0.00%   0.00%   0.01%
0         BGP Router
78       284296     1119907      253    0.00%   0.00%   0.00%
0         BGP I/O
79      8019956      163266    49122    0.00%   0.27%   0.35%
0         BGP Scanner
80           52         113      460    0.00%   0.01%   0.00%
2         Virtual Exec
82            0           5        0    0.00%   0.00%   0.00%
0         AAA Accounting
```

When the overall CPU utilization gets high, you can identify which process is using the most CPU cycles, and then focus your attention on that process. For example, if the IP-EIGRP CPU utilization runs high, you can determine that there is a problem within EIGRP, perhaps a routing loop or some other instability.

The second option, show processes memory, is used to associate memory utilization with the router's processes. Here is a sample output:

```
Router_D>show processes memory
Total: 52503792, Used: 45141524, Free: 7362268
 PID TTY Allocated    Freed    Holding   Getbufs
Retbufs Process
  0   0      54400      304    8898364        0
  0 *Init*
  0   0        632 3906083084     632        0
  0 *Sched*
  0   0 700723436 729437084     472484   1091352
  0 *Dead*
  1   0         96        0       6876        0
  0 SSCOP Input
  2   0          0        0       6780        0
  0 Check heaps
  3   0   17262036   152680       6916  12351248
260336 Pool Manager
  4   0        300      300       6780        0
  0 Timers
  5   0         96        0       3876        0
  0 OIR Handler
  6   0          0        0       6780        0
  0 IPC Zone
  7   0          0        0       6780        0
  0 IPC Realm
  8   0      60816    34504       7496        0
  0 IPC Seat
  9   0      14988   972016      91520
  0 ARP Input
 10   0         96        0       6876        0
  0 SERIAL detect
 11   0        228        0       7008        0
  0 Microcode
 12   0     112720   112136       7240        0
  0 ATM ILMI
```

```
13    0    2001476    3409452      7376           00
ILMI Process
14    0    244         0      7024         0
0 IP Crashinfo
```

The first line details the total, used, and free amounts of system memory. Following, you see the PID, allocated, freed, and holding memory. This means that the processor has allocated a given amount of memory to the process; if the process does not need all of that memory, it frees some of it and retains the rest.

Protocol Commands

At this point, we introduce only the protocol-related commands. We will discuss the specifics of the outputs in the following chapters, as we apply them in troubleshooting scenarios. There are many protocol-related commands. We'll discuss only the major protocol commands in this section.

The principal types of protocols that are discussed in this book are TCP/IP, HDLC, Frame Relay, X.25, ISDN, IPX, and AppleTalk. Because of the sheer number of show command options related to each of these protocols, it isn't logical to explain them all. We will briefly summarize the available commands for IP, IPX, and AppleTalk.

TCP/IP

The TCP/IP protocol suite includes many other protocols. This section summarizes the protocols and command options available.

Options associated with IP protocols are listed in Table 4.7.

TABLE 4.7   show ip protocol Command Options

show ip protocol Command Option	Protocol Description
BGP	BGP information and options
EIGRP	EIGRP information and options
IGMP	IGMP information
OSPF	OSPF information and options
TCP	TCP information

Each of these protocols has numerous show commands that are associated with it. To list the available options, execute the show ip <protocol> ? command from the command line on the router.

In addition to other protocols, there are several important options that are associated with IP alone. Table 4.8 lists the frequently used IP options.

TABLE 4.8 Frequently Used show IP Command Options

show ip Command Option	Option Description
access-lists	List IP access-lists
Accounting	The active IP accounting database
Interface	IP interface status and configuration
Route	IP routing table
Traffic	IP protocol statistics

IPX

There are fewer options associated with IPX than with IP. Some are protocol-related and others are IPX-specific. All of these options are listed in Table 4.9. (Further detail will be given in Chapter 9.)

TABLE 4.9 show IPX Command Options

show IPX Command Option	Description
Accounting	The active IPX accounting database
Eigrp	IPX EIGRP show commands
Interface	IPX interface status and configuration
Nlsp	Show NLSP information

TABLE 4.9 show IPX Command Options *(continued)*

show IPX Command Option	Description
Route	IPX routing table
Servers	SAP servers
Traffic	IPX protocol statistics

AppleTalk

AppleTalk has more options than IPX, but it has fewer than TCP/IP. The majority of these commands are AppleTalk-specific, but there is one protocol option. The options are shown in Table 4.10.

TABLE 4.10 show AppleTalk Command Options

show AppleTalk Command Option	Description
access-lists	AppleTalk access-lists
adjacent-routes	AppleTalk adjacent routes
Domain	AppleTalk Domain(s) information
Eigrp	AppleTalk/EIGRP show commands
Globals	AppleTalk global parameters
Interface	AppleTalk interface status and configuration
Neighbors	AppleTalk Neighboring router status
Route	AppleTalk routing table
Sockets	AppleTalk protocol processing information
Traffic	AppleTalk protocol statistics
Zone	AppleTalk Zone table information

debug Commands

The debug commands and options are very powerful tools. The messages produced by the debugging process give detailed information and provide insight into what is happening on a very low level.

This power does not come free of charge. Debugging requires every packet to be process-switched, meaning that the route processor has to look at every packet entering the router, if valid information is to be obtained. In addition, there are many other processes the router must run and manage. Debugging can cause a great deal of additional overhead on a router. Therefore, it is important to use the tool with discretion. It should be used to provide additional information on an existing problem, not used to monitor a router.

Because the majority of problems are reported while the network is in production, the last thing you want to do is crash a router or cause unnecessary overhead by using the debug tool. By focusing the application of the debug command by using various options and access lists, you can effectively troubleshoot problems without causing any additional ones. Always remember to turn the debugging function off after you obtain the necessary data. If left on, it can cause another network problem.

As with the show commands, there are global-, interface-, and protocol-debugging options. Because these tools/commands are used in detail in upcoming chapters, they are only summarized here according to usage.

Global Debugging

There are two "tricks" to successfully using the debug tool. First, make sure that your router is configured to apply timestamps to all messages. This is done with the following commands:

```
Router_A(config)#service timestamps debug datetime msec
localtime
Router_A(config)#service timestamps log datetime msec
localtime
```

Next, make sure that you see these messages. By default, error and debug messages are sent only to the console. If you are telneted to the router, you do not see the debug or log messages unless you issue the following command:

```
Router_A#terminal monitor
```

You can turn messages off by issuing the "no" form of the command. An example follows:

`Router_A#`**`terminal no monitor`**

If the output messages from the debug become excessive, it becomes difficult, if not impossible, to enter commands. If this happens, there are two commands that you can issue to stop the messages. The first one was already mentioned (the `terminal no monitor`–term no mon for short—command). You need to get used to shorthand when issuing router commands. If the route processor is busy processing packets, it is hard to enter commands. You type, but you don't see anything echo back. It can get confusing. Remember that the text messages that echo to the screen are not entered on the command line of the router. You can safely type **term no mon** and hit Enter, even with hundreds of messages scrolling past you on the screen. The router eventually recognizes and processes the command. That stops the messages from scrolling down the screen, but it does not stop the processor from looking at every packet.

To stop the debug process, the easiest way is to type the following command:

`Router_A#`**`un all`**

It is short and sweet, yet effective. It works especially well when the router seems to be having a runaway. This command stops all debug processes and all associated messages. This command can be entered safely while messages are scrolling wildly down the screen. It may take the router a few CPU cycles to accept the command and actually stop the debug process, so don't panic.

Some global `debug` commands are listed in Table 4.11. The table is not comprehensive; it is just a list of commonly used global `debug` commands. To obtain a comprehensive list of `debug` commands, issue the following command:

`Router_A#`**`debug ?`**

TABLE 4.11 Global debug Commands

Global debug Command	Description
Aaa	AAA Authentication, Authorization, and Accounting
adjacency	Adjacency
all	Enable all debugging

TABLE 4.11 Global debug Commands *(continued)*

Global debug Command	Description
Cbus	ciscoBus events
Cdp	CDP information
Chat	Chat scripts activity
Dhcp	DHCP client activity
Dialer	Dial on Demand
Domain	Domain Name System
Entry	Incoming queue entries
Snmp	SNMP information
Tacacs	TACACS authentication and authorization
Tbridge	Transparent bridging

Interface Debugging

Interface debugging is used to obtain information that is specific to interfaces, interface signaling, and interface processes. The same caution should be used with interface-related **debug** commands as with the global commands. The more focused the debug through the use of options, the easier it is to isolate the problem.

Interface-oriented commands are provided in Table 4.12. Again, each of these commands has additional options available. To see the related options, use the commands listed, followed by a question mark. Most of these commands will be described and applied in later chapters.

TABLE 4.12 Interface-Related debug Commands

debug Command	Description
Atm	ATM Interface information
Channel	Channel Interface information

TABLE 4.12 Interface-Related debug Commands *(continued)*

debug Command	Description
ethernet-interface	Ethernet network interface events
fastethernet	Fast Ethernet interface information
Serial	Serial interface information
Token	Token Ring information
Tunnel	Generic Tunnel Interface

Protocol Debugging

There are two protocol classes that may be debugged: desktop, or routed, protocols and routing protocols. There are several debug options for protocol information, and each protocol has its own associated debug options. These options can be obtained by using the command line help on the router.

Table 4.13 shows a list of the protocol-related **debug** commands available.

TABLE 4.13 Protocol-Related debug Commands

debug Command	Description
Apple	AppleTalk information
Arp	IP ARP and HP Probe transactions
Atm	ATM Signaling
broadcast	MAC broadcast packets
Decent	DECnet information
Dlsw	Data Link Switching (DLSw) events
Eigrp	EIGRP Protocol information

TABLE 4.13   Protocol-Related debug Commands *(continued)*

debug Command	Description
frame-relay	Frame Relay
Ip	IP information
Ipx	Novell/IPX information
Isis	IS-IS Information
Lane	LAN Emulation
Lat	LAT Information
Lex	LAN Extender protocol
llc2	LLC2 type II Information
Ppp	PPP (Point to Point Protocol) information
Qllc	qllc debug information
Sna	SNA Information
Spanning	Spanning-tree information
Sscop	SSCOP
telnet	Incoming telnet connections
translate	Protocol translation events
Vlan	VLAN information
X25	X.25 information

Executing a Router Core Dump

The information contained in a core dump can be useful for diagnosing router problems. A core dump contains an exact copy of the information that currently resides in system memory. Depending on the amount of RAM and the memory utilization, the core dump file can be very large. The information provided is normally used only by Cisco engineers.

There are two general methods for capturing the information contained in memory. In the first method, a router is configured to execute a core dump when the router crashes. The second method is to use a user privileged `exec` command from the command line.

exception Command

The `exception` command allows you to configure a router to execute a core dump if the router crashes. An integral part of the `exception` command is the TFTP, FTP, or RCP server. Here is a sample configuration:

```
Router_A#conf t
Enter configuration commands, one per line.  End with
CNTL/Z.
Router_A(config)#exception dump 172.16.10.10
Router_A(config)#^Z
Router_A#
```

The IP address in the command is the IP address of the TFTP, FTP, or RCP server. The router needs this address so it knows where to download the core dump. It uses any of the three protocols mentioned before.

Configuration varies, depending on which type of server is used. TFTP does not require any additional configuration than the example previously shown.

FTP and RCP require additional commands in order to support the file transfer. Here is an example:

```
Router_A#conf t
Enter configuration commands, one per line.  End with
CNTL/Z.
Router_A(config)#exception dump 172.16.10.11
Router_A(config)#ip ftp username kevin
Router_A(config)#ip ftp password aloha
Router_A(config)#ip ftp source-interface e0
Router_A(config)#exception protocol ftp
Router_A(config)#^Z
Router_A#
```

Because FTP servers require some type of username and password combination to allow access to the file system, they must be specified on the router. You can map the FTP server to the exiting interface on the router by using the `source-interface` command. This is just like a static route. If the route table did not have the route in its table, it would still know how to get to the FTP server. You must also specify which protocol is going to be used.

RCP requires configuration on the RCP server by editing the .rhosts files, as well as the router configuration. Here is a sample:

```
Router_A#conf t
Enter configuration commands, one per line.  End with
CNTL/Z.
Router_A(config)#exception protocol rcp
Router_A(config)#exception dump 172.16.10.12
Router_A(config)#ip rcmd remote-username kevin
Router_A(config)#ip rcmd rcp-enable
Router_A(config)#ip rcmd rsh-enable
Router_A(config)#ip rcmd remote-host kevin 172.16.10.12
kevin
Router_A(config)#^Z
Router_A#
```

The commands are mostly the same for the RCP server, as well. The remote-host command is configured by providing the local username, followed by the IP address for the RCP server and the remote username for the RCP server. This allows the router to log in on the RCP server and commence transferring the core dump.

write core Command

The write core command allows the user to execute a core dump without crashing the router. It is not advisable to use this command unless it is requested by Cisco TAC. Because it is copying the contents of memory via TFTP, it could have an adverse effect on the router. Here is a sample of the write core command:

```
Router_A#write core
Remote host? 172.16.10.10
Name of core file to write [Router_A-core]?
Write file Router_A-core on host 172.16.10.10? [confirm]
Writing Router_A-core !!!!! [OK]
Router_A#
```

The router output has been truncated in this example. You will see exclamation marks until the file is completely transferred. The more memory that needs to be copied, the longer it will take.

Again, this information will only be useful to Cisco engineers for diagnosing and resolving router problems.

ping Commands

The previous tools are in-depth tools used for problems that require very high granularity. This means that these tools are used to provide very detailed and specific information at a very low-level view. The `ping` command is a high-level simple tool. It is used to test for reachability and connectivity throughout a network.

This tool can be used to effectively isolate network problems. If certain machines on a network respond to the pings when others do not, this directs your efforts to focus more on the individual machines that are not responding.

Cisco provides two implementations of the `ping` command: the user and privileged levels. `ping` works for the following protocols on both levels:

- IP
- IPX
- AppleTalk
- CLNS
- Apollo
- VINES
- DECnet
- XNS

User EXEC Mode

The user mode for `ping` is restricted. Only the non-verbose method is allowed for the user level. We now discuss the user mode for IP, IPX, and AppleTalk.

IP

IP `ping` uses ICMP as the protocol to provide connectivity and reachability messages. It works on a simple principle: an ICMP echo message is sent to the specified IP address. If the address is reachable, the receiving station sends an ICMP echo-reply message back to the sending station.

It is important to be able to decipher the symbols that are echoed to the screen while a ping is taking place. By default and for user mode, five ICMP echo messages are sent. Let's look at a few samples:

```
Router_A>ping 172.16.1.10
Type escape sequence to abort.
Sending 5, 100-byte ICMP Echoes to 172.16.1.10, timeout is
2    seconds:
!!!!!
Success rate is 100 percent (5/5), round-trip min/avg/max
=    1/2/4 ms
Router_A>
Router_A>ping 172.16.2.130
Type escape sequence to abort.
Sending 5, 100-byte ICMP Echoes to 172.16.2.130, timeout
is    2 seconds:
.....
Success rate is 0 percent (0/5)
Router_A>
```

It looks good so far, but what do the different characters mean? Table 4.14 defines them.

TABLE 4.14   ping Character Map

Character	Explanation
!	Received an echo-reply message
.	Time out
U / H	Destination unreachable
N	Network unreachable
P	Protocol unreachable
Q	Source Quench
M	Unable to fragment
A	Administratively denied
?	Unknown packet-type

Now that the characters are defined, you can analyze the sample outputs. In the first ping, all five packets received echo-reply messages, which indicates that the host is reachable. Notice that the output gives a success percentage based on the five requests that were sent. It also gives the minimum, average, and maximum response times.

The second ping doesn't look so good. All five requests timed out. This means that each request waited two seconds for a response. When no response was received, a "." was echoed to the screen. It is possible that a request was received, but it was after the two-second waiting period. Either way, the host cannot be considered reachable.

IPX

The IPX ping uses functions within NLSP. It is important to note that the ping ipx command uses a Cisco proprietary Ping that actual Novell boxes do not respond to—only Cisco routers respond to the Cisco proprietary Ping. If you desire to ping a Novell box, you must configure the router to do so. In global configuration mode, enter the following command:

```
Router_B(config)# ipx ping-default novell
Router_B(config)# ^Z
Router_B#
```

Look at the ping IPX response. Following the output, refer to Table 4.15 for the character map definitions.

```
Router_B#ping ipx DD72C718.0e00.0f4a.64fe
Type escape sequence to abort.
Sending 5, 100-byte IPX cisco Echoes to
DD72C718.0e00.0f4a.64fe, timeout is 2 seconds:
!!!!!
Success rate is 100 percent (5/5), round-trip min/avg/max
=    8/8/8 ms
Router_B#
Router_B#ping ipx CD62F181.00f0.c044.18d4
Type escape sequence to abort.
Sending 5, 100-byte IPX cisco Echoes to
CD62F181.00f0.c044.18d4, timeout is 2 seconds:
.....
Success rate is 0 percent (0/5)
Router_B#
```

Most of the characters used by the `ping` IPX are the same as with `IP` `ping`. Table 4.15 defines the characters used with the `ping` IPX.

TABLE 4.15 IPX `ping` Message Explanation

Character	Explanation
!	Received an echo-reply message
.	Time out
U	Destination unreachable
C	Congestion
I	User interrupt
?	Unknown packet-type
&	TTL exceeded

AppleTalk

AppleTalk's version of ping uses the Apple Echo Protocol to send and receive reachability messages. Unlike IP, unless an interface is configured to listen to its own requests, `AppleTalk ping` does not work on the router interfaces.

You find the character map for AppleTalk echo messages in Table 4.16.

TABLE 4.16 AppleTalk `ping` Message Explanation

Character	Explanation
!	Received an echo-reply message
.	Time out
B	Bad echo packet
C	Bad DDP checksum
E	Transmission failed
R	No route to destination

Privileged EXEC Mode

The privileged mode for ping is known as an *extended ping*. This mode allows many options to aid in providing additional detailed information. The options are listed with each protocol, respectively.

IP

The functionality of the `ping` command is based on the same technology as with user mode. The extended ping offers options to change some of the ping settings.

The best way to explain it is to see it, so look at the following extended ping dialog:

```
Router_B #ping
Protocol [ip]:
Target IP address: 172.16.12.93
Repeat count [5]:
Datagram size [100]:
Timeout in seconds [2]:
Extended commands [n]: y
Source address or interface: 172.16.1.2
Type of service [0]:
Set DF bit in IP header? [no]:
Validate reply data? [no]:
Data pattern [0xABCD]:
Loose, Strict, Record, Timestamp, Verbose[none]: r
Number of hops [ 9 ]:
Loose, Strict, Record, Timestamp, Verbose[RV]:
Sweep range of sizes [n]:
Type escape sequence to abort.
Sending 5, 100-byte ICMP Echoes to 172.16.12.93, timeout
is 2 seconds:
Packet has IP options:  Total option bytes= 39, padded
length=40
 Record route: <*> 0.0.0.0 0.0.0.0 0.0.0.0 0.0.0.0
          0.0.0.0 0.0.0.0 0.0.0.0 0.0.0.0 0.0.0.0
Reply to request 0 (1 ms). Received packet has options
 Total option bytes= 40, padded length=40
```

```
 Record route: 172.16.1.2 172.16.0.13 172.16.12.1
172.16.12.93 172.16.0.14 172.16.0.21 172.16.1.2 <*>
0.0.0.0 0.0.0.0
 End of list
Reply to request 1 (4 ms). Received packet has options
 Total option bytes= 40, padded length=40
 Record route: 172.16.1.2 172.16.0.13 172.16.12.1
172.16.12.93 172.16.0.14 172.16.0.21 172.16.1.2 <*>
0.0.0.0 0.0.0.0
 End of list
Reply to request 2 (4 ms). Received packet has options
 Total option bytes= 40, padded length=40
 Record route: 172.16.1.2 172.16.0.13 172.16.12.1
172.16.12.93 172.16.0.14 172.16.0.21 172.16.1.2 <*>
0.0.0.0 0.0.0.0
 End of list
Reply to request 3 (1 ms). Received packet has options
 Total option bytes= 40, padded length=40
 Record route: 172.16.1.2 172.16.0.13 172.16.12.1
172.16.12.93 172.16.0.14 172.16.0.21 172.16.1.2 <*>
0.0.0.0 0.0.0.0
 End of list
Reply to request 4 (1 ms). Received packet has options
 Total option bytes= 40, padded length=40
 Record route: 172.16.1.2 172.16.0.13 172.16.12.1
172.16.12.93 172.16.0.14 172.16.0.21 172.16.1.2 <*>
0.0.0.0 0.0.0.0
 End of list
Success rate is 100 percent (5/5), round-trip min/avg/max
= 1/2/4 ms
Router_B#
```

The character echoes have the same meaning as with the user mode of the ping command. Let's discuss the extended dialog. The extended ping mode is accessed by just typing the word **ping**. The default protocol is IP. The next field is the target IP address. The default values are located within the brackets of each dialog question. The repeat count is five ICMP requests. The next field is the datagram size, followed by the timeout.

Additional commands are available by answering **yes** to the extended commands prompt. Extended options included the source IP address (it must be an IP address that is present on the router), type of service, don't fragment bit, data pattern, and header options.

Header options enable the route processor to analyze the packet header. There are five header options:

- Loose

- Strict

- Record

- Timestamp

- Verbose

The record option records the ICMP packets route to the destination address. It records up to nine hops. You can see the results of using the record packet header option in the previous output. The IP addresses are the addresses of the exiting interface. If you follow the route, you can see the packet leave the router and finally get to the destination on the fourth hop. But wait a minute—there are still more addresses. Yes, they are the addresses of the path back to the router. The path is recorded for both directions, not just to the destination.

There is a final option that allows the router to increment the packet size between 76 bytes and 18,024 bytes. Because it is an Ethernet interface, it does not exceed 1500 bytes.

IPX

The extended options for IPX are not as extensive as with IP. The following output depicts which options are available for an extended IPX ping:

```
Router_C#ping
Protocol [ip]: ipx
Target IPX address: C082B2B9.1171.587d.58fb
Repeat count [5]:
Datagram size [100]:
Timeout in seconds [2]:
Verbose [n]:
Novell Standard Echo [n]:
Type escape sequence to abort.
```

```
Sending 5, 100-byte IPX cisco Echoes to
C082B2B9.1171.587d.58fb, timeout is 2 seconds:
!!!!!
Success rate is 100 percent (5/5), round-trip min/avg/max
= 8/10/12 ms
Router_C#
Router_C#ping
Protocol [ip]: ipx
Target IPX address: C082B2B9.1171.587d.58fb
Repeat count [5]:
Datagram size [100]:
Timeout in seconds [2]:
Verbose [n]: y
Novell Standard Echo [n]:
Type escape sequence to abort.
Sending 5, 100-byte IPX cisco Echoes to
C082B2B9.1171.587d.58fb, timeout is 2 seconds:
0 in 12 ms
1 in 12 ms
2 in 12 ms
3 in 12 ms
4 in 12 ms
Success rate is 100 percent (5/5), round-trip min/avg/max
=    12/12/12 ms
Router_C#
```

If you answer **yes** to the Novell Standard Echo prompt, then Novell boxes can respond to the ping. The second ping is different from the first because the verbose option was selected. It displays the RTT for each packet separately.

AppleTalk

The extended options for AppleTalk are the same. The following dialog depicts the AppleTalk ping options:

```
Router_C#ping
Protocol [ip]: appletalk
Target AppleTalk address: 1.112
Repeat count [5]:
```

```
Datagram size [100]:
Timeout in seconds [2]:
Verbose [n]: y
Sweep range of sizes [n]:
Type escape sequence to abort.
Sending 5, 100-byte AppleTalk Echoes to 1.112, timeout is
2 seconds:
0 in 12 ms from 1.112 via 2 hops
1 in 12 ms from 1.112 via 2 hops
2 in 12 ms from 1.112 via 2 hops
3 in 12 ms from 1.112 via 2 hops
4 in 12 ms from 1.112 via 2 hops
Success rate is 100 percent (5/5), round-trip min/avg/max
= 12/12/12 ms
Router_C#
```

Because the verbose option was selected, the RTT along with the hop count are listed.

traceroute Command

The traceroute command is used for displaying the packet's path toward its destination. The functionality of the traceroute utility works on error messages that are generated by expired TTL values in the IP packet header. When the TTL value in an IP header reaches zero, the entire packet is discarded. At the same time, the IP host responsible for discarding the packet sends an error message to the source IP address in the header, informing the source that the packet was dropped. The TTL value is decremented by one every time the packet transits a router or IP host.

Traceroute capitalizes on this message exchange. When the traceroute function is used, the TTL in the IP header is set to a value of one. It then sends the packet to the specified destination. Because the next-hop decrements the TTL counter to zero, the packet is discarded and a message is sent back to the source address. The traceroute utility records the IP address from the error message and echoes it to the screen. An nslookup is performed on the IP address; if a result is received, the DNS name is displayed in addition to the IP address.

The TTL is then incremented to two and sent out. The packet transverses the first hop, the TTL is decremented to one, and it is forwarded on to the next-hop. When the second hop receives the packet, the TTL is decremented to zero and the error message is sent to the source address.

This process is followed until the destination host responds or until the TTL is exceeded. By default, the maximum TTL is 30. This means that if the destination host does not respond, the traceroute utility will attempt 30 times. Multiple requests are sent each attempt, which results in three RTT responses. In addition to the TTL error messages, port unreachable messages provide sufficient information for a path to the destination.

Table 4.17 lists the explanation for the response characters available within the traceroute utility.

TABLE 4.17   traceroute Response Meanings

Character	Explanation
xx msec	The RTT for each packet
*	Timeout
H	Host Unreachable
U	Port Unreachable
N	Network Unreachable
P	Protocol Unreachable
A	Administratively denied
Q	Source Quench
?	Unknown packet type

Successful functionality of the `traceroute` command depends on the IP configuration on each host along the path to the destination. It is possible that the IP configuration does not send error messages when the TTL expires, TTL is not decremented, or no port unreachable messages are sent. If any of these problems exist, you probably get timeout responses.

User EXEC Mode

The user mode of the traceroute command allows only the default options when using the command. Here is a sample output:

```
Router_B>traceroute www.netscape.com
Translating "www.netscape.com"...domain server
(172.16.4.2)    [OK]
Type escape sequence to abort.
Tracing the route to www-1d1.netscape.com (207.200.75.200)
1 172.16.2.1 0 msec 0 msec 0 msec
  2 172.16.4.53 [AS 209] 12 msec 8 msec 8 msec
  3 den-core-02.inet.qwest.net (205.171.16.137) [AS 209]
  12 msec 12 msec 8 msec
  4 sfo-core-02.inet.qwest.net (205.171.4.1) [AS 209]
  32 msec 36 msec 36 msec
  5 sjo-core-01.inet.qwest.net (205.171.4.101) [AS 209]
  36 msec 36 msec 40 msec
  6 sjo-core-03.inet.qwest.net (205.171.22.6) [AS 209]
  36 msec 36 msec 36 msec
  7 sjo-edge-05.inet.qwest.net (205.171.22.50) [AS 209]
  36 msec 40 msec 36 msec
  8 205.171.48.154 [AS 209] 36 msec 36 msec 36 msec
  9 h-207-200-69-241.netscape.com (207.200.69.241) [AS
  6992]    40 msec 40 msec 36 msec
  10 www-1d1.netscape.com (207.200.75.200) [AS 6992] 36
  msec    36 msec 36 msec
Router_B>
```

As you can see, the nslookup for the first two hops failed. The RTTs for the three probes follow. The times increment as the packet moves closer to the destination address. In addition to the DNS entry, IP address, and RTT, the AS number is also listed.

Here is another sample that includes timeouts and administratively denied probes:

```
Router_B>traceroute www.novell.com
Translating "www.novell.com"...domain server (172.16.4.2)
[OK]
Type escape sequence to abort.
```

```
Tracing the route to www.novell.com (137.65.2.5)
1 172.16.1.13 0 msec 0 msec 0 msec
 2 205.171.48.53 [AS 209] 8 msec 8 msec 12 msec
 3 den-core-01.inet.qwest.net (205.171.16.109) [AS 209]
 12 msec 8 msec 12 msec
 4 den-brdr-01.inet.qwest.net (205.171.16.114) [AS 209]
 8 msec 12 msec 12 msec
 5 s2-0-0.den-bb1.cerf.net (134.24.112.77) [AS 1740] 8
 msec    16 msec 12 msec
 6 s10-0-0.slc-bb1.cerf.net (134.24.46.98) [AS 1740]
 88 msec 84 msec 84 msec
 7 novell-gw.slc-bb1.cerf.net (134.24.116.54) [AS 1740]
 84 msec 84 msec 84 msec
 8 134.24.116.58 [AS 1740] 84 msec 84 msec 84 msec
 9  *   *  !A
Router_B>
```

Here, the probe made it to the destination address, but instead of receiving a TTL expired or port unreachable message, we get an administratively denied message.

Privileged EXEC Mode

The privileged mode has options that are similar to the ping privileged mode. The dialog contains several prompts that change the traceroute settings. The default settings are listed in the brackets. They can be selected by hitting Enter or changed by substituting a new value. Let's look at the privileged dialog, and then we can explain each of the prompts:

```
Router_B#traceroute
Protocol [ip]:
Target IP address: 137.65.2.11
Source address: 172.16.2.9
Numeric display [n]:
Timeout in seconds [3]:
Probe count [3]:
Minimum Time to Live [1]:
Maximum Time to Live [30]:
```

```
Port Number [33434]:
Loose, Strict, Record, Timestamp, Verbose[none]:
Type escape sequence to abort.
Tracing the route to www.novell.com (137.65.2.11)
1 172.16.0.1 0 msec 0 msec 0 msec
  2 205.171.48.53 [AS 209] 8 msec 8 msec 12 msec
  3 den-core-02.inet.qwest.net (205.171.16.137) [AS 209]
  12 msec 8 msec 12 msec
  4 den-brdr-01.inet.qwest.net (205.171.16.142) [AS 209]
  8 msec 12 msec 12 msec
  5 s2-0-0.den-bb1.cerf.net (134.24.112.77) [AS 1740]
  12 msec 12 msec 12 msec
  6 s10-0-0.slc-bb1.cerf.net (134.24.46.98) [AS 1740]
  84 msec 84 msec 88 msec
  7 novell-gw.slc-bb1.cerf.net (134.24.116.54) [AS 1740]
  84 msec 84 msec 84 msec
  8 134.24.116.58 [AS 1740] 84 msec 88 msec 84 msec
  9 134.24.116.58 [AS 1740] !A  *   *
Router_B#
```

Target IP address   The IP address of the destination host.

Source address   The IP address present on the router. This is used to select an address that is not directly connected to the next hop.

Numeric display   Disables nslookup on the IP address. Consequently, if this option is chosen, only the IP address is displayed.

Timeout   The threshold for response times for the returning error message.

Probe count   The number of probes sent at each TTL level.

Minimum TTL   The numerical value for the first TTL level.

Maximum TTL   The maximum TTL value; an equivalent of 30 hops is the default, and is the highest value possible.

Port Number   The port number used by UDP that creates a port unreachable error message.

Loose Source Routing   Specifies nodes that must be included in the path to the destination.

Strict Source Routing   Specifies the only nodes allowed in the path to the destination.

Record   Specifies the number of hops for the verbose path to display.

Timestamp   Specifies the number of timestamps to display.

Verbose   Automatically selected if any of the previous options are selected.

Summary

There are several commands that are supported by Cisco IOS, and it is important to understand what each tool does so you can effectively troubleshoot network problems.

Some of these tools can cause more overhead on the router compared to others. It is important that you judiciously use tools such as debug, so that no unnecessary problems are introduced into the network while you are troubleshooting.

Other tools, such as traceroute and ping, can be used with very little impact to the router, and provide global reachability and path connectivity. The show commands are abundant and are the most valuable tools in a troubleshooting situation.

The commands discussed in this chapter were the following:

- show (global, interface, protocol, and processes)

- debug

- ping

- traceroute

Information gathered from all of these commands can be forwarded to Cisco TAC if assistance is needed in resolving the problem.

We also discussed the different router architectures in order to gain a better understanding of the output from the listed troubleshooting commands.

Commands Used in This Chapter

The following list contains a summary of all the commands used in this chapter.

Command	Description
`exception dump`	Configures the router to perform a core dump via TFTP or FTP if and when the router crashes.
`Ping`	Initiates an ICMP echo request. There are two levels, User and Privileged. The IP protocol is used.
`ping appletalk`	Initiates an AppleTalk ping. There are two levels, User and Privileged.
`ping ipx`	Initiates an IPX ping. There are two levels, User and Privileged.
`show access-lists`	Displays the specified access list from the configuration.
`show arp`	Displays the contents of the ARP table as well as status.
`show buffers`	Displays buffer statistics for the router.
`show controllers cbus`	Displays the buffer information on line cards connected to the cbus.
`show interface`	Displays interface-specific settings and statistics.
`show interface accounting`	Displays statistical information regarding protocols on the interface.
`show logging`	Displays logs for the router including traps and system errors. Can also provide logs when logging access-lists.
`show memory`	Displays the statistics and status of the router's memory.

Command	Description
`show processes cpu`	Displays the router's processes and the percentage of CPU utilization over 5 seconds, 1 minute, and 5 minutes.
`show processes memory`	Displays the router's processes and the amount of memory allocated to each.
`show queue`	Displays interface-specific queuing information.
`show queueing`	Displays the configuration of queuing on the router.
`show running-config`	Displays the current configuration that is loaded into memory.
`show stacks`	Displays the router's stack information.
`show startup-config`	Displays the configuration version that is saved in NVRAM.
`show tech-support`	A comprehensive command that includes `show running-config`, `show version`, `show stacks`, `show processes cpu`, and `show processes memory`, along with many others.
`show version`	Displays the version of IOS, the reason for last reload, and the router's hardware configuration.
`terminal monitor`	Enables the router to echo console message to the active TTY port. This facilitates the debug tool.
`terminal no monitor`	Disables the echo.
`traceroute`	A hop-by-hop ICMP traceroute. This command has two levels, User and Privileged.
`un all`	Turns off all possible debugging.
`write core`	Initiates a core dump to the specified host.

Key Terms

Before you take the exam, be certain you are familiar with the following terms:

adjacency table

autonomous switching

Cisco Express Forwarding (CEF)

debug

distributed switching

extended ping

fast switching

Forwarding Information Base (FIB)

ignore

input queues

interface buffers

metrics

netflow switching

optimum switching

output queue

overrun

path determination

process switching

processes

routers

routing protocol

silicon switching

switching path

underrun

Review Questions

1. Which of the following are valid switching methods? (Choose all that apply.)

    A. Process switching

    B. Path switching

    C. Fast switching

    D. Cut-over switching

    E. Distributed switching

    F. Optimum switching

    G. Netflow switching

    H. Cisco Express Forwarding

2. What are the three buffer types used in a Cisco 7000 series router? (Choose three.)

    A. Input buffers

    B. Output buffers

    C. Hardware buffers

    D. Interface buffers

    E. System buffers

3. What are the four general categories for the Cisco show commands? (Choose four.)

    A. Process

    B. Queue

    C. Protocol

    D. Controller

    E. Global

    F. Interface

4. What information is provided by the `show logging` command? (Choose all that apply.)

   A. Access-list logs

   B. Debug messages

   C. Syslog messages

   D. Console messages

   E. None of the above

5. What information is provided by issuing the `show version` command? (Choose all that apply.)

   A. Hardware and software version

   B. Reason for last upgrade

   C. Reason for last reload

   D. Up time

   E. Configuration version

6. What information is provided by issuing the `show startup-config` command?

   A. The current configuration

   B. The configuration held in FLASH

   C. The configuration held in NVRAM

   D. The configuration held in RAM

7. What information is provided by issuing the `show running-config` command?

   A. The current configuration

   B. The configuration held in FLASH

   C. The configuration held in NVRAM

   D. The configuration held in RAM

8. What important information is provided by the `show buffers` command? (Choose all that apply.)

   A. Hits

   B. Misses

   C. Trims

   D. Created

   E. Failures

   F. Overruns

   G. Underruns

   H. Memory-allocation errors

9. Which Cisco IOS `show` command provides comprehensive information that is sent to the Cisco TAC?

   A. `show all`

   B. `show processes`

   C. `show tech-support`

   D. `show stacks`

10. What is the default Ethernet IP encapsulation on a Cisco router?

   A. SNAP

   B. ARPA

   C. Ethernet II

   D. Novell-Ether

11. What does `show interface <interface-type> <interface-number>` do? (Choose all that apply.)

   A. Interface description

   B. Interface status

   C. Statistical information

   D. Error statistics

   E. Layer 4 encapsulation type

   F. All of the above

12. What information is provided by the show arp command? (Choose all that apply.)

   A. Layer 3 address

   B. Layer 2 address

   C. Encapsulation

   D. Interface MAC address

   E. TTL timer

13. What information is provided by issuing the show processes cpu command? (Choose all that apply.)

   A. Memory utilization

   B. Processes

   C. CPU utilization percentages

   D. PID

   E. Free memory

14. What information is provided by issuing the show processes memory command? (Choose all that apply.)

   A. Free memory

   B. Used memory

   C. Total memory

   D. PID

   E. Memory allocated to the router's individual processes

15. What configuration changes should be added to a router to provide accurate debug information? (Choose all that apply.)

   A. Debug all

   B. Service timestamps debug datetime msec localtime

   C. Service timestamps log datetime msec localtime

   D. Service udp-small-servers

   E. Service tcp-small-servers

16. What command do you issue to view messages being sent to the console?

    A. `monitor terminal`

    B. `terminal monitor`

    C. `show console`

    D. `echo terminal`

17. What is the easiest way to turn off debugging?

    A. `no debug all`

    B. `no debug`

    C. `un all`

    D. `undebug all`

    E. All of the above

18. How are the **debug** commands categorized? (Choose all that apply.)

    A. Global

    B. Interface

    C. Protocol

    D. Process

19. What is the purpose of the `ping` command?

    A. Step-by-step connectivity

    B. Reachability and connectivity

    C. Test the ICMP protocol

    D. Test routing protocols

20. What is the purpose of the `traceroute` command?

    A. Step-by-step path connectivity

    B. Reachability and connectivity

    C. Test the ICMP protocol

    D. Test routing protocols

Answers to Review Questions

1. A, C, E, F, G, H. Path switching is a general term for the manner in which packets get from the incoming interface to the outgoing interface. Cut-over routing is not a valid term.

2. C, D, E. Input and output are general terms as well; all hardware, interface, and system buffers have input and output queues for directional buffering.

3. A, C, E, F. Queue and controller commands are specific commands for interfaces and global commands.

4. A, B, C, D. All of these messages are displayed by the command.

5. A, C, D. The command will not provide you with information regarding the reason for the last upgrade nor the version of configuration that resides on the router.

6. C. The start-up configuration is held in the NVRAM memory.

7. A. The running configuration is the configuration currently being run by the router.

8. A, B, C, D, E. Overruns and underruns deal with errors on interfaces. Memory allocation errors are seen using the show memory command.

9. C. show tech-support is the command that contains the information requested by TAC.

10. B. ARPA is the default encapsulation used by Cisco. The other three are valid encapsulation types, but are not turned on by default.

11. A, B, C, D. Layer 4 encapsulation is not included in the output of the above command.

12. A, B, C, D. The TTL timer is not shown in the show arp command.

13. B, C, D. Memory information is not displayed via this command.

14. A, B, C, D, E. All of the above information is provided by the specified command.

15. B, C. Timestamps are important to debugging so correlations can be made when events occur. `Debug all` is a command that implements debugging—it has nothing to do with how accurate the information is. D and E are commands that enable certain UDP and TCP services to the router. They have nothing to do with debug.

16. B. `Terminal monitor` is the correct command. `Term mon` can be used as a shorthand version of B.

17. C, D. `Un all` is a shortcut to turn off `debug`. The full command is `undebug all`.

18. A, B, C. All debugs are performed on processes. The processes must be categorized.

19. B. The ping packets are used to test for connectivity to a remote IP address.

20. A. Traceroute is used to map the hop path connectivity

Applying Cisco's Diagnostic Tools

TOPICS COVERED IN THIS CHAPTER INCLUDE:

✓ Using the troubleshooting tools you have learned thus far to diagnose and resolve network problems.

✓ Using the troubleshooting tools in a manner that will minimize their impact on the router's processor and data transfer.

✓ Using a protocol analyzer to collect information and then using that information to diagnose network problems.

In the previous chapters, you learned a great deal about Layer 2 and Layer 3 technologies and protocols. Additionally, you learned very useful information regarding router architecture and very detailed low-level information for understanding routing technology. With this knowledge, you will be able to better interpret the information provided by the troubleshooting tools and commands.

The time has come to implement all that you have learned, including applying the methodology from Chapter 1. Once you have the technical knowledge base, you must apply it by using a troubleshooting template if you are to efficiently and successfully troubleshoot network problems.

This chapter's format will be different from what you have seen up to now. Three different types of network problems will be outlined in detail, and each type will have two scenarios. The intent is for you to take the provided information and do the troubleshooting. You will see a great deal of router output and packet decodes from a protocol analyzer. The information is there for your reference and at times may not have a great deal of explanation. You must look at the output carefully in order to enable yourself to determine what is happening on the router or network.

For each scenario, you follow the steps outlined in Chapter 1 by listing observations, gathering facts, and proposing solutions. Because the book cannot be interactive, the scenarios are intended to accustom you to using the methodology, but you will not go so far as to actually verify that the proposed solution solved the network problem. Let's begin.

Identifying and Resolving Generic Router Problems

This section deals with Cisco routers and some simple generic problems that can be remedied easily, once they are identified. Each scenario will be accompanied by outputs from relevant diagnostic tools. The focus will be placed on the router itself because many other scenarios involve additional network equipment.

Scenario #1

You are installing a Cisco 2600 series router that was sent to you after headquarters entered the preliminary configuration. You are connected to the console port. You power on the router, and this is what you see as the router boots:

List Observations

```
System Bootstrap, Version 11.3(2)XA3, PLATFORM SPECIFIC
RELEASE SOFTWARE (fc1)
Copyright (c) 1998 by cisco Systems, Inc.
TAC:Home:SW:IOS:Specials for info
C2600 platform with 24576 Kbytes of main memory
program load complete, entry point: 0x80008000, size:
0x37b090
Self decompressing the image :
#######################################################
#######################################################
#######################################################
#######################################################
#######################################################
############################ [OK]
Restricted Rights Legend
Use, duplication, or disclosure by the Government is
subject to restrictions as set forth in subparagraph
(c) of the Commercial Computer Software - Restricted
Rights clause at FAR sec. 52.227-19 and subparagraph
(c) (1) (ii) of the Rights in Technical Data and Computer
Software clause at DFARS sec. 252.227-7013.

        cisco Systems, Inc.
        170 West Tasman Drive
        San Jose, California 95134-1706
```

```
Cisco Internetwork Operating System Software
IOS (tm) C2600 Software (C2600-D-M), Version 11.3(4)T1,
RELEASE SOFTWARE (fc1)
Copyright (c) 1986-1998 by cisco Systems, Inc.
Compiled Wed 01-Jul-98 11:42 by phanguye
Image text-base: 0x80008084, data-base: 0x8066A278

Cisco 2611 (MPC860) processor (revision 0x202) with
18432K/6144K bytes of memory
    .
Processor board ID JAB023601NE (1537311773)
M860 processor: part number 0, mask 32
Bridging software.
X.25 software, Version 3.0.0.
2 Ethernet/IEEE 802.3 interface(s)
1 Serial network interface(s)
32K bytes of non-volatile configuration memory.
8192K bytes of processor board System flash (Read/Write)




Press RETURN to get started!


%LINK-3-UPDOWN: Interface Ethernet0/0, changed state to up
%LINK-3-UPDOWN: Interface Ethernet0/1, changed state to up
%LINK-3-UPDOWN: Interface Serial0/0, changed state to down
Cisco Internetwork Operating System Software
IOS (tm) C2600 Software (C2600-D-M), Version 11.3(4)T1,
RELEASE SOFTWARE (fc1)
Copyright (c) 1986-1998 by cisco Systems, Inc.
Compiled Wed 01-Jul-98 11:42 by phanguye
%LINEPROTO-5-UPDOWN: Line protocol on Interface Ethernet0/
0, changed state to down
%LINEPROTO-5-UPDOWN: Line protocol on Interface Serial0/0,
changed state to down
```

Well, it looks like two interfaces on the router are down. So much for the preconfigured router. You change to the privileged level by entering the enable password. Here is where you need to start listing observations. The first one is that two of the interfaces on the router are down.

Before you look at the configuration or show commands, you check the cabling. Assuming that the cabling checks out, you should check the lights in the back of the router. Figure 5.1 shows the back of a 2611 router. The router comes with two Ethernet ports, a console port, an aux port, and a serial port. Each of the network interface ports (both Ethernet ports and the serial port) has a light next to it that indicates whether there is a physical connection. If any of these lights is not lit, there is a connectivity problem. In this example, assume that all three lights are lit.

FIGURE 5.1   Rear view of a Cisco 2611

Now that you observed the connectivity, you need to gather more information about the router's configuration. Go back to the console. You know that the problem deals with two interfaces: Ethernet 0/0 and Serial 0/0. For this example, don't use show running-config or show startup-config. Instead, use the interface-specific show commands.

The first command issued is show interface ethernet 0/0. Here are the results:

```
Router_A#show interface ethernet 0/0
Ethernet0/0 is up, line protocol is down
  Hardware is AmdP2, address is 0010.7bd9.2880      (bia
  0010.7bd9.2880)
  MTU 1500 bytes, BW 10000 Kbit, DLY 1000 usec,      rely
  128/255, load 1/255
  Encapsulation ARPA, loopback not set, keepalive set
  (10 sec)
  ARP type: ARPA, ARP Timeout 04:00:00
  Last input never, output 00:00:05, output hang never
  Last clearing of "show interface" counters never
```

```
Queueing strategy: fifo
Output queue 0/40, 0 drops; input queue 0/75, 0 drops
5 minute input rate 0 bits/sec, 0 packets/sec
5 minute output rate 0 bits/sec, 0 packets/sec
   0 packets input, 0 bytes, 0 no buffer
   Received 0 broadcasts, 0 runts, 0 giants, 0 throttles
   0 input errors, 0 CRC, 0 frame, 0 overrun, 0 ignored,
   0 abort
   0 input packets with dribble condition detected
   250 packets output, 15309 bytes, 0 underruns
   250 output errors, 0 collisions, 1 interface resets
   0 babbles, 0 late collision, 0 deferred
   250 lost carrier, 0 no carrier
   0 output buffer failures, 0 output buffers swapped
   out
Router_A#
```

The following outputs are from the show interface Ethernet 0/1 and show interface Serial 0/0 commands, respectively:

```
Ethernet0/1 is up, line protocol is up
  Hardware is AmdP2, address is 0010.7bd9.2881      (bia
  0010.7bd9.2881)
  Internet address is 172.16.20.5/24
  MTU 1500 bytes, BW 10000 Kbit, DLY 1000 usec,      rely
  128/255, load 1/255
  Encapsulation ARPA, loopback not set, keepalive set (10
  sec)
  ARP type: ARPA, ARP Timeout 04:00:00
  Last input never, output 00:00:02, output hang never
  Last clearing of "show interface" counters never
  Queueing strategy: fifo
  Output queue 0/40, 0 drops; input queue 0/75, 0 drops
  5 minute input rate 983450 bits/sec, 875 packets/sec
  5 minute output rate 435097 bits/sec, 357 packets/sec
     0 packets input, 0 bytes, 0 no buffer
     Received 0 broadcasts, 0 runts, 0 giants, 0 throttles
```

```
                      0 input errors, 0 CRC, 0 frame, 0 overrun, 0 ignored,
                      0 abort
                      0 input packets with dribble condition detected
                      274 packets output, 17062 bytes, 0 underruns
                      0 output errors, 0 collisions, 11 interface resets
                      0 babbles, 0 late collision, 0 deferred
                      0 lost carrier, 0 no carrier
                      0 output buffer failures, 0 output buffers swapped
                   out
Router_A#
Serial0/0 is administratively down, line protocol is down
   Hardware is PowerQUICC Serial
   Internet address is 172.16.20.5/30
   MTU 1500 bytes, BW 1544 Kbit, DLY 20000 usec,          rely
   255/255, load 1/255
   Encapsulation HDLC, loopback not set, keepalive set (10
   sec)
   Last input never, output never, output hang never
   Last clearing of "show interface" counters never
   Queueing strategy: fifo
   Output queue 0/40, 0 drops; input queue 0/75, 0 drops
   5 minute input rate 0 bits/sec, 0 packets/sec
   5 minute output rate 0 bits/sec, 0 packets/sec
                      0 packets input, 0 bytes, 0 no buffer
                      Received 0 broadcasts, 0 runts, 0 giants, 0 throttles
                      0 input errors, 0 CRC, 0 frame, 0 overrun, 0 ignored,
                      0 abort
                      0 packets output, 0 bytes, 0 underruns
                      0 output errors, 0 collisions, 8 interface resets
                      0 output buffer failures, 0 output buffers swapped
                   out
                      0 carrier transitions
                      DCD=down  DSR=down  DTR=down  RTS=down  CTS=down
Router_A#
```

What are your observations? Check your list with the following:

- No IP address is configured on Ethernet 0/0.

- Output packets generated on Ethernet 0/0 with the same number of output errors.

- The same number of lost carrier errors as the number of output errors.

- Serial 0/0 is administratively shut down.

- Ethernet 0/1 is up and up.

This list can contain more information regarding the interfaces, such as encapsulation types and so on. For clarity and simplicity, only the observations that are relevant to this scenario are listed.

After observations and fact-gathering are completed, it is time to formulate a problem description. Initially, from what you saw while the router booted, the problem description was vague. It could have been written something like this: "Interfaces Ethernet 0/0 and Serial 0/0 are down."

This is a good start, but it lacks detail. If this were a complicated problem, you could be troubleshooting for a long time because the description lacks focus.

Based on listed observations, you know exactly what the problem description is. Here is a sample of a focused and detailed problem statement or description: "Ethernet 0/0 is down because it doesn't have a carrier, and Serial 0/0 is down because it was administratively shut down."

With this problem statement, it should be obvious what needs to be done to fix the problems.

Propose Solutions

How did you do? Now that you observed these problems, what are the solutions? This relates to the "creating an action plan" part of the troubleshooting method. The more specific the problem statement, the more easily the solutions can be defined.

In the first scenario, there appear to be a few problems that need resolution. They are all simple solutions in this case:

- Check the cable and transceiver for the Ethernet port for a possible physical problem with the interface.

- Configure an IP address on Ethernet 0/0

- Turn up interface Serial 0/0.

With the proposed solutions, the only thing left is to implement them and see if they work, as follows:

```
Router_A#conf t
Enter configuration commands, one per line. End with CNTL/
Z.
Router_A(config)#interface ethernet 0/0
Router_A(config-if)#ip address 172.16.10.1 255.255.255.0
Router_A(config-if)#interface serial 0/0
Router_A(config-if)#no shut
172.16.20.5 overlaps with Ethernet0/1
Serial0/0: incorrect IP address assignment
Router_A(config-if)#^Z
Router_A#
```

It looks as if the Ethernet 0/0 interface is still not functional. We still need to check the cable and transceiver to try to isolate a physical problem. You test the cable and it is working properly so you swap the transceiver. Now let's check the interface status:

```
Ethernet0/0 is up, line protocol is up
Hardware is AmdP2, address is 0010.7bd9.2880      (bia
0010.7bd9.2880)
  MTU 1500 bytes, BW 10000 Kbit, DLY 1000 usec,     rely
128/255, load 1/255
  Encapsulation ARPA, loopback not set, keepalive set
(10 sec)
  ARP type: ARPA, ARP Timeout 04:00:00
  Last input never, output 00:00:05, output hang never
  Last clearing of "show interface" counters never
  Queueing strategy: fifo
  Output queue 0/40, 0 drops; input queue 0/75, 0 drops
  5 minute input rate 509000 bits/sec, 215 packets/sec
  5 minute output rate 1167000 bits/sec, 315 packets/sec
    12900 packets input, 10324500 bytes, 0 no buffer
    Received 235 broadcasts, 0 runts, 0 giants, 0
    throttles
```

```
0 input errors, 0 CRC, 0 frame, 0 overrun, 0 ignored,
0 abort
0 input packets with dribble condition detected
18903 packets output, 15198309 bytes, 0 underruns
283 output errors, 0 collisions, 2 interface resets
0 babbles, 0 late collision, 0 deferred
283 lost carrier, 0 no carrier
0 output buffer failures, 0 output buffers swapped
out
```

What happened to Serial 0/0? The console message stated that there was an address overlap with interface Ethernet 0/1, which means a duplicate IP address. The IP address on Ethernet 0/1 overlaps with the IP address on Serial 0/0. Let's look at the interface settings once more.

```
Router_A#show interface serial 0/0
Serial0/0 is administratively down, line protocol is down
  Hardware is PowerQUICC Serial
  Internet address is 172.16.20.5/30
  MTU 1500 bytes, BW 1544 Kbit, DLY 20000 usec, rely 255/
  255,      load 1/255
  Encapsulation HDLC, loopback not set, keepalive set (10
  sec)
  Last input never, output never, output hang never
  Last clearing of "show interface" counters never
  Queueing strategy: fifo
  Output queue 0/40, 0 drops; input queue 0/75, 0 drops
  5 minute input rate 0 bits/sec, 0 packets/sec
  5 minute output rate 0 bits/sec, 0 packets/sec
     0 packets input, 0 bytes, 0 no buffer
     Received 0 broadcasts, 0 runts, 0 giants, 0 throttles
     0 input errors, 0 CRC, 0 frame, 0 overrun, 0 ignored,
     0 abort
     0 packets output, 0 bytes, 0 underruns
     0 output errors, 0 collisions, 8 interface resets
     0 output buffer failures, 0 output buffers swapped
out
     0 carrier transitions
```

```
     DCD=down   DSR=down   DTR=down   RTS=down   CTS=down
Router_A#
```

This output indicates that the interface is still administratively down. You saw the `no shut` command issued in the previous screen capture, so why is it still in shutdown? Here is the answer. If an interface has a configuration conflict with another interface, it will not initialize. Because the serial interface was configured with a duplicate IP address, it wouldn't initialize. It remains in its previous state, shutdown. In order to activate the serial link we must do some more analysis.

Referring to the `show interface` results for Ethernet 0/1, you see that it does have the same address as Serial 0/0. This problem can easily be resolved, as long as you know which interface should have the `172.16.20.5` address. In this scenario, we will assume that Ethernet 0/1 has the incorrect IP address.

In essence, you have made additional observations.

- Serial 0/0 is configured with IP address `172.16.20.5/30`.

- Ethernet 0/1 is configured with IP address `172.16.20.5/24`.

- Cannot change administrative state for Serial 0/0 because of the IP address overlap with Ethernet 0/1.

Now, with these additional observations, new solutions must be proposed. Once the decision is made as to which IP address should be assigned to each interface, the problem should be resolved. The action plan is as follows:

- Leave IP address `172.16.20.5/30` to interface Serial 0/0.

- Assign IP address `172.16.30.1/24` to interface Ethernet 0/1.

- Remove the administrative shutdown from interface Serial 0/0.

Here is the configuration. Following the configuration, you see the `show interface` output for each interface. This is done to verify that all the changes that were made to the router fixed the problems that were observed.

```
Router_A#conf t
Enter configuration commands, one per line. End with CNTL/
Z.
Router_A(config-if)#interface ethernet 0/1
```

```
Router_A(config-if)#ip address 172.16.30.1 255.255.255.0
Router_A(config)#interface serial 0/0
Router_A(config-if)#no shutdown
Router_A(config-if)#^Z
Router_A#
Router_A#show interface ethernet 0/0
Ethernet0/0 is up, line protocol is up
  Hardware is AmdP2, address is 0010.7bd9.2880    (bia
  0010.7bd9.2880)
  Internet address is 172.16.10.1/24
  MTU 1500 bytes, BW 10000 Kbit, DLY 1000 usec, rely 255/
  255,    load 29/255
  Encapsulation ARPA, loopback not set, keepalive set (10
  sec)
  ARP type: ARPA, ARP Timeout 04:00:00
  Last input 00:00:00, output 00:00:00, output hang never
  Last clearing of "show interface" counters never
  Queueing strategy: fifo
  Output queue 0/40, 0 drops; input queue 1/75, 0    drops
  5 minute input rate 509000 bits/sec, 215 packets/sec
  5 minute output rate 1167000 bits/sec, 315 packets/sec
     25800 packets input, 20685400 bytes, 0 no buffer
     Received 3235 broadcasts, 0 runts, 0 giants
     6 input errors, 1 CRC, 5 frame, 0 overrun, 640
     ignored,        0 abort
     0 input packets with dribble condition detected
     37800 packets output, 30249800 bytes, 0 underruns
     283 output errors, 4 collisions, 2 interface
     resets
     0 babbles, 0 late collision, 0 deferred
     283 lost carrier, 0 no carrier
     0 output buffers copied, 0 interrupts, 0 failures
Router_A#show interface serial 0/0
Serial0/0 is up, line protocol is up
  Hardware is PowerQUICC Serial
  Internet address is 172.16.20.5/30
```

MTU 1500 bytes, BW 1544 Kbit, DLY 20000 usec, rely 255/255,   load 1/255

Encapsulation HDLC, loopback not set, keepalive set (10 sec)

Last input never, output never, output hang never

Last clearing of "show interface" counters never

Queueing strategy: fifo

Output queue 0/40, 0 drops; input queue 0/75, 0 drops

5 minute input rate 121000 bits/sec, 32 packets/sec

5 minute output rate 27000 bits/sec, 11 packets/sec

   960 packets input, 795680 bytes, 0 no buffer

   Received 0 broadcasts, 0 runts, 0 giants, 0 throttles

   0 input errors, 0 CRC, 0 frame, 0 overrun, 0 ignored, 0 abort

   330 packets output, 265640 bytes, 0 underruns

   0 output errors, 0 collisions, 22 interface resets

   0 output buffer failures, 0 output buffers swapped out

   0 carrier transitions

   DCD=up DSR=up DTR=down RTS=down CTS=up

Router_A#**show interface ethernet 0/1**

Ethernet0/1 is up, line protocol is up

  Hardware is AmdP2, address is 0010.7bd9.2881   (bia 0010.7bd9.2881)

  Internet address is 172.16.30.1/24

  MTU 1500 bytes, BW 10000 Kbit, DLY 1000 usec, rely 128/255,   load 1/255

  Encapsulation ARPA, loopback not set, keepalive set (10 sec)

  ARP type: ARPA, ARP Timeout 04:00:00

  Last input never, output 00:00:07, output hang never

  Last clearing of "show interface" counters never

  Queueing strategy: fifo

  Output queue 0/40, 0 drops; input queue 0/75, 0 drops

5 minute input rate 488000 bits/sec, 164 packets/sec

5 minute output rate 1473000 bits/sec, 297 packets/sec

   9840 packets input, 7815720 bytes, 0 no buffer

```
       Received 0 broadcasts, 0 runts, 0 giants, 0 throttles
       0 input errors, 0 CRC, 0 frame, 0 overrun, 0 ignored,
       0 abort
       0 input packets with dribble condition detected
       17820 packets output, 14352560 bytes, 0 underruns
       0 output errors, 0 collisions, 0 interface resets
       0 babbles, 0 late collision, 0 deferred
       0 lost carrier, 0 no carrier
       0 output buffer failures, 0 output buffers swapped
       out
Router_A#
```

From what you can see from the interface outputs, all interfaces are working properly. The changes made were effective, and they did not cause other network problems.

The final step is to document what was done:

- Added 172.16.10.1/24 to Ethernet 0/0.

- Left 172.16.20.5/30 on Serial 0/0.

- Changed administrative status for interface Serial 0/0 with the no shutdown command.

- Changed the IP address for interface Ethernet 0/1 from 172.16.20.5/30 to 172.16.30.1/24.

All of the necessary steps were taken to solve the observed problems. The first step was to record observations. Once the observations were made, a problem statement was written. Based on the problem statement, an action plan was devised to resolve the problems. After the first changes were made, interface Ethernet 0/0 came up. You saw that the router would not allow Serial 0/0 to be removed from administrative shutdown due to a duplicate IP address. The address conflicted with an IP address assigned to Ethernet 0/1. A new address was assigned to Ethernet 0/1, and Serial 0/0 was changed to an active state.

Scenario #2

This next scenario is a little more difficult. Look at Figure 5.2 to get a picture of the network that you will troubleshoot. Host Z is trying to FTP a file to Host A, but Host Z is unable to do so.

FIGURE 5.2 Network diagram for scenario #2

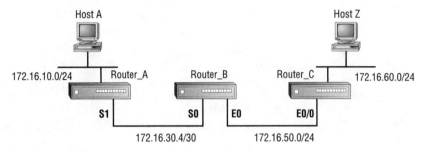

Let's move through the troubleshooting method to solve this problem. Start by listing your observations.

List Observations

As discussed in Chapter 1, you should define the boundary of dysfunctionality, which can be done in several ways. In this scenario, you test by attempting to FTP to Host A while observing the results.

The first test is an actual FTP attempt. Figure 5.3 shows the results of the FTP attempt. The software gives you a host unreachable error message, which is an ICMP response. EtherPeek was used to capture packets in this exchange. The first packet decode is Host Z sending an FTP connection request.

FIGURE 5.3 FTP attempt failure

```
connecting to 172.16.10.2:21
! Connection failed 172.16.10.2 - host unreachable
! Connection failed 172.16.10.2
```

```
        Flags:          0x00
        Status:         0x00
        Packet Length:66
        Timestamp:      22:11:39.486000 04/18/1999
    Ethernet Header
      Destination:   00:10:7b:d9:28:81   [0-5]
      Source:        00:a0:24:a5:06:57   [6-11]
      Protocol Type:08-00   IP   [12-13]
    IP Header - Internet Protocol Datagram
      Version:              4   [14 Mask 0xf0]
      Header Length:        5   [14 Mask 0xf]
      Precedence:           0   [15 Mask 0xe0]
      Type of Service:     %000   [15 Mask 0x1c]
      Unused:              %00   [15 Mask 0x3]
      Total Length:        48   [16-17]
      Identifier:          17152   [18-19]
      Fragmentation Flags:  %010  Do Not Fragment       [20
    Mask 0xe0]
      Fragment Offset:      0   [20-22 Mask 0x1fffff]
      Time To Live:        128
      IP Type:             0x06  TCP  [23]
      Header Checksum:     0x1923   [24-25]
      Source IP Address:   172.16.60.130   [26-29]
      Dest. IP Address:    172.16.10.2   [30-33]
      No Internet Datagram Options
    TCP - Transport Control Protocol
      Source Port:     1038   [34-35]
      Destination Port: 21  FTP Control - File Transfer
      Protocol  [36-37]
      Sequence Number:  6198340   [38-41]
      Ack Number:       0   [42-45]
      Offset:           7   [46 Mask 0xf0]
      Reserved:        %000000   [46 Mask 0xfc0]
      Code:            %000010   [47 Mask 0x3f]
                 Synch Sequence
      Window:           8192   [48-49]
```

Checksum: 0x2bb5 [50-51]
Urgent Pointer: 0 [52-53]
TCP Options: [54]
   Option Type: 2 *Maximum Segment Size* [55]
      Length: 4
        MSS: 1460 [56-58]
   Option Type: 1 *No Operation* [59]
   Option Type: 1 *No Operation* [60]
   Option Type: 4 [61]
      Length: 2
   No More FTP Command or Reply Data
Frame Check Sequence: 0x00000000

Everything looks fine with this packet. Now, look at the ICMP message received. Notice that the source IP address in the ICMP packet is from 172.16.60.1. That is the gateway address for Host Z.

Flags: 0x00
   Status: 0x00
   Packet Length:74
   Timestamp: 22:11:39.489000 04/18/1999
Ethernet Header
   Destination: 00:a0:24:a5:06:57 [0-5]
   Source: 00:10:7b:d9:28:81 [6-11]
   Protocol Type:08-00 IP [12-13]
IP Header - Internet Protocol Datagram
   Version: 4 [14 Mask 0xf0]
   Header Length: 5 [14 Mask 0xf]
   Precedence: 0 [15 Mask 0xe0]
   Type of Service: %000 [15 Mask 0x1c]
   Unused: %00 [15 Mask 0x3]
   Total Length: 56 [16-17]
   Identifier: 2815 [18-19]
   Fragmentation Flags: %000 [20 Mask 0xe0]
   Fragment Offset: 0 [20-22 Mask 0x1fffff]
   Time To Live: 255
   IP Type: 0x01 *ICMP* [23]

Header Checksum: 0xe021 [24-25]
Source IP Address: 172.16.60.1 [26-29]
Dest. IP Address: 172.16.60.130 [30-33]
No Internet Datagram Options
ICMP - Internet Control Messages Protocol [34]
  ICMP Type: 3 *Destination Unreachable* [35]
  Code: 1 *Host Unreachable*
  Checksum: 0x6439 [36-37]
  Unused (must be zero):0x00000000 [38-41]

Header of packet that caused error follows.
IP Header - Internet Protocol Datagram
  Version: 4 [42 Mask 0xf0]
  Header Length: 5 [42 Mask 0xf]
  Precedence: 0 [43 Mask 0xe0]
  Type of Service: %000 [43 Mask 0x1c]
  Unused: %00 [43 Mask 0x3]
  Total Length: 48 [44-45]
  Identifier: 17152 [46-47]
  Fragmentation Flags: %010 *Do Not Fragment*   [48 Mask 0xe0]
  Fragment Offset: 0 [48-50 Mask 0x1fffff]
  Time To Live: 127
  IP Type: 0x06 *TCP* [51]
  Header Checksum: 0x1a23 [52-53]
  Source IP Address: 172.16.60.130 [54-57]
  Dest. IP Address: 172.16.10.2 [58-61]
  No Internet Datagram Options
TCP - Transport Control Protocol
  Source Port: 1038 [62-63]
  Destination Port: 21 *FTP Control - File Transfer Protocol*   [64-65]
  Sequence Number: 6198340 [66-69]
  Ack Number: 0

The key information is provided under the ICMP header section. Notice the ICMP type of 3, which is equivalent to an unreachable destination—the code specifies that the host is not reachable. The ping command may be issued, but it will render the same information—host unreachable.

What other tool might be used to aid in defining the border of dysfunctionality? There are a couple of different directions that may be taken. One method is to try to FTP a file to hosts that do not reside on the 172.16.10.0/24 network. Another consists of running a traceroute to see where the path to Host A is failing.

Let's try the latter. Following are the results of a traceroute to Host A:

```
C:\WINDOWS>tracert 172.16.10.2
Tracing route to 172.16.10.2 over a maximum of 30 hops
1     5 ms      2 ms      4 ms   172.16.60.1
  2   172.16.60.1   reports: Destination host unreachable.
Trace complete.
```

These results indicate that Router C does not have a route to Host A. This allows you to draw the line of dysfunctionality to the boundary between Router C and Router B.

To further troubleshoot this problem, diagnostics must be executed from Router C. Let's bring up a console on Router C. The first command that should be issued is a show ip route. The results are as follows:

```
Router_C#show ip route
Codes: C - connected, S - static, I - IGRP, R - RIP, M -
mobile, B - BGP D - EIGRP, EX - EIGRP external, O - OSPF,
IA - OSPF inter area N1 - OSPF NSSA external type 1, N2 -
OSPF NSSA external type 2 E1 - OSPF external type 1, E2 -
OSPF external type 2, E - EGPi - IS-IS, L1 - IS-IS level-
1, L2 - IS-IS level-2, * - candidate default U - per-user
static route, o - ODR
Gateway of last resort is not set
172.16.0.0/24 is subnetted, 2 subnets
C       172.16.60.0 is directly connected, Ethernet0/1
C       172.16.50.0 is directly connected, Ethernet0/0
Router_C#
```

Router C knows only routes for networks that are directly connected. This points to problems with routing updates or routing protocols between Routers B and C. Let's take a look at the configuration on both routers:

```
Router_C#show running-config
Building configuration...
Current configuration:
!
version 11.3
no service password-encryption
!
hostname Router_C
!
enable password aloha
!
interface Ethernet0/0
 ip address 172.16.50.2 255.255.255.0
!
interface Serial0/0
 no ip address
 shutdown
!
interface Ethernet0/1
 ip address 172.16.60.1 255.255.255.0
!
router eigrp 100
 network 172.16.0.0
 no auto-summary
!
ip classless
!
line con 0
line aux 0
line vty 0 4
 password aloha
 login
```

```
!
end
Router_C#
```

The show interface results should be reviewed before the configuration of Router B is displayed. The only interface that is of concern is the one that connects the two routers—interface Ethernet 0/0. The results are shown as follows. As depicted, interface Ethernet 0/0 is up and functioning. This is proved by using the ping command.

```
Router_C>show interface ethernet0/0
Ethernet0/0 is up, line protocol is up
  Hardware is AmdP2, address is 0010.7bd9.2880 (bia
  0010.7bd9.2880)
  Internet address is 172.16.50.2/24
  MTU 1500 bytes, BW 10000 Kbit, DLY 1000 usec, rely 255/
  255,    load 1/255
  Encapsulation ARPA, loopback not set, keepalive set (10
  sec)
  ARP type: ARPA, ARP Timeout 04:00:00
  Last input 02:54:40, output 00:00:00, output hang never
  Last clearing of "show interface" counters never
  Queueing strategy: fifo
  Output queue 0/40, 0 drops; input queue 0/75, 0 drops
  5 minute input rate 0 bits/sec, 0 packets/sec
  5 minute output rate 0 bits/sec, 0 packets/sec
      1006 packets input, 90611 bytes, 0 no buffer
      Received 990 broadcasts, 0 runts, 0 giants, 0
      throttles
      0 input errors, 0 CRC, 0 frame, 0 overrun, 0 ignored,
      0 abort
      0 input packets with dribble condition detected
      4935 packets output, 402703 bytes, 0 underruns
      0 output errors, 0 collisions, 2 interface resets
      0 babbles, 0 late collision, 0 deferred
      0 lost carrier, 0 no carrier
      0 output buffer failures, 0 output buffers swapped
      out
```

```
Router_C>ping 172.16.50.1
Type escape sequence to abort.
Sending 5, 100-byte ICMP Echos to 172.16.50.1, timeout is
2  seconds:
.!!!!
Success rate is 80 percent (4/5), round-trip min/avg/max =
1/3/4 ms
Router_C>ping 172.16.50.1
Type escape sequence to abort.
Sending 5, 100-byte ICMP Echos to 172.16.50.1, timeout is
2   seconds:
!!!!!
Success rate is 100 percent (5/5), round-trip min/avg/max
=   4/4/4 ms
Router_C>
```

This output means that the routers are not sharing routing information. Something is causing the routing protocol to fail, but it is not because the interface is down. Before moving on, let's review our observations and make sure that the correct path is being followed.

- Host Z cannot FTP to Host A.

- Host Z cannot ping to Host A.

- Host Z cannot traceroute to Host A.

- ICMP "destination unreachable" responses were returned from the FTP request.

- Router C does not have a route to the destination network.

- Ethernet 0/0 is up and functioning.

- There is capability to ping Router B.

Before a problem definition statement can be devised, more information must be gathered from Router B. Let's Telnet to Router B. Something looks wrong:

```
Router_C>172.16.50.1
Trying 172.16.50.1 ... Open
User Access Verification
Password:
Router_B(boot)>
```

Instead of coming up with the normal prompt, the router is in boot mode, which explains why no routing is taking place. When a router is in boot mode, routing protocols do not work. This is the last key observation needed, and it allows you to define the problem.

Here is the problem statement: Router B is in boot mode, it does not route in this state, so Host Z cannot FTP to Host A. This statement lists the actual problem, as well as the reported problem.

Propose Solutions

With the observations made, and a detailed and focused problem statement, you can now move on to provide possible solutions to the problem. It is still important to consider the observations when determining the next action.

You know that the router is in boot mode, but what causes a router to be in boot mode? There are two simple reasons that a router may be in boot mode: lack of IOS on the system flash or the router is not looking for the IOS in the right location.

Let's look at the contents of Router B's flash. Then, look at the router's version information.

```
Router_B(boot)#show flash
System flash directory:
File  Length   Name/status
  1   4287696  c2500-i-1.112-15.bin
[4287760 bytes used, 4100848 available, 8388608 total]
8192K bytes of processor board System flash (Read/Write)
Router_B(boot)#
```

This shows one IOS image on the system flash. Now, you need to determine which version of IOS is running on the router:

```
Router_B(boot)#show version
Cisco Internetwork Operating System Software
IOS (tm) 3000 Bootstrap Software (IGS-BOOT-R), Version
11.0(10c)XB1, PLATFORM SPECIFIC RELEASE SOFTWARE (fc1)
Copyright (c) 1986-1996 by cisco Systems, Inc.
Compiled Wed 10-Sep-97 13:06 by phester
Image text-base: 0x01010000, data-base: 0x00001000
ROM: System Bootstrap, Version 11.0(10c)XB1, PLATFORM
SPECIFIC RELEASE SOFTWARE
```

```
(fc1)
Router_B uptime is 3 hours, 11 minutes
System restarted by reload
Running default software
cisco 2500 (68030) processor (revision A) with 4096K/2048K
bytes of memory.
Processor board ID 01229726, with hardware revision
00000000
X.25 software, Version 2.0, NET2, BFE and GOSIP compliant.
Cisco-ET Extended Temperature platform.
1 Ethernet/IEEE 802.3 interface.
2 Serial network interfaces.
32K bytes of non-volatile configuration memory.
8192K bytes of processor board System flash (Read/Write)
Configuration register is 0x2101
Router_B(boot)#
```

The response is that it is running a bootstrap version of IOS, which displays in the first few fields. From these two outputs, it can be deduced that the IOS contained in flash memory was not used to boot the router.

As previously mentioned, the IOS image could be corrupt, or the router is looking for the IOS in the wrong place. The router uses a configuration register to point to the location of the IOS image that it should load during the boot process.

For a full description of config-register settings, refer to CCO. To briefly explain, the config-register is a 16-bit number that controls the router's boot sequence. The lowest four bits indicate from where the system image, or IOS, will be loaded. If the value is 0000, then the router enters into ROM monitor mode. If the register is set to 0001, then the IOS will be loaded from the boot ROM.

In this case, the configuration register was set to the hex value of 0x2101, which tells the router to look for the system image on the boot ROM. Remember that it is only the first four bits that indicate the system image location.

The action plan for this scenario is to change the configuration register on Router B to load the image from system flash. The configuration changes follow. After the router reloads, a quick check can be made by issuing a show version command.

Router_B(boot)#**conf t**

Enter configuration commands, one per line. End with CNTL/ Z.

Router_B(boot)(config)#**config**

Router_B(boot)(config)#**config-register 0x2102**

Router_B(boot)(config)#**^Z**

Router_B(boot)#

Router_B(boot)#**reload**

Proceed with reload? [confirm]

 [Connection to 172.16.50.1 closed by foreign host]

Router_C>172.16.50.1

Trying 172.16.50.1 ... Open

User Access Verification

Password:

Router_B>en

Password:

Router_B#**show version**

Cisco Internetwork Operating System Software

IOS (tm) 2500 Software (C2500-I-L), Version 11.2(15), RELEASE SOFTWARE (fc1)

Copyright (c) 1986-1998 by cisco Systems, Inc.

Compiled Tue 07-Jul-98 21:51 by tmullins

Image text-base: 0x03022F80, data-base: 0x00001000

ROM: System Bootstrap, Version 11.0(10c)XB1, PLATFORM SPECIFIC RELEASE SOFTWARE(fc1)

BOOTFLASH: 3000 Bootstrap Software (IGS-BOOT-R), Version 11.0(10c)XB1, PLATFORM

SPECIFIC RELEASE SOFTWARE (fc1)

Router_B uptime is 2 minutes

System restarted by reload

System image file is "flash:c2500-i-l.112-15.bin", booted via flash

cisco 2500 (68030) processor (revision A) with 4096K/2048K bytes of memory.

Processor board ID 01229726, with hardware revision 00000000

Bridging software.

```
X.25 software, Version 2.0, NET2, BFE and GOSIP compliant.
Cisco-ET Extended Temperature platform.
1 Ethernet/IEEE 802.3 interface(s)
2 Serial network interface(s)
32K bytes of non-volatile configuration memory.
8192K bytes of processor board System flash (Read ONLY)
Configuration register is 0x2102
Router_B#
```

This time, the system image file is "flash:c2500-i-1.112-15.bin" booted from flash. This means that it is running the proper IOS. Now, look at the route table:

```
Router_B#show ip route
Codes: C - connected, S - static, I - IGRP, R - RIP, M -
mobile, B – BGP, D - EIGRP, EX - EIGRP external, O - OSPF,
IA - OSPF inter area N1 - OSPF NSSA external type 1, N2 -
OSPF NSSA external type 2 E1 - OSPF external type 1, E2 -
OSPF external type 2, E - EGPi - IS-IS, L1 - IS-IS level-
1, L2 - IS-IS level-2, * - candidate default
U - per-user static route, o - ODR
Gateway of last resort is not set
172.16.0.0/16 is variably subnetted, 2 subnets, 2 masks
D       172.16.60.0/24 [90/307200] via 172.16.50.2,
00:00:16, Ethernet0
D    172.16.10.0/24 [90/300200] via 172.16.30.5, 00:00:19,
Serial0
C       172.16.50.0/24 is directly connected, Ethernet0
C       172.16.30.4/30 is directly connected, Serial0
Router_B#
```

Now, the route to 172.16.10.0/24 is present in the route table. The next step is to look at the route table on Router C.

```
Router_C>sho ip route
Codes: C - connected, S - static, I - IGRP, R - RIP, M -
mobile, B – BGP, D - EIGRP, EX - EIGRP external, O - OSPF,
IA - OSPF inter area N1 - OSPF NSSA external type 1, N2 -
OSPF NSSA external type 2 E1 - OSPF external type 1, E2 -
OSPF external type 2, E - EGPi - IS-IS, L1 - IS-IS level-
```

```
1, L2 - IS-IS level-2, * - candidate defaultU - per-user
static route, o - ODR
Gateway of last resort is not set
172.16.0.0/16 is variably subnetted, 3 subnets, 2 masks
C       172.16.60.0/24 is directly connected, Ethernet0/1
C       172.16.50.0/24 is directly connected, Ethernet0/0
D       172.16.30.4/30 [90/2195456] via 172.16.50.1,
00:02:59, Ethernet0/0
D       172.16.10.0/24 [90/3295676] via 172.16.50.1,
00:02:59, Ethernet0/0
Router_C>
```

Everything looks as if it is in place, but the ultimate test is to FTP from Host Z to Host A. The connection was successful.

```
C:\WINDOWS>ftp 172.16.10.2
> ftp: connect :10061
ftp>
```

Let's review the steps taken. The observation was that Host Z could not FTP to Host A. The problem was isolated by using the ping and traceroute commands. After the problem was isolated, the correct observations were made that enabled a problem statement to be made. The problem was that Router B was in boot mode. This happened because the IOS image was loaded from the ROM instead of flash. The problem was remedied by changing the configuration register to indicate that the image should be loaded from the system flash.

The effect of the configuration changes was validated by showing the routes present on each router, as well as establishing an FTP session with Host A.

Troubleshooting Ethernet Problems

As the heading depicts, this section includes troubleshooting Ethernet-related problems. The examples are simple, and you need to use only Ethernet-related commands to effectively troubleshoot these problems.

Scenario #1

The problem here is that Host A cannot Telnet to Host Z. Figure 5.4 depicts the network that is used for this scenario. Troubleshooting will begin after the establishment of the boundary of dysfunctionality. You know that the problem exists between Router C and Host Z. Because this is a troubleshooting scenario for Ethernet, you know what to look for.

FIGURE 5.4 Network diagram for Ethernet scenario #1

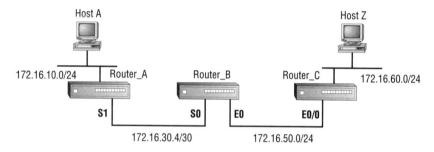

List Observations

The first thing to do is verify that Host Z is still unreachable. Let's look at the results of a ping test:

```
Router_C#ping 172.16.60.130
Type escape sequence to abort.
Sending 5, 100-byte ICMP Echos to 172.16.60.130, timeout
is 2 seconds:
.....
Success rate is 0 percent (0/5)
Router_C#
```

Because the ping test failed, the cause needs to be isolated. Let's look at the interface:

```
Router_C#show interface ethernet0/1
Ethernet0/1 is up, line protocol is up
  Hardware is AmdP2, address is 0010.7bd9.2881 (bia
0010.7bd9.2881)
```

```
    Internet address is 172.16.60.1/24
    MTU 1500 bytes, BW 10000 Kbit, DLY 1000 usec, rely 255/
255,    load 1/255
    Encapsulation ARPA, loopback not set, keepalive set (10
sec)
    ARP type: ARPA, ARP Timeout 04:00:00
    Last input 00:41:42, output 00:00:00, output hang never
    Last clearing of "show interface" counters never
    Queueing strategy: fifo
    Output queue 0/40, 0 drops; input queue 0/75, 0 drops
    5 minute input rate 0 bits/sec, 0 packets/sec
    5 minute output rate 0 bits/sec, 0 packets/sec
        147 packets input, 9568 bytes, 0 no buffer
        Received 5 broadcasts, 0 runts, 0 giants, 0 throttles
      0 input errors, 0 CRC, 0 frame, 0 overrun, 0 ignored,
0 abort
        0 input packets with dribble condition detected
        2009 packets output, 162455 bytes, 0 underruns
        0 output errors, 0 collisions, 2 interface resets
        0 babbles, 0 late collision, 0 deferred
        0 lost carrier, 0 no carrier
        0 output buffer failures, 0 output buffers swapped
out
Router_C#
```

Everything looks good, except for the fact that no traffic is being sent across the interface. That can be another indication that there is a problem between the router and Host Z. Now, look at the ARP table:

```
Router_C>show arp
Protocol  Address      Age (min) Hardware Addr  Type  Interface
Internet  172.16.60.1    -       0010.7bd9.2881 ARPA  Ethernet0/1
Internet  172.16.50.2    -       0010.7bd9.2880 ARPA  Ethernet0/0
Internet  172.16.50.1    0       0000.0c09.99cc ARPA  Ethernet0/0
Router_C>
```

The address of interest is not listed in the ARP table, which means that Router C does not know where to send the Layer 2 PDU. A trace using Ether-Peek shows the router sending out an ARP broadcast:

```
Flags:          0x00
  Status:        0x00
  Packet Length:64
  Timestamp:     11:30:42.713000 04/19/1999
Ethernet Header
  Destination:  ff:ff:ff:ff:ff:ff Ethernet Brdcast  [0-5]
  Source:        00:10:7b:d9:28:81  [6-11]
  Protocol Type:08-06  IP ARP  [12-13]
ARP - Address Resolution Protocol
  Hardware:                   1  Ethernet (10Mb)  [14-15]
  Protocol:                   08-00  IP  [16-18]
  Hardware Address Length:  6  [19]
  Protocol Address Length:  4
  Operation:                  1  ARP Request  [20-21]
  Sender Hardware Address:  00:10:7b:d9:28:81  [22-27]
  Sender Internet Address:  172.16.60.1  [28-31]
  Target Hardware Address:  00:00:00:00:00:00  (ignored)
  [32-37]
  Target Internet Address:  172.16.60.130  [38-41]
Extra bytes (Padding):
  ...............  00 00 00 00 00 00 00 00 00 00 00 00 00
00 00 00   [42-57]
  ..                  00 00   [58-59]
Frame Check Sequence:  0x00000000
```

No response was received from this broadcast. Let's list the facts that you have gathered:

- Router C cannot ping Host Z.

- Interface Ethernet 0/1 is up and line protocol is up.

- There are no collisions on the Ethernet interface.

- No traffic is transiting the Ethernet 0/1 interface.

- There is no listing for Host Z in the ARP table.

- An ARP broadcast was sent out Ethernet 0/1, but no response was received from Host Z.

The problem statement is that Ethernet 0/1 is functioning properly, but it cannot communicate with Host Z. There is no listing for Host Z in the ARP table.

It is simpler to decide the possible causes and create an action plan by focusing on the ARP table. What possible reasons are there for Host Z not to be listed in the ARP table? Some reasons are as follows:

- Failed host

- Cabling failures

- Bad Ethernet NIC on Host Z

- Mismatching frame encapsulation type

Propose Solutions

You verified that the host is not down. No traffic is transiting the Ethernet interface on the router. This indicates that the Ethernet card is not starting to fail, but could have completely failed. Cabling is probably not the issue because you would see interface resets or carrier transitions. None of those symptoms are indicated on the interface. This leaves us with mismatching encapsulation type as the probable problem.

The easiest way to test it is to ping Router C from Host Z. The results follow:

```
C:\WINDOWS>ping 172.16.60.1
Pinging 172.16.60.1 with 32 bytes of data:
Reply from 172.16.60.1: bytes=32 time=7ms TTL=255
Reply from 172.16.60.1: bytes=32 time=1ms TTL=255
Reply from 172.16.60.1: bytes=32 time=2ms TTL=255
Reply from 172.16.60.1: bytes=32 time=4ms TTL=255
Ping statistics for 172.16.60.1:
    Packets: Sent = 4, Received = 4, Lost = 0 (0% loss),
Approximate round trip times in milli-seconds:
    Minimum = 1ms, Maximum =  7ms, Average =  3ms
C:\WINDOWS>
```

The ping was successful. Why is it that Router C can ping Host Z, but Host Z cannot ping Router C? Let's go back to the router. Look at the ARP table now.

```
Router_C>show arp
Protocol   Address      Age (min) Hardware Addr  Type   Interface
Internet   172.16.60.130 1      00a0.24a5.0657 SNAP   Ethernet0/1
Internet   172.16.60.1   -      0010.7bd9.2881 ARPA   Ethernet0/1
Internet   172.16.50.2   -      0010.7bd9.2880 ARPA   Ethernet0/0
Internet   172.16.50.1   111    0000.0c09.99cc ARPA   Ethernet0/0
Router_C>
```

Wait a minute! Host Z is listed in the table now. How did that happen? You must remember that although Cisco understands several different encapsulation types, its default is ARPA. When the router sent the ARP request, it was sent using ARPA. Host Z does not understand ARPA, and so it did not respond to the ARP request.

The process works differently on a Cisco router. When Host Z sent an ARP broadcast, it was sent with SNAP encapsulation. The difference is that the router understood the broadcast, recorded the encapsulation type, and entered it into the router's ARP table, as seen previously. The type allows the router to override the default encapsulation. Now, when the router needs to send a frame to Host Z, it uses SNAP encapsulation. Let's test it:

```
Router_C#ping 172.16.60.130
Type escape sequence to abort.
Sending 5, 100-byte ICMP Echos to 172.16.60.130, timeout
is 2 seconds:
!!!!!
Success rate is 100 percent (5/5), round-trip min/avg/max
= 4/4/8 ms
Router_C#
```

It worked great because the router now knows which encapsulation type must be used when communicating with Host Z. This problem has been resolved temporarily. To solve it permanently, you must manually change the encapsulation type used for the interface that Host Z connects to. Now, let's move on to the next one.

Scenario #2

This is another simple Ethernet problem. Using the example network depicted in Figure 5.5, you will attempt to solve a less tangible network problem. The user at Host A complains of very slow throughput to Host Z. He is able to ping and Traceroute to the destination, but file transfers experience very slow transfer times.

FIGURE 5.5 Network diagram for Ethernet scenario #2

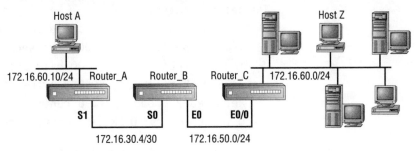

List Observations

List the observations given you by the user, and then move on to other fact-gathering procedures:

- Large transfer times
- Slow throughput
- Can ping and traceroute to host

The fact that ping and traceroute work indicates that the routing between Host A and Host Z is intact. There must be something that causes latency somewhere along the line. Again, start at the far end of the problem.

The following outputs are several `show interface` outputs of the same interface over an extended period of time. Look at them all and see if you can see the problem.

```
Router_C#show int ethernet 0/1
Ethernet0/1 is up, line protocol is up
  Hardware is Lance, address is 0000.0c47.abea (bia
  0000.0c47.abea)
  Internet address is 172.16.60.1/24
  MTU 1500 bytes, BW 10000 Kbit, DLY 1000 usec, rely 255/
  255,    load 46/255
  Encapsulation ARPA, loopback not set, keepalive set (10
  sec)
  ARP type: ARPA, ARP Timeout 04:00:00
  Last input 00:00:00, output 00:00:00, output hang never
```

```
Last clearing of "show interface" counters 00:00:05
Queueing strategy: fifo
Output queue 0/40, 0 drops; input queue 0/75, 0 drops
5 minute input rate 1259000 bits/sec, 629 packets/sec
5 minute output rate 1822000 bits/sec, 486 packets/sec
    3476 packets input, 455808 bytes, 0 no buffer
    Received 2 broadcasts, 0 runts, 0 giants
    0 input errors, 0 CRC, 0 frame, 0 overrun, 0 ignored,
    0 abort
    0 input packets with dribble condition detected
    1165 packets output, 1667097 bytes, 0 underruns
    0 output errors, 175 collisions, 0 interface resets
    0 babbles, 0 late collision, 182 deferred
    0 lost carrier, 0 no carrier
    0 output buffer failures, 0 output buffers swapped
    out
Router_C#show int ethernet 0/1
Ethernet0/1 is up, line protocol is up
  Hardware is Lance, address is 0000.0c47.abea (bia
  0000.0c47.abea)
  Internet address is 172.16.60.1/24
  MTU 1500 bytes, BW 10000 Kbit, DLY 1000 usec, rely 255/
  255,    load 46/255
  Encapsulation ARPA, loopback not set, keepalive set (10
  sec)
  ARP type: ARPA, ARP Timeout 04:00:00
  Last input 00:00:00, output 00:00:00, output hang never
  Last clearing of "show interface" counters 00:00:16
  Queueing strategy: fifo
  Output queue 0/40, 0 drops; input queue 0/75, 0 drops
  5 minute input rate 1243000 bits/sec, 627 packets/sec
  5 minute output rate 1826000 bits/sec, 484 packets/sec
      9872 packets input, 1760499 bytes, 0 no buffer
      Received 4 broadcasts, 0 runts, 0 giants
      0 input errors, 0 CRC, 0 frame, 0 overrun, 0 ignored,
      0 abort
      0 input packets with dribble condition detected
```

```
    2858 packets output, 3943213 bytes, 0 underruns
    0 output errors, 443 collisions, 0 interface resets
    0 babbles, 0 late collision, 471 deferred
    0 lost carrier, 0 no carrier
    0 output buffer failures, 0 output buffers swapped
    out
Router_C#show int ethernet 0/1
Ethernet0/1 is up, line protocol is up
  Hardware is Lance, address is 0000.0c47.abea (bia
  0000.0c47.abea)
  Internet address is 172.16.60.1/24
  MTU 1500 bytes, BW 10000 Kbit, DLY 1000 usec, rely 255/
  255,    load 46/255
  Encapsulation ARPA, loopback not set, keepalive set (10
  sec)
  ARP type: ARPA, ARP Timeout 04:00:00
  Last input 00:00:00, output 00:00:00, output hang never
  Last clearing of "show interface" counters 00:00:37
  Queueing strategy: fifo
  Output queue 0/40, 0 drops; input queue 0/75, 0 drops
  5 minute input rate 1209000 bits/sec, 620 packets/sec
  5 minute output rate 1819000 bits/sec, 477 packets/sec
    21386 packets input, 3979009 bytes, 0 no buffer
    Received 9 broadcasts, 0 runts, 0 giants
    0 input errors, 0 CRC, 0 frame, 0 overrun, 0 ignored,
    0 abort
    0 input packets with dribble condition detected
    5590 packets output, 8237684 bytes, 0 underruns
    0 output errors, 889 collisions, 0 interface resets
    0 babbles, 0 late collision, 1006 deferred
    0 lost carrier, 0 no carrier
    0 output buffer failures, 0 output buffers swapped
    out
Router_C#show int ethernet 0/1
Ethernet0/1 is up, line protocol is up
  Hardware is Lance, address is 0000.0c47.abea (bia
  0000.0c47.abea)
```

```
Internet address is 172.16.60.1/24
MTU 1500 bytes, BW 10000 Kbit, DLY 1000 usec, rely 255/
255,    load 46/255
Encapsulation ARPA, loopback not set, keepalive set (10
sec)
ARP type: ARPA, ARP Timeout 04:00:00
Last input 00:00:00, output 00:00:00, output hang never
Last clearing of "show interface" counters 00:00:50
Queueing strategy: fifo
Output queue 0/40, 0 drops; input queue 0/75, 0 drops
5 minute input rate 1209000 bits/sec, 620 packets/sec
5 minute output rate 1819000 bits/sec, 477 packets/sec
    21386 packets input, 3979009 bytes, 0 no buffer
    Received 9 broadcasts, 0 runts, 0 giants
    0 input errors, 0 CRC, 0 frame, 0 overrun, 0 ignored,
    0 abort
    0 input packets with dribble condition detected
    6000 packets output, 8237684 bytes, 0 underruns
    0 output errors, 1020 collisions, 0 interface resets
    0 babbles, 0 late collision, 1006 deferred
    0 lost carrier, 0 no carrier
    0 output buffer failures, 0 output buffers swapped
    out
```

So, what do you think? What are your observations? This exercise was designed specifically to educate you about Ethernet capabilities. The principal observation that you should have made was the increasing number of collisions on the interface.

Collisions are a normal occurrence for CSMA/CD protocols. The fact that a connection is not full duplex creates the opportunity for collisions. Although collisions are normal, excessive collisions can be detrimental to a network. Once collisions exceed 5 to 8 percent of the output packets, the interface becomes very ineffective. The higher the collision rate, the more packets that have to be retransmitted.

The output queue for the Ethernet interface doesn't stop filling up just because of collisions on the line. Therefore, not only does the interface have to transmit the normal queue of packets, it has to retransmit all of the frames that were lost due to collisions. The number of packets that need to be transmitted can grow exponentially. Let's calculate the collision percentage for the four show interface outputs:

- 175 collisions/1165 output packets = 15.02% collisions

- 443 collisions/2858 output packets = 15.5% collisions

- 889 collisions/5590 output packets = 15.9% collisions

- 1020 collisions/6000 output packets = 17.0% collisions

All of these values are well in excess of 5 to 8 percent. It looks like a key observation has been made, and now the problem statement can be written. The collision percentage on Ethernet 0/1 exceeds healthy values and can be blamed for causing slow network throughput.

Propose Solutions

The hard part is to determine what is causing the collisions. In this scenario, solutions will be tried from Layer 1 up to Layer 2. Following are possible solutions:

- Replace a faulty cable

- Replace a faulty transceiver

- Replace a faulty interface by changing the router

The proposed solutions are to test the cable—if the cable passes, then change the transceiver. If that doesn't help, assume that the interface on the router has gone bad. If the latter is the problem, the problem may be solved by moving the connection to another interface on the same router or to a different interface on a different router.

Figure 5.6 depicts the physical hardware involved in this scenario. The cable connects to the hub and to a transceiver that is connected to the router's AUI interface.

FIGURE 5.6 Ethernet physical hardware

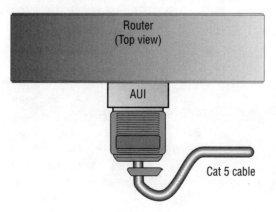

You tested the cable and it passed, so you then change transceivers and look at the interface status again.

```
Router_C#show interface ethernet 0/1
Ethernet0/1 is up, line protocol is up
  Hardware is Lance, address is 0000.0c47.abea (bia
  0000.0c47.abea)
  Internet address is 172.16.60.1/24
  MTU 1500 bytes, BW 10000 Kbit, DLY 1000 usec, rely 255/
  255,    load 28/255
  Encapsulation ARPA, loopback not set, keepalive set (10
  sec)
  ARP type: ARPA, ARP Timeout 04:00:00
  Last input 00:00:00, output 00:00:00, output hang never
  Last clearing of "show interface" counters 00:00:11
  Queueing strategy: fifo
  Output queue 0/40, 0 drops; input queue 0/75, 0 drops
  5 minute input rate 1381000 bits/sec, 723 packets/sec
  5 minute output rate 1126000 bits/sec, 418 packets/sec
     8291 packets input, 1933415 bytes, 0 no buffer
     Received 3 broadcasts, 0 runts, 0 giants
     0 input errors, 0 CRC, 0 frame, 0 overrun, 0 ignored,
     0 abort
     0 input packets with dribble condition detected
     7172 packets output, 1446188 bytes, 0 underruns
     0 output errors, 251 collisions, 0 interface resets
     0 babbles, 0 late collision, 265 deferred
     0 lost carrier, 0 no carrier
     0 output buffer failures, 0 output buffers swapped
     out
Router_C#
Router_C#show interface ethernet 0/1
Ethernet0/1 is up, line protocol is up
  Hardware is Lance, address is 0000.0c47.abea (bia
  0000.0c47.abea)
  Internet address is 172.16.60.1/24
  MTU 1500 bytes, BW 10000 Kbit, DLY 1000 usec, rely 255/
  255,    load 28/255
```

Encapsulation ARPA, loopback not set, keepalive set (10 sec)

ARP type: ARPA, ARP Timeout 04:00:00

Last input 00:00:00, output 00:00:00, output hang never

Last clearing of "show interface" counters 00:00:49

Queueing strategy: fifo

Output queue 0/40, 0 drops; input queue 0/75, 0 drops

5 minute input rate 1392000 bits/sec, 735 packets/sec

5 minute output rate 1114000 bits/sec, 425 packets/sec

    39411 packets input, 8957876 bytes, 0 no buffer

    Received 14 broadcasts, 0 runts, 0 giants

    0 input errors, 0 CRC, 0 frame, 0 overrun, 0 ignored, 0 abort

    0 input packets with dribble condition detected

    38944 packets output, 6409017 bytes, 0 underruns

    0 output errors, 1556 collisions, 0 interface resets

    0 babbles, 0 late collision, 1368 deferred

    0 lost carrier, 0 no carrier

    0 output buffer failures, 0 output buffers swapped out

Router_C#

Router_C#**show interface ethernet 0/1**

Ethernet0/1 is up, line protocol is up

Hardware is Lance, address is 0000.0c47.abea (bia 0000.0c47.abea)

Internet address is 172.16.60.1/24

MTU 1500 bytes, BW 10000 Kbit, DLY 1000 usec, rely 255/255,   load 28/255

Encapsulation ARPA, loopback not set, keepalive set (10 sec)

ARP type: ARPA, ARP Timeout 04:00:00

Last input 00:00:00, output 00:00:00, output hang never

Last clearing of "show interface" counters 00:01:16

Queueing strategy: fifo

Output queue 0/40, 0 drops; input queue 0/75, 0 drops

5 minute input rate 1396000 bits/sec, 742 packets/sec

5 minute output rate 1110000 bits/sec, 434 packets/sec

    60752 packets input, 13691996 bytes, 0 no buffer

```
        Received 22 broadcasts, 0 runts, 0 giants
        0 input errors, 0 CRC, 0 frame, 0 overrun, 0 ignored,
        0 abort
        0 input packets with dribble condition detected
        65212 packets output, 10035669 bytes, 0 underruns
        0 output errors, 2466 collisions, 0 interface resets
        0 babbles, 0 late collision, 2163 deferred
        0 lost carrier, 0 no carrier
        0 output buffer failures, 0 output buffers swapped
        out
Router_C#
Router_C#show interface ethernet 0/1
Ethernet0/1 is up, line protocol is up
  Hardware is Lance, address is 0000.0c47.abea (bia
  0000.0c47.abea)
  Description: 10BaseT to Core3
  Internet address is 172.16.60.1/24
  MTU 1500 bytes, BW 10000 Kbit, DLY 1000 usec, rely 255/
  255,    load 28/255
  Encapsulation ARPA, loopback not set, keepalive set (10
  sec)
  ARP type: ARPA, ARP Timeout 04:00:00
  Last input 00:00:00, output 00:00:00, output hang never
  Last clearing of "show interface" counters 00:01:42
  Queueing strategy: fifo
  Output queue 0/40, 0 drops; input queue 0/75, 0 drops
  5 minute input rate 1415000 bits/sec, 753 packets/sec
  5 minute output rate 1135000 bits/sec, 442 packets/sec
      81784 packets input, 18845458 bytes, 0 no buffer
      Received 29 broadcasts, 0 runts, 0 giants
      0 input errors, 0 CRC, 0 frame, 0 overrun, 0 ignored,
      0 abort
      0 input packets with dribble condition detected
      97408 packets output, 14297058 bytes, 0 underruns
      0 output errors, 3498 collisions, 0 interface resets
      0 babbles, 0 late collision, 2986 deferred
      0 lost carrier, 0 no carrier
      0 output buffer failures, 0 output buffers swapped
      out
Router_C#
```

Collision percentage calculations result in an average of 3.72 percent collisions. This is much better than the 15 percent you saw previously. In this scenario, a bad transceiver was to blame for the excessive collisions.

Troubleshooting Token Ring Problems

The Token Ring scenarios in this section focus on troubleshooting Token Ring problems. Both scenarios may be effectively solved by using generic Cisco troubleshooting commands.

Scenario #1

Figure 5.7 displays the Token Ring network that is used for this scenario. You can see Routers A and B connected via Token Ring interfaces.

FIGURE 5.7 Network diagram for Token Ring scenario #1 and #2

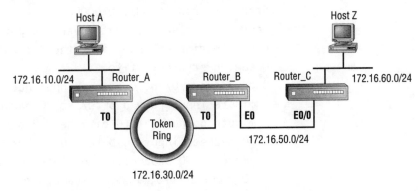

You are connecting Router A to Router B via the Token Ring interfaces, and you cannot get the interfaces to come up. You have console access to both routers.

List Observations

You must now gather information from both routers that will allow you to create a problem statement. You start by gathering information from Router A.

```
Router_A#show int to0
TokenRing0 is up, line protocol is down
  Hardware is TMS380, address is 0007.787c.e14b (bia
  0007.787c.e14b)
  Internet address is 172.16.30.1, subnet mask is
  255.255.255.0
  MTU 4464 bytes, BW 4000 Kbit, DLY 630 usec, rely 255/
  255,    load 1/255
  Encapsulation SNAP, loopback not set, keepalive set (10
  sec)
  ARP type: SNAP, ARP Timeout 04:00:00
  Ring speed: 4 Mbps
  Single ring node, Source Route Transparent Bridge
  capable
  Ethernet Transit OUI: 0x000000
  Last input never, output never, output hang never
  Last clearing of "show interface" counters never
  Queueing strategy: fifo
  Output queue 0/40, 0 drops; input queue 0/75, 0 drops
  5 minute input rate 0 bits/sec, 0 packets/sec
  5 minute output rate 0 bits/sec, 0 packets/sec
     0 packets input, 0 bytes, 0 no buffer
     Received 0 broadcasts, 0 runts, 0 giants
     0 input errors, 0 CRC, 0 frame, 0 overrun, 0 ignored,
     0 abort
     0 packets output, 0 bytes, 0 underruns
     0 output errors, 0 collisions, 0 interface resets
     0 output buffer failures, 0 output buffers swapped
     out
     1 transition
```

Nothing looks wrong, so get a copy of the configuration.

```
Router_A#show running-config
```

```
Building configuration...
Current configuration:
!
version 11.2
no service password-encryption
no service udp-small-servers
service tcp-small-servers
!
hostname Router_A
!
enable password aloha
!
interface Ethernet0
 no ip address
 shutdown
!
interface Serial0
 ip address 172.16.20.6 255.255.255.252
 shutdown
 clockrate 4000000
 dce-terminal-timing-enable
!
interface Serial1
 no ip address
 shutdown
!
interface TokenRing0
 ip address 172.16.30.1 255.255.255.0
 ring-speed 4
!
router eigrp 100
 network 172.16.0.0
!
ip classless
!
line con 0
line aux 0
 transport input all
line vty 0 4
```

```
    password aloha
    login
    !
   end
   Router_A#
```

Everything seems to be configured properly. Now, move on to the console of Router B. First, issue a show interface command:

```
Router_B#show interface to0
TokenRing0 is up, line protocol is down
  Hardware is TMS380, address is 0007.787c.e1cb (bia
  0007.787c.e1cb)
  Internet address is 172.16.30.2, subnet mask is
  255.255.255.0
  MTU 4464 bytes, BW 16000 Kbit, DLY 630 usec, rely 255/
  255,    load 1/255
  Encapsulation SNAP, loopback not set, keepalive set (10
  sec)
  ARP type: SNAP, ARP Timeout 04:00:00
  Ring speed: 16 Mbps
  Single ring node, Source Route Transparent Bridge
  capable
  Ethernet Transit OUI: 0x000000
  Last input never, output never, output hang never
  Last clearing of "show interface" counters never
  Queueing strategy: fifo
  Output queue 0/40, 0 drops; input queue 0/75, 0 drops
  5 minute input rate 0 bits/sec, 0 packets/sec
  5 minute output rate 0 bits/sec, 0 packets/sec
     0 packets input, 0 bytes, 0 no buffer
     Received 0 broadcasts, 0 runts, 0 giants
     0 input errors, 0 CRC, 0 frame, 0 overrun, 0 ignored,
     0 abort
     0 packets output, 0 bytes, 0 underruns
     0 output errors, 0 collisions, 0 interface resets
     0 output buffer failures, 0 output buffers swapped
     out
     2 transitions
```

Now, you should be able to distinguish some differences and pinpoint the problem. There are two fields within this output that differ from the output from Router A. The first hint is to look at the interface metrics. The second hint is to look at the ring speed.

Now, list the observations:

- The Token Ring interfaces on Routers A and B are in an up/down state.

- Router A ring speed is set to 4Mbps.

- Router B ring speed is set to 16Mbps.

The problem statement is "The ring speeds for Routers A and B are different."

Propose Solutions

The solution for this case is straightforward. Change the ring speed on Router A to match the ring speed on Router B. The configuration follows:

```
Router_A(config)#interface to0
Router_A(config-if)#ring-speed 16
Router_A(config-if)#^Z
Router_A#
```

Now, verify the interface status. The interface should be in an up and up state:

```
Router_A#show interface to0
TokenRing0 is up, line protocol is up
  Hardware is TMS380, address is 0007.787c.e14b (bia
  0007.787c.e14b)
  Internet address is 172.16.30.1, subnet mask is
  255.255.255.0
  MTU 4464 bytes, BW 16000 Kbit, DLY 630 usec, rely 255/
  255,    load 1/255
  Encapsulation SNAP, loopback not set, keepalive set (10
  sec)
  ARP type: SNAP, ARP Timeout 04:00:00
  Ring speed: 16 Mbps
  Single ring node, Source Route Transparent Bridge
  capable
  Ethernet Transit OUI: 0x000000
  Last input never, output never, output hang never
```

```
Last clearing of "show interface" counters never
Queueing strategy: fifo
Output queue 0/40, 0 drops; input queue 0/75, 0 drops
5 minute input rate 0 bits/sec, 0 packets/sec
5 minute output rate 0 bits/sec, 0 packets/sec
    0 packets input, 0 bytes, 0 no buffer
    Received 0 broadcasts, 0 runts, 0 giants
    0 input errors, 0 CRC, 0 frame, 0 overrun, 0 ignored,
    0 abort
    0 packets output, 0 bytes, 0 underruns
    0 output errors, 0 collisions, 0 interface resets
    0 output buffer failures, 0 output buffers swapped
    out
    3 transitions
```

The interface is now up, and you can ping the interface on Router B:

```
Router_A#ping 172.16.30.2
Type escape sequence to abort.
Sending 5, 100-byte ICMP Echos to 172.16.30.2, timeout is
2   seconds:
!!!!!
Success rate is 100 percent (5/5)
```

Scenario #2

Use the same network diagram found in Figure 5.7. The scenario is the same in that you cannot get the interface on Router A or B to initialize. The problem is different, so use Token Ring commands to find and solve the problem.

List Observations

The first command you issue on Router A is a show interface to0. The results follow:

```
Router_A#show interface to0
TokenRing0 is down, line protocol is down
   Hardware is TMS380, address is 0007.787c.e14b (bia
   0007.787c.e14b)
```

```
Internet address is 172.16.30.1, subnet mask is
255.255.255.0
MTU 4464 bytes, BW 16000 Kbit, DLY 630 usec, rely 255/
255,    load 1/255
Encapsulation SNAP, loopback not set, keepalive set (10
sec)
ARP type: SNAP, ARP Timeout 04:00:00
Ring speed: 16 Mbps
Single ring node, Source Route Transparent Bridge
capable
Ethernet Transit OUI: 0x000000
Last input never, output never, output hang never
Last clearing of "show interface" counters never
Queueing strategy: fifo
Output queue 0/40, 0 drops; input queue 0/75, 0 drops
5 minute input rate 0 bits/sec, 0 packets/sec
5 minute output rate 0 bits/sec, 0 packets/sec
    0 packets input, 0 bytes, 0 no buffer
    Received 0 broadcasts, 0 runts, 0 giants
    0 input errors, 0 CRC, 0 frame, 0 overrun, 0 ignored,
    0 abort
    0 packets output, 0 bytes, 0 underruns
    0 output errors, 0 collisions, 0 interface resets
    0 output buffer failures, 0 output buffers swapped
    out
    5 transitions
```

The fact that the physical interface is down indicates a Layer 1 or Layer 2 problem. The line protocol indicates a Layer 2 or Layer 3 problem. In this case, if there is a Physical layer problem, the upper layers do not work. Troubleshooting the upper layers is a waste of time until the lower layer problems are resolved.

Propose Solutions

The principal observation is that there is a physical problem with the interface. Review the Token Ring architecture so you can create an action plan. Figure 5.8 depicts the manner in which a station connects via Token Ring.

FIGURE 5.8 Token Ring topology

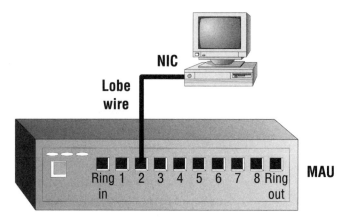

You can see that from the Token Ring NIC on the station, the lobe wire connects to a multistation access unit, or MAU. The MAU is similar to an Ethernet hub. Therefore, there are three physical pieces to look at: NIC, cable, and MAU.

The action plan is to inspect each of these elements. Start with the easiest part—inspect the cable, inspect the MAU, and then inspect the NIC.

Assume that the NIC is functioning properly, and the cable tested clean. That leaves the MAU. There can be two problems: the cable connection between the NIC and MAU was not connected properly, or there can be something wrong with the MAU itself. The MAU can have a variety of problems—it can have a bad port or it may not have been initialized.

The action plan is to reconnect the cable, change ports on the MAU, and verify that the MAU has been initialized.

Once the physical problem is resolved, the interface should change to interface up. The line protocol status depends on whether there are existing problems with the configuration.

Summary

The chapter was dedicated to exposing you to common problems that you can encounter with routers, Ethernet, and Token Ring. These scenarios all dealt with configuration problems or physical media issues. Although the majority of problems were found to be on Layer 2 and Layer 1, some were Layer 3 problems.

Here is a summary of the problems encountered and how they were solved:

Interfaces in the up/down state   Remove the administrative shutdown, add IP addresses, and eliminate duplicate IP addresses.

The router was in boot mode   Change the configuration register to indicate that the system image should be loaded from flash.

Ethernet frame encapsulation mismatch   Allow the host machine to ARP for the router. The router then records the frame type in the ARP table for future communication.

High number of collisions   Replace the transceiver. It is important to note that collisions aren't excessive until they are over 5 to 8 percent.

Token Ring interface in an up/down state   Ring speed mismatch. Adjust the ring speeds to match.

Token Ring interface in a down/down state   This is a Physical layer problem. Replace the cable or check the MAU.

Commands Used in This Chapter

The following list contains a summary of all the commands used in this chapter.

Command	Description
ping	Executes the ICMP reachability test.
show arp	Displays the contents of the ARP table.
show flash	Displays the contents of the system flash, such as the IOS and any other files that may be present.
show interface	Lists the configuration details, status, and statistics for the interface.
show ip route	Displays the contents of the IP route table as well as the default gateway for the router.

Command	Description
show running-config	Displays the contents of the running configuration of the router.
show version	Displays the current IOS, hardware configuration, reason for last reload, and system uptime.
tracert	The trace command used in the Windows operating system. Provides a step-by-step ICMP trace from source to destination.

Review Questions

1. What do the following lines mean?

   ```
   Router_A#show interface ethernet 0/0
   Ethernet0/0 is up, line protocol is down
   ```

   A. The physical interface is receiving keepalive packets from the transceiver.

   B. The interface is actually down because the line protocol is down.

   C. The interface will work on Layer 2.

   D. None of the above.

2. What do the following lines mean? (Choose all that apply.)

   ```
   Router_A>show int serial 0/0
   Serial0/0 is administratively down, line protocol is
   down
   ```

   A. The interface is experiencing trouble and needs the administrator to investigate.

   B. The interface was placed in shutdown through the `Interface configuration` command within the interface.

   C. The interface is experiencing a Layer 2 problem.

   D. The interface is experiencing a Layer 3 problem.

3. What command is used to display the ARP table? (Choose all that apply.)

   A. `show ip arp`

   B. `show Ethernet arp`

   C. `show interface arp`

   D. `show arp`

4. Which generic troubleshooting tool is used to test for reachability and connectivity?

   A. Traceroute

   B. Debug

   C. Ping

   D. None of the above

5. What does it mean when the router is in "boot" mode?

   A. The IOS system image was loaded from the boot ROM or from BootFLASH.

   B. The IOS system image was loaded from RAM.

   C. The IOS system image was loaded from flash.

   D. The IOS system image was loaded from a bootP server.

6. How can the router be removed from boot mode?

   A. Reboot it.

   B. Change the configuration register so the system image is loaded from a source other than the boot ROM.

   C. Change the configuration by adding the `no system boot` command.

   D. None of the above.

7. Which of the following statements is accurate about a router that is in boot mode?

   A. It will route traffic as usual.

   B. It will not route traffic.

   C. It will not allow you to change the configuration register.

   D. Only traffic with high priority and established flows will be routed.

8. Which ARP types does a Cisco router recognize? (Choose all that apply.)

   A. ARPA

   B. SNAP

   C. HP

   D. Probe

9. How can the ARP type be changed on a Cisco router?

   A. By using the global command `arp type <type>`

   B. By issuing the interface command `arp <type>`

   C. By issuing the interface command `arp type <type>`

   D. By issuing the global command `arp <type>`

10. How do you calculate the collision percentage for an Ethernet interface?

    A. (collisions/input packets) * 100

    B. (collisions/interface resets) *100

    C. (collisions/output packets) * 100

    D. (collisions/output rate bps) * 100

11. What physical device can be responsible for excessive collisions? (Choose all that apply.)

    A. Transceiver

    B. CSU/DSU

    C. Ethernet interface

    D. None of the above

12. What are the two ring speeds allowed for Token Ring? (Choose two.)

    A. 2Mbps

    B. 4Mbps

    C. 8Mbps

    D. 16Mbps

13. How is the ring speed changed on the token ring interface?

    A. By issuing the global command `ring speed <4 or 16>`

    B. By issuing the interface command `ring speed <4 or 16>`

    C. By issuing the global command `ring-speed <4 or 16>`

    D. By issuing the interface command `ring-speed <4 or 16>`

14. What could the following lines mean?

```
Router_A#show int to0
TokenRing0 is down, line protocol is down
```

    A. Bad cable

    B. Bad MAU port

    C. MAU not initialized

    D. All of the above

15. What troubleshooting tool is used to test for step-by-step path connectivity?

    A. Debug

    B. Ping

    C. Traceroute

    D. CDP

16. What is the purpose of listing observations? (Choose all that apply.)

    A. To define the problem

    B. To create an action plan

    C. To diagnose the problem

    D. To resolve the problem

17. What is the purpose of proposing solutions?

    A. It is equivalent to considering possibilities.

    B. It is equivalent to creating an action plan.

    C. It is equivalent to defining the problem.

    D. It is equivalent to the iteration process.

18. Why should you clear the counters on an interface you are troubleshooting? (Choose all that apply.)

    A. By clearing the counters, you may clear the problem that you are investigating.

    B. Clearing the counters flushes any corrupt packets from the interface.

    C. Clearing the counters creates a reference point.

    D. The `show interface` command will not work if the interface isn't cleared first.

19. What can cause an ARP entry to appear in the ARP table only after a ping is sent to the router from the host?

    A. The Ethernet encapsulation used on the remote device does not match the default encapsulation setting on the Ethernet interface on the router.

    B. The Ethernet encapsulation used on the remote device is not recognized by the encapsulation used on the Ethernet interface on the router.

    C. The Ethernet segment is faulty.

    D. The router cannot reach the host.

20. When should the number of collisions be considered excessive?

    A. Greater than 10–12 percent

    B. Greater than 4–5 percent

    C. Greater than 15 percent

    D. Greater than 5–8 percent

Answers to Review Questions

1. B. Even though the interface says that it is up, if the line protocol is down, the interface will not function and therefore is actually down.

2. B. The interface is administratively down, therefore, it had to have been done through the interface configuration.

3. A, D. Both of these commands may be used to display the ARP table.

4. C. Ping is the tool that is used specifically to test for reachability and connectivity.

5. A. Boot mode is caused when the image has to be loaded from the boot ROM and no other images are available or the configuration register was set to read only from the boot ROM.

6. B. Rebooting will not help if the configuration register is still set to tell the router to only boot from the boot ROM. Option C is invalid syntax and is not allowed to be input on the router.

7. B. No routing protocols run on the boot image for a router, therefore, it is unable to route traffic.

8. A, B, D. The valid ARP types are ARPA, SNAP, and Probe.

9. B. The correct syntax is described by B.

10. C. Collisions are based on output packets.

11. A, C. Collisions are characteristics of the Ethernet protocol. Any devices involved in an Ethernet connection can contribute to collisions.

12. B, D. The two valid ring speeds are 4Mbps and 16Mbps.

13. D. D represents the correct syntax for changing the ring speed.

14. D. All of these options can cause the Token Ring interface to go down.

15. C. Traceroute, or trace, is the tool used to test for each hop in the path to the destination.

16. A. Listing observations is similar to gathering facts. Fact gathering is done to aid in the formation of a problem statement, therefore defining the problem.

17. B. Proposing solutions is the same as creating an action plan of possible solutions.

18. C. It is easier to watch for incrementing counters when they have been reset to zero.

19. A. Once the router receives the ICMP request, it can identify the encapsulation type used by the host and can enter that in the ARP table for future reference. The host cannot adapt to the encapsulation used by the router, therefore it must send something to the router so the router may adapt.

20. D. Once collisions exceed 5 to 8 percent, there is a significant problem that should be investigated further.

Chapter

6

Troubleshooting TCP/IP Connectivity

TOPICS COVERED IN THIS CHAPTER INCLUDE:

✓ Analyzing symptoms and then implementing solutions to resolve problems in IP-based networks.

✓ Gaining a complete understanding of the TCP/IP suite and how to best troubleshoot problems common to TCP/IP networks.

✓ Implementing the problem resolution techniques learned thus far.

✓ Troubleshooting TCP/IP on machines using the Windows operating system.

This chapter is dedicated to covering essential TCP/IP trouble-shooting skills and tools. Generic commands such as `ping` and `traceroute` will be applied to network problems. We will also use the `debug` command to provide insight into router interaction regarding the TCP/IP suite.

Problem isolation techniques that are used in troubleshooting LAN, WAN, and routing protocols will be outlined and implemented. Routing protocols that will be covered include RIP, IGRP, EIGRP, and OSPF.

In addition to detailed problem-solving techniques, quick reference summary charts are located at the end of the chapter. These tables help to quickly associate a cause to many TCP/IP symptoms.

TCP/IP Router Diagnostic Tools

Several tools exist to aid in detecting and isolating TCP/IP suite problems. Some of these tools were mentioned in previous chapters, and some are new as they apply to the TCP/IP suite.

Because the TCP/IP suite of protocols is so extensively used, numerous troubleshooting targets can be identified and analyzed. Each of these targets requires a different set of diagnostic tools to effectively identify and isolate failures.

ping and *traceroute* **Commands**

These tools can easily be used in TCP/IP networks to test for reachability and hop-by-hop path connectivity. It is important to use these two tools in conjunction. It may be possible to ping a certain device, but perhaps the ICMP requests are taking the wrong route to the host.

Figure 6.1 depicts how this can happen. Host A is able to ping Host B without a problem. However, if the `traceroute` command is used to provide further information, the packet actually goes through five routers. According to the topology, the traceroute should need to transit only two routers in order to arrive at Host B.

FIGURE 6.1   ping vs. traceroute

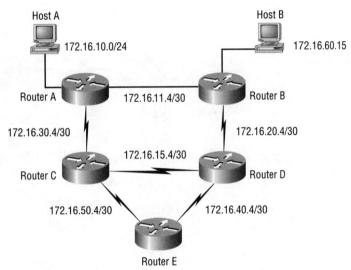

Let's look at the results as seen from Host A. First, you see the results of the ping command, followed by the traceroute results.

```
Host_A > ping 172.16.60.15
172.16.60.15 is alive

Host_A > traceroute Host_B
traceroute to Host_B (172.16.60.15), 30 hops max, 40 byte
packets
  1  Router_A (172.16.10.1)  1 ms  0 ms  0 ms
  2  Router_C (172.16.30.6)  1 ms  1 ms  1 ms
  3  Router_E (172.16.50.6)  1 ms  1 ms  1 ms
  4  Router_D (172.16.40.6)  1 ms  1 ms  1 ms
  5  Router_B (172.16.20.5)  1 ms  2 ms  3 ms
  6  Host_B (172.16.60.15)  2 ms  2 ms  2 ms
Host_A >
```

This information indicates that there is a problem with the link between Router A and Router B. Figure 6.2 shows that the link between the two routers is down. If only ping were used, the fact that the link between Routers A and B was down would take much longer to isolate.

FIGURE 6.2 Link failure detected by using the traceroute utility

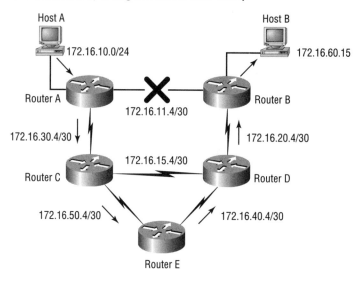

It is important to use ping and traceroute commands in conjunction when you troubleshoot network problems. Relying on only one of the utilities can mislead you.

Although `ping` and `traceroute` are designed to provide detailed feedback, this doesn't always work. A perfect example is when `ping` or `traceroute` packets have been administratively denied. If the receiving host is configured to not send a deny response, `ping` and `traceroute` indicate that the attempt timed out. There are times when one type or the other will be denied, but not both. Therefore, if you make sure to use both utilities, you are more likely to get usable information.

The previous examples are only two of many. The `ping` and `traceroute` utilities may be used on Cisco routers to aid in diagnosing routing problems as well as reachability problems.

By understanding exactly how each of these utilities works, the information provided by them can be invaluable. By using both tools, you can isolate a router that has lost its default gateway (gateway of last resort). The following command line output indicates that a router is not reachable using the `ping` command. The `traceroute` command indicates that there is a route to the router, but the requests are timing out. Figure 6.3 depicts the network topology.

FIGURE 6.3 Using `ping` and `traceroute` to isolate a router with no default network

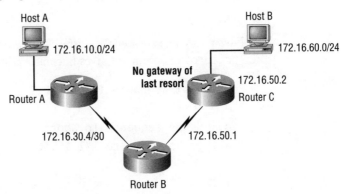

The first command—`ping`–fails. Figure 6.4 represents what happened. Five individual probes were sent to Router C and none of them returned, so the machine is unreachable.

FIGURE 6.4 The ping utility indicates that Router C is unreachable

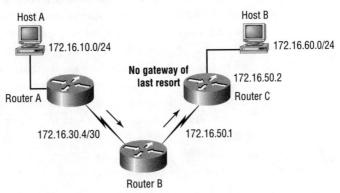

Here is the output of the ping command from Router A:

```
Router_A>ping 172.16.30.6

Type escape sequence to abort.
Sending 5, 100-byte ICMP Echos to 172.16.30.6, timeout is
2 seconds:
.....
Success rate is 0 percent (0/5)
Router_A>
```

Now that you have seen the output from the ping command, look at what the traceroute command gives back as a result:

```
Router_A#traceroute 172.16.50.2

Type escape sequence to abort.
Tracing the route to 172.16.50.2

 1 172.16.30.6 4 msec 0 msec 4 msec
 2 * * *
 3 * * *
 4 * ^C
Router_A#
```

Figure 6.5 gives more insight to what happened with the traceroute command. The arrows on the diagram represent the sequence and direction in which the ICMP requests are sent. The first request is sent to Router B. Router B responds. The third arrow indicates that the ICMP request is sent to Router C. As you can see, there is no arrow indicating that a response is sent to Router A. This diagram shows that the ICMP request did get to Router C, but that a response was not sent back to Router A. This indicates that Router C does not know how to return the response, indicating that Router C has not learned the route to Router A, and it has lost its gateway of last resort.

FIGURE 6.5 Stepping through the traceroute process

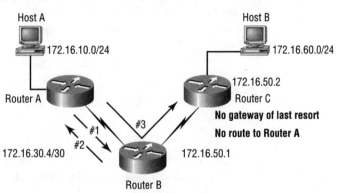

This can be proved by moving one hop closer to Router C. The `ping` and
`traceroute` commands use the interface closest to the next hop. Because
directly connected addresses are automatically placed in the route table,
Router B has a route to Router C, and vice versa. Look at the route table for
both routers:

```
Router_B>show ip route
Codes: C - connected, S - static, I - IGRP, R - RIP, M -
mobile, B - BGP
    D - EIGRP, EX - EIGRP external, O - OSPF, IA - OSPF
    inter area
    N1 - OSPF NSSA external type 1, N2 - OSPF NSSA
external type 2
    E1 - OSPF external type 1, E2 - OSPF external type 2,
    E - EGP
     i - IS-IS, L1 - IS-IS level-1, L2 - IS-IS level-2,
     *    - candidate
default U - per-user static route, o - ODR

Gateway of last resort is not set

     172.16.0.0/24 is subnetted, 3 subnets
D       172.16.60.0 [90/307200] via 172.16.50.2, 00:00:01,
Ethernet0
C       172.16.30.4/30 is directly connected, Serial0
C       172.16.50.0 is directly connected, Ethernet0
Router_B>
```

```
Router_C>show ip route
Codes: C - connected, S - static, I - IGRP, R - RIP, M -
mobile, B - BGP
    D - EIGRP, EX - EIGRP external, O - OSPF, IA - OSPF
    inter area
    N1 - OSPF NSSA external type 1, N2 - OSPF NSSA
    external type 2
    E1 - OSPF external type 1, E2 - OSPF external type 2,
    E - EGP
    i - IS-IS, L1 - IS-IS level-1, L2 - IS-IS level-2,
    * - candidate
default U - per-user static route, o - ODR

Gateway of last resort is not set

    172.16.0.0/24 is subnetted, 2 subnets
C       172.16.50.0 is directly connected, Ethernet0/0
C       172.16.60.0 is directly connected, Ethernet0/1
Router_C>
```

As suspected, Router C does not know a route to Router A, and it has no gateway of last resort. This explains why the ICMP request was not sent back to Router A.

These examples show how useful the ping and traceroute commands are when troubleshooting TCP/IP router and network problems. Be sure to use them in conjunction for the best results.

show Commands

The show commands provide router- and interface-specific information. Several show commands were discussed in previous chapters. Due to the number of show commands available on the router, they must be discussed within the context they are used.

Each troubleshooting session requires the use of different show commands. The common show commands used to troubleshoot TCP/IP commands are listed as follows:

show ip interface This command provides information specific to the TCP/IP configuration of the specified interface. Information regarding the interface status, IP address, subnet mask, broadcast address, and applied access lists is all contained in the `show ip interface` command. A sample output follows:

```
Router_B#show ip interface serial 0
Serial0 is up, line protocol is up
  Internet address is 172.16.30.6/30
  Broadcast address is 255.255.255.255
  Address determined by non-volatile memory
  MTU is 1500 bytes
  Helper address is not set
  Directed broadcast forwarding is enabled
  Multicast reserved groups joined: 224.0.0.10
  Outgoing access list is not set
  Inbound  access list is not set
  Proxy ARP is enabled
  Security level is default
  Split horizon is enabled
  ICMP redirects are always sent
  ICMP unreachables are always sent
  ICMP mask replies are never sent
  IP fast switching is enabled
  IP fast switching on the same interface is enabled
  IP multicast fast switching is enabled
  Router Discovery is disabled
  IP output packet accounting is disabled
  IP access violation accounting is disabled
  TCP/IP header compression is disabled
  Probe proxy name replies are disabled
  Gateway Discovery is disabled
  Policy routing is disabled
  Network address translation is disabled
Router_B#
```

show ip access-list   This command provides information regarding a specified access list, or all access lists that fall within the 1–199 range.

When different access lists are configured on the router, the show ip access-list command shows NAMED IP access lists only. From the following sample output, you can see that it lists both standard and extended lists:

```
Standard IP access list 5
    permit 172.16.14.2
    permit 172.16.91.140
    permit 172.16.10.51
    permit 172.16.1.7
    permit 172.16.155.0, wildcard bits 0.0.0.255
Extended IP access list 152
    deny ip any 172.16.91.0 0.0.0.63 log (268436 matches)
    deny ip any host 172.16.91.66 log (81058 matches)
    permit tcp any any established (8809 matches)
    permit ip host 172.16.2.55 any
    permit ip host 172.60.22.10 any (2194226 matches)
    permit ip host 172.140.64.8 any (7930443 matches)
    permit ip 172.16.10.0 0.0.255.255 any (9076 matches)
```

show ip protocols This command provides information about the IP routing protocols that run on the router. The sample output includes only EIGRP information because that is all that is being run on the router. As you can see, global filters are not applied. Metric values are displayed for each individual routing protocol. Route redistribution information is also provided.

```
Router_B#show ip protocols
Routing Protocol is "eigrp 100"
  Outgoing update filter list for all interfaces is not
  set
  Incoming update filter list for all interfaces is not
  set
  Default networks flagged in outgoing updates
  Default networks accepted from incoming updates
  EIGRP metric weight K1=1, K2=0, K3=1, K4=0, K5=0
  EIGRP maximum hopcount 100
  EIGRP maximum metric variance 1
```

```
    Redistributing: eigrp 100
    Automatic network summarization is not in effect
    Routing for Networks:
      172.16.0.0
    Routing Information Sources:
      Gateway           Distance        Last Update
    Distance: internal 90 external 170
Router_B#
```

show ip traffic   This command returns information pertaining to IP traffic statistics. When the command is issued, the output is organized according to the IP protocol. Here is a sample:

```
Router_B#show ip traffic
IP statistics:
    Rcvd:  400 total, 400 local destination
           0 format errors, 0 checksum errors,
           0 bad hop count
           0 unknown protocol, 0 not a gateway
           0 security failures, 0 bad options,
           0 with options
    Opts:  0 end, 0 nop, 0 basic security,
           0 loose source  route
           0 timestamp, 0 extended security, 0 record route
           0 stream ID, 0 strict source route, 0 alert,
           0 cipso
           0 other
    Frags: 0 reassembled, 0 timeouts, 0 couldn't reassemble
           0 fragmented, 0 couldn't fragment
    Bcast: 0 received, 0 sent
    Mcast: 398 received, 401 sent
    Sent:  404 generated, 0 forwarded
           0 encapsulation failed, 0 no route

ICMP statistics:
    Rcvd: 0 format errors, 0 checksum errors, 0 redirects, 0
    unreachable
```

                    0 echo, 0 echo reply, 0 mask requests, 0 mask
                    replies, 0 quench
                    0 parameter, 0 timestamp, 0 info request, 0 other
                    0 irdp solicitations, 0 irdp advertisements
             Sent: 0 redirects, 0 unreachable, 0 echo, 0 echo reply
                    0 mask requests, 0 mask replies, 0 quench, 0
                    timestamp
                    0 info reply, 0 time exceeded, 0 parameter problem
                    0 irdp solicitations, 0 irdp advertisements

        UDP statistics:
          Rcvd: 0 total, 0 checksum errors, 0 no port
          Sent: 0 total, 0 forwarded broadcasts

        TCP statistics:
          Rcvd: 0 total, 0 checksum errors, 0 no port
          Sent: 0 total

        Probe statistics:
          Rcvd: 0 address requests, 0 address replies
                0 proxy name requests, 0 where-is requests, 0
                other
          Sent: 0 address requests, 0 address replies (0 proxy)
                0 proxy name replies, 0 where-is replies

        EGP statistics:
          Rcvd: 0 total, 0 format errors, 0 checksum errors, 0 no
          listener
          Sent: 0 total

        IGRP statistics:
          Rcvd: 0 total, 0 checksum errors
          Sent: 0 total

        OSPF statistics:
          Rcvd: 0 total, 0 checksum errors
                0 Hello, 0 database desc, 0 link state req
                0 link state updates, 0 link state acks

```
   Sent: 0 total

IP-IGRP2 statistics:
  Rcvd: 402 total
  Sent: 406 total

PIMv2 statistics: Sent/Received
  Total: 0/0, 0 checksum errors, 0 format errors
  Registers: 0/0, Register Stops: 0/0

IGMP statistics: Sent/Received
  Total: 0/0, Format errors: 0/0, Checksum errors: 0/0
  Host Queries: 0/0, Host Reports: 0/0, Host Leaves: 00
  DVMRP: 0/0, PIM: 0/0

ARP statistics:
  Rcvd: 0 requests, 0 replies, 0 reverse, 0 other
  Sent: 1 requests, 5 replies (0 proxy), 0 reverse
Router_B#
```

show ip route   This command returns information stored in the IP
route table. The command can be issued as a general command, and all IP
routes and corresponding information will be displayed. Additionally, a
given network may be specified, and the command will return information regarding that network only. Here are two samples. Notice that the
two outputs are different. The general command provides summary information for every IP route in the route table. However, when a network is
specified, the results are much more detailed. Information such as the
exact routing protocol responsible for learning the route, the source interface, and the next hop router's IP address is all included.

```
Router_A>sho ip route
Codes: C - connected, S - static, I - IGRP, R - RIP, M -
mobile, B - BGP
```

```
                D - EIGRP, EX - EIGRP external, O - OSPF, IA - OSPF
                inter area
                N1 - OSPF NSSA external type 1, N2 - OSPF NSSA
                external type 2
                E1 - OSPF external type 1, E2 - OSPF external type 2,
                E - EGP
                i - IS-IS, L1 - IS-IS level-1, L2 - IS-IS level-2, *
                   - candidate default
        U - per-user static route, o - ODR

        Gateway of last resort is not set

                172.16.0.0/16 is variably subnetted, 2 subnets, 2
        masks
        D         172.16.50.0/24 [90/2195456] via 172.16.30.6,
        00:00:19, Serial1
        C         172.16.30.4/30 is directly connected, Serial1
        Router_A>

        Router_A>sho ip route 172.16.50.0
        Routing entry for 172.16.50.0/24
          Known via "eigrp 100", distance 90, metric 2195456, type
        internal
          Redistributing via eigrp 100
          Last update from 172.16.30.6 on Serial1, 00:02:03 ago
          Routing Descriptor Blocks:
          * 172.16.30.6, from 172.16.30.6, 00:02:03 ago, via
        Serial1
              Route metric is 2195456, traffic share count is 1
              Total delay is 21000 microseconds, minimum bandwidth
              is 1544 Kbit
              Reliability 128/255, minimum MTU 1500 bytes
              Loading 1/255, Hops 1

        Router_A>
```

show ip arp This command provides information contained in the router's ARP cache. Information includes the IP address, MAC address, encapsulation type, and interface that it learned the MAC from. Here is a sample:

```
Router_C#show ip arp
Protocol  Address            Age (min)  Hardware Addr  Type
Interface
Internet  172.16.60.1            -      0010.7bd9.2881  ARPA
Ethernet0/1
Internet  172.16.50.2            -      0010.7bd9.2880  ARPA
Ethernet0/0
Internet  172.16.50.1            6      0000.0c09.99cc  ARPA
Ethernet0/0
Router_C#
```

debug Commands

Just as with the show commands, there are numerous debug commands and options. The problem being analyzed will dictate which IP debug commands need to be used. Table 6.1 lists most of the available debug commands and options within IP. The first command, arp, is not an IP-specific command, yet it provides valuable IP information.

TABLE 6.1   IP debug Commands and Options

Command	Description
arp	IP ARP and HP Probe transactions
bgp	BGP information
cache	IP cache operations
cef	IP CEF operations
cgmp	CGMP protocol activity
drp	Director response protocol
dvrmp	DVMRP protocol activity

TABLE 6.1 IP debug Commands and Options *(continued)*

Command	Description
egp	EGP information
eigrp	IP EIGRP information
error	IP error debugging
ftp	FTP dialogue
http	HTTP connections
icmp	ICMP transactions
igmp	IGMP protocol activity
igrp	IGRP information
mbgp	MBGP information
mcache	IP multicast cache operations
mds	IP distributed multicast information
mobile	Mobility protocols
mpacket	IP multicast packet debugging
mrouting	IP multicast routing table activity
msdp	Multicast Source Discovery Protocol (MSDP)
mtag	IP multicast tagswitching activity
nat	NAT events
ospf	OSPF information
packet	General IP debugging and IPSO security transactions
peer	IP peer address activity

TABLE 6.1   IP debug Commands and Options *(continued)*

Command	Description
pim	PIM protocol activity
policy	Policy routing
rip	RIP protocol transactions
routing	Routing table events
rsvp	RSVP protocol activity
rtp	RTP information
sd	Session Directory (SD)
security	IP security options
socket	Socket event
tcp	TCP information
trigger-authentication	Trigger authentication
udp	UDP-based transactions
wccp	WCCP information

You can use any of these commands. The `debug ip packets` command contains an option to provide an access list, which narrows the scope of the debug even more. There are some prerequisites, though. In order to properly use `debug ip packets`, the packets must be process-switched, which means that all switching types must be turned off. Fast, optimum, and other switching types do not provide the necessary information regarding the IP transactions.

Problem Isolation in TCP/IP Networks

Chapter 1 described three methods of attack for isolating network problems. Here's a quick review:

Outside-In This approach entails starting troubleshooting at the remote system and working back to the local host, one hop at a time.

Divide-by-Half This approach works by starting the troubleshooting in the middle. From there, divide the isolated area in half again, and continue the troubleshooting until the problem is isolated.

Inside-Out This approach entails starting with the local host, and then working your way to the remote host, one hop at a time.

All of these methods are effective because they are all systematic approaches. When troubleshooting, it is very important to be systematic. By following systematic procedures while troubleshooting, you can better manage the situation. If the correct process is followed, you will have documentation that records all attempts made to fix the problem. This can stop you from chasing your tail.

The outside-in method will be used in this section. Certain steps should be followed when trying to isolate the problem. The easiest step is to use built-in tools such as `ping` and `traceroute`. These commands are designed specifically to test reachability and path connectivity. Many problems can be isolated by analyzing the output of these two commands.

As shown in Figure 6.6, a good first step for isolating a problem between Host A and Host C would be to ping Host C. This test indicates whether Host C is reachable. If the ping fails, the next step would be to traceroute to Host C. The results of the traceroute indicate where the problem is most likely occurring.

FIGURE 6.6 TCP/IP network failure isolation

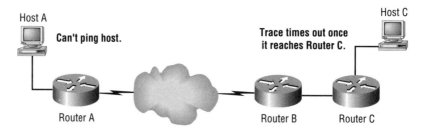

For a simple example, Host A cannot ping Host C. The traceroute stops at Router C, indicating that the problem can be said to be on or behind Router C. With the problem thus isolated, troubleshooting can be concentrated in that area.

Although further isolation can be done via the show commands previously mentioned, no matter where the problem lies, the next step is the same—fix it.

Many times, the problem you have isolated is on a system to which you do not have access. A perfect example is a WAN link. You were notified that a remote site is unreachable. Upon further investigation, you isolate the problem to the local carrier. You don't have access to run any diagnostics on their equipment, so your hands are tied. The only thing you can do in this case is to notify the carrier that a problem exists in their network.

Figure 6.7 depicts a flowchart with simple TCP/IP fault isolation steps. It is important to remember that you need to deal with host configurations, as well as router configurations, when troubleshooting TCP/IP failures.

FIGURE 6.7   TCP/IP isolation flowchart

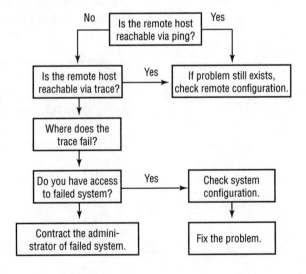

Problem Isolation for Windows 95/98/NT

Different traffic types may exist when sending Windows 95/98/NT client/server information through a Cisco router or switch. Router configurations change, depending on what traffic types need to be supported. Some examples of the traffic types are NetBEUI, transparent or source route bridging, Novell type 20 NetBIOS, Microsoft TCP/IP stack, and UDP NetBIOS broadcasts.

Proper troubleshooting requires diagnostic information from the host, router, and server. The Cisco troubleshooting tools can be used to gather information concerning the router. Windows provides diagnostic tools to enable you to obtain the information necessary to isolate and diagnose Windows 95/98/NT problems. Table 6.2 contains some of the diagnostic tools available in Windows 95/98/NT.

TABLE 6.2 Windows 95/98/NT TCP/IP Diagnostic Tools

Tool	Description
Ipconfig	IP information for all interfaces, including IP address, subnet mask, DNS server, DHCP information, and some NetBIOS (available only in Windows 98/NT)
Winipcfg	IP information for Windows 95 interfaces
event viewer	System log containing TCP/IP or DHCP events, among others (available only in Windows 98/NT)
Ping	TCP/IP ICMP utility
Tracert	ICMP utility, same as traceroute
telnet	Allows for IP testing
Nbstat	NetBIOS statistics

Here is a sample output of the `ipconfig /all` command issued in an MS-DOS window:

```
C:\WINDOWS>ipconfig /all

Windows 98 IP Configuration

        Host Name . . . . . . . . . : loco.somewhere.com
        DNS Servers . . . . . . . : 172.16.1.2
        Node Type . . . . . . . . . : Broadcast
        NetBIOS Scope ID. . . . . . :
        IP Routing Enabled. . . . . : No
        WINS Proxy Enabled. . . . . : No
        NetBIOS Resolution Uses DNS : Yes

0 Ethernet adapter :

        Description . . . . . . . . : PPP Adapter.
        Physical Address. . . . . . : 45-44-35-45-00-00
        DHCP Enabled. . . . . . . . : Yes
        IP Address. . . . . . . . . : 172.16.50.101
        Subnet Mask . . . . . . . . : 255.255.255.0
        Default Gateway . . . . . . : 172.16.50.101
        DHCP Server . . . . . . . . : 255.255.255.255
        Primary WINS Server . . . . :
        Secondary WINS Server . . . :
        Lease Obtained. . . . . . . : 01 01 80 12:00:00 AM
        Lease Expires . . . . . . . : 01 01 80 12:00:00 AM

1 Ethernet adapter :


        Description . . . . . . . . : ELPC3R Ethernet Adapter

        Physical Address. . . . . . : 00-A0-24-A5-06-57
```

```
DHCP Enabled. . . . . . . . : No
IP Address. . . . . . . . . : 172.16.40.130
Subnet Mask . . . . . . . . : 255.255.255.0
Default Gateway . . . . . . : 172.16.40.1
Primary WINS Server . . . . :
Secondary WINS Server . . . :
Lease Obtained. . . . . . . :
Lease Expires . . . . . . . :
```

C:\WINDOWS>

You can review similar information on Windows 95/NT clients and servers. Verify that the host is configured properly, and then you can eliminate it as a suspect.

Depending on the traffic type transiting the router, you can check several different configuration settings. If NetBEUI traffic is running across the router, make sure that the router is properly configured for transparent or source-route bridging (SRB). If Novell type 20 NetBIOS is being used, make sure that the router has the command ipx type-20-propagation. If clients reside on a network different from the server's network, IP helper addresses and protocol forwarding must be enabled on the router.

Three elements need to be verified when troubleshooting Windows 95/NT TCP/IP problems: the host, the router, and the server.

LAN Connectivity Problems

Troubleshooting LAN connectivity was covered in part through the discussion of troubleshooting Ethernet and Token Ring problems. Those are LAN technologies. This section deals with host connectivity in relation to Cisco routers.

Obtaining an IP Address

Hosts can obtain an IP address in one of two ways: statically or dynamically. Once an IP address is configured on a host, it is assigned to that machine until the administrator removes it. Assuming that the address, mask, and gateway were configured correctly, and that it is not a duplicate IP address, the host will not have any problems connecting to the LAN that could be attributed to its IP address and configuration.

There are two protocols used to allow hosts to obtain their IP address dynamically: *Bootstrap Protocol (BootP)* and *Dynamic Host Configuration Protocol (DHCP)*.

DHCP

DHCP is a superset of the Bootstrap Protocol (BootP). This means that it uses the same protocol structure as BootP, but it has enhancements added. Both of these protocols use servers that dynamically configure clients when requested. The two major enhancements are address pools and lease times.

The process for each differs somewhat. DHCP clients broadcast a Discover message that contains the MAC address, hostname, and other options. The broadcast is sent from UDP port 67 to UDP port 68. Servers respond by sending from UDP port 68 destined to UDP port 67. When the server sends the response, it is called an Offer. The Offer includes the information sent in the client's Discover request, IP configuration information, and lease information. If the client chooses to accept the offer, it sends a Request that includes the Offer information, as well as the original Discover information. If the DHCP server is still able to grant the Offer configuration, it will send an acknowledgment to the client. If it cannot grant the Offer, it sends a Decline message to the client. Figure 6.8 gives a clearer picture of these transactions.

FIGURE 6.8 DHCP client/server sequence

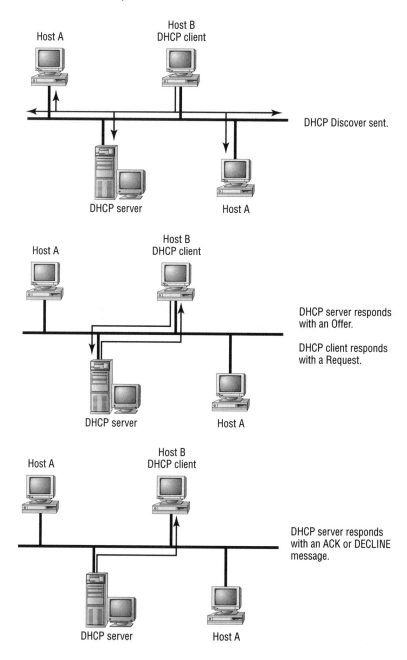

Lease information is one of the enhancements of DHCP. It allows an IP address to be assigned for a preconfigured amount of time. When the lease expires, the IP address is added back to the available address pool. Each host tries to renew the lease when the time is half-expired.

BootP

The BootP process is much simpler. When a host tries to obtain an IP address, it sends a bootrequest, which contains the client's MAC address. When the BootP server receives the request, it checks its database for the MAC address. If it finds an entry, then a bootreply, which contains the IP address and other configuration settings, is sent. If the BootP server does not find the client's MAC address in its database, it does not respond.

Troubleshooting DHCP and BootP

Because these protocols are dynamic, there may be times when they fail or when an end user is unable to connect to the network. If you have a protocol analyzer, you could capture the DHCP and BootP sequences to make sure that the clients and servers are talking.

You can also use the show commands available to aid in troubleshooting DHCP on Cisco routers.

```
Router_C#show dhcp server
DHCP Proxy Client Status:
   DHCP server: ANY (255.255.255.255)
      Leases:    0
      Offers:    0      Requests: 0      Acks: 0      Naks: 0
      Declines: 0      Releases: 0      Bad:  0

Router_C#
```

If the router is configured to use DHCP, you can also get information regarding the lease by issuing the show dhcp lease command.

ARP

Address Resolution Protocol maps Layer 2 MAC addresses to Layer 3 IP addresses. An ARP table is built on the router through the exchange of ARP requests and replies. Here is a sample ARP table:

```
Router_C>show arp
Protocol  Address          Age (min)  Hardware Addr   Type   Interface
Internet  172.16.60.1         -       0010.7bd9.2881  ARPA
    Ethernet0/1
Internet  172.16.50.2         -       0010.7bd9.2880  ARPA
    Ethernet0/0
Internet  172.16.50.1        108      0000.0c09.99cc  ARPA
    Ethernet0/0
Router_C>
```

Notice the Age field in the ARP table. ARP entries are stored or cached for future use. This allows a router to look up the MAC address, instead of having to send a broadcast to learn it again. However, the ARP entry does not stay in the table indefinitely.

Several problems could occur if a MAC address were permanently mapped to an IP address. You learned that DHCP can assign a given IP address to any requesting host, if it is available. In this scenario, the IP address could be assigned to different MAC addresses. If this were to happen, any existing entry in an ARP table would be invalidated. If a NIC is replaced on a host, the MAC address is changed as well. If the ARP cache wasn't cleared and updated, the IP address would still be mapped to the old MAC address. You get the picture. These mappings are not permanent, so the cache entries cannot be permanent either.

Sometimes problems occur within a network because of ARP problems. The best way to troubleshoot these issues is by looking at the ARP table on the router with the show arp command and (if necessary) using the debug arp tool. Problems may be fixed by simply clearing the ARP cache and allowing the router to rebuild the table.

WAN Access Problems

The function of a *wide area network (WAN)* is to connect multiple local area networks (LANs). There are several technologies and topologies for connecting LANs. Here are a few examples:

- Serial lines
- HSSI (High-Speed Serial Lines)
- ATM
- ISDN
- Frame Relay
- DDR
- POSIP (Packet over Sonet IP)

No matter what physical media, technology, or topology is used, one thing remains constant: For information to get from one LAN to another, the data has to be routed.

In order for data to be routed, certain components must be configured and must work properly. The components that will be discussed are default gateways, and static and dynamic routing. Troubleshooting methods for each of these components will be addressed in their corresponding sections.

Default Gateways

The capability of a router to route or forward data depends on its knowledge of the world around it. This knowledge comes in the form of a route table. The route table is populated by the router's own networks, as well as by advertisements received from neighboring routers. This will be covered in detail when static and dynamic routing is discussed.

What happens if a router doesn't have a route to a destination? There are two possibilities. If the router is configured to do so, it will send the packet to a neighboring router that is considered to be the default gateway, with the hope that the default gateway will know where to send the packet. If the router is not configured to do that, it will simply drop the packet.

How do you configure a router to send packets to a neighbor without a route? That is where the gateway of last resort comes in. A gateway of last resort tells the router that if it doesn't have a route to a given network, it should send the packet out the specified interface, or default gateway.

The purpose of a default gateway is somewhat of a last-ditch effort to forward a packet. Look at Figure 6.9. In this example, Router A receives a packet from Host A that is destined for network 10.1.2.0. The problem is that Router A does not have a route for 10.1.2.0. The only chance of getting the packet forwarded to network 10.1.2.0 is to send it to Router B and hope that Router B has a route to network 10.1.2.0. Router A considers Router B as its default gateway, so it sends the packet to Router B. For this example, assume that Router B does have the route and sends the packet on its way.

FIGURE 6.9 Default gateways

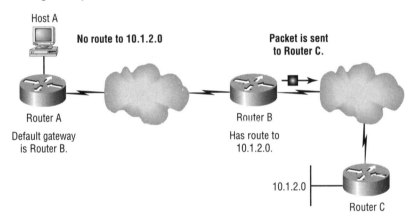

TCP/IP hosts also have default gateways set. If the default gateway for a router or a host is configured improperly, data will not be routed. Default gateways are used on TCP/IP hosts so they do not have to keep individual route tables. All hosts need to point to a router on the same network to be used as the default gateway.

When the default gateway is not working properly, whether it is on a host or on a router, the problem is probably caused by incorrect configuration.

To check for proper configuration on Windows, issue the ipconfig /all command from a DOS prompt. Here is a sample:

```
1 Ethernet adapter :

        Description . . . . . . . . : ELPC3R Ethernet Adapter
        Physical Address. . . . . . : 00-A0-24-A5-06-57
        DHCP Enabled. . . . . . . . : No
        IP Address. . . . . . . . . : 172.16.50.130
        Subnet Mask . . . . . . . . : 255.255.255.0
        Default Gateway . . . . . . : 172.16.50.1
        Primary WINS Server . . . . :
        Secondary WINS Server . . . :
        Lease Obtained. . . . . . . :
        Lease Expires . . . . . . . :
```

C:\WINDOWS>

The way to check for a default gateway on a Cisco router is to use the show ip route command. The output follows:

```
Router_C#show ip route
Codes: C - connected, S - static, I - IGRP, R - RIP, M -
mobile, B - BGP
    D - EIGRP, EX - EIGRP external, O - OSPF, IA - OSPF
    inter area
    E1 - OSPF external type 1, E2 - OSPF external type 2,
    E - EGP
    i - IS-IS, L1 - IS-IS level-1, L2 - IS-IS level-2, *
    - candidate default
        U - per-user static route

Gateway of last resort is 172.16.50.2 to network 10.1.2.0

        172.16.0.0/16 is variably subnetted, 2 subnets, 2
        masks
C       172.16.50.0/24 is directly connected, Ethernet0/0
```

```
D        172.16.30.4/30 [90/2195456] via 172.16.50.1,
00:00:18, Ethernet0/0
Router_C#

Router_B#sho ip route
Codes: C - connected, S - static, I - IGRP, R - RIP, M -
mobile, B - BGP
    D - EIGRP, EX - EIGRP external, O - OSPF, IA - OSPF
    inter area
    N1 - OSPF NSSA external type 1, N2 - OSPF NSSA
    external type 2
    E1 - OSPF external type 1, E2 - OSPF external type 2,
    E - EGP
    i - IS-IS, L1 - IS-IS level-1, L2 - IS-IS level-2, *
    - candidate default
        U - per-user static route, o - ODR

Gateway of last resort is 172.16.50.2 to network 0.0.0.0

    172.16.0.0/16 is variably subnetted, 2 subnets, 2
masks
C        172.16.50.0/24 is directly connected, Ethernet0
C        172.16.30.4/30 is directly connected, Serial0
S*  0.0.0.0/0 [1/0] via 172.16.50.2
Router_B#
```

The difference between the two examples is that one is dynamically set by using the ip default-network command, and the other is set by using a static route. Both methods end with the same results. If Router B does not have a route for a requested destination, it forwards the packet to the next hop of 172.16.50.2.

An example was given previously that demonstrated the importance of having a default gateway configured. The ping and traceroute commands can be used to isolate default gateway problems. When the router uses a dynamic method of selecting a default gateway, there is a greater possibility that it may fail.

Static and Dynamic Routing

Static routing depends solely on a manual input of routes. If you do not want to enable a routing protocol on the router, you can manually enter all the routes that you believe will be necessary; for everything else, the default gateway is used. This is a very cumbersome and poor way to configure a router. Static routes are only used locally and are not advertised to neighboring routers unless they are redistributed into a routing protocol session.

Dynamic routing is based on active routing protocols that share route information with one another. When a destination is no longer reachable, the route is removed from the routing table and the change is propagated throughout the network. If a new destination becomes available, the router adds the information into the route table and propagates the change throughout the network.

This approach is much better than static routes. If a host that is entered in the route table via a static route fails, the route remains in the route table, but the source interface changes to Null 0. If static routes are redistributed, other routers would still learn the route and send traffic there. Once the packets reach the router with the static address, the packet will be sent to Null 0—in other words, dropped.

By issuing the show ip route command, you can tell which routes are learned dynamically and which are learned statically. Here is an example:

```
Router_B>show ip route
Codes:  C-  connected, S- static, I- IGRP, R - RIP, M -
mobile, B - BGP
     D - EIGRP, EX - EIGRP external, O - OSPF, IA - OSPF
     inter area
     N1 - OSPF NSSA external type 1, N2 - OSPF NSSA
     external type 2
        E1 - OSPF external type 1, E2 - OSPF external type
        2, E - EGP
        i - IS-IS, L1 - IS-IS level-1, L2 - IS-IS level-2,
        *    - candidate default
     U - per-user static route, o - ODR

Gateway of last resort is 172.16.50.2 to network 0.0.0.0
```

```
         172.16.0.0/16 is variably subnetted, 3 subnets, 2
         masks
C        172.16.50.0/24 is directly connected, Ethernet0
D        172.16.60.0/24 [90/2195456] via 172.16.50.2,
00:31:39, Ethernet0
C        172.16.30.4/30 is directly connected, Serial0
S*   0.0.0.0/0 [1/0] via 172.16.50.2
Router_B>
```

The "S" indicates that the route is a static route. The other routes are either directly connected or learned via a routing protocol—in this case, EIGRP.

IP Access Lists

Troubleshooting access lists is a very simple task if you understand how they are written and if you are familiar with the different protocols that can be managed by using extended access lists.

Standard Access Lists

A *standard access list* is a sequential list of permit or deny statements that are based on the source IP address of a packet. When a packet reaches a router, the packet has to follow a different procedure, based on whether it's trying to enter or leave an interface. If there's an access list on the interface, the packet must go through every line in it until the packet matches the specified criteria. If the packet goes through the entire list without a match, it is dropped. For the packet to be forwarded, there has to be a permit statement at the end of the list allowing that, or else the packet will simply be dropped.

In Cisco IOS, there's an implied deny statement at the end of the access list, so if the purpose of your access list is to deny a few criteria but forward everything else, you must include a permit statement as the final line of the access list. However, you don't have to end the access list with a deny statement if the list's purpose is to permit only certain criteria and drop the rest—this is automatically understood.

Figure 6.10 shows a flowchart that describes the steps taken when a packet enters or leaves an interface.

FIGURE 6.10 Flowchart process of a standard access list

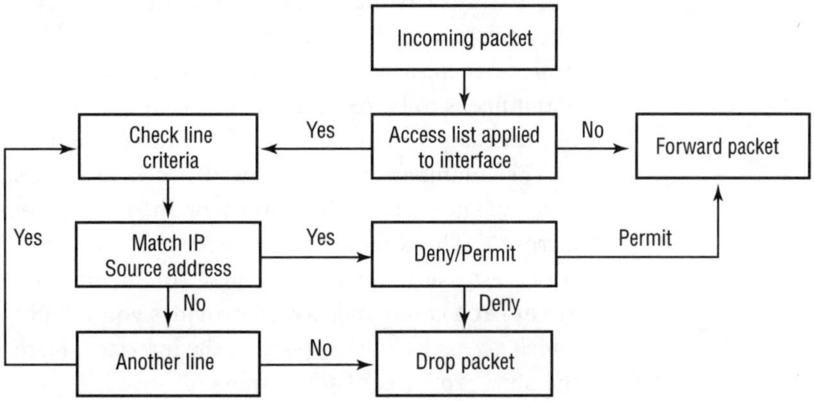

Stepping through the flowchart, you can see that the packet arrives at the specific interface through which it must enter or leave. The router's first step is to check whether there is an access list applied to the interface. If so, it passes through each line of the access list until the packet's source address matches one of the source addresses listed. If the packet fails to match any of the source addresses, it is denied. However, if the packet's source address does find a match in the list, the packet is then subjected to any condition applied on that line of the access list. The two conditional possibilities are to deny the packet or permit it. When a packet is denied, it's dropped; when it's permitted, it's forwarded to the next hop.

Exiting packets are first routed to the exiting interface and then verified by the access list, which determines whether the packet will be dropped or forwarded through the interface. Incoming packets arrive from the forwarding machine or router, and are then checked against the access list. If the packet is permitted by the list, the packet is accepted through the interface and forwarded to the exit interface.

This is important information to understand when troubleshooting any access list. It does depend on whether the packet is incoming or outgoing, so you can tell which interfaces to look at and analyze access lists for.

Troubleshooting standard access lists is very simple because they are based on only one criterion, the source IP address. The basic method of troubleshooting an access list is to read it line-by-line, and analyze it to determine whether any lines are out of order or typed incorrectly.

If, after analyzing the access list, you can't see any problems but the problem is still occurring, you can temporarily remove the access list from the interface to see what effect this has on the problem. If the problem disappears after the access list is removed, something is wrong with the access list and it needs to be fixed. If the problem does not go away with the removal of the access list from the interface, you can eliminate it as a possible cause.

The commands used to view IP access lists are simply show running-config, show startup-config, or show ip access-list <access-list number>. These commands provide the information regarding each line of the access list. In addition to these commands, you can issue the show ip interface command, which provides you with information regarding which access lists are applied to the interface. Here is a sample output from the show ip interface command:

```
Router_B>show ip interface
Ethernet0 is up, line protocol is up
  Internet address is 172.16.50.1/24
  Broadcast address is 255.255.255.255
  Address determined by non-volatile memory
  MTU is 1500 bytes
  Helper address is not set
  Directed broadcast forwarding is disabled
  Multicast reserved groups joined: 224.0.0.10
  Outgoing access list is not set
  Inbound  access list is not set
  Proxy ARP is enabled
  Security level is default
  Split horizon is enabled
  ICMP redirects are always sent
  ICMP unreachables are always sent
  ICMP mask replies are never sent
  IP fast switching is enabled
  IP fast switching on the same interface is disabled
  IP multicast fast switching is disabled
  Router Discovery is disabled
  IP output packet accounting is disabled
  IP access violation accounting is disabled
```

```
TCP/IP header compression is disabled
Probe proxy name replies are disabled
Gateway Discovery is disabled
Policy routing is disabled
```

As you can see from this output, interface Ethernet0 does not have any access lists applied to it.

Extended Access Lists

Extended access lists offer filtering on port numbers, session-layer protocols, and destination addresses, in addition to filtering by source address. Although all these extended filtering features make this kind of access list much more powerful, they can also be more difficult to troubleshoot because of their potential complexity.

A packet must follow the same basic process when arriving at an interface with an extended access list applied to it as it does when confronting an interface with an applied standard list. Figure 6.11 illustrates the procedure that a packet follows when being compared against an extended list—the only difference is the much greater scope of criteria that are specifiable.

FIGURE 6.11   Packet processing through an extended access list

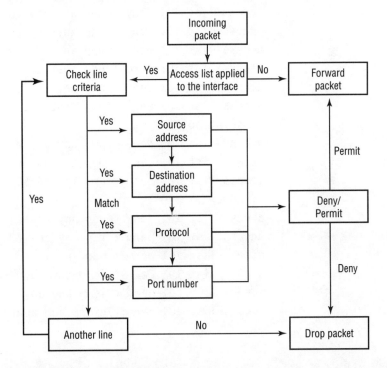

The same procedures and commands that are used to analyze standard access lists apply to extended access lists. The only difference is the different criteria that can be used with extended access lists.

In addition to correctly analyzing the lines of the access list, you must know which way the list is applied to the interface. By conceptualizing the packet flow through an interface and the subsequent access list, you will be successful in troubleshooting access list–related problems. Here is a sample extended access list:

```
access-list 101 deny    tcp any any eq chargen
access-list 101 deny    tcp any any eq daytime
access-list 101 deny    tcp any any eq discard
access-list 101 deny    tcp any any eq echo
access-list 101 deny    tcp any any eq finger
access-list 101 deny    tcp any any eq kshell
access-list 101 deny    tcp any any eq klogin
access-list 101 deny    tcp any any eq 37
access-list 101 deny    tcp any any eq uucp
access-list 101 deny    udp any any eq biff
access-list 101 deny    udp any any eq bootpc
access-list 101 deny    udp any any eq bootps
access-list 101 deny    udp any any eq discard
access-list 101 deny    udp any any eq netbios-dgm
access-list 101 deny    udp any any eq netbios-ns
access-list 101 permit udp host 172.16.10.2 any eq snmp
access-list 101 deny    udp any any eq snmp
access-list 101 permit udp host 172.16.10.2 any eq
    snmptrap
access-list 101 deny    udp any any eq snmptrap
access-list 101 deny    udp any any eq who
access-list 101 permit udp 172.16.50.0 0.0.0.255 any eq
    xdmcp
access-list 101 deny    udp any any eq xdmcp
access-list 101 permit tcp any any
access-list 101 permit udp any any
access-list 101 permit icmp any any
access-list 101 permit igmp any any
access-list 101 permit eigrp any any
```

As you can see, there are many line options that need to be understood when troubleshooting extended access lists. Not only do you have to understand the significance of the line, but you have to be familiar with the protocol you are troubleshooting. If necessary, debug options can be used in conjunction with access lists to isolate and diagnose network failures.

ICMP Messages

*I*nternet Control Message Protocol is used to provide information to TCP/IP devices regarding packet status, errors, and overall network congestion. This is the protocol used by `ping` and `traceroute`.

These messages are useful because they explain what is happening on the network. If you try to connect to a remote host and get a Destination Unreachable or Port Unreachable message, it is ICMP informing you that it was unable to connect to the remote host.

ICMP uses several different packet types and codes. Table 6.3 lists some of the types and their corresponding meanings. Some types have subsets called codes; they are listed below their corresponding ICMP types.

TABLE 6.3   ICMP Types and Codes

ICMP Type	ICMP Code	Description
0		Echo Reply
3		Destination Unreachable
	0	Net Unreachable
	1	Host Unreachable
	2	Protocol Unreachable
	3	Port Unreachable
	4	Fragmentation Needed and Don't Fragment Was Set
	5	Source Route Failed
	6	Destination Network Unknown
	7	Destination Host Unknown

TABLE 6.3 ICMP Types and Codes *(continued)*

ICMP Type	ICMP Code	Description
	8	Source Host Isolated
	9	Communication with Destination Network Is Administratively Prohibited
	10	Communication with Destination Host is Administratively Prohibited
	11	Destination Network Unreachable for Type of Service
	12	Destination Host Unreachable for Type of Service
	13	Communication Administratively Prohibited
	14	Host Precedence Violation
	15	Precedence Cutoff in Effect
4		Source Quench
5		Redirect
	0	Redirect Datagram for the Network
	1	Redirect Datagram for the Host
	2	Redirect Datagram for the Type of Service and Network
	3	Redirect Datagram for the Type of Service and Host
6		Alternate Host Address
8		Echo
9		Router Advertisement
10		Router Selection
11		Time Exceeded
30		traceroute

These types and codes allow ICMP to communicate network status and information among hosts and routers. ICMP is a very useful protocol in the troubleshooting arsenal.

Troubleshooting RIP

RIP was first designed for Xerox. The protocol, known as *routed*, was later used in UNIX. Thereafter, RIP was implemented as a TCP/IP routing protocol. RIP is used by most versions of Novell NetWare for routing. Other protocols have been derived from RIP.

RIP1 and RIP2

The original version of RIP (RIP1) had several limitations that restricted its use and scalability. Problems such as the frequent routing updates and limited hop-count needed to be overcome.

RIP uses UDP broadcasts to flood route updates. Every router floods the network with its update. RIP also features split horizon and poison reverse updates to prevent routing loops. RIP updates every 30 seconds and has a hop-count limit of 16 hops.

RIP2 functions in much the same way as RIP1, but with a few enhancements. RIP2 supports classless routing (CIDR), route summarization, and variable length subnet masks (VLSM).

show Commands

The show commands that are useful for troubleshooting RIP1 and RIP2 are listed in Table 6.4.

TABLE 6.4 RIP-Related show Commands

Command	Description
show ip route rip	Displays the RIP route table
show ip route	Displays the IP route table
show ip interface	Displays IP interface configuration
show running-config	Displays the running configuration

debug Commands

The `debug` command should always be used with caution and, in many circumstances, as a last resort. If the previous `show` commands do not provide you with enough information to isolate and resolve the RIP problem, you can enable the debug tool.

The syntax for the debug mode in RIP is `debug ip rip events`. If you need even more general RIP information, use the global form of the command, `debug ip rip`. This command provides you with all possible RIP protocol information.

Typical Problems

Because RIP uses UDP broadcasts by default, it can cause network congestion or broadcast storms if not configured correctly. The way to avoid this problem is to configure RIP to allow unicast updates. This is done with the `neighbor` statement from within the RIP protocol configuration mode. In addition to using the `neighbor` statement, specified interfaces can be made `passive-interfaces`. This means that routing updates are not sent out to the specified interfaces. Frequent routing updates can also cause network congestion. This can be controlled or remedied by adjusting the various RIP timers.

Problems can also occur due to version mismatches. By default, Cisco routers can understand both versions, but they advertise and forward data using RIP1. It is possible to configure interfaces to send and receive only one version. The problem occurs when the RIP versions on the two connected interfaces do not match.

For example, if Router A's interfaces are configured to send and receive only RIP2, and Router B's interfaces are configured to listen and speak RIP1, the two routers won't be able to share RIP information. This problem can be resolved by analyzing the interface configuration on both routers and changing them so they match.

Troubleshooting IGRP

IGRP is a Cisco proprietary routing protocol that uses a distance vector algorithm because it uses a vector (a one-dimensional array) of information to calculate the best path. This vector consists of four elements:

- Bandwidth
- Delay
- Load
- Reliability

MTU, or maximum transmission unit, information is included in the final route information, but it's not used as part of the vector of metrics. Each element will be described in detail in a little while.

IGRP is intended to replace RIP and create a stable, quickly converging protocol that scales with increased network growth. As mentioned, it's preferable to implement a link-state protocol in large networks because of the high overhead and delay that result from using a distance vector protocol.

IGRP has several features included in the algorithm—these features and a brief description of each can be found in Table 6.5. These features were added to make IGRP more stable, and a few were created to deal with routing updates and to make network convergence happen more quickly.

TABLE 6.5   IGRP Features

Feature	Description
Configurable metrics	Metrics (or variables in the equation) may be configured by the user.
Flash updates	Updates are sent out prior to the default time setting. Updates occur when the metrics for a route change.
Poison reverse updates	These are implemented to prevent routing loops. The updates place a route in holddown. (Holddown means that the router won't accept any new route information on a given route for a certain period of time.)
Unequal-cost load balancing	This feature allows packets to be shared/distributed across multiple paths.

IGRP is a classfull protocol, which means that it doesn't include any subnet information about the network with route information. Three types of routes are recognized by IGRP:

Interior   Networks that are directly connected to a router interface.

System   Routes are advertised by other IGRP neighbors within the same AS (autonomous system). The AS number identifies the IGRP session because it's possible for a router to have multiple IGRP sessions.

Exterior   Routes are learned via IGRP from a different AS number, which provides information used by the router to set the gateway of last resort. (The gateway of last resort is the path a packet takes if a specific route isn't found on the router.)

show Commands

The show commands that are useful for troubleshooting IGRP are listed in Table 6.6.

TABLE 6.6   IGRP show Commands

Command	Description
show running-config	Displays the current configuration
show ip route igrp	Displays IGRP routes only
show ip route	Displays the entire route table

debug Commands

IGRP events—as well as the protocol itself—can be analyzed by the debug tool. To watch IGRP events and protocol communications, you can enter the following debug commands:

- debug ip igrp events
- debug ip igrp transactions

Depending on the problem or the activity within IP, these commands can produce a great number of messages being logged to the console and the router's logging buffer.

Typical Problems

Because IGRP is a distance-vector protocol, you will not encounter problems with neighbor relationships or different databases that link-state protocols use.

For IGRP, the most typical problems are caused by access lists, improper configuration, or the line to an adjacent router being down. The easiest way to tell if the router is receiving and sending IGRP information is to use the two debugging tools.

The primary symptom of a problem with IGRP is the lack of IGRP learned routes. This can be verified through the use of the show commands listed in Table 6.6.

Troubleshooting EIGRP

Enhanced IGRP was created to resolve some of the problems with IGRP. These problems include the fact that the entire route table is sent when changes are made in the network, and that there is a lack of formal neighbor relationships with connected routers. EIGRP is a hybrid of both link-state and distance-vector routing algorithms, which brings the best of both worlds together.

EIGRP allows for equal-cost load balancing, incremental routing updates, and formal neighbor relationships, overcoming the limitations of IGRP. This enhanced version uses the same distance-vector information as IGRP, yet with a different algorithm. EIGRP uses DUAL (diffused update algorithm) for metric calculation.

EIGRP's specific features are detailed in Table 6.7. The features offered by EIGRP make it a stable and scalable protocol. EIGRP is also a Cisco proprietary protocol.

TABLE 6.7 EIGRP Features

Feature	Description
Route tagging	Distinguishes routes learned via different EIGRP sessions.
Formal neighbor relationships	Uses the Hello protocol to establish peering.

TABLE 6.7 EIGRP Features *(continued)*

Feature	Description
Incremental routing updates	Advertises only changes, instead of the entire route table.
Classless routing	Supports subnet and VLSM information.
Configurable metrics	Allows metric information to be set through configuration commands.
Equal-cost load balancing	Allows traffic to be sent equally across multiple connections.

To aid in the calculation of the best route and load sharing, EIGRP utilizes several databases of information. These databases are as follows:

- The route database, where the best routes are stored

- The topology database, where all route information resides

- A neighbor table that is used to house information concerning other EIGRP neighbors

Each of these databases exists for IP-EIGRP, IPX-EIGRP, and AT-EIGRP or AppleTalk-EIGRP. Therefore, it is possible for EIGRP to have nine active databases when all three protocols are configured on the router.

Neighbor Formation

The manner in which EIGRP establishes and maintains neighbor relationships is derived through its link-state properties. EIGRP uses the Hello protocol (similar to OSPF) to establish and maintain peering relationships with directly connected routers. Hello packets are sent between EIGRP routers to determine the state of the connection between them. Once the neighbor relation is established via the Hello protocol, the routers can exchange route information.

Each router establishes a neighbor table, in which it stores important information regarding the neighbors that are directly connected. The information consists of the neighbor's IP address, hold time interval, smooth round-trip timer (SRTT), and queue information. These data are used to help determine when the link state changes.

When two routers initialize communication, their entire route tables are shared. Thereafter, only changes to the route table are propagated. These changes are shared with all directly connected EIGRP-speaking routers. Each of these steps is summarized below.

1. Hello packets are multicast out all of the router's interfaces.

2. Replies to the Hello packets include all routes in the neighbor router's topology database, including the metrics. Routes that are learned from the originating router are not included in the reply.

3. The originating router acknowledges the update to each neighbor via an ACK packet.

4. The topology database is then updated with the newly received information.

5. Once the topology database is updated, the originating router then advertises its entire table to all the new neighbors.

6. Neighbor routers acknowledge the receipt of the route information from the originating router by sending back an ACK packet.

These steps are used in the initialization of EIGRP neighbors and change somewhat only when updates are sent to existing neighbors.

show Commands

Due to the complexity of EIGRP, there are several more show commands available to aid in troubleshooting EIGRP problems. The majority of the commands are listed in Table 6.8.

TABLE 6.8 EIGRP show Commands

Command	Description / Output
show running-config	Displays the current configuration.
show ip route	Displays the full IP route table.
show ip route eigrp	Displays the EIGRP routes.
show ip eigrp interfaces	Displays EIGRP peer information for that interface.
show ip eigrp neighbors	Displays all EIGRP neighbors, along with summary information about each neighbor.
show ip eigrp topology	Displays the contents of the EIGRP topology table.
show ip eigrp traffic	Displays a summary of EIGRP routing statistics, such as the number of Hellos and routing updates.
show ip eigrp events	Displays a log of the most recent EIGRP protocol events. This information includes the insertion and removal of routes from the route table, updates, and neighbor status.

debug Commands

There are also several debug commands within EIGRP that allow you to specify what processes you want to debug. Here is a list of commands:

- debug ip eigrp <AS number>

- debug ip eigrp neighbor

- debug ip eigrp notifications

- debug ip eigrp summary

- debug ip eigrp

Here is a sample of the information that can be obtained by using these commands:

```
Router_C#debug ip eigrp
IP-EIGRP Route Events debugging is on
IP-EIGRP: Processing incoming QUERY packet
IP-EIGRP: Int 172.16.30.4/30 M 4294967295 - 0 4294967295
SM 4294967295 - 0 4294967295
IP-EIGRP: 172.16.30.4/30 routing table not updated
IP-EIGRP: 172.16.30.4/30, - do advertise out Ethernet0/0
IP-EIGRP: Int 172.16.30.4/30 metric 4294967295 - 1657856
4294967295
IP-EIGRP: Processing incoming UPDATE packet
IP-EIGRP: Int 172.16.30.4/30 M 2195456 - 1657856 537600 SM
2169856 - 1657856 512000
IP-EIGRP: Int 172.16.30.4/30 metric 2195456 - 1657856
537600
IP-EIGRP: Processing incoming QUERY packet
IP-EIGRP: Int 172.16.30.4/30 M 4294967295 - 0 4294967295
SM 4294967295 - 0 4294967295
IP-EIGRP: 172.16.30.4/30 routing table not updated
IP-EIGRP: 172.16.30.4/30, - do advertise out Ethernet0/0
IP-EIGRP: Int 172.16.30.4/30 metric 4294967295 - 1657856
4294967295
IP-EIGRP: Processing incoming UPDATE packet
IP-EIGRP: Int 172.16.30.4/30 M 2195456 - 1657856 537600 SM
2169856 - 1657856 512000
IP-EIGRP: Int 172.16.30.4/30 metric 2195456 - 1657856
537600
```

You can see from this information when routes are removed from the route table and they are no longer advertised. Once the route is advertised to the router, it inserts the route back into the route table and commences advertisement.

Typical Problems

Some of the typical problems with EIGRP are the loss of neighbor adjacencies, lost routes in earlier versions of IOS™, and lost default gateways.

Neighbor failures can be attributed to link failures, just as much as they can be attributed to software problems. If a neighbor relation has problems establishing, use the proper debug command to see what is occurring between both routers.

When troubleshooting an EIGRP problem, it is always a good idea to get a picture of the network. The most relevant picture is provided by the show ip eigrp neighbors command. This command shows all adjacent routers that share route information within a given autonomous system. If neighbors are missing, check the configuration and link status on both routers to verify that the protocol has been configured correctly.

If all neighbors are present, verify the routes learned. By executing the show ip route eigrp command, you gain a quick picture of the routes in the route table. If the route does not appear in the route table, verify the source of the route. If the source is functioning properly, check the topology table.

The topology table is displayed by using the show ip eigrp topology command. If the route is in the topology table, it is safe to assume that there is a problem between the topology database and the route table. There must be a reason why the topology database is not injecting the route into the route table.

Other commands, such as show ip eigrp traffic, can be used to see whether updates are being sent. If the counters for EIGRP input and output packets don't increase, no EIGRP information is being sent between peers.

The show ip eigrp events command is an undocumented command. This command displays a log of every EIGRP event—when routes are injected and removed from the route table, and when EIGRP adjacencies reset or fail. This information can be used to see whether there are routing instabilities in the network.

Troubleshooting OSPF

OSPF differs from IGRP and Enhanced IGRP because it is a pure link-state routing technology. Also, it is an open standard routing protocol, which means that it was not developed solely by Cisco. OSPF was designed and developed by the IETF to provide a scalable, quickly converging, and efficient routing protocol that can be used by all routing equipment. Complete details for OSPF are found in RFC2178.

Areas are used within OSPF to define a group of routers and networks belonging to the same OSPF session. Links connect routers, and the information about each link is defined by its link state. On each broadcast or multi-access network segment, two routers must be assigned the responsibilities of designated router (DR) and backup designated router (BDR).

Like EIGRP, OSPF maintains three databases: adjacency, topology, and route. The adjacency database is similar to the neighbor database used by EIGRP. It contains all information about OSPF neighbors and the links connecting them. The topology database maintains all route information. The best routes from the topology database are placed in the route database, or route table.

Neighbor and Adjacency Formation

The Hello protocol is used to establish peering sessions between routers. Hello packets are multicast out every interface. The information that is multicast includes the router ID, timing intervals, existing neighbors, area identification, router priority, designated and backup router information, authentication password, and stub area information. All this information is used when establishing new peers. Descriptions of each element can be found in Table 6.9.

TABLE 6.9 OSPF Multicast Information

Information	Description
Router ID	Highest active IP address on the router.
Time intervals	Intervals between Hello packets, and the allowed dead time interval.
Existing neighbors	Addresses for any existing OSPF neighbors.

TABLE 6.9 OSPF Multicast Information *(continued)*

Information	Description
Area identification	OSPF area number and link information, which must be the same for a peering session to be established.
Router priority	Value assigned to a router and used when choosing the DR and BDR.
DR and BDR	If they have already been chosen, their Router ID and address is contained in the Hello packet.
Authentication password	All peers must have the same authentication password if authentication is enabled.
Stub area flag	This is a special area—two routers must share the same stub information. This is not necessary to initiate a regular peering session with another OSPF router.

Figure 6.12 displays a flowchart that depicts each step of the initialization process. The process starts by sending out Hello packets. Every listening router then adds the originating router to the adjacency database. The responding routers reply with all of their Hello information so that the originating router can add them to its adjacency table.

FIGURE 6.12 OSPF peer initialization

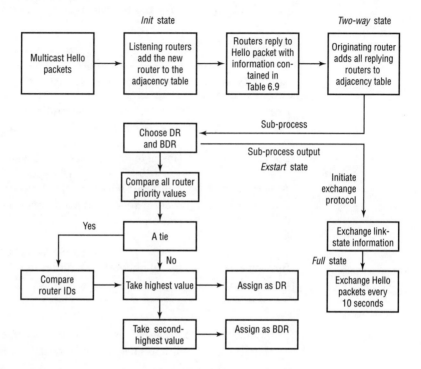

OSPF Area Types

OSPF uses areas in place of an autonomous system. An OSPF area consists of a group of routers or interfaces on a router that is assigned to a common area.

OSPF also allows and uses different area types. When deploying OSPF, there must be a backbone area. Standard and stub areas connect to the backbone area. Below is a list of each router type, followed by a short description of the area type.

Backbone   This area accepts all LSAs and is used to connect multiple areas.

Stub   This area does not accept any external routing update, but it accepts summary LSAs.

Totally Stub   These areas are closed off from accepting external or summary advertisements.

Standard   This is the normal area that accepts internal and external LSAs, and summary information.

Multiple router types can exist within an OSPF area. Table 6.10 lists all of the OSPF router types and the role that each plays within the area.

TABLE 6.10 OSPF Router Types

Router Type	Description of Responsibility
Internal	All interfaces are defined on the same area. All internal routers have an identical link-state database.
Backbone	Has at least one interface assigned to area 0.
Area Border Router (ABR)	Interfaces are connected to multiple OSPF areas. Information specific to each area is stored on this type of router.
Autonomous System Border Router (ASBR)	This type of router has an interface connected to an external network or a different AS.

In addition to the previous responsibilities, a router can also be assigned additional responsibilities. These additions are assumed when a router is assigned the role of DR or BDR.

show Commands

Due to the complexity of OSPF, several show commands are available to provide information regarding the configuration and functionality of OSPF on a router. Table 6.11 lists most of the available OSPF-related show commands.

TABLE 6.11 OSPF show Commands

Command	Description / Output
show running-config	Displays the current router configuration.
show ip route	Displays the entire IP route table.
show ip route ospf	Displays OSPF routes.
show ip ospf	Displays information for OSPF.

TABLE 6.11 OSPF show Commands *(continued)*

Command	Description / Output
show ip ospf <process-id>	Displays information relevant to the specified process ID.
show ip ospf border-routers	Displays the routers that join different areas, or border routers.
show ip ospf database	Provides an OSPF database summary.
show ip ospf interface	Displays OSPF information on a interface.
show ip ospf neighbor	Displays OSPF neighbor information.
show ip ospf request-list	Displays link-state request list.
show ip ospf retransmission list	Displays link-state retransmission list.
show ip ospf summary-address	Displays summary-address redistribution information.
show ip ospf virtual-links	Displays virtual link information.
show ip interface	Displays IP interface settings.

These commands provide you with a great amount of information valuable for troubleshooting OSPF routing problems.

debug Commands

OSPF runs many processes to maintain all of its databases, routing updates, and peering connections. Most of these processes use Link-State Advertisements (LSAs) to share information.

Let's briefly explore the different types of Link-State Advertisements. LSAs are the heart of OSPF's information exchange. Different types of LSAs represent different types of route information. All of the LSA types are summarized in Table 6.12.

TABLE 6.12 OSPF LSA Types

LSA Type	Description of LSA
(1) Router link entry	This LSA is broadcast only within its defined area. The LSA contains all of the default link-state information.
(2) Network entry	This LSA is multicast to all area routers by the DR. This update contains network-specific information.
(3/4) Summary entry	Type 3 LSAs contain route information for internal networks and are sent to backbone routers. Type 4 LSAs contain information about ASBRs. Summary information is multicast by the ABR, and the information reaches all backbone routers.
(5) Autonomous system entry	As the name indicates, these advertisements originate from the ASBR. These packets contain information about external networks.
(7) NSSA autonomous system entry	Not So Stubby Area (NSSA) permits Type 7 AS external routers to be imported inside the NSSA area by redistribution.

Different LSA types represent the type of route that is being advertised, and they assist in restricting the number and types of routes that are accepted by a given area. As is shown in the table, an LSA of type 5 is only sent by the Autonomous System Border Router.

Now, let's look at the available debug options for OSPF:

debug ip ospf adj   Provides debug information about events concerning adjacency relationships with other OSPF routers.

debug ip ospf events   Provides debug information for all OSPF events.

debug ip ospf flood   Provides information about OSPF flooding. (Flooding is the way that an OSPF router sends updates.) It broadcasts a change in its route table, and all other members of the OSPF area receive the update.

debug ip ospf lsa-generation   Gives detailed information regarding the generation of LSA messages.

debug ip ospf packet   Gives detailed information regarding OSPF packets.

debug ip ospf retransmission   If OSPF has to retransmit information, it triggers a retransmission event that debug captures and echoes to the console.

debug ip ospf spf   Provides debug information for all SPF transactions. By enabling SPF debugging, OSPF events debugging is also turned on.

debug ip ospf tree   Provides information for the OSPF database tree.

Following is a debug ip ospf trace. Notice that OSPF event debugging was turned on as well (lines 2 through 3 of the output). SPF is an algorithm used to select the best route to each destination.

```
Router_A#debug ip ospf spf
OSPF spf intra events debugging is on
OSPF spf inter events debugging is on
OSPF spf external events debugging is on
Router_A#
%LINEPROTO-5-UPDOWN: Line protocol on Interface Serial1,
changed state to down
%LINK-3-UPDOWN: Interface Serial1, changed state to down
OSPF: running SPF for area 0
OSPF: Initializing to run spf
```

```
It is a router LSA 172.16.40.1. Link Count 1
  Processing link 0, id 172.16.30.4, link data
255.255.255.252, type 3
  Add better path to LSA ID 172.16.30.7, gateway
172.16.30.4, dist 64
  Add path fails: no output interface to 172.16.30.4,
next hop 0.0.0.0
OSPF: Adding Stub nets
OSPF: Path left undeleted to 172.16.30.4
OSPF: Entered old delete routine
OSPF: No ndb for STUB NET old route 172.16.60.0, mask /24,
next hop 172.16.30.6
OSPF: No ndb for STUB NET old route 172.16.30.4, mask /30,
next hop 172.16.30.5
OSPF: No ndb for NET old route 172.16.50.0, mask /24, next
hop 172.16.30.6
OSPF: delete lsa id 172.16.60.255, type 0, adv rtr
172.16.60.1 from delete list
OSPF: delete lsa id 172.16.30.7, type 0, adv rtr
172.16.40.1 from delete list
OSPF: delete lsa id 172.16.50.1, type 2, adv rtr
172.16.50.1 from delete list
OSPF: running spf for summaries area 0
OSPF: sum_delete_old_routes area 0
OSPF: Started Building Type 5 External Routes
OSPF: ex_delete_old_routes
OSPF: Started Building Type 7 External Routes
OSPF: ex_delete_old_routes
%LINK-3-UPDOWN: Interface Serial1, changed state to up
%LINEPROTO-5-UPDOWN: Line protocol on Interface Serial1,
changed state to up
OSPF: running SPF for area 0
OSPF: Initializing to run spf
 It is a router LSA 172.16.40.1. Link Count 1
  Processing link 0, id 172.16.30.4, link data
255.255.255.252, type 3
  Add better path to LSA ID 172.16.30.7, gateway
172.16.30.4, dist 64
  Add path: next-hop 172.16.30.5, interface Serial1
OSPF: Adding Stub nets
```

```
OSPF: insert route list LS ID 172.16.30.7, type 0, adv rtr
172.16.40.1
OSPF: Entered old delete routine
OSPF: running spf for summaries area 0
OSPF: sum_delete_old_routes area 0
OSPF: Started Building Type 5 External Routes
OSPF: ex_delete_old_routes
OSPF: Started Building Type 7 External Routes
OSPF: ex_delete_old_routes
```

This is a lot of information over a very short period. You can get an idea of what the CPU goes through when there is a link-state change in a OSPF network.

Typical Problems

Because of the great number of processes and calculations that the CPU has to make when changes occur in an OSPF network, the router can become overwhelmed with all the processing that has to be done. The bigger the OSPF network, the more calculations have to be done, not to mention the greater probability of changes that need to be propagated throughout the network.

A general rule of thumb is to not add more than 100 routers per area, and to not have more than 700 routers throughout the network. It is possible to have smaller or larger networks, but the numbers here are given simply as a guideline.

The more links that exist in a network, the greater the probability of instability. When a large network experiences instability, the routers have to spend a great deal of time and CPU cycles processing link and route updates.

Another problem common to OSPF is wrongly configured wildcard masks in the OSPF network statements. OSPF uses wildcard bits to specify the networks that should be advertised instead of using multiple network statements. Either approach works, but be aware of the wildcard mask problems.

Redistribution of Routing Protocols

When multiple routing protocols are used within a network and they need to be redistributed into one another, it is important that it be done correctly by assigning the proper metrics through the redistribution. If protocols are redistributed without metric adjustment, many networking problems can occur.

Although redistribution allows multiple protocols to share routing information, it can result in routing loops, slow convergence, and inconsistent route information. This is caused by the different algorithms and methods used by each protocol. It is not a good practice to redistribute bidirectionally (if, for example, you have both IGRP 100 and EIGRP 200 routing sessions running on your router). Bidirectional redistribution occurs if you enter redistribution commands under each protocol session. Here is an example:

```
Router_A#config t
Enter configuration commands, one per line.  End with
CNTL/Z.
Router_A(config)#router igrp 100
Router_A(config-router)#redistribute eigrp 200
Router_A(config-router)#router eigrp 200
Router_A(config-router)#redistribute igrp 100
Router_A(config-router)#^Z
Router_A#
```

When a route from RIP, IGRP, or OSPF is injected into another routing protocol, the route loses its identity and its metrics are converted from the original format to the other protocol's format. This can cause confusion within the router. The method of ensuring that the metric is converted properly is done through metric commands.

Dealing with Routing Metrics

The router in which multiple protocols or sessions meet is called the *autonomous system boundary router (ASBR)*. When routes from one protocol or session are injected or redistributed into another protocol or session, the routes are tagged as external routes. Let's look at a simple example of a route table that has external routes:

```
Router_X#sho ip route eigrp
     172.16.0.0/16 is variably subnetted, 301 subnets, 10
     masks
D EX    172.16.27.230/32
             [170/24827392] via 172.16.131.82, 02:33:32,
             ATM6          0/0.3114
D EX    172.16.237.16/29
             [170/40542208] via 172.16.131.82, 23:40:32,
             ATM6          0/0.3114
             [170/40542208] via 172.16.131.74, 23:40:32,
             ATM6          0/0.3113
D EX    172.16.237.24/29
             [170/40542208] via 172.16.131.82, 23:40:32,
             ATM6          0/0.3114
             [170/40542208] via 172.16.131.74, 23:40:32,
             ATM6          0/0.3113
D EX    172.16.52.192/26
         [170/2202112] via 172.16.131.82, 23:40:27, ATM6
         0/0.3114
D EX    172.16.41.216/29
             [170/46232832] via 172.16.131.82, 23:40:28,
             ATM6          0/0.3114
D EX    172.16.38.200/30
         [170/2176512] via 172.16.131.82, 23:40:27, ATM6
         0/0.3114
D EX    172.16.237.0/29
             [170/40542208] via 172.16.131.82, 23:40:32,
             ATM6          0/0.3114
             [170/40542208] via 172.16.131.74, 23:40:32,
             ATM6          0/0.3113
D       172.16.236.0/24
         [90/311808] via 172.16.131.82, 23:40:32, ATM6/0
         0.3114
         [90/311808] via 172.16.131.74, 23:40:32, ATM6/0
         0.3113
D       172.16.235.0/24
         [90/311808] via 172.16.131.82, 23:40:32, ATM6/0
         0.3114
```

IGRP and EIGRP

Each protocol has its own method of route redistribution. You must be familiar with each protocol's implementation of route redistribution and default-metric settings.

IGRP and EIGRP use the same command to adjust metrics. It is done through the `default-metric` command. Here is an example:

`default-metric` *bandwidth delay reliability load MTU*

This command takes the metrics for the protocol being injected into IGRP or EIGRP, and converts them directly to values that IGRP or EIGRP can use. The *bandwidth* is the capacity of the link; *delay* is the time in microseconds; *reliability* and *load* are values from 1 to 255; and *MTU* is the maximum transmission unit in bytes.

Finally, you can also change the distance values that are assigned to EIGRP (90 internal; 170 external). The distance value tells the router which protocol to believe. The lower the distance value, the more believable the protocol. The administrative distance values for EIGRP are changed with the following command from within the EIGRP session:

`distance eigrp` *internal-distance external-distance*

Internal distance and external distance have a range of values from 1 to 255.

Remember that a value of 255 tells the router to ignore the route. So, unless you want the routes from the protocol to be ignored, never use the value of 255.

This can be a source of problems when troubleshooting routing problems. If multiple protocols advertise the same routes, it is possible that differences in the administrative distance may cause the route to be learned by the wrong protocol, and thus it is not propagated correctly throughout the network.

Metrics used by EIGRP are the same as those used by IGRP. As with IGRP, metrics decide how the routes are selected. The higher the metric associated with a route, the less desirable the route is. The overall metric assigned to a route is created by the Bellman-Ford algorithm, using the following equation:

$$CM = [\frac{K_1}{Be} + (K_2 \times Dc)]\, r$$

In this equation,

- *CM* is the composite metric assigned to the route.

- K_1 and K_2 are equation constants.

- *Be* is the bandwidth capacity. This is the capacity without any traffic.

- *Dc* is the delay associated with the link to the next hop in the path to the network.

- *r* is the reliability of the physical link. If a circuit has several outages, this is calculated into the composite metric.

Just as with IGRP, you can set these metrics manually from within the Configuration mode. Details on how to change metrics will be explained after we discuss how EIGRP is configured.

OSPF

The metrics associated with OSPF are different from those associated with IGRP and EIGRP. OSPF uses bandwidth as the main metric in selecting a route. The cost is calculated by using the bandwidth for the link. The equation is 100,000 divided by the bandwidth. You may change bandwidth on the individual interface.

The cost is manipulated by changing the value to a number within the range of 1 to 65,535. Because the cost is assigned to each link, the value must be changed on each interface. The command to do this follows:

```
ip ospf cost
```

Cisco bases link cost on bandwidth. Other vendors may use other metrics to calculate the link's cost. When connecting links between routers from different vendors, you may have to adjust the cost to match the other router. Both routers must assign the same cost to the link for OSPF to work.

You can configure the OSPF distance with the following command:

```
distance ospf [external | Intra-area | Inter-area]
distance
```

This command allows the distance metric to be defined for external OSPF, and intra-area and inter-area routes. (Intra-area and inter-area routes are discussed in the "Configuring OSPF" subsection.) Distance values range from 1 to 255—and the lower the distance, the better.

Other values important to OSPF's operation are not actually metrics, but can be configured as well. Values such as the router ID and router priority are important in router initialization and for DR and BDR selection. You can change these values with some minor configuration changes.

To change the router priority, use the following command on the desired interface:

```
ip ospf priority number
```

The *number* can range from 0 to 255—the higher value indicates a higher priority when choosing the DR and BDR for the area.

Just as with EIGRP, new metrics must be assigned to route information that is injected into the OSPF session. The command is much simpler than the command used when assigning metrics for EIGRP or IGRP—it is almost the same, but only one metric is assigned. The value of the metric is the cost for the route.

```
default-metric cost
```

Distribute Lists

Distribute lists are access lists applied to an interface from within a routing protocol. The purpose of a distribute list is to control which routes are advertised to adjacent routers.

Problems can occur if distribute lists are missing or improperly configured. Figure 6.13 shows a picture of three meshed routers. Undesired routing can occur if the advertised routes are not controlled through the use of distribute lists.

FIGURE 6.13 Distribute lists to prevent routing loops

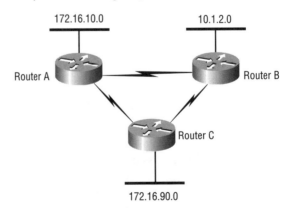

Router A and Router B are core level routers. Router C is a small access router. The potential problem is that Router A could learn about network 10.1.2.0 via Router C instead of Router B, if no distribute lists are used to control what routes are advertised from Router C.

If all of Router A's traffic destined for 10.1.2.0 were routed through Router C, it could easily overwhelm the small router. In this scenario, we only want Router C to have redundant links to the core, and not let the core transit an access router to reach another core router.

The problem can be solved or avoided by configuring an access list that permits only networks connected to Router C. The access list would be applied outbound to the interfaces connecting Routers A and B with the `distribute-list` command. The command is issued from within the routing protocol configuration mode.

Distribute lists can solve problems as well as cause problems. If the downstream routers are configured to learn their default gateway dynamically, the router must have the default network in the route table. If the route is not present, the router will lose the gateway of last resort. When a distribute list is applied, you must verify that it allows route advertisement of the default network, as well as any other crucial routes.

Route Maps

Route maps are used to manipulate routing. They are small scripts that can contain multiple instances and multiple conditions for each instance. Route maps are somewhat like access lists if you specify that the packet must match an access list. In addition to the capability of permitting or denying the packet, you can define what is done before the packet is forwarded.

Route maps can be used to set metrics for route updates, set a command to its default value, and so on. Table 6.13 gives a list of what a route map can do.

TABLE 6.13 Route Map Configuration Commands

Command	Description
default	Set a command to its defaults.
exit	Exit from route-map configuration mode.

TABLE 6.13 Route Map Configuration Commands *(continued)*

Command	Description
help	Description of the interactive help system.
match	Match values from routing table.
no	Negate a command or set its defaults.
set	Set values in destination routing protocol.

Here is a sample route map:

```
route-map test permit 10
 match ip address 1
 set metric-type type-2
!
route-map test permit 20
 match ip address 2
 set metric-type type-1
!
route-map test permit 30
 set metric 100
```

The router runs through this route map, just as it runs through an access list. The only difference is that there are commands that the router performs instead of simply forwarding or dropping the packet. In this example, any packet matching the addresses listed in the IP access list 1 has its metric set as an OSPF type-2 metric. Any packet matching the addresses specified in access list 2 has its OSPF metric set to type-1. The final instance of the route map "test" is to set the metric of the route update to 100.

TCP/IP Symptoms and Problems: Summary Sheet

Table 6.14 lists several common TCP/IP symptoms and their probable causes.

TABLE 6.14   TCP/IP Symptoms and Causes

Symptom	Problems
Local host cannot communicate with a remote host	(a) DNS not working properly (b) no route to remote host (c) missing default gateway (d) administrative denial (access lists)
Certain applications won't work properly	(a) administrative denial (access lists) (b) network not configured to handle the application
Booting failures	(a) BootP server did not have an entry for the MAC address (b) missing IP helper-address (c) access lists (d) change in the NIC or MAC address (e) duplicate IP address (f) improper IP configuration
Can't ping a remote station	(a) access lists (b) no route to host (c) no default gateway set (d) remote host down
Missing routes	(a) improper routing protocol configuration (b) distribute lists (c) passive interface (doesn't receive updates) (d) neighbor not advertising routes (e) protocol version mismatch (f) neighbor relation not established

TABLE 6.14   TCP/IP Symptoms and Causes *(continued)*

Symptom	Problems
Adjacencies not forming	(a) improper routing protocol configuration (b) improper IP configuration (c) misconfigured network or neighbor statements (d) mismatched Hello timers (e) mismatched area ID
High CPU utilization	(a) several routing updates due to instabilities (b) debug wasn't turned off (c) a process gone amok
Route stuck in active mode	(a) misconfigured timers (b) hardware problems (c) unstable link

TCP/IP Symptoms and Action Plans: Summary Sheet

Table 6.15 contains action plans for each of the problems outlined in Table 6.14.

TABLE 6.15   Action Plans for Common TCP/IP Problems

Problem	Action Plan
DNS not working properly	Check the DNS configuration on host and DNS server. May use the nslookup utility to verify functionality of the DNS server.
No route to remote host	This can be caused by several different things: 1. Check the default gateway using the `ipconfig / all` or `winipcfg` command if you are on a Windows machine. 2. Using the `show ip route` command, check to see whether the router has a route.

T A B L E 6.15 Action Plans for Common TCP/IP Problems *(continued)*

Problem	Action Plan
	3. If the router doesn't have a route, use the show ip route command to see whether a gateway of last resort is set.
	4. If there is a gateway, check the next hop in the path toward the destination. If there is not a gateway, fix the problem or investigate why the router does not have a route.
Access Lists	If you isolate the problem to an access list you need to analyze the list, rewrite it correctly, and then apply the new access list.
Network not configured to handle the application	When applications use NetBIOS, NetBEUI, IPX, or other non-IP applications, verify that the routers involved are configured to properly handle them by using transparent bridging, SRB, tunneling, and so on.
Booting failures	1. Check the DHCP or BootP server, and verify that it has an entry for the MAC address of the problem station.
	2. Use debug ip udp to verify that packets are being received from the host.
	3. Verify that the helper addresses are correctly configured.
	4. Check for access lists that might be denying the packets.
	5. Make the necessary changes.
Missing routes	1. Look on the first router to see what routes are being learned. Issue the show ip route command.
	2. Depending on the routing protocol, verify that adjacencies have been formed with neighboring routers.

TABLE 6.15 Action Plans for Common TCP/IP Problems *(continued)*

Problem	Action Plan
	3. Using the `show running-config` command, look at the router's configuration and verify that the routing protocol has the proper network or neighbor statements.
	4. When troubleshooting OSPF, verify that the wildcard mask permits the correct routes.
	5. Check the distribute lists that are applied to the interfaces. Analyze the inbound filters.
	6. Verify that both neighbors have the correct IP configuration.
	7. Verify the metric if routes are being redistributed.
	8. Verify that the routes are being redistributed properly.
Adjacencies not forming	1. Perform a `show ip <protocol> neighbors` command to list the adjacencies that have formed.
	2. Look at the protocol configuration to confirm which adjacencies have not formed.
	3. Check the network statements in the protocol configuration.
	4. Show the `ip <protocol>` interface to obtain interface-specific information such as Hello timers.
	5. Once you have isolated the problem, make the necessary changes.

Summary

This chapter dealt with aspects of troubleshooting TCP/IP networks. It covered everything from the tools used to troubleshoot to a summary of what to do when you see a specific problem. Here's what was covered:

- TCP/IP diagnostic commands (such as `ping`, `traceroute`, `debug`, and all of the `show` commands), which can be used to troubleshoot TCP/IP-related problems.

- Common LAN and WAN access problems that may be encountered, as well as methods for troubleshooting TCP/IP hosts in addition to routers.

- Access lists, which may be used in conjunction with the debug tool. They may also be the cause of some network failures. It is important to understand the criteria used and how the criteria is compared to the packets.

- Several routing protocols, each one with its own set of `show` and `debug` commands that can be used when troubleshooting routing problems.

Commands Used in This Chapter

The following list contains a summary of all the commands used in this chapter.

Command	Description
`debug ip eigrp`	Causes a general debug to be performed on all EIGRP.
`debug ip eigrp <AS number>`	Debugs EIGRP for the specified AS.
`debug ip eigrp neighbor`	Debugs the transactions and exchanges among EIGRP neighbors.

Command	Description
`debug ip eigrp notifications`	Provides detailed information about neighbor notifications.
`debug ip eigrp summary`	Provides summarized information during a debug.
`debug ip igrp events`	Provides information regarding IGRP events (protocol-related).
`debug ip igrp transactions`	Provides more detailed information regarding IGRP events (protocol-related).
`debug ip ospf adj`	Provides debug information about events concerning adjacency relationships with other OSPF routers.
`debug ip ospf events`	Provides debug information for all OSPF events.
`debug ip ospf flood`	Provides information about OSPF flooding. (Flooding is the way that OSPF router sends updates.) It broadcasts a change in its route table and all other members of the OSPF area receive the update.
`debug ip ospf lsa-generation`	Gives detailed information regarding the generation of LSA messages.
`debug ip ospf packet`	Gives detailed information regarding OSPF packets.
`debug ip ospf retransmission`	When OSPF has to retransmit information, this command triggers a retransmission event that debug captures and echoes to the console.

Command	Description
debug ip ospf spf	Provides debug information for all SPF transactions. By enabling SPF debugging, OSPF events debugging is also turned on.
debug ip ospf tree	Provides information for the OSPF database tree.
debug ip rip	Provides you with all possible RIP protocol information.
debug ip rip events	Provides output regarding RIP protocol events.
ipconfig /all	(Windows 98 command.) Provides interface configuration for the host.
Ping	Initiates an ICMP echo request. There are two levels, User and Privileged. The IP protocol is used.
show dhcp servers	Shows information regarding the DHCP servers.
show ip access-list	Displays information regarding access lists within the IP value range.
show ip arp	Provides information contained in the router's ARP cache.
show ip eigrp events	Displays a log of the most recent EIGRP protocol events. This information includes the insertion and removal of routes from the route table, updates, and neighbor status.
show ip eigrp interfaces	Displays EIGRP peer information for that interface.

Command	Description
`show ip eigrp neighbors`	Displays all EIGRP neighbors, along with summary information about each neighbor.
`show ip eigrp topology`	Displays the contents of the EIGRP topology table.
`show ip eigrp traffic`	Displays a summary of EIGRP routing statistics, such as the number of Hellos and routing updates.
`show ip interface`	Displays the interface's status as well as the IP configuration and settings for the interface.
`show ip ospf`	Displays information for OSPF.
`show ip ospf <process-id>`	Process ID number. Displays information relevant to the specified process ID.
`show ip ospf border-routers`	Displays the routers that join different areas, or border routers.
`show ip ospf database`	Provides an OSPF database summary.
`show ip ospf interface`	Displays OSPF information on a interface.
`show ip ospf neighbor`	Displays OSPF neighbor information.
`show ip ospf request-list`	Displays link-state request list.
`show ip ospf retransmission list`	Displays link-state retransmission list.
`show ip ospf summary-address`	Displays summary-address redistribution information.
`show ip ospf virtual-links`	Displays virtual link information.

Command	Description
show ip protocols	Provides information about the IP routing protocols that run on the router.
show ip route	Displays the contents of the IP route table as well as the default gateway for the router.
show ip route eigrp	Displays the EIGRP routes.
show ip route igrp	Displays IGRP routes only.
show ip route ospf	Displays OSPF routes.
show ip route rip	Displays the RIP route table.
show ip traffic	Returns information pertaining to IP traffic statistics.
show running-config	Displays the running configuration.
traceroute	Performs a hop-by-hop ICMP traceroute. This command has two levels, User and Privileged.

Key Terms

Before you take the exam, be certain you are familiar with the following terms:

autonomous system boundary router (ASBR)

Bootstrap Protocol (BootP)

distribute lists

Dynamic Host Configuration Protocol (DHCP)

extended access lists

Internet Control Message Protocol

route maps

standard access list

wide area network (WAN)

Review Questions

1. What is the difference between the ping and traceroute utilities?

    A. Ping is an end-to-end test and traceroute is a step-by-step test.

    B. Ping uses ICMP and traceroute uses UDP.

    C. They are the same ICMP message type.

    D. Ping tests for IP connectivity and traceroute tests for TCP connectivity.

2. Choose four common IP show commands.

    A. `show ip route`

    B. `show ip interface`

    C. `show running-config`

    D. `show ip access-lists`

    E. `show ip default-gateway`

    F. `show ip mrm`

3. Which debug command can be used to provide important IP information, and yet is not part of the IP debug commands?

    A. `debug ospf`

    B. `debug eigrp`

    C. `debug arp`

    D. `debug ip arp`

4. What are the three methods that can be used to isolate problems in TCP/IP networks? (Choose three.)

    A. Divide and conquer

    B. Divide by half

    C. Inside-out

    D. Outside-in

5. What does the output of the following command display?

`ipconfig /all`

   A. IP information for all interfaces, including IP address, subnet mask, DNS server, DHCP information, and some NetBIOS

   B. All Layer 3 information

   C. IP address and subnet mask only

   D. None of the above

6. What is the BootP server's response if it receives a bootrequest, but it cannot find the MAC address in the database?

   A. It sends a deny message to the client.

   B. It sends an ARP request, so it can add the MAC address to the database.

   C. It checks the databases on other BootP or DHCP servers.

   D. It does nothing.

7. When are ARP cache table entries cleared? (Choose all that apply.)

   A. Upon the issuance of the `clear arp-cache` command

   B. Upon reload

   C. When the timers expire

   D. Never

8. What is the function of a default gateway?

   A. It is a default next hop if the router or host does not know a route to the destination.

   B. It is used to provide the default network.

   C. It provides the method of returning network management information to a router.

   D. None of the above.

9. What are the methods of setting the gateway of last resort on a Cisco router? (Choose two.)

   A. Configure `ip default-route`

   B. Configure `ip default neighbor`

   C. Configure a static route

   D. Configure an IP default-network

10. What criterion/criteria is used when comparing a packet against a standard access list?

    A. Destination address

    B. Source address

    C. Source and destination address

    D. All of the above

11. What commands can be used to see the contents of an IP access list?

    A. `show access-lists`

    B. `show ip access-lists`

    C. `show running-config`

    D. All of the above

12. Which commands can be used to verify the interfaces that an IP access list is applied to? (Choose all that apply.)

    A. `show access-lists`

    B. `show interface <interface-type> <interface number>`

    C. `show ip interfaces`

    D. `show running-config`

    E. All of the above

13. Match each command with its corresponding output. The output choices are as follows: (1) Displays IP; (2) Displays the running configuration; (3) Displays the RIP route table; (4) Displays the IP route table.

    A. `show ip route rip`

    B. `show ip route`

    C. `show ip interface`

    D. `show running-config`

14. Match each command with its corresponding output. The output choices are as follows: (1) Displays IGRP routes only; (2) Displays the entire route table; (3) Displays the current configuration.

    A. `show running-config`

    B. `show ip route igrp`

    C. `show ip route`

15. Match each command with its corresponding output. The output choices are as follows: (1) Displays EIGRP peer information for that interface; (2) Displays a summary of EIGRP routing statistics, such as the number of Hellos and routing updates; (3) Displays the contents of the EIGRP topology table; (4) Displays the EIGRP routes; (5) Displays a log of most recent EIGRP protocol events (including the insertion and removal of routes from the route table, updates, and neighbor status); (6) Displays all EIGRP neighbors, along with summary information about each neighbor.

    A. `show ip route eigrp`

    B. `show ip eigrp interfaces`

    C. `show ip eigrp neighbors`

    D. `show ip eigrp topology`

    E. `show ip eigrp traffic`

    F. `show ip eigrp events`

16. Match each command with its corresponding output. The output choices are as follows: (1) Displays OSPF routes; (2) Displays the routers that join different areas or border routers; (3) Displays OSPF neighbor information; (4) Displays summary-address redistribution information; (5) Displays information for OSPF; (6) Displays process ID number that displays information relevant to the specified process ID; (7) Displays link-state request list; (8) Displays link-state retransmission list; (9) Provides an OSPF database summary; (10) Displays Virtual link information; (11) Displays OSPF information on an interface.

    A. `show ip route ospf`

    B. `show ip ospf`

    C. `show ip ospf <process-id>`

    D. `show ip ospf border-routers`

    E. `show ip ospf database`

    F. `show ip ospf interface`

    G. `show ip ospf neighbor`

    H. `show ip ospf request-list`

    I. `show ip ospf retransmission list`

    J. `show ip ospf summary-address`

    K. `show ip ospf virtual-links`

17. Where are distribute lists applied?

    A. Directly to the interface

    B. To the interface via the routing protocol

    C. To the routing protocol

    D. None of the above

18. What command(s) is/are used to see the contents of a route map? (Choose all that apply.)

   A. `show running-config`

   B. `show ip route-map`

   C. `show route-map`

   D. `show ip interface`

19. What is the difference between a route map and an access list?

   A. There is no difference.

   B. Access lists have greater impact on the router's CPU.

   C. The route map allows actions other than forwarding or dropping the packet.

   D. None of the above.

20. Why should metrics be set properly when redistributing routing protocols?

   A. To avoid confusion.

   B. So the protocol receiving the injected routes can propagate the correct information.

   C. Routing won't work without them.

   D. None of the above.

Answers to Review Questions

1. A. The characteristics of ping tests are to determine reachability. traceroute characteristics are meant to provide hop-by-hop information.

2. A, B, C, D. `show ip default-gateway` is not a valid command, and `show ip mrm` is only used when working with multicast issues.

3. C. The `debug arp` command provides important IP information even though it is not part of the IP debug set.

4. B, C, D. These methods are the three discussed in the text, Chapters 1 and 6.

5. A. The command is issued on a Windows 98 host and provides the information specified in A.

6. D. It cannot respond, so it does nothing.

7. A, B, C. These are all valid scenarios in which the ARP table entries are cleared.

8. A. The default gateway indicates the next hop for packets with no route to the destination address.

9. C, D. These are the valid methods, though not stated here in the exact syntax. The first two answers are invalid as to both method and syntax.

10. B. Standard access lists compare only the source address.

11. D. All of the above commands can display the contents of an IP access list.

12. C, D. The correct syntax is given by C and D.

13. A (3), B (4), C (1), D (2). IP-related information for an interface is given by the `show ip interface` command.

14. A (3), B (1), C (2). The current configuration is also known as the running configuration.

15. A (4), B (1), C (6), D (3), E (2), F (5). These are all EIGRP-related commands. They can be verified by logging onto the router and experimenting with the output of each of these commands.

16. A (1), B (5), C (6), D (2), E (9), F (11), G (3), H (7), I (8), J (4), K (10). These are all OSPF-related commands and can be verified by logging onto a router and experimenting with the output of each of these commands.

17. B. The list must be applied to an interface fromÅ within the routing protocol.

18. A, C. Route maps are not IP specific.

19. C. Route maps use access lists to match a packet. After a match is made, many different actions may be taken.

20. B. Different protocols do not share the same metric values. A translation has to occur for the injected routes to be understood by the new protocol. This is done via setting default metrics.

Troubleshooting Serial Line and Frame Relay Connectivity

TOPICS COVERED IN THIS CHAPTER INCLUDE:

✓ Analyzing Frame Relay, X.25, and general serial line problem symptoms.

✓ Using Cisco IOS commands that will aid in problem isolation and the ability to identify WAN and Frame Relay problems.

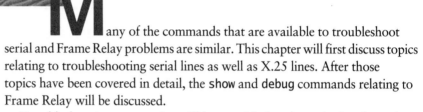

any of the commands that are available to troubleshoot serial and Frame Relay problems are similar. This chapter will first discuss topics relating to troubleshooting serial lines as well as X.25 lines. After those topics have been covered in detail, the show and debug commands relating to Frame Relay will be discussed.

Troubleshooting summaries will be provided at the end of each section. These summaries will be valuable as quick-reference guides when isolating and diagnosing serial line and Frame Relay problems.

Troubleshooting Serial Lines

There are numerous commands available to aid in troubleshooting serial lines. Some of them are show commands; others are debug commands. Here is a list of the commands that will be covered in this section:

- clear counters serial
- show interface serial
- show controllers serial
- show buffers
- debug serial interface
- debug serial packet

An integral part of serial connections is the hardware involved. Look at Figure 7.1. In this graphic, you see Router A connected to a channel service unit/digital service unit (CSU/DSU), through a serial cable that is connected to another CSU/DSU, and then connected to Router B.

FIGURE 7.1   Serial line setup

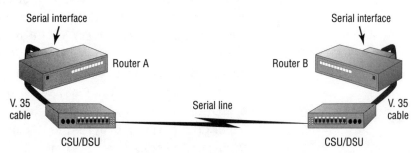

HDLC Encapsulation

High-level Data Link Control (HDLC) is an encapsulation method used by serial links. You learned in Chapter 2 that HDLC provides a 32-bit checksum and three different transfer modes: normal, asynchronous response, and asynchronous balanced.

HDLC is used by default on Cisco serial interfaces. The first important point of troubleshooting serial line problems is to verify that both sides of the link are using the same encapsulation types. Here is a look at a serial interface from a Cisco 2501. Notice that the encapsulation type is HDLC:

```
Router_A>show interface serial0
Serial0 is administratively down, line protocol is down
  Hardware is HD64570
  Internet address is 172.16.20.6/30
  MTU 1500 bytes, BW 1544 Kbit, DLY 20000 usec, rely 255/
  255, load 1/255
  Encapsulation HDLC, loopback not set, keepalive set (10
  sec)
  Last input never, output never, output hang never
  Last clearing of "show interface" counters never
  Input queue: 0/75/0 (size/max/drops); Total output
  drops: 0
  Queueing strategy: weighted fair
```

```
    Output queue: 0/1000/64/0 (size/max total/threshold/
drops)
        Conversations  0/0/256 (active/max active/max total)
        Reserved Conversations 0/0 (allocated/max allocated)
    5 minute input rate 0 bits/sec, 0 packets/sec
    5 minute output rate 0 bits/sec, 0 packets/sec
        0 packets input, 0 bytes, 0 no buffer
        Received 0 broadcasts, 0 runts, 0 giants, 0 throttles
        0 input errors, 0 CRC, 0 frame, 0 overrun, 0 ignored,
        0 abort
        0 packets output, 0 bytes, 0 underruns
        0 output errors, 0 collisions, 1 interface resets
        0 output buffer failures, 0 output buffers swapped
        out
        0 carrier transitions
        DCD=down  DSR=down  DTR=down  RTS=down  CTS=down
Router_A>
```

Other encapsulations may be used on serial interfaces, but HDLC is used for synchronous data link control.

show interface serial Command

The show interface serial commands provide you with a great deal of information to help you when you troubleshoot serial line and other serial interface-related problems, such as Frame Relay. However, in order to get correct information, you should first clear the counters for the interface of interest.

Before you do so, look at the output of the show interface serial 1 command:

```
Router_A>show interface serial 1
Serial1 is up, line protocol is up
  Hardware is HD64570
  Internet address is 172.16.30.5/30
  MTU 1500 bytes, BW 1544 Kbit, DLY 20000 usec, rely 255/
255, load 1/255
  Encapsulation HDLC, loopback not set, keepalive set (10
sec)
```

```
    Last input 00:00:08, output 00:00:07, output hang never
    Last clearing of "show interface" counters never
    Input queue: 0/75/0 (size/max/drops);
Total output drops: 0
    Queueing strategy: weighted fair
    Output queue: 0/1000/64/0 (size/max total/threshold/
drops)
        Conversations  0/1/256 (active/max active/max total)
        Reserved Conversations 0/0 (allocated/max allocated)
    5 minute input rate 0 bits/sec, 0 packets/sec
    5 minute output rate 0 bits/sec, 0 packets/sec
        1307 packets input, 85380 bytes, 0 no buffer
        Received 695 broadcasts, 0 runts, 0 giants, 0
throttles
        0 input errors, 0 CRC, 0 frame, 0 overrun, 0 ignored,
        0 abort
        1308 packets output, 85652 bytes, 0 underruns
        0 output errors, 0 collisions, 116 interface resets
        0 output buffer failures, 0 output buffers swapped
        out
        238 carrier transitions
        DCD=up  DSR=up  DTR=up  RTS=up  CTS=up
Router_A>
```

The output tells you that the interface is up and the line protocol is also up. The information contained in the show interface serial command will be discussed in more detail in just a moment. For now, it is important to recognize that many of the counters have elevated numbers. Also, notice that the seventh line of the output declares that the counters were never cleared.

You cannot effectively troubleshoot if you do not have accurate data returned through the many diagnostic commands. One way to ensure that the data you are analyzing is accurate and directly applies to the problem at hand is to perform the clear counters serial <number> command, which resets the interface counters to zero. This ensures that the data retrieved from the interface command is representative of what is happening at that moment on the network.

Here is how it is done and what the interface looks like after the command has been issued:

```
Router_A#clear counters serial 1
Clear "show interface" counters on this interface
[confirm]
%CLEAR-5-COUNTERS: Clear counter on interface Serial1 by
console
Router_A#show interface serial 1
Serial1 is up, line protocol is up
  Hardware is HD64570
  Internet address is 172.16.30.5/30
  MTU 1500 bytes, BW 1544 Kbit, DLY 20000 usec, rely 255/
255, load 51/255
  Encapsulation HDLC, loopback not set,
  keepalive set (10  sec)
  Last input 00:00:00, output 00:00:00, output hang never
  Last clearing of "show interface" counters 00:28:48
  Input queue: 1/75/0 (size/max/drops);
Total output drops: 0
  Queueing strategy: weighted fair
  Output queue: 0/1000/64/0 (size/max total/threshold/
drops)
     Conversations  0/2/256 (active/max active/max total)
     Reserved Conversations 0/0 (allocated/max allocated)
  5 minute input rate 321000 bits/sec, 48 packets/sec
  5 minute output rate 320000 bits/sec, 48 packets/sec
     12439 packets input, 13257786 bytes, 0 no buffer
     Received 202 broadcasts, 0 runts, 0 giants, 0
throttles
     0 input errors, 0 CRC, 0 frame, 0 overrun, 0 ignored,
     0 abort
     12438 packets output, 13256434 bytes, 0 underruns
     0 output errors, 0 collisions, 0 interface resets
     0 output buffer failures, 0 output buffers swapped
     out
     0 carrier transitions
     DCD=up  DSR=up  DTR=up  RTS=up  CTS=up
Router_A#
```

Notice the seventh line of the output. It says that the counters were cleared 28 minutes before. After the counters are cleared, you can associate any new data with current network events. If you try to associate current network events with inaccurate data, you will never find the problem.

Now let's go through the available data provided by the `show interface serial` command. Refer to the output previously listed.

The first line provides information regarding the status of the interface and the line protocol:

```
Serial1 is up, line protocol is up
```

In this case, both are up and functional. If the interface is down, the line protocol must also be down.

Cabling problems, carrier problems, or hardware problems can all be reasons for a serial interface to report as down. These problems can be addressed by verifying proper cable connectivity, replacing hardware (including cables), and checking the CSU/DSU for carrier signal. If you cannot resolve the problem by using these techniques, you can and should contact the local carrier, who can verify the carrier service.

Another possibility for the interface status is that the interface is up, but the line protocol is down. When this happens, it can be a variety of problems, as follows:

- Failed CSU/DSU

- Router interface problems

- Mismatched timing on CSU/DSU or carrier network

- Misconfigured interface

- Keepalive signals not received from remote router

- Carrier problem

You should verify that the local interface and the remote interface are properly configured. Loopback tests can be performed. These tests will be discussed in the CSU/DSU section of the chapter.

Continuing with the description of the output of the `show interface serial` command, you see that the second line of the output displays the hardware type of the interface:

```
Hardware is HD64570
```

The third line shows the Layer 3 IP address with the associated subnet mask:

```
Internet address is 172.16.30.5/30
```

Line 4 contains all of the information needed to create a route metric for the interface. The data includes MTU, bandwidth, delay, reliability, and load.

```
MTU 1500 bytes, BW 1544 Kbit, DLY 20000 usec, rely 255/
255, load 51/255
```

Line 5 indicates the type of encapsulation that is being used on the line, as well as loopback and keepalive information:

```
Encapsulation HDLC, loopback not set, keepalive set (10
sec)
```

The sixth line displays the last time the interface saw any traffic:

```
Last input 00:00:00, output 00:00:00, output hang never
```

Again, the seventh line shows the time that transpired since the last time the interface counters were cleared:

```
Last clearing of "show interface" counters 00:28:48
```

Lines 8 through 12 contain information regarding the buffers on the interface:

```
Input queue: 1/75/0 (size/max/drops);
Total output drops: 0
  Queueing strategy: weighted fair
  Output queue: 0/1000/64/0 (size/max total/threshold/
  drops)
    Conversations  0/2/256 (active/max active/max total)
    Reserved Conversations 0/0 (allocated/max allocated)
```

Lines 13 and 14 display the five-minute average for input and output bits per second, and packets per second on the interface:

```
5 minute input rate 321000 bits/sec, 48 packets/sec
5 minute output rate 320000 bits/sec, 48 packets/sec
```

Beginning with line 15 and until line 17, the output displays interface input information. The first line is a counter that keeps track of the number of incoming packets on the interface. Because it is a counter, it will reach a maximum value, and then reset. The next line displays information for broadcast, runt, giant, and throttled packets. The last line (line 17) displays any input, CRC, frame, overrun, ignored, or abort errors:

```
12439 packets input, 13257786 bytes, 0 no buffer
     Received 202 broadcasts, 0 runts, 0 giants,
     0 throttles
     0 input errors, 0 CRC, 0 frame, 0 overrun, 0 ignored,
     0 abort
```

The output interface statistics begin with line 18 and end on line 21. This data reflects the number of output packets, underruns, output errors, collisions, interface resets, output buffer failures, swapped output buffers, and carrier transitions:

```
12438 packets output, 13256434 bytes, 0 underruns
     0 output errors, 0 collisions, 0 interface resets
     0 output buffer failures,
     0 output buffers swapped out
     0 carrier transitions
```

Interface resets should be warning flags. If you see a large number of interface resets after clearing the counter, you should be concerned. Interface resets are caused by the following:

- Queued packets not sent for several seconds

- Hardware problems (for example, router interface, cable, or CSU/DSU)

- Mismatched clocking signals

- Looped interface

- Interface shut down

- Line protocol down and the interface resetting periodically

The next warning flag should be carrier transitions. This counter counts the number of times that the DCD (data carrier detect) signal changes state. If the carrier keeps fluctuating, you do not have a stable circuit. This is often a carrier problem, and the local carrier must be contacted.

The final line of the show interface serial command displays carrier-specific information:

```
DCD=up  DSR=up  DTR=up  RTS=up  CTS=up
```

show controllers Command

The show controllers command is used to display interface status and whether a cable is connected to the interface. Let's look at a couple of different outputs from the show controllers command.

The first output is from interface serial 0. There is no cable attached to the interface:

```
Router_A#show controllers serial 0
HD unit 0, idb = 0x94AEC, driver structure at 0x99870
buffer size 1524  HD unit 0, No cable, clockrate 4000000
cpb = 0x41, eda = 0x4940, cda = 0x4800
RX ring with 16 entries at 0x414800
 .
 . {some output omitted}
 .
TX ring with 2 entries at 0x415000
 .
 . {some output omitted}
 .
0 missed datagrams, 0 overruns
0 bad datagram encapsulations, 0 memory errors
0 transmitter underruns
0 residual bit errors

Router_A#
```

The second output is from interface serial 1, which does have a cable connected and is functioning properly:

```
Router_A#show controllers serial 1
HD unit 1, idb = 0x9D4E0, driver structure at 0xA2260
buffer size 1524  HD unit 1, V.35 DCE cable, clockrate
4000000
cpb = 0x42, eda = 0x3104, cda = 0x3118
RX ring with 16 entries at 0x423000
```

```
.
.   {some output omitted}
.
TX ring with 2 entries at 0x423800
.
.   {some output omitted}
.
0 missed datagrams, 0 overruns
0 bad datagram encapsulations, 0 memory errors
0 transmitter underruns
0 residual bit errors

Router_A#
```

The basic information provided by this command is the interface status regarding missed datagrams, overruns, bad encapsulation, memory errors, underruns, and bit errors. In addition, it indicates the interface clock rate, as well as the cable type that is connected to the interface.

If you don't see a cable connected to the interface, verifying that a cable is properly connected is a good item to include in a troubleshooting action plan. If there are excessive errors on the interface, it can be faulty hardware.

show buffers Command

The show buffers command can be used to look at system buffer pools, but it also provides information regarding interface buffers. Look at the sample output from a 2514 router:

```
Router_B>show buffers
Buffer elements:
    500 in free list (500 max allowed)
    52587626 hits, 0 misses, 0 created

Public buffer pools:
Small buffers, 104 bytes (total 50, permanent 50):
    50 in free list (20 min, 150 max allowed)
    7709985 hits, 0 misses, 0 trims, 0 created
    0 failures (0 no memory)
```

```
Middle buffers, 600 bytes (total 25, permanent 25):
     24 in free list (10 min, 150 max allowed)
     2045756 hits, 0 misses, 0 trims, 0 created
     0 failures (0 no memory)
Big buffers, 1524 bytes (total 50, permanent 50):
     50 in free list (5 min, 150 max allowed)
     2541768 hits, 774 misses, 217 trims, 217 created
     24 failures (0 no memory)
VeryBig buffers, 4520 bytes (total 10, permanent 10):
     10 in free list (0 min, 100 max allowed)
     52464 hits, 0 misses, 0 trims, 0 created
     0 failures (0 no memory)
Large buffers, 5024 bytes (total 0, permanent 0):
     0 in free list (0 min, 10 max allowed)
     0 hits, 0 misses, 0 trims, 0 created
     0 failures (0 no memory)
Huge buffers, 18024 bytes (total 0, permanent 0):
     0 in free list (0 min, 4 max allowed)
     0 hits, 0 misses, 0 trims, 0 created
     0 failures (0 no memory)

Interface buffer pools:
Ethernet0 buffers, 1524 bytes (total 32, permanent 32):
     5 in free list (0 min, 32 max allowed)
     255684 hits, 64696 fallbacks
     8 max cache size, 5 in cache
Ethernet1 buffers, 1524 bytes (total 32, permanent 32):
     0 in free list (0 min, 32 max allowed)
     300993 hits, 1024384 fallbacks
     8 max cache size, 6 in cache
Serial0 buffers, 1524 bytes (total 32, permanent 32):
     7 in free list (0 min, 32 max allowed)
     25 hits, 0 fallbacks
     8 max cache size, 8 in cache
Serial1 buffers, 1524 bytes (total 32, permanent 32):
     7 in free list (0 min, 32 max allowed)
     25 hits, 0 fallbacks
     8 max cache size, 8 in cache
```

Notice that the interface buffers are listed at the end of the output. This information can be useful to troubleshoot serial interface problems. It is important to look at the number of free buffers. These numbers indicate the memory that is available on the interface for buffering incoming and outgoing packets.

debug serial interface Command

As always with debug tools, you must exercise caution. When executing a serial debug or Frame Relay debug, the router can generate large amounts of data that can encumber the router. Make sure that the specific command is used when possible. debug can be used in conjunction with access lists to focus the application of the debug tool.

The debug of a serial interface displays HDLC or Frame Relay communication messages. A sample follows that includes Frame Relay information. It is important to understand that the output of this command varies with the encapsulation type used on the interface:

```
Router_A#debug serial interface
Serial network interface debugging is on
Serial0(out): StEnq, myseq 135, yourseen 134, DTE up
Serial0(in): Status, myseq 135
Serial1(out): StEnq, myseq 2, yourseen 8, DTE up
Serial1(in): Status, myseq 2
Serial2(out): StEnq, myseq 247, yourseen 247, DTE up
Serial2(in): Status, myseq 247
Serial3(out): StEnq, myseq 30, yourseen 28, DTE up
Serial3(in): Status, myseq 30
Serial0(out): StEnq, myseq 136, yourseen 135, DTE up
Serial0(in): Status, myseq 136
Serial1(out): StEnq, myseq 3, yourseen 9, DTE up
Serial1(in): Status, myseq 3
Serial2(out): StEnq, myseq 248, yourseen 248, DTE up
Serial2(in): Status, myseq 248
Serial3(out): StEnq, myseq 31, yourseen 29, DTE up
Serial3(in): Status, myseq 31
Serial0(out): StEnq, myseq 137, yourseen 136, DTE up
```

```
Serial0(in): Status, myseq 137
Serial1(out): StEnq, myseq 4, yourseen 10, DTE up
Serial1(in): Status, myseq 4
Serial2(out): StEnq, myseq 249, yourseen 249, DTE up
Serial2(in): Status, myseq 249
Serial3(out): StEnq, myseq 32, yourseen 30, DTE up
Serial3(in): Status, myseq 32
```

This sample includes output from many interfaces. The boldface type is used to highlight interface serial 0. Here is the definition of what you see:

StEnq This is an LMI status enquiry sent from the router to the Frame Relay switch.

Status This is the reply sent to the router from the Frame Relay switch.

mysec This is the local keepalive number. The value is the sequence identifier.

yourseen This is the keepalive sent by the other side of the serial connection.

DTE This is the data-termination equipment status. In this example, it is up.

The in and out specify the directions that the packets are sent. The outbound packets are keepalives sent by the local side, whereas the inbound packets are the keepalives sent from the other end.

If the sequence numbers for a given interface don't increment, then there is probably a timing or line problem at one end or the other of the connection. The line will reset if two out of six consecutive keepalive packets fail to increment. Although the Layer 3 protocol considers the line protocol to be down, the Layer 2 protocol continues to send keepalive messages. Once the Layer 2 protocol achieves three consecutive sequences, the line protocol is brought back up.

Here is a sample of HDLC communication:

```
Router_A#debug serial interface
Serial network interface debugging is on
Serial0: HDLC myseq 172188, mineseen 172188*, yourseen
172326, line up
```

```
Serial0: HDLC myseq 172189, mineseen 172189*, yourseen
172327, line up
Serial0: HDLC myseq 172190, mineseen 172190*, yourseen
172328, line up
Serial0: HDLC myseq 172191, mineseen 172191*, yourseen
172329, line up
Router_A#
```

The field values are very similar to the field values in the Frame Relay output. Here are the field definitions:

mysec   This is the local keepalive number. The value is the sequence identifier.

yourseen   This is the keepalive sent by the other side of the serial connection.

mineseen   This is the value of the keepalive sent by the local interface seen by the remote side.

debug serial packet Command

The debug serial packet command is used to provide additional information regarding serial interfaces. According to information contained in CCO UniverCD, the debug serial packet only provides information for interfaces that use SMDS encapsulation.

A sample output is not shown here because the information included in the output is useful only when you have an understanding of the SMDS protocol, which has not been discussed in this book.

CSU/DSU Loopback Tests

Loopback tests aid in physically isolating serial line and Frame Relay problems. Four different loopback tests can be performed to troubleshoot the circuit. You can perform two of them, and the local provider has access to perform the other two. Here is a list of four loopback tests:

- Local loopback on the local CSU/DSU

- Local loopback on the remote CSU/DSU

- Remote loopback from the local NIU to the remote CSU/DSU

- Remote loopback from the remote NIU to the local CSU/DSU

Look at Figure 7.2 to see how the tests are performed.

FIGURE 7.2   CSU/DSU loopback tests

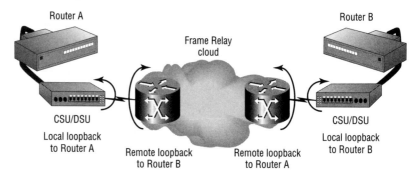

The tests that you can perform are the two local loopback tests. You can perform these tests because you have access to the equipment. The local provider has to perform the remote loopback tests because it has access to the equipment within the cloud.

When using loopback tests for troubleshooting, you should follow these steps:

1. Perform the local loopback test for the local router (Router A in this example).

2. Verify the line status. This means to check for LMI status when using Frame Relay on the interface.

3. Perform the local loopback test for the remote router, Router B.

4. Verify the line status. This means to check for LMI status when using Frame Relay on the interface.

5. If you see LMI, but cannot get remote connectivity, contact your local service provider, who can run the remote loopback tests.

Remember that LMI stands for Local Management Interface. When you see LMI up on a router interface during a loopback test, it means that the protocol is working locally, but not necessarily working remotely. By putting a CSU/DSU into loopback, the signal is sent back to the interface, so the line protocol shows up. For end-to-end connectivity, both end sites must have LMI up status. In addition, all of the Frame Relay switches that participate in the PVC must be working properly. Remote loopback tests confirm the functionality of the circuit.

Serial Line Summary

Several encapsulations and protocols may be used over serial lines. Because of this variety, many different problems can occur. It is also important to realize that the output of many show commands may differ, depending on the interface configuration.

To aid you in diagnosing and resolving serial line problems, this section includes two quick reference tables for your convenience.

Symptoms and Problems

Table 7.1 lists several common serial line conditions and their related possible problems.

TABLE 7.1 Serial Line Symtoms and Problems

Symptom or Condition	Associated Problem(s)
Interface is administratively down; line protocol is down	(a) The interface has been placed in shutdown via a configuration command (b) Duplicate IP addresses are not allowed and one of the two interfaces with the same IP address will be shut down
Interface is down; line protocol is down	(a) Improper cabling (b) No carrier signal from local provider. (c) Hardware failure (interface or CSU/DSU, cabling)
Interface is up; line protocol is down	(a) Misconfigured interface, local or remote (b) Local provider problem (c) Keepalive sequencing not incrementing (d) Hardware failures (local or remote interfaces and CSU/DSU) (e) Noisy line (f) Timing mismatches
Interface is up; line protocol is up (looped)	(a) The circuit is in loopback

TABLE 7.1 Serial Line Symtoms and Problems *(continued)*

Symptom or Condition	Associated Problem(s)
Incrementing carrier transition counter	(a) Unstable signaling coming from the local provider (b) Faulty cabling (c) Failing hardware (for example, interface or CSU/DSU)
Incrementing interface resets	(a) Faulty cabling, causing the loss of the CD signal (b) Hardware failure (c) Line congestion
Input drops, errors, CRC, and framing errors	(a) Line speed oversubscribes the router interface capacity (b) Local provider problem (c) Noisy line (d) Faulty cabling (e) Improper cabling (f) Failing hardware
Output drops	(a) The interface is capable of transmitting at higher than line speed

Problems and Action Plans

Now that you have seen the list of symptoms with their problems, you need a quick reference for resolving the problems. Table 7.2 provides summary action plans for resolving the listed serial line problems.

TABLE 7.2 Action Plans for Common Serial Line Problems

Problem	Resolution Action Plan
Local provider problems	1. Check the CSU/DSU for a CD signal. Check for other signals, such as RX and TX, to see if the circuit is transmitting and receiving information. 2. If you do not get a CD signal or have other problems, contact the local service provider to troubleshoot and fix the problem.

TABLE 7.2   Action Plans for Common Serial Line Problems *(continued)*

Problem	Resolution Action Plan
Improper or faulty cabling	1. Make sure that you are using the proper cable for the equipment being used.
	2. Use a breakout box to check the control leads.
	3. Swap faulty cables.
Misconfigured interface	1. View the interface configuration using the show running-config command.
	2. Make sure that the same encapsulation type is used at both ends of the circuit by using the show interface command.
Keepalive problems	1. Verify that keepalives are being sent. You can check this via the router configuration or by using the show interface command.
	2. If the configuration says that keepalives are being sent, you may want to enable debug serial interface for the interface.
	3. Verify that the sequence numbers are incrementing.
	4. If they don't increment, run loopback tests on the local and remote sites.
	5. If the sequences don't increment, even when the CSU/DSU is in loopback, you have a hardware problem.
	6. Replace faulty hardware.
Hardware failure	1. Replace the hardware.

T A B L E   7 . 2   Action Plans for Common Serial Line Problems *(continued)*

Problem	Resolution Action Plan
Interface is in loopback mode	1. Check the interface configuration. 2. If there is a loopback entry in the interface configuration, remove it with the no form of the command. 3. If the interface configuration is clean, check the CSU/DSU to see if it is placed in loopback. 4. If it is, remove the CSU/DSU from loopback mode. 5. If the CSU/DSU is not in loopback mode, contact the local provider; it may have placed the circuit in loopback.
Interface is administratively down	1. Check the configuration. Verify that the IP address is not a duplicate. 2. Enter the configuration mode and issue the no shutdown command within the interface.
Line speed is larger than the interface capacity	1. Reduce input queue size by using the hold-queue in command. 2. Increase output queues on exiting interfaces.
Interface speed is larger than the line speed	1. Reduce broadcast traffic. 2. Increase output queue. 3. Implement queuing algorithms, if necessary.

Troubleshooting X.25

Troubleshooting X.25 is accomplished the same way as serial line and Frame Relay troubleshooting. The following sections will discuss the commands used to troubleshoot X.25. In addition to the commands, the output of the respective command will also be discussed.

show interface serial Commands

When a serial interface is configured to use X.25, the show interface serial command provides information specific to the X.25 protocol. Here is a sample of an X.25 interface:

```
Router_A#show interface serial 1
Serial1 is up, line protocol is up
  Hardware is HD64570
  Internet address is 172.16.30.5/30
  MTU 1500 bytes, BW 1544 Kbit, DLY 20000 usec, rely 255/
255, load 51/255
  Encapsulation X25, loopback not set
LAPB DTE, state CONNECT, modulo 8, k 7, N1 12043, N2 10
T1 3000, interface outage (partial T3) 0, T4 0
VS 1, VR 1, Remote VR 1, Retransmissions 0
  IFRAMEs 1/1 RNRs 0/0 REJs 0/0 SABM/Es 1/0 FRMRs 0/0
DISCs 0/0
X25 DTE, address 190118, state R1, modulo 8, timer 0
Defaults: cisco encapsulation, idle 0, nvc 1
Input/output window sizes 2/2, packet sizes 128/128
Timers: T20 180, T21 200, T22 180, T23 180, TH 0
Channels: Incoming-only none, Two-way 5-1024, Outgoing-
only none
RESTARTs 1/1 CALLs 0+0/0+0/0+0 DIAGs 0/0
  Last input 00:00:00, output 00:00:00, output hang never
  Last clearing of "show interface" counters 00:28:48
  Input queue: 1/75/0 (size/max/drops);
  Total output drops: 0
  Queueing strategy: weighted fair
```

```
Output queue: 0/1000/64/0 (size/max total/threshold/
drops)
    Conversations  0/2/256 (active/max active/max total)
    Reserved Conversations 0/0 (allocated/max allocated)
5 minute input rate 321000 bits/sec, 48 packets/sec
5 minute output rate 320000 bits/sec, 48 packets/sec
    12439 packets input, 13257786 bytes, 0 no buffer
    Received 202 broadcasts, 0 runts, 0 giants,
    0 throttles
    0 input errors, 0 CRC, 0 frame, 0 overrun, 0 ignored,
    0 abort
    12438 packets output, 13256434 bytes, 0 underruns
    0 output errors, 0 collisions, 0 interface resets
    0 output buffer failures, 0 output buffers swapped
    out
    0 carrier transitions
    DCD=up  DSR=up  DTR=up  RTS=up  CTS=up
Router_A#
```

The output contains all of the relevant serial data, as well as all of the LAPB and X.25 information. Following are explanations of these new fields:

RNRs Number of Receiver Not Ready events

REJs Number of rejects

SABMs Number of Set Asynchronous Balance Mode requests

FRMRs Number of protocol frame errors

DISCs Number of disconnects

RESTARTs Number of restarts

For more detailed information about LAPB or X.25, the **debug** command must be used.

debug Commands

There are several debug commands associated with X.25. A few of them are debug x25 all, debug x25 events, debug x25 vc, debug x25 interface, and debug lapb. The two that will be discussed in this section are the debug x25 events and debug lapb.

debug x25 events

When the events option is used, the output does not contain any information regarding data or Receive Ready (RR) flow control packets. Calls and other data flow packets are not recorded because of the large amount of output they generate.

debug lapb

This tool can be used when X.25 interfaces experience frequent restarts and instability. X.25 relies on LAPB Layer 2 protocol for stable data link. If there are problems with the LAPB protocol, it propagates to the X.25 protocol and interface. The output from LAPB debugging contains information regarding all packets and traffic that use LAPB encapsulation.

Complete documentation regarding the output from the LAPB debug trace can be found within the documentation included in the UniverCD.

X.25 Link Summary

This section includes the quick reference guide for recognizing, diagnosing, isolating, and resolving X.25 problems.

Symptoms and Problems

Table 7.3 contains common symptoms and their corresponding problems.

TABLE 7.3 X.25 Symptoms and Problems

Symptom or Condition	Associated Problem(s)
X.25 connection failures	(a) Link is down
	(b) Faulty hardware

TABLE 7.3 X.25 Symptoms and Problems *(continued)*

Symptom or Condition	Associated Problem(s)
	(c) Incorrect or faulty wiring
	(d) Improper interface configuration
Excessive errors	(a) Faulty hardware
	(b) Incorrect or faulty wiring

Problems and Action Plans

Table 7.4 summarizes the action plans that are necessary to resolve the problems listed in Table 7.3. The table is meant only as an overall guideline for resolving X.25 problems.

TABLE 7.4 Action Plans for Common X.25 Problems

Problem	Resolution Action Plan
Link down	Follow steps for troubleshooting serial lines.
Faulty hardware or cabling	1. Check the interface status. Verify that the LAPB is in CONNECT state.
	2. If it is not in CONNECT state, use the debug LAPB command.
	3. If there is a definite problem, check the cabling and hardware. Replace equipment as needed.
Misconfigured interfaces or protocol	1. Verify the current configuration by using the show running-config command.
	2. If needed, use debug LAPB to look for SABMs. If no SABMs are sent, change the debugging to debug x25 events.
	3. Watch for RESTART messages and also check the LAPB parameters on the interface.

Troubleshooting Frame Relay

Frame Relay is a popular WAN solution in many networks. Frame Relay supports PVCs and switched virtual circuits (SVCs). These virtual circuits are built by using DLCI numbers. A *Data-Link Connection Identifier (DLCI)* is used to identify the virtual circuits in a Frame Relay cloud. Figure 7.3 depicts a Frame Relay network. Notice the DLCI numbers assigned to the different interfaces throughout the network.

FIGURE 7.3   Frame Relay network

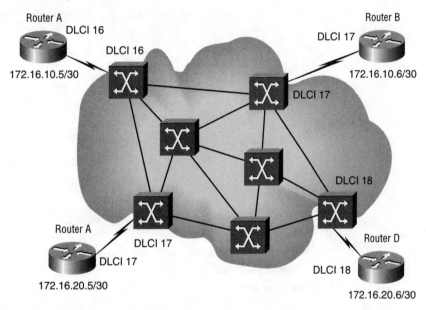

It is important to remember that the DLCI is only locally significant. The DLCI maps to Layer 3 IP addresses, as shown in Figure 7.3. The IP addresses given on the diagram suggest the PVCs that exist through the Frame Relay cloud.

When Frame Relay problems occur, you follow this troubleshooting checklist:

1. Check Layer 1, the Physical layer, for any cabling or interface problems.

2. Check the interface encapsulation.

3. Check the LMI type.

4. Verify the DLCI-to-IP address mapping.

5. Verify the Frame Relay PVCs.

6. Verify the Frame Relay LMI.

7. Verify the Frame Relay Map.

8. Verify the loopback tests, as described in the CSU/DSU Loopback Tests section.

The following commands describe how to execute each of these steps.

Frame Relay *show* Commands

Here is a list of the show commands that will be covered in this section:

- show interface
- show frame-relay lmi
- show frame-relay pvc
- show frame-relay map

You probably noticed a term you didn't recognize. *LMI (Local Management Interface)* provides support for keepalive devices to verify data flow. You will see this term a great deal when dealing with Frame Relay troubleshooting.

show interface

The show interface command is used to provide information on serial lines. In addition to normal serial line information, Frame Relay information is included in the output if the interface is configured for Frame Relay.

Line-by-line detail has already been given for a normal serial interface. Therefore, only the fields relating to Frame Relay are listed. Here is a sample of a Frame Relay interface output:

```
Router_A#show interface serial0
Serial0 is up, line protocol is up
  Hardware is HD64570
  MTU 1500 bytes, BW 1544 Kbit, DLY 20000 usec, rely 255/
  255, load 1/255
  Encapsulation FRAME-RELAY, loopback not set, keepalive
  set (10 sec)
  LMI enq sent  823406, LMI stat recvd 823403, LMI upd
  recvd 507, DTE LMI up
```

LMI enq recvd 0, **LMI stat sent** 0, **LMI upd sent** 0
LMI DLCI 1023 **LMI type** is CISCO **frame relay** DTE
Broadcast queue 0/64, broadcasts sent/dropped 0/0,
interface broadcasts 36752578
Last input 00:00:00, output 00:00:00, output hang never
Last clearing of "show interface" counters never
Input queue: 0/75/0 (size/max/drops); Total output
drops: 0
Queueing strategy: weighted fair
Output queue: 0/64/0 (size/threshold/drops)
    Conversations 0/20 (active/max active)
    Reserved Conversations 0/0 (allocated/max allocated)
5 minute input rate 5000 bits/sec, 6 packets/sec
5 minute output rate 5000 bits/sec, 6 packets/sec
    134880248 packets input, 102288228 bytes, 0 no buffer
    Received 823910 broadcasts, 0 runts, 0 giants
    1 input errors, 1 CRC, 0 frame, 0 overrun, 0 ignored,
    1 abort
    136835759 packets output, 3397101778 bytes, 0
    underruns
    0 output errors, 0 collisions, 14 interface resets
    0 output buffer failures, 0 output buffers swapped
    out
    2 carrier transitions
    DCD=up DSR=up DTR=up RTS=up CTS=up
Router_A#**show interface serial 0.2**
Serial0.2 is up, line protocol is up
  Hardware is HD64570
  Internet address is 172.16.30.6/30
  MTU 1500 bytes, BW 1544 Kbit, DLY 20000 usec, rely 255/
  255, load 1/255
  Encapsulation FRAME-RELAY
Router_A#

Let's highlight the relevant Frame Relay terms:

Encapsulation   Cisco routers support two types of Frame Relay: Cisco and IETF.

LMI enq sent   This is the number of LMI enquiries sent.

LMI stat recvd   This is the number of LMI status packets received.

LMI upd recvd   This is the number of LMI updates received.

DTE LMI   This is the status of the DTE Local Management Interface.

LMI enq recvd   This is the number of LMI enquiries received.

LMI stat sent   This is the number of LMI status packets sent.

LMI upd sent   This is the number of LMI updates sent.

LMI DLCI   This is the DLCI number used for LMI. Cisco LMI type uses DLCI 1023. When ANSI is used, the LMI DLCI is 0.

LMI type   This is the LMI type used by the interface. Default is Cisco. The other two types are ANSI and ITU-T. The LMI type must match on the router and the Frame Relay switch. Simply put, LMI type must match on the DTE and DCE equipment.

show frame-relay lmi

The show frame-relay lmi command displays LMI-relevant information. The output contains the LMI type, enquiry, update, and status information:

```
Router_B#show frame-relay lmi
LMI Statistics for interface Serial0 (Frame Relay DTE) LMI
TYPE = CISCO
  Invalid Unnumbered info 0    Invalid Prot Disc 0
  Invalid dummy Call Ref 0     Invalid Msg Type 0
  Invalid Status Message 0     Invalid Lock Shift 0
  Invalid Information ID 0     Invalid Report IE Len 0
  Invalid Report Request 0     Invalid Keep IE Len 0
  Num Status Enq. Sent 823406    Num Status msgs Rcvd
  823403
  Num Update Status Rcvd 507    Num Status Timeouts 3
```

show frame-relay pvc

When you issue the `show frame-relay pvc` command, you get output that contains the LMI status of every DLCI on the router, or you may be more specific and check only certain PVCs.

There are two types of DLCI usage: local DTE and switched. Things to check for in the output of the command include dropped frames, congestion notifications, and discard-eligible packets.

Here is a sample output. The data provided includes PVC information. It has the input and output packets for the interface, as well as FECN and BECN packet information. These statistics are available for every DLCI PVC on the router. Here, only two PVCs are shown:

```
Router_A#show frame-relay pvc

PVC Statistics for interface Serial0 (Frame Relay DTE)

DLCI = 18, DLCI USAGE = LOCAL, PVC STATUS = ACTIVE,
INTERFACE = Serial0.4

input pkts 37515875 output pkts 38589330 in bytes
4113557032
out bytes 2755391175 dropped pkts 16 in FECN pkts 0
in BECN pkts 0 out FECN pkts 0 out BECN pkts 0
in DE pkts 315420 out DE pkts 0
pvc create time 13w4d, last time pvc status changed
06:40:12

DLCI = 19, DLCI USAGE = UNUSED, PVC STATUS = ACTIVE,
INTERFACE = Serial0

input pkts 38 output pkts 0 in bytes 8372
out bytes 0 dropped pkts 0 in FECN pkts 0
in BECN pkts 0 out FECN pkts 0 out BECN pkts 0
in DE pkts 0 out DE pkts 0
pvc create time 13w4d, last time pvc status changed 7w4d
Num Pkts Switched 0
```

Problems can be detected by watching the number of FECN or BECN packets increase, which indicates line congestion. Forward explicit congestion notification, FECN, notifies the receiving station (DTE) that congestion was experienced en route to the destination. Backward explicit congestion notification, BECN, notifies the sending station that congestion was experienced. FECN messages are sent in the direction of the congestion, and BECN messages are sent in the opposite direction of the congestion.

show frame-relay map

The show frame-relay map command contains information about the DLCI numbers and the encapsulation of all Frame Relay interfaces. The status of the interface is indicated with the up or down state found within the parentheses. The next field indicates the type of interface: point-to-point or multipoint. The DLCI for the interface and the encapsulation type are also included in the output. Here is a sample:

```
Router_B#show frame-relay map
Serial0.10 (down): point-to-point dlci, dlci
24(0x18,0x480), broadcast, IETF, BW = 1024000 status
defined, inactive
Serial0.7 (down): point-to-point dlci, dlci
21(0x15,0x450), broadcast, IETF, BW = 1024000 status
defined, inactive
Serial0.5 (up): point-to-point dlci, dlci 20(0x14,0x440),
broadcast, IETF, BW = 1024000 status defined, active
Serial0.6 (up): point-to-point dlci, dlci 30(0x1E,0x4E0),
broadcast, IETF, BW = 48000 status defined, active
Serial0.4 (up): point-to-point dlci, dlci 18(0x12,0x420),
broadcast, IETF, BW = 1024000 status defined, active
Serial0.2 (up): point-to-point dlci, dlci 27(0x1B,0x4B0),
broadcast, IETF, BW = 48000 status defined, active
Serial0.11 (up): point-to-point dlci, dlci 31(0x1F,0x4F0),
broadcast, IETF, BW = 48000 status defined, active
Serial0.9 (up): point-to-point dlci, dlci 29(0x1D,0x4D0),
broadcast, IETF, BW = 48000 status defined, active
Serial0.12 (up): point-to-point dlci, dlci 32(0x20,0x800),
broadcast, IETF, BW = 48000 status defined, active
Serial0.8 (up): point-to-point dlci, dlci 28(0x1C,0x4C0),
broadcast, IETF, BW = 48000 status defined, active
Serial1.1 (up): point-to-point dlci, dlci 16(0x10,0x400),
broadcast, IETF, BW = 1024000 status defined, active
```

Frame Relay *debug* Commands

As always, you must exercise caution when using debug commands, due to the amount of output they can generate. The more traffic that exists on an interface, the more output that will be generated on the router. The commands that will be discussed in this section are as follows:

- debug frame-relay lmi
- debug frame-relay events

debug frame-relay lmi

An LMI Frame Relay debug displays LMI exchange information. The exchange consists of LMI status enquiries and responses, including sequencing numbers. Here is a sample:

```
Router_B#debug frame-relay lmi
Frame Relay LMI debugging is on
Displaying all Frame Relay LMI data
Serial0(out): StEnq, myseq 142, yourseen 141, DTE up
datagramstart = 0x40081DA0, datagramsize = 13
FR encap = 0xFCF10309
00 75 01 01 01 03 02 8E 8D
Serial0(in): Status, myseq 142
RT IE 1, length 1, type 1
KA IE 3, length 2, yourseq 142, myseq 142
Serial1(out): StEnq, myseq 9, yourseen 15, DTE up
datagramstart = 0x40000528, datagramsize = 13
FR encap = 0xFCF10309
00 75 01 01 01 03 02 09 0F

Serial1(in): Status, myseq 9
RT IE 1, length 1, type 1
KA IE 3, length 2, yourseq 16, myseq 9
Serial2(out): StEnq, myseq 254, yourseen 254, DTE up
datagramstart = 0x40000528, datagramsize = 13
FR encap = 0xFCF10309
00 75 01 01 01 03 02 FE FE
```

The StEnq, myseq, and yourseen are similar to the data provided by the serial debug command. The newly introduced fields are as follows:

RT IE This is a Report Type Information Element.

KA IE This is a Keepalive Information Element.

This debug command does not generate a great deal of output, as you can see. Therefore, it can be used even during high traffic times. Some outputs will include more information than the sample displayed previously. Additional information includes clocking, PVC, and Committed Information Rate detail.

debug frame-relay events

Data provided by this command is useful because it gives details about protocols and applications using the DLCI. A sample follows. The (i) and (o) specify inbound and outbound traffic:

```
Router_A#debug frame-relay events
Serial3(i): dlci 1023(0xFCF1), pkt type 0x309,
datagramsize 13
Serial3.6(o): dlci 1023(0xFCF1), pkt type 0x309,
datagramsize 13
Serial3(i): dlci 1023(0xFCF1), pkt type 0x309,
datagramsize 13
Serial3.6(o): dlci 1023(0xFCF1), pkt type 0x309,
datagramsize 13
Serial0.2(o): dlci 1023(0xFCF1), pkt type 0x309,
datagramsize 13
Serial3(i): dlci 1023(0xFCF1), pkt type 0x309,
datagramsize 13
```

The pkt type is used to distinguish the packet type that transits the DLCI. Several different packet types may appear in the pkt type field. The packet type tells you which applications are on the circuit.

Frame Relay Summary

This summary includes tables that can be used for quick reference when diagnosing, isolating, and resolving Frame Relay problems.

Symptoms and Problems

Table 7.5 includes Frame Relay symptoms and their related problems.

TABLE 7.5   Frame Relay Symptoms and Problems

Symptom or Condition	Associated Problem(s)
Frame Relay link is down.	(a) Faulty cabling
	(b) Faulty hardware
	(c) Local service provider problem
	(d) LMI type mismatch
	(e) Keepalives not being sent
	(f) Encapsulation type
	(g) DLCI mismatch
Cannot ping remote host across a Frame Relay network.	(a) DLCI assigned to wrong subinterface
	(b) Encapsulation mismatch
	(c) Access list problem
	(d) Interface misconfiguration

Problems and Action Plans

Table 7.6 includes the resolution action plans for the problems listed in Table 7.5.

T A B L E 7 . 6 Action Plans for Common Frame Relay Problems

Problem	Resolution Action Plan
Faulty cabling	1. Check the cabling and use a breakout box to test the control leads.
	2. Replace cabling as needed.
Faulty hardware	1. You can isolate hardware problems by performing loopback tests.
	2. Change the cable to a new interface on the router, and configure the new interface to match the configuration of the old interface. If the link comes up, you know that you must replace the hardware.
Local service provider problem	1. If loopback tests bring the LMI state up, but you cannot connect to the remote site, contact the local carrier.
	2. Problems can include carrier problems as well as Frame Relay misconfiguration, such as DLCI mismatch or encapsulation mismatch.
LMI type mismatch	1. Verify that the LMI type on the router matches the LMI type for every device in the PVC.
	2. You won't have access to see the LMI information inside a public provider network; you need to contact the carrier.
Keepalive problems	1. Use the show interface command to see whether keepalives are disabled or are configured properly.

TABLE 7.6 Action Plans for Common Frame Relay Problems *(continued)*

Problem	Resolution Action Plan
	2. If the keepalive is not set, enter the configuration mode and enter the keepalive interval on the proper interface.
Encapsulation type	1. Verify that the encapsulation type is the same on both routers. If non-Cisco equipment is used, the encapsulation must be set for IETF. You can display this information by using the show frame-relay map command.
	2. The encapsulation can be changed by using the encapsulation frame-relay ietf command.
DLCI mismatch	1. Use the show running-config command to display the DLCI number assigned to the proper interface. The show frame-relay pvc command can also display the DLCI assigned to the interface.
	2. If the correct DLCI number is configured on the proper interface, contact the local carrier to verify that it has the same DLCI configured on the Frame Relay switch.
Access List problem	1. Use the show ip interface command to display the access list applied to the interface.
	2. Analyze the access list, and then remove and modify it, if necessary.

Summary

Several troubleshooting methods presented in this chapter can be used to resolve many different types of serial line problems.

show interface can be used to provide information relevant to serial line, X.25, and Frame Relay interfaces. The command output varies, depending on the way the interface was configured.

debug serial interface is similar because it can provide information that is relevant to all types of serial troubleshooting scenarios.

CSU/DSU loopback tests can be used in many scenarios to isolate hardware and software problems encountered with serial lines.

debug commands can be very useful, but it is important to use them with caution because of the large amount of output that they generate. Some information provided by the **debug** commands is hard to understand, so knowledge of the protocol is necessary.

Summary tables were provided for serial, X.25, and Frame Relay troubleshooting. The problems listed in these tables are common ones and should be straightforward to resolve.

Many times, it will be necessary to contact the local service provider to aid in troubleshooting failed links. It is important that you run all of the diagnostics available to you to isolate the problem before you call. If you have done a lot of the groundwork, the carrier will be more willing to run tests within its network.

Commands Used in This Chapter

The following list contains a summary of all the commands used in this chapter.

Command	Description
clear counters serial	Clears the statistical counters on the interface.
debug frame-relay events	Gives details about protocols and applications using the DLCI.

Command	Description
`debug frame-relay lmi`	Displays LMI exchange information. The exchange consists of LMI status enquiries and responses, including sequencing numbers.
`debug lapb`	Contains information regarding all packets and traffic that use LAPB encapsulation.
`debug serial interface`	Displays signaling information for the interface.
`debug serial packet`	Displays information regarding serial packets.
`debug x25 events`	Displays X.25 events in detail.
`show buffers`	Displays buffer statistics for the router.
`show controllers serial`	Shows specific hardware information regarding the serial controller.
`show frame-relay lmi`	Displays LMI-relevant information. The output contains the LMI type, enquiry, update, and status information.
`show frame-relay map`	Contains information about the DLCI numbers and the encapsulation of all Frame Relay interfaces. The status of the interface is indicated with the up or down state found within the parentheses.

Command	Description
`show frame-relay pvc`	Contains the LMI status of every DLCI on the router, or you may be more specific and check only certain PVCs.
`show interface serial`	The `show interface` command executed on a serial interface. Provides important information regarding serial interfaces, including IP, encapsulation, and line statistics.

Key Terms

Before you take the exam, be certain you are familiar with the following terms:

Data-Link Connection Identifier (DLCI)

Local Management Interface

loopback tests

Review Questions

1. What is the output of the `clear counters` command?

   A. It displays all counters for the specified interface, and then resets the counters.

   B. It displays the value of the counters before the last time the interface was reset.

   C. There is no output.

   D. It clears the statistical counter on the specified interface.

2. Which of the following elements are displayed by using the `show interface serial` command? (Choose all that apply.)

   A. Frame Relay information

   B. Encapsulation type

   C. Interface error information

   D. IOS version number

3. Which of the following elements are displayed by using the `show controller serial` command? (Choose all that apply.)

   A. Encapsulation type

   B. LMI type

   C. Clock rate

   D. Cable type

   E. Cable connection status

   F. Error information

4. Which of the following elements are displayed by using the `show buffers` command? (Choose all that apply.)

   A. Interface buffers (on low-level routers)

   B. Very huge buffers

   C. Huge buffers

   D. Tiny buffers

5. Which of the following information fields are displayed by using the `debug serial interface` command? (Choose all that apply.)

    A. myseq

    B. yourseen

    C. mineseen

    D. StEnq

6. What are two of the four CSU/DSU loopback tests? (Choose two.)

    A. Local loopback at local site

    B. Remote loopback from remote site

    C. Local remote loopback from local site

    D. Remote local loopback from remote site

7. Which of the following fields are X.25-related from the `show interface serial` command?

    A. RNRs

    B. REJs

    C. LMI type

    D. SABMs

    E. FRMRs

    F. DLCI

    G. DISCs

    H. RESTARTs

8. Which of the following fields are LAPB-related from the `show interface serial` command? (Choose all that apply.)

    A. RNRs

    B. REJs

    C. LMI type

    D. SABMs

9. Which of the following fields are Frame Relay/LMI-related from the `show interface serial` command? (Choose all that apply.)

   A. LMI enq sent

   B. LMI stat recvd

   C. RESTARTs

   D. LMI encapsulation

10. Which of the following fields are Frame Relay/LMI-related from the `show interface serial` command? (Choose all that apply.)

    A. LMI upd recvd

    B. DTE LMI

    C. LMI enq recvd

    D. Frame Relay enq sent

11. Which of the following fields are Frame Relay/LMI-related from the `show interface serial` command? (Choose all that apply.)

    A. LMI stat sent

    B. LMI upd sent

    C. LMI DLCI

    D. LMI type

12. Which command(s) display the LMI type? (Choose all that apply.)

    A. `show interface serial`

    B. `show frame-relay map`

    C. `show frame-relay pvc`

    D. `show frame-relay lmi`

13. Which of the following information fields are displayed by the `show frame-relay pvc` command? (Choose all that apply.)

A. BECN statistics

B. FECN statistics

C. Configuration register setting

D. VPI number

14. Which of the following commands provide the DLCI number of the serial interface? (Choose all that apply.)

A. `show running-config`

B. `show frame-relay map`

C. `show serial dlci`

D. `show frame-relay lmi`

15. What property must the DLCI number have?

A. It must match the DLCI on the other end of the PVC.

B. It must be between 0 and 16.

C. It has only local significance.

D. All of the above.

16. Which of the following statements is true of the LMI type on the router? (Choose all that apply.)

A. It must match the remote end.

B. It must have the same DLCI.

C. It can be set to Cisco.

D. It can be set to ANSI.

17. Which statements are true regarding the encapsulation used when connecting a Cisco router to a non-Cisco router?

    A. It must be Cisco.

    B. It must be ANSI.

    C. It must be IETF.

    D. It must be ITU.

18. Which statements are true regarding the encapsulation on the router's interface? (Choose all that apply.)

    A. Both sides of the PVC must be using the same type.

    B. Encapsulation is local to the router.

    C. ITU-T is a valid encapsulation type.

    D. IETF is a valid encapsulation type.

19. Which of the following debug commands can be detrimental to a router?

    A. `frame-relay packets`

    B. `frame-relay events`

    C. `frame-relay lmi`

    D. None of the above

20. The `debug frame-relay lmi` command does not generate a large amount of output. Why?

    A. Infrequent LMI exchanges between the router and switch

    B. Small amounts of data in each LMI packet

    C. Non-detailed information provided

    D. None of the above

Answers to Review Questions

1. C. Other than the dialog of the command, there is no output.

2. A, B, C. All of these elements are displayed using the show interface serial command.

3. C, D, E, F. A and B are displayed using the show interface serial command.

4. A, C. B and D are not valid names for the buffer pools. There are others, but they are not listed here.

5. A, B, C, D. All of these fields are available via the output from the `debug serial interface` command

6. A, B. A loopback test is either local or remote.

7. H. RESTARTs can be seen on an X.25 `show interface serial` command.

8. A, B, D. All of these fields can be seen from the command. There are more, but they are not listed here.

9. A, B. These are the Frame Relay/LMI-related fields. There are more, but they are not listed here.

10. A, B, C. These are also valid Frame Relay/LMI fields.

11. A, B, C, D. As you can see, a great number of fields are related to Frame Relay/LMI via the `show interface serial` command.

12. A, D. These are the two commands that can provide information regarding the LMI type.

13. A, B. These, along with other statistics can be found via the `show frame-relay pvc` command.

14. A, B. These are two commands that provide DLCI number information. There are additional commands, but they are not shown here.

15. C. The DLCI does have a limit in values, but it is of local significance only. It does not need to match.

16. A, C, D. It doesn't matter what type is set, as long as both ends of the PVC are configured to use the same type.

17. C. It must be IETF, because non-Cisco equipment will not understand Cisco-specific encapsulation.

18. A, D. IETF and Cisco are valid encapsulations. They must be the same on both sides of the connection.

19. A. The `frame-relay packets debug` can be very detrimental due to the fact that every packet would be analyzed by the debug process.

20. A. The data provided by the `debug` command is summarized and exchanges are not as frequent as Frame Relay packets are.

Chapter 8

Troubleshooting ISDN

TOPICS COVERED IN THIS CHAPTER INCLUDE:

✓ Learning the troubleshooting tools and commands that will enable you to isolate and resolve ISDN problems.

✓ Covering the basics of ISDN technology and familiarizing yourself with the troubleshooting targets within ISDN BRI.

"It still does nothing."

"Yes, this is the phone company. May I please speak with Mr. Isdn?"

The jokes and stories regarding Integrated Services Digital Networks (ISDN) have been merciless and, in some cases, more prevalent than the service itself.

Although it is true that ISDN is difficult to order and configure, ISDN is an important option for administrators to consider when designing networks. Frame Relay and xDSL are strong contenders, but ISDN's availability and cost advantages in certain situations are difficult to ignore. In addition, the difficulties in configuration have been removed to a large degree as the service becomes better known.

Some of the commands listed in this chapter are unavailable on certain Cisco routers because of hardware and software considerations. The Cisco 804 router with internal ISDN BRI was used to provide the screen output for this chapter.

ISDN Fundamentals

ISDN was developed in large part from the phone company's conversion to digital networks from analog switches. This conversion, which started in the 1960s, resulted in the following features:

- Clearer, cleaner signals
- Compressible voice, resulting in better trunking utilization
- Longer distances between switching devices
- Value-added features, including caller ID and three-way calling
- Greater bandwidth—a single connection to the phone company can service more than one phone number
- Elimination of load coils and amplifiers in the network

The concept of ISDN was originally conceived as a means to move the digital network into the home, where a single ISDN connection would provide two standard phone lines and digital services for data. This migration from the analog phone would continue to use the existing copper wire plant, while adding services that would ultimately increase revenues.

Unfortunately, users failed to accept ISDN in the numbers desired. This was especially true in the United States, where installation problems, service availability, and pricing all conspired to hinder acceptance.

In the late 1990s, ISDN was finding a new marketplace. Always On ISDN uses the D channel to replace legacy X.25 networks, especially in point-of-sale transactions. (A description of the B and D channels is included later in this chapter.) Standard ISDN service is popular for videoconferencing and as a residential connection to the Internet. Cable modems and xDSL technologies will probably replace this market in the 21st century, however.

Common ISDN Problems

As with problems affecting other protocols and networking devices, ISDN problems appear in certain common areas. Some frequently encountered problems are presented in this section for administrators to consider when evaluating real-world issues. Later in this chapter, the commands that are appropriate for troubleshooting these problems with Cisco routers will be presented.

ISDN problems may be divided into three general categories: misconfigured routers, physical wiring and ISDN protocol issues, and misconfigured switches. You will learn about each type of problem in this section.

Misconfigured Routers

The router configuration is one of many areas that can require attention when researching ISDN problems. Misconfiguration issues can happen due to a variety of reasons, including typographical errors, erroneous information from service providers, and failure to correctly configure the router itself.

Service Profile Identifiers (SPIDs)

The *Service Profile Identifiers*, or SPIDs, are analogous to phone numbers in the analog phone environment. The numbers usually include the telephone number with area code and, occasionally, extra digits used by the switch. This results in a SPID of 41555512340101, for example, which corresponds to number 415-555-1234, with additional parameters of 0101. The local service provider should document these numbers for the administrator.

ISDN is unique in that the local device must learn its identifying number. This is contrasted with analog phones, which remain unaware of their actual phone number—relying on a switch to trigger the ringer.

SPIDs are used only in North America, and the integration of the phone number into the SPID is most applicable for public ISDN installations. Private ISDN networks usually use SPIDs without a phone number.

It is surprisingly common for administrators to assign IP addresses within two different subnets on ISDN interfaces that connect to each other. It is important to consider each end of an ISDN DDR connection to be part of a single subnet. From a Layer 3 perspective, they are the same as any other point-to-point WAN connection.

Challenge Handshake Authentication Protocol (CHAP)

ISDN provides the capability to control access by requiring authentication, which helps to make use of the public network acceptable from a business/security perspective.

The inner workings of the *Challenge Handshake Authentication Protocol (CHAP)* are beyond the scope of this chapter; basically, CHAP is used to provide a layer of security on inbound connections. When troubleshooting, it is important to confirm that the CHAP configuration on both routers matches. As noted in the output that follows, Cisco also supports the Microsoft CHAP and PAP protocols. MS-CHAP was added in IOS 12.

CHAP authentication requires the point-to-point protocol (PPP). This is enabled on the interface with the command encapsulation ppp.

```
Top(config-if)#ppp auth ?
  chap    Challenge Handshake Authentication Protocol
  (CHAP)
  ms-chap Microsoft Challenge Handshake Authentication
  Protocol (MS-CHAP)
  pap     Password Authentication Protocol (PAP)
```

When troubleshooting, remember that it is quite common for the username parameters that define the passwords to be set incorrectly, including a typo in the password itself or an omitted username. With encrypted passwords, this is made more difficult to research. If a password problem is suspected, an administrator should enable the debug ppp authentication function. As shown in the output that follows (italics added), the authentication failed, due to an incorrect password.

```
Bottom#debug ppp authentication
PPP authentication debugging is on
Bottom#ping 10.1.1.1
Type escape sequence to abort.
Sending 5, 100-byte ICMP Echos to 10.1.1.1, timeout is 2
seconds:
01:54:14: %LINK-3-UPDOWN: Interface BRIO:1, changed state
to up.
```

```
01:54:14: BR0:1 PPP: Treating connection as a callout
01:54:14: BR0:1 PPP: Phase is AUTHENTICATING, by both
01:54:14: BR0:1 CHAP: O CHALLENGE id 7 len 27 from
"Bottom"
01:54:14: BR0:1 CHAP: I CHALLENGE id 7 len 24 from "Top"
01:54:14: BR0:1 CHAP: O RESPONSE id 7 len 27 from "Bottom"
01:54:14: BR0:1 CHAP: I FAILURE id 7 len 25 msg is "MD/DES
compare failed"
01:54:15: %ISDN-6-DISCONNECT: Interface BRIO:1
disconnected from 18008358661 , call lasted 1 seconds
01:54:15: %LINK-3-UPDOWN: Interface BRIO:1, changed state
to down.
01:54:18: %LINK-3-UPDOWN: Interface BRIO:1, changed state
to up.
01:54:18: BR0:1 PPP: Treating connection as a callout
01:54:18: BR0:1 PPP: Phase is AUTHENTICATING, by both
01:54:18: BR0:1 CHAP: O CHALLENGE id 8 len 27 from
"Bottom"
01:54:18: BR0:1 CHAP: I CHALLENGE id 8 len 24 from "Top"
01:54:18: BR0:1 CHAP: O RESPONSE id 8 len 27 from "Bottom"
01:54:18: BR0:1 CHAP: I FAILURE id 8 len 25 msg is "MD/DES
compare failed"
01:54:19: %ISDN-6-DISCONNECT: Interface BRIO:1
disconnected    from 18008358661 , call lasted 1 seconds
01:54:19: %LINK-3-UPDOWN: Interface BRIO:1, changed state
to down.
01:54:22: %LINK-3-UPDOWN: Interface BRIO:1, changed state
to up.
```

Dialer Map Entries

Dialer map statements relate upper-layer addresses to their associated phone numbers. Therefore, it is critical that these entries contain valid IP addresses and numbers. Note that individual dialer map statements are needed for each protocol, as follows:

```
dialer map ip 10.11.3.20 name Top broadcast 18005551212
dialer map appletalk 310.10 name Top broadcast 18005551212
```

Some ISDN switches require the area code and escape character, even when the phone numbers are in the same area code. Thus, it is recommended that dialer-map entries always include the full 11-digit number (North American Dialing Plan).

Access Lists

Access lists are commonly used in ISDN connections to prevent certain types of traffic from triggering a connection. Most frequently, this is done to save money because ISDN is frequently tariffed on a per-minute, per-B-channel basis. As of this writing, some providers offered Centrix ISDN and other options that circumvented this issue, but it is common for Frame Relay and other technologies to provide the same or greater bandwidth at lower cost. This is usually true after approximately 40 hours per month or utilization on the B channels. The xDSL technologies are quickly gaining market share at an unlimited usage tariff, as well.

To control usage, administrators frequently configure an access list based on permitted functions only, and all other services are denied. This causes problems when a new service is added that is not explicitly added to the list. Troubleshooting any ISDN configuration that worked in the past should include a thorough review of all access lists, including the dialer lists.

```
Bottom(config)#dialer-list 1 protocol ip ?
  deny     Deny specified protocol
  list     Add access list to dialer list
  permit   Permit specified protocol
```

A dialer list to provide IP, IPX ,and AppleTalk services is shown as follows:

```
dialer-list 1 protocol ip permit
dialer-list 1 protocol appletalk permit
dialer-list 1 protocol ipx permit
```

Point-to-Point Protocol

Although the point-to-point protocol (PPP) is recommended for ISDN connectivity, there are other options available, including the default HDLC. PPP is recommended in large part to provide security via CHAP, described previously in this chapter.

In troubleshooting, the PPP protocol provides additional information regarding the connection, including the protocol type. This rarely presents itself in a manner that is usable to administrators, however. Rather, an understanding of the protocol and its capability to provide useful functions, including CHAP, is often more helpful to administrators. Note that the PPP protocol is the same for analog or ISDN connections, so the configuration of PPP on a workstation using an analog modem requires PPP encapsulation on an ISDN host router. PPP also supports compression.

PPP contains protocol field values that document the upper layer information included in the datagram. A list of some protocol field values is given in Table 8.1.

TABLE 8.1 Point-to-Point Protocol Field Values

Hex Value of Field	Protocol
0021	IP
0029	AppleTalk
002B	IPX
003D	Multilink
0201	802.1d Hellos
0203	Source Route Bridging Bridge Protocol Data Units
8021	IPCP
8029	ATCP
802B	IPXCP
C223	CHAP
C023	PAP

The debug ppp output later in this chapter provides additional magic number information.

Physical Layer Connections

It is important to consider the Physical layer when troubleshooting, especially in new installations. Wiring is particularly important when connecting ISDN videoconferencing equipment to internal PBX equipment. Some administrators use Category 5 wiring for internal ISDN connections, although Category 3 is acceptable. This chapter focuses on the Basic Rate Interface, which operates over standard copper pairs.

The Basic Rate Interface

Most installations of ISDN in the field are Basic Rate Interface (BRI). This differs from the available primary rate interface (PRI), which uses a T1 as the conduit. The primary rate of telecommunications connections is usually measured in DS-1 increments. A DS-1, or T1, is equivalent to 24T1 voice channels. The basic rate for a voice connection is referred to as a DS-0, or a single 64Kbit channel of the T1. In ISDN, this refers to the single B-channel capacity of the circuit. The formal description of BRI is specified in I.430, whereas the I.431 specification addresses PRI ISDN.

ISDN BRI was designed to provide digital services over existing pairs of copper. The service is used for videoconferencing, voice services, data, and out-of-band management. In addition, the D-channel function of BRI is used for replacement of legacy X.25 networks.

The ISDN BRI Channels

ISDN BRI is a 192Kbps circuit that is divided into three distinct channels. The two primary data channels are the B channels. Each B channel provides 64Kbps. The third channel provides 16Kbps of bandwidth for commands and signaling, and is referred to as the D channel. The remaining bandwidth of 48Kbps is overhead.

The physical frame in ISDN BRI is 48 bits, and the circuit sends 4,000 frames per second.

Services are available to send data over the D channel. These services are often referred to as *always on*, reflecting the non-demand nature of this channel. Always on services are often used to replace X.25 point-of-sale circuits and are provisioned to offer 9.6Kbit bandwidth to the application.

The Local Loop

Although the majority of administrators troubleshoot only the local side of the ISDN circuit, there is a remote side that is critical to the successful operation of ISDN.

The local loop refers to the circuit between the customer premises and the central office (CO). This may include an access layer, referred to as an RT, which permits digital connections to be greater distances from the central office. The local loop interconnects the ISDN device to an ISDN switch—a DMS-100, for example. Note that all digital services are sensitive to the distance between the switch and end device.

The Physical Layer

In order to properly troubleshoot ISDN, it is very important that you have a good understanding of its technology, terminology, architecture, and functionality. Here is a list of some terms used with ISDN that you should familiarize yourself with:

LT/ET The line termination and exchange termination points are called LT and ET, respectively. They handle the termination of the local loop and switching functions.

NT1 The NT1 is the network termination point. It is often the demarc.

TE1 A device with a four-wire, twisted-pair digital interface is referred to as terminal equipment type one. Most modern ISDN devices are of this type.

TE2 Terminal equipment type two devices do not contain ISDN interfaces. A terminal adapter (TA) is required.

R reference point Devices without internal ISDN functions are called TE2s, and require a connection to a TA for operation in ISDN networks. There is no standard connection between these devices, however—the connection is referred to as the R reference point.

S reference point   The S reference point is the interface between the ISDN router (or other user equipment) and the NT2 or NT1. Note that the user equipment is referred to as the TE1 or TA.

T reference point   The interface between the NT1, or the local loop termination point, and the NT2, or customer site switching equipment, is referred to as the T reference point. This point, along with the S reference point, is within the customer premises, and faulty wiring may be the cause of a problem within this context.

U reference point   The U reference point is between the NT1 and the LE. It is normally serviced on a single pair to reduce costs and simplify installations.

Layer 1 S/T Interface   This connection uses a physical connector of RJ-45, as defined in ISO 8877. A straight-through pin configuration connects the terminal end point (TE) to the network termination (NT). Table 8.2 reflects the specific pinning.

TABLE 8.2   The RJ-45 ISDN S/T Interface

Pin	Terminal End-Point (TE)	Network Termination (NT)
1	Power +	Power +
2	Power -	Power -
3	Transmit +	Receive +
4	Receive +	Transmit +
5	Receive -	Transmit -
6	Transmit -	Receive -
7	Power -	Power -
8	Power +	Power +

Some installers use RJ-11 or RJ-14 connections for ISDN terminations. Although these connections work, it is recommended that RJ-45 be used in all circumstances. Wires 1, 2, 7, and 8 may be used for alternate mark inversion (AMI) encoding, and RJ-45 connections provide a visual variance from standard phone jacks.

Misconfigured Phone Switches

Administrators must consider the possibility that the service provider failed to properly configure the ISDN switch. Although this is a very rare occurrence, the possibility exists and should be considered, especially in new installations.

An understanding of ISDN as it relates to the OSI model can greatly assist the network troubleshooter in locating problem causes. In addition, administrators must be aware of the ISDN switch types and their impact on connectivity.

Troubleshooting Layer 2

There are two Layer 2 troubleshooting targets that should be identified and analyzed when working on ISDN networks: the q.921 protocol and PPP.

q.921

ISDN maps well with the OSI reference model. Layer 2 is defined in *q.921*.

The q.921 signaling is carried over the D channel by using *Link Access Procedure protocol, or LAPD.* This connection between the central office switch (or the Teltone ILS-2000 in this test network) and the router must occur and complete before Layer 3 connections are possible.

Troubleshooting q.921 problems is most frequently handled with the `debug isdn q921` command. Often, problems relate to the terminal end point identifier, or TEI. This value uniquely identifies each terminal in the network, and a TEI of 128 represents a broadcast. TEIs 64 through 126 are reserved for assignment during the activation of a Layer 2 ISDN connection. This assignment is dynamic.

TEI has different message types that allow the engineer to identify what type of information is being exchanged, thus identifying any failures in the TEI process. Refer to Table 8.3 for descriptions of these types.

TABLE 8.3   TEI Message Types

Type Number	Type Description
1	ID Request
2	ID Assigned
3	ID Denied
4	ID Check Request
5	ID Check Response
6	ID Remove
7	ID Verify

By using these references, you will be able to understand the exchanges during the TEI process.

Administrators may also need to review the SAPI, or service access point identifier. This field may include a SAPI of 0, which represents that Layer 3 signaling is present. Such signaling is provided by q.931. Other values may include 63, which is a management SAPI for the assignment of the TEI values, or 64, which is used for call control.

One last target to check while troubleshooting the q.921 with the `debug isdn q.921` command is the SABME messages. The SABME is exchanged along with the ID verify messages. If the SABME fails and sends a disconnect response, no further link establishment will occur, and you should investigate the reason for the SABME failure. If the SABME succeeds, an acknowledgment is sent and the Layer 2 connection is complete, and the TE will begin to send INFO frames.

Sample outputs for the `show interface` and `debug isdn q921`

PPP

Troubleshooting targets within the PPP protocol are also important when trying to isolate and resolve ISDN BRI problems. The targets are the steps in PPP and CHAP negotiation. Let's look at the steps taken by PPP to establish a link.

1. LCP at the router (TE) sends a configuration request known as a CONFREQ. Options are specified by the requesting router.

2. The request is either accepted or denied. If it is accepted, an acknowledgment, known as a CONFACK, is returned to the TE. If the request is denied, a negative CONFACK is returned. The difference between a normal and a negative CONFACK is the acceptance or denial of the request. If the CONFREQ was not recognized by the remote TE, a configuration reject message, known as a CONFREJ, is sent to the requesting TE.

3. If the CONFREQ was recognized and accepted and CHAP is being used for authentication, the process continues with the three-way handshake.

    A. Challenge is sent to the remote TE.

    B. The remote TE responds.

    C. If the values match, authentication is given.

The troubleshooting targets in this process are the request/response sequence between the peers as well as all of the CHAP targets.

Troubleshooting Layer 3

The third layer of ISDN is addressed in the ITU-T I.451 specification, which is also called *q.931*. This protocol includes several message commands, which are viewed with the debug isdn q931 command. These commands include call setup, connect, release, cancel, status, disconnect, and user information.

The output of the show and debug commands will be covered later in the chapter. It is important to identify the troubleshooting targets that exist in Layer 3 for ISDN BRI. It is important to recognize that the Layer 3 connection is between the local router (TE) and the remote ISDN switch (ET).

Just as the q.931 operates on the D channel, so does all debugging. Troubleshooting targets include the call reference flag, message types, and information elements. Tables 8.4, 8.5, and 8.6 provide summaries for the messages and their meaning.

TABLE 8.4 Call Reference Flag Definitions

Field Value	Definition
0	From call originator
1	To call originator

TABLE 8.5 q.931 Message Types

Field Value	Definition
0x05	Setup
0x45	Disconnect
0x7d	Status

TABLE 8.6 q.931 Information Elements

Field Value	Definition
0x04	Bearer capability
0x2c	Keypad facility
0x6c	Calling party number
0x70	Called party number
0x3a	SPID

Again, all of this information is provided by the debug isdn q931 command. A sample output is provided later in the chapter. The easiest way to keep track of the different calls is with the call reference number indicated in the output of the debug command. This way you will be able to follow the same call all the way through the process.

Note that these messages are carried on the D channel and are not end-to-end. Rather, they are for connections and setup between the central office switch and the router. The B channel is then available for data transfer.

ISDN calls are established between the router and the local switch over the D channel. The local switch establishes a separate connection to the remote switch, which is responsible for the call setup to the remote router or other ISDN device.

Now let's discuss the call setup on Layer 3 via q.931. It will aid you in troubleshooting and isolating ISDN BRI network problems. This information is provided by the debug isdn q931 command.

1. **SETUP:** The SETUP process sends information elements; this occurs between the local TE and the remote TE.

2. **CALL_PROC:** The call proceeding signal is given; this occurs between the ET and the TE.

3. **ALERT:** The remote TE alerts the local TE via a ring back.

4. **CONNECT:** The remote TE answers, thus stopping the local ring back.

5. **CONNECT_ACK:** A message from the remote ET to the remote TE is sent, acknowledging that the setup is complete.

This is the process that must be followed. You can use the output of the debug isdn q931 to verify that the process is happening correctly.

Switch Types

Recall that ISDN is a connection between the ISDN router and the phone company's central office switch. Therefore, it is important to define the type of switch in use to the router. This is configured with the isdn switch-type command. The isdn switch ? command reports the available switch types and their usual country or continent for the Cisco router.

```
Top(config)#isdn switch-type ?
  basic-1tr6     1TR6 switch type for Germany
  basic-5ess     AT&T 5ESS switch type for the U.S.
  basic-dms100   Northern DMS-100 switch type
  basic-net3     NET3 switch type for UK and Europe
```

```
basic-ni       National ISDN switch type
basic-ts013    TS013 switch type for Australia
ntt            NTT switch type for Japan
vn3            VN3 and VN4 switch types for France
```

If the switch type is unknown (North America), an administrator may wish to use the auto-configuration command. The command is `isdn autodetect`. If the SPID is unknown, the command `isdn spidn 0` may be used. Some administrators prefer to specify this information manually. Please be advised that this option is not available on many routers; however, it is available on the Cisco 804 router, and it may be helpful in new installations. It is likely that Cisco will add this function to new products.

It is important to note that the switch type is specific to the local loop switch, and not the remote connection or entire connection. For example, when connecting a router in North America to use for connections to Europe, the North American router is likely to be set to basic-dms100, for example. The European router is set to basic-net3.

Different switch types and configurations may set each B channel at 56Kbps, instead of the potentially available 64Kbps. Failure to match speeds causes connectivity problems.

ISDN Troubleshooting Commands

The Cisco IOS provides a broad range of troubleshooting commands to assist administrators in the deployment and configuration of ISDN, including the common problems noted previously. Although many of these commands are common to other typologies and protocols (`ping`, for example), other commands are specific to ISDN, including `debug isdn q931`.

ping

As with non dial-on-demand (DDR) connections, the `ping` command is one of the most useful troubleshooting tools. `ping` verifies routes and other connections; in DDR, the command triggers a call.

```
Bottom#ping 10.1.1.1
Type escape sequence to abort.
Sending 5, 100-byte ICMP Echos to 10.1.1.1, timeout is 2
seconds:
.
00:37:12: %LINK-3-UPDOWN: Interface BRI0:1, changed state
to up
00:37:13: %LINEPROTO-5-UPDOWN: Line protocol on Interface
BRI0:1, changed state to up.!!!
Success rate is 60 percent (3/5), round-trip min/avg/max =
32/38/48 ms
Bottom#
00:37:14: %LINK-3-UPDOWN: Interface BRI0:2, changed state
to up
00:37:15: %LINEPROTO-5-UPDOWN: Line protocol on Interface
BRI0:2, changed state to up
```

Note that the five Pings generated by the router completed before the second B channel came up. The `ping` command is perhaps the most common troubleshooting tool in TCP/IP networks.

 It is quite common for the first three Pings to fail in DDR ISDN connections. This is due to the two- to three-second delay in establishing the connection. It is usually not an indication of a problem.

Figure 8.1 diagrams the network used for this chapter.

FIGURE 8.1   ISDN Troubleshooting network design

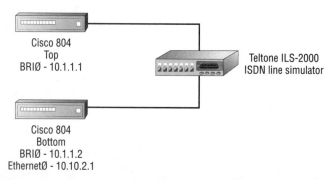

clear interface bri n

The `clear interface bri n` command resets the various counters that are available on the interface and terminates a connection on the interface. The `n` value should equal the port, or port and slot, of the interface. This command is most useful for clearing a call that was activated by a dialer-map or other catalyst, which may be desired when configuring and testing new access lists and other call triggers.

```
Bottom#clear int bri0
Bottom#
00:26:158913789951: %ISDN-6-DISCONNECT: Interface BRI0:2
disconnected from 8358663 , call lasted 104 seconds
00:26:154624128828: %LINK-3-UPDOWN: Interface BRI0:2,
changed state to down
00:26:36: %ISDN-6-LAYER2UP: Layer 2 for Interface BR0, TEI
92 changed to up
00:26:36: %ISDN-6-LAYER2UP: Layer 2 for Interface BR0, TEI
93 changed to up
00:26:37: %LINEPROTO-5-UPDOWN: Line protocol on Interface
BRI0:2, changed state to down
```

show interface bri n

Information regarding the ISDN BRI D channel is available with the `show interface bri n` command. Note that the command reports the B channel's status, as well as spoofing on the interface. This is due to the dynamic nature of DDR connections—they are only up when necessary. In addition, note that the interface was not configured for point-to-point protocol (PPP), but is using the default encapsulation of HDLC.

It is important for administrators to review the output of the `show interface` command, especially when researching user reports of slow performance. For example, the `txload` and `rxload` parameters provide a strong indication of bandwidth loads. Observe the (spoofing) tag in the following output as well. This indicates that the router is maintaining the link as though it was always active, even though ISDN is dynamic.

```
Bottom#show int bri0
BRI0 is up, line protocol is up (spoofing)
  Hardware is BRI with U interface and POTS
  Internet address is 10.1.1.2/24
  MTU 1500 bytes, BW 64Kbit, DLY 20000 usec,
      reliability 255/255, txload 1/255, rxload 1/255
  Encapsulation HDLC, loopback not set
  Last input 00:00:05, output 00:00:05, output hang never
  Last clearing of "show interface" counters never
  Input queue: 0/75/0 (size/max/drops); Total output
drops: 0
  Queueing strategy: weighted fair
  Output queue: 0/1000/64/0 (size/max total/threshold/
drops)
      Conversations  0/1/256 (active/max active/max total)
      Reserved Conversations 0/0 (allocated/max allocated)
  5 minute input rate 0 bits/sec, 0 packets/sec
  5 minute output rate 0 bits/sec, 0 packets/sec
      85 packets input, 791 bytes, 0 no buffer
      Received 4 broadcasts, 0 runts, 0 giants, 0 throttles
      0 input errors, 0 CRC, 0 frame, 0 overrun, 0 ignored,
      0 abort
      92 packets output, 701 bytes, 0 underruns
      0 output errors, 0 collisions, 4 interface resets
      0 output buffer failures, 0 output buffers swapped
out
      1 carrier transitions
```

show interface bri n 1 2

The show interface bri1 2 *n* command is used to display a single B channel of the BRI interface. In this example, the circuit is down.

Although this command can be important when isolating an individual B channel problem, the show interface bri n command usually suffices for the majority of troubleshooting processes.

```
Bottom#show interface bri0 1
BRIO:1 is down, line protocol is down
  Hardware is BRI with U interface and POTS
  MTU 1500 bytes, BW 64Kbit, DLY 20000 usec,
      reliablility 255/255, txload 1/255, rxload 1/255
  Encapsulation PPP, loopback not set, keepalive set (10
  sec)
  LCP Closed, multilink Closed
  Closed: BACP, CDPCP, IPCP
  Last input 00:02:09, output 00:02:09, output hang never
  Last clearing of "show interface" counters never
  Queueing strategy: fifo
  Output queue 0/40, 0 drops; input queue 0/75, 0 drops
  5 minute input rate 0 bits/sec, 0 packets/sec
  5 minute output rate 0 bits/sec, 0 packets/sec
     219 packets input, 3320 bytes, 0 no buffer
     Received 219 broadcasts, 0 runts, 0 giants, 0
     throttles
     146 input errors, 9 CRC, 59 frame, 0 overrun, 0
     ignored, 78 abort
     279 packets output, 16195 bytes, 0 underruns
     0 output errors, 0 collisions, 0 interface resets
     0 output buffer failures, 0 output buffers swapped
     out
     15 carrier transitions
```

show controller bri

The interface hardware controller information is displayed with the show controller bri command. This command is most useful for troubleshooting with Cisco's TAC, but some information can assist the administrator. Most important, the status of the interface, in this case a U type connection, and the superframe error counter are available in this show command.

```
Bottom#show controller bri
BRI unit 0:BRI unit 0 with U interface and POTS:
Layer 1 internal state is ACTIVATED
```

```
Layer 1 U interface is ACTIVATED.
ISDN Line Information:
    Current EOC commands:
        RTN - Return to normal
    Received overhead bits:
     AIB=1, UOA=1, SCO=1, DEA=1, ACT=1, M50=1, M51=1,
     M60=1, FEBE=1
    Errors:  [FEBE]=0, [NEBE]=0
    Errors:  [Superframe Sync Loss]=0, [IDL2 Data
Transparency Loss]=0
             [M4 ACT 1 -> 0]=0
BRI U MLT Timers:  [TPULSE]=0, [T75S]=0
. . . some output omitted . . .
 0 missed datagrams, 0 overruns
 0 bad datagram encapsulations, 0 memory errors
 0 transmitter underruns
```

show isdn status

The show isdn status command is one of the more significant troubleshooting commands because the output reports not only the status of the interface, but a breakdown of each layer. As shown in the first screen, the router has established a connection at Layer 1, but Layer 2 either remains in a negotiation mode or has failed to negotiate due to an improperly set switch or router.

```
Top#show isdn status
Global ISDN Switchtype = basic-ni
ISDN BRI0 interface
dsl 0, interface ISDN Switchtype = basic-ni
    Layer 1 Status:
ACTIVE
    Layer 2 Status:
TEI = 79, Ces = 1, SAPI = 0, State = MULTIPLE_FRAME_
ESTABLISHED
    Spid Status:
TEI 79, ces = 1, state = 8(established)
```

```
    spid1 configured, no LDN, spid1 NOT sent, spid1 NOT
    valid
TEI Not Assigned, ces = 2, state = 1(terminal down)
    spid2 configured, no LDN, spid2 NOT sent, spid2 NOT
    valid
    Layer 3 Status:
0 Active Layer 3 Call(s)
    Activated dsl 0 CCBs = 1
CCB:callid=0x0, sapi=0x0, ces=0x1, B-chan=0 calltype =
INTERNAL
Total Allocated ISDN CCBs = 1
```

The following display reports a correctly configured router and switch. Note that the SPIDs are confirmed and all layers are active on both B channels.

```
Top#show isdn status
Global ISDN Switchtype = basic-ni
ISDN BRIO interface
dsl 0, interface ISDN Switchtype = basic-ni
    Layer 1 Status:
ACTIVE
    Layer 2 Status:
TEI = 83, Ces = 1, SAPI = 0, State = MULTIPLE_FRAME_
ESTABLISHED
TEI = 84, Ces = 2, SAPI = 0, State = MULTIPLE_FRAME_
ESTABLISHED
    Spid Status:
TEI 83, ces = 1, state = 5(init)
    spid1 configured, no LDN, spid1 sent, spid1 valid
    Endpoint ID Info: epsf = 0, usid = 1, tid = 1
TEI 84, ces = 2, state = 5(init)
    spid2 configured, no LDN, spid2 sent, spid2 valid
    Endpoint ID Info: epsf = 0, usid = 3, tid = 1
    Layer 3 Status:
0 Active Layer 3 Call(s)
    Activated dsl 0 CCBs = 0
Total Allocated ISDN CCBs = 0
```

Although this command is most frequently used for new installations, field installations and SOHO (small office, home office) installations frequently find the ISDN device turned off when not in use. This is usually caused by the router being plugged into a power strip attached to a PC.

When the router is disconnected from the ISDN circuit, the D channel (which is always "on") suddenly disconnects. Some phone companies view this as an error, and disconnect the circuit on the central office switch. When the user returns power to the circuit, this prevents connectivity because the switch no longer expects a connection. The show isdn status command provides an indication of problems that require contacting the phone company, and this should be considered if the user has disconnected the power or the ISDN phone cable. It is recommended that administrators instruct users to never disconnect the cable or power.

show dialer

The show dialer command reports information regarding the DDR connections, including the number dialed, the success of the connection, the idle timers that control the duration of a DDR connection without data packets, and the number of calls that were screened or rejected due to administrative policy.

This command is useful for verifying a previous connection or checking the number called. Note that dialer map statements, which link network addresses to ISDN numbers, can be implemented incorrectly. For example, IP address one is linked to number B instead of A. Although the router dials and the ISDN connection may succeed, it cannot pass packets due to Layer 3 mismatches. Note the Idle timer (120 secs) notation, which reflects the default Idle timer of two minutes for each B channel. The Idle timer shuts down the connection when no packets have traversed the link.

```
Bottom#show dialer
BRI0 - dialer type = ISDN
Dial String      Successes    Failures    Last called      Last status
   18008358661                2        0    00:02:49      successful
0 incoming call(s) have been screened.
0 incoming call(s) rejected for callback.
BRI0:1 - dialer type = ISDN
Idle timer (120 secs), Fast idle timer (20 secs)
Wait for carrier (30 secs), Re-enable (15 secs)
Dialer state is idle
```

```
BRIO:2 - dialer type = ISDN
Idle timer (120 secs), Fast idle timer (20 secs)
Wait for carrier (30 secs), Re-enable (15 secs)
Dialer state is idle
```

show ppp multilink

Multilink is an extended portion of the point-to-point protocol. As shown in the following, the service is configured with the ppp multilink bap and ppp bap commands (italicized below).

```
interface BRIO
  ip address 10.1.1.2 255.255.255.0
  no ip directed-broadcast
  encapsulation ppp
  dialer map ip 10.1.1.1 name Top broadcast 18008358661
  dialer-group 1
  isdn switch-type basic-ni
  isdn spid1 0835866201
  isdn spid2 0835866401
  ppp multilink bap
  ppp bap call accept
  ppp bap timeout pending 20
  hold-queue 75 in
```

Debugging ISDN

The debug commands in ISDN are extremely helpful for researching problem causes and resolving them. This section addresses the commands and provides some useful methods for employing them, and attempts to provide scenarios where such commands may be needed.

The debug command is assigned a high CPU priority and can generate a high processor load. Always use caution when using a debug command. The resulting processor load and output can degrade router performance or render the system unusable.

It is recommended that routers be configured with timestamps for debug and log output. Use the `service timestamps debug datetime msec show-timezone localtime` command to provide debug time information.

debug bri

The debug bri command provides information regarding the B channels of the BRI. An example of the command's output is provided below. Note that bandwidth information is also provided.

The B channels of the BRI are the data-carrying channels; therefore, an error in the activation of a B channel prevents data flow. It is also possible for the router to command one B channel to connect while the other B channel fails, which may be due to a misconfigured SPID or configuration problem. This command provides some insight into this potential problem.

```
Bottom#debug bri
Basic Rate network interface debugging is on
Bottom#ping 10.1.1.1
Type escape sequence to abort.
Sending 5, 100-byte ICMP Echos to 10.1.1.1, timeout is 2
seconds:
00:29:48: BRI: enable channel B1
00:29:48: BRIO:MC145572 state handler current state 3
actions 1 next state 3
00:29:48: BRIO:Starting activation
00:29:48: %LINK-3-UPDOWN: Interface BRIO:1, changed state
to up.
00:29:49: BRI 0 B1: Set bandwidth to 64Kb
```

```
00:29:50: %LINEPROTO-5-UPDOWN: Line protocol on Interface
BRIO:1, changed state to up
00:29:50: BRI 0 B2: Set bandwidth to 64Kb
00:29:50: BRI: enable channel B2
00:29:50: BRIO:MC145572 state handler current state 3
actions 1 next state 3
00:29:50: BRIO:Starting activation
00:29:50: %LINK-3-UPDOWN: Interface BRIO:2, changed state
to up.!!!
Success rate is 60 percent (3/5), round-trip min/avg/max =
36/41/52 ms
00:29:50: BRI: enable channel B2
00:29:50: BRIO:MC145572 state handler current state 3
actions 1 next state 3
00:29:50: BRIO:Starting activation
00:29:50: BRI 0 B2: Set bandwidth to 64Kb
00:29:51: %LINEPROTO-5-UPDOWN: Line protocol on Interface
BRIO:2, changed state to up
```

debug isdn q921

The q.921 protocol addresses Layer 2 of the OSI model and its relationship to ISDN. Information regarding the D channel interface is available via the debug isdn q921 command.

The D channel is always connected in ISDN, and the channel is used for signaling between the switch and local ISDN device. Connections over the B channels cannot occur without signaling commands on the D channel. Administrators should use this command to monitor the proper flow of messages when calls do not connect. It is recommended that a baseline debug be performed and recorded to compare against suspected problem debug output.

```
Bottom#debug isdn q921
ISDN Q921 packets debugging is on
00:19:15: ISDN BRO: TX -> RRp sapi = 0  tei = 92 nr = 12
00:19:64424550400: ISDN BRO: RX <- RRf sapi = 0  tei = 92
nr = 12
Bottom#ping 10.1.1.1
Type escape sequence to abort.
Sending 5, 100-byte ICMP Echos to 10.1.1.1, timeout is 2
seconds:
.
```

```
00:19:23: ISDN BR0: TX ->  INFOc sapi = 0  tei = 92  ns =
12    nr = 12  i = 0x080
10305040288901801832C0B3138303038333538363631
00:19:98789554100: ISDN BR0: RX <-  INFOc sapi = 0  tei =
92    ns = 12  nr = 13
i =
0x08018302180189952A1B809402603D8307383335383636318E0B2054
454C544F4E45203120
00:19:23: ISDN BR0: TX ->  RRr sapi = 0  tei = 92  nr = 13
00:19:103079256064: ISDN BR0: RX <-  INFOc sapi = 0  tei =
92  ns = 13  nr = 13
 i = 0x08018307
00:19:24: ISDN BR0: TX ->  RRr sapi = 0  tei = 92  nr = 14
00:19:24: %LINK-3-UPDOWN: Interface BRI0:1, changed state
to up
00:19:24: ISDN BR0: TX ->  INFOc sapi = 0  tei = 92  ns =
13    nr = 14  i = 0x080
1030F
00:19:103079215104: ISDN BR0: RX <-  RRr sapi = 0  tei =
92    nr = 14
00:19:25: %LINEPROTO-5-UPDOWN: Line protocol on Interface
BRI0:1, changed state to up
00:19:107379488692: ISDN BR0: RX <-  UI sapi = 0  tei -
127    i = 0x08010A05040288
9018018A3401403B0282816C09418138333538363637008C138333538
36   3632
00:19:25: %LINK-3-UPDOWN: Interface BRI0:2, changed state
t.!!!
Success rate is 60 percent (3/5), round-trip min/avg/max =
32/38/48 ms
Bottom#o up
00:19:25: ISDN BR0: TX ->  INFOc sapi = 0  tei = 92  ns =
14    nr = 14  i = 0x080
18A0718018A
00:19:107374223360: ISDN BR0: RX <-  INFOc sapi = 0  tei =
92  ns = 14  nr = 15
 i = 0x08010A0F
00:19:25: ISDN BR0: TX ->  RRr sapi = 0  tei = 92  nr = 15
```

```
00:19:27: %LINEPROTO-5-UPDOWN: Line protocol on Interface
BRI0:2, changed state to up
00:19:36: ISDN BR0: TX ->  RRp sapi = 0  tei = 93 nr = 0
00:19:154618822656: ISDN BR0: RX <-  RRf sapi = 0  tei =
93    nr = 0
```

debug ppp negotiation

When the router is configured for point-to-point protocol, the debug ppp negotiation command provides real-time information about the establishment of a session. This is useful if connections are possible with the HDLC protocol and failures with the PPP protocol. There is a great deal of information provided by the following command. However, it can be used to verify the PPP negotiation described earlier in the chapter. You should use this output to verify the troubleshooting targets in PPP negotiation.

```
Bottom#debug ppp negotiation
PPP protocol negotiation debugging is on
Bottom#ping 10.1.1.1
Type escape sequence to abort.
Sending 5, 100-byte ICMP Echos to 10.1.1.1, timeout is 2
seconds:
00:22:28: %LINK-3-UPDOWN: Interface BRI0:1, changed state
to    up
00:22:28: BR0:1 PPP: Treating connection as a callout
00:22:28: BR0:1 PPP: Phase is ESTABLISHING, Active Open
00:22:28: BR0:1 LCP: O CONFREQ [Closed] id 3 len 10
00:22:28: BR0:1 LCP:    MagicNumber 0x50239604
(0x050650239604)
00:22:28: BR0:1 LCP: I CONFREQ [REQsent] id 13 len 10
00:22:28: BR0:1 LCP:    MagicNumber 0x5023961F
(0x05065023961F)
00:22:28: BR0:1 LCP: O CONFACK [REQsent] id 13 len 10
00:22:28: BR0:1 LCP:    MagicNumber 0x5.023961F
(0x05065023961F)
00:22:28: BR0:1 LCP: I CONFACK [ACKsent] id 3 len 10
00:22:28: BR0:1 LCP:    MagicNumber 0x50239604
(0x050650239604)
```

```
00:22:28: BR0:1 LCP: State is Open
00:22:28: BR0:1 PPP: Phase is UP
00:22:28: BR0:1 CDPCP: O CONFREQ [Closed] id 3 len 4
00:22:28: BR0:1 IPCP: O CONFREQ [Closed] id 3 len 10
00:22:28: BR0:1 IPCP:    Address 10.1.1.2 (0x03060A010102)
00:22:28: BR0:1 CDPCP: I CONFREQ [REQsent] id 3 len 4
00:22:28: BR0:1 CDPCP: O CONFACK [REQsent] id 3 len 4
00:22:28: BR0:1 IPCP: I CONFREQ [REQsent] id 3 len 10
00:22:28: BR0:1 IPCP:    Address 10.1.1.1 (0x03060A010101)
00:22:28: BR0:1 IPCP: O CONFACK [REQsent] id 3 len 10
00:22:28: BR0:1 IPCP:    Address 10.1.1.1 (0x03060A010101)
00:22:28: BR0:1 CDPCP: I CONFACK [ACKsent] id 3 len 4
00:22:28: BR0:1 CDPCP: State is Open
00:22:28: BR0:1 IPCP: I CONFACK [ACKsent] id 3 len 10
00:22:28: BR0:1 IPCP:    Address 10.1.1.2 (0x03060A010102)
00:22:28: BR0:1 IPCP: State is Open
00:22:28: BR0 IPCP: Install route to 10.1.1.1
00:22:2.!!!
Success rate is 60 percent (3/5), round-trip min/avg/max =
32/38/48 ms
Bottom#9: %LINEPROTO-5-UPDOWN: Line protocol on Interface
BRI0:1, changed state to up
00:22:29: %LINK-3-UPDOWN: Interface BRI0:2, changed state
to   up
00:22:29: BR0:2 PPP: Treating connection as a callin
00:22:29: BR0:2 PPP: Phase is ESTABLISHING, Passive Open
00:22:29: BR0:2 LCP: State is Listen
00:22:30: BR0:2 LCP: I CONFREQ [Listen] id 3 len 10
00:22:30: BR0:2 LCP:    MagicNumber 0x50239CC8
(0x050650239CC8)
00:22:30: BR0:2 LCP: O CONFREQ [Listen] id 3 len 10
00:22:30: BR0:2 LCP:    MagicNumber 0x50239CDA
(0x050650239CDA)
00:22:30: BR0:2 LCP: O CONFACK [Listen] id 3 len 10
00:22:30: BR0:2 LCP:    MagicNumber 0x50239CC8
(0x050650239CC8)
00:22:30: BR0:2 LCP: I CONFACK [ACKsent] id 3 len 10
```

```
00:22:30: BR0:2 LCP:    MagicNumber 0x50239CDA
(0x050650239CDA)
00:22:30: BR0:2 LCP: State is Open
00:22:30: BR0:2 PPP: Phase is UP
00:22:30: BR0:2 CDPCP: O CONFREQ [Closed] id 3 len 4
00:22:30: BR0:2 IPCP: O CONFREQ [Closed] id 3 len 10
00:22:30: BR0:2 IPCP:    Address 10.1.1.2 (0x03060A010102)
00:22:30: BR0:2 CDPCP: I CONFREQ [REQsent] id 3 len 4
00:22:30: BR0:2 CDPCP: O CONFACK [REQsent] id 3 len 4
00:22:30: BR0:2 IPCP: I CONFREQ [REQsent] id 3 len 10
00:22:30: BR0:2 IPCP:    Address 10.1.1.1 (0x03060A010101)
00:22:30: BR0:2 IPCP: O CONFACK [REQsent] id 3 len 10
00:22:30: BR0:2 IPCP:    Address 10.1.1.1 (0x03060A010101)
00:22:30: BR0:2 CDPCP: I CONFACK [ACKsent] id 3 len 4
00:22:30: BR0:2 CDPCP: State is Open
00:22:30: BR0:2 IPCP: I CONFACK [ACKsent] id 3 len 10
00:22:30: BR0:2 IPCP:    Address 10.1.1.2 (0x03060A010102)
00:22:30: BR0:2 IPCP: State is Open
00:22:31: %LINEPROTO-5-UPDOWN: Line protocol on Interface
BRI0:2, changed state to up
00:21:22: BR0:1 LCP: O ECHOREQ [Open] id 12 len 12 magic
0x5020C645
00:21:22: BR0:1 LCP: echo_cnt 1, sent id 12, line up
00:21:22: BR0:1 PPP: I pkt type 0xC021, datagramsize 16
00:21:22: BR0:1 LCP: I ECHOREP [Open] id 12 len 12 magic
0x5020C654
00:21:22: BR0:1 LCP: Received id 12, sent id 12, line up
00:21:22: BR0:2 LCP: O ECHOREQ [Open] id 12 len 12 magic
0x5020CD1B
00:21:22: BR0:2 LCP: echo_cnt 1, sent id 12, line up
00:21:22: BR0:2 PPP: I pkt type 0xC021, datagramsize 16
00:21:22: BR0:2 LCP: I ECHOREP [Open] id 12 len 12 magic
0x5020CD0D
00:21:22: BR0:2 LCP: Received id 12, sent id 12, line up
00:21:23: BR0:1 PPP: I pkt type 0xC021, datagramsize 16
00:21:23: BR0:1 LCP: I ECHOREQ [Open] id 12 len 12 magic
0x5020C654
```

```
00:21:23: BRO:1 LCP: O ECHOREP [Open] id 12 len 12 magic
0x5020C645
00:21:23: BRO:2 PPP: I pkt type 0xC021, datagramsize 16
00:21:23: BRO:2 LCP: I ECHOREQ [Open] id 12 len 12 magic
0x5020CD0D
00:21:23: BRO:2 LCP: O ECHOREP [Open] id 12 len 12 magic
0x5020CD1B
00:21:24: BRO:2 PPP: I pkt type 0x0207, datagramsize 15
00:21:25: BRO:2 PPP: I pkt type 0x0207, datagramsize 312
00:21:25: %ISDN-6-DISCONNECT: Interface BRIO:1
disconnected from 18008358661 To p, call lasted 120
seconds
00:21:25: %LINK-3-UPDOWN: Interface BRIO:1, changed state
to down
00:21:107379488949: %ISDN-6-DISCONNECT: Interface BRIO:2
disconnected from 8358 663 , call lasted 120 seconds
00:21:25: %LINK-3-UPDOWN: Interface BRIO:2, changed state
to down
00:21:26: %LINEPROTO-5-UPDOWN: Line protocol on Interface
BRIO:1, changed state to down
00:21:26: %LINEPROTO-5-UPDOWN: Line protocol on Interface
BRIO:2, changed state to down
```

debug isdn q931

The q.931 specification addresses Layer 3 of the OSI model for ISDN. Events occurring at Layer 3 may be monitored with the debug isdn q931 command. In the following output, the two B channels are disconnected.

The output from this command is best compared to a baseline debug captured on a working connection. However, administrators may use the output to verify acknowledgments and messages without a complete understanding of the protocol. There is a great deal of information provided by the following command. However, it can be used to verify the Layer 3 (q.931) setup described earlier in the chapter.

```
Bottom#debug isdn q931
ISDN Q931 packets debugging is on
00:15:184683593728: ISDN BRO: RX <-  STATUS_ENQ pd = 8
callref = 0x82
```

00:15:43: ISDN BRO: TX -> STATUS pd = 8 callref = 0x02

00:15:43:   Cause i = 0x809E - Response to STATUS
ENQUIRY or number unassigned

00:15:43:   Call State i = 0x0A

00:15:188978601984: ISDN BRO: RX <- STATUS_ENQ pd = 8
callref = 0x06

00:15:44: ISDN BRO: TX -> STATUS pd = 8 callref = 0x86

00:15:44:   Cause i = 0x809E - Response to STATUS
ENQUIRY or number unassigned

00:15:44:   Call State i = 0x0A

00:16:55834615808: ISDN BRO: RX <- STATUS_ENQ pd = 8
callref = 0x82

00:16:13: ISDN BRO: TX -> STATUS pd = 8 callref = 0x02

00:16:13:   Cause i = 0x809E - Response to STATUS
ENQUIRY or number unassigned

00:16:13:   Call State i = 0x0A

00:16:60129583104: ISDN BRO: RX <- STATUS_ENQ pd = 8
callref = 0x06

00:16:14: ISDN BRO: TX -> STATUS pd = 8 callref = 0x86

00:16:14:   Cause i = 0x809E - Response to STATUS
ENQUIRY or number unassigned

00:16:14:   Call State i = 0x0A

00:16:188978601984: ISDN BRO: RX <- DISCONNECT pd = 8
callref = 0x82

00:16:188978561024:   Cause i = 0x8290 - Normal call
clearing

00:16:188978601984:   Signal i = 0x3F - Tones off

00:16:44: %ISDN-6-DISCONNECT: Interface BRIO:1
disconnected   from 18008358661 To p, call lasted 120
seconds

00:16:44: %LINK-3-UPDOWN: Interface BRIO:1, changed state
to down

00:16:44: ISDN BRO: TX -> RELEASE pd = 8 callref = 0x02

00:16:188978601984: ISDN BRO: RX <- RELEASE_COMP pd = 8
callref = 0x82

00:16:188978561024: %ISDN-6-DISCONNECT: Interface BRIO:2
disconnected from 8358 663 , call lasted 120 seconds

00:16:44: ISDN BRO: TX -> DISCONNECT pd = 8 callref =
0x86

```
00:16:44:          Cause i = 0x8090 - Normal call clearing
00:16:188978561024: ISDN BRO: RX <-  RELEASE pd = 8
callref   = 0x06
00:16:44: %LINK-3-UPDOWN: Interface BRIO:2, changed state
to down
00:16:44: ISDN BRO: TX -> RELEASE_COMP pd = 8  callref =
0x86
00:16:45: %LINEPROTO-5-UPDOWN: Line protocol on Interface
BRIO:1, changed state to down
00:16:45: %LINEPROTO-5-UPDOWN: Line protocol on Interface
BRIO:2, changed state to down
```

debug ppp packet

The debug ppp packet command reports real-time PPP packet flow, including the type of packet and the specific B channel used. Although this command generates a significant amount of output, it is quite useful for locating errors that involve upper-layer protocols.

As with other debug packet commands, the debug ppp packet command records each packet that moves through the router using PPP. As such, the administrator can monitor traffic flows as if they had a protocol analyzer attached to the interface. This may be useful for troubleshooting Application layer problems, but a formal protocol analyzer is highly recommended.

```
Bottom#debug ppp packet
PPP packet display debugging is on
Bottom#ping 10.1.1.1
Type escape sequence to abort.
Sending 5, 100-byte ICMP Echos to 10.1.1.1, timeout is 2
seconds:
00:24:49: %LINK-3-UPDOWN: Interface BRIO:1, changed state
to up.
00:24:50: BRO:1 LCP: O CONFREQ [Closed] id 4 len 10
00:24:50: BRO:1 LCP:    MagicNumber 0x5025BF23
(0x05065025BF23)
00:24:50: BRO:1 PPP: I pkt type 0xC021, datagramsize 14
00:24:50: BRO:1 PPP: I pkt type 0xC021, datagramsize 14
00:24:50: BRO:1 LCP: I CONFREQ [REQsent] id 14 len 10
```

```
00:24:50: BR0:1 LCP:    MagicNumber 0x5025BF46
(0x05065025BF46)
00:24:50: BR0:1 LCP: O CONFACK [REQsent] id 14 len 10
00:24:50: BR0:1 LCP:    MagicNumber 0x5025BF46
(0x05065025BF46)
00:24:50: BR0:1 LCP: I CONFACK [ACKsent] id 4 len 10
00:24:50: BR0:1 LCP:    MagicNumber 0x5025BF23
(0x05065025BF23)
00:24:50: BR0:1 PPP: I pkt type 0x8207, datagramsize 8
00:24:50: BR0:1 PPP: I pkt type 0x8021, datagramsize 14
00:24:50: BR0:1 CDPCP: O CONFREQ [Closed] id 4 len 4
00:24:50: BR0:1 PPP: I pkt type 0x8207, datagramsize 8
00:24:50: BR0:1 IPCP: O CONFREQ [Closed] id 4 len 10
00:24:50: BR0:1 IPCP:    Address 10.1.1.2 (0x03060A010102)
00:24:50: BR0:1 CDPCP: I CONFREQ [REQsent] id 4 len 4
00:24:50: BR0:1 CDPCP: O CONFACK [REQ.!!!
Success rate is 60 percent (3/5), round-trip min/avg/max =
36/41/52 ms
. . . some output omitted . . .
00:25:03: BR0:2 LCP: O ECHOREP [Open] id 2 len 12 magic
0x5025C605undebug all
All possible debugging has been turned off
Bottom#
```

debug dialer

The debug dialer command provides information regarding the cause of a dialing connection and the status of the connection. Note in the following output that an IP packet caused the dial to occur. This information can provide assistance for tuning connections. Administrators frequently do this to limit the use of an ISDN circuit when charged on distance and per-minute tariffs.

```
Bottom#debug dialer
Dial on demand events debugging is on
Bottom#ping 10.1.1.1
Type escape sequence to abort.
Sending 5, 100-byte ICMP Echos to 10.1.1.1, timeout is 2
seconds:
```

```
00:27:26: BRIO: Dialing cause ip (s=10.1.1.2, d=10.1.1.1)
00:27:26: BRIO: Attempting to dial 18008358661
00:27:27: %LINK-3-UPDOWN: Interface BRIO:1, changed state
to up.
00:27:27: dialer Protocol up for BRO:1
00:27:28: %LINEPROTO-5-UPDOWN: Line protocol on Interface
BRIO:1, changed state to up
00:27:29: %LINK-3-UPDOWN: Interface BRIO:2, changed state
to up.!!!
Success rate is 60 percent (3/5), round-trip min/avg/max =
32/37/48 ms
Bottom#
00:27:29: dialer Protocol up for BRO:2
00:27:30: %LINEPROTO-5-UPDOWN: Line protocol on Interface
BRIO:2, changed state to up
```

Summary

In this chapter, some of the common issues confronting administrators in ISDN networks were presented, including encapsulation, SPID configuration, and Physical layer connections. In addition, the tools necessary for analyzing and resolving these problems were presented as they relate to the Cisco IOS.

Other troubleshooting elements covered in this chapter include:

- Router configurations
- Physical wiring
- Switch configurations
- Cisco IOS commands for troubleshooting ISDN environments
- The Basic Rate Interface (BRI) and the B and D channels
- ISDN protocols—q.921 and q.931

Commands Used in This Chapter

The following list contains a summary of all the commands used in this chapter.

Command	Description
clear interface bri n	Resets the various counters that are available on the Basic Rate Interface (BRI) and terminates a connection on the interface.
debug bri	Provides information regarding the B channels of the interface.
debug dialer	Provides information regarding the cause of a dialing connection and the status of the connection.
debug isdn q921	Gives details regarding the Layer 2 connection sequence for ISDN.
debug isdn q931	Gives details regarding the Layer 3 connection sequence for ISDN.
debug ppp authentication	Gives details regarding the PPP / CHAP authentication connection sequence.
debug ppp negotiation	Provides real-time information about the establishment of a session.
debug ppp packet	Reports real-time PPP packet flow, including the type of packet and the specific B channel used.
ping	Initiates an ICMP echo request. There are two levels, User and Privileged. The IP protocol is used.
show controller bri	Displays the interface status and the superframe error counter.

Command	Description
show dialer	Reports information regarding the DDR connections, including the number dialed, the success of the connection, the idle timers that control the duration of a DDR connection without data packets, and the number of calls that were screened or rejected due to administrative policy.
show interface bri n	Reports the B channel's status, as well as spoofing on the interface.
show interface bri1 2 n	Displays a single B channel of the BRI interface.
show isdn status	Reports the status of the interface, as well as a breakdown of each layer.
show ppp multilink	Displays configuration settings for PPP Multilink.

Key Terms

Before you take the exam, be certain you are familiar with the following terms:

access lists

Challenge Handshake Authentication Protocol (CHAP)

dialer map statements

ISDN BRI

Layer 1 S/T Interface

Link Access Procedure Protocol(LAPD)

LT/ET

NT1

q.921

q.931

R reference point

S reference point

Service Profile Identifiers

T reference point

TE1

TE2

U reference point

Review Questions

1. Where does the q.931 signaling operate?

   A. At Layer 3 of the OSI model on the B channel

   B. At Layer 2 of the OSI model on the B channel

   C. At Layer 3 of the OSI model on the D channel

   D. At Layer 2 of the OSI model on the D channel

   E. On all channels of the BRI

2. What does the Basic Rate Interface (BRI) provide?

   A. 64Kbps of bandwidth in each direction

   B. 192Kbps of user bandwidth

   C. Two 64Kbps data channels and one management channel of 16Kbps

   D. Two 64Kbps data channels

   E. 128Kbps for user data

3. The remote router is connected to a DMS-100 switch using the basic-dms100 setting. The local router would be configured with what command?

   A. `isdn switch-type basic-dms100`

   B. `isdn switch-type basic-basic-ni1`

   C. `isdn switch basic dms100`

   D. Answer cannot be determined from the information given

4. Challenge Handshake Authentication Protocol requires which of the following? (Choose all that apply.)

A. ISDN

B. PPP

C. A defined username

D. Encrypted passwords on the router

E. An external server running TACACS+

5. Router_A is configured for ISDN BRI and PPP, with an IP address of 192.168.10.1 and a subnet mask of 255.255.255.252. Router_B would be configured with which of the following?

A. 192.168.10.254

B. 192.168.10.2

C. 192.168.10.3

D. `ip unnumbered`

E. Answer cannot be determined from the information given

6. An ISDN call initially succeeds, but Pings and other packets fail. What is the likely cause? (Choose all that apply.)

A. A faulty cable

B. A misconfiguration of CHAP

C. Incorrect speeds between the switch and router

D. An incorrect route or missing route

7. An administrator finds that an ISDN router does not dial. What are the possible causes? (Choose all that apply.)

   A. A misconfigured dialer map

   B. A dialer list filter

   C. Incorrect switch type

   D. Incorrect SPIDs

8. What does the `clear interface bri` n command disconnect?.

   A. The interface counters for interface *n*

   B. All calls on the router

   C. The active calls on interface *n*

   D. None of the above

9. What are the advantages of CHAP? (Choose all that apply.)

   A. Password authentication

   B. Compression

   C. Encryption of data packets

   D. Encryption of the authentication process

10. The command(s) to restrict dialing on an ISDN router can include which of the following?

   A. `dialer-list 1 protocol ip list 101`

   B. `dialer list 1 protocol ip list 110`

   C. `access-list 200 permit ip any any`

   D. `dialer-map deny packet bri0`

11. Which of the following is required for CHAP services?

   A. TCP/IP

   B. PPP

   C. PAP

   D. TACACS+

   E. Radius

12. Which channels must be active in order for ISDN BRI to send packets?

   A. Both B channels

   B. One B channel and the D channel

   C. Both B channels and the D channel

   D. All 24 B channels

13. Which of the following commands provides information regarding superframe sync loss?

   A. `show interface bri`

   B. `show controller bri`

   C. `show isdn sync`

   D. `show isdn controller`

14. In North America, a SPID might appear as which of the following?

   A. 10.1.1.1

   B. e415.5551.2120

   C. 41555512120101

   D. 5551212

15. To verify all three layers of an ISDN circuit prior to dialing, an administrator should use which of the following commands?

   A. `show ppp multilink`

   B. `show dialer`

   C. `debug bri`

   D. `show isdn status`

16. How long is the default ISDN idle timer for each B channel?

    A. 30 seconds

    B. 60 seconds

    C. 90 seconds

    D. 120 seconds

    E. 300 seconds

17. Layer 3 of ISDN (q.931) is responsible for which of the following?

    A. Determining the switch type

    B. Call setup and disconnect

    C. Assignment of the TEI

    D. Encapsulation of packets on the B channel

18. What is the D channel used for? (Choose all that apply.)

    A. q.921 messages

    B. q.931 messages

    C. TCP/IP

    D. AppleTalk

19. If the switch type is unknown, which command may the administrator use?

    A. `isdn switch type 0`

    B. `isdn auto switch`

    C. `isdn autodetect`

    D. `isdn switch generic`

    E. None of the above

20. An administrator has a non-ISDN device (TE2). Which of the following is required to connect the device to the ISDN network?

A. A terminal adapter (TA)

B. Category 5 wiring

C. Category 3 wiring

D. A codec

E. Device cannot be connected

Answers to Review Questions

1. C. q.931 runs on the D channel and is located at Layer 3.

2. C. While D and E are partially correct, the BRI includes both B channels and the D channel.

3. D. More information is needed before the switch-type is configured.

4. B, C. PPP is required for CHAP to work on ISDN. Usernames must be defined on the routers for authentication purposes. The other options are not required for proper CHAP operation.

5. B. The subnet mask indicates only two hosts on the network. The only other host allowed is 192.168.10.2.

6. B, D. A faulty cable can be eliminated because the call would not succeed if there were a cable fault. Speeds are default.

7. A, B, C, D. Any of these can be cause of the router not dialing.

8. C. The interface must be specified to clear the call.

9. A, D. CHAP was intended for password authentication and encryption.

10. A. The correct syntax requires a hyphen.

11. B. PPP is a required protocol for CHAP to function.

12. B. One B channel may be used without the use of the other. The D channel must be active to handle the call.

13. B. The controller command shows the superframe information.

14. C. The SPID is appended to the 10-digit phone number.

15. D. The status command provides the necessary information.

16. D. The timer is set for 2 minutes idle time.

17. B. q.931 is responsible for the call setup and disconnect, since this occurs on Layer 3.

18. A, B. The D channel is used for administration and not data (payload) transfers.

19. C. Autodetect tells the router to listen for the switch type and set it accordingly.

20. A. A terminal adapter is required for a non-ISDN device.

Chapter

9

Troubleshooting Novell Connectivity

TOPICS COVERED IN THIS CHAPTER INCLUDE:

- ✓ Learning to recognize problem symptoms that relate to IPX and learning what must be done to resolve those problems utilizing the troubleshooting method.

- ✓ Learning the inner workings of Novell IPX, such as the connection sequences.

- ✓ Learning which troubleshooting tools will be useful in identifying and solving Novell IPX network problems.

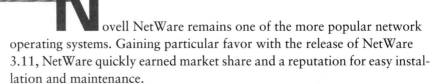

ovell NetWare remains one of the more popular network operating systems. Gaining particular favor with the release of NetWare 3.11, NetWare quickly earned market share and a reputation for easy installation and maintenance.

Part of this reputation is due to the simplicity of NetWare's network protocol—IPX (Internetwork Packet Exchange). IPX removed many of the client-configuration issues that were inherent in other protocols.

With the release of NetWare 5.0, Novell departed from the IPX/SPX (Sequenced Packet Exchange) protocol in favor of the more universal TCP/IP. This was due in large part to the growth of the Internet and the advantages of using a single network protocol. There are many legacy applications and networks that still make use of IPX, however, and there are still advantages to using it. There are also specific issues that arise in NetWare environments that require troubleshooting by the network administrator.

In this chapter, troubleshooting commands, connection sequences, and diagnostic tools will be presented as they relate to an IPX environment. This includes an overview of IPX networks and addressing. In this chapter, too, you will be provided the opportunity to work on some labs that will allow you to troubleshoot general problems as well as IPX-specific symptoms.

IPX Networking Fundamentals

Although IPX operates at the Network layer of the OSI model and shares addressing concepts with IP, it is much easier to configure and administer. IPX addresses appear in the format `network.node`, where the network is an administrator-assigned address of four octets. This address is combined with the MAC layer address of the node, creating a ten-octet address. This system greatly reduces the administrative overhead at the network node—workstation, printer, or other device. In addition, the addressing scheme is independent of the IP subnet mask concept, and any number of nodes can belong to an IPX network within the constraints of the medium and the broadcast limitations of IPX itself.

As with TCP/IP addresses, IPX addresses can be written in several formats. Most often, they're written in hexadecimal—for example, 00007C80.0000.8609.33E9. The first eight hex digits (00007C80) represent the network portion of the address; the remaining 12 hex digits (0000.8609.33E9) represent the node portion and are the MAC address of the workstation. When referring to the IPX network, it's a common IPX custom to drop leading 0s. Thus, the above network address is referred to as IPX network 7C80. The node portion is commonly divided into three sections of four hex digits that are divided by periods, as shown.

Many networks use both IP and IPX concurrently. A common convention is to use the IP decimal or hex values to make up the IPX network number; thus, 10.11.10.0 becomes IPX network 10d11d10 or 10d0Bd10 (the "d" is for "dot"). Some network administrators alter this convention in favor of a frame type–location–segment format. For example, F4150001 could refer to the first IPX network using the Ethernet II frame type in the San Francisco office (area code 415). Please note that IPX network numbers must be unique within the entire internetwork.

IPX simplifies functions for the network and server administrators, in that the IP functions of DHCP, ARP, and DNS/WINS are included in the base functionality of the protocol. ARP packets are unnecessary because the MAC address is part of the overall network address. Address assignment (the DHCP function in IP) is also handled by IPX because all MAC addresses are unique, by design. The network number is presumed unique as a function of both the internetwork design and the administrator's policies. Finally, name resolution is a function of the SAP (service advertising protocol) process, which automatically updates all resources with the address and socket of all services. This simplification is not without its penalties, because IPX and its higher-level protocol SPX have a reputation for being chattier than TCP/IP.

Connecting to a Novell Network

Although a myriad of problems can confront network administrators in NetWare environments, a significant percentage of issues includes the initial connection between the client and server. This connection, by its very nature, may be the first indication of an erred configuration or other problem within the network.

Connecting to a NetWare server first requires an administrator to select an encapsulation method for the network. Once connectivity is established at this layer, service broadcasts begin. This section covers the following issues related to IPX:

- Encapsulation

- Get Nearest Server

- Service Advertising Protocol

Encapsulation

In NetWare, *encapsulation and framing* refer to the method used to take an IPX datagram, a Layer 3 element, and add it to an appropriate Layer 2 frame. In this section, the framing process is outlined as it relates to Ethernet. Framing is also relevant in Token Ring and FDDI topologies, however.

Encapsulation is one of the more common troubleshooting problems in NetWare networks. If the frame type does not match on all network resources, the various components cannot communicate. This is akin to speaking a different language from everyone else in the room—communication is impossible without a translator. If client A speaks SNAP and the server speaks 802.3, they do not understand each other. They must both speak either 802.3 or SNAP.

The four Ethernet IPX frame options are 802.3, 802.2, SNAP, and Ethernet II. Note that Cisco refers to these Novell names with different terminology, as shown in Table 9.1.

TABLE 9.1 Novell Ethernet Encapsulations

NetWare Frame Type	Features	Cisco Term
Ethernet_802.3	Default IPX frame type through NetWare 3.11. 802.3 supports only IPX and contains a length field after the source MAC address. It is available only on Ethernet.	novell-ether
Ethernet_802.2	Default IPX frame type since NetWare 3.12. This frame type is supported for Ethernet, FDDI, and Token Ring. It is recommended in environments that have a combination of physical media.	sap or iso1
Ethernet_II	Supports both TCP/IP and IPX. The ether type is placed after the source MAC address. IPX uses 8137 for the ether type; IP uses 0800.	arpa
Ethernet_SNAP	AppleTalk, IPX, and TCP/IP are supported on Token Ring, Ethernet, and FDDI. It includes a SNAP header.	snap

It was noted earlier that all resources need to use the same frame type on the network. There are times, however, when more than one frame type might be supported on a particular segment. This may be during a transition from one frame type to another, or to support a specific hardware or software platform. This usually involves configuring the server and/or router for all applicable frame types, and it adds a great deal of unnecessary overhead for both the server and the network. It is recommended that administrators select one frame type for new installations and remove as many frame types as possible in legacy installations.

Although the default protocol for NetWare 5.0 is IP, the IPX default (when used) is Ethernet 802.2, and 802.2 has been the default since Net-Ware 3.12. Prior to version 3.12, Novell used Ethernet 802.3, or raw Ethernet. This frame type supports only IPX, and places a length field after the source MAC address in an Ethernet frame. As noted in Table 9.1, the selection of frame type is dependent on existing network applications and configurations, as well as on the features needed.

WARNING   IPX external network numbers must be unique for each frame type used, even if two frame types are bound to the same physical network.

Get Nearest Server

Before connecting to a Novell server, clients must locate an appropriate resource. This is accomplished with the *GNS (get nearest server)* request that is specified within the SAP. The next section addresses the SAP process specifically, whereas the focus of this section is the GNS process itself.

GNS is a broadcast datagram that is answered by any IPX server on the network. If there are multiple servers on a network segment, the client receives a response from each one and accepts the first one for the rest of the initialization process. Note that the first server may not be the preferred server listed in the client's configuration file.

When a client wishes to connect to a network resource, it uses the GNS broadcast, which is captured with an EtherPeek analyzer, as follows. In this example, the workstation's MAC address is 00:60:08:9e:2e:44 and the first packet is the client's GNS request.

```
Flags:  0x80 802.3
 Status:  0x00
 Packet Length:64
 Timestamp: 22:56:14.565643 10/07/1998
802.3 Header
Destination: ff:ff:ff:ff:ff:ff Ethernet Brdcast
```

Source: 00:60:08:9e:2e:44

LLC Length: 38

802.2 Logical Link Control (LLC) Header

Dest. SAP: 0xe0 NetWare

Source SAP: 0xe0 NetWare Individual LLC Sublayer
Management Function

Command: 0x03 Unnumbered Information

IPX - NetWare Protocol

Checksum: 0xffff

Length: 34

Transport Control:

Reserved: %0000

Hop Count: %0000

Packet Type: 0 Novell

Destination Network: 0x00000000

Destination Node: ff:ff:ff:ff:ff:ff Ethernet Brdcast

Destination Socket: 0x0452 Service Advertising Protocol

Source Network: 0xf3df9b36

Source Node: 00:60:08:9e:2e:44

Source Socket: 0x4000 IPX Ephemeral

SAP - Service Advertising Protocol

Operation: 3 NetWare Nearest Service Query

Service Type: 4 File Server

Extra bytes (Padding):

....   00 04 00 04 00 04 00 04 00

Frame Check Sequence: 0x00000000

Novell networking adheres to a client-server model in almost all cases. As
such, servers are strictly servers and clients are resources that use the services provided by servers. This differs from AppleTalk and Microsoft networking, where clients can be servers as well.

Note that the GNS request is a broadcast and is not forwarded by a router.
Although this might lead an administrator to believe that an IPX server needs to
be installed on each network segment, this is not the case. IPX places a GNS

listener on each IPX network. The router also contains a SAP table and responds as necessary to GNS requests.

Cisco routers do not respond to a GNS request if a NetWare server is on the segment.

In the next capture, the Ecorp server responded to the GNS broadcast sent previously, and is providing the client with its IPX network address and status as a file server:

```
Flags:  0x80 802.3
 Status:  0x00
 Packet Length:118
 Timestamp: 22:56:14.565643 10/07/1998
802.3 Header
 Destination: 00:60:08:9e:2e:44
 Source:  00:60:08:9d:2a:8e
 LLC Length: 99
802.2 Logical Link Control (LLC) Header
 Dest. SAP: 0xe0 NetWare
 Source SAP: 0xe0 NetWare Group LLC Sublayer Management
Function
 Command:  0x03 Unnumbered Information
IPX - NetWare Protocol
 Checksum:   0xffff
 Length:   96
 Transport Control:
 Reserved:  %0000
 Hop Count:  %0000
 Packet Type:  4 PEP
 Destination Network: 0xf3df9b36
 Destination Node:  00:60:08:9e:2e:44
 Destination Socket: 0x4000 IPX Ephemeral
 Source Network:  0xf3df9b36
 Source Node:  00:60:08:9d:2a:8e
 Source Socket:  0x0452 Service Advertising Protocol
```

```
SAP - Service Advertising Protocol
 Operation:  4 NetWare Nearest Service Response
Service Advertising Set #1
 Service Type:  4 File Server
 Service Name:
 ECORP.....................................
 Network Number: 0x34b62f24
 Node Number:  00:00:00:00:00:01
 Socket Number: 0x0451
 Hops to Server: 1
 Extra bytes (Padding):
   .    00
Frame Check Sequence: 0x00000000
```

The return packet from Ecorp is a unicast back to the requesting client. This is more efficient than a broadcast-based return, and the packet includes information about the services provided and the internal network number.

At this point in the connection, the client has no knowledge of the services available—the SAP table that contains the information about all servers was not sent to the client. Rather, the client has a single server from which to obtain this information. The GNS process presumes that the first server to respond to the GNS request is the closest (or least busy) of equally preferable servers.

Following the GNS response, the client requests routing information from the router. Once this information is provided, the client establishes a direct connection to the server.

Figure 9.1 provides a visual representation of the GNS process in an IPX network where the server is separated from the client by a router. The first two transmissions from the client are broadcasts, whereas the responses are unicasts. NCP (NetWare Control Protocol) is a connection-oriented protocol that is used for primary Novell functions. Once the client and server establish an NCP session, the client proceeds to the login phase.

FIGURE 9.1 The Novell connection sequence with a remote server

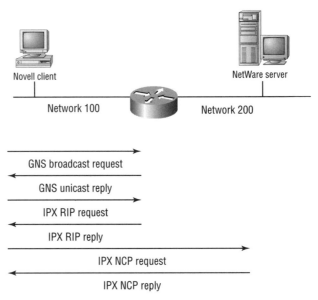

Service Advertising

NetWare servers advertise their services by sending *SAP (service advertising protocol)* broadcasts. These advertisements are sent every 60 seconds by default, and are heard by all servers and routers. In order for clients to find their desired resource initially, the nearest server needs to have an entry in its SAP table for that resource. The advantage to the SAP system is that all servers (barring access lists) are aware of all resources in the internetwork, and the client can obtain the information from any server. The disadvantage is that the SAP process doesn't scale well—the server's processor and the network itself must transmit and process all the information about all the resources. This can reduce overall network availability for user functions. These issues will be reviewed later in this chapter.

It is important to note that services are learned and incorporated into each individual IPX resource's SAP table. This summarized information is then re-sent out each interface on the router or server to populate all other resources. This is an important consideration in troubleshooting because a problem in forwarding or storing the SAP table on any server or router can cause services to be unavailable.

Because SAP information is shared among all servers, the servers eventually become aware of all available services and are thereby equipped to respond to client GNS requests. As new services are introduced, they're automatically added to local SAP tables and added to new broadcasts to populate other servers.

Unless the configuration is modified, SAPs are sent from each IPX router interface at 60-second intervals—identical to NetWare servers. This is a significant point, especially with WAN links, where bandwidth may be limited. The router isolates SAP broadcasts to individual segments and passes along only the summarized information to each segment.

A SAP broadcast decodes with an EtherPeek analyzer, as follows:

```
Flags:      0x00
 Status:      0x00
 Packet Length:306
 Timestamp:  23:48:36.362000 06/28/1998
Ethernet Header
 Destination: ff:ff:ff:ff:ff:ff Ethernet Brdcast
 Source:      00:80:5f:ad:14:e4
 Protocol Type:81-37 NetWare
IPX - NetWare Protocol
 Checksum:        0xffff
 Length:          288
 Transport Control:
  Reserved:       %0000
  Hop Count:      %0000
 Packet Type:     4 PEP
 Destination Network: 0xcc715b00
 Destination Node:    ff:ff:ff:ff:ff:ff Ethernet Brdcast
 Destination Socket:  0x0452 Service Advertising Protocol
 Source Network:      0xcc715b00
 Source Node:         00:80:5f:ad:14:e4
 Source Socket:       0x0452 Service Advertising Protocol
SAP - Service Advertising Protocol
 Operation:       2 NetWare General Service Response
```

```
Service Advertising Set #1
 Service Type:    263 NetWare 386
 Service Name:
        BORDER3...................................
 Network Number:  0x12db8494
 Node Number:     00:00:00:00:00:01
 Socket Number:   0x8104
 Hops to Server:  1
Service Advertising Set #2
 Service Type:    4 File Server
 Service Name:
        BORDER3...................................
 Network Number:  0x12db8494
 Node Number:     00:00:00:00:00:01
 Socket Number:   0x0451
 Hops to Server:  1
Service Advertising Set #3
 Service Type:    632
 Service Name:    BORDER_____R.S.I@@@@@D.PJ..
 Network Number:  0x12db8494
 Node Number:     00:00:00:00:00:01
 Socket Number:   0x4006
 Hops to Server:  1
Service Advertising Set #4
 Service Type:    993
 Service Name:
        BORDER3...................................
 Network Number:  0x12db8494
 Node Number:     00:00:00:00:00:01
 Socket Number:   0x9056
 Hops to Server:  1
Frame Check Sequence: 0x00000000
```

This SAP is from a NetWare server named Border3. Four services were offered. Each service, as well as its address and socket information, is included in the SAP table of all IPX-enabled devices attached to this network (including routers) and rebroadcast.

When troubleshooting, especially in unfamiliar networks, remember that SAP announcements are occasionally filtered with access lists. This may be for traffic management or to establish a security policy. Researching a service unavailable–type problem should include a review of the access lists on all intermediate routers.

Novell Router Diagnostic Tools

A wide variety of troubleshooting commands is available within the Cisco IOS for resolving IPX networking problems. Although it is important to use all available tools to resolve a network problem—including protocol analyzers, workstation and server applications—most troubleshooting steps are augmented by the IOS commands. As such, there is an emphasis on the following commands and their capabilities to assist as part of an overall problem-resolution strategy:

The most widely used commands include the following:

- ping commands
- show commands
- debug commands

ping Commands

Cisco routers provide a Ping utility for troubleshooting IPX connectivity problems, much like the IP Ping utility. This utility can be used to verify that the routing tables are being updated correctly, and that all interfaces and segments are available.

Novell IPX resources do not respond to the Cisco IPX Ping without the configuration command ipx ping-default novell or the Novell Standard Echo.

The following example demonstrates an IPX Ping to a Cisco router's network 200 interface:

```
Router_A#ping ipx 200.0000.30c0.9690
Type escape sequence to abort.
```

```
Sending 5, 100-byte IPX cisco Echoes to
200.0000.30c0.9690,    timeout is 2 seconds
:
!!!!!
Success rate is 100 percent (5/5), round-trip min/avg/max
=    16/20/32 ms
```

In the following example, the Novell Standard Echo option and verbose were selected by using the extended commands:

```
Router_A#ping
Protocol [ip]: ipx
Target IPX address: 200.0000.30c0.9690
Repeat count [5]:
Datagram size [100]:
Timeout in seconds [2]:
Verbose [n]: y
Novell Standard Echo [n]: y
Type escape sequence to abort.
Sending 5, 100-byte IPX Novell Echoes to
200.0000.30c0.9690, timeout is 2 seconds:
0 in 20 ms
1 in 20 ms
2 in 20 ms
3 in 16 ms
4 in 20 ms
Success rate is 100 percent (5/5), round-trip min/avg/max
=    16/19/20 ms
```

show Commands

The Cisco router's show commands provide a great deal of information regarding IPX. This output is available from the show ipx ? command. As presented in Table 9.2, the show ipx command provides information regarding routing and routing protocols, in addition to NetWare servers.

TABLE 9.2 The IPX Show Options

Show IPX Option	Brief Description
Accounting	The active IPX accounting database
Cache	IPX fast-switching cache
Compression	IPX compression information
Eigrp	IPX EIGRP show commands
Interface	IPX interface status and configuration
Nasi	NetWare Asynchronous Services Interface status
Nhrp	NHRP information
Nlsp	Show NLSP information
Route	IPX routing table
Servers	SAP servers
spx-protocol	Sequenced Packet Exchange protocol status
spx-spoof	SPX Spoofing table
traffic	IPX protocol statistics

Some commands have additional options. Due to changes in different versions of the IOS, it is recommended that administrators use the ? command to review.

show ipx interface

The show ipx interface command provides information on all IPX-configured interfaces. The output appears in the format shown below. In this example, the router has a high-speed serial interface (HSSI) that is configured for IPX. In addition to show running-config, this command is useful for locating IPX access lists that may block SAP traffic.

As indicated previously, out-of-date access lists are a frequent cause of network problems. Access lists serve as a powerful tool for network management and security, but misunderstood or forgotten lists can prevent connectivity when needed.

The output from this command also provides information about NetBIOS over IPX (type 20) packets, the number of packets sent and received for IPX RIP and SAP, and the status of watchdog and SPX spoof functions.

```
Router_A#show ipx interface
Hssi3/0 is up, line protocol is up
IPX address is F100.0010.0d28.6760 [up] line-up, RIPPQ: 0,
SAPPQ: 0
Delay of this IPX network, in ticks is 1 throughput 0 link
delay 0
 IPXWAN processing not enabled on this interface.
 IPX SAP update interval is 1 minute(s)
 IPX type 20 propagation packet forwarding is disabled
 Incoming access list is not set
 Outgoing access list is not set
 IPX helper access list is not set
 SAP GNS processing enabled, delay 0 ms, output filter
 list is not set
 SAP Input filter list is not set
 SAP Output filter list is not set
 SAP Router filter list is not set
 Input filter list is not set
 Output filter list is not set
 Router filter list is not set
 Netbios Input host access list is not set
 Netbios Input bytes access list is not set
 Netbios Output host access list is not set
 Netbios Output bytes access list is not set
 Updates each 60 seconds, aging multiples RIP: 3 SAP: 3
 SAP interpacket delay is 55 ms, maximum size is 480 bytes
 RIP interpacket delay is 55 ms, maximum size is 432 bytes
```

```
Watchdog spoofing is disabled, SPX spoofing is disabled,
idle time 60
IPX accounting is disabled
IPX fast switching is configured (enabled)
RIP packets received 3228022, RIP packets sent 121313
SAP packets received 3507665, SAP packets sent 3003606
```

show ipx route

The show ipx route command is useful for reviewing the state of the Net-Ware network, and it should be used to confirm that a path exists to the desired resource. The output reports connected IPX RIP, NLSP and IPX EIGRP routes, in addition to IPXWAN and static routes.

The following example includes routers for the connected IPX network 200 on the FDDI 8/0 interface; and three routes to networks 1, 101 and 201, reachable via 100.0060.833c.4d49 on Hs3/0. The interface is using the FDDI SNAP-frame type and the routes were learned via IPX RIP.

```
Router_A#show ipx route
Codes: C - Connected primary network
c - Connected secondary network, S - Static, F - Floating
static, L - Local (internal), W - IPXWANR - RIP, E -
EIGRP, N - NLSP, X - External,
A - Aggregate
  s - seconds, u - uses
128 Total IPX routes. Up to 3 parallel paths and 16 hops
allowed.
No default route known.
C    200 (SNAP),      Fd8/0
R      1 [03/02] via   100.0060.833c.4d49,   8s, Hs3/0
R    101 [04/03] via   100.0060.833c.4d49,   8s, Hs3/0
R    201 [04/03] via   100.0060.833c.4d49,   8s, Hs3/0
```

WARNING   Please do not confuse the IPX RIP protocol with the RIP routing protocol in TCP/IP. Both are routing protocols and there are similarities, but they are different protocols.

show ipx servers

The show ipx servers command displays all servers known to the router through SAP advertisements. Recall that, in the absence of filters, this list should include all resources in the internetwork. If elements are missing, there may be an issue with access lists, down interfaces, down networks, congestion, or frame types.

This command is also useful for locating duplicate network numbers:

```
Router_A#show ipx servers
Codes: S - Static, P - Periodic, E - EIGRP, N - NLSP,
 H - Holddown, + = detail
117 Total IPX Servers
Table ordering is based on routing and server info
Type Name        Net Address        Port  Route Hops Itf
P+ 4 SRV-00001   1.0000.0000.0001:0451  4/03  3    Hs3/0
P+ 4 SRV-00002   2.0000.0000.0001:0451  4/03  3    Hs3/0
```

Note that the MAC addresses in this display are 00:00:00:00:00:01. This is the internal IPX network address indicator; and the first server, SRV-00001, has an internal IPX network number of 1.

show ipx traffic

The show ipx traffic command reports information about the IPX packets transmitted and received. This breakdown includes information regarding IPX SAPs and watchdog packets, as well as IPX RIP, IPX EIGRP, and NLSP routing packets. A sample of this information is presented as follows:

```
Router_A#show ipx traffic
System Traffic for 0.0000.0000.0001 System-Name: Router_
ARcvd:  92678244 total, 158 format errors, 0 checksum
errors, 0 bad hop count,1677 packets pitched, 65955970
local destination, 0 multicast
Bcast: 65957365 received, 63751306 sent
Sent:  75752069 generated, 26672221 forwarded
     50141 encapsulation failed, 1465 no route
SAP:  48 SAP requests, 0 SAP replies, 399 servers
     58523476 SAP advertisements received, 61481958 sent
```

0 SAP flash updates sent, 6 SAP format errors, last
seen from 500.0010.0b4f.2660
RIP: 48 RIP requests, 0 RIP replies, 128 routes
7432398 RIP advertisements received, 2261621 sent
8498 RIP flash updates sent, 0 RIP format errors
Echo: Rcvd 0 requests, 0 replies
Sent 0 requests, 0 replies
0 unknown: 0 no socket, 0 filtered, 0 no helper
0 SAPs throttled, freed NDB len 0
Watchdog:
0 packets received, 0 replies spoofed
Queue lengths:
IPX input: 0, SAP 0, RIP 0, GNS 0
SAP throttling length: 0/(no limit), 0 nets pending
lost route reply
Delayed process creation: 0
EIGRP: Total received 0, sent 0
Updates received 0, sent 0
Queries received 0, sent 0
Replies received 0, sent 0
SAPs received 0, sent 0
NLSP: Level-1 Hellos received 0, sent 0
PTP Hello received 0, sent 0
Level-1 LSPs received 0, sent 0
LSP Retransmissions: 0
LSP checksum errors received: 0
LSP HT=0 checksum errors received: 0
Level-1 CSNPs received 0, sent 0
Level-1 PSNPs received 0, sent 0
Level-1 DR Elections: 0
Level-1 SPF Calculations: 0
Level-1 Partial Route Calculations: 0

debug Commands

As with other network protocols, there is a wide variety of IPX **debug** commands available within the Cisco IOS. The **debug** IPX commands provide the administrator with a means to view Novell traffic in real-time as it enters or leaves the router.

The debug command is assigned a high CPU priority and can generate a high processor load. Always use caution when using a debug command. The resulting processor load and output can degrade router performance or render the system unusable.

debug ipx routing

The **debug ipx routing** command reports all IPX routing processes at the router, including IPX RIP, IPX EIGRP, and NLSP. The first line reports the standard IPX RIP broadcast, whereas the remainder demonstrate the events related to the recovery of an interface configured for IPX. In this case, the TO0 interface cable was reinserted:

```
*Mar 1 00:34:26.515 UTC: IPXRIP: sending update to
0.ffff.ffff.ffff via [all]
*Mar 1 00:38:43.455 UTC: IPX: Setting state of [itf]:[net]
To0:D to [up]:[down]
*Mar 1 00:38:43.455 UTC: IPX: cache flush
*Mar 1 00:38:43.459 UTC: IPXRIP: Marking network D for
Flash Update
*Mar 1 00:38:43.459 UTC: IPXRIP: Deleting network D
*Mar 1 00:38:43.463 UTC: IPX: cache flush
*Mar 1 00:38:43.467 UTC: IPX: Setting state of [itf]:[net]
To0:D to [up]:[up]
*Mar 1 00:38:43.467 UTC: IPX: cache flush
*Mar 1 00:38:43.467 UTC: IPXRIP: Marking network D for
Flash Update
```

debug ipx packet

The debug `ipx packet` command displays all IPX traffic that enters or leaves the router. Thus, this command can generate a great deal of output, and its use is recommended only with caution.

IPX packets that are fast-switched are not captured by the debug `ipx packet` command. In order to view all packets, add the `no ipx route-cache` command to each interface that you wish to include in the debug capture. If the initial problem is related to fast switching, this may lead to erroneous troubleshooting results.

The following example contains the entry of a packet destined for server 130—internal network number. The response was sent to the gateway on network 120:

```
IPX: src=100.0000.0c4c.42fa, dst=130.0000.0000.0001,
packet     received
IPX: src=100.0000.0c4c.42fa,
dst=130.0000.0000.0001,gw=120.0000.0ca3.1bd0, sending
packet
```

debug ipx sap activity

As previously reviewed, SAP traffic provides the foundation for all Novell functions. Incorrect functioning of the SAP process can prevent access to services and cause other connectivity problems. As such, the debug `ipx sap activity` command provides an administrator with additional information and possible indications of problem causes:

```
Router_A#debug ipx sap activity
IPX service debugging is on
Feb 1 10:08:38.424:  type 0x30C, "PTR_1",
105.0006.0d86.5380(401C), 4 hops
Feb 1 10:08:38.424:  type 0x30C, "PTR_2",
105.0006.0d6e.1a65(400C), 4 hops
Feb 1 10:08:38.648:  type 0x44C, "AR3",
102.0000.0000.0001(8600), 3 hops
Feb 1 10:08:38.648:  type 0x23F, "SRL03",
102.0000.0000.0001(907B), 3 hops
```

```
Feb 1 10:08:38.704: IPXSAP: at 690465B4:
I SAP Response type 0x2 len 480 src:100.0060.837b.4a19
dest:100.ffff.ffff.ffff(452)
```

debug ipx sap events

The debug ipx sap events command appears to include the same information as the debug ipx sap activity command. However, the router defines events as interesting, and the events keyword limits the output of information. Although limited, there are times when events may provide sufficient data for problem resolution. A sample of the output is provided as follows. (Note that there are two SAP broadcasts.)

```
Router_A#debug ipx sap event
IPX service events debugging is on
Feb 17 11:09:13.556: IPXSAP: at 608FD48C:
O SAP Update type 0x2 len 480 src:200.0006.c13e.b20c
dest:200.ffff.ffff.ffff(452)
Feb 17 11:09:13.556:  type 0x4, "SRV-NDS",
101.0000.0000.0001(451), 3 hops
Feb 17 11:09:13.556:  type 0x4, "SRV-NMS",
701.0000.0000.0001(451), 3 hops
Feb 17 11:09:13.556:  type 0x4, "SRV-ORD",
801.0000.0000.0001(451), 3 hops
Feb 17 11:09:13.556:  type 0x4, "SRV-SAA",
501.0000.0000.0001(451), 3 hops
Feb 17 11:09:13.560: IPXSAP: at 608BD614:
O SAP Update type 0x2 len 480 src:500.0006.c13e.b20c
dest:500.ffff.ffff.ffff(452)
Feb 17 11:09:13.560:  type 0x4, "SRV-NDS",
101.0000.0000.0001(451), 3 hops
Feb 17 11:09:13.560:  type 0x4, "SRV-NMS",
701.0000.0000.0001(451), 3 hops
Feb 17 11:09:13.560:  type 0x4, "SRV-ORD",
801.0000.0000.0001(451), 3 hops
Feb 17 11:09:13.560:  type 0x4, "SRV-SAA",
501.0000.0000.0001(451), 3 hops
```

WARNING Remember to use the undebug all or no debug commands to shut down debug sessions. Failure to shut down debug sessions can cause performance degradation.

Common Novell Troubleshooting Issues

Standard troubleshooting procedures can and should be used when approaching a NetWare-related issue, as they would be used for any other network problem. This includes identifying and defining the problem, fact gathering, assessing possible solutions, creating an action plan, and implementing that plan. Based on the results, the problem may be resolved, new information may be added to the assessment, or another action plan may be needed.

There are some common issues that present themselves in NetWare networks, however. For example, the router may not correctly propagate SAP updates, which are very important in NetWare. Causes for this may include access lists, duplicate network numbers, incorrect frame types, timing problems, or incorrectly set timers.

Although the **debug** and show commands can provide a great deal of information that is useful for resolving the problem, protocol analyzers and knowledge of the server and client platforms should also be used to provide rapid resolutions.

In NetWare, most problems can be isolated by doing the following:

- Check the client configuration. This includes the frame type, hardware (IRQ/DMA settings), and physical connectivity.

- Review the router and any local server configurations. Although this chapter focuses on Cisco routers, it is important to confirm the internal and external IPX network numbers on the server, in addition to the frame type. Novell documentation addresses other concerns, including network interface cards, overloaded processors, licenses, and drive space. All should be included in the troubleshooting process.

- Verify that non-IPX problems are not the cause. This can include over-loaded segments or down links. Note that many IPX environments today are also using IP and AppleTalk.

Ethernet Encapsulation Mismatches and Network Settings

As noted previously, Novell networks and their clients can use any of four different frame types in Ethernet. A client, server, and router all must use the same frame type in order to communicate, however. The IOS commands `write terminal` or `show running-config` are useful for reviewing the encapsulation settings. Note that in this example there are no settings to reflect the frame type. The router is using the Cisco default of novell-ether or Ethernet 802.3 on all interfaces. It is important for the administrator to realize that although the default does not have a command in the IOS configuration file, it may differ from the server default or setting.

```
Router_A#write terminal
Building configuration...
Current configuration:
!
version 11.1
service timestamps debug datetime localtime show-timezone
service timestamps log datetime localtime show-timezone
!
service password-encryption
service udp-small-servers
service tcp-small-servers
!
hostname Router_A
!
ipx routing 0010.0d28.6710
ipx maximum-paths 3
!
interface Ethernet0
 mtu 1500
 ip address 10.11.10.1 255.255.255.0
 ipx network 10
```

```
!
interface Ethernet1
 ip address 10.11.20.1 255.255.255.0
 no keepalive
 ipx network 2000
!
end
```

In this example, the router interface is displayed with the show ipx interface command, and the interface is FDDI with the default SNAP frame type in use:

```
Router_A#show ipx interface
Fddi0 is up, line protocol is up
 IPX address is 100000.0060.837c.4d31, SNAP [up] line-up,
RIPPQ: 0, SAPPQ: 0
```

In addition to frame type, a common issue with interconnectivity is incorrectly configured network addresses. All servers and routers on an IPX network must be manually configured with the same external IPX network number. A typical problem scenario occurs as follows:

After realizing that at least one server on the network is unreachable, the administrator notes the following error on the router console or in the router log. A similar message may appear on the server console:

```
00:60:08:40:1F:1C claims network 100 should be 200
```

In addition to confirming that the frame type of all network resources is set to the same value, all servers and routers also need to have their external IPX network numbers set to the same value. In this case, the unreachable server is configured for IPX network 200, where the router has been configured for network 100. After the correct network number is determined, the incorrect setting should be modified.

Problems Attaching to Remote Servers

Frequently, IPX networks are designed without a locally attached server. The file server may be installed on another local segment or may be remotely connected via a serial connection.

Although this serial connection may be a T1, many sites still use 56Kbps DDS circuits or low CIR (committed information rate) frame-relay connections.

As a NetWare network grows, the volume of RIP and SAP traffic also grows. Eventually, a 56Kbps connection (or Frame Relay connection) will be overwhelmed with RIP and SAP updates, to the point where user data can no longer be transferred. A saturated T1 may also have difficulty providing adequate bandwidth to support large RIP and SAP updates.

In addition, the connection to a file server from the client requires a response to the GNS broadcast described previously. Although the router responds in the absence of a server, the subsequent connections may fail due to timeouts or other issues. In addition, the server or client may be overloaded. A protocol analyzer is a good way to review this issue, although `debug` commands can be used with caution. If the issue involved is an overloaded server, a solution may involve use of the `ipx gns-round-robin` configuration command. If more than one NetWare server is listed in the SAP table as being an equal distance away, this command provides a limited form of load balancing.

Conversely, there may be times when the router responds to the client too quickly. Although this is a rare occurrence in modern networks, the default delay of 0ms can be changed with the `ipx gns-response-delay` configuration command.

There is also a scenario referred to as the *backdoor bridge*. In this example, a bridge connects two IPX networks and leaks routing information. The `show ipx traffic` command should be used to determine whether the bad hop counter is incrementing. If it is, a protocol analyzer should be used to find a source address that matches the remote node and not the router.

SAP Congestion Management in IPX RIP

Service advertisements can generate a significant amount of traffic in medium-scale networks. In large networks, they can cause high processor utilization and overall degradation of the network.

Without using NetWare's NLSP to control IPX RIP and SAP datagrams, an administrator may use access lists to block SAP traffic from crossing an interface. This solution does have shortcomings, however. Any resource that is restricted by an access list is unavailable to the opposing portion of the network.

In many large networks, this solution is quite appropriate—even considering the negatives. Users in Chicago rarely need to print files in San Francisco, and users in London may not need files in Tokyo. By reviewing the business needs of the users, a balance between filter restrictions and service can be obtained. In addition to traffic management, an administrator may also use the filtering of certain IPX packets for network security.

An IPX access list is not dissimilar to an IP access list. Both standard and extended access lists are available. Standard IPX access lists are numbered from 800 to 899, and extended lists are numbered from 900 to 999. As with IP, more options are available with extended access lists, and a list is applied with the `access-group` command on the interface.

Standard IPX Access Lists

The syntax of the standard IPX access list is presented for review:

```
access-list access-list-number [deny | permit] source-
network[.source-node [source-node-mask]] [destination-
network[.destination-node [destination-node-mask]]]
```

There are few parameters that can be used in standard access lists. Packets can be filtered based on the source and destination address information only. To filter on socket numbers, extended access lists must be used. It is recommended that standard lists be used only when configuring small networks—most administrators find that eventually they need the flexibility of extended access lists.

Extended IPX Access Lists

An extended IPX access list filters on source and destination address information as standard lists do. Extended lists may also be used to filter on:

- Source network/node

- Destination network/node

- IPX protocol (SAP, SPX, etc.)

- IPX socket

The syntax of the command provides a number of options, including the use of masks for both the network and node sections of the packet:

```
access-list access-list-number [deny|permit] protocol
[source-network][[[.source-node] source-node-mask] |
[.source-node source-network-mask.source-node-mask]]
  [source-socket]
  [destination.network][[[.destination-node] destination-
  node-mask] | [.destination-node destination-network-
  mask.destination-nodemask]] [destination-socket]
```

As an example, a simple extended access list is presented by using the format `access-list [number] [permit|deny] [protocol] [source] [socket][destination] [socket]`. As shown previously, this format can be expanded with additional masks.

```
RouterA#config t
Enter configuration commands, one per line. End with CNTL/Z.
RouterA(config)#access-list 910 deny -1 50 0 10 0
RouterA(config)#access-list 910 permit -1 -1 0 -1 0
RouterA(config)#int e0
RouterA(config-if)#ipx access-group 910 out
RouterA(config-if)#^Z
```

The any command word may be used in place of the –1 network parameter, depending on the IOS version in use. Also, some versions of the IOS may report an "unrecognized command" error from the command `access-list 910 deny -1 ?`. Administrators should use the online help and test configuration commands within the specific IOS installed.

Extended access list 910 is configured to deny all IPX protocols from network 50 that are destined for network 10. Using a -1 in the protocol section of the command serves as a wildcard for all protocols. Use of a -1 in the source or destination field serves as a wildcard for all networks. Recall that access lists include an implicit deny—access list 910 negates this deny by permitting all packets to pass that were not denied previously.

Online help is available by typing **?** and should be referenced when using any unfamiliar command.

SAP Access Lists

Although standard and extended access lists are useful for blocking traffic between IPX networks, Cisco provides a better solution for filtering the SAP traffic between networks. The 1000–1099 range of access lists may be used to permit or block SAP packets specifically, as compared to the general IPX traffic filtering that is available from the standard and extended lists.

Using the syntax access-list [number] [permit/deny] [source] [service type], access list 1010 is configured to permit all SAP traffic from the server. Service type zero represents all service types. Service type four is used for file servers, and type seven represents print servers. This access list was configured on interface e0 as an input SAP filter—all SAP traffic from server 11 (internal IPX network number) is permitted, and all other SAPs are denied.

```
RouterA#config t
Enter configuration commands, one per line. End with CNTL/
Z.
RouterA(config)#access-list 1010 permit 11.0000.0000.0001
0
RouterA(config)#int e0
RouterA(config-if)#ipx input-sap-filter 1010
RouterA(config-if)#^Z
```

When troubleshooting, remember to use the following commands to quickly disable IPX access lists. (They need to be reinstated when troubleshooting is complete.)

- no ipx access-group access-group number

- no ipx input-sap-filter access-list number

- no ipx output-sap-filter access-list number

It is possible to alter the default 60-second SAP timer with the ipx sap-interval command. The improper use of this command can cause significant problems with SAP updates, and can cause servers to appear and disappear in the SAP table.

Debugging Scalable NetWare Protocols

Although NetWare's RIP and SAP are fine for smaller networks, they do not scale well. As networks increase in size, the broadcast traffic generated by these processes can quickly overwhelm the network. In addition, RIP is slow to converge and is limited regarding redundant network paths. Because convergence and redundancy are important considerations as the network expands, it becomes important to consider the scalable IPX protocols: IPX EIGRP and NLSP. Note that Cisco routers automatically redistribute IPX EIGRP and NLSP to IPX RIP. The redistribution of NLSP routing information into IPX EIGRP requires manual configuration.

IPX EIGRP

Cisco's EIGRP is a good choice for building scalability into IPX networks. The protocol is proprietary, however, and administrators need to commit to an all-Cisco environment when choosing this solution. Table 9.3 contrasts IPX RIP with IPX EIGRP.

TABLE 9.3 IPX RIP and IPX EIGRP Compared

	IPX RIP	IPX EIGRP
Network diameter	15	224
Convergence	Slow	Fast
Bandwidth	High	Low
Updates	60 seconds	As needed

The Cisco IOS provides information regarding EIGRP with the show ipx eigrp commands, identified with the following output:

```
Router_A#show ipx eigrp ?
  interfaces  IPX EIGRP Interfaces
  neighbors   IPX EIGRP Neighbors
  topology    IPX EIGRP Topology Table
  traffic     IPX EIGRP Traffic Statistics
```

show ipx eigrp neighbors

Router_A is running IPX EIGRP process 10, and is connected to IPX network B via its Ethernet1 interface and IPX network D via its Token Ring 0 interface. This command is most beneficial for verifying initial EIGRP configurations, and an example follows:

```
Router_A#show ipx eigrp neighbors
IPX EIGRP Neighbors for process 10
H  Address
1  B.0000.0c1b.367c
0  D.0000.30da.5842
```

show ipx eigrp topology

Router_C is connected to Router_A via a Token Ring connection, IPX network D. Networks B and A are available via Router_A—Router_B has a connection to IPX network A. Note the higher metric for network A.

```
Router_C#show ipx eigrp topology
IPX EIGRP Topology Table for process 10
Codes: P - Passive, A - Active, U - Update, Q - Query, R -
Reply, r - Reply status
P A, 1 successors, FD is 323328
      via D.0000.30e8.6d0f (323328/307200), TokenRing0
P B, 1 successors, FD is 297728
      via D.0000.30e8.6d0f (297728/281600), TokenRing0
P D, 1 successors, FD is 176128
      via Connected, TokenRing0
```

show ipx route

The show ipx route command provides information on static, IPX RIP, NLSP, and IPX EIGRP routes in the network. Note that the following example contains a single connected route, in addition to an IPX EIGRP route. Also, note that only one parallel path is permitted, according to this example. Reviewing this output is recommended, following the use of the ipx maximum-paths command. The default behavior of a Cisco router is to consider only one IPX route. The ipx maximum-paths command changes this default.

```
Router_C#show ipx routes
Codes: C - Connected primary network, c - Connected
secondary network, S - Static,  F - Floating static, L -
Local (internal),  W – IPXWAN, R - RIP, E - EIGRP, N -
NLSP,  X - External, A - Aggregate
  s - seconds,  u - uses
2 Total IPX routes. Up to 1 parallel paths and 16 hops
allowed.
No default route known.
C D (SAP),    To0
E B [297728/0] via D.0000.30e8.6d0f, age 00:02:30, 1u, To0
```

In addition to network D, this routing table was populated via IPX EIGRP with network B. Network D is connected to Token Ring 0, and network B is accessible through router D.0000.30e8.6d0f. There is only one known route to network B.

NLSP and IPXWAN

NLSP, or NetWare Link Services Protocol, affords network designers and administrators some advantages over IPX RIP, in the same way that IP RIP networks benefit by changing to IGRP and EIGRP.

Like IP RIP, IPX RIP supports networks of no more than 15 hops. NLSP expands the routing diameter to 127 hops. In addition, NLSP's link state packets, LSPs, are sent only when there are changes to the routing topology—unlike IPX RIP packets, which are sent every 60 seconds. This greatly reduces the impact of updates on slower WAN links. Cisco routers automatically redistribute information learned from NLSP to IPX RIP on non-NLSP segments. It is important to use care when using NLSP on a non-WAN point-to-point link, because NLSP-only segments do not contain the IPX RIP information needed for non-NLSP resources.

NLSP provides the capability to remove IPX SAP from a network segment by handling updates via NLSP. The protocol reduces both IPX RIPs and SAPs by sending updates on changes to the database, rather than updating every 60 seconds. NLSP also requires use of the `ipx internal-network` command, unlike IPX RIP and IPX EIGRP.

To enable NLSP, type the `ipx nlsp enable` command. This is configured on each interface that will run NLSP. If there are routing problems and the network is supposed to use NLSP, manually verify this command on each interface and on each network resource.

Unlike IPX RIP, NLSP will send an update only if there is a change to the routing topology. If no modifications occur for two hours, NLSP sends an update to all neighbors. Also, NLSP is configured with an area address, which is defined in the command area-address address mask. Using an address and mask of zero defines that all IPX networks belong to the NLSP area. Typically, administrators disable IPX RIP when enabling NLSP.

Additional information about NLSP configuration is available in the *CCNP: Advanced Cisco Router Configuration Study Guide* by Todd Lammle, Kevin Hales, and Donald Porter (ISBN 0-7821-2403-8, Sybex, Inc., 1999).

An NLSP Hello packet is sent regularly to inform neighbor routers of its status. An Ethernet example appears, as follows:

```
Flags:      0x80 802.3
 Status:     0x00
 Packet Length:92
 Timestamp:  00:55:25.715452 10/21/1998
802.3 Header
 Destination: ff:ff:ff:ff:ff:ff Ethernet Brdcast
 Source:     00:00:0c:3e:82:2a
 Length:     74
IPX - NetWare Protocol
 Checksum:        0xffff
 Length:          73
 Transport Control:
  Reserved:       %0000
  Hop Count:      %0000
 Packet Type:     0 Novell
 Destination Network: 0x00000000
 Destination Node:   ff:ff:ff:ff:ff:ff Ethernet Brdcast
 Destination Socket:  0x9001 IPX Static
 Source Network:     0x00000010
 Source Node:        00:00:0c:3e:82:2a
 Source Socket:      0x9001 IPX Static
```

IPX Data Area:

```
.............>.*.  83 1b 02 00 0f 01 00 00 11 00 00 0c 3e
82 2a 00
..+@...>.*. ....  01 00 2b 40 00 00 0c 3e 82 2a 01 c0 08
00 00 00
..... ...       00 00 00 00 00 c5 04 00 00
```

Extra bytes (Padding):

```
.  .            05 dc 06
```

Frame Check Sequence: 0x00000000

A functional NLSP network presents different routing table entries than a network using IPX RIP.

```
Router_C#show ipx route
Codes: C - Connected primary network,
       c - Connected secondary network
       S - Static, F - Floating static, L - Local
       (internal), W - IPXWAN
       R - RIP, E - EIGRP, N - NLSP, X - External,
       A - Aggregate
       s - seconds, u - uses
7 Total IPX routes. Up to 1 parallel paths and 16 hops
allowed.
No default route known.
L C is the internal network
C 40 (HDLC),     Se0
C 50 (NOVELL-ETHER), Et0
N A  [72][13/02] via B.0000.0000.0001,   1990s, Se0
N B  [27][02/01] via B.0000.0000.0001,   1991s, Se0
N 10 [72][12/02] via B.0000.0000.0001,   1991s, Se0
N 30 [27][01/01] via B.0000.0000.0001,   1991s, Se0
```

There are four NLSP routes displayed, in addition to two connected networks and the internal IPX network of the router. Also note that the list of servers is different under NLSP.

```
Router_C#show ipx servers
Codes: S - Static, P - Periodic, E - EIGRP, N - NLSP, H -
Holddown, + = detail
```

```
3 Total IPX Servers
Table ordering is based on routing and server info
Type Name    Net Address        Port Route  Hops Itf
N    4 server1 10.0000.0000.0001:0000 12/02  3    Se0
N    4 server2 10.0000.0000.0002:0000 12/02  3    Se0
N    4 server3 10.0000.0000.0003:0000 12/02  3    Se0
```

show ipx nlsp neighbors

The show ipx nlsp neighbors command displays all NLSP neighbors. A *neighbor* is defined as an NLSP resource that is directly connected—NLSP packets traverse only the local segment because they are not forwarded by the router.

```
Router_A#show ipx nlsp neighbors
NLSP Level-1 Neighbors: Tag Identifier = notag
System Id Interface State Holdtime Priority  Circuit Id
Router_B  Se0      Up    55       0         04
```

Router_A has one NLSP neighbor, Router_B. By adding the detail command, the output includes the IPX internal network number and the uptime.

```
Router_A#show ipx nlsp neighbors detail
NLSP Level-1 Neighbors: Tag Identifier = notag
System Id Interface State Holdtime Priority Circuit Id
Router_B  Se0      Up    43       0        04
  IPX Address: B.0000.0000.0001
  IPX Areas: 00000000/00000000
  Uptime: 01:13:09
```

show ipx nlsp database

This command provides data regarding the local NLSP process. The LSPID (link state protocol identifier) comprises the system identifier, the pseudonode circuit identifier, and the fragment number. LSP (link state protocol) is the foundation of NLSP, and the show ipx nlsp database command reports significant information, including the last sequence number, the checksum, and the LSP holdtime. The *hold timer* reflects the times in seconds before the information expires, assuming that Hello packets are received.

ATT and OL refer to the L2 attached and overload bits; the P bit (partition) is not used.

```
Router_A#show ipx nlsp database
NLSP Level-1 Link State Database
LSPID            LSP Seq Num LSP Checksum LSP Holdtime ATT/P/OL
Router_A.00-00 * 0x00000003  0xF99B          7443        0/0/0
Router_A.04-00 * 0x00000002  0x9F16          7441        0/0/0
Router_B.00-00   0x00000003  0x1C33          7423        0/0/0
Router_B.03-00   0x00000002  0x9DE9          7421        0/0/0
Router_C.00-00   0x00000002  0x459D          7440        0/0/0
```

debug ipx ipxwan

The debug ipx ipxwan command produces information during state changes and the start-up of serial interfaces configured for ipxwan. Although it is seldom used in Cisco networks, ipxwan is defined in RFC 1634, and may be required for connecting IPX resources on WAN links. This is especially true when connecting to non-Cisco devices.

Summary

In this chapter, common NetWare network problems were presented, along with generalized troubleshooting commands and recommendations to assist in preparing for the CIT examination and for use in real-world problem resolution. These troubleshooting tools included the use of the Cisco IOS show, debug, and Ping commands, and summaries of problems that include GNS and SAP failures.

Readers should also understand the IPX addressing scheme; the initial client-connection process; encapsulation; access lists; service advertisements; and the benefits of scalable NetWare protocols, including IPX EIGRP and NLSP.

Commands Used in This Chapter

The following list contains a summary of all the commands used in this chapter.

Command	Description
debug ipx ipxwan	Produces information during state changes and the start-up of serial interfaces configured for ipxwan.
debug ipx packet	Displays all IPX traffic that enters or leaves the router.
debug ipx routing	Reports all IPX routing processes at the router, including IPX RIP, IPX EIGRP, and NLSP.
debug ipx sap activity	Provides an administrator with additional information and possible indications of problem causes.
debug ipx sap events	Displays events as *interesting*, and the events keyword limits the output of information.
ping ipx	Initiates an IPX Ping. Allows for User and Privileged level execution.
show ipx eigrp neighbors	Provides detailed IPX EIGRP neighbor information.
show ipx eigrp topology	Displays multiple paths to IPX EIGRP learned routes.
show ipx interface	Provides information on all IPX-configured interfaces.
show ipx nlsp database	Reports significant information, including the last sequence number, the checksum, and the LSP holdtime.
show ipx nlsp neighbors	Displays all NLSP neighbors.

Command	Description
`show ipx route`	Displays the state of the NetWare network, and it should be used to confirm that a path exists to the desired resource. The output reports connected IPX RIP, NLSP and IPX EIGRP routes, in addition to IPXWAN and static routes.
`show ipx servers`	Displays all servers known to the router through SAP advertisements.
`show ipx traffic`	Reports information about the IPX packets transmitted and received. This breakdown includes information regarding IPX SAPs and watchdog packets, as well as IPX RIP, IPX EIGRP, and NLSP routing packets.

Key Terms

Before you take the exam, be certain you are familiar with the following terms:

encapsulation and framing

GNS (get nearest server)

SAP (service advertising protocol)

Laboratory Exercise

In this exercise, three routers will be connected via their Ethernet interfaces. Configure the routers with the following commands to set up NLSP. Figure 9.2 illustrates the connections.

FIGURE 9.2   Network configuration for the NLSP laboratory

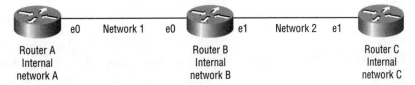

Router A
Internal
network A

Router B
Internal
network B

Router C
Internal
network C

```
Router_A#conf t
Enter configuration commands, one per line. End with CNTL/Z.
Router_A(config)#ipx routing
Router_A(config)#ipx internal-network A
Router_A(config)#int e0
Router_A(config-if)#ipx network 1
Router_A(config-if)#ipx nlsp enable
Router_A(config-if)#^Z
Router_A#wr t


Router_B#conf t
 Enter configuration commands, one per line. End with CNTL/Z.
Router_B(config)#ipx routing
Router_B(config)#ipx internal-network B
Router_B(config)#int e0
Router_B(config-if)#ipx network 1
Router_B(config-if)#ipx nlsp enable
Router_B(config-if)#int e1
Router_B(config-if)#ipx network 2
Router_B(config-if)#ipx nlsp enable
Router_B(config-if)#^Z
Router_B#wr t
```

```
Router_C#conf t
 Enter configuration commands, one per line. End with CNTL/Z.
Router_C(config)#ipx routing
Router_C(config)#ipx internal-network C
Router_C(config)#int e1
Router_A(config-if)#ipx network 2
Router_C(config-if)#ipx nlsp enable
Router_C(config-if)#^Z
Router_C#wr t
```

Does NLSP work? What commands were used to determine that NLSP was working? What changes to the configuration are needed, if any?

Review Questions

1. What command would provide the administrator with a list of Novell servers on the network?

   A. `show ipx route`

   B. `show ipx servers`

   C. `show ipx traffic`

   D. `debug ipx ipxwan`

2. When does a Cisco router respond to a GNS request?

   A. For every GNS unicast request.

   B. For every GNS broadcast request.

   C. For every GNS broadcast request when there is no local server on the network segment.

   D. A Cisco router does not respond to GNS requests.

3. A Novell client is configured for the Ethernet II frame type. The Cisco router needs which encapsulation type(s)? (Choose all that apply.)

   A. `Ethernet II`

   B. `802.3`

   C. `arpa`

   D. `iso1`

4. When IPX clients first attempt to locate services, how do they find them?

   A. SAP

   B. RIP

   C. NLSP

   D. GNS

5. Duplicate network numbers are suspected as a cause of problems in the network. What command is used to locate the problem?

   A. show ipx servers

   B. debug ipx sap events

   C. debug ipx ipxwan

   D. show int e0

6. The default interval between SAP packets is how long?

   A. 300 seconds.

   B. 10 seconds.

   C. 60 seconds.

   D. There is no interval—SAP packets are sent only when needed.

7. An IPX RIP network is limited to how many network hops?

   A. 3.

   B. 15.

   C. 127.

   D. There is no limit.

8. Which of the following are problems with RIP and SAP? (Choose all that apply.)

   A. TCP/IP incompatibility

   B. AppleTalk incompatibility

   C. Convergence time

   D. Bandwidth utilization

   E. Scalability

9. All IPX networks need to be included in NLSP. Which of the following is the correct command?

   A. area-address 0 FFFFFFFF

   B. area-address 0 0

   C. network FFFFFFFF

   D. ipx nlsp rip on

10. IPX EIGRP is available on which of the following platforms?

   A. Novell servers

   B. Cisco routers

   C. Ascend routers

   D. Windows NT servers

   E. All of the above

11. To permit all SAP traffic from the Novell server, an access list with which command is needed?

   A. `access-list 1080 permit 1.0000.0000.0001 0`

   B. `access list 1080 permit 1.0000.0000.0001 0`

   C. `access-list 910 permit 1.FFFF.FFFF.FFFF 0`

   D. `access-list 910 deny neq 1.0000.0000.0001`

   E. `access-list 1080 permit 1.0000.0000.0001 FFFFFFFF`

12. To block all IPX traffic from network 50 destined for network 30 and permit all other IPX traffic, the access list needs to be which of the following?

   A. `access-list 940 deny 50 -1 0 30 -1 0,access-list 940 permit -1 -1`

   B. `access-list 940 deny FFFFFFFF 50 30`

   C. `access-list 940 deny -1 50 0 30 0`

   D. `access-list 940 permit -1 30 0 50 0`

   E. `access-list 940 deny -1 50 0 30 0, access-list 940 permit -1 -1 0 -1 0`

13. IPX extended access lists filter on what? (Choose all that apply.)

   A. IPX socket

   B. IPX protocol

   C. RTMP

   D. Source network/node

   E. Destination network/node

14. How are standard IPX access lists numbered?

    A. 1–99

    B. 1000–1099

    C. 800–899

    D. 900–999

    E. 500–599

15. On Ethernet, when do IPX devices send an ARP request?

    A. Locating the nearest server.

    B. Locating the local router.

    C. Locating a remote server.

    D. IPX does not use ARP.

    E. The ARP process in IPX is handled by NLSP.

16. Which of the following are valid IPX network addresses? (Choose all that apply.)

    A. 2.14

    B. 2.0000.0000.0001

    C. 2.1

    D. 2.0000.0C04.0311

    E. FACE.0000.0C04.0311

    F. Server_A.0000.0000.0001

17. There are two frame types on the same physical interface of the router, and the router is running NLSP and IPX RIP. A total of how many network numbers are needed?

    A. None

    B. One

    C. Two

    D. Three

    E. Four

18. When using the `debug ipx packet` command, the administrator should consider using which of the following?

   A. `no ipx route-cache`

   B. `no ipx sap`

   C. `debug all`

   D. `debug ipx sap-input-filter all`

   E. None of the above

19. The SAP interpacket delay is available from which of the following commands?

   A. `debug ipx sap`

   B. `debug ipx sap delay brief`

   C. `show ipx interface`

   D. `show sap interpacket delay`

20. To view the available options for IPX debugging, type which of the following?

   A. ipx debug ?

   B. debug ipx ?

   C. debug all

   D. ipx debug help

   E. ipx debug options

Answers to Review Questions

1. B. The correct command for server information is given by B.

2. C. If there is no local server, the router will respond as the server. If there is a local server, the router will not respond.

3. A, C. Ethernet II and ARPA are synonymous. Novell calls it Ethernet II while Cisco calls it ARPA. Therefore, the encapsulation is the same.

4. D. Before a client can locate services, it needs to know where the servers are. This is done with the GNS request.

5. A. The show ipx servers output provides specific enough information that duplicate networks can be found.

6. C. The default setting is 60 seconds.

7. B. Somewhat similar to an IP RIP hop count, there is a 15-hop limit with IPX RIP.

8. C, D, E. TCP/IP and AppleTalk have nothing to do with SAP, and RIP is compatible with TCP/IP and AppleTalk.

9. B. This command provides the right network and mask.

10. B. Since EIGRP is Cisco proprietary, it can only be on Cisco routers.

11. A. This provides the correct syntax, network, and mask.

12. E. Recall that access lists have implicit deny statements, therefore C would block all IPX traffic.

13. A, B, D, E. These are the valid criteria for extended access list filtering.

14. C. 800–899 is the defined range for standard IPX access lists.

15. D. IPX does not use ARP.

16. B, D, E. There must be four octets, in hex, that specify the network and node.

17. D. There must be two for the external networks and one for the internal network required by NLSP.

18. A. If the packets are route-cached (i.e., switched), they will not cross the processor—thus, debug will not be able to see them.

19. C. The configured value appears when using this command.

20. B. This answer provides the correct syntax.

Chapter

10

Troubleshooting AppleTalk Connectivity

TOPICS COVERED IN THIS CHAPTER INCLUDE:

- ✓ Learning the connection sequences associated with AppleTalk.
- ✓ Identifying troubleshooting targets within AppleTalk and being able to efficiently utilize the targets in problem resolution.

In the 1980s, Apple Computer released the Macintosh—a platform that would later be regarded with almost religious reverence. The Mac has certainly established a niche for itself, and all but controls the education and desktop publishing environments. It is also frequently found in businesses, especially in smaller companies.

Although an all-Macintosh network traditionally used the AppleTalk network protocol, the explosive growth of the Internet has generated a need for TCP/IP, as well. With the latest releases of the Macintosh OS and Apple-Share IP, many administrators, especially those in combined Mac and PC environments, have migrated away from AppleTalk in favor of IP only.

To its credit, AppleTalk does simplify administration, as compared to TCP/IP. Further, some applications will continue to need AppleTalk, and there are still good reasons to understand and use this protocol. This chapter addresses many of the troubleshooting issues commonly found in AppleTalk networks.

The AppleTalk Protocol

The AppleTalk protocol is designed primarily for ease of administration. In fact, small networks can be created with virtually no formal training and little administration. This is made possible by the following protocols that are part of AppleTalk:

AppleTalk Address Resolution Protocol AARP performs two different functions in AppleTalk. First, it is responsible for mapping AppleTalk addresses to hardware addresses. This Layer 3 to Layer 2 mapping is similar to the ARP process in IP. Second, AARP handles the dynamic assignment of node addresses. (This will be covered in greater detail later in this chapter.)

Datagram Delivery Protocol   *DDP* provides unique addressing of all nodes on the AppleTalk internetwork, and is responsible for connectionless delivery of datagrams between nodes.

Name Binding Protocol   *NBP* provides name-to-address resolution that is similar to DNS in TCP/IP; it also handles additional functions.

Routing Table Maintenance Protocol   AppleTalk's default routing protocol is *RTMP*. Updates are sent every 10 seconds, and routes are aged out of the table after 20 seconds. This can result in route flapping on congested segments as the RTMP updates are dropped.

Zone Information Protocol   Zones are logical divisions of AppleTalk resources. *ZIP* maps zone names to network addresses. Although nodes belong to one zone, zones can span multiple physical networks.

AppleTalk Addressing

An AppleTalk address contains network and node information in the format *network.node*. This is similar to the IPX protocol—there is no subnet as with IP. The administrator defines the network portion of the address by defining a cable range. This range varies in size, depending on the phase (version) of AppleTalk and the needs of the network. The network portion of the address is composed of a 16-bit number, whereas the node is defined with eight bits.

AppleTalk Cable Range

AppleTalk networks define their network numbers by assigning a cable range. This range, in the more common AppleTalk *phase two*, can be very large in scope—accommodating a virtually unlimited number of nodes. AppleTalk *phase one* is capable only of addressing one cable number, and it is further restricted to 127 hosts. Table 10.1 presents the differences between AppleTalk phases one and two.

TABLE 10.1 Comparison of AppleTalk Phase One and AppleTalk Phase Two

	AppleTalk Phase One	**AppleTalk Phase Two**
Number of network addresses per segment	1	65,279
Number of host addresses per network	254—127 servers, 127 hosts	253 per network address, Virtually unlimited
Number of zones per network	1	255

Table 10.1 presents AppleTalk phase two as being virtually unlimited in terms of host addresses. This is due to the theoretical capability of AppleTalk to consider cable range 1–65,279 as one network, with 253 hosts per single cable range (cable range 1–1, for example). Thus, the true number of maximum nodes in an AppleTalk network is approximately 16 million. Although possible, this is well beyond the broadcast and physical limitations of most networks, and most cable ranges do not span more than 10 digits (10–19, for example).

A cable range is defined at an AppleTalk router, and it provides the network portion of the address. In phase one, this range consists of a single number (five, for example). In phase two, this number can span any sequential set of numbers. For example, a valid network in phase two AppleTalk is 10–17. This range provides for 2,024 nodes. Note that there are no subnet masks or other IP-style parameters.

AppleTalk Routing

By default, AppleTalk uses RTMP and ZIP, which are protocols that contribute to AppleTalk's chatty reputation. RTMP updates are sent every 10 seconds; by default, routes are aged out after 20 seconds. This results in a high volume of traffic and an extreme sensitivity to congestion—a route announcement may not be sent due to other traffic.

Networks using Cisco routers can also use AT EIGRP, which provides significant advantages in terms of the bandwidth required. As with IP EIGRP and IPX EIGRP, the protocol is proprietary and can require a significant amount of processor and memory on the router. Because non-Cisco devices cannot use the EIGRP protocol, its use is usually limited to WAN and backbone links. This assumes that RTMP is disabled on the segment. This is accomplished with the `no appletalk protocol rtmp` command. Cisco routers automatically redistribute RTMP and AT EIGRP.

AppleTalk Update-Based Routing Protocol (AURP) is a method of encapsulating AppleTalk traffic. This occurs within the header of another protocol, usually TCP/IP. The resulting connection is referred to as an AURP tunnel. AURP maintains routing table information and permits AppleTalk networks to span WANs that do not service the AppleTalk protocol. While AURP is considered an AppleTalk routing protocol, this chapter will focus on RTMP and AT EIGRP.

Unlike IP and IPX EIGRP, which use an autonomous system number or process number, AT EIGRP uses a router number. This number must be unique for each router in the network.

AppleTalk *ping* Command

The AppleTalk `ping` command is used for troubleshooting, in much the same way as the TCP/IP `ping` command is used. This command is useful for verifying connectivity if the administrator knows the AppleTalk address or node name.

A command line `ping` is displayed as follows:

```
Router_C#ping apple 1.87
Type escape sequence to abort.
Sending 5, 100-byte AppleTalk Echos to 1.87, timeout is 2
seconds:
!!!!!
Success rate is 100 percent (5/5), round-trip min/avg/max
=    1/2/4 ms
```

The extended `ping` option with verbose mode selected is as follows:

```
Router_C#ping
```

```
Protocol [ip]: apple
Target AppleTalk address: 1.87
Repeat count [5]:
Datagram size [100]:
Timeout in seconds [2]:
Verbose [n]: y
Sweep range of sizes [n]:
Type escape sequence to abort.
Sending 5, 100-byte AppleTalk Echos to 1.87, timeout is 2
seconds:
0 in 4 ms from 1.87 via 1 hop
1 in 4 ms from 1.87 via 1 hop
2 in 4 ms from 1.87 via 1 hop
3 in 4 ms from 1.87 via 1 hop
4 in 4 ms from 1.87 via 1 hop
Success rate is 100 percent (5/5), round-trip min/avg/max
=    4/4/4 ms
```

AppleTalk *show* Commands

As with other protocols, the Cisco IOS show commands provide a wealth of information regarding AppleTalk, including routing, zone, and cache data. A list of options is displayed as follows with the show appletalk ? command. Many options have suboptions—use the ? command to review further.

```
Router_C#show appletalk ?
  access-lists      AppleTalk access lists
  adjacent-routes   AppleTalk adjacent routes
  arp               AppleTalk arp table
  aurp              AURP information
  cache             AppleTalk fast-switching cache
  domain            AppleTalk Domain(s) information
  eigrp             AppleTalk/EIGRP show commands
  globals           AppleTalk global parameters
  interface         AppleTalk interface status and
                    configuration
  macip-clients     Mac IP clients
```

macip-servers	Mac IP servers
macip-traffic	Mac IP traffic
name-cache	AppleTalk name cache
nbp	AppleTalk NBP name table
neighbors	AppleTalk Neighboring router status
remap	AppleTalk remap table
route	AppleTalk routing table
sockets	AppleTalk protocol processing information
static	AppleTalk static table
traffic	AppleTalk protocol statistics
zone	AppleTalk Zone table information

show appletalk interface

The show appletalk interface command displays the interface status, cable range, and network and node address, in addition to the zone name and route cache status. In this example, the zone name is "one" and the interface is 1.230. AppleTalk also verifies the configuration of the port—in this case, router 1.87 performed this function.

```
Router_C#show appletalk interface
TokenRing0 is up, line protocol is up
  AppleTalk cable range is 1-1
  AppleTalk address is 1.230, Valid
  AppleTalk zone is "one"
  AppleTalk port configuration verified by 1.87
  AppleTalk address gleaning is disabled
  AppleTalk route cache is enabled
```

Note that in troubleshooting, there may be cause to use the clear appletalk commands, which includes the clear appletalk interface option. A list of the clear appletalk options is included as follows.

WARNING

The clear appletalk interface command resets the specified interface(s), disrupting connectivity.

```
Router_C#clear appletalk ?
  arp           Reset AppleTalk information
  eigrp         Clear AppleTalk/EIGRP
  interface     Clear & restart AppleTalk interface
  nbp           Reset AppleTalk NBP cache information
  neighbor      Reset AppleTalk down neighbor information
  route         Reset AppleTalk routing table
  route-cache   Reset AppleTalk fast-switching cache(s)
  traffic       Reset AppleTalk traffic counters
```

show appletalk route

The show appletalk route command provides a summary of all known routes and the protocol that distributed them. In addition, the primary zone of each network is displayed. Recall that a network can contain up to 255 zones in AppleTalk phase two. Although the example here displays the zone names "one" and "Two," most administrators will name zones for the workgroup served—"Marketing Zone," for example. Note that zone names are also case-sensitive.

```
Router_C#show appletalk route
Codes: R - RTMP derived, E - EIGRP derived, C - connected,
A - AURP, S - static  P - proxy
2 routes in internet
The first zone listed for each entry is its default
(primary) zone.
C Net 1-1 directly connected, TokenRing0, zone one
R Net 2-2 [1/G] via 1.87, 9 sec, TokenRing0, zone Two
```

show appletalk zone

The show appletalk zone command displays the zone names and networks that are known to the router through ZIP updates. This command is most useful for troubleshooting reports of "missing" zones.

As noted previously, zones are the logical definitions of network resources. For example, a zone called "Marketing" can be used to define those resources (including file servers and printers) that are used by the marketing group. This is also a better name than "Zone1" because the name denotes the department or other business boundary. Naming zones for groups of users can greatly simplify troubleshooting and assist users because they will select resources based on the zone name first.

Zone names are useful in grouping geographically separated workgroups, as well. The Marketing zone may include cable range 5–10 when initially created, but a new marketing group in another building may be needed. This group can be placed on cable range 1000–1005, yet remain in the Marketing zone.

AppleTalk does not provide a mechanism for updating zone names. For example, if an administrator changes the zone name from "Finance" to "Marketing," the local router zone name changes, but the remote routers continue to reference "Finance." This is referred to as a *ghost zone*. It is recommended that administrators disable all networks that are related to the zone name being changed. This ages out the routing table; upon reinstatement, the routers learn the route and new zone name information.

The output of the `show appletalk zone` command follows:

```
Router_C#show appletalk zone
Name                           Network(s)
one                            1-1
Two                            2-2
Dilbert                        14000-14005
Kenny                          22638-22639
Total of 4 zones
```

show appletalk access-lists

Access lists are usually configured to restrict access to various resources within the network. This may be for broadcast control, data security, or other considerations. Regarding AppleTalk, access lists are numbered from 600 to 699. In addition, the Cisco IOS filters zone and network information simultaneously. Because administrators may wish to write lists that block certain traffic and permit all other traffic, it is important to consider both the `access-list permit other-access` and `access-list permit additional-zones` statements. As with other access lists, implicit denies are automatically assumed at the end of an AppleTalk access list. In the example, `access-list 605` demonstrates the more common AppleTalk access list, in which certain packets are permitted and all items not permitted are denied. This is a default behavior of `AppleTalk access-lists`, but is explicitly restated in this example.

```
Router_C#show appletalk access-lists
AppleTalk access list 605:
  permit zone Padjen
  permit zone Robert
  permit zone Tyler
  permit zone Kristie
  permit zone Eddie
  permit zone Dilbert
  permit zone Cessna
  deny additional-zones
  deny other-access
```

show appletalk adjacent-routes

The show appletalk adjacent-routes command shows connected and one-hop-away routes that are known to the router. Two examples of the command are displayed:

```
Router_A#show appletalk adjacent-routes
Codes: R - RTMP derived, E - EIGRP derived, C - connected,
A – AURP, S - static  P - proxy
796 routes in internet

The first zone listed for each entry is its default
(primary) zone.

C Net 144-144 directly connected, FastEthernet0/0, zone
This
C Net 147-147 directly connected, Ethernet1/2, zone That
C Net 148-148 directly connected, Ethernet4/5, zone The
Other
R Net 151-151 [1/G] via Router_C.Ethernet5, 8 sec,
Ethernet4/2, Zone: "Backbone"
Router_C#show appletalk adjacent-routes
Codes: R - RTMP derived, E - EIGRP derived, C - connected,
A – AURP, S - static  P - proxy
2 routes in internet
The first zone listed for each entry is its default
(primary) zone.
C Net 1-1 directly connected, TokenRing0, zone one
R Net 2-2 [1/G] via 1.87, 5 sec, TokenRing0, zone Two
```

show appletalk arp

The show appletalk arp command displays the ARP cache of the router for all AppleTalk addresses. This is populated by the AppleTalk Address Resolution Protocol (AARP). Address resolution is needed to link the MAC layer address to the Layer 3 address.

```
Router_C#show appletalk arp
Address  Age (min) Type      Hardware Addr       Encap
Interface
1.87     7         Dynamic   0000.30e8.6d0f.0000 SNAP
TokenRing0
1.230    -         Hardware  0000.30da.5842.0000 SNAP
TokenRing0
```

The ARP cache can be cleared with the clear appletalk arp command. This may be useful if a corrupt ARP cache is suspected when troubleshooting.

show appletalk globals

This command is one of the most valuable in AppleTalk troubleshooting. The show appletalk globals command provides information about phase one compatibility, ZIP, RTMP, AARP, and DDP functions. In addition, routing information is displayed.

```
Router_C#show appletalk globals
AppleTalk global information:
  Internet is compatible with older, AT Phase1, routers.
  There are 2 routes in the internet.
  There are 2 zones defined.
  Logging of significant AppleTalk events is disabled.
  ZIP resends queries every 10 seconds.
  RTMP updates are sent every 10 seconds.
  RTMP entries are considered BAD after 20 seconds.
  RTMP entries are discarded after 60 seconds.
  AARP probe retransmit count: 10, interval: 200 msec.
  AARP request retransmit count: 5, interval: 1000 msec.
```

```
DDP datagrams will be checksummed.
RTMP datagrams will be strictly checked.
RTMP routes may not be propagated without zones.
Routes will be distributed between routing protocols.
Routing between local devices on an interface will not
be performed.
IPTalk uses the udp base port of 768 (Default).
AppleTalk EIGRP is not enabled.
Alternate node address format will not be displayed.
Access control of any networks of a zone hides the zone.
```

show appletalk name-cache

The show appletalk name-cache displays a list of NBP services from other AppleTalk routers and devices that support NBP. The output, as shown, includes the network, address, socket information, and NBP type.

```
Router_C#show appletalk name-cache
AppleTalk Name Cache:
Net Adr Skt Name                        Type        Zone
144  46 254 Router_C.FastEthernet0/0 ciscoRouter  Dilbert
147  96 254 Router_C.Ethernet1/2      ciscoRouter  Robert
148 252 254 Router_C.Ethernet4/5      ciscoRouter  Piper
157  93 254 Router_C.Ethernet4/2      ciscoRouter  Info
157 102 254 Router_A.Ethernet         ciscoRouter  Info
157 188 254 Router_B.Ethernet5        ciscoRouter  Info
```

show appletalk traffic

The show appletalk traffic command summarizes all AppleTalk traffic that enters or leaves the router—including erred packets, routing counters, and broadcast information. This information can be very useful for obtaining a quick overview of the state of the AppleTalk protocol. Although a baseline is valuable for comparison, the counters presented in this command usually present an indication of errors that need resolution.

The output of the command is shown as follows:

```
Router_C#show appletalk traffic
AppleTalk statistics:
  Rcvd:  167 total, 0 checksum errors, 0 bad hop count
    167 local destination, 0 access denied
      0 for MacIP, 0 bad MacIP, 0 no client
      0 port disabled, 109 no listener
      0 ignored, 0 martians
  Bcast: 0 received, 52 sent
  Sent:  53 generated, 0 forwarded, 0 fast forwarded, 0
  loopback
      0 forwarded from MacIP, 0 MacIP failures
      0 encapsulation failed, 0 no route, 0 no source
  DDP:   167 long, 0 short, 0 macip, 0 bad size
  NBP:   10 received, 0 invalid, 0 proxies
      0 replies sent, 10 forwards, 10 lookups, 0 failures
  RTMP:  45 received, 0 requests, 0 invalid, 0 ignored
      45 sent, 0 replies
  ATP:   0 received
  ZIP:   7 received, 3 sent, 5 netinfo
  Echo:  0 received, 0 discarded, 0 illegal
      0 generated, 0 replies sent
  Responder:  0 received, 0 illegal, 0 unknown
      0 replies sent, 0 failures
  AARP:  1 requests, 0 replies, 10 probes
      0 martians, 0 bad encapsulation, 0 unknown
  AppleTalk statistics:
      11 sent, 0 failures, 0 delays, 0 drops
  Lost: 0 no buffers
  Unknown: 0 packets
  Discarded: 0 wrong encapsulation, 0 bad SNAP
  discriminator
  AURP: 0 Open Requests, 0 Router Downs
      0 Routing Information sent, 0 Routing Information
      received
```

```
0 Zone Information sent, 0 Zone Information
received
0 Get Zone Nets sent, 0 Get Zone Nets received
0 Get Domain Zone List sent, 0 Get Domain Zone
List    received
0 bad sequence
```

show appletalk neighbors

To view information about directly connected AppleTalk routers, use the show appletalk neighbors command. This command provides information about the AppleTalk address, the routing protocol that connects the two routers, and the local interface.

```
Router_C#show appletalk neighbors
AppleTalk neighbors:
1.87          TokenRing0, uptime 00:07:31, 1 sec
Neighbor is reachable as a RTMP peer
```

show appletalk nbp

The output of the show appletalk nbp command is similar to the output from the show appletalk name-cache command because both are populated from the same function. In this example, the Type field includes ciscoRouter and SNMP Agent. The command displays the contents of the NBP registration table.

```
Router_C#show appletalk nbp
  Net Adr Skt  Name                     Type        Zone
  17   93 254 Router_C.Ethernet4/2      ciscoRouter Dilbert
  186 181 254 Router_C.FastEthernet6/1 ciscoRouter Kenny
  144  46 254 Router_C.FastEthernet0/0 ciscoRouter Info
  144  46   8 Router_C                  SNMP Agent  Info
  186 181   8 Router_C                  SNMP Agent  Piper
```

AppleTalk *test* Commands

The test commands are not limited to AppleTalk. They include AppleTalk, EIGRP, Banyan Vines, and interfaces. As shown in the following output, the test apple command includes specific sequences for ARP, AT EIGRP, and NBP.

```
Router_C#test apple
Router_C(atalk test)#?
  arp    APPLETALK ARP test commands
  eigrp  APPLETALK EIGRP test commands
  end    Exit AppleTalk test mode
  nbp    AppleTalk NBP test commands
```

Please note that most of these commands include further options.

Use of the following commands requires entering test apple mode. The prompt will change to (atalk test).

The NBP tests are perhaps the most beneficial for testing. The options include confirm, lookup, parameters, and poll. The parameters command sets options for the other commands and is rarely necessary.

The test appletalk nbp suboptions are listed as follows:

```
Router_C(atalk test)#nbp ?
  confirm     Confirm NBP
  lookup      Send NBP Lookup
  parameters  Set NBP timeouts
  poll        Poll all devices in internet
```

NBP Poll

Within the test apple syntax, it is possible to send an NBP poll. This command searches for all devices in all zones. A brief example is included as follows:

```
Router_C(atalk test)#nbp poll
poll: sent 2 lookups
(1n,230a,254s)[1]:   'Router_C.TokenRing0:ciscoRouter@one'
(2n,111a,254s)[1]:   'Router_A.Ethernet1:ciscoRouter@Two'
NBP polling completed.
Processed 2 replies, 2 events
```

WARNING   Use the nbp poll command with caution. It generates a great deal of traffic on the entire network.

A more extensive example is included here. Note that non-Cisco router types were also discovered.

```
Router_C(atalk test)#nbp poll
poll:  sent 439 lookups
(449n,48a,136s)[4]:    'Server02:DceDspRpc Endpoint
Mapper@Corp'
(449n,160a,2s)[1]:     'Server31@Server02:Microsoft:A8
Windows NT:AA Prt 4.00@ Dilbert'
(595n,30a,254s)[1]:    'lear.Ethernet3/5:ciscoRouter@
Kenny'
(43199n,145a,244s)[0]:    'what:AFPServer@Piper'
(455n,121a,254s)[1]:    'widget.Ethernet0:ciscoRouter@
Kenny'
```

NBP Lookup

The NBP lookup command can be used to provide the AppleTalk address of a known NBP service. The syntax is nbp lookup object:type@zone.

NBP Confirm

The nbp confirm command is seldom used in production environments because the show and ping commands are more familiar to administrators. Since IOS release 11.1, however, the command has been available to verify the AppleTalk address against its name and zone information. The syntax is nbp confirm appletalk-address [:skt] object: type@zone. In the following example, the NBP confirm was responded to with the socket information included.

```
Router(atalk test)#nbp confirm 19.71
server:AFPServer@Dilbert
confirmed server:AFPServer@Dilbert at 19n,71a,250s
```

NBP Parameters

The NBP parameters permit control over retransmissions, replies, and intervals used by the other NBP test commands. Table 10.2 defines the values that are entered in the syntax nbp parameters [retransmissions] [replies] [interval].

TABLE 10.2   NBP Parameter Values

Option	Definition	Range of Values	Default
Retransmissions	Maximum number of lookup retransmissions	1 to 5	5
Replies	Maximum number of replies per lookup	1 to 500	1
Interval	Number of seconds between each retry	1 to 60	5

AppleTalk *debug* Commands

The AppleTalk debug commands are helpful for isolating and resolving network problems by providing the administrator with real-time data. Care must be exercised in using these commands, however, because they may disrupt network handling by the router. Also, there are instances when a protocol analyzer may be a better troubleshooting tool; and, as with all troubleshooting procedures, it is helpful to understand the client, server, and network components. A listing of the debug apple commands from the ? option is listed as follows:

```
Router_C#debug apple ?
  arp                   Appletalk address resolution
protocol
  aurp-connection       AURP connection
  aurp-packet           AURP packets
  aurp-update           AURP routing updates
  domain                AppleTalk Domain function
  eigrp-all             All AT/EIGRP functions
```

eigrp-external	AT/EIGRP external functions
eigrp-hello	AT/EIGRP hello functions
eigrp-packet	AT/EIGRP packet debugging
eigrp-query	AT/EIGRP query functions
eigrp-redistribution	AT/EIGRP route redistribution
eigrp-request	AT/EIGRP external functions
eigrp-target	Appletalk/EIGRP for targeting address
eigrp-update	AT/EIGRP update functions
errors	Information about errors
events	Appletalk special events
fs	Appletalk fast-switching
iptalk	IPTalk encapsulation and functionality
load-balancing	AppleTalk load-balancing
macip	MacIP functions
nbp	Name Binding Protocol (NBP) functions
packet	Per-packet debugging
redistribution	Route Redistribution
remap	AppleTalk Remap function
responder	AppleTalk responder debugging
routing	(RTMP&EIGRP) functions
rtmp	(RTMP) functions
zip	Zone Information Protocol functions

WARNING The debug command is assigned a high-CPU priority and can generate a high processor load. Always use caution when using a debug command. The resulting processor load and output can degrade router performance or render the system unusable.

debug apple arp

The ARP process is responsible for resolving Layer 3 addresses to their Layer 2 devices. The debug appletalk arp command reports all real-time events that are related to this process.

In the following example, the ARP table is displayed with the show appletalk arp command. There are two entries in the table: the remote router interface at 1.87 and the local AppleTalk interface at 1.230. The table is then cleared with the clear arp command.

```
Router_C#debug appletalk arp
AppleTalk ARP debugging is on
Router_C#show appletalk arp
Address   Age (min) Type     Hardware Addr     Encap   Interface
1.87      10        Dynamic  0000.30e8.6d0f.0000  SNAP  TokenRing0
1.230     -         Hardware 0000.30da.5842.0000  SNAP  TokenRing0
Router_C#clear arp
Router_C#
TokenRing0: AARP: Removing entry for 1.87(0000.30e8.6d0f)
TokenRing0: AARP: Removing entry for 1.230(0000.30da.5842)
AARP: creating entry for TokenRing0, 1.230(0000.30da.5842)
TokenRing0: AARP aarp_insert, initial NULL entry
AARP: aarp_insert, entry 60C57FD8 for node 1.230(0000.30da.5842)
added on TokenRing0
```

debug apple errors

AppleTalk errors, including incorrect encapsulation, invalid Ping packets, NetInfoReply errors, configuration mismatch problems, and bad responder packet types are all presented by the debug apple errors command.

Decoding of the debug apple errors command usually is helped with reference to CCO (Cisco Connections Online). This support tool is very helpful and provides the latest information available.

```
Router_C#debug apple errors
AppleTalk packet errors debugging is on
TokenRing0: input AT packet: enctype SNAP, size 65
```

```
C00040000000000030E86D0FAAAA03080007809B|00418B4700000001F
F575858580205EDAC
00000000000000000000000000000010001000C010001000000000F02
04000C0001000100
TokenRing0: input AT packet: enctype SNAP, size 65
C00040000000000030E86D0FAAAA03080007809B|00418B4700000001F
F575858580205EDAC
00000000000000000000000000000010001000C010001000000000F02
04000C0001000100
TokenRing0: input AT packet: enctype SNAP, size 65
C00040000000000030E86D0FAAAA03080007809B|00418B4700000001F
F575858580205EDAC
00000000000000000000000000000010001000C010001000000000F02
04000C0001000100
TokenRing0: input AT packet: enctype SNAP, size 65
C00040000000000030E86D0FAAAA03080007809B|00418B4700000001F
F575858580205EDAC
00000000000000000000000000000010001000C010001000000000F02
04000C0001000100
```

debug apple events

The debug apple events command reports AppleTalk special events, including interfaces going up or down, and neighbor unreachability. In a stable network, this command produces no output.

Although Cisco recommends that administrators enable this command prior to making configuration changes, few administrators heed this advice. Many sites do use the apple event-logging command, however, which reports special events to a syslog server.

Note that when the command is used during configuration changes (specifically, the enabling of a new router interface), the following sequence should be observed:

- Line down

- Restarting

- Probing—this is an AARP process to find its address

- Acquiring via GetNetInfo requests

- Sending ZIP requests for a list of zones on the cable

- Verification that the router's configuration matches the information received from the previous requests; note that an error at this point will result in a port configuration mismatch

- Zone verification to confirm that the router's zone list is valid

- Operational status and interface up

debug apple nbp

The debug apple nbp command should be used to confirm receipt of valid NBP updates. This is usually warranted after a problem viewed with the show appletalk nbp command.

```
Router_A# debug apple nbp
AT: NBP ctrl = LkUp, ntuples = 1, id = 77
AT: 410.19, skt 2, enum 0, name: =:ciscoRouter@Lab
AT: LkUp =:ciscoRouter@Lab
AT: NBP ctrl = LkUp-Reply, ntuples = 1, id = 77
AT: 4160.154, skt 254, enum 1, name:
lestat.Ether0:ciscoRouter@Lab
AT: NBP ctrl = LkUp, ntuples = 1, id = 78
AT: 410.19, skt 2, enum 0, name: =:IPADDRESS@Lab
AT: NBP ctrl = LkUp, ntuples = 1, id = 79
AT: 410.19, skt 2, enum 0, name: =:IPGATEWAY@Lab
AT: NBP ctrl = LkUp, ntuples = 1, id = 83
AT: 410.19, skt 2, enum 0, name: =:ciscoRouter@Lab
AT: LkUp =:ciscoRouter@LabAT: NBP ctrl = LkUp, ntuples =
1, id = 84
AT: 410.19, skt 2, enum 0, name: =:IPADDRESS@Lab
AT: NBP ctrl = LkUp, ntuples = 1, id = 85
AT: 410.19, skt 2, enum 0, name: =:IPGATEWAY@Lab
AT: NBP ctrl = LkUp, ntuples = 1, id = 85
AT: 410.19, skt 2, enum 0, name: =:IPGATEWAY@Lab
```

debug apple packet

This command reports all inbound and outbound AppleTalk datagrams at the router. Although this command can be very useful when troubleshooting, it is recommended that care be used. A protocol analyzer may prove to be a more useful diagnostic tool.

As displayed in the following, the output includes RTMP and other AppleTalk packets that can be displayed with more limiting **debug** commands.

```
Router_C#debug apple packet
AppleTalk packets debugging is on
TokenRing0: input AT packet: enctype SNAP, size 29
C00040000000000030E86D0FAAAA03080007809B|001DD8F900000001F
F5701010100010857
00018000018200028000028201FF570101010001085700018000018200
0280000282B73A6E
TokenRing0: input AT packet: enctype SNAP, size 29
C00040000000000030E86D0FAAAA03080007809B|001DD8F900000001F
F5701010100010857
00018000018200028000028201FF570101010001085700018000018200
0280000282B73A6E
TokenRing0: input AT packet: enctype SNAP, size 65
C00040000000000030E86D0FAAAA03080007809B|00418B4700000001F
F575858580205EDAC
00000000000000000000000000000010001000C010001000000000F02
04000C0001000100
TokenRing0: encap'ed output packet AT packet: enctype
SNAP, size 45
00000000000000000000000000000000000000000|0040C000400000000
00030DA5842AAAA03
080007809B$0017BEE200000001FFE6010101000108E6000180000182D
1000000000000000
AT: src=TokenRing0:1.230, dst=1-1, size=10, 0 rtes, RTMP
pkt sentg all
```

debug apple routing

The debug apple routing command displays transaction information on all RTMP and AppleTalk EIGRP packets. This example includes the report (italic) that network 2-2 is no longer available. A disconnected wire caused this outage.

```
Router_C#debug apple routing
AppleTalk RTMP routing debugging is on
AppleTalk EIGRP routing debugging is on
Router_C#
```

```
AT: src=TokenRing0:1.230, dst=1-1, size=10, 0 rtes, RTMP
pkt sent
AT: Route ager starting on Main AT RoutingTable (2 active
nodes)
AT: Route ager finished on Main AT RoutingTable (2 active
nodes)
AT: RTMP from 1.87 (new 0,old 1,bad 0,ign 0, dwn 0)
AT: src=TokenRing0:1.230, dst=1-1, size=10, 0 rtes, RTMP
pkt sent
AT: Route ager starting on Main AT RoutingTable (2 active
nodes)
AT: Route ager finished on Main AT RoutingTable (2 active
nodes)
AT: RTMP from 1.87 (new 0,old 1,bad 0,ign 0, dwn 0)
AT: src=TokenRing0:1.230, dst=1-1, size=10, 0 rtes, RTMP
pkt sent
AT: Route ager starting on Main AT RoutingTable (2 active
nodes)
AT: Route ager finished on Main AT RoutingTable (2 active
nodes)
%AT-6-PATHNOTIFY: TokenRing0: AppleTalk RTMP path to 2-2
down; reported bad by 1.87
AT: RTMP from 1.87 (new 0,old 0,bad 0,ign 0, dwn 1)
AT: src=TokenRing0:1.230, dst=1-1, size=10, 0 rtes, RTMP
pkt sent
```

debug apple zip

As presented previously, zone updates are critical to the proper functioning of
AppleTalk networks. The debug apple zip command reports all ZIP packet
information in real time for troubleshooting zone problems. The following
output includes the response to a ZIP query on network 2-2. Note the "name
Two" entry within the output.

```
Router_C#debug apple zip
AppleTalk ZIP Packets debugging is on
AT: NextNbrZipQuery: [2-2] zoneupdate 0 gw: 1.87 n: 1.87
AT: NextNbrZipQuery: r->rpath.gwptr: 60C60D20, n: 60C60D20
AT: maint_SendNeighborQueries, sending 1 queries to 1.87
```

```
AT: 1 query packet sent to neighbor 1.87
AT: Recvd ZIP cmd 2 from 1.87-6
AT: 1 zones in ZIPreply pkt, src 1.87
AT: net 2, zonelen 3, name Two
AT: in CancelZoneRequest, cancelling req on 2-
2...succeeded
AT: atzip_GC() called
```

Common AppleTalk Troubleshooting Issues

As with most networks, AppleTalk nets are prone to common issues that prompt troubleshooting. This section addresses these common problems and outlines their resolutions in the context of the Cisco IOS show and debug commands.

Note that the following section should not take the place of a methodical troubleshooting procedure. In AppleTalk, this process should include verifying the local configuration and/or outlining the scope of the problem. This includes determining whether the problem affects more than one system or location.

Further generic troubleshooting should also include the verification of the local router and the impact of any access lists. Non-AppleTalk issues should also be reviewed, including high utilization and error rates. In summary, the main troubleshooting targets for AppleTalk are as follows:

- Local host configuration

- Routers connected to AppleTalk networks

- Remote host configuration

It is important to realize that these are very general and high-level troubleshooting targets, and that each one has several more low-level targets.

ZIP Storms

A ZIP storm can occur when a zone name does not map to an AppleTalk route. Although storms are prevented by the Cisco IOS, other routers can permit this problem. Because AppleTalk has no mechanism for alerting stations to changes in the zone list, routers request ZIP updates upon learning about a new route.

When troubleshooting ZIP storms, use the `show appletalk traffic` command. Evidence of a storm can be found by reviewing the number of ZIP requests over a period of 30 seconds, and noting a higher than normal increment. Although `debug` commands can provide further troubleshooting information, it is recommended that a protocol analyzer be used. This is because of the high processor utilization that the `debug` command requires and other network issues that are usually associated with ZIP storms.

Higher than normal assumes that the administrator has established a baseline for the network. This is a troubleshooting step that occurs before an incident. By comparing the network when it is operating correctly to the degraded network metrics, a course of action should become clear.

AARP Broadcast Frames

When connecting to an AppleTalk network, the workstation (or other device) sends AARP probe frames to verify that its address is unique. On Ethernet and Token Ring, the station sends 10 broadcasts. If there is a response, the workstation must send another set of AARP broadcasts with a different address to find an available address. On networks with a low number of available addresses, this can result in a significant amount of traffic.

Prevention of this problem can be more beneficial than detection. When setting up networks, make certain that there is sufficient growth room for addresses. If troubleshooting, use the `show appletalk traffic` command to review the status of AARP broadcast frames.

Phase One/Phase Two Compatibility Problems

Although this problem is very unlikely in most modern networks, the differences between the versions of the AppleTalk protocol can create significant service disruptions.

The Cisco IOS has supported phase two since version 8.2, and few administrators have any reason to not use phase two throughout the network. However, it is possible that a legacy or misconfigured router can cause a phase one/phase two mismatch. The `show appletalk globals` command provides the administrator with a simple method of troubleshooting this potential cause. If the `show appletalk globals` command reports incompatibility with a phase one device, the `show appletalk neighbors` and `show appletalk route` commands should provide sufficient information for resolution.

Duplicate or Crossed Network Numbers

It is very easy for an administrator to use the same cable range on two physical media or to cross address ranges on different media. For example, placing cable range 5–10 on the Ethernet interface of Router_A and 5–10 on the FDDI interface results in a duplicate network number. It is even more common for an administrator to accidentally use 5–10 for one network and 7–12 for another. Because of the overlap, the route table becomes unstable. In troubleshooting, it is helpful to disable the suspected duplicate interface, and then use the show appletalk route command to confirm that the network still exists.

It is possible to simplify administration by using seed routers. A seed router provides all other routers with the AppleTalk network information needed to function. Setting the cable range to 0–0 places the router into AppleTalk discovery mode. One router needs to be configured with a real cable range and zone per physical media.

Overloaded Network

As with all other protocols, it is possible for AppleTalk to be affected by an overloaded segment or router. This may be due to other traffic or traffic within the AppleTalk network itself. It is also possible for the overload to be a function of ZIP or RTMP traffic within AppleTalk.

Troubleshooting should begin with the show interface command. Note that this is sans physical or protocol parameters because initially the overload itself is only being researched. At the initial troubleshooting point, it is not possible to specify a specific protocol or interface. If an interface (or interfaces) shows high loads, the administrator should use a protocol analyzer to further determine the cause. Although debug and show commands may be used as well, caution must be exercised with the debug command in this situation.

No Resources Listed in Chooser

The Chooser is the Macintosh application that users use to select file and print services. Frequently, the help desk will receive a report that there are no resources available—sometimes only reported as an unavailable service.

Although the resource becoming unavailable or a down network can cause this problem, it is also possible for the cause to be an access list or workstation problem.

To troubleshoot an access list issue or other restriction, the administrator should use the `show appletalk access-list` command to review any filters and the `no appletalk access-group` command to disable the list for testing. After locating the offending access list, the administrator will likely wish to reconfigure the list with appropriate permit and deny statements, as warranted by security policies.

However, it is also possible that the problem is isolated to the workstation. Ideally, help desk staff will have performed a preliminary assessment of the problem, which should include asking the caller if other users are currently experiencing the problem. If the problem does not affect other users, it is possible that the workstation itself has a disconnected cable or that the internal network configuration has changed. Macintosh systems can use a network card for their network connections or the serial port, with the default being a serial port connection. This should be checked by using the AppleTalk control panel.

A specific type of access list is available to limit zone information. Applied to individual interfaces, the administrator may use the `appletalk getzonelist-filter 610` command. This command would apply access list 610 to any zone updates composed by the router. Such an access list would be a likely candidate for missing resources in the Chooser.

Summary

This chapter addressed troubleshooting connectivity issues in AppleTalk networks. It reviewed the AppleTalk addressing scheme, including phase one and phase two network addresses. In addition, the chapter covered AppleTalk zones, overlapping cable ranges, NBP issues, and RTMP limitations.

It is hoped that administrators reading this chapter have also noted the importance of good documentation, large cable range definitions for scalability, and the use of descriptive zone names to assist in user acceptance and troubleshooting.

Commands Used in This Chapter

The following list contains a summary of all the commands used in this chapter.

Command	Description
debug apple arp	Reports all real-time events that are related to the process of resolving Layer 3 addresses to Layer 2 devices.
debug apple errors	Reports AppleTalk errors, including incorrect encapsulation, invalid ping packets, NetInfoReply errors, configuration mismatch problems, and bad responder packet types.
debug apple events	Reports AppleTalk special events, including interfaces going up or down, and neighbor unreachability.
debug apple nbp	Confirms receipt of valid NBP updates.
debug apple packet	Reports all inbound and outbound AppleTalk datagrams at the router.
debug apple routing	Displays transaction information on all RTMP and AppleTalk EIGRP packets.
debug apple zip	Reports all ZIP packet information in real time for troubleshooting zone problems.
nbp confirm appletalk-address [:skt] object: type@zone	Verifies the AppleTalk address against its name and zone information.
nbp lookup object:type@zone	Provides the AppleTalk address of a known NBP service.

Command	Description
`nbp parameters`	Permits control over retransmissions, replies, and intervals used by the other NBP `test` commands.
`NBP Poll`	Searches for all devices in all zones.
`ping apple`	Pings Apple addresses.
`show appletalk access-lists`	Displays the AppleTalk access lists.
`show appletalk adjacent-routes`	Shows connected and one-hop-away routes that are known to the router.
`show appletalk arp`	Displays the ARP cache of the router for all AppleTalk addresses.
`show appletalk globals`	Provides information about phase one compatibility, ZIP, RTMP, AARP, and DDP functions. In addition, displays routing information.
`show appletalk interface`	Shows the AppleTalk settings for the interface.
`show appletalk name-cache`	Cache displays a list of NBP services from other AppleTalk routers and devices that support NBP.
`show appletalk nbp`	Displays a list of NBP services from other AppleTalk routers and devices that support NBP.
`show appletalk neighbors`	Provides information about the AppleTalk address, the routing protocol that connects the two routers, and the local interface.
`show appletalk route`	Provides a summary of all known routes and the protocol that distributed them.

Command	Description
show appletalk traffic	Summarizes all AppleTalk traffic that enters or leaves the router, including erred packets, routing counters, and broadcast information.
show appletalk zone	Displays the zone names and networks that are known to the router through ZIP updates.
test appletalk	Enables the testing mode for AppleTalk.

Key Terms

Before you take the exam, be certain you are familiar with the following terms:

AppleTalk Address Resolution Protocol (AARP)

Datagram Delivery Protocol (DDP)

Name Binding Protocol (NBP)

Routing Table Maintenance Protocol (RTMP)

Zone Information Protocol (ZIP)

Review Questions

1. AppleTalk addresses appear in what format?

    A. workstation@applezone

    B. 172.16.2.56

    C. 5.42

    D. 82.000C.3090.8730

    E. http://www.aeroventure.com

2. On a Cisco router, a phase one cable range (or compatible cable range) is which of the following?

    A. 172.16.2.0/24

    B. 5–10

    C. 5–5

    D. ZoneOne

3. An AppleTalk node can do which of the following?

    A. It can belong to a single zone.

    B. It cannot belong to multiple zones.

    C. It cannot belong to multiple zones as long as it is a server.

    D. It cannot belong to a zone.

4. What protocol associates an AppleTalk address with a MAC layer address?

    A. NBP

    B. AARP

    C. RTMP

    D. ZIP

5. Which of the following steps occur(s) during AppleTalk node address assignments? (Choose all that apply.)

   A. Conflicting address sends a conflict message indicating a problem.

   B. The node chooses a new address.

   C. The node chooses a network address.

   D. The node chooses its first network node address.

   E. The node checks to see whether a network address is in use.

6. AppleTalk can be routed with which of the following? (Choose all that apply.)

   A. Static

   B. AURP

   C. RIP

   D. RTMP

   E. EIGRP

   F. OSPF

   G. IGRP

7. Zone Widget can belong to which cable ranges?

   A. 1–1, 5–5, 6–6

   B. 1–1

   C. 1–6

   D. 1–6, 200–300

   E. All of the above

   F. None of the above

8. Which AppleTalk protocol is used to establish and maintain routing tables?

   A. ZIP

   B. NBP

   C. RTMP

   D. IGRP

9. Which protocol in AppleTalk is most similar to TCP/IP DNS?

   A. RTMP

   B. AT DNS

   C. NBP

   D. AURP

   E. AT EIGRP

10. Which of the following probably causes user inability to see zones or services outside of their own network?

   A. Clients not configured with a default gateway

   B. Phase one, phase two incompatibility

   C. Incorrect AppleTalk encapsulation

   D. Too many zones configured for a single network

11. The AppleTalk access lists are defined by which of the following?

   A. 500–599

   B. 600–699

   C. 900–999

   D. 100–199

12. Which of the following protocols is part of AppleTalk? (Choose all that apply.)

   A. AARP

   B. DDP

   C. ZIP

   D. RTMP

   E. RIP

   F. NBP

   G. All of the above

13. A Macintosh user uses which of the following application(s) to select resources?

    A. The Control Panel

    B. The Finder

    C. The Chooser

    D. The Selector

    E. Network Neighborhood

    F. NIS+

14. A Macintosh can bind AppleTalk to which of the following interfaces? (Choose all that apply.)

    A. The modem serial port

    B. The printer serial port

    C. An Ethernet card in the workstation

    D. Macintosh systems running MacTalk

    E. All of the above

15. Which command is used on an AppleTalk network to find problems when neighbors become reachable or unreachable, and interfaces come up or down?

    A. `show apple rtmp`

    B. `debug apple traffic`

    C. `protocol apple verbose`

    D. `debug apple events`

16. Why is AppleTalk easy to administer?

    A. All frames are 53 bytes long.

    B. The administrator controls addressing.

    C. Many functions are handled automatically by the protocol.

    D. DNS is easier than NBP.

17. Which command can be used to record significant changes to interfaces?

   A. `debug apple routing`

   B. `apple event-logging`

   C. `debug apple significant event`

   D. `debug apple all`

   E. `debug apple nbp`

18. Based on the `debug apple zip` command that follows, what is the network number for the zone named Dilbert?

```
AT: Sent GetNetInfo request broadcast on Ether1
AT: Recvd ZIP cmd 6 from 10.152-6
AT: 3 query packets sent to neighbor 10.251
AT: 1 zones for 700, ZIP XReply, src 10.251
AT: net 700, zonelen 7, name Dilbert
```

   A. 10

   B. 251

   C. 700

   D. Cannot be determined from the information given

19. Which protocol is responsible for establishing unique addressing?

   A. RTMP

   B. TACACS+

   C. ZIP

   D. DDP

   E. AT EIGRP

20. To review AppleTalk access lists on the router, type which of the following commands?

   A. `show appletalk access lists`

   B. `show access-lists appletalk`

   C. `debug apple access-lists`

   D. `show appletalk access-lists`

Answers to Review Questions

1. C. AppleTalk addresses have the form *network.node* with only one decimal point in the address.

2. C. Phase one allowed for only one cable range per segment or network.

3. A. Nodes can only belong to a single zone.

4. B. Just as ARP works with IP to provide address resolution, AARP resolves the AppleTalk address to a MAC address.

5. A, B, C, D, E. Each one of the answers is part of the sequence of obtaining a node address.

6. A, B, D, E. These protocols route AppleTalk.

7. E. A zone can belong to or have many cable ranges.

8. C. RTMP deals with AppleTalk routes and route tables.

9. C. NBP is the protocol most similar to TCP/IP's DNS.

10. B. If the addressing is incompatible, routing cannot take place. Therefore anything outside of a given cable range would not be reachable.

11. B. The range for AppleTalk access lists is from 600 to 699.

12. A, B, C, D, F. RIP is not part of AppleTalk.

13. C. The Chooser is the application that provides selection of the servers and print services.

14. A, B, C. All of these connections are valid connection media for AppleTalk.

15. D. The events debug allows the administrator to view when interfaces change state.

16. C. AppleTalk was developed to not require much administrative overhead.

17. B. Logging records messages, and the correct syntax is indicated by the answer B.

18. C. The network is identified with the field AT: `net 700`.

19. D. DDP is used for establishing addressing.

20. D. The correct syntax is shown by D.

Chapter 11

Troubleshooting Switched Ethernet

TOPICS COVERED IN THIS CHAPTER INCLUDE:

✓ Learning which diagnostic tools to apply to Catalyst 5000 problems.

✓ Learning which diagnostic tools to apply to VLAN configuration problems.

✓ Learning the similarities between Cisco IOS router troubleshooting commands and Catalyst 5000 switched troubleshooting commands and how to use them both in conjunction to solve switched and VLAN problems.

✓ Performing labs that troubleshoot problems (hardware, software, or configuration bugs), then correcting these bugs to restore full network operations.

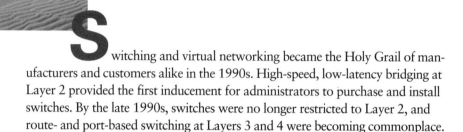

Switching and virtual networking became the Holy Grail of manufacturers and customers alike in the 1990s. High-speed, low-latency bridging at Layer 2 provided the first inducement for administrators to purchase and install switches. By the late 1990s, switches were no longer restricted to Layer 2, and route- and port-based switching at Layers 3 and 4 were becoming commonplace.

Switching provides many significant advantages, including greater aggregate bandwidth at lower cost and collision (full-duplex) control. The downside frequently includes a forklift upgrade in the wiring closet and slightly modified troubleshooting procedures. For example, it is not possible to simply plug a protocol analyzer into a port and see all traffic on the segment.

The Cisco Catalyst product line includes Ethernet, FDDI, Token Ring, and ATM switching. Although this section focuses primarily on the Catalyst 5000 product line, other Catalyst products are capable of additional functions, including voice switching and Layer 3 processing.

Switches, Bridges, and Hubs

An understanding of switches and their functions requires an understanding of the differences between broadcast and collision domains.

The *broadcast domain* defines the scope of broadcasts within the network. Usually, this is equal to the diameter of the subnet because most upper-layer protocols rely on broadcasts to function. As such, the broadcast domain is usually controlled by routers.

Collision domains are defined by the scope of impact that a collision may have. With hubs, this scope is equal to all stations connected to the shared media; as the number of nodes and traffic load increases, collisions become a more significant problem for administrators and designers. Switches reduce this scope to two: the switch port and the end node. By using full-duplex Ethernet, which is an option available on most switches and newer NICs, collisions are no longer a factor.

On an Ethernet hub, the collision domain and the broadcast domain are the same—all ports receive all frames and the receivers are required to analyze the destination address. If the frame is a broadcast or a unicast to the station (omitting multicasts), the frame will be processed further. The negative to this is unnecessary processing at all the workstations for which the frames were not intended. The collision domain on a hub is inclusive of all ports and stations on that hub. The broadcast domain on a hub is identical to the collision domain, although this assumes that a single hub represents the entire network or that a single hub is the only device connected to the router port. Technically, routers contain the broadcast domain. All other stations will hear any frame sent from a station on the hub.

The collision domain on a switch is limited to the individual port on the switch and its directly connected resource (workstation or other device). This greatly reduces workstation overhead because the frames received by the workstation should be intended for that station. In addition, the switch can provide a dedicated pipe to the workstation. Thus, a 10Mbit network interface card can provide 10Mbit, rather than sharing that bandwidth with all other stations. A small 12-port Ethernet switch provides a theoretical 120Mbit of bandwidth, compared to the 10Mbit provided by an Ethernet hub.

Table 11.1 compares the differences between switches and hubs.

TABLE 11.1   Comparison of Switches and Hubs

Type	Switch	Hub
Unicasts	Sent only to destination port.	Sent to all ports.
Broadcasts	Sent to all ports defined to the same VLAN.	Sent to all ports.
Aggregate Bandwidth	Equal to bandwidth of each port times number of ports. A 12-port Ethernet switch is capable of providing a total bandwidth of 120Mbit. (Note that backplane, processor, and other factors may change this simplification.)	Equal to speed of medium—an Ethernet hub would provide a total of 10Mbit.

TABLE 11.1 Comparison of Switches and Hubs *(continued)*

Type	Switch	Hub
Full/half duplex	Full duplex connections available.	Half duplex only.
Support for mixed media—Token Ring, Ethernet, FDDI, and so on	Depending on the switch, translations may occur between frame types or physical media.	Supports single media.

Table 11.2 contrasts the differences between switches and bridges.

TABLE 11.2 Switches and Bridges

Specification	Switches	Bridges
Support for mixed media	Usually	Depends on bridge configuration
Processing of frames	Hardware (ASIC)	Software or generic hardware
Number of ports	From 12 to over 100	Usually under 16; sometimes only two
Frame type translation	Usually	Depends on bridge configuration.

Catalyst Troubleshooting Tools

The Catalyst system provides for significant diagnostic and administrative tools. These are included in the CLI (command line interface) and CWSI (CiscoWorks for Switched Internetworks). Troubleshooting switched networks frequently includes correlating Layer 2 addressing to Layer 3, and researching Physical layer problems. Although this section focuses primarily on the tools and commands themselves, a review of standards and typical problems will be presented later in the chapter.

Catalyst Command Line Interface

Many administrators prefer the command line interface, especially if they are already experienced with the Cisco IOS. Although the GUI applications can simplify many functions, and (in some cases) address functions not available from the command line interface (CLI), they fail to provide the speed and simplicity of CLI.

The CLI provides a wealth of configuration and diagnostic tools for the administrator. Commands include the set and clear options that are used to configure the switch, and the show commands to monitor the current settings.

The show commands, displayed in enable mode with the show ? command, include the following:

```
show alias          Show aliases for commands
show arp            Show ARP table
show bridge         Show bridge information
show cam            Show CAM table
show cdp            Show Cisco Discovery Protocol
                    Information
show cgmp           Show CGMP info
show config         Show system configuration
show drip           Show DRiP Information
show fddi           Show FDDI module entries
show fddicam        Show FDDI module CAM table
show flash          Show system flash information
show help           Show this message
show interface      Show network interfaces
show ip             Show IP Information
show log            Show log information
show logging        Show system logging information
show mac            Show MAC information
show microcode      Show microcode versions
show module         Show module information
show multicast      Show multicast information
show netstat        Show network statistics
show ntp            Show ntp statistics
show port           Show port information
```

```
show rif           Show Routing Information Field
(RIF)Table
show rsmautostate  Show RSM derived interface state
                   enabled/disabled
show snmp          Show SNMP information
show span          Show switch port analyzer information
show spantree      Show spantree information
show station       Show Tokenring Station info
show summertime    Show state of summertime information
show system        Show system information
show tacacs        Show TACACS information
show test          Show results of diagnostic tests
show time          Show time of day
show timezone      Show the current timezone offset
show tokenring     Show tokenring information
show trunk         Show trunk ports
show users         Show active Admin sessions
show version       Show version information
show vlan          Show Virtual LAN information
show vmps          Show VMPS information
show vtp           Show VTP information
```

show system

The show system command provides high-level summary information regarding the switch, including the status of power supplies, uptime and administrative settings, and the percentage of traffic on the backplane.

```
Switch_A> (enable) show system
```

PS1-Status	PS2-Status	Fan-Status	Temp-Alarm	Sys-Status	Uptime d,h:m:s	Logout
ok	ok	ok	off	ok	153,19:29:57	none

PS1-Type	PS2-Type	Modem	Baud	Traffic	Peak	Peak-Time
WS-C5008B	WS-C5008B	disable	9600	0%	0%	Tue Feb 22 2000, 12:14:38

System Name	System Location	System Contact
Switch_A	Maui, Hawaii	Robert Padjen

show port

The show port commands provide specific information about ports or all ports on a module. This includes commands that are available from other show commands, including show mac, for example.

```
Switch_A> (enable) show port ?
Usage: show port
        show port <mod_num>
        show port <mod_num/port_num>
Show port commands:
show port broadcast        Show port broadcast information
show port cdp              Show port CDP information
show port channel         Show port channel information
show port counters        Show port counters
show port fddi            Show port FDDI information
show port filter          Show Token Ring port filtering
                          information
show port help            Show this message
show port mac             Show port MAC counters
show port multicast       Show port multicast information
show port security        Show port security information
show port spantree        Show port spantree information
show port status          Show port status
show port trap            Show port trap information
show port trunk           Show port trunk information
```

The show port command output appears as follows. Note that VLAN membership, port speed and configuration, and error statistics are available.

```
Switch_A> (enable) show port 3/20
Port  Name      Status     Vlan Level  Duplex Speed  Type
----- --------- ---------- ---- ------ ------ ------ -------
3/20 connected 1 normal half 10 10BaseT


Port Security Secure-Src-Addr Last-Src-Addr Shutdown Trap
---- -------- --------------- ------------- -------- --------
3/20 disabled No disabled


Port     Broadcast-Limit Broadcast-Drop
-------- --------------- --------------
3/20                   -              0


Port  Align Err  FCS-Err    Xmit-Err   Rcv-Err    UnderSize
----- ---------- ---------- ---------- ---------- ---------
 3/20          0          0          0          0          0


Port  Single-Col Multi-Coll Late-Coll  Excess-Col Carri-Sen Runts     Giants
----- ---------- ---------- ---------- ---------- --------- --------- ---------
3/20        3922        703          0          0         0         0         0
```

show log

The show log command does not report events the same way that a Cisco router does. The command reports significant events, including reboots of all modules, traps, and power supply failures. Note that the following output reports four power supply failures in the period that may be useful information for the administrator if users report intermittent connectivity problems.

```
Switch_A> (enable) show log
Network Management Processor (ACTIVE NMP) Log:
  Reset count:   4
 Re-boot History:  Sep 22 1998 23:06:05 0, Sep 17 1998
11:28:27 0
                Sep 16 1998 18:48:02 0, Sep 14 1998
12:18:05 0
  Bootrom Checksum Failures:      0
```

UART Failures:	0
Flash Checksum Failures:	0
Flash Program Failures:	0
Power Supply 1 Failures:	4
Power Supply 2 Failures:	0
Swapped to CLKA:	0
Swapped to CLKB:	0
Swapped to Processor 1:	0
Swapped to Processor 2:	0
DRAM Failures:	0

```
Exceptions:                        4
  Last Exception occurred on  ...
  Software version = 3.2(1b)
  Error Msg:
  PID = 0 Kernel
  PC: 10000D0C, Status: 2704, Vector: 007C
  sp+00: 27041000 0D0C007C 2604101F 0D3A007C
  sp+10: 00000000 101785A2 00000030 102FB11C
  sp+20: 10FFFF9C 10179C06 10357A90 102FB11C
  sp+30: 10FFFFA8 101FB86E 00000000 10FFFFE8
  sp+40: 101FC0D4 00000000 10278814 00002000
  sp+50: 00000080 0000101F B9862078 01000001
  sp+60: 1CD80000 001E0000 00010000 00000000
  sp+70: 00000000 00000000 00000007 68000000
  sp+80: 00000000 00000000 00000000 00000000
  sp+90: 00000000 103FFFEC 10000420 100009C2
  sp+A0: 10000940 10000A4E 10001030 10001030
  sp+B0: 10001030 10001030 10000BD0 10000AD0
  sp+C0: 10000B28 10001030 10001030 10001030
  sp+D0: 10001030 10001030 10001030 10001030
  sp+E0: 10001030 10001030 10001030 10001030
  sp+F0: 10001030 10001030 10001030 493798E4
  D0: 00000000, D1: 00002604, D2: 00000030, D3: 00005C05
  D4: 11000000, D5: 11000000, D6: 10FF0008, D7: 11000000
  A0: 68000000, A1: 00000000, A2: 10357A90, A3: 103C182C
```

```
        A4: 103C182C, A5: 64000000, A6: 10FFFF8C, sp: 10FFFF6C

NVRAM log:


Module 2 Log:
  Reset Count:    4
  Reset History: Tue Sep 22 1998, 23:07:05
                 Thu Sep 17 1998, 11:29:27
                 Wed Sep 16 1998, 18:49:01
                 Mon Sep 14 1998, 12:19:05


Module 3 Log:
  Reset Count:    4
  Reset History: Tue Sep 22 1998, 23:07:05
                 Thu Sep 17 1998, 11:29:27
                 Wed Sep 16 1998, 18:49:01
                 Mon Sep 14 1998, 12:19:29

 Module 4 Log:
  Reset Count:    4
  Reset History: Tue Sep 22 1998, 23:07:05
                 Thu Sep 17 1998, 11:29:27
                 Wed Sep 16 1998, 18:49:01
                 Mon Sep 14 1998, 12:19:30
```

show interface

The show interface command reports the IP configuration of the Supervisor module. Although SLIP (serial line interface protocol) connection is configured on sl0, most installations use the in-band sc0 connection. As shown, it belongs to VLAN 1, which always exists on the switch.

```
Switch_A> (enable) show interface
sl0: flags=51<UP,POINTOPOINT,RUNNING>
        slip 0.0.0.0 dest 0.0.0.0
sc0: flags=63<UP,BROADCAST,RUNNING>
        vlan 1 inet 10.11.10.1 netmask 255.255.255.0
broadcast 10.11.10.255
```

show cdp

Cisco Discovery Protocol is an incredibly powerful troubleshooting tool. Available on all Cisco routers and switches, the protocol operates between Cisco devices on media that support SNAP. The protocol has been available since IOS 10.3.

CDP packets are sent as a multicast and are not forwarded by the router or switch.

Following is a sample of the CDP report on a Catalyst 5505 switch with three neighbors:

```
Switch_A> (enable) show cdp neighbor detail
Device-ID: Router_A.domain.com
Device Addresses:
  IP Address: 10.1.1.1
Holdtime: 142 sec
Capabilities: ROUTER
Version:
  Cisco Internetwork Operating System Software
  IOS (tm) 4500 Software (C4500-J-M), Version 11.2(15a)P,
  P RELEASE SOFTWARE (fc1)
  Copyright (c) 1986-1998 by cisco Systems, Inc.
Platform: cisco 4700
Port-ID (Port on Device): FastEthernet0
Port (Our Port): 2/1
```

```
Device-ID: Router_B.domain.com
Device Addresses:
  IP Address: 10.1.2.1
Holdtime: 130 sec
Capabilities: ROUTER
Version:
  Cisco Internetwork Operating System Software
  IOS (tm) 4500 Software (C4500-J-M), Version 11.2(15a)P,
  P    RELEASE SOFTWARE (fc1)
```

```
    Copyright (c) 1986-1998 by cisco Systems, Inc.
Platform: cisco 4700
Port-ID (Port on Device): FastEthernet0
Port (Our Port): 2/2
```

```
Device-ID: Router_C.domain.com
Device Addresses:
  IP Address: 10.10.1.1
Holdtime: 177 sec
Capabilities: ROUTER SR_BRIDGE
Version:
  Cisco Internetwork Operating System Software
  IOS (tm) C2600 Software (C2600-JS-M), Version 12.0(2a),
  RELEASE SOFTWARE (fc1)
  Copyright (c) 1986-1999 by cisco Systems, Inc.
Platform: cisco 2612
Port-ID (Port on Device): Ethernet1/0
Port (Our Port): 2/17
```

A CDP datagram decodes with EtherPeek, as follows:

```
Packet 3 captured at 02/22/1999 09:08:57 AM; Packet size
is   302(0x12e)bytes
      Relative time: 000:00:01.473
      Delta time: 0.042.868
Ethernet Protocol
      Address: 00-00-0C-1B-63-97 --->01-00-0C-CC-CC-CC
      Length: 288
Logical Link Control
      SSAP Address: 0xAA, CR bit = 0 (Command)
      DSAP Address: 0xAA, IG bit = 0 (Individual address)
      Unnumbered frame: UI
SubNetwork Access Protocol
      Organization code: 0x00000c
      Type: Custom Defined
Flags:        0x80   802.3
```

```
Status:        0x00
Packet Length:339
Timestamp:     16:40:23.689000 03/16/1999
```
802.3 Header
```
Destination:   01:00:0c:cc:cc:cc
Source:        00:00:0c:17:b6:f2
LLC Length:    321
```
802.2 Logical Link Control (LLC) Header
```
Dest. SAP:     0xaa   SNAP
Source SAP:    0xaa   SNAP
Command:       0x03   Unnumbered Information
Protocol:      00-00-0c-20-00
```
Packet Data:
```
. _'....Router_A  01 b4 9e 27 00 01 00 0c 52 6f 75 74 65
72 5f 41
...6............  00 02 00 36 00 00 00 03 01 01 cc 00 04
0a 02 01
... ...._7.....  01 02 08 aa aa 03 00 00 00 81 37 00 0a
00 00 00
..... ...  ...._  0b 00 00 0c 17 b6 f2 02 08 aa aa 03 00
00 00 80
 ....o....Ethern  9b 00 03 00 02 6f 00 03 00 0d 45 74 68
65 72 6e
et1.......... C   65 74 31 00 04 00 08 00 00 00 01 00 05
00 d0 43
isco Internetwor  69 73 63 6f 20 49 6e 74 65 72 6e 65 74
77 6f 72
k Operating Syst  6b 20 4f 70 65 72 61 74 69 6e 67 20 53
79 73 74
em Software .IOS  65 6d 20 53 6f 66 74 77 61 72 65 20 0a
49 4f 53
 (tm) 4000 Softw  20 28 74 6d 29 20 34 30 30 30 20 53 6f
66 74 77
are (XX-J-M), Ve  61 72 65 20 28 58 58 2d 4a 2d 4d 29 2c
20 56 65
rsion 11.0(17),   72 73 69 6f 6e 20 31 31 2e 30 28 31 37
29 2c 20
RELEASE SOFTWARE  52 45 4c 45 41 53 45 20 53 4f 46 54 57
41 52 45
```

```
 (fc1).Copyright   20 28 66 63 31 29 0a 43 6f 70 79 72 69
67 68 74

 (c) 1986-1997 b   20 28 63 29 20 31 39 38 36 2d 31 39 39
37 20 62

y cisco Systems,   79 20 63 69 73 63 6f 20 53 79 73 74 65
6d 73 2c

 Inc..Compiled T   20 49 6e 63 2e 0a 43 6f 6d 70 69 6c 65
64 20 54

hu 04-Sep-97 14:   68 75 20 30 34 2d 53 65 70 2d 39 37 20
31 34 3a

44 by richv....c   34 34 20 62 79 20 72 69 63 68 76 00 06
00 0e 63

isco 4000          69 73 63 6f 20 34 30 30 30
Frame Check Sequence:   0x00000000
```

show config

The show config command is similar to the show running-config command on Cisco routers. The command provides all configuration settings on the switch for all modules, with a few exceptions for certain modules such as the RSM (Route Switch Module).

The output of the command appears as follows:

```
Switch_A> (enable) show config
.....
.........
.........
.........
.........
..

begin
set password $1$Oo6Z$GChAFNM/MGi
set enablepass $1$CeBqb$zRTAOr.Cukh/
set prompt Switch_A>
set length 24 default
set logout 0
set banner motd ^C
```

```
This is Switch_A. For additional information contact an
administrator.
^C
!
#system
set system baud   9600
set system modem disable
set system name   Switch_A
set system location Maui, Hawaii
set system contact  Robert Padjen
!
#snmp
set snmp community read-only       public
set snmp community read-write       private
set snmp community read-write-all all
set snmp rmon disable
set snmp trap enable  module
set snmp trap enable  chassis
set snmp trap enable  bridge
set snmp trap enable  repeater
set snmp trap enable  vtp
set snmp trap enable  auth
set snmp trap enable  ippermit
set snmp trap enable  vmps
!
#ip
set interface sc0 1 10.1.2.10 255.255.255.0 10.1.2.255
set interface sl0 0.0.0.0 0.0.0.0
set arp agingtime 1200
set ip redirect    enable
set ip unreachable    enable
set ip fragmentation enable
set ip route 0.0.0.0          10.1.2.1   0
set ip alias default          0.0.0.0
!
```

```
#Command alias
!
#vmps
set vmps server retry 3
set vmps server reconfirminterval 60
set vmps tftpserver 0.0.0.0 vmps-config-database.1
set vmps state disable

!
#dns
set ip dns disable
!
#tacacs+
set tacacs attempts 3
set tacacs directedrequest disable
set tacacs timeout 5
set authentication login tacacs disable
set authentication login local enable
set authentication enable tacacs disable
set authentication enable local enable
!
#bridge
set bridge ipx snaptoether    8023raw
set bridge ipx 8022toether    8023
set bridge ipx 8023rawtofddi snap
!
#vtp
set vtp domain Global
set vtp mode transparent
set vtp v2 disable
set vtp pruneeligible 2-1000
clear vtp pruneeligible 1001-1005
set vlan 1 name default type ethernet mtu 1500 said 100001
state active
set vlan 1002 name fddi-default type fddi mtu 1500 said
101002 state active
```

```
set vlan 1004 name fddinet-default type fddinet mtu 1500
said 101004 state active bridge 0x0 stp ieee
set vlan 1005 name trnet-default type trbrf mtu 1500 said
101005 state active bridge 0x0 stp ieee
set vlan 1003 name Token-Ring-default type trcrf mtu 1500
said 101003 state active parent 0 ring 0x0 mode srb
aremaxhop 7 stemaxhop 7
!
#spantree
#uplinkfast groups
set spantree uplinkfast disable
#vlan 1
set spantree enable      1
set spantree fwddelay 15     1
set spantree hello    2      1
set spantree maxage   20     1
set spantree priority 32768 1
#vlan 1003
set spantree enable      1003
set spantree fwddelay 4      1003
set spantree hello    2      1003
set spantree maxage   10     1003
set spantree priority 32768 1003
set spantree portstate 1003 auto 0
set spantree portcost 1003 80
set spantree portpri  1003 4
set spantree portfast 1003 disable
#vlan 1005
set spantree enable      1005
set spantree fwddelay 15     1005
set spantree hello    2      1005
set spantree maxage   20     1005
set spantree priority 32768 1005
set spantree multicast-address 1005 ieee
!
#cgmp
set cgmp disable
```

```
set cgmp leave disable
!
#syslog
set logging console enable
set logging server disable
set logging level cdp 2 default
set logging level cgmp 2 default
set logging level disl 5 default
set logging level dvlan 2 default
set logging level earl 2 default
set logging level fddi 2 default
set logging level ip 2 default
set logging level pruning 2 default
set logging level snmp 2 default
set logging level spantree 2 default
set logging level sys 5 default
set logging level tac 2 default
set logging level tcp 2 default
set logging level telnet 2 default
set logging level tftp 2 default
set logging level vtp 2 default
set logging level vmps 2 default
set logging level kernel 2 default
set logging level filesys 2 default
set logging level drip 2 default
set logging level pagp 5 default
!
#ntp
set ntp broadcastclient disable
set ntp broadcastdelay 3000
set ntp client disable
set timezone PST 0 0
set summertime disable
!
#permit list
set ip permit disable
```

```
!
#drip
set tokenring reduction enable
set tokenring distrib-crf disable
!
#module 1 : 2-port 100BaseFX MM Supervisor
set module name    1
set vlan 1    1/1-2
set port channel 1/1-2 off
set port channel 1/1-2 auto
set port enable      1/1-2
set port level       1/1-2  normal
set port duplex      1/1-2  half
set port trap        1/1-2  enable
set port name        1/1-2
set port security    1/1-2  disable
set port broadcast   1/1-2  100%
set port membership 1/1-2   static
set cdp enable       1/1-2
set cdp interval 1/1-2 60
set trunk 1/1   auto 1-1005
set trunk 1/2   auto 1-1005
set spantree portfast     1/1-2 disable
set spantree portcost     1/1-2 19
set spantree portpri      1/1-2 32
set spantree portvlanpri 1/1  0
set spantree portvlanpri 1/2  0
set spantree portvlancost 1/1  cost 18
set spantree portvlancost 1/2  cost 18
!
#module 2 : 24-port 10/100BaseTX Ethernet
set module name    2
set module enable  2
set vlan 1    2/1-24
set port enable      2/1-24
set port level       2/1-24  normal
```

```
set port speed       2/3-24  auto
set port speed       2/1-2 100
set port duplex      2/1-2  full
set port trap        2/1-24  enable
set port name        2/1-24
set port security    2/1-24  disable
set port broadcast   2/1-24  0
set port membership  2/1-24  static
set cdp enable    2/1-24
set cdp interval 2/1-24 60
set spantree portfast      2/1-24 disable
set spantree portcost      2/9  100
set spantree portcost      2/10 100
set spantree portcost      2/11 100
set spantree portcost      2/12 100
set spantree portcost      2/17 100
set spantree portcost      2/18 100
set spantree portcost      2/19 100
set spantree portcost      2/21 100
set spantree portcost      2/1-8,2/13-16,2/20,2/22-24 19
set spantree portpri       2/1-24 32
!
. . . some output omitted . . .

#switch port analyzer
set span disable
!
#cam
set cam agingtime 1,1003,1005 300
end
```

show test

The status of the switch, including interface cards, power supplies, and memory, is available by using the show test command.

Observe that the first show test output reports only the status of the supervisor module and no information specific to the other modules.

```
Switch_A> (enable) show test
Environmental Status (. = Pass, F = Fail, U = Unknown)
  PS (3.3V):   .  PS (12V): .  PS (24V):   .  PS1: .
  PS2: .
  Temperature: .  Fan:       .  Clock(A/B): A   Chassis-
  Ser-  EEPROM: .

Module 1 : 2-port 100BaseFX MM Supervisor
Network Management Processor (NMP) Status: (. = Pass, F =
Fail, U = Unknown)
  ROM:   .  Flash-EEPROM: .  Ser-EEPROM: .  NVRAM: .  MCP
  Comm: .

  EARL Status :
          NewLearnTest:         .
          IndexLearnTest:       .
          DontForwardTest:      .
          MonitorTest           .
          DontLearn:            .
          FlushPacket:          .
          ConditionalLearn:     .
          EarlLearnDiscard:     .
          EarlTrapTest:         .


LCP Diag Status for Module 1  (. = Pass, F = Fail, N = N/A)
CPU       : .  Sprom    : .  Bootcsum : .  Archsum  : N
RAM       : .  LTL : .  CBL    : .  DPRAM    : .SAMBA : .
Saints    : .  Pkt Bufs : .  Repeater : N   FLASH   :   N
```

```
              MII Status:
              Ports 1  2
              -----------
                      N  N

              SAINT/SAGE Status :
              Ports 1  2  3
              --------------
                      .  .  .

              Packet Buffer Status :
              Ports 1  2  3
              --------------
                      .  .  .

              Loopback Status [Reported by Module 1] :
              Ports  1  2  3
              --------------
                      .  .  .

              Channel Status :
              Ports  1  2
              -----------
                      .  .
```

The following output provides the test results from module three of a Catalyst 5505. The module has 48 ports providing 10Mbit Ethernet. By using the show test 3 command, the switch reports the test results of the entire card, including the SAINT and EARL ASICs. These ASICs (Application Specific Integrated Circuits) will be reviewed later in this chapter.

```
Switch_A> (enable) show test 3

Module 3 : 48-port 10BaseT Ethernet

LCP Diag Status for Module 3  (. = Pass, F = Fail, N = N/A)
CPU         : .  Sprom   : .  Bootcsum : .  Archsum  : .
```

```
RAM         : .   LTL      : .   CBL      : N   DPRAM    : N   SAMBA : .
Saints      : .   Pkt Bufs : .   Repeater : N   FLASH    : .

SAINT/SAGE Status :
Ports 1  2  3  4  5  6  7  8  9  10 11 12 13 14 15 16 17  18 19 20 21 22 23 24
-----------------------------------------------------------  ------------------
      .  .  .  .  .  .  .  .  .  .  .  .  .  .  .  .  .   .  .  .  .  .  .  .

25 26 27 28 29 30 31 32 33 34 35 36 37 38 39 40 41 42 43 44 45 46 47 48
----------------------------------------------------------------------
 .  .  .  .  .  .  .  .  .  .  .  .  .  .  .  .  .  .  .  .  .  .  .  .

Packet Buffer Status :
Ports 1  2  3  4  5  6  7  8  9  10 11 12 13 14 15 16 17   18 19 20 21 22 23 24
------------------------------------------------------------------------
 .  .  .  .  .  .  .  .  .  .  .  .  .  .  .  .  .  .   .  .  .  .  .  .  .
25 26 27 28 29 30 31 32 33 34 35 36 37 38 39 40 41 42 43 44 45 46 47 48
            ----------------------------------------------------------------
 .  .  .  .  .  .  .  .  .  .  .  .  .  .  .  .  .  .  .  .  .  .  .  .

Loopback Status [Reported by Module 1] :
Ports 1  2  3  4  5  6  7  8  9   10 11 12 13 14 15 16 17 18 19 20 21 22 23 24
------------------------------------------------------------------------------
 .  .  .  .  .  .  .  .  .   .  .  .  .  .  .  .  .  .  .  .  .  .  .  .
Ports 25 26 27 28 29 30 31 32 33 34 35 36 37 38 39 40 41 42 43 44 45 46 47 48
-----------------------------------------------------------------------
 .  .  .  .  .  .  .  .  .  .  .  .  .  .  .  .  .  .  .  .  .  .  .  .
```

show mac

The following output is provided from the show mac command. Although it is quite long, it was truncated from the original capture. For highly populated switches, this command requires a capturing program for later analysis. Note that numerous counters are maintained in normal operation, including the frame traffic per port; the total number of incoming frames, including discards; and the total number of transmits and aborts due to excessive deferral or MTU violations. Broadcast counters are also maintained in addition to discards due to EARL page full errors. (EARL is covered in greater detail later in this chapter.) In some cases, an administrator may find the show port command more helpful in troubleshooting.

The following output has been slightly modified for space considerations. RCV-M is representative of RCV-Multi. Xmit-M is used in place of Xmit-Multi, and Dcrd is used for Discard.

```
Switch_A> (enable) show mac
```

MAC	Rcv-Frms	Xmit-Frms	Rcv-M	Xmit-M	Rcv-Broad	Xmit-Broad
1/1	0	0	0	0	0	0
1/2	0	0	0	0	0	0
2/1	1840	1997	53	136	8	91
2/2	941	1026	56	133	4	95
2/3	6001	6489	0	187	26	73
2/4	776	1179	0	187	1	98
2/5	4951	6115	0	187	0	99
2/6	0	0	0	0	0	0
2/7	26	301	0	187	1	98
2/8	246	524	0	187	0	99
2/9	0	0	0	0	0	0

MAC	Dely-Exced	MTU-Exced	In-Dcrd	Lrn-Dcrd	In-Lost	OutLost
1/1	0	0	0	0	0	0
1/2	0	0	0	0	0	0
2/1	0	0	0	0	0	0
2/2	0	0	0	0	0	0
2/3	0	0	0	0	0	0
2/4	0	0	0	0	0	0
2/5	0	0	0	0	0	0
2/6	0	0	0	0	0	0
2/7	0	0	0	0	0	0
2/8	0	0	0	0	0	0
2/9	0	0	0	0	0	0

```
. . . some output omitted . . .
```

Port	Rcv-unicast	Rcv-Multicast	Rcv-Broadcast
1/1	0	0	0
1/2	0	0	0
2/1	1814	56	8

Port			
2/2	882	58	8
2/3	5996	0	26
2/4	793	0	2
2/5	5099	0	0
2/6	0	0	0
2/7	26	0	1
2/8	252	0	0
2/9	0	0	0

. . . some output omitted . . .

Port	Xmit-Unicast	Xmit-Multicast	Xmit-Broadcast
1/1	0	0	0
1/2	0	0	0
2/1	1819	141	97
2/2	798	140	101
2/3	6260	195	83
2/4	921	195	107
2/5	6104	195	109
2/6	0	0	0
2/7	16	195	108
2/8	242	195	109
2/9	0	0	0

. . . some output omitted . . .

Port	Rcv-Octet	Xmit-Octet
1/1	0	0
1/2	0	0
2/1	445231	405059
2/2	208680	300413
2/3	2935182	2876636
2/4	61427	114408
2/5	716265	601719
2/6	0	0
2/7	3125	53564
2/8	36993	96826
2/9	0	0

. . . some output omitted . . .

Last-Time-Cleared

Tue Feb 22 2000, 12:14:38

show vtp domain

The VLAN Trunk Protocol (VTP) is designed to simplify the introduction of VLANs in multi-switch networks. Within the management domain, a new VLAN is only specified once, and the configuration is propagated throughout the network. The configuration information includes the parameters needed for differing topologies within the switched network.

The show vtp domain command provides the following status information. Note that VTP updates are sent over VLAN 1 when troubleshooting VTP issues.

```
Switch_A> (enable)  show vtp domain
Domain Name                        Domain Index VTP Version
Local Mode   Password
---------------------------------- ------------ -----------
------------ --------
Global                             1            2
Transparent -

Vlan-count Max-vlan-storage Config Revision Notifications
---------- ---------------- --------------- -------------
5          1023             0               enabled

Last Updater    V2 Mode  Pruning  PruneEligible on Vlans
--------------- -------- -------- ----------------------
-
10.1.2.20       disabled disabled 2-1000
```

show cam

Switches operate at Layer 2 of the OSI model, so MAC addresses are the basis for forwarding decisions. Although VLANs are typically assigned on Layer 3 boundaries, the switch directs unicast frames in the same manner as a bridge.

The show cam command reports the MAC address associated with the ports of the switch, as follows. Note the specifications that must be included with the command in the first output, followed by the actual MAC list in the second.

```
Switch_A> (enable)  show cam
Usage: show cam [count] <dynamic|static|permanent|system>
[vlan]
       show cam <dynamic|static|permanent> <mod_num/port_
num>
       show cam <mac_addr> [vlan]
       show cam agingtime
```

```
Switch_A> (enable) show cam dynamic 1
VLAN   Dest MAC/Route Des   Destination Ports or VCs
1      00-80-2f-9f-54-5f    2/3
1      00-08-27-ca-c9-cd    3/18
1      00-08-27-ca-cd-da    3/23
1      00-08-27-ca-d1-20    3/27
1      00-08-27-29-89-80    3/44
1      00-08-27-29-88-a7    4/41
1      00-08-27-d2-ce-43    4/1
1      00-08-27-9a-0e-e9    3/13
1      00-08-27-ca-db-5e    4/38
1      00-08-27-ca-db-70    4/30
1      00-08-27-29-82-5d    2/22
1      00-08-27-8c-fd-e5    3/7
1      00-08-27-8c-fc-c0    3/32
1      00-08-27-d2-f8-10    4/43
1      00-08-27-ca-e0-47    4/29
1      00-08-27-ca-e0-6c    2/20
1      00-08-27-d2-fd-ab    3/2
1      00-08-27-d2-fe-4a    4/36
1      00-08-27-d2-fe-f5    2/24
1      00-08-27-d2-ff-c7    2/23
1      00-08-27-d2-ff-dd    4/45
1      00-08-27-d2-f1-87    2/8
Total Matching CAM Entries Displayed = 21
```

Duplicate MAC Addresses

Some network devices may be configured with the same MAC address on each interface, including certain dual-homed UNIX workstations. This is a common event that can create substantial problems in the network. The show cam command is one of the best methods for finding this issue, although prevention via communication and change control can be more beneficial. If the administration of workstations and network services is divided in an administrator's organization, it is recommended that this issue be reviewed and that duplicate MAC addresses be used only when required. Documentation of the installation should accompany such a decision.

show spantree

Although the spanning tree process is covered later in this chapter, the use of spanning trees is crucial to the successful running of switched networks where loops may occur. The show spantree command reports the status of the spanning tree process for each VLAN, when enabled as follows:

```
Switch_A> (enable) show spantree
VLAN 1
Spanning tree enabled
Spanning tree type          ieee

Designated Root             00-90-86-fc-48-00
Designated Root Priority    32768
Designated Root Cost        0
Designated Root Port        1/0
Root Max Age    20 sec    Hello Time 2  sec   Forward Delay  15 sec

Bridge ID MAC ADDR          00-90-86-fc-48-00
Bridge ID Priority          32768
Bridge Max Age 20 sec     Hello Time 2  sec   Forward Delay  15 sec

Port    Vlan  Port-State     Cost   Priority Fast-Start Group-method
------- ----  -------------  -----  -------- ---------- ---------
 1/1     1    not-connected   19      32      disabled
 1/2     1    not-connected   19      32      disabled
 2/1     1    forwarding      19      32      disabled
 2/2     1    forwarding      19      32      disabled
 2/3     1    forwarding      19      32      disabled
 2/4     1    forwarding      19      32      disabled
 2/5     1    forwarding      19      32      disabled
 2/6     1    not-connected   19      32      disabled
 2/7     1    forwarding      19      32      disabled
 2/8     1    forwarding      19      32      disabled
 2/9     1    not-connected  100      32      disabled
. . . some output omitted . . .
```

show flash

Cisco switches operate with software that is very similar to the Cisco IOS on routers. This software is stored and may be upgraded in flash stored on the Supervisor module. The show flash command reports the space required for the installed software and the version of code.

```
Switch_A> (enable) show flash
File          Version  Sector    Size Built
c5000 nmp     3.2(1b)  02-11  1571059 05/04/98 22:37:19
      epld    3.2      30       72920 05/04/98 22:37:23
      lcp atm 3.2(1)   12-15    23822 05/04/98 15:29:01
      lcp tr  3.2      12-15    29016 05/04/98 15:30:46
      lcp c5ip 3.2     12-15    23744 05/04/98 15:33:40
      lcp 64k 3.2      12-15    57046 05/04/98 15:32:12
      atm/fddi 3.2     12-15    24507 05/04/98 15:27:10
      lcp 360 3.2(1)   12-15   123108 05/04/98 15:37:04
      lcp     3.2      12-15    27561 05/04/98 15:25:48
      smcp    3.2      12-15    34155 05/04/98 15:22:38
      mcp     3.2      12-15    26378 05/04/98 15:24:20
```

show version

The show version command provides hardware and software version numbers, in addition to memory and system uptime statistics. The output of the command appears as follows:

```
Switch_A> (enable) show version
WS-C5505 Software, Version McpSW: 3.2(1) NmpSW: 3.2(1b)
Copyright (c) 1995-1998 by Cisco Systems
NMP S/W compiled on May  4 1998, 15:20:25
MCP S/W compiled on May 04 1998, 15:22:38

System Bootstrap Version: 3.1(2)

Hardware Version: 1.0  Model: WS-C5505  Serial #: 066911349

Module Ports Model     Serial #   Hw   Fw      Fw1     Sw
1      2     WS-X5506 009071826 2.3  3.1(2)  2.4(1) 3.2(1b)
2      24    WS-X5224 006711612 1.4  3.1(1)         3.2(1)
```

```
3      48     WS-X5012 010128192 2.3  2.3(2)        3.2(1)
4      48     WS-X5012 010127211 2.3  2.3(2)        3.2(1)


       DRAM                    FLASH              NVRAM
Module Total  Used  Free   Total Used  Free   Total Used  Free
1      16384K 7846K 8538K  8192K 3840K 4352K  256K  107K  149K


Uptime is 171 days, 8 hours, 23 minutes
```

CiscoWorks for Switched Internetworks

CiscoWorks for Switched Internetworks (CWSI) can augment HP OpenView, SunNet Manager, or NetView/AIX, in addition to running as a stand-alone application on NT or UNIX—including Solaris, HP-UNIX, and AIX. The application includes a number of tools for installation, monitoring, and troubleshooting. Table 11.3 documents some of the more relevant functions within CWSI.

TABLE 11.3 CWSI Applications Matrix

Application	Function
CiscoView	A graphical application that provides virtual chassis viewing, configuration tools, performance monitoring, and minor troubleshooting functions.
VlanDirector	Switching is most useful when combined with virtual LANs. The VlanDirector application provides a graphical administration tool for adding users, assigning ports, and changing associations.
TrafficDirector	RMON, or remote monitoring, is one of the best baselining and troubleshooting tools in switched environments. TrafficDirector provides a united view of the switched network, including trunk links and switch ports.
AtmDirector	In Asynchronous Transfer Mode networks, this tool eases installation and administration.
User Tracking	Cisco switches permit VLAN assignments based on dynamic parameters, including the MAC layer address. User Tracking defines these dynamic VLANs and tracks stations within the network.

RMON

Modern network devices provide greater visibility into the functioning of the network. Simple Network Management Protocol (SNMP) and *Remote Monitoring (RMON)* provide much of this visibility. RMON is another method for obtaining environmental and statistical information from devices. Much of the RMON technology implementation is based on the deployment of RMON probes that gather the information from the circuit (physical media) because the router or switch may not support all levels of RMON information.

Catalyst 5000 series switches provide internal support for four of the nine RMON groups defined in RFC 1757. These groups include port utilization and error statistics, historical statistics, alarm notification, and event logging. Additional monitoring may use the Switched Port Analyzer (SPAN) function, which is also referred to as *port mirroring*. Cisco's SwitchProbe product line can provide access to the other five layers of RMON in addition to the RMON2 groups. Examples of the commands used to configure a SPAN port appear later in this chapter.

Indicator Lights

In addition to the command line interface and the functions of CWSI, the Catalyst provides diagnostic information via LEDs on the line modules and the Supervisor engine.

The Supervisor engine includes load LEDs that indicate the current utilization of the switch. A high load (over 80 percent) may indicate a network problem, including a broadcast storm or the need for review of the network design. This set of lights is useful when troubleshooting in the main equipment room or wiring closet.

Following start-up, during which the LEDs will flash, the LEDs should appear steady green. An orange LED may indicate a problem; a red LED may indicate a failure.

Controlling Recurring Paths with Spanning Tree

Although there are differences, switches share many common positives and negatives with bridges. For example, bridges frequently hide larger network problems and are invisible to the administrator. This differs significantly from routers, which are visible through increments in hop counters and MAC address changes in each frame. Bridges do not modify the frame in any way, so a frame may traverse multiple bridges with no changes to the frame. A changing frame provides indications that facilitate troubleshooting.

One of the more common problems in bridged networks involves loops, or a situation in which a single frame can continuously traverse the network. Note again that a bridge does not increment a counter—specifically, a time-to-live (TTL) value—in the packet to differentiate frame A from frame A the seventh time crossing the bridge. Such recurring paths can and should be controlled. The most common method of control is referred to as *spanning tree*. The spanning tree algorithm is defined in 802.1d and is used to control recurring paths among multiple switches, thus avoiding loops in the network.

If switches failed to prevent multiple forwardings of the same packet, and an administrator interconnects multiple switches (or bridges) between two segments, a loop can occur. This loop could theoretically take a single broadcast packet, which a bridge would automatically forward, and then resend it hundreds of times. Referring to Figure 11.1, Station A sends a broadcast. Switch One forwards the packet to the yellow cable, and Switch Two sends the broadcast back to the blue cable. Switch One then receives a forwarded broadcast packet that is in turn forwarded to the yellow cable. This continues infinitely without some type of intervention or control built into the software on the switch.

FIGURE 11.1 A simple bridge/switch loop configuration

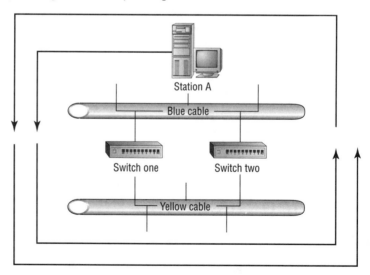

Note that although Figure 11.1 denotes a single flow of packets that move counterclockwise, in a real loop, the initial broadcast is also forwarded clockwise. Although different cable colors have been used in this example, both cables are within the same VLAN.

Although Figure 11.1 reflects shared media connected to switches, a switch/bridge loop can occur in an all-switched network. This diagram simplifies the physical connections involved by moving them "outside the box."

Logically, an administrator could avoid the entire loop issue by removing one of the two bridges/switches. Because only one path would exist, no loop is created. However, there are advantages to installing multiple switches or bridges. By installing multiple switches/bridges, the network can incorporate some degree of fault tolerance.

Troubleshooting Spanning Tree Problems

There are several troubleshooting targets for isolating and resolving spanning tree protocol problems in a switched network. The most essential aspect of troubleshooting spanning tree problems is to understand the spanning tree protocol. It is also important to pay attention to indicators that there may be loops in the network. A simple indicator is the LED on the Supervisor engine: If the LED shows around 80% load, this may be a signal that loops are occurring.

Proper spanning tree functionality requires that there is only one unique bridge ID for each VLAN. You must also be aware that trunk ports on the Catalyst 5000 may belong to multiple spanning trees. This can cause the problem that if loops occur on one, the other spanning trees may be adversely affected. The show spantree command will display this information.

When the Cisco port-fast and uplink-fast modes are enabled on ports, some of the transitions of the spanning tree protocol are skipped. This could add to the potential of loops in the network. The show spantree command also shows whether the fast-start option has been enabled on a port-by-port basis.

The Catalyst 5000 Internal Structure

There are four significant components of the Catalyst 5000 system that manage the switching functions: *SAMBA*, *SAINT*, *SAGE*, and *EARL*. Each of these components is described in detail below. A clear understanding of these components is useful for overall troubleshooting of the Catalyst system in switched networks. This is especially true when evaluating different switches and options, such as the different Supervisor engines, and the RSM and NetFlow features. This is also beneficial when isolating hardware-caused problems.

The Catalyst system uses a management bus to direct the switching process, whereas the actual data packets use a separate 1.2Gb backplane. The management bus operates at 761Kbps. These buses interconnect various cards within the chassis for Ethernet, Token Ring, FDDI, and, in some cases, ATM.

SAMBA

The *SAMBA ASIC* is located on line modules and on the Supervisor modules. On the line cards, this chip is responsible for broadcast suppression, based on thresholds established by the administrator. This ASIC also maintains statistics on packets.

From a troubleshooting perspective, the SAMBA ASIC proves to be most useful for obtaining various metrics to evaluate packet flow through the switch. In addition, there may be instances when administrators wish to suppress broadcast traffic on a threshold basis. Note that filtering broadcasts on a port basis may cause problems for upper-layer protocols.

Cisco's SAMBA should not be confused with the SAMBA utility for providing SMB (Windows NT) services on UNIX platforms.

SAINT

The *SAINT (Synergy Advanced Interface and Network Termination)* handles Ethernet switching on the Catalyst 5000 platform, and it also handles ISL encapsulation. Each Ethernet port has an independent 192KB buffer for inbound and outbound packets, which is divided to provide 168KB to outbound traffic and 24KB for inbound frames.

The ISL functionality is covered in another section of this chapter. Although the buffer arrangement controlled by the SAINT has proven itself in hundreds of networks and rarely presents a troubleshooting issue, administrators must always consider buffer overflows and underruns as a factor. Again, capturing the appropriate counters with the show commands provides the administrator with troubleshooting tools.

SAGE

Although the *SAGE (Synergy Advanced Gate-Array Engine)* is similar to the SAINT, it is used for non-Ethernet applications—including FDDI, ATM LANE, Token Ring, and the Network Management Processor on the Supervisor engine.

From a troubleshooting perspective, there is little direct control that an administrator has over this ASIC. The `show test` command can verify problems indicated by various symptoms, including errors in Token Ring switching.

EARL

No kingdom is complete without an EARL, and, building on Cisco's apparent pun, the Catalyst 5000 is no different. In switching, however, *EARL* refers to the *Encoded Address Recognition Logic ASIC*. This chip works with the bus arbitration system to control access to the data-switching bus. EARL also controls the destination ports of packet transfers.

More specifically, the EARL monitors frame flow and compiles the list of MAC addresses, as related to port numbers and VLAN ID. In addition, the ASIC determines the destination port of frames and maintains the timer for aging entries out of the forwarding table. By default, entries are discarded after 300 seconds, although the administrator can change this value. Valid parameters are limited between 1 and 20 minutes. The EARL can maintain a table of up to 128,000 addresses. As such, the EARL handles forwarding and filtering decisions within the switch.

Administrators do not troubleshoot the EARL, per se. Rather, issues with MAC address and port mappings controlled by EARL are more a part of the diagnostic process. Understanding the significant function of the EARL in the Catalyst line and its role in all switching can assist in hardware-related debugging.

Virtual LANs

In their simplest forms, *virtual LANs* (or *VLANs*) are no different from traditional LANs. The virtual component comes from the capability to define memberships based on individual ports, as administered by either a physical port or a dynamic relationship to the MAC address.

VLANs can potentially reduce the costs associated with moves, adds, and changes, in addition to reducing the costs for unused ports on non-VLAN hubs and switches. However, VLAN technology adds to the initial costs and may require additional training.

It is not uncommon to find a single switch serving more than one subnetwork. This logical segmentation of ports can create its own set of troubleshooting issues.

However, the increased port utilization and other cost savings will more than offset these issues.

Administrators unaccustomed to segmented switches may find VLANs confusing. With hubs, all ports are part of the same network, and most networks are configured with a separate hub for each subnet—even if that subnet contains as few as two devices. Switches with VLAN capabilities, with their higher port cost and management systems, may have three or four subnets connected into the same chassis. In troubleshooting, it is important to have an accurate understanding of the current switch configuration and VLAN definitions, and—more importantly—verification that the end nodes match those definitions. It is not uncommon for a port to be defined to VLAN 1, where the workstation is configured with an IP address and default gateway matching VLAN 5. Under such circumstances, the workstation support staff will believe that the configuration is correct, and the network administrator will document that the port is correct. In addition to the show port command, it is important to have valid documentation of all VLANs and the associated network configurations for each VLAN.

Inter-Switch Link (ISL)

It is not possible for a switch to forward datagrams from one VLAN to another without a router or routing function. Recall that switches operate at Layer 2 of the OSI model, and although switches are available with routing engines and even Layer 4 processors, this section will retain a definition limited to Layer 2.

Inter-switch Link (ISL) is a Cisco proprietary method of interconnecting two devices that support VLANs. These connections provide the administrator with a cost-effective option in deploying switches and VLANs in the network. For example, a normal switch installation requires a single port in each VLAN to be connected to the corresponding router interface, assuming a typical installation in which each VLAN is a logical extension of a subnet. This requires N ports on the router, in addition to the same number of ports on the switch.

Although this solution is easy to install and provides each VLAN with a dedicated 10- or 100Mbit port on the router, it also greatly increases the costs and fails to account for differences in local and remote traffic. Recall that networks were historically designed with 80 percent of the traffic remaining on the local subnet. Although the percentage of local traffic is significantly lower today, you would still be unlikely to find all traffic leaving the subnet.

What would happen if N VLANs on the switch could share a single 100Mbit connection to the router? The number of ports used for connectivity would equal two, as opposed to (N*2), and the available number of ports for servers and workstations would increase substantially.

> In this section, the use of ISL was defined with a switch to router connection. ISL should also be considered when the administrator wishes to connect multiple switches that are members of the same VLAN.

Administrators must keep the following issues in mind when considering ISL:

- ISL is available only on products that support ISL. Although a number of other vendors have licensed ISL technology (including Intel), the standard is proprietary to Cisco, and fewer vendors support the ISL standard compared to 802.1q. In addition, with the release of 802.1q and gigabit interfaces, Cisco has altered the default trunk encapsulation in favor of 802.1q. Gigabit EtherChannel trunk links default to 802.1q, whereas non-EtherChannel gigabit ports negotiate ISL or 802.1q. FastEthernet ports, as of this writing, continue to default to ISL.

- ISL links must be point-to-point.

- ISL should only be used on 100Mbit full-duplex or greater connections. Although it is possible to use ISL on 10Mbit links, the limited bandwidth and other considerations make such a plan impractical.

- ISL may require an upgrade of the IOS or memory on the router.

- ISL can encapsulate Token Ring. This is referred to as ISL+.

- ISL adds 30 octets to the original frame, which is encapsulated without modification.

- ISL includes a CRC value at the end of the frame.

Because ISL is an encapsulation of the original frame, an administrator must consider the overhead generated to support the encapsulation. Frequently, the available bandwidth is more than sufficient to cover this additional load. ISL adds 30 octets to the length of the original frame. In the case of Ethernet, this results in a frame 1,548 octets long.

The ISL frame is shown in Figure 11.2.

FIGURE 11.2 The ISL encapsulation

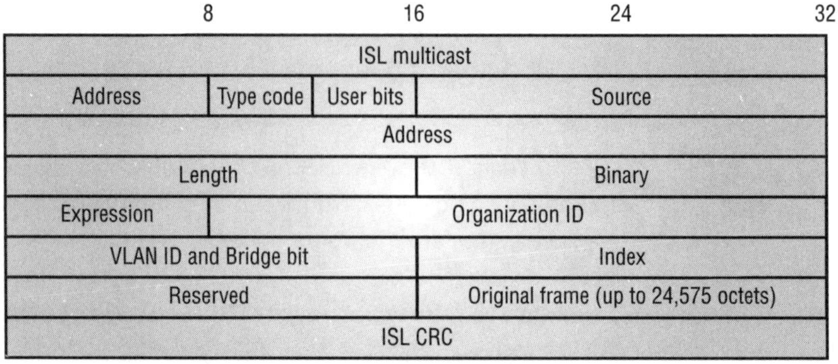

Figure 11.2 is indexed in Table 11.4.

TABLE 11.4 Key for Figure 11.2

Figure Symbol	Definition
ISL multicast address	The ISL multicast address of 01:00:0C:00:00. **Note that this is a 40-bit value.**
Type code	The encapsulated frame's type code. For Ethernet, this is 0000. Token Ring frames are defined with 0001 and FDDI is marked with 0010. ATM has been reserved for 0011 as a type code.
User bits	The user-defined bits are used to mark the encapsulated frame's priority. Frames marked 0000 are processed as normal priority, whereas 0011 marks the frame as high priority.
Source address	This is the 48-bit MAC address of the source port.

TABLE 11.4   Key for Figure 11.2 *(continued)*

Figure Symbol	Definition
Length	The length field defines the length of the ISL frame minus the multicast address, the type and user-defined bits, and the source address of the ISL packet. The length field also omits its own length and the CRC from the 16-bit value. Thus, the length is always equal to the length of the ISL frame minus 18 octets.
Binary expression	ISL frames use SNAP LLC, and the binary expression noted in the table above decodes to AA:AA:03, which is the same as the SNAP header.
Organization ID	The Organization ID bits provide the unique organization identifier of the source address. This is equal to the first three octets of the MAC address.
VLAN ID, Bridge bit	The VLAN identifier is a 15-bit value that identifies the VLAN membership of the frame. Cisco uses only 10 bits in this header to support up to 1,024 virtual LANs. The bridge bit is set for all encapsulated bridge protocol frames, including spanning tree updates, in addition to Cisco's CDP and VTP (VLAN Trunking Protocol) packets.
Index	The index field may be useful for troubleshooting and contains the source port value of the frame.

TABLE 11.4   Key for Figure 11.2 *(continued)*

Figure Symbol	Definition
Reserved	The reserved bits are set to zero for Ethernet frames. However, when ISL encapsulates Token Ring, the access control (AC) and frame information (FC) octets are duplicated here. When encapsulating FDDI, the frame control octet is prefixed with 0x00 and copied in this field.
Original frame	The original frame field may be 24,575 octets long and includes Ethernet, Token Ring, or FDDI frames—along with the original CRC value for the encapsulated frame.
ISL CRC	The ISL CRC field is a new 32-bit CRC that is calculated for the entire ISL frame. It is calculated from the entire ISL frame, including the original frame.

802.1q Trunking

Although the *IEEE 802.1q* standard is similar to the Cisco proprietary ISL protocol in terms of function, as a standard it may be used to connect non-Cisco trunks to Cisco equipment. Note that the 802.1q encapsulation is accessed with the command encapsulation dot1Q, which is available in IOS versions 12.0.1(t) and higher on routers and IOS 4.1 on the Catalyst 5000 switches.

ISL provides additional functions, when compared with 802.1q. For example, spanning trees are handled somewhat better in ISL. However, 802.1q should be recommended in any network that does not adhere to a strict Cisco-only policy, given the proprietary concerns.

From a troubleshooting perspective, 802.1q requires the same understanding of the VLAN's relationships to the subnets that are beneficial in all switching diagnostics. The 802.1q header differs from the ISL header, in that only 4 octets are added to the frame, as compared to the 30 added in ISL. Also, the 802.1q information is not wrapped around the original packet—the VLAN information is inserted into the frame, following the destination and source addresses in the original packet. This lack of overhead is another benefit of 802.1q.

Although most protocol analyzers provide decode filters for 802.1q in their current releases, administrators should check with their vendor. It is rare that the problem is directly related to the tag information itself, although administrators should consider this in researching trunk problems. Rather, most trunking problems, along with 802.1q, result from misconfiguration of the VLANs or mismatches between two sides of the trunk. Although they serve similar functions, ISL cannot connect to 802.1q on the same link.

VLAN Trunking Protocol (VTP)

VLAN Trunking Protocol (VTP) is a protocol that uses multicast messages to inform all other switches in the VTP domain about the VLANs within the domain. This domain is a management domain that allows control of the VTP multicast updates. A switch may be configured with three different VTP settings.

VTP Server   The server maintains the VLAN information for the VTP domain. When a change is detected, it is propagated throughout the domain. Manual manipulation of the VLAN table may be performed on a VTP Server. Trunk ports are then reconfigured to allow traffic from the new VLAN.

VTP Client   The client also maintains a copy of the VLAN information for the domain. It will transmit any changes to its known VLANs. When a change is detected, the trunk ports are then reconfigured to allow traffic from the new VLAN.

VTP Transparent   When a switch is in transparent mode, it chooses not to allow the reconfiguration of the new VLAN. It does, however, continue to forward VTP advertisements.

Cabling Issues

Today's networks operate at higher speeds than ever before. Bandwidth is measured in gigabits, with individual workstations accessing 100Mb connections or faster. Only recently it was still common to find a hundred stations sharing a 10Mbit segment.

Higher speeds bring added complexity at the Physical layer of the network. Installations must adhere to strict tolerances regarding distance, cable type, and installation to permit proper operation. This creates new troubleshooting issues for the administrator.

Frequently, an administrator will convert a workstation to 100Mbit (Fast) Ethernet, and will find an excessive number of errors that degrade performance so much that the link becomes unusable. The type of cable or the distance between the switch and workstation may cause this. For example, perhaps the original installation used Category 3 cable. Although satisfactory for 10Mbit Ethernet, 100Mbit Ethernet requires the higher-capacity Category 5. Also, although the distance for both 10- and 100Mbit Ethernet on copper media is 100 meters, it is possible to use longer lengths for 10Mbit without degradation. When converting to 100Mbit, problems may become evident. Consideration of the Physical layer is imperative when troubleshooting switched networks. Table 11.5 presents the Physical layer limitations.

TABLE 11.5 Physical Layer Standards

Cable	10Mbit	100Mbit
Distance with Category 3 copper	100 meters	Not available per 100BaseTX standard
Distance with Category 5 copper	100 meters	100 meters
Distance with Multi Mode fiber	2,000 meters	2,000 meters
Distance with Single Mode fiber	10,000 meters	10,000 meters

Half-duplex Fast Ethernet implementations limit the Multi Mode fiber distance to 400 meters to allow for the round-trip time of the packet transmission.

Cable Problems

Cable problems may appear as intermittent issues or as a single failure. Clearly, the intermittent issues provide greater challenges, especially if the duration of the problem is very short. An intermittent cable problem may appear as slow performance or failure of the workstation, which requires a reboot.

An analyzer may be the best method for finding cable problems, and administrators should be familiar with the operation of an available cable tester, time domain reflectometer (TDR), or handheld analyzer. Even when certified by the cable installer, cables may break or develop problems during subsequent activity in the conduit or at the jack.

In addition to a tester, it is a good idea to have spare cables and a crimp set to quickly re-terminate circuits when troubleshooting.

Cross-Over Cables

A surprising number of network administrators have not used cross-over cables, particularly when their previous experience is from the workstation installation and configuration segments of Information Services or other Information Technology departments. In other companies, such cables are used only when absolutely necessary and with a great deal of documentation, including highly recommended color-coding.

Normally, a workstation is connected to a hub that does not require the cross-over of the transmit and receive pairs in the wire. However, there are times when a connection is needed and the pairs must be crossed. This occurs when connecting two 10BaseT workstations together without a hub or when connecting two network devices. Note that some devices provide a button or other administrator-selectable setting to enable or disable the function. Small hubs frequently provide this with an "uplink" port.

Connectivity problems may result when the wrong type of cable is installed or when a selectable port is set incorrectly. This may be masked by link lights and other indications that the connection is correct. The only way to isolate this problem is to look at the colors in the cube (the RJ-45 connector) and verify that they are correct. It may be appropriate when troubleshooting to swap the original cable for another of the opposite type. This provides a quick check of the cable, and substituting a straight-through cable for a cross-over cable may lead to evidence of equipment that is mislabeled or misconfigured. Note that Ethernet uses wires 1, 2, 3, and 6. While T1 circuits on RJ-45 use wires 1, 2, 4, and 5. Swapping different cross-over cables will also lead to problems—for example, if a T1 cross-over is used for an Ethernet connection.

Troubleshooting Switched Connections

Switched networks incorporate a number of unique problems for administrators, including the use of port mirroring for protocol analysis, and routing and trunking. Routing and trunking within the Catalyst system may include an RSM, or route switch module, which is a 400Mbit 7500 series router on a card that operates within the Catalyst chassis. Trunking may incorporate one of many protocols, including ISL, 802.10, 802.1q, and ATM LANE. The effect of trunking is the same, however. A single physical medium may be used to connect multiple VLANs (or ELANs) between switches and routers.

The Switched Port Analyzer

This chapter previously noted that one of the difficulties in troubleshooting switched networks is the port isolation inherent in switches. Such isolation prevents the use of a protocol analyzer in a switched environment, without connecting directly to the wire between the switch and workstation, and such a connection cannot be full-duplex, as a general rule.

Cisco addresses this problem with SPAN, or the Switched Port Analyzer. Other vendors may refer to this function as *port mirroring*. Effectively, the switch is commanded to copy all packets that would be sent to the workstation interface to another port as well. This port is not assigned a VLAN—it takes on the identity of the original port.

To configure the switch for SPAN, use the following commands:

```
set span enable|disable
set span <src_module/src_port> <dest_module/dest_port>
[rx|tx|both]
set span <src_VLAN> <dest_module/dest_port> [rx|tx|both]
```

Note that traffic may be monitored on the receive or transmit channels, or both. The administrator may select to mirror a single port within the VLAN or have all traffic within the VLAN copied onto the mirroring port. It is important for the administrator to understand the problem's scope and the network topology before attempting to troubleshoot problems with the SPAN function.

The Route Switch Module and Catalyst Routing

The route switch module, or RSM, is a Cisco router on a card within the Catalyst chassis. This card may be configured to provide routing between VLANs. With an external router, companies often incur additional expense and complexity—the RSM virtually attaches to VLANs, and as such does not occupy a port as an ISL or 802.1q-linked external router would. Of course, there are times when an external router is required. The performance of the 7513 is faster and a greater number of interface types are supported. However, when combined with the NetFlow Feature Card (NFFC or NFFC II), the RSM and Catalyst can provide powerful Layer 2 and 3 switching.

The configuration of the RSM is very similar to the Cisco router platform. As shown in the following output, the router module supports IOS features, including password encryption and HSRP. Note that the interfaces are defined as VLAN1 and VLAN2. Unlike the router, the RSM is virtually connected to the VLANs via the backplane. This connection is 400Mbit half-duplex.

To connect to the RSM, administrators typically connect to the Supervisor engine CLI and use the `session` command to attach to the RSM. For example, if the RSM card were in slot 4, the command would read `session 4`.

```
Building configuration...



Current configuration:

!

version 11.3
service timestamps debug uptime
service timestamps log uptime
no service password-encryption
```

```
!

hostname RSM_A
!
interface Vlan1
 description Admin VLAN
 ip address 10.1.1.3 255.255.255.0
 no ip redirects
 standby 1 timers 5 15
 standby 1 priority 10
 standby 1 preempt
 standby 1 ip 10.1.1.1
!
interface Vlan2
 description User VLAN
 ip address 10.1.2.1 255.255.255.0
!
```

The show port command provides the following information regarding the RSM:

```
4/1  RSM_A       connected  trunk      normal  half   400
Route Switch
```

As noted previously, an external router may be used to connect VLANs on the Catalyst switch. This usually occurs through a single connection configured for ISL or another trunking protocol. Fast Ethernet and Gigabit Ethernet connections are common for this configuration.

When configuring the router for this type of connection, each VLAN must be defined to a subinterface, and the main interface must be configured without a configuration. This usually appears as follows:

```
interface fastethernet 0/0
no ip address
no shutdown
full-duplex
interface fastethernet 0/0.1
description vlan1
ip address 10.1.1.1 255.255.255.0
encapsulation isl 1
```

The `encapsulation isl 1` command defines that VLAN1 is using this physical interface and is trunked via ISL. This command is placed on each subinterface. Use the `set trunk` and `clear trunk` commands on the switch to configure the switch side of the connection.

VLANs across Routers and Switches

VLAN implementation has been described on Catalyst switches and Catalyst switches with Route Switch Modules. One VLAN implementation is left, using a router and a switch.

The router plays many important roles in the implementation of VLANs throughout a network. The overall role of a router is to provide communication among VLANs. Also, routers are able to perform many functions that add to the flexibility and scalability of VLAN deployment. Some of these major functions are broadcast management, routing, policy control, VLAN switching, and VLAN translation. Others include QoS management, redundancy, hierarchical design, and traffic shaping and management.

Broadcast Management

Simply put, routers will not forward broadcasts. Switches also control broadcasts by forwarding only to ports that are members of the source VLAN. This property allows routers to lower broadcast traffic on the network backbone.

Policy Control

Switches do not have the capability to apply policy control to individual ports or VLANs on the switch. Use of a router provides the means to implement security and policy control to and from connected VLANs. Access lists may be written and applied to the VLAN subinterface on the router to provide this capability.

VLAN Switching

VLAN switching occurs when a packet destined for the same VLAN on a different interface crosses the router. The header remains intact and the frame is switched at Layer 2 to the destination interface where the VLAN resides.

VLAN Translation

Translation must occur in two scenarios. The first scenario occurs when VLAN A uses a different VLAN protocol than VLAN B. For example, VLAN A uses ISL for its VLAN protocol, whereas VLAN B uses 802.1q. In order for these two VLANs to communicate, the router must perform protocol translation. This occurs at Layer 2 and the frame headers are changed to accommodate the change in protocol.

The second scenario is when a VLAN protocol must be translated into a non-VLAN Layer 2 protocol. An example of this is when VLAN A (using ISL or 802.1q) needs to communicate with a Layer 2 destination that does not use any VLAN protocol. The router then translates the VLAN header into a header such as 802.10 so the two can communicate.

Routing

To enable communication between different VLANs or non-VLAN networks (Layer 3), routing must occur. The router maintains routes for the subnets/networks that belong to each VLAN. When VLAN A needs to reach VLAN B, a route lookup is performed and the packets are routed on Layer 3.

When a machine on a VLAN wants to communicate to a host on any other destination not on a local VLAN, routing is performed as well. It is important to realize that translation is not occurring because routing is a Layer 3 function, whereas translation occurs at Layer 2.

Troubleshooting VLANs on Routers

Some commands are similar across the IOS for the routers and the software running on the switches. It is important, however, to know which commands provide unique output and should be executed on a router rather than on a switch.

The following commands provide additional information regarding the VLANs from the router:

- `show vlans`
- `show spanning-tree`
- `show arp`
- `show interface`
- `show cdp neighbor`
- `debug vlan packet`
- `debug spantree`

Some of these commands have been covered in previous chapters and will not be repeated here. The commands that have not been discussed are covered below. The debug commands provide debug information with respect to VLAN packets and the spanning tree protocol.

show vlans

This command is executed from the router and it displays the details about the VLANs configured on the router. The detail includes the VLAN name, the interface, and the IP address used. It also includes the VLAN protocol (encapsulation) and interface protocol such as IP or IPX. Here is a sample:

```
Router_A#show vlans

Virtual LAN ID:  1 (Inter Switch Link Encapsulation)

   vLAN Trunk Interface:    FastEthernet1/0.1

   Protocols Configured:   Address:          Received:
Transmitted:
         IP              172.16.1.1        4236441842
854332923

Virtual LAN ID:  2 (Inter Switch Link Encapsulation)

   vLAN Trunk Interface:    FastEthernet1/0.2

   Protocols Configured:   Address:          Received:
Transmitted:
         IP              172.16.2.1        3002644583
2325942305

Router_A#
```

show spanning-tree

For IOS revisions prior to 12.0T, this command was known as show span (not to be confused with the similar command for switches). In the 12.0T IOS release the command was changed to show spanning-tree. This command displays spanning tree information for the router.

VLAN Design Issues and Troubleshooting

Although VLANs must adhere to most of the basic network design rules, there are a number of new issues for administrators to consider with Catalyst switches.

First, the network diameter should be less than eight switches. This limitation is mostly related to spanning tree concerns; however, it is also a good rule of thumb for manageability.

Second, VLANs must be numbered within certain limitations, and each VLAN needs to adhere to MTU considerations. Although a large MTU is desirable for FDDI and Token Ring, the Ethernet MTU limitation of 1500 is recommended for all interfaces. This is partly due to the Catalyst backplane and the conversions that are needed between different Physical layers.

The default configuration of the switch includes the following VLANs, as shown in Table 11.6.

TABLE 11.6 The Default Switch VLAN Configuration

VLAN Name	Type of VLAN	MTU	ISL VLAN ID	802.10 VLAN ID (SAID)
Default	ethernet	1500	0001	100001
Fddi-default	fddi	1500	1002	101002
Token Ring default	token-ring	4472	1003	101003
Fddinet-de-fault	fddi-net	1500	1004	101004
Trnet-default	tr-net	4472	1005	101005

When troubleshooting switches and routers, administrators should consider each element in the network by using a layered approach. For example, configuring a bridge to link two ISL trunks could cause spanning-tree problems. In addition, there are two spanning-tree protocols available on the switch: IEEE and DEC. Failure to use the same protocol will again cause spanning-tree issues.

In addition, general routing rules apply to VLANs and the RSM module. For example, a default router is still required on all devices, and all VLANs must have a router to go from one VLAN to another.

For example, to display the physical interfaces, the administrator would use show port on the switch, as opposed to show interface, which is used on the router. The show interface command on the switch is used to check the SL0 and SC0 interfaces.

Remember that most troubleshooting is actually isolation. View the network from each layer and work through the system. For example, is there a link light denoting Layer 1 connectivity? Is the port configured for the same speed and duplex on each end? These basic questions, along with the Cisco debug and show commands, frequently provide the proper clues to isolate problems.

Although available, the use of automatic speed and duplex configuration settings is not recommended. Most administrators prefer the control and manageability that is available from manually configuring these settings. Administrators should familiarize themselves with the proper commands on various platforms. For example, NT usually permits the modification of this setting from the network control panel, but some installations may require registry modification. On Solaris, the /kernel/drv/hme.conf file is modified when using that type of NIC.

Summary

This chapter addressed the generic aspects of switching, and the specific functions and commands available on the Cisco Catalyst switches. Common problems in switched networks were also addressed, including duplicate MAC addresses and cabling requirements that frequently accompany the higher bandwidth configurations available with switches. An overview of the difficulties facing administrators in switched networks was also presented.

This chapter also covered the Command Line Interface for Catalyst 5000s, CiscoWorks for Switched Internetworks, and RMON, in addition to the RSM module and the use of Cisco routers with the Catalyst platform.

Commands Used in This Chapter

The following list contains a summary of all the commands used in this chapter.

Command	Description
show system	Provides high-level summary information regarding the switch, including the status of power supplies, uptime and administrative settings, as well as the percentage of traffic on the backplane.
show port	Provides information about specific ports or all ports on a module. VLAN membership, port speed and configuration, and error statistics are available.
show log	Reports significant events, including reboots of all modules, traps, and power supply failures.
show interface	Reports the IP configuration of the supervisor module.
show cdp	Displays the Cisco neighbors.
show config	Similar to the show running-config command on Cisco routers. Provides all configuration settings on the switch for all modules, with a few exceptions for certain modules such as the RSM (Route Switch Module).
show test	The status of the switch, including interface cards, power supplies, and available memory.

Command	Description
`show mac`	Maintains numerous counters in normal operation, including the frame traffic per port; the total number of incoming frames, including discards; and the total number of transmits and aborts due to excessive deferral or MTU violations. Broadcast counters are also maintained in addition to discards due to EARL page full errors.
`show vtp domain`	Provides status information for the VTP domain configured on the switch. Note that VTP updates are sent over VLAN 1 when troubleshooting.
`show cam`	Reports the MAC address associated with the ports of the switch. These addresses are stored in the CAM table; this command accesses that table.
`show spantree`	Reports the status of the spanning tree process for each VLAN, when spanning-tree has been enabled on the switch.
`show flash`	Reports the space required for the installed software and the version of code.
`show version`	Provides hardware and software version numbers, in addition to memory and system uptime statistics.
`show vlans`	Provides VLAN information and status from the router.

Command	Description
`show span`	Shows spanning tree information from the router. Very different from a show span on a switch.
`show bridge {vlan number}`	Shows which bridging encapsulations are enabled.
`show arp`	Displays the ARP information for the router.
`debug vlan packet`	Debugs VLAN packets.
`debug span`	Debugs spanning tree.

Key Terms

Before you take the exam, be certain you are familiar with the following terms:

802.1q

broadcast domain

Cisco Discovery Protocol

collision domain

EARL (Encoded Address Recognition Logic ASIC)

Inter-switch Link (ISL)

Remote Monitoring (RMON)

SAGE (Synergy Advanced Gate-Array Engine)

SAINT (Synergy Advanced Interface and Network Termination)

SAMBA ASIC

spanning tree

Virtual LANs (VLANs)

VLAN Trunking Protocol (VTP)

Laboratory Exercise

This lab exercise does not necessarily require access to a Catalyst switch.

1. The administrator finds that devices on at least one VLAN cannot communicate with devices on other VLANs. In addition, some devices within the VLAN cannot reach other intra-VLAN devices. Name at least five areas to examine and the commands needed to isolate these issues.

Review Questions

1. Catalyst 5000 switches are which one of the following?

   A. Devices that operate at Layer 2 of the OSI model

   B. Limited to 16 ports

   C. Limited to only one physical media

   D. Available for Ethernet only

   E. Available for ATM only

2. 100BaseTX requires which of the following?

   A. Category 1 cables

   B. Category 3 cables

   C. Category 5 cables

   D. Fiber cables

3. Which of the following does the SAINT handle? (Choose all that apply.)

   A. Token Ring

   B. Ethernet

   C. ISL

   D. ATM

   E. FDDI

4. Which of the following is true about VLANs?

   A. They define the broadcast domain.

   B. They define the collision domain.

   C. They are unique to each workstation.

   D. They are available only on Ethernet.

   E. They require the use of ISL or 802.1q.

   F. They require the use of 802.1d or spanning tree.

5. ISL is useful for which one of the following?

   A. Trunking between non-Cisco switches

   B. Trunking between Cisco switches

   C. Configuring VLANs

   D. Quadrupling the bandwidth between switches

6. Which of the following are the same encapsulation type? (Choose all that apply.)

   A. 802.1Q

   B. ISL

   C. 802.3

   D. 802.1D

   E. None of the above

7. The Catalyst command to display information on neighboring Cisco devices is which of the following?

   A. `show neighbors cdp`

   B. `display cisco neighbors`

   C. `show cdp neighbors all`

   D. `show cdp neighbors detail`

   E. `show neighboring cdp details`

8. Spanning tree provides which one of the following?

   A. A single path through multiple subnets

   B. Redundant paths while preventing loops

   C. Trunking multiple VLANs onto FDDI interfaces

   D. MAC layer address translation

9. In order to connect the Marketing VLAN to the Payroll VLAN, which one of the following must be true about a packet?

   A. It must use ISL.

   B. It must be forwarded at least once by a router.

   C. It must be greater than 1,024 octets long.

   D. The packet cannot go from the Marketing VLAN to the Payroll VLAN.

   E. It must be converted into ATM cells.

10. Which of the following commands provides system uptime?

   A. `show version`

   B. `show config`

   C. `uptime`

   D. `show flash`

11. Switch utilization is available from which of the following?

   A. LEDs on the supervisor module

   B. Cisco WAN Manager

   C. CLI

   D. `show snmp utilization`

12. VLANs control the scope of which one of the following?

   A. The collision domain

   B. The broadcast domain

   C. Conversion from half to full duplex

   D. Port mirroring for troubleshooting with SPANs

13. Which of the following applications provides a graphical method for assigning virtual LAN ports?

   A. VLANWorks

   B. LANDesigner

   C. TrafficDirector

   D. PortMapper

   E. VLANDirector

14. Cisco Discovery Protocol provides which of the following?

   A. Ping services for Cisco devices

   B. Automatic VLAN configuration services

   C. VLAN security by controlling the ARP discovery process

   D. Network management information regarding Cisco products

   E. Automatic ISL and 802.1q services

15. Token Ring frames are handled by which of the following? (Choose all that apply.)

   A. SAINT

   B. SAGE

   C. EARL

   D. SAMBA

16. Which of the following commands provides information regarding individual ports on the switch? (Choose all that apply.)

A. `show all ports`

B. `show port <mod/port>`

C. `show port detail <mod/port>`

D. `show switch port <port/mod>`

17. An administrator adds a VLAN to Switch_A, which is connected to Switch_B and Switch_C. Which of the following will be true about the VLAN?

A. It will need to be added manually to each switch in the network.

B. It will need to be added manually to each switch in the network that participates in the VLAN, but no others.

C. It will automatically be added to each switch in the subnet.

D. It will automatically be added to each switch in the VTP domain.

E. It will automatically be added via the TrafficDirector tool.

18. How many VLANs can be active on a single non-trunk port?

A. Two

B. One

C. Multiple

D. None

19. How many VLANs can be present on an ISL port?

A. Multiple

B. Only one

C. None

D. Two

20. Collisions are possible on which of the following connections?

A. FDDI

B. Token Ring

C. Fast Ethernet

D. Full duplex Ethernet

Answers to Review Questions

1. A. Switches operate at Layer 2 of the OSI model. The Catalyst 5000 has a variety of interfaces and media configurations.

2. C. Category 5 cables are required to ensure sufficient pairs of copper for the transmit and receive signals as well as to provide the electrical characteristics needed.

3. B, C. The SAINT handles Ethernet protocol as well as ISL VLAN encapsulation.

4. A. The collision domain is controlled by the switch port. A VLAN can exist on multiple machines.

5. B. Because ISL is a Cisco proprietary encapsulation, it does not work with non-Cisco switches.

6. E. None of these encapsulations are the same, and 802.1D is not a real frame encapsulation type.

7. D. The correct syntax is given by the answer D.

8. B. The main function of spanning tree is to prevent loops in a switched network.

9. B. In order for different VLANs to communicate, the packets must be routed.

10. A. The `show version` command displays the system's uptime.

11. A, C. Both of these, along with CWSI, allow the user to check the switch utilization.

12. B. VLANs control broadcast domains. Collisions, duplex, and mirroring are all done by the switch.

13. E. This is the proper software for VLAN configuration and management.

14. D. CDP discovers and retains information regarding directly connected Cisco devices.

15. B, C, D. The SAGE handles non-Ethernet frames, but all frames are handled by the EARL and SAMBA ASICs.

16. B. The correct syntax for the command that provides port information is given in B.

17. D. VLAN information is automatically propagated via the VTP protocol within the domain. Each switch can only belong to one domain.

18. B. One VLAN per non-trunking port. When a port is a trunk port, it handles all VLANs.

19. A. An ISL port has the same function as a trunking port.

20. C. Collisions are possible if there are multiple workstations on a switched port or the port is configured to half duplex instead of full duplex.

Chapter 12

Cisco Support Functions

TOPICS COVERED IN THIS CHAPTER INCLUDE:

✓ Familiarizing yourself with the types of information you should provide Cisco for optimal support when reporting problems.

✓ Learning what resources are available to you via CCO (CD and Web site) that will aid you in your troubleshooting endeavors.

✓ Learning the escalation method when working with Cisco support services.

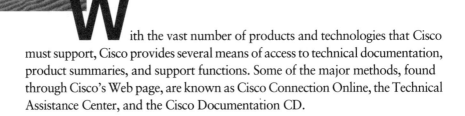

With the vast number of products and technologies that Cisco must support, Cisco provides several means of access to technical documentation, product summaries, and support functions. Some of the major methods, found through Cisco's Web page, are known as Cisco Connection Online, the Technical Assistance Center, and the Cisco Documentation CD.

Cisco Connection Family

Cisco Connection Family is a collection of interactive electronic media that is intended to provide technical assistance and support for Cisco products and networking technologies. There are five members of the Cisco Connection family:

- Cisco Connection Online (CCO)
- Cisco Technical Assistance and Software Center
- Cisco Connection Consultant Tools CD-ROM
- Cisco Commerce Agents
- Cisco MarketPlace

Cisco Connection Online (CCO)

The *Cisco Web site,* known as *CCO (Cisco Connection Online),* is the repository for information regarding Cisco products, networking technology, configuration examples, troubleshooting tools, and network planning.

CCO has two access levels. The first is guest privilege, which does not require a login account. This level provides general product and company information. The second level is for registered Cisco users who purchased a Cisco support contract or are sponsored by a Cisco Authorized Partner. This level provides all information available to the guest level, in-depth detailed technical documentation, access to download Cisco IOS images, trouble ticket queries, and so on.

There are a few subtle differences between the guest page and the user page. The significant changes are under the Service and Support category. The guest has access only to see the Online Support benefits, whereas the user actually has access to the online support.

If you follow the Software Center link under guest access, you notice that it does not allow Cisco IOS image downloads. You have to be a registered user to have access to download Cisco IOS.

Online Information

The front page of CCO offers links to many different types of information. Network solutions, product and network technologies, corporate news, product ordering, and information about Cisco-related events are all available from CCO.

The network solutions section provides explanations about technology and how it can be used in many scenarios. Its examples range from people interested in Cisco equipment to companies looking for enterprise-wide network solutions. Case studies are provided for businesses ranging from home offices to large enterprises.

Cisco customers are also able to access all of Cisco's product documentation, as well as industry technologies. This information can be used to choose the right equipment for the technologies that are planned for implementation.

Ordering information and product purchases can be made through the Web site, as well. Purchasing is handled by the Networking Products MarketPlace.

Information for Cisco Partners and Resellers is also accessible through CCO. Finally, recent and historical corporate news and information are available through the Corporate News and Information Menu. This menu has information regarding Cisco acquisitions, investor information, and information on contacting Cisco Systems.

Features and Electronic Services

Cisco provides several electronic services and features within the menus of CCO. Many of the features can be considered to be services, as well. Some of the most prominent features and services along with their description are as follows:

Software Center   The Software Center is an interactive site that allows the user to go directly to the software image that is needed. Alternatively, it has several categories that help the user select the IOS image that is best suited for the network resources and requirements. The subcategories are broken down by product type. The software center also provides an IOS upgrade planner. Patches to IOS bugs and the latest feature set are available through the Software Center.

Online Technical Support   This menu provides links to several electronic services and features. Here is a list of some of the services and features accessible from the Online Technical Support site:

- Open Q&A Forum
- Software Bug Toolkit
- Technical Tips
- IP Subnet Calculator
- TAC Case Management
- TAC Processes and Competencies
- Memory Calculator
- Bug Watcher

The Open Q&A Forum allows a user to browse through previous technical questions and answers or post a new question. A search engine is available for locating specific topics or technologies. Questions are answered by anyone holding a CCIE certification.

If you have questions about an IOS bug or a problem you think may be a bug, you can use the Software Bug Toolkit. This allows the registered user to provide IOS revision information and search for bugs that are associated with a specified release of IOS.

The Bug Watcher is part of the Bug Toolkit. The Bug Watcher allows a user to identify the different bugs that are present in current IOS releases, track them, and update the user about the current status of the bug.

Technical Tips hosts information regarding different IOS versions, hardware platforms, and configuration guides. When new technologies are implemented, the Cisco Technical Tips page will have information to walk you through the configuration.

Special features include the IP Subnet and Memory Calculators. The IP Subnet Calculator is an interactive page that asks for user input, and then returns subnet information based on that input.

TAC Case Management involves querying, opening, updating, and closing Cisco TAC cases. All of these processes may be accomplished by using CCO.

Troubleshooting Engine

The *Troubleshooting Engine* is part of the Online Technical Support menu. This tool can be used to help isolate and diagnose many networking problems, based on user input and the Cisco database.

This interactive tool starts by asking the user to have a hard copy of the configuration in question, in addition to an accurate network topology. With these items in hand, the page lists a number of technology categories. Here are the categories currently available with troubleshooting engine support:

IBM/SNA   Provides support for BSTUN, CIP, DLSw, QLLC, SRB, and transparent bridging.

IP   Support for RIP, IGRP, EIGRP, OSPF, BGP, IP/TV applications, and IP performance issues.

LAN   Support for AppleTalk Routing, ATM, IPX, and LAN-switching issues.

Network Management   Provides support for CiscoWorks and Cisco-Works 2000.

Platform Help   Provides support for low-level routers: 1600, 2500, and 3600 series.

Voice   Provides support for voice on 2600, 3600, 3810, and 5300 routers, as well as issues related to VoIP (Voice over IP). Provides support for WAN-switching equipment.

WAN and Access Services Provides Access dial-up, ISDN, PPP, TACACS, radius, and AAA issues. Frame Relay and WAN-switching is also supported.

Let's work through an IP example. You select the IP Step-by-Step link and proceed to the Troubleshooting Assistant, which allows you to specify a specific problem:

- Problems with configuring IP addressing
- Local host cannot access remote host
- Local client/server cannot access local router
- Connections fail with certain applications
- Problems with forwarding BootP and other UDP broadcasts
- Problems with RIP/IGRP
- Problems with OSPF
- Problems with EIGRP
- Problems with BGP performance

Click the Next button, and the Troubleshooting Assistant asks you questions that are more specific. The process then moves through a series of Yes/No questions, trying to diagnose the problem that you are experiencing. Once the Assistant decides that it has enough information to diagnose your problem, it will suggest various solutions.

If you cannot remember which questions were asked or how you answered them, you can review the Q&A session by clicking the session log button on the left side of the screen.

If the information suggested by the Troubleshooting Assistant doesn't solve your problem, you can also open a TAC case from the troubleshooting engine's screen by selecting the Open a Case button on the left side of the page.

Additional problems can be analyzed by selecting the Start Over button.

Cisco Connection Documentation

Cisco's *Cisco Connection Documentation CD-ROM* is the collection of technical documentation, available on CCO as well as on the Documentation CD, which accompanies new Cisco equipment purchases. Both forms of the technical documentation are very helpful for providing critical information regarding Cisco products, networking technologies, and configuration examples.

CCO

The CCO version of Cisco Connection Documentation CD-ROM may be accessed through the front page of CCO by using the Technical Documents link. The Documentation home page has links discussing the CD-ROM, Cisco product documentation, router configuration tools, technology information, and other information.

Documentation for Cisco products and technology available on the CCO Web site include:

- Cisco IOS Software configuration
- 10/100 Hubs
- CDDI/FDDI Adapters and concentrators
- Multi-layer LAN switches
- ATM adapters and switching
- Access servers and routers
- Core and High-end routers
- FastHub Repeaters
- Network management
- 10BaseT hubs
- Layer 3 switching
- Internet service unit
- Cisco WAN switching
- Broadband/Cable solutions
- DSL products
- Telephony

Cisco Connection Documentation CD-ROM

The Cisco Connection Documentation CD-ROM accompanies new Cisco equipment purchases. The information on the CD-ROM is updated as changes are made to IOS features and configuration options.

The CD-ROM contains all of the same information as the Web site, except for the documentation on telephony. The CD-ROM also includes technology information and router configuration tools.

The CD-ROM has the following technology information:

- Internetworking technology overview

- Troubleshooting internetwork systems

- Internetworking terms and acronyms

- Internetworking case studies

- Internetworking design guide

- Cisco site preparation guide

- Internetwork troubleshooting guide

- Remote configuration guide

These same topics are covered on the CCO Web site. Additional information shared by the CCO Web site and the Cisco Connection Documentation CD-ROM is in the Cisco product catalog. The product quick reference guide is available only from the CCO Web site.

CD-ROM navigation is best done by using existing menus. The search function on the Documentation CD-ROM is not as effective as navigating the menus provided.

For example, if you need to know how to configure ISDN BRI, the quickest way to get to it is to select the Cisco IOS Software Configuration link on the home page for the Documentation information. Next, you select the correct version of IOS—use 11.3 for this example. After selecting 11.3, the CD-ROM gives a summary of all the topics covered under IOS version 11.3. Select the first line ➤ Cisco IOS 11.3 Configuration Guides ➤ Command References. Upon selecting the configuration guide, you see a list of configuration topics.

To successfully navigate through the topics, you need to spend time investigating what technologies belong to which topic. In this scenario, you need to select the Dial Solutions Configuration Guide. Next, because you want information on how to configure a port, choose the Dial-in Port Setup. In this menu, you find the topic on Setting Up ISDN Basic Rate Services. By selecting that link, you get the file that details how to configure ISDN BRI services.

If you enter a search on the keywords **ISDN BRI** from the home page, you get thousands of responses, with none of the top 10 being relevant to what you are trying to do.

The CD-ROM is an invaluable tool because it is mobile and does not require a network connection. This is important if you are installing a router at a remote site, and don't yet have a network connection.

Cisco's Technical Assistance Center (TAC)

When you need additional resources to solve network failures, you can contact the *Cisco Technical Assistance Center,* or *TAC.* The TAC is accessible by phone, the CCO Web site, fax, or e-mail.

The TAC provides support for Cisco contract holders, gives warranty service, and can even bill you directly if you do not have a Cisco maintenance contract.

If you can solve the network problem yourself, you can avoid the time that it takes to contact and receive assistance from the TAC. However, the TAC has access to information that the end user does not have. Often, this information proves invaluable for solving the problem. You also need to contact them if the problem is faulty hardware—the TAC can send you replacement equipment, if needed.

You need to give some basic information when contacting the TAC to open a case. First, the Customer Response Center operator asks you for a serial number or a contract number. (The Customer Response Center is the central point for incoming calls.) In addition to your contract or serial number, they ask you for your name and company name. They verify your address, phone number, and e-mail address. They take preliminary information and prioritize the case, and then forward the case to the proper engineering group. You should make sure to record the ticket number for future reference.

When you open your ticket, you can specify the priority of your case. There are *four priorities* to choose from:

Priority 1   Production network down

Priority 2   Production network performance seriously degraded

Priority 3   Network performance degraded

Priority 4   Information needed on Cisco products

If you choose to categorize your ticket as a Priority 1, the engineer is required to stay on the phone with you until the problem is resolved or the case priority is downgraded.

The TAC is divided into several engineering groups, so that the engineers that handle the case can specialize in a given area. For example, there is an ATM group, a routing protocols group, an NMS group, and so on. Once an engineer gets the case, they need more information from you.

You should be able to provide the engineer with a `show tech-support` output from all affected equipment. In addition to the `show tech-support` information, you should be able to provide information regarding recent configuration changes, debug, or third-party protocol analyzer information.

After you open a ticket, you receive automated updates on the status of your case. If you need to add information to your ticket, you can send e-mail to the engineer working on the case, or you can go to the Web site and add it to the case by using the CCO Case Management Toolkit.

The TAC engineer works with you on your case to implement necessary changes and then observe the results. This process is followed until the problem is resolved.

Let's summarize the steps of opening a case with the Cisco TAC.

1. Gather relevant information about your problem. This includes a `show tech-support` from all affected devices, recent configuration changes, debug, and protocol analyzer information.

2. Give the Customer Response Center the necessary contract or serial number. In addition, provide your name and company name, and verify the address, phone number, and e-mail.

3. Give a brief description of the problem and assign the case the correct priority. You will be given a case number. Record it.

4. Your case will be forwarded to the appropriate TAC engineering group.

5. Use the Case Management Toolkit to add more information, close the case, or open a new case.

6. Work with the engineer to make the necessary changes to resolve the problem, and then observe results to verify that the problem is solved. If the problem gets worse, you can upgrade the case priority.

Other Cisco Documentation

Cisco has other methods of providing information to Cisco users. It provides seminars and presentations regarding new products and new network solutions.

Cisco also publishes Cisco books in a collection called Cisco Press. The books are written by Cisco to provide more information on products, technologies, case studies, and implementation. These books can be found on CCO at `http://www.cisco.com/cpress/home/home.htm`.

Summary

Cisco provides several means of getting important information. The Cisco Connection Family is designed to perform two functions: prevent problems from occurring, and resolve them when they do occur. It achieves these goals in the following ways:

- Cisco provides product and technology documentation, including configuration guides online and on CD-ROM. It also allows the user to purchase needed equipment using Cisco MarketPlace, Pricing Agent, and the Configuration Agent.

- The Software Agent provides access to IOS images, as well as planning tools to make sure that the correct version and feature set are chosen for the right router or switch. Patches are also available when necessary.

To help correct problems after they occur, Cisco has several online services besides the TAC:

- Bug Navigator, Bug Alerts, and Bug Watcher are tools available to the user to track IOS bug information.

- The Troubleshooting Engine and Assistant can be used to solve simple network problems. It is an interactive tool that allows the user to provide symptoms and answer questions to aid in isolating and potentially resolving network failures.

- TAC is available for users via phone, e-mail, CCO, and fax. By providing the necessary information, you can work with a Cisco engineer to solve your problem.

- Mailing lists, as well as the Cisco Open Forum, provide responses to "real-life" network failures and problems.

Commands Used in This Chapter

The following list contains a summary of all the commands used in this chapter.

Command	Description
show tech-support	A comprehensive command that includes show running-config, show version, show stacks, show processes cpu, and show processes memory, along with many others.

Key Terms

Before you take the exam, be certain you are familiar with the following terms:

CCO (Cisco Connection Online)

Cisco Connection Documentation CD-ROM

Cisco Connection Family

Cisco Technical Assistance Center (TAC)

Cisco Web site

four priorities

Priority 1

Priority 2

Priority 3

Priority 4

Troubleshooting Engine

Review Questions

1. Which of the following are members of the Cisco Connection Family? (Choose all that apply.)

    A. Cisco Connection Online (CCO)

    B. CiscoWorks

    C. Cisco Technical Assistance and Software Center

    D. Cisco Connection Consultant Tools CD-ROM

2. Which of the following are valid access levels for CCO? (Choose all that apply.)

    A. Account holder

    B. Guest

    C. VIP

    D. User

3. Which of the following allow a guest to register for user access? (Choose all that apply.)

    A. Service contract number

    B. Purchasing Cisco equipment

    C. Referral of a Cisco employee

    D. Proof of Cisco equipment on the premises.

4. Which of the following features does the Software Center provide? (Choose all that apply.)

   A. Direct access to IOS images

   B. Automated upgrade service

   C. IOS upgrade planner

   D. Free upgrades for existing IOS

5. Which of the following are part of the Online Technical Support? (Choose all that apply.)

   A. Technical Tips

   B. IP Subnet Calculator

   C. Decimal to Hex address converter

   D. Memory Calculator

   E. All of the above

6. What resources are available through the Open Q&A Forum? (Choose all that apply.)

   A. Posting technical answers

   B. Searching for technical documentation

   C. Searching the forum for past questions

   D. Answering questions

7. Which of the following are components of the Software Bug Toolkit? (Choose all that apply.)

   A. Latest IOS revisions

   B. Bug Watcher

   C. Free upgrades

   D. IOS Planner

8. Which of the following categories can be found in the LAN category of the Troubleshooting Engine? (Choose all that apply.)

   A. ATM

   B. IP

   C. LAN switching

   D. Network Management

9. What topics are supported in the WAN and Access category? (Choose all that apply.)

   A. PPP

   B. IP routing protocols

   C. VOIP

   D. Low-end router platforms

   E. High-end router support

   F. WAN switching

10. Which of the following is the correct method for displaying the question-and-answer dialog box from the TroubleShooting assistant?

   A. Select the Session Log button.

   B. Select the Feedback button.

   C. Select the Open a Case button.

   D. None of the above.

11. Which forms of electronic media are used to provide access to Cisco's Documentation CD-ROM? (Choose all that apply.)

   A. CCO

   B. Fax

   C. E-mail

   D. Cisco Connection Documentation CD-ROM

12. What is the easiest way to navigate the Cisco Connection Documentation CD-ROM?

   A. Use the search engine provided.

   B. Use the existing menu structure.

   C. Use Netscape as your browser.

   D. Use the CCO search engine.

13. What information is provided on CCO version of the Cisco Documentation that is not found on the CD-ROM version?

A. Cisco IOS configuration guides

B. Network Management

C. DSL products

D. Telephony

14. How many priority levels exist for a Cisco TAC case?

A. 1

B. 3

C. 4

D. 5

15. What information do you need to provide when opening a TAC case? (Choose all that apply.)

A. Contract number

B. Unit serial number

C. `show proc cpu` information

D. IANA handle

E. Company name

16. Which of the following are valid descriptions for the four priority levels? If you are able to, you can also associate a description with the priority level. (Choose all that apply.)

A. Production network performance severely degraded

B. Information on products or configuration issues

C. Production network down

D. Network performance degraded

E. Network performance somewhat degraded

17. What is the online tool available for Cisco Case Management?

    A. Case Management Toolkit

    B. CCO Case Manager

    C. CCO TAC Manager

    D. None of the above

18. Via which means is the Cisco TAC accessible? (Choose all that apply.)

    A. Phone

    B. E-mail

    C. CCO

    D. Fax

    E. Online chat

    F. AOL

19. Which of the following are methods Cisco uses to notify users of problems with new technologies? (Choose all that apply.)

    A. Phone calls

    B. CD distribution

    C. Mailing lists

    D. Web site

20. Which of the following are valid points when working on a case with Cisco TAC? (Choose all that apply.)

A. Work with the engineer to make the necessary changes to resolve the problem, and then observe results to verify that the problem is solved. If the problem gets worse, you can upgrade the case priority.

B. Use the Case Management Toolkit to add more information, close the case, or open a new case.

C. Give a brief description of the problem and assign the case the correct priority. You will be given a case number. Record it.

D. Give the Customer Response Center the necessary contract or serial number. In addition, provide your name and company name, and verify the address, phone number, and e-mail.

E. Gather relevant information about your problem. This includes a `show tech-support` from all affected devices, recent configuration changes, debug, and protocol analyzer information.

Answers to Review Questions

1. A, C, D. There are five members of the Cisco Connection Family; not all were listed here. CiscoWorks is a software package.

2. B, D. These are the two valid access levels for non-Cisco employees.

3. A, B. Either of these forms will allow a guest the ability to apply for user status. There are other valid methods that were not listed.

4. A, C. Cisco doesn't provide automated upgrade service. You must have a maintenance contract to get "free" IOS upgrades. There are other features to the Software Center, as covered in this chapter.

5. A, B, D. There are many features, only a portion were listed. There is no Decimal to Hex converter.

6. C. Users are not allowed to post answers. Technical documentation is provided through other resources.

7. B. The Bug Watcher and interim patches are available via the toolkit.

8. A, C. These are topics within the LAN category. There are also two others: IPX/SPX and AppleTalk Routing.

9. A, F. There are several others that were not listed. Here is a complete list: Dial-up services, Authentication, Cable technologies, DSL, Frame Relay, PPP, TACACS, WAN, WAN switching.

10. A. This will display the questions asked and your responses to those questions.

11. A, D. These are the two methods Cisco uses to provide the documentation from Cisco Connection Documentation CD-ROM.

12. B. Due to the vast amount of data on the CD and discrepancies with the search engine, the most efficient way to access the information is via the menu structure.

13. D. Telephony is only available via the Web site.

14. C. There are only four priorities at this point.

15. A, B, E. The complete list of what needs to be given consists of the following: contract number, serial number, `show tech-support` output, name, phone number, e-mail, company name.

16. A, B, C, D. These are all valid descriptions. They are listed as Priority 2, 4, 1, 3, respectively.

17. A. The Case Management Toolkit is the tool designed to provide online case management.

18. A, B, C, D. These are valid methods of contacting and working with the TAC.

19. C, D. These methods are used to notify customers of any major recent problems or bugs that have surfaced.

20. A, B, C, D, E. All of these are valid points when working with TAC.

Appendix

A

Practice Exam

Practice Exam Questions

1. Place the eight steps of the troubleshooting method in the order they are performed.

   A. Document Changes

   B. Define the Problem

   C. Implement Action Plan

   D. Gather Facts

   E. Iterate as Needed

   F. Observe Results

   G. Consider Possible Causes

   H. Create Action Plan

2. Which method of problem isolation is the most effective?

   A. Divide-by-half

   B. Inside-out

   C. Outside-in

   D. All of the above

3. Which of the following are characteristics of a good action plan? (Choose all that apply.)

A. Make one change at a time.

B. Make non-impacting changes.

C. Be careful not to create security holes while making changes.

D. Create a plan to back out of the changes.

4. Which of the following components belong in a network baseline? (Choose all that apply.)

A. Network topology

B. Active network and routing protocols

C. History of network problems

D. Network device configurations

E. Device passwords

5. What name does Cisco use for Novell 802.3 raw frames?

A. ARPA

B. SNAP

C. Novell-Ether

D. IEEE 802.3

6. Which IPX Ethernet frame type is configured by default on Cisco routers?

A. ARPA

B. Novell-Ether

C. SNAP

D. Ethernet II

7. Which is the correct definition of CSMA/CD?

    A. Carrier System Management Algorithm / Carrier Detection

    B. BCarrier Sense Multiple Access / Carrier Detection

    C. Collision Sensing Multiple Access / Collision Detection

    D. Carrier Sense, Multiple Access / Collision Detection

8. What information is located in the token frame for Token Ring?

    A. Data

    B. Data and control information

    C. Control information

    D. Nothing—it is nothing but zero values

9. Which OSI layers correspond to the Novell NetWare protocol? (Choose all that apply.)

    A. Layer 1

    B. Layer 2

    C. Layer 3

    D. Layer 4

    E. Layer 5

    F. Layer 6

    G. Layer 7

10. Which of the following protocols use tokens? (Choose all that apply.)

    A. FDDI

    B. Frame Relay

    C. CSMA/CD

    D. Token Ring

11. Where is the best location for a protocol analyzer to be placed when attempting to collect data?

    A. Connected to the nearest router

    B. Connected to the same classfull network

    C. On the same segment where the devices of interest reside

    D. Remotely

12. What advantage(s) do TDRs have over normal cable testers? (Choose all that apply.)

    A. They can determine the location of the fault.

    B. They perform the same operations, just faster.

    C. They can be used on fiber optic cable as well as copper.

    D. They are less expensive.

13. Based on the following output from a protocol analyzer, what can you determine about the frame? (Choose all that apply.)

```
Flags:        0x00
  Status:       0x00
  Packet Length:99
  Timestamp:    14:48:51.539000 03/22/1999
Ethernet Header
  Destination: 01:a1:32:5a:a6:f1  [0-5]
  Source:      08:00:02:32:1f:f2  [6-11]
  Protocol Type:08-00  IP  [12-13]
IP Header - Internet Protocol Datagram
  Version:            4  [14 Mask 0xf0]
  Header Length:      5  [14 Mask 0xf]
  Precedence:         0  [15 Mask 0xe0]
  Type of Service:  %000  [15 Mask 0x1c]
  Unused:           %00  [15 Mask 0x3]
  Total Length:      81  [16-17]
  Identifier:      6039  [18-19]
  Fragmentation Flags: %010  Do Not Fragment   [20
```

Mask 0xe0]
  Fragment Offset: 0 [20-22 Mask 0x1fffff]
  Time To Live: 255
  IP Type: 0x06 *TCP* [23]
  Header Checksum: 0xd488 [24-25]
  Source IP Address: 172.16.12.10 [26-29]
  Dest. IP Address: 172.16.12.130 [30-33]
  No Internet Datagram Options
TCP - Transport Control Protocol
  Source Port: 110 *POP3* [34-35]
  Destination Port: 1324 [36-37]
  Sequence Number: 3712383331 [38-41]
  Ack Number: 31151113 [42-45]
  Offset: 5 [46 Mask 0xf0]
  Reserved: %000000 [46 Mask 0xfc0]
  Code: %011000 [47 Mask 0x3f]
        Ack is valid
        Push Request
  Window: 8760 [48-49]
  Checksum: 0x2d24 [50-51]
  Urgent Pointer: 0 [52-53]
  No TCP Options
POP - Post Office Protocol
  POP Reply: +OK *Positive Reply* [54-56]
  Comment: [57]
  POP3 mail.somewhere.com 50 45 50 33 21 68 61 6d 2f
  75 65   6e 2d 6e 72 67   [58-73]
   v6.50 server re   21 76 36 2a 35 30 21 73 65 72 77
  65 78   20 72 65   [74-89]
  ady   61 46 80   [90-92]
  Newline Sequence: 0x0d0a [93-94]
Frame Check Sequence: 0xffff00cd

A. It is a POP3 packet.

B. It uses TCP as its transport protocol.

C. TCP options were specified.

D. It is a connectionless packet.

14. Identify any NMS attributes. (Choose all that apply.)

    A. Security

    B. Quality of Service

    C. Inventory management

    D. Traffic analysis

15. Why is it necessary to disable cached switching (fast switching, silicon switching, optimum switching, etc.) when running the debug process?

    A. Running caching and debugging at the same time produces too much overhead for the processor.

    B. If caching is used, the packets may not be processed by the route processor, thus not allowing debug to see the packet.

    C. The IOS only allows one process or the other to run at a time.

    D. Debugging corrupts the caches and therefore interrupts the switching process, and packets are subsequently dropped.

16. Choose the best description of an overrun.

    A. The number of packets being transferred from the interface exceeds the number of packets the link can receive.

    B. The processor is overrun by requests to process switch packets.

    C. The interface receiver receives packets faster than it can transfer them to the hardware buffer.

    D. None of the above.

17. Choose the best description of an underrun.

    A. The transmitter runs at a higher rate than the packets sent from the hardware buffer.

    B. The interface receiver does not receive packets fast enough to transfer them to the hardware buffer to keep it full.

    C. The hardware buffer can't keep up with the requests from the output queue.

    D. None of the above.

18. Where do input and output queues exist, and what are they used for?

    A. Queues reside on each individual interface and are used to avoid interface congestion.

    B. Queues reside in the CxBus or CyBus and are used to avoid collisions on the backplane.

    C. Queues reside in RAM and store input and output statistics for all interfaces.

    D. Queues reside on the RP, and they are used to link the SP buffers to the RP buffers.

19. What information determines a "flow" in Netflow switching? (Choose all that apply.)

    A. Source and destination IP addresses

    B. Source and destination MAC addresses

    C. Protocol

    D. Source and destination ports

    E. Incoming interface

    F. Switching cache used

20. What can be determined from the following lines of a packet decode? (Choose all that apply.)

```
IP Header - Internet Protocol Datagram
  Version:                4  [14 Mask 0xf0]
  Header Length:          5  [14 Mask 0xf]
  Precedence:             0  [15 Mask 0xe0]
  Type of Service:        %000  [15 Mask 0x1c]
  Unused:                 %00  [15 Mask 0x3]
  Total Length:           56  [16-17]
  Identifier:             2815  [18-19]
  Fragmentation Flags:    %000  [20 Mask 0xe0]
  Fragment Offset:        0  [20-22 Mask 0x1fffff]
  Time To Live:           255
  IP Type:                0x01  ICMP  [23]
  Header Checksum:        0xe021  [24-25]
  Source IP Address:      172.16.60.1  [26-29]
  Dest. IP Address:       172.16.60.130  [30-33]
  No Internet Datagram Options
ICMP - Internet Control Messages Protocol  [34]
  ICMP Type:              3  Destination Unreachable
  [35]
  Code:                   1  Host Unreachable
  Checksum:               0x6439  [36-37]
  Unused (must be zero):0x00000000  [38-41]
```

A. This is an SNMP packet.

B. This is an ICMP packet.

C. This is a type 3 ICMP packet.

D. The source IP address is 172.16.60.130.

21. What can be determined from the following lines of a packet decode? (Choose all that apply.)

```
TCP - Transport Control Protocol
    Source Port:       1038  [34-35]
    Destination Port:  21  FTP Control - File Transfer
    Protocol  [36-37]
    Sequence Number:   6198340  [38-41]
    Ack Number:        0  [42-45]
    Offset:            7  [46 Mask 0xf0]
    Reserved:          %000000  [46 Mask 0xfc0]
    Code:              %000010  [47 Mask 0x3f]
              Synch Sequence
    Window:            8192  [48-49]
    Checksum:          0x2bb5  [50-51]
    Urgent Pointer:    0  [52-53]
```

   A. This is an FTP packet.

   B. The transfer is occurring on port 21.

   C. The packet is out of sequence.

   D. All of the above.

22. Which of the following can cause a Token Ring interface to not function? (Choose all that apply.)

   A. Ring speed mismatch

   B. Lobe wire fault

   C. Too many tokens on the ring at one time

   D. All of the above

23. What can you determine from the following router output? (Choose all that apply.)

Router_B(boot)#**show version**

Cisco Internetwork Operating System Software

IOS (tm) 3000 Bootstrap Software (IGS-BOOT-R), Version 11.0(10c)XB1, PLATFORM SPECIFIC RELEASE SOFTWARE (fc1)

Copyright (c) 1986-1996 by cisco Systems, Inc.

Compiled Wed 10-Sep-97 13:06 by phester

Image text-base: 0x01010000, data-base: 0x00001000

ROM: System Bootstrap, Version 11.0(10c)XB1, PLATFORM SPECIFIC RELEASE SOFTWARE

(fc1)

Router_B uptime is 3 hours, 11 minutes

System restarted by reload

Running default software

cisco 2500 (68030) processor (revision A) with 4096K/ 2048K bytes of memory.

Processor board ID 01229726, with hardware revision 00000000

X.25 software, Version 2.0, NET2, BFE and GOSIP compliant.

Cisco-ET Extended Temperature platform.

1 Ethernet/IEEE 802.3 interface.

2 Serial network interfaces.

32K bytes of non-volatile configuration memory.

8192K bytes of processor board System flash (Read/ Write)

Configuration register is 0x2101

A. The router is in boot mode.

B. The configuration register is set to 0x2101.

C. The last time the system was started was 3 hours 11 minutes ago.

D. There are three interfaces on this router.

24. What can you determine from the following router output? (Choose all that apply.)

```
Router_C#ping
Protocol [ip]:
Target IP address: 172.16.60.130
Repeat count [5]: 20
Datagram size [100]:
Timeout in seconds [2]:
Extended commands [n]:
Sweep range of sizes [n]:
Type escape sequence to abort.
Sending 20, 100-byte ICMP Echos to 172.16.60.130,
timeout is 2 seconds: 172.16.60.130
Type escape sequence to abort.
!!!!!.!..!!!!...!!!!
Success rate is 30 percent (6/20), round-trip min/avg/
max = 4/500/2000 ms
Router_C#
```

A. There is 70 percent packet loss on this interface.

B. The interface is down.

C. There are several collisions on the interface.

D. The average RTT was 500 ms.

25. Which command was used to produce the following output?

```
P 172.16.165.0/24, 1 successors, FD is 3609600
        via 172.16.247.122 (3609600/3097600), Serial4/
7.2
P 172.16.135.48/30, 1 successors, FD is 388608
        via 172.16.247.18 (388608/30208), BVI1
P 0.0.0.0/0, 1 successors, FD is 3101696
        via 172.16.247.6 (3101696/3099648), ATM2/0.8
P 172.16.177.0/24, 1 successors, FD is 2199552
        via 172.16.0.17 (2199552/2197504), ATM0/0.2
P 172.16.33.156/30, 1 successors, FD is 20480
        via 172.16.231.2 (20480/18432), ATM2/0.2
P 172.16.189.0/24, 1 successors, FD is 2199552
        via 172.16.0.17 (2199552/2197504), ATM0/0.2
```

A. show ip eigrp neighbors

B. show ip eigrp events

C. show ip eigrp topology

D. show ip route eigrp

26. Which command was issued to produce the following output?

```
ATM0/0.1 is up, line protocol is up
  Internet address is 172.16.0.10/30
  Broadcast address is 255.255.255.255
  Address determined by non-volatile memory
  MTU is 4470 bytes
  Helper address is not set
  Directed broadcast forwarding is disabled
  Multicast reserved groups joined: 224.0.0.10
  Outgoing access list is not set
  Inbound  access list is not set
  Proxy ARP is enabled
  Security level is default
  Split horizon is disabled
  ICMP redirects are always sent
  ICMP unreachables are always sent
  ICMP mask replies are never sent
  IP fast switching is enabled
  IP fast switching on the same interface is disabled
  IP Flow switching is disabled
  IP Fast switching turbo vector
  IP Null turbo vector
  IP multicast fast switching is enabled
  IP multicast distributed fast switching is disabled
  Router Discovery is disabled
  IP output packet accounting is disabled
  IP access violation accounting is disabled
  TCP/IP header compression is disabled
  RTP/IP header compression is disabled
  Probe proxy name replies are disabled
  Policy routing is disabled
  Network address translation is disabled
  WCCP Redirect outbound is disabled
  WCCP Redirect exclude is disabled
  BGP Policy Mapping is disabled
```

A. show interface atm0/0.1

B. show ip configuration

C. show ip interface atm0/0.1

D. show ipx interface atm0/0.1

27. Which command provided the following output?

```
Routing Protocol is "eigrp 100"
  Outgoing update filter list for all interfaces is
    ATM0/0.2 filtered by 2 (per-user), default is 2
  Default networks flagged in outgoing updates
  Default networks accepted from incoming updates
  EIGRP metric weight K1=1, K2=0, K3=1, K4=0, K5=0
  EIGRP maximum hopcount 100
  EIGRP maximum metric variance 1
  Redistributing: static, eigrp 100
  Automatic network summarization is not in effect
  Routing for Networks:
      172.16.0.0
  Routing Information Sources:
    Gateway          Distance       Last Update
    172.16.247.70       90          00:02:18
    (this router)        5          7w4d

Routing Protocol is "bgp 110"
  Sending updates every 60 seconds, next due in 0
  seconds
  Outgoing update filter list for all interfaces is
  Incoming update filter list for all interfaces is
  IGP synchronization is disabled
  Automatic route summarization is enabled
  Aggregate Generation:

  Neighbor(s):
    Address          FiltIn FiltOut DistIn DistOut
```

```
Weight RouteMap
    172.16.58.1              1
    172.16.205.128                  2
    172.16.24.248
Routing for Networks:
Routing Information Sources:
  Gateway          Distance       Last Update
```

A. show ip eigrp

B. show ip bgp

C. show protocols

D. show ip protocols

28. Which command produced the following output?

```
IP statistics:
  Rcvd:  1831527162 total, 84211470 local destination
         2 format errors, 0 checksum errors, 3768517
         bad hop count
         379 unknown protocol, 0 not a gateway
         0 security failures, 0 bad options, 235102
         with options
  Opts:  7194 end, 110313 nop, 433 basic security, 1647
loose source route
         0 timestamp, 0 extended security, 827 record
         route
         0 stream ID, 0 strict source route, 222718
         alert, 0 cipso
         0 other
  Frags: 2091 reassembled, 0 timeouts, 0 couldn't
reassemble
         31638 fragmented, 551 couldn't fragment
  Bcast: 1141692 received, 77 sent
  Mcast: 51561848 received, 69917527 sent
  Sent:  108224695 generated, 1673287491 forwarded
  Drop:  10593027 encapsulation failed, 0 unresolved, 0
```

no adjacency
            2725 no route, 0 unicast RPF, 0 forced drop

ICMP statistics:
  Rcvd: 8 format errors, 529 checksum errors, 27
  redirects, 1973 unreachable
            715642 echo, 1992 echo reply, 8 mask requests,
0 mask replies, 574 quench
            0 parameter, 0 timestamp, 0 info request, 0
            other
            0 irdp solicitations, 0 irdp advertisements
  Sent: 553 redirects, 5046681 unreachable, 2469 echo,
715642 echo reply
            0 mask requests, 0 mask replies, 0 quench, 0
            timestamp
            0 info reply, 3735885 time exceeded, 0
            parameter problem
            0 irdp solicitations, 0 irdp advertisements

UDP statistics:
  Rcvd: 13440570 total, 0 checksum errors, 1065848 no
  port
  Sent: 12413099 total, 0 forwarded broadcasts

TCP statistics:
  Rcvd: 4360344 total, 11 checksum errors, 117397 no
  port
  Sent: 4368739 total

A. show ip protocols

B. show ip traffic

C. debug ip traffic

D. debug ip protocols

29. Which command produced the following output?

```
Protocol  Address              Age(min)    Hardware Addr
Type    Interface
Internet  205.124.112.200           0    00a0.c9f6.2cd9
ARPA    Ethernet5/0
Internet  205.124.235.66           50    0000.0c47.abea
ARPA    Ethernet5/4
Internet  205.124.235.65            -    0090.923f.40a4
ARPA    Ethernet5/4
Internet  205.124.240.1             -    0090.923f.4062
ARPA    Ethernet3/2
```

A. show mac-address

B. show arp

C. show ip-arp table

D. show arp-table

30. Which of the following information fields are displayed by the show frame-relay pvc command? (Choose all that apply.)

A. Last time the counters were cleared

B. DE statistics

C. DLCI number

D. Interface statistics

31. Which command provided the following output?

Serial0(out): StEnq, myseq 135, yourseen 134, DTE up
Serial0(in): Status, myseq 135
Serial1(out): StEnq, myseq 2, yourseen 8, DTE up
Serial1(in): Status, myseq 2
Serial2(out): StEnq, myseq 247, yourseen 247, DTE up
Serial2(in): Status, myseq 247
Serial3(out): StEnq, myseq 30, yourseen 28, DTE up
Serial3(in): Status, myseq 30
Serial0(out): StEnq, myseq 136, yourseen 135, DTE up
Serial0(in): Status, myseq 136

A. show frame-relay pvc

B. debug serial interface

C. debug frame-relay

D. show serial interface

32. Which command provided the following output?

Serial0 is administratively down, line protocol is down
  Hardware is HD64570
  Internet address is 172.16.20.6/30
  MTU 1500 bytes, BW 1544 Kbit, DLY 20000 usec, rely
  255/ 255, load 1/255
  Encapsulation HDLC, loopback not set, keepalive set
  (10 sec)
  Last input never, output never, output hang never
  Last clearing of "show interface" counters never
  Input queue: 0/75/0 (size/max/drops); Total output
  drops: 0
  Queueing strategy: weighted fair
  Output queue: 0/1000/64/0 (size/max total/threshold/
  drops)
    Conversations 0/0/256 (active/max active/max
    total)
    Reserved Conversations 0/0 (allocated/max

```
allocated)
5 minute input rate 0 bits/sec, 0 packets/sec
5 minute output rate 0 bits/sec, 0 packets/sec
   0 packets input, 0 bytes, 0 no buffer
   Received 0 broadcasts, 0 runts, 0 giants, 0
   throttles
   0 input errors, 0 CRC, 0 frame, 0 overrun, 0
   ignored, 0      abort
   0 packets output, 0 bytes, 0 underruns
   0 output errors, 0 collisions, 1 interface resets
   0 output buffer failures, 0 output buffers swapped
   out
   0 carrier transitions
   DCD=down   DSR=down   DTR=down   RTS=down   CTS=down
```

A. show interface serial *<number>*

B. show ip interface serial *<number>*

C. show frame-relay interface *<number>*

D. debug serial interface

33. What can be determined from the following router output?

```
Serial1 is up, line protocol is up
  Hardware is HD64570
  Internet address is 172.16.30.5/30
  MTU 1500 bytes, BW 1544 Kbit, DLY 20000 usec, rely
  255/  255, load 51/255
  Encapsulation X25, loopback not set
LAPB DTE, state CONNECT, modulo 8, k 7, N1 12043, N2 10
T1 3000, interface outage (partial T3) 0, T4 0
VS 1, VR 1, Remote VR 1, Retransmissions 0
  IFRAMEs 1/1 RNRs 0/0 REJs 0/0 SABM/Es 1/0 FRMRs 0/0
```

```
DISCs 0/0
X25 DTE, address 190118, state R1, modulo 8, timer 0
Defaults: cisco encapsulation, idle 0, nvc 1
Input/output window sizes 2/2, packet sizes 128/128
Timers: T20 180, T21 200, T22 180, T23 180, TH 0
Channels: Incoming-only none, Two-way 5-1024, Outgoing-
only none
RESTARTs 1/1 CALLs 0+0/0+0/0+0 DIAGs 0/0
  Last input 00:00:00, output 00:00:00, output hang
never
  Last clearing of "show interface" counters 00:28:48
  Input queue: 1/75/0 (size/max/drops); Total output
drops: 0
  Queueing strategy: weighted fair
  Output queue: 0/1000/64/0 (size/max total/threshold/
drops)
    Conversations  0/2/256 (active/max active/max
    total)
    Reserved Conversations 0/0 (allocated/max
    allocated)
  5 minute input rate 321000 bits/sec, 48 packets/sec
  5 minute output rate 320000 bits/sec, 48 packets/sec
    12439 packets input, 13257786 bytes, 0 no buffer
    Received 202 broadcasts, 0 runts, 0 giants, 0
    throttles
    0 input errors, 0 CRC, 0 frame, 0 overrun, 0
    ignored, 0      abort
    12438 packets output, 13256434 bytes, 0 underruns
    0 output errors, 0 collisions, 0 interface resets
    0 output buffer failures, 0 output buffers swapped
    out
    0 carrier transitions
    DCD=up  DSR=up  DTR=up  RTS=up  CTS=up
```

A. This is a Frame Relay interface.

B. This is an X.25 interface.

C. This is an HDLC-encapsulated X.25 interface.

D. X.25 is default for Cisco serial interfaces.

34. Which command produced the following output?

```
LMI Statistics for interface Serial0 (Frame Relay DTE)
LMI TYPE = CISCO
   Invalid Unnumbered info 0    Invalid Prot Disc 0
   Invalid dummy Call Ref 0     Invalid Msg Type 0
   Invalid Status Message 0     Invalid Lock Shift 0
   Invalid Information ID 0      Invalid Report IE Len 0
   Invalid Report Request 0     Invalid Keep IE Len 0
   Num Status Enq. Sent 823406    Num Status msgs Rcvd
   823403
   Num Update Status Rcvd 507    Num Status Timeouts 3
```

A. show frame-relay

B. show lmi

C. show frame-relay lmi

D. show DLCI lmi

35. Choose one of the three **debug** commands that should be used when troubleshooting the connection between the local TE and the remote TE.

A. debug q931

B. debug q921

C. debug isdn

D. debug isdn q931

E. debug isdn q921

36. Choose one of the three **debug** commands that should be used when troubleshooting the connection between the local TE and remote TE.

A. debug ppp negotiation

B. debug ppp

C. debug isdn q921

D. debug negotiation

37. Choose one of the three **debug** commands that should be used when troubleshooting the connection between the local TE and remote TE.

   A. debug chap negotiation

   B. debug isdn q921

   C. debug ppp authentication

   D. debug ppp chap

38. Choose one of the two **debug** commands that should be used when troubleshooting the connection between the TE and the LT/ET.

   A. debug isdn q921

   B. debug isdn bri *n*

   C. debug ppp negotiation

   D. debug isdn q931

39. Choose one of the two **debug** commands that should be used when troubleshooting the connection between the TE and the LT/ET.

   A. debug isdn bri *n*

   B. debug ppp chap

   C. debug serial interface

   D. debug dialer

40. Which command produced the following output?

```
Hssi3/0 is up, line protocol is up
IPX address is F100.0010.0d28.6760 [up] line-up, RIPPQ:
0, SAPPQ: 0
Delay of this IPX network, in ticks is 1 throughput 0
link delay 0
 IPXWAN processing not enabled on this interface.
 IPX SAP update interval is 1 minute(s)
 IPX type 20 propagation packet forwarding is disabled
 Incoming access list is not set
 Outgoing access list is not set
 IPX helper access list is not set
 SAP GNS processing enabled, delay 0 ms, output filter
list  is not set
 SAP Input filter list is not set
 SAP Output filter list is not set
 SAP Router filter list is not set
 Input filter list is not set
 Output filter list is not set
 Router filter list is not set
 Netbios Input host access list is not set
 Netbios Input bytes access list is not set
 Netbios Output host access list is not set
 Netbios Output bytes access list is not set
 Updates each 60 seconds, aging multiples RIP: 3 SAP: 3
 SAP interpacket delay is 55 ms, maximum size is 480
bytes
 RIP interpacket delay is 55 ms, maximum size is 432
bytes
 Watchdog spoofing is disabled, SPX spoofing is
disabled,  idle time 60
 IPX accounting is disabled
 IPX fast switching is configured (enabled)
 RIP packets received 3228022, RIP packets sent 121313
 SAP packets received 3507665, SAP packets sent 3003606
```

A. show interface hssi3/0

B. debug ipx interface hssi3/0

C. show ipx interface hssi3/0

D. show ipx protocol interface hssi3/0

41. What command produced the following output?

```
Codes: S - Static, P - Periodic, E - EIGRP, N - NLSP,
 H - Holddown, + = detail
117 Total IPX Servers
Table ordering is based on routing and server info
Type Name      Net Address          Port  Route Hops Itf
P+ 4 SRV-00001  1.0000.0000.0001:0451  4/03   3    Hs3/0
P+ 4 SRV-00002  2.0000.0000.0001:0451  4/03   3    Hs3/0
```

A. debug ipx server

B. show ipx server

C. show ipx route

D. show ipx sap

42. Which command produced the following output?

```
System Traffic for 0.0000.0000.0001 System-Name:
Router_ARcvd:  92678244 total, 158 format errors, 0
checksum errors, 0 bad hop count,1677 packets pitched,
65955970 local destination, 0 multicast
Bcast: 65957365 received, 63751306 sent
Sent:  75752069 generated, 26672221 forwarded
     50141 encapsulation failed, 1465 no route
SAP:  48 SAP requests, 0 SAP replies, 399 servers
     58523476 SAP advertisements received, 61481958 sent
   0 SAP flash updates sent, 6 SAP format errors, last
   seen from 500.0010.0b4f.2660
RIP:  48 RIP requests, 0 RIP replies, 128 routes
     7432398 RIP advertisements received, 2261621 sent
     8498 RIP flash updates sent, 0 RIP format errors
Echo:  Rcvd 0 requests, 0 replies
     Sent 0 requests, 0 replies
     0 unknown: 0 no socket, 0 filtered, 0 no helper
     0 SAPs throttled, freed NDB len 0
Watchdog:
     0 packets received, 0 replies spoofed
Queue lengths:
     IPX input: 0, SAP 0, RIP 0, GNS 0
     SAP throttling length: 0/(no limit), 0 nets pending
```

```
lost route reply
    Delayed process creation: 0
EIGRP: Total received 0, sent 0
    Updates received 0, sent 0
    Queries received 0, sent 0
    Replies received 0, sent 0
    SAPs received 0, sent 0
NLSP:  Level-1 Hellos received 0, sent 0
    PTP Hello received 0, sent 0
    Level-1 LSPs received 0, sent 0
    LSP Retransmissions: 0
    LSP checksum errors received: 0
    LSP HT=0 checksum errors received: 0
    Level-1 CSNPs received 0, sent 0
    Level-1 PSNPs received 0, sent 0
    Level-1 DR Elections: 0
    Level-1 SPF Calculations: 0
    Level-1 Partial Route Calculations: 0
```

A. debug ipx nlsp

B. debug ipx eigrp

C. show ipx route

D. show ipx traffic

43. What can be determined from the following output? (Choose all that apply.)

```
access-list 1060 permit 7593729 4
access-list 1060 permit 7593729 107
access-list 1060 permit 7593729 26B
access-list 1060 permit 7593729 278
access-list 1060 deny FFFFFFFF
```

A. Uses a SAP filter

B. Permits services 4, 107, 26b, 278

C. Denies all other

D. Permits all

44. Which command produced the following output?

```
IPX EIGRP Topology Table for process 10
Codes: P - Passive, A - Active, U - Update, Q - Query,
R - Reply, r - Reply status
P A, 1 successors, FD is 323328
       via D.0000.30e8.6d0f (323328/307200), TokenRing0
P B, 1 successors, FD is 297728
       via D.0000.30e8.6d0f (297728/281600), TokenRing0
P D, 1 successors, FD is 176128
       via Connected, TokenRing0
```

A. debug ipx events

B. show ipx eigrp events

C. show ipx eigrp topology

D. show ipx eigrp neighbors

45. Which command produced the following output?

```
AppleTalk global information:
  Internet is compatible with older, AT Phase1,
routers.
  There are 2 routes in the internet.
  There are 2 zones defined.
  Logging of significant AppleTalk events is disabled.
  ZIP resends queries every 10 seconds.
  RTMP updates are sent every 10 seconds.
  RTMP entries are considered BAD after 20 seconds.
  RTMP entries are discarded after 60 seconds.
  AARP probe retransmit count: 10, interval: 200 msec.
  AARP request retransmit count: 5, interval: 1000
msec.
  DDP datagrams will be checksummed.
  RTMP datagrams will be strictly checked.
  RTMP routes may not be propagated without zones.
  Routes will be distributed between routing protocols.
  Routing between local devices on an interface will
```

```
not be performed.
IPTalk uses the udp base port of 768 (Default).
AppleTalk EIGRP is not enabled.
Alternate node address format will not be displayed.
Access control of any networks of a zone hides the
zone.
```

A. show appletalk interface

B. show appletalk information

C. show appletalk global information

D. show appletalk globals

46. Which command produced the following output?

```
TokenRing0 is up, line protocol is up
  AppleTalk cable range is 1-1
  AppleTalk address is 1.230, Valid
  AppleTalk zone is "one"
  AppleTalk port configuration verified by 1.87
  AppleTalk address gleaning is disabled
  AppleTalk route cache is enabled
```

A. show appletalk interface

B. show appletalk globals

C. show token-ring interface

D. show running-configuration

47. When should you use the debug apple events? (Choose all that apply.)

A. To test for neighbor state changes

B. To see all packets exchanged between two AppleTalk peers

C. To view interface transitions

D. To debug routing synchronization

48. Which command(s) will allow you to see zone information? (Choose all that apply.)

A. show appletalk interface

B. show zones

C. show appletalk zone

D. show appletalk route

49. Which command produced the following output?

```
AT: NextNbrZipQuery: [2-2] zoneupdate 0 gw: 1.87 n:
1.87
AT: NextNbrZipQuery: r->rpath.gwptr: 60C60D20, n:
60C60D20
AT: maint_SendNeighborQueries, sending 1 queries to
1.87
AT: 1 query packet sent to neighbor 1.87
AT: Recvd ZIP cmd 2 from 1.87-6
AT: 1 zones in ZIPreply pkt, src 1.87
AT: net 2, zonelen 3, name Two
AT: in CancelZoneRequest, cancelling req on 2-
2...succeeded
AT: atzip_GC() called
```

A. debug appletalk zip

B. debug apple zip

C. debug nbp

D. debug appletalk nbp

50. Switch utilization is available from which of the following? (Choose all that apply.)

A. LEDs on the supervisor module

B. show version

C. CWSI

D. show utilization

E. An external RMON probe only

51. Which of the following functions do routers provide for the switched network? (Choose all that apply.)

    A. Collision domain

    B. Broadcast domain

    C. Policy control

    D. Hierarchical topology

52. Which command will provide the MAC address of the workstations connected to the switch?

    A. show arp

    B. show cam dynamic

    C. show mac

    D. show mac dynamic

53. Which of the following are valid VTP configurations? (Choose all that apply.)

    A. Server

    B. Master

    C. Slave

    D. Client

    E. Transparent

54. What is the maximum recommended diameter of a switched network?

    A. Three

    B. Ten

    C. Eight

    D. Seven

55. Which of the following are valid members of the Cisco Connection Family? (Choose all that apply.)

    A. Cisco Commerce Agents

    B. Cisco MarketPlace

    C. CCO

    D. Cisco Connection Documentation CD-ROM

56. Which of the following allow(s) a guest to register for user access? (Choose all that apply.)

  A. Cisco Reseller or Certified Partner

  B. Customer of a Cisco Certified Partner

  C. Planning to purchase Cisco equipment

  D. Evaluating Cisco equipment

57. Which of the following features does the Software Center provide? (Choose all that apply.)

  A. Product pricing calculator

  B. Product configurator

  C. Patches for some IOS versions

  D. Discount IOS sales

58. Which of the following are part of the Online Technical Support? (Choose all that apply.)

  A. Open Q&A Forum

  B. Software Bug Toolkit

  C. IOS debugging

  D. All of the above

59. What resources are available through the Open Q&A Forum? (Choose all that apply.)

  A. Posting technical questions

  B. Posting sales questions

  C. Asking for product testimonials

  D. Posting technical documentation

Answers to Practice Exam

1. Steps should be performed in this order: B, D, G, H, C, F, E (if needed), then A.

2. D. All three methods are effective methods for problem isolation. Depending on where the problem is, one method may be faster than the others, but all are effective.

3. A, B, C, D. These are the four characteristics that should be present in a good action plan.

4. A, B, C, D. Device passwords do not affect network problems, nor do they contribute to providing information on the state of the network.

5. C. The standard name is Novell 802.3; however, Cisco refers to it as Novell-Ether.

6. A, D. These frame types are identical—the term Novell uses is Ethernet II, while Cisco uses the term ARPA.

7. D.

8. C. Tokens contain control information about which station has the token as well as additional control information.

9. C, D, E, F, G. NetWare corresponds to the top five layers of the OSI model.

10. A, D. FDDI and Token Ring both use tokens to control transmission on the ring.

11. C. You will need to place the analyzer on the same segment as the one where the problem is occurring. If you connect remotely you will not be able to capture the data of interest. None of the other options are feasible or effective.

12. A. TDRs specialize in locating the fault, not just identifying it. Other cable testers cannot determine fault location. OTDRs must be used on optic cable.

13. A, B. Because POP3 uses TCP as its transport protocol, it is not a connectionless packet. No TCP options were specified in this packet.

14. A, B, D. An NMS may have the ability to maintain inventory information, but it is not one of the five necessary attributes.

15. B. Debug only sees packets that are process switched. Therefore, all other forms of switching must be disabled on the interface.

16. C. There are numerous reasons why the receiver can't transfer the packets fast enough; regardless of the reason, the condition causes an overrun.

17. A. If the transmitter attempts to transfer packets faster than the hardware buffer can send them to the transmitter, an underrun occurs.

18. D. These queues hold copies of packets before and after the RP has processed them.

19. A, C, D, E. MAC addresses cannot be used since the Layer 2 headers change at every hop. The switching type is not used.

20. B, C. The packet is a type 3, as indicated by the number next to the "Destination Unreachable."

21. A, B. The application sources the connection via 1038, but the destination port is the significant port—the host will listen for FTP on port 21.

22. A, B. Either of these items can cause the interface not to function.

23. A, B, C, D. All of these statements are true. There are one Ethernet interface and two Serial interfaces.

24. A, D. If the success rate was only 30 percent of the packets getting through, then 70 percent of the packets were dropped.

25. C. The output seen is from the show ip eigrp topology.

26. C. This output contains the IP configuration of the interface.

27. D. This command lists all IP protocols configured on the router.

28. B. All IP traffic statistics are displayed with this command.

29. B. The other commands are invalid commands.

30. B, C, D. These along with other statistics can be found via the `show frame-relay pvc` command.

31. B. The output is produced by the `debug` command.

32. A. This is the normal view of a serial interface, not the IP version.

33. B. X.25 is the encapsulation type for this serial interface.

34. C. Since LMI is part of Frame Relay, the correct syntax includes both.

35. D. q.931 is the Layer 3 protocol that is used from end to end. D shows the correct syntax.

36. A. PPP negotiation is an end-to-end protocol.

37. D. CHAP is an end-to-end negotiation and D shows the proper syntax.

38. A. q.921 is used between the TE and the LT/ET on Layer 2.

39. C. Along with `debug isdn q921`, this command can provide information regarding the connection between the TE and the LT/ET. The `debug` dialer only provides information on the local router.

40. C. The show ipx interface command produces the above output

41. B. `show ipx server` provides information regarding the servers and the network they reside on.

42. D. This output shows all protocols that are related to IPX.

43. A, B, C. This list permits certain services and denies all others.

44. C. This output shows information regarding the topology table for IPX-EIGRP.

45. D. This is the correct syntax for the command that produced the information.

46. A. show appletalk interface displays the AppleTalk configuration for the specified interface.

47. A, C. Events are considered to be interface transitions and neighbor transitions.

48. A, C, D. All these commands provide some information on Apple-Talk zones; however, the show appletalk zone command is the most comprehensive.

49. B. This is the correct syntax to enable ZIP debugging.

50. A, C. These, along with the CLI show commands, provide switch utilization.

51. B, C, D. Routing provides a hierarchy for switched networks. Routers also allow access lists to be applied to the interface.

52. B. The cam table holds the MAC addresses of all the workstations connected to the switch.

53. A, D, E. A switch may be a server, a client, and a transparent member of the VTP domain.

54. D. The recommended size is less than eight, therefore seven or fewer switches.

55. A, B, C. There are five members of the Cisco Connection Family; not all were listed here. Cisco Connection Documentation CD-ROM is part of the CCO member.

56. A, B. These are another two forms of obtaining a user account for CCO Web site, as discussed in this chapter.

57. C. There are other valid features that were not listed.

58. A, B. There are many features; only a few were listed.

59. A. The forum is where you receive answers to technical questions and search the database of past answers and questions.

Appendix B

Commands in This Study Guide

This appendix is a compilation of the "Commands Used in this Chapter" sections at the end of the chapters.

Command	Description	Chapter(s)
clear counters serial	Clears the statistical counters on the interface.	7
clear interface bri n	Resets the various counters that are available on the basic rate interface (BRI) and terminates a connection on the interface.	8
debug apple arp	Reports all real-time events that are related to the process of resolving Layer 3 addresses to Layer 2 devices.	10
debug apple errors	Reports AppleTalk errors, including incorrect encapsulation, invalid ping packets, NetInfoReply errors, configuration mismatch problems, and bad responder packet types.	10
debug apple events	Reports AppleTalk special events, including interfaces going up or down, and neighbor unreachability.	10
debug apple nbp	Confirms receipt of valid NBP updates.	10
debug apple packet	Reports all inbound and outbound AppleTalk datagrams at the router.	10
debug apple routing	Displays transaction information on all RTMP and AppleTalk EIGRP packets.	10
debug apple zip	Reports all ZIP packet information in real time for troubleshooting zone problems.	10
debug bri	Provides information regarding the B channels of the interface.	8
debug dialer	Provides information regarding the cause of a dialing connection and the status of the connection.	8
debug frame-relay events	Gives details about protocols and applications using the DLCI.	7

Command	Description	Chapter(s)
`debug frame-relay lmi`	Displays LMI exchange information. The exchange consists of LMI status enquiries and responses, including sequencing numbers.	7
`debug ip eigrp`	Causes a general debug to be performed on all EIGRP.	6
`debug ip eigrp <AS number>`	Debugs EIGRP for the specified AS.	6
`debug ip eigrp neighbor`	Debugs the transactions and exchanges among EIGRP neighbors.	6
`debug ip eigrp notifications`	Provides detailed information about neighbor notifications.	6
`debug ip eigrp summary`	Provides summarized information during a debug.	6
`debug ip igrp events`	Provides information regarding IGRP events (protocol-related).	6
`debug ip igrp transactions`	Provides more-detailed information regarding IGRP events (protocol-related).	6
`debug ip ospf adj`	Provides debug information about events concerning adjacency relationships with other OSPF routers.	6
`debug ip ospf events`	Provides debug information for all OSPF events.	6
`debug ip ospf flood`	Provides information about OSPF flooding. (Flooding is the way that OSPF router sends updates.) It broadcasts a change in its route table and all other members of the OSPF area receive the update.	6
`debug ip ospf lsa-generation`	Gives detailed information regarding the generation of LSA messages.	6
`debug ip ospf packet`	Gives detailed information regarding OSPF packets.	6

Command	Description	Chapter(s)
debug ip ospf retransmission	When OSPF has to retransmit information, this command triggers a retransmission event that debug captures and echoes to the console.	6
debug ip ospf spf	Provides debug information for all SPF transactions. By enabling SPF debugging, OSPF events debugging is also turned on.	6
debug ip ospf tree	Provides information for the OSPF database tree.	6
debug ip rip	Provides you with all possible RIP protocol information.	6
debug ip rip events	Provides output regarding RIP protocol events.	6
debug ipx ipxwan	Produces information during state changes and the start-up of serial interfaces configured for IPXWAN.	9
debug ipx packet	Displays all IPX traffic that enters or leaves the router.	9
debug ipx routing	Reports all IPX routing processes at the router, including IPX RIP, IPX EIGRP, and NLSP.	9
debug ipx sap activity	Provides an administrator with additional information and possible indications of problem causes.	9
debug ipx sap events	Displays events as interesting, and the events keyword limits the output of information.	9
debug isdn q921	Gives details regarding the Layer 2 connection sequence for ISDN.	8
debug isdn q931	Gives details regarding the Layer 3 connection sequence for ISDN.	8
debug lapb	Contains information regarding all packets and traffic that use LAPB encapsulation.	7

Command	Description	Chapter(s)
`debug ppp authentication`	Gives details regarding the PPP/CHAP authentication connection sequence.	8
`debug ppp negotiation`	Provides real-time information about the establishment of a session.	8
`debug ppp packet`	Reports real-time PPP packet flow, including the type of packet and the specific B channel used.	8
`debug serial interface`	Displays signaling information for the interface.	7
`debug serial packet`	Displays information regarding serial packets.	7
`debug snmp packets`	Provides detail for snmp packets destined for the router.	3
`debug span`	Debugs spanning tree.	11
`debug vlan packet`	Debugs VLAN packets.	11
`debug x25 events`	Displays X.25 events in detail.	7
`exception dump`	Configures the router to perform a core dump via TFTP or FTP if and when the router crashes.	4
`ipconfig /all`	(Windows 98 command) Provides interface configuration for the host.	6
`nbp confirm appletalk-address [:skt] object: type@zone`	Verifies the AppleTalk address against its name and zone information.	10
`nbp lookup object:type@zone`	Provides the AppleTalk address of a known NBP service.	10
`nbp parameters`	Permits control over retransmissions, replies, and intervals used by the other NBP `test` commands.	10
`NBP Poll`	Searches for all devices in all zones.	10
`ping`	Initiates an ICMP echo request. There are two levels, User and Privileged. The IP protocol is used.	4, 5, 6, 8

Command	Description	Chapter(s)
`ping appletalk`	Initiates an AppleTalk ping. There are two levels, User and Privileged.	4, 10
`ping ipx`	Initiates an IPX ping. There are two levels, User and Privileged.	4, 9
`show access-list`	Displays the specified access list from the configuration.	4
`show appletalk access-lists`	Displays the AppleTalk access lists.	10
`show appletalk adjacent-routes`	Shows connected and one-hop-away routes that are known to the router.	10
`show appletalk arp`	Displays the ARP cache of the router for all AppleTalk addresses.	10
`show appletalk globals`	Provides information about phase one compatibility, ZIP, RTMP, AARP, and DDP functions. In addition, displays routing information.	10
`show appletalk interface`	Shows the AppleTalk settings for the interface.	10
`show appletalk name-cache`	Cache displays a list of NBP services from other AppleTalk routers and devices that support NBP.	10
`show appletalk nbp`	Displays a list of NBP services from other AppleTalk routers and devices that support NBP.	10
`show appletalk neighbors`	Provides information about the AppleTalk address, the routing protocol that connects the two routers, and the local interface.	10
`show appletalk route`	Provides a summary of all known routes and the protocol that distributed them.	10
`show appletalk traffic`	Summarizes all AppleTalk traffic that enters or leaves the router, including erred packets, routing counters, and broadcast information.	10

Command	Description	Chapter(s)
show appletalk zone	Displays the zone names and networks that are known to the router through ZIP updates.	10
show arp	Displays the contents of the ARP table as well as status.	4, 5
show arp	Displays the ARP information for the router.	11
show bridge {vlan number}	Shows which bridging encapsulations are enabled.	11
show buffers	Displays buffer statistics for the router.	4, 7
show cam	Reports the MAC address associated with the ports of the switch. These addresses are stored in the CAM table; this command accesses that table.	11
show cdp	Displays the Cisco neighbors.	11
show config	Similar to the show running-config command on Cisco routers. Provides all configuration settings on the switch for all modules, with a few exceptions for certain modules such as the RSM (Route Switch Module).	11
show controller bri	Displays the interface status and the superframe error counter.	8
show controllers cbus	Displays the buffer information on line cards connected to the cbus.	4
show controllers serial	Shows specific hardware information regarding the serial controller.	7
show dhcp servers	Shows information regarding the DHCP servers.	6
show dialer	Reports information regarding the DDR connections, including the number dialed, the success of the connection, the idle timers that control the duration of a DDR connection without data packets, and the number of calls that were screened or rejected due to administrative policy.	8

Command	Description	Chapter(s)
show flash	Displays the contents of the system flash, such as the IOS™ and any other files that may be present.	5, 11
show frame-relay lmi	Displays LMI-relevant information. The output contains the LMI type, enquiry, update, and status information.	7
show frame-relay map	Contains information about the DLCI numbers and the encapsulation of all Frame Relay interfaces. The status of the interface is indicated with the up or down state found within the parentheses.	7
show frame-relay pvc	Contains the LMI status of every DLCI on the router, or you may be more specific and check only certain PVCs.	7
show interface	Lists the configuration details, status, and statistics for the interface.	4, 5, 11
show interface accounting	Displays statistical information. regarding protocols on the interface.	4
show interface bri *n*	Reports the B channel's status, as well as spoofing on the interface.	8
show interface bri *n* 1 2	Displays a single B channel of the BRI interface.	8
show interface serial	The show interface command executed on a serial interface. Provides important information regarding serial interfaces, including IP, encapsulation, and line statistics.	7
show ip access-list	Displays information regarding access lists within the IP value range.	6
show ip arp	Provides information contained in the router's ARP cache.	6
show ip eigrp events	Displays a log of the most recent EIGRP protocol events. This information includes the insertion and removal of routes from the route table, updates, and neighbor status.	6

Command	Description	Chapter(s)
`show ip eigrp interfaces`	Displays EIGRP peer information for that interface.	6
`show ip eigrp neighbors`	Displays all EIGRP neighbors, along with summary information about each neighbor.	6
`show ip eigrp topology`	Displays the contents of the EIGRP topology table.	6
`show ip eigrp traffic`	Displays a summary of EIGRP routing statistics, such as the number of Hellos and routing updates.	6
`show ip interface`	Displays the interface's status as well as the IP configuration and settings for the interface.	6
`show ip ospf`	Displays information for OSPF.	6
`show ip ospf <process-id>`	Process ID number. Displays information relevant to the specified process ID.	6
`show ip ospf border-routers`	Displays the routers that join different areas, or border routers.	6
`show ip ospf database`	Provides an OSPF database summary.	6
`show ip ospf interface`	Displays OSPF information on a interface.	6
`show ip ospf neighbor`	Displays OSPF neighbor information.	6
`show ip ospf request-list`	Displays link-state request list.	6
`show ip ospf retransmission list`	Displays link-state retransmission list.	6
`show ip ospf summary-address`	Displays summary-address redistribution information.	6
`show ip ospf virtual-links`	Displays virtual link information.	6
`show ip protocols`	Provides information about the IP routing protocols that run on the router.	6
show ip route	Displays the contents of the IP route table as well as the default gateway for the router.	5, 6

Command	Description	Chapter(s)
`show ip route eigrp`	Displays the EIGRP routes.	6
`show ip route igrp`	Displays IGRP routes only.	6
`show ip route ospf`	Displays OSPF routes.	6
`show ip route rip`	Displays the RIP route table.	6
`show ip traffic`	Returns information pertaining to IP traffic statistics.	6
`show ipx eigrp neighbors`	Provides detailed IPX EIGRP neighbor information.	9
`show ipx eigrp topology`	Displays multiple paths to IPX EIGRP learned routes.	9
`show ipx interface`	Provides information on all IPX-configured interfaces.	9
`show ipx nlsp database`	Reports significant information, including the last sequence number, the checksum, and the LSP holdtime.	9
`show ipx nlsp neighbors`	Displays all NLSP neighbors.	9
`show ipx route`	Displays the state of the NetWare network, and it should be used to confirm that a path exists to the desired resource. The output reports connected IPX RIP, NLSP and IPX EIGRP routes, in addition to IPXWAN and static routes.	9
`show ipx servers`	Displays all servers known to the router through SAP advertisements.	9
`show ipx traffic`	Reports information about the IPX packets transmitted and received. This breakdown includes information regarding IPX SAPs and watchdog packets, as well as IPX RIP, IPX EIGRP, and NLSP routing packets.	9
`show isdn status`	Reports the status of the interface, as well as a breakdown of each layer.	8

Command	Description	Chapter(s)
show log	Reports significant events, including reboots of all modules, traps, and power supply failures.	11
show logging	Displays logs for the router including traps and system errors. Can also provide logs when logging access lists.	4
show mac	Maintains numerous counters in normal operation, including the frame traffic per port; the total number of incoming frames, including discards; and the total number of transmits and aborts due to excessive deferral or MTU violations. Broadcast counters are also maintained in addition to discards due to EARL page full errors.	11
show memory	Displays the statistics and status of the router's memory.	4
show port	Provides information about specific ports or all ports on a module. VLAN membership, port speed and configuration, and error statistics are available.	11
show ppp multilink	Displays configuration settings for PPP Multilink.	8
show processes cpu	Displays the router's processes and the percentage of CPU utilization over 5 seconds, 1 minute, and 5 minutes.	4
show processes memory	Displays the router's processes and the amount of memory allocated to each.	4
show queue	Displays interface-specific queuing information.	4
show queueing	Displays the configuration of queuing on the router.	4
show running-config	Displays the contents of the running configuration of the router.	4, 5, 6

Command	Description	Chapter(s)
show span	Shows spanning tree information from the router. Very different from a show span on a switch.	11
show spantree	Reports the status of the spanning tree process for each VLAN, when spanning-tree has been enabled on the switch.	11
show stacks	Displays the router's stack information.	4
show startup-config	Displays the configuration version that is saved in NVRAM.	4
show system	Provides high-level summary information regarding the switch, including the status of power supplies, uptime and administrative settings, as well as the percentage of traffic on the backplane.	11
show tech-support	A comprehensive command that includes show running-config, show version, show stacks, show processes cpu, and show processes memory, along with many others.	4, 12
show test	The status of the switch, including interface cards, power supplies, and available memory.	11
show version	Displays the version of IOS, the reason for last reload, and the router's hardware configuration.	4, 5, 11
show vlans	Provides VLAN information and status from the router.	11

Command	Description	Chapter(s)
show vtp domain	Provides status information for the VTP domain configured on the switch. Note that VTP updates are sent over VLAN 1 when troubleshooting.	11
terminal monitor	Enables the router to echo console message to the active TTY port. This facilitates the debug tool.	4
terminal no monitor	Disables the echo.	4
test appletalk	Enables the testing mode for AppleTalk.	10
traceroute	Performs a hop-by-hop ICMP trace. This command has two levels, User and Privileged.	4, 6
tracert	The trace command used in the Windows operating system. Provides a step-by-step ICMP trace from source to destination.	5
un all	Turns off all possible debugging.	4
write core	Initiates a core dump to the specified host.	4

Glossary

10BaseT Part of the original IEEE 802.3 standard, 10BaseT is the Ethernet specification of 10Mbps baseband that uses two pairs of twisted-pair, Category 3, 4, or 5 cabling—using one pair to send data and the other to receive. 10BaseT has a distance limit of about 100 meters per segment. *See also: Ethernet* and *IEEE 802.3.*

100BaseT Based on the IEEE 802.3u standard, 100BaseT is the Fast Ethernet specification of 100Mbps baseband that uses UTP wiring. 100BaseT sends link pulses (containing more information than those used in 10BaseT) over the network when no traffic is present. *See also: 10BaseT, Fast Ethernet,* and *IEEE 802.3.*

100BaseTX Based on the IEEE 802.3u standard, 100BaseTX is the 100Mbps baseband Fast Ethernet specification that uses two pairs of UTP or STP wiring. The first pair of wires receives data; the second pair sends data. To ensure correct signal timing, a 100BaseTX segment cannot be longer than 100 meters.

802.1q *See: IEEE 802.1*

A&B bit signaling Used in T1 transmission facilities and sometimes called "24th channel signaling." Each of the 24 T1 subchannels in this procedure uses one bit of every sixth frame to send supervisory signaling information.

AAL ATM Adaptation Layer: A service-dependent sublayer of the Data-Link layer which accepts data from other applications and brings it to the ATM layer in 48-byte ATM payload segments. CS and SAR are the two sublayers that form AALs. Currently, the four types of AAL recommended by the ITU-T are AAL1, AAL2, AAL3/4, and AAL5. AALs are differentiated by the source-destination timing they use, whether they are CBR or VBR, and whether they are used for connection-oriented or connectionless mode data transmission. *See also: AAL1, AAL2, AAL3/4, AAL5, ATM,* and *ATM layer.*

AAL1 ATM Adaptation Layer 1: One of four AALs recommended by the ITU-T, it is used for connection-oriented, time-sensitive services that need constant bit rates, such as isochronous traffic and uncompressed video. *See also: AAL.*

AAL2 ATM Adaptation Layer 2: One of four AALs recommended by the ITU-T, it is used for connection-oriented services that support a variable bit rate, such as voice traffic. *See also: AAL.*

AAL3/4 ATM Adaptation Layer 3/4: One of four AALs (a product of two initially distinct layers) recommended by the ITU-T, supporting both connectionless and connection-oriented links. Its primary use is in sending SMDS packets over ATM networks. *See also: AAL.*

AAL5 ATM Adaptation Layer 5: One of four AALs recommended by the ITU-T, it is used to support connection-oriented VBR services primarily to transfer classical IP over ATM and LANE traffic. This least complex of the AAL recommendations uses SEAL, offering lower bandwidth costs and simpler processing requirements but also providing reduced bandwidth and error-recovery capacities. *See also: AAL.*

AARP AppleTalk Address Resolution Protocol: The protocol in an AppleTalk stack that maps data-link addresses to network addresses.

AARP probe packets Packets sent by the AARP to determine whether a given node ID is being used by another node in a nonextended AppleTalk network. If the node ID is not in use, the sending node appropriates that node's ID. If the node ID is in use, the sending node will select a different ID and then send out more AARP probe packets. *See also: AARP.*

ABM Asynchronous Balanced Mode: When two stations can initiate a transmission, ABM is an HDLC (or one of its derived protocols) communication technology that supports peer-oriented, point-to-point communications between both stations.

ABR Area Border Router: An OSPF router that is located on the border of one or more OSPF areas. ABRs are used to connect OSPF areas to the OSPF backbone area.

access layer One of the layers in Cisco's three-layer hierarchical model. The access layer provides users with access to the internetwork.

access link Is a link used with switches and is only part of one Virtual LAN (VLAN). Trunk links carry information from multiple VLANs.

access list A set of test conditions kept by routers that determines "interesting traffic" to and from the router for various services on the network.

access method The manner in which network devices approach gaining access to the network itself.

access server Also known as a "network access server," it is a communications process connecting asynchronous devices to a LAN or WAN through network and terminal emulation software, providing synchronous or asynchronous routing of supported protocols.

acknowledgment Verification sent from one network device to another signifying that an event has occurred. May be abbreviated as ACK. *Contrast with: NAK.*

ACR allowed cell rate: A designation defined by the ATM Forum for managing ATM traffic. Dynamically controlled using congestion control measures, the ACR varies between the minimum cell rate (MCR) and the peak cell rate (PCR). *See also: MCR and PCR.*

action plan A list of steps or procedures used to resolve a network problem. This plan should possess four characteristics: make one change at a time, make non-impacting changes, do not compromise security, and have a procedure to back out of any changes made.

active monitor The mechanism used to manage a Token Ring. The network node with the highest MAC address on the ring becomes the active monitor and is responsible for management tasks such as preventing loops and ensuring tokens are not lost.

address learning Used with transparent bridges to learn the hardware addresses of all devices on an internetwork. The switch then filters the network with the known hardware (MAC) addresses.

address mapping By translating network addresses from one format to another, this methodology permits different protocols to operate interchangeably.

address mask A bit combination descriptor identifying which portion of an address refers to the network or subnet and which part refers to the host. Sometimes simply called the mask. *See also: subnet mask.*

address resolution The process used for resolving differences between computer addressing schemes. Address resolution typically defines a method for tracing Network layer (Layer 3) addresses to Data-Link layer (Layer 2) addresses. *See also: address mapping.*

adjacency The relationship made between defined neighboring routers and end nodes, using a common media segment, to exchange routing information.

adjacency table The adjacency table is a table that contains all active/existing adjacencies of neighboring routers.

administrative distance A number between 0 and 225 that expresses the value of trustworthiness of a routing information source. The lower the number, the higher the integrity rating.

administrative weight A value designated by a network administrator to rate the preference given to a network link. It is one of four link metrics exchanged by PTSPs to test ATM network resource availability.

ADSU ATM Data Service Unit: The terminal adapter used to connect to an ATM network through an HSSI-compatible mechanism. *See also: DSU.*

advertising The process whereby routing or service updates are transmitted at given intervals, allowing other routers on the network to maintain a record of viable routes.

AEP AppleTalk Echo Protocol: A test for connectivity between two AppleTalk nodes where one node sends a packet to another and receives an echo, or copy, in response.

AFI Authority and Format Identifier: The part of an NSAP ATM address that delineates the type and format of the IDI section of an ATM address.

AFP AppleTalk Filing Protocol: A Presentation-layer protocol, supporting AppleShare and Mac OS File Sharing, that permits users to share files and applications on a server.

AIP ATM Interface Processor: Supporting AAL3/4 and AAL5, this interface for Cisco 7000 series routers minimizes performance bottlenecks at the UNI. *See also: AAL3/4 and AAL5.*

algorithm   A set of rules or process used to solve a problem. In networking, algorithms are typically used for finding the best route for traffic from a source to its destination.

alignment error   An error occurring in Ethernet networks, in which a received frame has extra bits; that is, a number not divisible by eight. Alignment errors are generally the result of frame damage caused by collisions.

all-routes explorer packet   An explorer packet that can move across an entire SRB network, tracing all possible paths to a given destination. Also known as an all-rings explorer packet. *See also: explorer packet, local explorer packet,* and *spanning explorer packet.*

AM   Amplitude Modulation: A modulation method that represents information by varying the amplitude of the carrier signal. *See also: modulation.*

AMI   Alternate Mark Inversion: A line-code type on T1 and E1 circuits that shows zeros as "01" during each bit cell, and ones as "11" or "00," alternately, during each bit cell. The sending device must maintain ones density in AMI but not independently of the data stream. Also known as binary-coded, alternate mark inversion. *Contrast with: B8ZS. See also: ones density.*

amplitude   An analog or digital waveform's highest value.

analog transmission   Signal messaging whereby information is represented by various combinations of signal amplitude, frequency, and phase.

ANSI   American National Standards Institute: The organization of corporate, government, and other volunteer members that coordinates standards-related activities, approves U.S. national standards, and develops U.S. positions in international standards organizations. ANSI assists in the creation of international and U.S. standards in disciplines such as communications, networking, and a variety of technical fields. It publishes over 13,000 standards, for engineered products and technologies ranging from screw threads to networking protocols. ANSI is a member of the IEC and ISO.

anycast   An ATM address that can be shared by more than one end system, allowing requests to be routed to a node that provides a particular service.

AppleTalk   Currently in two versions, the group of communication protocols designed by Apple Computer for use in Macintosh environments. The earlier Phase 1 protocols support one physical network with only one network number that resides in one zone. The later Phase 2 protocols support more than one logical network on a single physical network, allowing networks to exist in more than one zone. *See also: zone, AARP (AppleTalk Address Resolution Protocol).*

Application layer   Layer 7 of the OSI reference network model, supplying services to application procedures (such as electronic mail or file transfer) that are outside the OSI model. This layer chooses and determines the availability of communicating partners along with the resources necessary to make the connection, coordinates partnering applications, and forms a consensus on procedures for controlling data integrity and error recovery.

ARA   AppleTalk Remote Access: A protocol for Macintosh users establishing their access to resources and data from a remote AppleTalk location.

area   A logical, rather than physical, set of segments (based on either CLNS, DECnet, or OSPF) along with their attached devices. Areas are commonly connected to others using routers to create a single autonomous system. *See also: autonomous system.*

ARM   Asynchronous Response Mode: An HDLC communication mode using one primary station and at least one additional station, in which transmission can be initiated from either the primary or one of the secondary units.

ARP   Address Resolution Protocol: Defined in RFC 826, the protocol that traces IP addresses to MAC addresses. *See also: RARP.*

ASBR   Autonomous System Boundary Router: An area border router placed between an OSPF autonomous system and a non-OSPF network that operates both OSPF and an additional routing protocol, such as RIP. ASBRs must be located in a non-stub OSPF area. *See also: ABR, non-stub area,* and *OSPF.*

ASCII American Standard Code for Information Interchange: An 8-bit code for representing characters, consisting of seven data bits plus one parity bit.

ASICs Application-Specific Integrated Circuits: Used in Layer-2 switches to make filtering decisions. The ASIC looks in the filter table of MAC addresses and determines which port the destination hardware address of a received hardware address is destined for. The frame will be allowed to traverse only that one segment. If the hardware address is unknown, the frame is forwarded out all ports.

ASN.1 Abstract Syntax Notation One: An OSI language used to describe types of data that is independent of computer structures and depicting methods. Described by ISO International Standard 8824.

ASP AppleTalk Session Protocol: A protocol employing ATP to establish, maintain, and tear down sessions, as well as sequence requests. *See also: ATP.*

AST Automatic Spanning Tree: A function that supplies one path for spanning explorer frames traveling from one node in the network to another, supporting the automatic resolution of spanning trees in SRB networks. AST is based on the IEEE 802.1 standard. *See also: IEEE 802.1 and SRB.*

asynchronous transmission Digital signals sent without precise timing, usually with different frequencies and phase relationships. Asynchronous transmissions generally enclose individual characters in control bits (called start and stop bits) that show the beginning and end of each character. *Contrast with: isochronous transmission and synchronous transmission.*

ATCP AppleTalk Control Program: The protocol for establishing and configuring AppleTalk over PPP, defined in RFC 1378. *See also: PPP.*

ATDM Asynchronous Time-Division Multiplexing: A technique for sending information, it differs from normal TDM in that the time slots are assigned when necessary rather than preassigned to certain transmitters. *Contrast with: FDM, statistical multiplexing, and TDM.*

ATG Address Translation Gateway: The mechanism within Cisco DECnet routing software that enables routers to route multiple, independent DECnet networks and to establish a user-designated address translation for chosen nodes between networks.

ATM Asynchronous Transfer Mode: The international standard, identified by fixed-length 53-byte cells, for transmitting cells in multiple service systems, such as voice, video, or data. Transit delays are reduced because the fixed-length cells permit processing to occur in the hardware. ATM is designed to maximize the benefits of high-speed transmission media, such as SONET, E3, and T3.

ATM ARP server A device that supplies logical subnets running classical IP over ATM with address-resolution services.

ATM endpoint The initiating or terminating connection in an ATM network. ATM endpoints include servers, workstations, ATM-to-LAN switches, and ATM routers.

ATM Forum The international organization founded jointly by Northern Telecom, Sprint, Cisco Systems, and NET/ADAPTIVE in 1991 to develop and promote standards-based implementation agreements for ATM technology. The ATM Forum broadens official standards developed by ANSI and ITU-T and creates implementation agreements before official standards are published.

ATM layer A sublayer of the Data-Link layer in an ATM network that is service independent. To create standard 53-byte ATM cells, the ATM layer receives 48-byte segments from the AAL and attaches a 5-byte header to each. These cells are then sent to the Physical layer for transmission across the physical medium. *See also: AAL.*

ATMM ATM Management: A procedure that runs on ATM switches, managing rate enforcement and VCI translation. *See also: ATM.*

ATM user-user connection A connection made by the ATM layer to supply communication between at least two ATM service users, such as ATMM processes. These communications can be uni- or bidirectional, using one or two VCCs, respectively. *See also: ATM layer and ATMM.*

ATP AppleTalk Transaction Protocol: A transport-level protocol that enables reliable transactions between two sockets, where one requests the other to perform a given task and to report the results. ATP fastens the request and response together, assuring a loss-free exchange of request-response pairs.

attenuation   In communication, weakening or loss of signal energy, typically caused by distance.

AURP   AppleTalk Update-based Routing Protocol: A technique for encapsulating AppleTalk traffic in the header of a foreign protocol that allows the connection of at least two noncontiguous AppleTalk internetworks through a foreign network (such as TCP/IP) to create an AppleTalk WAN. The connection made is called an AURP tunnel. By exchanging routing information between exterior routers, the AURP maintains routing tables for the complete AppleTalk WAN. *See also: AURP tunnel.*

AURP tunnel   A connection made in an AURP WAN that acts as a single, virtual link between AppleTalk internetworks separated physically by a foreign network such as a TCP/IP network. *See also: AURP.*

authority zone   A portion of the domain-name tree associated with DNS for which one name server is the authority. *See also: DNS.*

auto duplex   A setting on Layer-1 and -2 devices that sets the duplex of a switch or hub port automatically.

automatic call reconnect   A function that enables automatic call rerouting away from a failed trunk line.

autonomous confederation   A collection of self-governed systems that depend more on their own network accessibility and routing information than on information received from other systems or groups.

autonomous switching   The ability of Cisco routers to process packets more quickly by using the cisco-Bus to switch packets independently of the system processor.

autonomous system (AS)   A group of networks under mutual administration that share the same routing methodology. Autonomous systems are subdivided by areas and must be assigned an individual 16-bit number by the IANA. *See also: area.*

autoreconfiguration   A procedure executed by nodes within the failure domain of a Token Ring, wherein nodes automatically perform diagnostics, trying to reconfigure the network around failed areas.

auxiliary port   The console port on the back of Cisco routers that allows you to dial the router and make console configuration settings.

B8ZS   Binary 8-Zero Substitution: A line-code type, interpreted at the remote end of the connection, that uses a special code substitution whenever eight consecutive zeros are transmitted over the link on T1 and E1 circuits. This technique assures ones density independent of the data stream. Also known as bipolar 8-zero substitution. *Contrast with: AMI. See also: ones density.*

backbone   The basic portion of the network that provides the primary path for traffic sent to and initiated from other networks.

back end   A node or software program supplying services to a front end. *See also: server.*

bandwidth   The gap between the highest and lowest frequencies employed by network signals. More commonly, it refers to the rated throughput capacity of a network protocol or medium.

baseband   A feature of a network technology that uses only one carrier frequency, for example Ethernet. Also named "narrowband." *Compare with: broadband.*

baseline   Baseline information includes historical data about the network and routine utilization information. This information can be used to determine whether there were recent changes made to the network that may contribute to the problem at hand.

Basic Management Setup   Used with Cisco routers when in setup mode. Only provides enough management and configuration to get the router working so someone can telnet into the router and configure it.

baud   Synonymous with bits per second (bps), if each signal element represents one bit. It is a unit of signaling speed equivalent to the number of separate signal elements transmitted per second.

B channel   Bearer channel: A full-duplex, 64Kbps channel in ISDN that transmits user data. *Compare with: D channel, E channel, and H channel.*

beacon An FDDI device or Token Ring frame that points to a serious problem with the ring, such as a broken cable. The beacon frame carries the address of the station thought to be down. *See also: failure domain.*

BECN Backward Explicit Congestion Notification: BECN is the bit set by a Frame Relay network in frames moving away from frames headed into a congested path. A DTE that receives frames with the BECN may ask higher-level protocols to take necessary flow-control measures. *Compare with: FECN.*

BGP4 Border Gateway Protocol Version 4: Version 4 of the interdomain routing protocol most commonly used on the Internet. BGP4 supports CIDR and uses route-counting mechanisms to decrease the size of routing tables. *See also: CIDR.*

binary A two-character numbering method that uses ones and zeros. The binary numbering system underlies all digital representation of information.

BIP Bit Interleaved Parity: A method used in ATM to monitor errors on a link, sending a check bit or word in the link overhead for the previous block or frame. This allows bit errors in transmissions to be found and delivered as maintenance information.

BISDN Broadband ISDN: ITU-T standards created to manage high-bandwidth technologies such as video. BISDN presently employs ATM technology along SONET-based transmission circuits, supplying data rates between 155Mbps and 622Mbps and beyond. Contrast with N-ISDN. *See also: BRI, ISDN, and PRI.*

bit-oriented protocol Regardless of frame content, the class of Data-Link layer communication protocols that transmits frames. Bit-oriented protocols, as compared with byte-oriented, supply more efficient and trustworthy, full-duplex operation. *Compare with: byte-oriented protocol.*

Boot ROM Used in routers to put the router into bootstrap mode. Bootstrap mode then boots the device with an operating system. The ROM can also hold a small Cisco IOS.

bootstrap protocol A protocol used to dynamically assign IP address and gateway to requesting clients.

border gateway A router that facilitates communication with routers in different autonomous systems.

boundary of dysfuntionality The limit or scope of the network problem. This boundary lies between areas where the network is functioning properly and where it ceases to function.

BPDU Bridge Protocol Data Unit: A Spanning-Tree Protocol initializing packet that is sent at definable intervals for the purpose of exchanging information among bridges in networks.

breakout boxes These items are used to verify pin-outs (e.g., TD—transmit data, RD—receive data, CTS—clear to send) for all types of serial and parallel connections.

BRI Basic Rate Interface: The ISDN interface that facilitates circuit-switched communication between video, data, and voice; it is made up of two B channels (64Kbps each) and one D channel (16Kbps). *Compare with: PRI. See also: BISDN.*

bridge A device for connecting two segments of a network and transmitting packets between them. Both segments must use identical protocols to communicate. Bridges function at the Data-Link layer, Layer 2 of the OSI reference model. The purpose of a bridge is to filter, send, or flood any incoming frame, based on the MAC address of that particular frame.

broadband A transmission methodology for multiplexing several independent signals onto one cable. In telecommunications, broadband is classified as any channel with bandwidth greater than 4kHz (typical voice grade). In LAN terminology, it is classified as a coaxial cable on which analog signaling is employed. Also known as wideband. *Contrast with: baseband.*

broadcast A data frame or packet that is transmitted to every node on the local network segment (as defined by the broadcast domain). Broadcasts are known by their broadcast address, which is a destination network and host address with all the bits turned on. Also called "local broadcast." *Compare with: directed broadcast.*

broadcast domain A group of devices receiving broadcast frames initiating from any device within the group. Because they do not forward broadcast frames, broadcast domains are generally surrounded by routers.

broadcast storm An undesired event on the network caused by the simultaneous transmission of any number of broadcasts across the network segment. Such an occurrence can overwhelm network bandwidth, resulting in time-outs.

buffer A storage area dedicated to handling data while in transit. Buffers are used to receive/store sporadic deliveries of data bursts, usually received from faster devices, compensating for the variations in processing speed. Incoming information is stored until everything is received prior to sending data on. Also known as an information buffer.

bus topology A linear LAN architecture in which transmissions from various stations on the network are reproduced over the length of the medium and are accepted by all other stations. *Compare with: ring* and *star.*

bus Any physical path, typically wires or copper, through which a digital signal can be used to send data from one part of a computer to another.

BUS broadcast and unknown servers: In LAN emulation, the hardware or software responsible for resolving all broadcasts and packets with unknown (unregistered) addresses into the point-to-point virtual circuits required by ATM. *See also: LANE, LEC, LECS,* and *LES.*

BX.25 AT&T's use of X.25. *See also: X.25.*

bypass mode An FDDI and Token Ring network operation that deletes an interface.

bypass relay A device that enables a particular interface in the Token Ring to be closed down and effectively taken off the ring.

byte-oriented protocol Any type of data-link communication protocol that, in order to mark the boundaries of frames, uses a specific character from the user character set. These protocols have generally been superseded by bit-oriented protocols. *Compare with: bit-oriented protocol.*

cable range In an extended AppleTalk network, the range of numbers allotted for use by existing nodes on the network. The value of the cable range can be anywhere from a single to a sequence of several touching network numbers. Node addresses are determined by their cable range value.

cable testers This is a family of apparatus that are used to verify media integrity and connectivity. Several different devices can be considered cable testers

CAC Connection Admission Control: The sequence of actions executed by every ATM switch while connection setup is performed in order to determine if a request for connection is violating the guarantees of QoS for established connections. Also, CAC is used to route a connection request through an ATM network.

call admission control A device for managing of traffic in ATM networks, determining the possibility of a path containing adequate bandwidth for a requested VCC.

call priority In circuit-switched systems, the defining priority given to each originating port; it specifies in which order calls will be reconnected. Additionally, call priority identifies which calls are allowed during a bandwidth reservation.

call set-up time The length of time necessary to effect a switched call between DTE devices.

CBR Constant Bit Rate: An ATM Forum QoS class created for use in ATM networks. CBR is used for connections that rely on precision clocking to guarantee trustworthy delivery. *Compare with: ABR* and *VBR.*

CCO Cisco Connection Online: The *Cisco Web site,* CCO, is the repository for information regarding Cisco products, networking technology, configuration examples, troubleshooting tools, and network planning. CCO has two access levels. The first is guest privilege, which does not require a login account. This level provides general product and company information. The second level is for registered Cisco users who have purchased a Cisco support contract, or are sponsored by a Cisco Authorized Partner. This level provides all information available to the guest level, in-depth detailed technical documentation, access to download Cisco IOS images, trouble ticket queries, and so on.

CD Carrier Detect: A signal indicating that an interface is active or that a connection generated by a modem has been established.

CDP Cisco Discovery Protocol: Cisco's proprietary protocol that is used to tell a neighbor Cisco device about the type of hardware, software version, and active interfaces that the Cisco device is using. It uses a SNAP frame between devices and is not routable.

CDVT Cell Delay Variation Tolerance: A QoS parameter for traffic management in ATM networks specified when a connection is established. The allowable fluctuation levels for data samples taken by the PCR in CBR transmissions are determined by the CDVT. *See also: CBR and PCR.*

cell In ATM networking, the basic unit of data for switching and multiplexing. Cells have a defined length of 53 bytes, including a 5-byte header that identifies the cell's data stream and 48 bytes of payload. *See also: cell relay.*

cell payload scrambling The method by which an ATM switch maintains framing on some medium-speed edge and trunk interfaces (T3 or E3 circuits). Cell payload scrambling rearranges the data portion of a cell to maintain the line synchronization with certain common bit patterns.

cell relay A technology that uses small packets of fixed size, known as cells. Their fixed length enables cells to be processed and switched in hardware at high speeds, making this technology the foundation for ATM and other high-speed network protocols. *See also: cell.*

Centrex A local exchange carrier service, providing local switching that resembles that of an on-site PBX. Centrex has no on-site switching capability. Therefore, all customer connections return to the CO. *See also: CO.*

CER Cell Error Ratio: The ratio in ATM of transmitted cells having errors to the total number of cells sent in a transmission within a certain span of time.

channelized E1 Operating at 2.048Mpbs, an access link that is sectioned into 29 B-channels and one D-channel, supporting DDR, Frame Relay, and X.25. *Compare with: channelized T1.*

channelized T1 Operating at 1.544Mbps, an access link that is sectioned into 23 B-channels and 1 D-channel of 64Kbps each, where individual channels

or groups of channels connect to various destinations, supporting DDR, Frame Relay, and X.25. *Compare with: channelized E1.*

CHAP Challenge Handshake Authentication Protocol: Supported on lines using PPP encapsulation, it is a security feature that identifies the remote end, helping keep out unauthorized users. After CHAP is performed, the router or access server determines whether a given user is permitted access. It is a newer, more secure protocol than PAP. *Compare with: PAP.*

checksum A test for ensuring the integrity of sent data. It is a number calculated from a series of values taken through a sequence of mathematical functions, typically placed at the end of the data from which it is calculated, and then recalculated at the receiving end for verification. *Compare with: CRC.*

choke packet When congestion exists, it is a packet sent to inform a transmitter that it should decrease its sending rate.

CIDR Classless Interdomain Routing: A method supported by classless routing protocols, such as OSPF and BGP4, based on the concept of ignoring the IP class of address, permitting route aggregation and VLSM that enable routers to combine routes in order to minimize the routing information that needs to be conveyed by the primary routers. It allows a group of IP networks to appear to other networks as a unified, larger entity. In CIDR, IP addresses and their subnet masks are written as four dotted octets, followed by a forward slash and the numbering of masking bits (a form of subnet notation shorthand). *See also: BGP4.*

CIP Channel Interface Processor: A channel attachment interface for use in Cisco 7000 series routers that connects a host mainframe to a control unit. This device eliminates the need for an FBP to attach channels.

CIR Committed Information Rate: Averaged over a minimum span of time and measured in bps, a Frame Relay network's agreed-upon minimum rate of transferring information.

circuit switching Used with dial-up networks such as PPP and ISDN. Passes data, but needs to set up the connection first—just like making a phone call.

Cisco Connection Documentation CD-ROM The CD is the collection of technical documentation, available on CCO as well as the Documentation CD, which accompanies new Cisco equipment purchases. Both forms of the technical documentation are very helpful for providing critical information regarding Cisco products, networking technologies, and configuration examples.

Cisco Connection Family The Cisco Connection Family is a collection of interactive electronic media that is intended to provide technical assistance and support for Cisco products and networking technologies. There are five members of the Cisco Connection family: Cisco Connection Online (CCO), Cisco Technical Assistance and Software Center, Cisco Connection Consultant Tools CD-ROM, Cisco Commerce Agents, and Cisco MarketPlace.

Cisco Express Fowarding Cisco Express Forwarding (CEF) is a switching function, designed for high-end backbone routers. It functions on Layer 3 of the OSI model, and its biggest asset is the capability to remain stable in a large network. However, it's also more efficient than both the fast and optimum default switching paths.

Cisco FRAD Cisco Frame-Relay Access Device: A Cisco product that supports Cisco IPS Frame Relay SNA services, connecting SDLC devices to Frame Relay without requiring an existing LAN. May be upgraded to a fully functioning multiprotocol router. Can activate conversion from SDLC to Ethernet and Token Ring, but does not support attached LANs. *See also: FRAD.*

CiscoFusion Cisco's name for the internetworking architecture under which its Cisco IOS operates. It is designed to "fuse" together the capabilities of its disparate collection of acquired routers and switches.

Cisco IOS software Cisco Internet Operating System software. The kernel of the Cisco line of routers and switches that supplies shared functionality, scalability, and security for all products under its Cisco-Fusion architecture. *See also: CiscoFusion.*

Cisco Technical Assistance Center The TAC provides support for Cisco contract holders, gives warranty service, and can even bill you directly if you do not have a Cisco maintenance contract.

CiscoView GUI-based management software for Cisco networking devices, enabling dynamic status, statistics, and comprehensive configuration information. Displays a physical view of the Cisco device chassis and provides device-monitoring functions and fundamental troubleshooting capabilities. May be integrated with a number of SNMP-based network management platforms.

Class A network Part of the Internet Protocol hierarchical addressing scheme. Class A networks have only 8 bits for defining networks and 24 bits for defining hosts on each network.

Class B network Part of the Internet Protocol hierarchical addressing scheme. Class B networks have 16 bits for defining networks and 16 bits for defining hosts on each network.

Class C network Part of the Internet Protocol hierarchical addressing scheme. Class C networks have 24 bits for defining networks and only 8 bits for defining hosts on each network.

classical IP over ATM Defined in RFC 1577, the specification for running IP over ATM that maximizes ATM features. Also known as CIA.

classless routing Routing that sends subnet mask information in the routing updates. Classless routing allows Variable-Length Subnet Mask (VLSM) and supernetting. Routing protocols that support classless routing are RIP version 2, EIGRP, and OSPF.

CLI Command-Line Interface: Allows you to configure Cisco routers and switches with maximum flexibility.

CLP Cell Loss Priority: The area in the ATM cell header that determines the likelihood of a cell being dropped during network congestion. Cells with CLP = 0 are considered insured traffic and are not apt to be dropped. Cells with CLP = 1 are considered best-effort traffic that may be dropped during congested episodes, delivering more resources to handle insured traffic.

CLR Cell Loss Ratio: The ratio of discarded cells to successfully delivered cells in ATM. CLR can be designated a QoS parameter when establishing a connection.

CO Central Office: The local telephone company office where all loops in a certain area connect and where circuit switching of subscriber lines occurs.

collapsed backbone A nondistributed backbone where all network segments are connected to each other through an internetworking device. A collapsed backbone can be a virtual network segment at work in a device such as a router, hub, or switch.

collision The effect of two nodes sending transmissions simultaneously in Ethernet. When they meet on the physical media, the frames from each node collide and are damaged. *See also: collision domain.*

collision domain The network area in Ethernet over which frames that have collided will spread. Collisions are propagated by hubs and repeaters, but not by LAN switches, routers, or bridges. *See also: collision.*

composite metric Used with routing protocols, such as IGRP and EIGRP, that use more than one metric to find the best path to a remote network. IGRP and EIGRP both use bandwidth and delay of the line by default. However, Maximum Transmission Unit (MTU), load, and reliability of a link can be used as well.

configuration register A 16-bit configurable value stored in hardware or software that determines how Cisco routers function during initialization. In hardware, the bit position is set using a jumper. In software, it is set by specifying specific bit patterns used to set start-up options, configured using a hexadecimal value with configuration commands.

congestion Traffic that exceeds the network's ability to handle it.

congestion avoidance To minimize delays, the method an ATM network uses to control traffic entering the system. Lower-priority traffic is discarded at the edge of the network when indicators signal it cannot be delivered, thus using resources efficiently.

congestion collapse The situation that results from the retransmission of packets in ATM networks where little or no traffic successfully arrives at destination points. It usually happens in networks made of switches with ineffective or inadequate buffering capabilities combined with poor packet discard or ABR congestion feedback mechanisms.

connection ID Identifications given to each Telnet session into a router. The `show sessions` command will give you the connections a local router will have to a remote router. The `show users` command will show the connection IDs of users telnetted into your local router.

connectionless Data transfer that occurs without the creating of a virtual circuit. No overhead, best-effort delivery, not reliable. *Contrast with: connection-oriented. See also: virtual circuit.*

connection-oriented Data transfer method that sets up a virtual circuit before any data is transferred. Uses flow and error control for reliable data transfer. *Contrast with: connectionless. See also: virtual circuit.*

console port Typically an RJ-45 port on a Cisco router and switch that allows Command-Line Interface capability.

control direct VCC One of three control connections defined by Phase I LAN Emulation; a bi-directional virtual control connection (VCC) established in ATM by an LEC to an LES. *See also: control distribute VCC.*

control distribute VCC One of three control connections defined by Phase 1 LAN Emulation; a unidirectional virtual control connection (VCC) set up in ATM from an LES to an LEC. Usually, the VCC is a point-to-multipoint connection. *See also: control direct VCC.*

convergence The process required for all routers in an internetwork to update their routing tables and create a consistent view of the network, using the best possible paths. No user data is passed during a convergence time.

core layer Top layer in the Cisco three-layer hierarchical model, which helps you design, build, and maintain Cisco hierarchical networks. The core layer passes packets quickly to distribution-layer devices only. No packet filtering should take place at this layer.

cost Also known as path cost, an arbitrary value, based on hop count, bandwidth, or other calculation, that is typically assigned by a network administrator and used by the routing protocol to compare different routes through an internetwork. Routing protocols use cost values to select the best path to a certain destination: the lowest cost identifies the best path. Also known as path cost. *See also: routing metric.*

count to infinity A problem occurring in routing algorithms that are slow to converge where routers keep increasing the hop count to particular networks. To avoid this problem, various solutions have been implemented into each of the different routing protocols. Some of those solutions include defining a maximum hop count (defining infinity), route poisoning, poison reverse, and split horizon.

CPCS Common Part Convergence Sublayer: One of two AAL sublayers that is service-dependent, it is further segmented into the CS and SAR sublayers. The CPCS prepares data for transmission across the ATM network; it creates the 48-byte payload cells that are sent to the ATM layer. *See also: AAL* and *ATM layer.*

CPE Customer Premises Equipment: Items such as telephones, modems, and terminals installed at customer locations and connected to the telephone company network.

crankback In ATM, a correction technique used when a node somewhere on a chosen path cannot accept a connection setup request, blocking the request. The path is rolled back to an intermediate node, which then uses GCAC to attempt to find an alternate path to the final destination.

CRC Cyclical Redundancy Check: A methodology that detects errors, whereby the frame recipient makes a calculation by dividing frame contents with a prime binary divisor and compares the remainder to a value stored in the frame by the sending node. *Contrast with: checksum.*

CSMA/CD Carrier Sense Multiple Access Collision Detection. A technology defined by the Ethernet IEEE 802.3 committee. Each device senses the cable for a digital signal before transmitting. Also, CSMA/CD allows all devices on the network to share the same cable, but one at a time. If two devices transmit at the same time, a frame collision will occur and a jamming pattern will be sent; the devices will stop transmitting, wait a predetermined amount of time, and then try to transmit again.

CSU Channel Service Unit: A digital mechanism that connects end-user equipment to the local digital telephone loop. Frequently referred to along with the data service unit as CSU/DSU. *See also: DSU.*

CTD Cell Transfer Delay: For a given connection in ATM, the time period between a cell exit event at the source user-network interface (UNI) and the corresponding cell entry event at the destination. The CTD between these points is the sum of the total inter-ATM transmission delay and the total ATM processing delay.

cut-through frame switching A frame-switching technique that flows data through a switch so that the leading edge exits the switch at the output port before the packet finishes entering the input port. Frames will be read, processed, and forwarded by devices that use cut-through switching as soon as the destination address of the frame is confirmed and the outgoing port is identified.

dialer map statements Configuration statements that link network addresses to ISDN numbers.

data direct VCC A bidirectional point-to-point virtual control connection (VCC) set up between two LECs in ATM and one of three data connections defined by Phase 1 LAN Emulation. Because data direct VCCs do not guarantee QoS, they are generally reserved for UBR and ABR connections. *Compare with: control distribute VCC* and *control direct VCC.*

data frame Protocol Data Unit encapsulation at the Data-Link layer of the OSI reference model. Encapsulates packets from the Network layer and prepares the data for transmission on a network medium.

datagram A logical collection of information transmitted as a Network layer unit over a medium without a previously established virtual circuit. IP datagrams have become the primary information unit of the Internet. At various layers of the OSI reference model, the terms *cell, frame, message, packet,* and *segment* also define these logical information groupings.

data link control layer Layer 2 of the SNA architectural model, it is responsible for the transmission of data over a given physical link and compares somewhat to the Data-Link layer of the OSI model.

Data-Link layer Layer 2 of the OSI reference model, it ensures the trustworthy transmission of data across a physical link and is primarily concerned with physical addressing, line discipline, network topology, error notification, ordered delivery of frames, and flow control. The IEEE has further segmented this layer into the MAC sublayer and the LLC sublayer. Also known as the Link layer. Can be compared somewhat to the data link control layer of the SNA model. *See also: Application layer, LLC, MAC, Network layer, Physical layer, Presentation layer, Session layer,* and *Transport layer.*

DCC Data Country Code: Developed by the ATM Forum, one of two ATM address formats designed for use by private networks. *Compare with: ICD.*

DCE data communications equipment (as defined by the EIA) or data circuit-terminating equipment (as defined by the ITU-T): The mechanisms and links of a communications network that make up the network portion of the user-to-network interface, such as modems. The DCE supplies the physical connection to the network, forwards traffic, and provides a clocking signal to synchronize data transmission between DTE and DCE devices. *Compare with: DTE.*

D channel (1) Data channel: A full-duplex, 16Kbps (BRI) or 64Kbps (PRI) ISDN channel. *Compare with: B channel, E channel,* and *H channel. (2)* In SNA, anything that provides a connection between the processor and main storage with any peripherals.

DDP Datagram Delivery Protocol: Used in the AppleTalk suite of protocols as a connectionless protocol that is responsible for sending datagrams through an internetwork.

DDR dial-on-demand routing: A technique that allows a router to automatically initiate and end a circuit-switched session per the requirements of the sending station. By mimicking keepalives, the router fools the end station into treating the session as active. DDR permits routing over ISDN or telephone lines via a modem or external ISDN terminal adapter.

DE Discard Eligibility: Used in Frame Relay networks to tell a switch that a frame can be discarded if the switch is too busy. The DE is a field in the frame that is turned on by transmitting routers if the Committed Information Rate (CIR) is oversubscribed or set to 0.

debug The Cisco IOS command that provides the administrator with low-level, detailed information about processes that run on the router.

default route The static routing table entry used to direct frames whose next hop is not spelled out in the dynamic routing table.

delay The time elapsed between a sender's initiation of a transaction and the first response they receive. Also, the time needed to move a packet from its source to its destination over a path. *See also: latency.*

demarc The demarcation point between the customer premises equipment (CPE) and the telco's carrier equipment.

demodulation A series of steps that return a modulated signal to its original form. When receiving, a modem demodulates an analog signal to its original digital form (and, conversely, modulates the digital data it sends into an analog signal). *See also: modulation.*

demultiplexing The process of converting a single multiplex signal, comprising more than one input stream, back into separate output streams. *See also: multiplexing.*

designated bridge In the process of forwarding a frame from a segment to the route bridge, the bridge with the lowest path cost.

designated port Used with the Spanning-Tree Protocol (STP) to designate forwarding ports. If there are multiple links to the same network, STP will shut a port down to stop network loops.

designated router An OSPF router that creates LSAs for a multi-access network and is required to perform other special tasks in OSPF operations. Multi-access OSPF networks that maintain a minimum of two attached routers identify one router that is chosen by the OSPF Hello protocol, which makes possible a decrease in the number of adjacencies necessary on a multi-access network. This in turn reduces the quantity of routing protocol traffic and the physical size of the database.

destination address   The address for the network devices that will receive a packet.

DHCP   Dynamic Host Configuaration Protocol; DHCP is a superset of the BootP protocol. This means that it uses the same protocol structure as BootP, but it has enhancements added. Both of these protocols use servers that dynamically configure clients when requested. The two major enhancements are address pools and lease times.

directed broadcast   A data frame or packet that is transmitted to a specific group of nodes on a remote network segment. Directed broadcasts are known by their broadcast address, which is a destination subnet address with all the bits turned on.

discovery mode   Also known as dynamic configuration, this technique is used by an AppleTalk interface to gain information from a working node about an attached network. The information is subsequently used by the interface for self-configuration.

distance-vector routing algorithm   In order to find the shortest path, this group of routing algorithms repeats on the number of hops in a given route, requiring each router to send its complete routing table with each update, but only to its neighbors. Routing algorithms of this type tend to generate loops, but they are fundamentally simpler than their link-state counterparts. *See also: link-state routing algorithm and SPF.*

distribute lists   These lists are references to access-lists and are applied to interfaces via a routing protocol.

distributed switching   Distributed switching happens on the VIP (Versatile Interface Processor) cards (which have a switching processor onboard), so it's very efficient. All required processing is done right on the VIP processor, which maintains a copy of the router's routing cache.

distribution layer   Middle layer of the Cisco three-layer hierarchical model, which helps you design, install, and maintain Cisco hierarchical networks. The distribution layer is the point where access layer devices connect. Routing is performed at this layer.

divide-by-half troubleshooting   Troubleshooting method in which a point between two ends of a network problem is used as a troubleshooting reference point. Either half may be investigated first, thus narrowing down the trouble location.

DLCI   Data-Link Connection Identifier: Used to identify virtual circuits in a Frame Relay network.

DNS   Domain Name System: Used to resolve host names to IP addresses.

DSAP   Destination Service Access Point: The service access point of a network node, specified in the destination field of a packet. *See also: SSAP and SAP.*

DSR   Data Set Ready: When a DCE is powered up and ready to run, this EIA/TIA-232 interface circuit is also engaged.

DSU   Data Service Unit: This device is used to adapt the physical interface on a data terminal equipment (DTE) mechanism to a transmission facility such as T1 or E1 and is also responsible for signal timing. It is commonly grouped with the channel service unit and referred to as the CSU/DSU. *See also: CSU.*

DTE   data terminal equipment: Any device located at the user end of a user-network interface serving as a destination, a source, or both. DTE includes devices such as multiplexers, protocol translators, and computers. The connection to a data network is made through data channel equipment (DCE) such as a modem, using the clocking signals generated by that device. *See also: DCE.*

DTR   data terminal ready: An activated EIA/TIA-232 circuit communicating to the DCE the state of preparedness of the DTE to transmit or receive data.

DUAL   Diffusing Update Algorithm: Used in Enhanced IGRP, this convergence algorithm provides loop-free operation throughout an entire route's computation. DUAL grants routers involved in a topology revision the ability to synchronize simultaneously, while routers unaffected by this change are not involved. *See also: Enhanced IGRP.*

DVMRP   Distance Vector Multicast Routing Protocol: Based primarily on the Routing Information Protocol (RIP), this Internet gateway protocol implements a common, condensed-mode IP multicast scheme, using IGMP to transfer routing datagrams between its neighbors. *See also: IGMP.*

DXI Data Exchange Interface: Described in RFC 1482, DXI defines the effectiveness of a network device such as a router, bridge, or hub to act as an FEP to an ATM network by using a special DSU that accomplishes packet encapsulation.

dynamic entries Used in Layer-2 and -3 devices to create a table of either hardware addresses or logical addresses dynamically.

dynamic routing Also known as adaptive routing, this technique automatically adapts to traffic or physical network revisions.

dynamic VLAN An administrator will create an entry in a special server with the hardware addresses of all devices on the internetwork. The server will then assign dynamically used VLANs.

E1 Generally used in Europe, a wide-area digital transmission scheme carrying data at 2.048Mbps. E1 transmission lines are available for lease from common carriers for private use.

E.164 (1) Evolved from standard telephone numbering system, the standard recommended by ITU-T for international telecommunication numbering, particularly in ISDN, SMDS, and BISDN. (2) Label of field in an ATM address containing numbers in E.164 format.

E channel Echo channel: A 64Kbps ISDN control channel used for circuit switching. Specific description of this channel can be found in the 1984 ITU-T ISDN specification, but was dropped from the 1988 version. *See also: B, D,* and *H channels.*

EARL Encoded Address Recognition Logic ASIC: This chip works with the bus arbitration system to control access to the data-switching bus. EARL also controls the destination ports of packet transfers.

edge device A device that enables packets to be forwarded between legacy interfaces (such as Ethernet and Token Ring) and ATM interfaces based on information in the Data-Link and Network layers. An edge device does not take part in the running of any Network layer routing protocol; it merely uses the route description protocol in order to get the forwarding information required.

EEPROM Electronically Erasable Programmable Read-Only Memory: Programmed after their manufacture, these nonvolatile memory chips can be erased if necessary using electric power and reprogrammed. *See also: EPROM, PROM.*

EFCI Explicit Forward Congestion Indication: A congestion feedback mode permitted by ABR service in an ATM network. The EFCI may be set by any network element that is in a state of immediate or certain congestion. The destination end-system is able to carry out a protocol that adjusts and lowers the cell rate of the connection based on value of the EFCI. *See also: ABR.*

EIGRP *See: Enhanced IGRP.*

EIP Ethernet Interface Processor: A Cisco 7000 series router interface processor card, supplying 10Mbps AUI ports to support Ethernet Version 1 and Ethernet Version 2 or IEEE 802.3 interfaces with a high-speed data path to other interface processors.

ELAN Emulated LAN: An ATM network configured using a client/server model in order to emulate either an Ethernet or Token Ring LAN. Multiple ELANs can exist at the same time on a single ATM network and are made up of a LAN emulation client (LEC), a LAN Emulation Server (LES), a Broadcast and Unknown Server (BUS), and a LAN Emulation Configuration Server (LECS). ELANs are defined by the LANE specification. *See also: LANE, LEC, LECS,* and *LES.*

ELAP EtherTalk Link Access Protocol: In an EtherTalk network, the link-access protocol constructed above the standard Ethernet Data-Link layer.

encapsulation The technique used by layered protocols in which a layer adds header information to the protocol data unit (PDU) from the layer above. As an example, in Internet terminology, a packet would contain a header from the Physical layer, followed by a header from the Network layer (IP), followed by a header from the Transport layer (TCP), followed by the application protocol data.

encryption The conversion of information into a scrambled form that effectively disguises it to prevent unauthorized access. Every encryption scheme uses some well-defined algorithm, which is reversed at the receiving end by an opposite algorithm in a process known as decryption.

Enhanced IGRP Enhanced Interior Gateway Routing Protocol: An advanced routing protocol created by Cisco, combining the advantages of link-state and distance-vector protocols. Enhanced IGRP has superior convergence attributes, including high operating efficiency. *See also: IGP, OSPF,* and *RIP.*

enterprise network A privately owned and operated network that joins most major locations in a large company or organization.

EPROM Erasable Programmable Read-Only Memory: Programmed after their manufacture, these nonvolatile memory chips can be erased if necessary using high-power light and reprogrammed. *See also: EEPROM, PROM.*

error control The control mechanism for verification of contiguous and non-erroneous packets.

ESF Extended Superframe: Made up of 24 frames with 192 bits each, with the 193rd bit providing other functions including timing. This is an enhanced version of SF. *See also: SF.*

Ethernet A baseband LAN specification created by the Xerox Corporation and then improved through joint efforts of Xerox, Digital Equipment Corporation, and Intel. Ethernet is similar to the IEEE 802.3 series standard and, using CSMA/CD, operates over various types of cables at 10Mbps. *Also called: DIX (Digital/Intel/Xerox) Ethernet. See also: 10BaseT, Fast Ethernet,* and *IEEE.*

EtherTalk A data-link product from Apple Computer that permits AppleTalk networks to be connected by Ethernet.

excess rate In ATM networking, traffic exceeding a connection's insured rate. The excess rate is the maximum rate less the insured rate. Depending on the availability of network resources, excess traffic can be discarded during congestion episodes. *Compare with: maximum rate.*

expansion The procedure of directing compressed data through an algorithm, restoring information to its original size.

expedited delivery An option that can be specified by one protocol layer, communicating either with other layers or with the identical protocol layer in a different network device, requiring that identified data be processed faster.

explorer packet An SNA packet transmitted by a source Token Ring device to find the path through a source-route-bridged network.

extended addressing The technique used by AppleTalk Phase 2 to assign multiple network addresses to a single segment.

extended IP access list IP access list that filters the network by logical address, protocol field in the Network layer header, and even the port field in the Transport layer header.

extended IPX access list IPX access list that filters the network by logical IPX address, protocol field in the Network layer header, and even the socket number in the Transport layer header.

Extended Setup Used in setup mode to configure the router with more detail than Basic Setup mode. Allows multiple-protocol support and interface configuration.

extended ping The enhanced version of PING that allows user interaction to choose options when executing the PING command. This resource requires enable access to the router.

fact gathering The process of using diagnostic tools to collect information specific to the network and network devices involved in a problem. Additional information should include data that excludes other possibilities and helps pinpoint the actual problem.

failure domain The region in which a failure has occurred in a Token Ring. When a station gains information that a serious problem, such as a cable break, has occurred with the network, it sends a beacon frame that includes the station reporting the failure, its NAUN, and everything between. This defines the failure domain. Beaconing then initiates the procedure known as autoreconfiguration. *See also: autoreconfiguration* and *beacon.*

fallback In ATM networks, this mechanism is used for scouting a path if it isn't possible to locate one using customary methods. The device relaxes requirements for certain characteristics, such as delay, in an attempt to find a path that meets a certain set of the most important requirements.

Fast Ethernet Any Ethernet specification with a speed of 100Mbps. Fast Ethernet is ten times faster than 10BaseT, while retaining qualities like MAC mechanisms, MTU, and frame format. These similarities make it possible for existing 10BaseT applications and management tools to be used on Fast Ethernet networks. Fast Ethernet is based on an extension of IEEE 802.3 specification (IEEE 802.3u). *Compare with: Ethernet. See also: 100BaseT, 100BaseTX, and IEEE.*

fast switching   A Cisco feature that uses a route cache to speed packet switching through a router. *Contrast with: process switching.*

FDM   Frequency-Division Multiplexing: A technique that permits information from several channels to be assigned bandwidth on one wire based on frequency. *See also: TDM, ATDM, and statistical multiplexing.*

FDDI   Fiber Distributed Data Interface: A LAN standard, defined by ANSI X3T9.5 that can run at speeds up to 200Mbps and uses token-passing media access on fiber-optic cable. For redundancy, FDDI can use a dual-ring architecture.

FECN   Forward Explicit Congestion Notification: A bit set by a Frame Relay network that informs the DTE receptor that congestion was encountered along the path from source to destination. A device receiving frames with the FECN bit set can ask higher-priority protocols to take flow-control action as needed. *See also: BECN.*

FEIP   Fast Ethernet Interface Processor: An interface processor employed on Cisco 7000 series routers, supporting up to two 100Mbps 100BaseT ports.

FIB   Forwarding Information Base: The FIB consists of information duplicated from the IP route table. Every time the routing information changes, the changes are propagated to the FIB.

firewall   A barrier purposefully erected between any connected public networks and a private network, made up of a router or access server or several routers or access servers, that uses access lists and other methods to ensure the security of the private network.

Flash   Electronically Erasable Programmable Read-Only Memory (EEPROM). Used to hold the Cisco IOS in a router by default.

flash memory   Developed by Intel and licensed to other semiconductor manufacturers, it is nonvolatile storage that can be erased electronically and reprogrammed, physically located on an EEPROM chip. Flash memory permits software images to be stored, booted, and rewritten as needed. Cisco routers and switches use flash memory to hold the IOS by default. *See also: EPROM, EEPROM.*

flat network   Network that is one large collision domain and one large broadcast domain.

flooding   When traffic is received on an interface, it is then transmitted to every interface connected to that device with exception of the interface from which the traffic originated. This technique can be used for traffic transfer by bridges and switches throughout the network.

flow control   A methodology used to ensure that receiving units are not overwhelmed with data from sending devices. Pacing, as it is called in IBM networks, means that when buffers at a receiving unit are full, a message is transmitted to the sending unit to temporarily halt transmissions until all the data in the receiving buffer has been processed and the buffer is again ready for action.

FRAD   Frame Relay Access Device: Any device affording a connection between a LAN and a Frame Relay WAN. *See also: Cisco FRAD, FRAS.*

fragment   Any portion of a larger packet that has been segmented into smaller pieces. A packet fragment does not necessarily indicate an error and can be intentional. *See also: fragmentation.*

fragmentation   The process of intentionally segmenting a packet into smaller pieces when sending data over an intermediate network medium that cannot support the larger packet size.

FragmentFree   LAN switch type that reads into the data section of a frame to make sure fragmentation did not occur. Sometimes called modified cut-through.

frame   A logical unit of information sent by the Data-Link layer over a transmission medium. The term often refers to the header and trailer, employed for synchronization and error control, that surround the data contained in the unit.

Frame Relay   A more efficient replacement of the X.25 protocol (an unrelated packet relay technology that guarantees data delivery). Frame Relay is an industry-standard, shared-access, best-effort, switched Data-Link layer encapsulation that services multiple virtual circuits and protocols between connected mechanisms.

Frame Relay bridging Defined in RFC 1490, this bridging method uses the identical spanning-tree algorithm as other bridging operations but permits packets to be encapsulated for transmission across a Frame Relay network.

framing Encapsulation at the Data-Link layer of the OSI model. It is called framing because the packet is encapsulated with both a header and a trailer.

FRAS Frame Relay Access Support: A feature of Cisco IOS software that enables SDLC, Ethernet, Token Ring, and Frame Relay-attached IBM devices to be linked with other IBM mechanisms on a Frame Relay network. *See also: FRAD.*

frequency The number of cycles of an alternating current signal per time unit, measured in hertz (cycles per second).

FSIP Fast Serial Interface Processor: The Cisco 7000 routers' default serial interface processor, it provides four or eight high-speed serial ports.

FTP File Transfer Protocol: The TCP/IP protocol used for transmitting files between network nodes, it supports a broad range of file types and is defined in RFC 959. *See also: TFTP.*

full duplex The capacity to transmit information between a sending station and a receiving unit at the same time. *See also: half duplex.*

full mesh A type of network topology where every node has either a physical or a virtual circuit linking it to every other network node. A full mesh supplies a great deal of redundancy but is typically reserved for network backbones because of its expense. *See also: partial mesh.*

GNS Get Nearest Server: On an IPX network, a request packet sent by a customer for determining the location of the nearest active server of a given type. An IPX network client launches a GNS request to get either a direct answer from a connected server or a response from a router disclosing the location of the service on the internetwork to the GNS. GNS is part of IPX and SAP. *See also: IPX and SAP.*

GRE Generic Routing Encapsulation: A tunneling protocol created by Cisco with the capacity for encapsulating a wide variety of protocol packet types inside IP tunnels, thereby generating a virtual point-to-point

connection to Cisco routers across an IP network at remote points. IP tunneling using GRE permits network expansion across a single-protocol backbone environment by linking multiprotocol subnetworks in a single-protocol backbone environment.

guard band The unused frequency area found between two communications channels, furnishing the space necessary to avoid interference between the two.

half duplex The capacity to transfer data in only one direction at a time between a sending unit and receiving unit. *See also: full duplex.*

handshake Any series of transmissions exchanged between two or more devices on a network to ensure synchronized operations.

H channel High-speed channel: A full-duplex, ISDN primary rate channel operating at a speed of 384Kbps. *See also: B, D, and E channels.*

HDLC High-level Data Link Control: Using frame characters, including checksums, HDLC designates a method for data encapsulation on synchronous serial links and is the default encapsulation for Cisco routers. HDLC is a bit-oriented synchronous Data-Link layer protocol created by ISO and derived from SDLC. However, most HDLC vendor implementations (including Cisco's) are proprietary. *See also: SDLC.*

helper address The unicast address specified, which instructs the Cisco router to change the client's local broadcast request for a service into a directed unicast to the server.

hierarchical addressing Any addressing plan employing a logical chain of commands to determine location. IP addresses are made up of a hierarchy of network numbers, subnet numbers, and host numbers to direct packets to the appropriate destination.

HIP HSSI Interface Processor: An interface processor used on Cisco 7000 series routers, providing one HSSI port that supports connections to ATM, SMDS, Frame Relay, or private lines at speeds up to T3 or E3.

holddown The state a route is placed in so that routers can neither advertise the route nor accept advertisements about it for a defined time period. Holddown is used to surface bad information about a route from all routers in the network. A route is generally placed in holddown when one of its links fails.

hop   The movement of a packet between any two network nodes. *See also: hop count.*

hop count   A routing metric that calculates the distance between a source and a destination. RIP employs hop count as its sole metric. *See also: hop and RIP.*

host address   Logical address configured by an administrator or server on a device. Logically identifies this device on an internetwork.

HSCI   High-Speed Communication Interface: Developed by Cisco, a single-port interface that provides full-duplex synchronous serial communications capability at speeds up to 52Mbps.

HSRP   Hot Standby Router Protocol: A protocol that provides high network availability and provides nearly instantaneous hardware fail-over without administrator intervention. It generates a Hot Standby router group, including a lead router that lends its services to any packet being transferred to the Hot Standby address. If the lead router fails, it will be replaced by any of the other routers—the standby routers—that monitor it.

HSSI   High-Speed Serial Interface: A network standard physical connector for high-speed serial linking over a WAN at speeds of up to 52Mbps.

hubs   Physical-layer devices that are really just multiple port repeaters. When an electronic digital signal is received on a port, the signal is reamplified or regenerated and forwarded out all segments except the segment from which the signal was received.

ICD   International Code Designator: Adapted from the subnetwork model of addressing, this assigns the mapping of Network layer addresses to ATM addresses. HSSI is one of two ATM formats for addressing created by the ATM Forum to be utilized with private networks. *See also: DCC.*

ICMP   Internet Control Message Protocol: Documented in RFC 792, it is a Network layer Internet protocol for the purpose of reporting errors and providing information pertinent to IP packet procedures.

IEEE   Institute of Electrical and Electronics Engineers: A professional organization that, among other activities, defines standards in a number of fields within computing and electronics, including networking and communications. IEEE standards are the predominant LAN standards used today throughout the industry. Many protocols are commonly known by the reference number of the corresponding IEEE standard.

IEEE 802.1   The IEEE committee specification that defines the bridging group. The specification for STP (Spanning-Tree Protocol) is IEEE 802.1d. The STP uses SPA (spanning-tree algorithm) to find and prevent network loops in bridged networks. The specification for VLAN trunking is IEEE 802.1q.

IEEE 802.3   The IEEE committee specification that defines the Ethernet group, specifically the original 10Mbps standard. Ethernet is a LAN protocol that specifies Physical layer and MAC sublayer media access. IEEE 802.3 uses CSMA/CD to provide access for many devices on the same network. FastEthernet is defined as 802.3u, and Gigabit Ethernet is defined as 802.3q. *See also: CSMA/CD.*

IEEE 802.5   IEEE committee specification that defines Token Ring media access.

IGMP   Internet Group Management Protocol: Employed by IP hosts, the protocol that reports their multicast group memberships to an adjacent multicast router.

ignore   A Cisco IOS command, which can be caused in three ways: the hardware buffer fills up and it signals to the transmitting interface to throttle down, the interface is receiving frames faster than the SP can pull them off, and when the CxBus is so busy that the interface processor is unable to copy the packet from the hardware buffer to the SP buffers.

IGP   Interior Gateway Protocol: Any protocol used by the Internet to exchange routing data within an independent system. Examples include RIP, IGRP, and OSPF.

IGRP Interior Gateway Routing Protocol: a Cisco proprietary routing protocol that uses a distance-vector algorithm. It uses a vector (a one-dimensional array) of information to calculate the best path. This vector consists of four elements: bandwidth, delay, load, reliability.

ILMI Integrated (or Interim) Local Management Interface. A specification created by the ATM Forum, designated for the incorporation of network-management capability into the ATM UNI. Integrated Local Management Interface cells provide for automatic configuration between ATM systems. In LAN emulation, ILMI can provide sufficient information for the ATM end station to find an LECS. In addition, ILMI provides the ATM NSAP (Network Service Access Point) prefix information to the end station.

in-band management In-band management is the management of a network device "through" the network. Examples include using Simple Network Management Protocol (SNMP) or Telnet directly via the local LAN. *Compare with: out-of-band management.*

input queues These queues reside on the RP, and they are used to link the SP buffers to the RP buffers. The queue reserves RP buffer space for a packet that was forwarded from the SP/SSP. If the Router Processor doesn't process the queued packets at the same rate, the queue fills up and the incoming packets are dropped.

inside-out troubleshooting This method of troubleshooting directs the troubleshooter to start near the user and work their way toward the far end of the area of dysfunctionality.

insured burst In an ATM network, it is the largest temporarily permitted data burst exceeding the insured rate on a PVC and not tagged by the traffic policing function for being dropped if network congestion occurs. This insured burst is designated in bytes or cells.

interarea routing Routing between two or more logical areas. *Contrast with: intra-area routing. See also: area.*

interface buffer A buffer used for intermediate storage. Packets from all of the hardware buffers are copied to the interface buffers. The switch processor houses the intermediate buffers by using 512KB for

the SP board memory. This memory is also shared with the autonomous switching cache.

interface processor Any of several processor modules used with Cisco 7000 series routers. *See also: AIP, CIP, EIP, FEIP, HIP, MIP, and TRIP.*

Internet The global "network of networks," whose popularity has exploded in the last few years. Originally a tool for collaborative academic research, it has become a medium for exchanging and distributing information of all kinds. The Internet's need to link disparate computer platforms and technologies has led to the development of uniform protocols and standards that have also found widespread use within corporate LANs. *See also: TCP/IP and MBONE.*

internet Before the rise of the Internet, this lowercase form was shorthand for "internetwork" in the generic sense. Now rarely used. *See also: internetwork.*

Internet protocol Any protocol belonging to the TCP/IP protocol stack. *See also: TCP/IP.*

internetwork Any group of private networks interconnected by routers and other mechanisms, typically operating as a single entity.

internetworking Broadly, anything associated with the general task of linking networks to each other. The term encompasses technologies, procedures, and products. When you connect networks to a router, you are creating an internetwork.

intra-area routing Routing that occurs within a logical area. *Contrast with: interarea routing.*

Inverse ARP Inverse Address Resolution Protocol: A technique by which dynamic mappings are constructed in a network, allowing a device such as a router to locate the logical network address and associate it with a permanent virtual circuit (PVC). Commonly used in Frame Relay to determine the far-end node's TCP/IP address by sending the Inverse ARP request to the local DLCI.

IP Internet Protocol: Defined in RFC 791, it is a Network layer protocol that is part of the TCP/IP stack and allows connectionless service. IP furnishes an array of features for addressing, type-of-service specification, fragmentation and reassembly, and security.

IP address Often called an Internet address, this is an address uniquely identifying any device (host) on the Internet (or any TCP/IP network). Each address consists of four octets (32 bits), represented as decimal numbers separated by periods (a format known as "dotted-decimal"). Every address is made up of a network number, an optional subnetwork number, and a host number. The network and subnetwork numbers together are used for routing, while the host number addresses an individual host within the network or subnetwork. The network and subnetwork information is extracted from the IP address using the subnet mask. There are five classes of IP addresses (A–E), which allocate different numbers of bits to the network, subnetwork, and host portions of the address. *See also: CIDR, IP,* and *subnet mask.*

IPCP IP Control Program: The protocol used to establish and configure IP over PPP. *See also: IP* and *PPP.*

IP multicast A technique for routing that enables IP traffic to be reproduced from one source to several endpoints or from multiple sources to many destinations. Instead of transmitting only one packet to each individual point of destination, one packet is sent to a multicast group specified by only one IP endpoint address for the group.

IPX Internetwork Packet Exchange: Network layer protocol (Layer 3) used in Novell NetWare networks for transferring information from servers to workstations. Similar to IP and XNS.

IPXCP IPX Control Program: The protocol used to establish and configure IPX over PPP. *See also: IPX and PPP.*

IPXWAN Protocol used for new WAN links to provide and negotiate line options on the link using IPX. After the link is up and the options have been agreed upon by the two end-to-end links, normal IPX transmission begins.

ISDN Integrated Services Digital Network: Offered as a service by telephone companies, a communication protocol that allows telephone networks to carry data, voice, and other digital traffic. *See also: BISDN, BRI, and PRI.*

ISDN BRI ISDN Basic Rate Interface: ISDN BRI was designed to provide digital services over existing pairs of copper. The service is used for videoconferencing, voice services, data, and out-of-band management. In addition, the D-channel function of BRI is used for replacement of legacy X.25 networks. *ISDN BRI* is a 192Kbps circuit that is divided into three distinct channels. The two primary data channels are the B channels. Each B channel provides 64Kbps. The third channel provides 16Kbps of bandwidth for commands and signaling, and is referred to as the D channel.

ISL routing Inter-Switch Link routing is a Cisco proprietary method of frame tagging in a switched internetwork. Frame tagging is a way to identify the VLAN membership of a frame as it traverses a switched internetwork.

isochronous transmission Asynchronous data transfer over a synchronous data link, requiring a constant bit rate for reliable transport. *Compare with: asynchronous transmission* and *synchronous transmission.*

iteration This is the repetition of certain steps within the troubleshooting model. Certain steps may need to be repeated in order to solve the problem at hand.

ITU-T International Telecommunication Union Telecommunication Standardization Sector: This is a group of engineers that develops worldwide standards for telecommunications technologies.

LAN Local Area Network: Broadly, any network linking two or more computers and related devices within a limited geographical area (up to a few kilometers). LANs are typically high-speed, low-error networks within a company. Cabling and signaling at the Physical and Data-Link layers of the OSI are dictated by LAN standards. Ethernet, FDDI, and Token Ring are among the most popular LAN technologies. *Compare with: MAN.*

LANE LAN emulation: The technology that allows an ATM network to operate as a LAN backbone. To do so, the ATM network is required to provide multicast and broadcast support, address mapping (MAC-to-ATM), SVC management, in addition to an operable packet format. Additionally, LANE defines Ethernet and Token Ring ELANs. *See also: ELAN.*

LAN switch A high-speed, multiple-interface transparent bridging mechanism, transmitting packets between segments of data links, usually referred to specifically as an Ethernet switch. LAN switches transfer traffic based on MAC addresses. Multilayer switches are a type of high-speed, special-purpose, hardware-based router. *See also: multilayer switch,* and *store-and-forward packet switching.*

LAPB Link Accessed Procedure, Balanced: A bit-oriented Data-Link layer protocol that is part of the X.25 stack and has its origin in SDLC. *See also: SDLC and X.25.*

LAPD Link Access Procedure on the D channel. The ISDN Data-Link layer protocol used specifically for the D channel and defined by ITU-T Recommendations Q.920 and Q.921. LAPD evolved from LAPB and is created to comply with the signaling requirements of ISDN basic access.

latency Broadly, the time it takes a data packet to get from one location to another. In specific networking contexts, it can mean either (1) the time elapsed (delay) between the execution of a request for access to a network by a device and the time the mechanism actually is permitted transmission, or (2) the time elapsed between when a mechanism receives a frame and the time that frame is forwarded out of the destination port.

Layer 1 S/T Interface This connection uses a physical connector of RJ-45, as defined in ISO 8877. A straight-through pin configuration connects the terminal end point (TE) to the network termination (NT).

Layer-3 switch *See: multilayer switch.*

layered architecture Industry standard way of creating applications to work on a network. Layered architecture allows the application developer to make changes in only one layer instead of the whole program.

LCP Link Control Protocol: The protocol designed to establish, configure, and test data link connections for use by PPP. *See also: PPP.*

leaky bucket An analogy for the basic cell rate algorithm (GCRA) used in ATM networks for checking the conformance of cell flows from a user or network. The

bucket's "hole" is understood to be the prolonged rate at which cells can be accommodated, and the "depth" is the tolerance for cell bursts over a certain time period.

learning bridge A bridge that transparently builds a dynamic database of MAC addresses and the interfaces associated with each address. Transparent bridges help to reduce traffic congestion on the network.

LE ARP LAN Emulation Address Resolution Protocol: The protocol providing the ATM address that corresponds to a MAC address.

leased lines Permanent connections between two points leased from the telephone companies.

LEC LAN Emulation Client: Software providing the emulation of the link layer interface that allows the operation and communication of all higher-level protocols and applications to continue. The LEC client runs in all ATM devices, which include hosts, servers, bridges, and routers. The LANE client is responsible for address resolution, data transfer, address caching, interfacing to the emulated LAN, and driver support for higher-level services. *See also: ELAN and LES.*

LECS LAN Emulation Configuration Server: An important part of emulated LAN services, providing the configuration data that is furnished upon request from the LES. These services include address registration for Integrated Local Management Interface (ILMI) support, configuration support for the LES addresses and their corresponding emulated LAN identifiers, and an interface to the emulated LAN. *See also: LES and ELAN.*

LES LAN Emulation Server: The central LANE component that provides the initial configuration data for each connecting LEC. The LES typically is located on either an ATM-integrated router or a switch. Responsibilities of the LES include configuration and support for the LEC, address registration for the LEC, database storage and response concerning ATM addresses, and interfacing to the emulated LAN. *See also: ELAN, LEC, and LECS.*

link-state routing algorithm A routing algorithm that allows each router to broadcast or multicast information regarding the cost of reaching all its neighbors to every node in the internetwork. Link-state algorithms provide a consistent view of the network and are therefore not vulnerable to routing loops. However, this is achieved at the cost of somewhat greater difficulty in computation and more widespread traffic (compared with distance-vector routing algorithms). *See also: distance-vector routing algorithm.*

LLAP LocalTalk Link Access Protocol: In a LocalTalk environment, the data link–level protocol that manages node-to-node delivery of data. This protocol provides node addressing and management of bus access, and it also controls data sending and receiving to assure packet length and integrity.

LLC Logical Link Control: Defined by the IEEE, the higher of two Data-Link layer sublayers. LLC is responsible for error detection (but not correction), flow control, framing, and software-sublayer addressing. The predominant LLC protocol, IEEE 802.2, defines both connectionless and connection-oriented operations. *See also: Data-Link layer and MAC.*

LMI Local Management Interface: An enhancement to the original Frame Relay specification. Among the features it provides are a keepalive mechanism, a multicast mechanism, global addressing, and a status mechanism.

LNNI LAN Emulation Network-to-Network Interface: In the Phase 2 LANE specification, an interface that supports communication between the server components within one ELAN.

local explorer packet In a Token Ring SRB network, a packet generated by an end system to find a host linked to the local ring. If no local host can be found, the end system will produce one of two solutions: a spanning explorer packet or an all-routes explorer packet.

local loop Connection from a demarcation point to the closest switching office.

LocalTalk Utilizing CSMA/CD, in addition to supporting data transmission at speeds of 230.4Kbps, LocalTalk is Apple Computer's proprietary baseband protocol, operating at the Data-Link and Physical layers of the OSI reference model.

loopback tests These tests aid in physically isolating serial line and Frame Relay problems. Four different loopback tests can be performed to troubleshoot the circuit: local loopback on the local CSU/DSU, local loopback on the remote CSU/DSU, remote loopback

from the local NIU to the remote CSU/DSU, and remote loopback from the remote NIU to the local CSU/DSU.

LSA link-state advertisement: Contained inside of link-state packets (LSPs), these advertisements are usually multicast packets, containing information about neighbors and path costs, that are employed by link-state protocols. Receiving routers use LSAs to maintain their link-state databases and, ultimately, routing tables.

LT/ET The line termination and exchange termination points are called LT and ET, respectively. They handle the termination of the local loop and switching functions.

LUNI LAN Emulation User-to-Network Interface: Defining the interface between the LAN Emulation Client (LEC) and the LAN Emulation Server, LUNI is the ATM Forum's standard for LAN Emulation on ATM networks. *See also: LES and LECS.*

MAC Media Access Control: The lower sublayer in the Data-Link layer, it is responsible for hardware addressing, media access, and error detection of frames. *See also: Data-Link layer and LLC.*

MAC address A Data-Link layer hardware address that every port or device needs in order to connect to a LAN segment. These addresses are used by various devices in the network for accurate location of logical addresses. MAC addresses are defined by the IEEE standard and their length is six characters, typically using the burned-in address (BIA) of the local LAN interface. Variously called hardware address, physical address, burned-in address, or MAC-layer address.

MacIP In AppleTalk, the Network layer protocol encapsulating IP packets in Datagram Delivery Protocol (DDP) packets. MacIP also supplies substitute ARP services.

MAN Metropolitan-Area Network: Any network that encompasses a metropolitan area; that is, an area typically larger than a LAN but smaller than a WAN. *See also: LAN.*

Manchester encoding A method for digital coding in which a mid-bit-time transition is employed for clocking, and a 1 (one) is denoted by a high voltage level during the first half of the bit time. This scheme is used by Ethernet and IEEE 802.3.

maximum burst Specified in bytes or cells, the largest burst of information exceeding the insured rate that will be permitted on an ATM permanent virtual connection for a short time and will not be dropped even if it goes over the specified maximum rate. *Compare with: insured burst. See also: maximum rate.*

maximum rate The maximum permitted data throughput on a particular virtual circuit, equal to the total of insured and uninsured traffic from the traffic source. Should traffic congestion occur, uninsured information may be deleted from the path. Measured in bits or cells per second, the maximum rate represents the highest throughput of data the virtual circuit is ever able to deliver and cannot exceed the media rate. *Compare with: excess rate. See also: maximum burst.*

MBS Maximum Burst Size: In an ATM signaling message, this metric, coded as a number of cells, is used to convey the burst tolerance.

MBONE multicast backbone: The multicast backbone of the Internet, it is a virtual multicast network made up of multicast LANs, including point-to-point tunnels interconnecting them.

MCDV Maximum Cell Delay Variation: The maximum two-point CDV objective across a link or node for the identified service category in an ATM network. The MCDV is one of four link metrics that are exchanged using PTSPs to verify the available resources of an ATM network. Only one MCDV value is assigned to each traffic class.

MCLR Maximum Cell Loss Ratio: The maximum ratio of cells in an ATM network that fail to transit a link or node compared with the total number of cells that arrive at the link or node. MCDV is one of four link metrics that are exchanged using PTSPs to verify the available resources of an ATM network. The MCLR applies to cells in VBR and CBR traffic classes whose CLP bit is set to zero. *See also: CBR, CLP, and VBR.*

MCR Minimum Cell Rate: A parameter determined by the ATM Forum for traffic management of the ATM networks. MCR is specifically defined for ABR transmissions and specifies the minimum value for the allowed cell rate (ACR). *See also: ACR and PCR.*

MCTD Maximum Cell Transfer Delay: In an ATM network, the total of the maximum cell delay variation and the fixed delay across the link or node. MCTD is one of four link metrics that are exchanged using PNNI topology state packets to verify the available resources of an ATM network. There is one MCTD value assigned to each traffic class. *See also: MCDV.*

metrics These measurements are associated with each route that is present in the route table. Metrics are calculated by the routing protocol to define a cost of getting to the destination address. Some algorithms use hop count (the number of routers between it and the destination address), whereas others use a vector of values.

MIB Management Information Base: Used with SNMP management software to gather information from remote devices. The management station can poll the remote device for information, or the MIB running on the remote station can be programmed to send information on a regular basis.

MIP Multichannel Interface Processor: The resident interface processor on Cisco 7000 series routers, providing up to two channelized T1 or E1 connections by serial cables connected to a CSU. The two controllers are capable of providing 24 T1 or 30 E1 channel groups, with each group being introduced to the system as a serial interface that can be configured individually.

mips millions of instructions per second: A measure of processor speed.

MLP Multilink PPP: A technique used to split, recombine, and sequence datagrams across numerous logical data links.

MMP Multichassis Multilink PPP: A protocol that supplies MLP support across multiple routers and access servers. MMP enables several routers and access servers to work as a single large dial-up pool with one network address and ISDN access number. MMP successfully supports packet fragmenting and reassembly when the user connection is split between two physical access devices.

modem modulator-demodulator: A device that converts digital signals to analog and vice-versa so that digital information can be transmitted over analog communication facilities, such as voice-grade telephone lines. This is achieved by converting digital signals at the source to analog for transmission and reconverting the analog signals back into digital form at the destination. *See also: modulation* and *demodulation.*

modem eliminator A mechanism that makes possible a connection between two DTE devices without modems by simulating the commands and physical signaling required.

modulation The process of modifying some characteristic of an electrical signal, such as amplitude (AM) or frequency (FM), in order to represent digital or analog information. *See also: AM.*

MOSPF Multicast OSPF: An extension of the OSPF unicast protocol that enables IP multicast routing within the domain. *See also: OSPF.*

MPOA Multiprotocol over ATM: An effort by the ATM Forum to standardize how existing and future Network-layer protocols such as IP, Ipv6, AppleTalk, and IPX run over an ATM network with directly attached hosts, routers, and multilayer LAN switches.

MTU maximum transmission unit: The largest packet size, measured in bytes, that an interface can handle.

multicast Broadly, any communication between a single sender and multiple receivers. Unlike broadcast messages, which are sent to all addresses on a network, multicast messages are sent to a defined subset of the network addresses; this subset has a group multicast address, which is specified in the packet's destination address field. *See also: broadcast, directed broadcast.*

multicast address A single address that points to more than one device on the network by specifying a special non-existent MAC address specified in that particular multicast protocol. Identical to group address. *See also: multicast.*

multicast send VCC A two-directional point-to-point virtual control connection (VCC) arranged by an LEC to a BUS, it is one of the three types of informational link specified by phase 1 LANE. *See also: control distribute VCC* and *control direct VCC.*

multilayer switch A highly specialized, high-speed, hardware-based type of LAN router, the device filters and forwards packets based on their Layer 2 MAC addresses and Layer 3 network addresses. It's possible that even Layer 4 can be read. Sometimes called a Layer 3 switch. *See also: LAN switch.*

multimeters Hardware used measure voltage, resistance, and current. They work with electrical-based cabling and can be used to test for physical connectivity.

multiplexing The process of converting several logical signals into a single physical signal for transmission across one physical channel. *Contrast with: demultiplexing.*

NAK negative acknowledgment: A response sent from a receiver, telling the sender that the information was not received or contained errors. *Compare with: acknowledgment.*

NAT Network Address Translation: An algorithm instrumental in minimizing the requirement for globally unique IP addresses, permitting an organization whose addresses are not all globally unique to connect to the Internet, regardless, by translating those addresses into globally routable address space.

NBP Name Binding Protocol: In AppleTalk, the transport-level protocol that interprets a socket client's name, entered as a character string, into the corresponding DDP address. NBP gives AppleTalk protocols the capacity to discern user-defined zones and names of mechanisms by showing and keeping translation tables that map names to their corresponding socket addresses.

neighboring routers Two routers in OSPF that have interfaces to a common network. On networks with multi-access, these neighboring routers are dynamically discovered using the Hello protocol of OSPF.

NetBEUI NetBIOS Extended User Interface: An improved version of the NetBIOS protocol used in a number of network operating systems including LAN Manager, Windows NT, LAN Server, and Windows for Workgroups, implementing the OSI LLC2 protocol. NetBEUI formalizes the transport frame not standardized in NetBIOS and adds more functions. *See also: OSI.*

NetBIOS Network Basic Input/Output System: The API employed by applications residing on an IBM LAN to ask for services, such as session termination or information transfer, from lower-level network processes.

netflow switching Collects detailed data for use with circuit accounting and application-utilization information. Because of all the additional data that Netflow collects (and may export), expect an increase in router overhead—possibly as much as a five-percent increase in CPU utilization.

NetView A mainframe network product from IBM, used for monitoring SNA (Systems Network Architecture) networks. It runs as a VTAM (Virtual Telecommunications Access Method) application.

NetWare A widely used NOS created by Novell, providing a number of distributed network services and remote file access.

network address Used with the logical network addresses to identify the network segment in an internetwork. Logical addresses are hierarchical in nature and have at least two parts: network and host. An example of a hierarchical address is 172.16.10.5, where 172.16 is the network and 10.5 is the host address.

network analyzer Also known as protocol analyzers. A device that collects and analyzes data on a connected broadcast domain. The information provided is a packet decode of data transiting the network. This data is used to troubleshoot network problems.

Network layer In the OSI reference model, it is Layer 3—the layer in which routing is implemented, enabling connections and path selection between two end systems. *See also: Application layer, Data-Link layer, Physical layer, Presentation layer, Session layer, and Transport layer.*

Network Monitor This software-based tool simply monitors the network. It can do this in several ways, including the Simple Network Management Protocol (SNMP) and the Internet Control Message Protocol (ICMP).

NFS Network File System: One of the protocols in Sun Microsystems' widely used file system protocol suite, allowing remote file access across a network.

The name is loosely used to refer to the entire Sun protocol suite, which also includes RPC, XDR (External Data Representation), and other protocols.

NHRP Next Hop Resolution Protocol: In a non-broadcast multi-access (NBMA) network, the protocol employed by routers in order to dynamically locate MAC addresses of various hosts and routers. It enables systems to communicate directly without requiring an intermediate hop, thus facilitating increased performance in ATM, Frame Relay, X.25, and SMDS systems.

NHS Next Hop Server: Defined by the NHRP protocol, this server maintains the next-hop resolution cache tables, listing IP-to-ATM address maps of related nodes and nodes that can be reached through routers served by the NHS.

NIC network interface card: An electronic circuit board placed in a computer. The NIC provides network communication to a LAN.

NLSP NetWare Link Services Protocol: Novell's link-state routing protocol, based on the IS-IS model.

NMP Network Management Processor: A Catalyst 5000 switch processor module used to control and monitor the switch.

NMS Network Management Systems: A software/hardware package that is used to monitor availability, network performance, security, services, and policies.

node address Used to identify a specific device in an internetwork. Can be a hardware address, which is burned into the network interface card or a logical network address, which an administrator or server assigns to the node.

nondesignated port The Spanning-Tree Protocol tells a port on a Layer-2 switch to stop transmitting and creating a network loop. Only designated ports can send frames.

non-stub area In OSPF, a resource-consuming area carrying a default route, intra-area routes, interarea routes, static routes, and external routes. Non-stub areas are the only areas that can have virtual links configured across them and exclusively contain an anonymous system boundary router (ASBR). *Compare with: stub area. See also: ASBR and OSPF.*

NRZ Nonreturn to Zero: One of several encoding schemes for transmitting digital data. NRZ signals sustain constant levels of voltage with no signal shifting (no return to zero-voltage level) during a bit interval. If there is a series of bits with the same value (1 or 0), there will be no state change. The signal is not self-clocking. *See also: NRZI.*

NRZI Nonreturn to Zero Inverted: One of several encoding schemes for transmitting digital data. A transition in voltage level (either from high to low or vice-versa) at the beginning of a bit interval is interpreted as a value of 1; the absence of a transition is interpreted as a 0. Thus, the voltage assigned to each value is continually inverted. NRZI signals are not self-clocking. *See also: NRZ.*

NT1 network termination 1: Is an ISDN designation to devices that understand ISDN standards.

NT2 network termination 2: Is an ISDN designation to devices that do not understand ISDN standards. To use an NT2, you must use a terminal adapter (TA).

NVRAM Non-Volatile RAM: Random-access memory that keeps its contents intact while power is turned off.

observing results Using the exact same methods and commands that were used to obtain information in order to define the problem and see whether the changes implemented were effective.

OC Optical Carrier: A series of physical protocols, designated as OC-1, OC-2, OC-3, and so on, for SONET optical signal transmissions. OC signal levels place STS frames on a multimode fiber optic line at various speeds, of which 51.84Mbps is the lowest (OC-1). Each subsequent protocol runs at a speed divisible by 51.84. *See also: SONET.*

octet Base-8 numbering system used to identify a section of a dotted decimal IP address. Also referred to as a byte.

ones density Also known as pulse density, this is a method of signal clocking. The CSU/DSU retrieves the clocking information from data that passes through it. For this scheme to work, the data needs to be encoded to contain at least one binary 1 for each eight bits transmitted. *See also: CSU and DSU.*

optimum switching Switching method that replaced fast switching on higher-end Cisco routers.

Switching is done by comparing incoming packets against the optimum switching cache.

OSI Open System Interconnection: International standardization program designed by ISO and ITU-T for the development of data networking standards that make multivendor equipment interoperability a reality.

OSI reference model Open System Interconnection reference model: A conceptual model defined by the International Organization for Standardization (ISO), describing how any combination of devices can be connected for the purpose of communication. The OSI model divides the task into seven functional layers, forming a hierarchy with the applications at the top and the physical medium at the bottom, and it defines the functions each layer must provide. *See also: Application layer, Data-Link layer, Network layer, Physical layer, Presentation layer, Session layer,* and *Transport layer.*

OSPF Open Shortest Path First: A link-state, hierarchical IGP routing algorithm derived from an earlier version of the IS-IS protocol, whose features include multipath routing, load balancing, and least-cost routing. OSPF is the suggested successor to RIP in the Internet environment. *See also: Enhanced IGRP, IGP,* and *IP.*

OUI Organizationally Unique Identifier: Is assigned by the IEEE to an organization that makes network interface cards. The organization then puts this OUI on each and every card they manufacture. The OUI is 3 bytes (24 bits) long. The manufacturer then adds a 3-byte identifier to uniquely identify the host on an internetwork. The total length of the address is 48 bits (6 bytes) and is called a hardware address or MAC address.

out-of-band management Management "outside" of the network's physical channels. For example, using a console connection not directly interfaced through the local LAN or WAN or a dial-in modem. *Compare with: in-band management.*

out-of-band signaling Within a network, any transmission that uses physical channels or frequencies separate from those ordinarily used for data transfer. For example, the initial configuration of a Cisco Catalyst switch requires an out-of-band connection via a console port.

output queue   This queue resides on the RP and is used to hold the packet until the packet can be copied to the buffers on the SP/SSP. From there, it is forwarded to the specified interface processor.

outside-in troubleshooting   Troubleshooting method that consists of choosing the opposite end of the connection and working back toward you or the user that reported the problem.

overrun   Phenomenon that occurs when the receiver receives packets faster than it can transfer them to the hardware buffer.

packet   In data communications, the basic logical unit of information transferred. A packet consists of a certain number of data bytes, wrapped or encapsulated in headers and/or trailers that contain information about where the packet came from, where it's going, and so on. The various protocols involved in sending a transmission add their own layers of header information, which the corresponding protocols in receiving devices then interpret.

packet switch   A physical device that makes it possible for a communication channel to share several connections. Its functions include finding the most efficient transmission path for packets.

packet switching   A networking technology based on the transmission of data in packets. Dividing a continuous stream of data into small units—packets—enables data from multiple devices on a network to share the same communication channel simultaneously but also requires the use of precise routing information.

PAP   Password Authentication Protocol: In Point-to-Point Protocol (PPP) networks, a method of validating connection requests. The requesting (remote) device must send an authentication request, containing a password and ID, to the local router when attempting to connect. Unlike the more secure CHAP (Challenge Handshake Authentication Protocol), PAP sends the password unencrypted and does not attempt to verify whether the user is authorized to access the requested resource; it merely identifies the remote end. *See also: CHAP.*

parity checking   A method of error-checking in data transmissions. An extra bit (the parity bit) is

added to each character or data word so that the sum of the bits will be either an odd number (in odd parity) or an even number (even parity).

partial mesh   A type of network topology in which some network nodes form a full mesh (where every node has either a physical or a virtual circuit linking it to every other network node), but others are attached to only one or two nodes in the network. A typical use of partial-mesh topology is in peripheral networks linked to a fully meshed backbone. *See also: full mesh.*

path determination   Condition where the router is aware of a route that leads to the desired destination address.

PCR   Peak Cell Rate: As defined by the ATM Forum, the parameter specifying, in cells per second, the maximum rate at which a source may transmit.

PDN   Public Data Network: Generally for a fee, a PDN offers the public access to computer communication network operated by private concerns or government agencies. Small organizations can take advantage of PDNs, to aid them in creating WANs without their having to invest in long-distance equipment and circuitry.

PGP   Pretty Good Privacy: A popular public-key/private-key encryption application offering protected transfer of files and messages.

Physical layer   The lowest layer—Layer 1—in the OSI reference model, it is responsible for converting data packets from the Data-Link layer (Layer 2) into electrical signals. Physical-layer protocols and standards define, for example, the type of cable and connectors to be used, including their pin assignments and the encoding scheme for signaling 0 and 1 values. *See also: Application layer, Data-Link layer, Network layer, Presentation layer, Session layer,* and *Transport layer.*

physical test equipment   A genre of testing equipment including multi-meters, cable testers, TDRs, and OTDRs. Used for testing cable integrity and end-to-end physical connectivity.

ping   packet Internet groper: A Unix-based Internet diagnostic tool, consisting of a message sent to test the accessibility of a particular device on the IP network.

The acronym (from which the "full name" was formed) reflects the underlying metaphor of submarine sonar. Just as the sonar operator sends out a signal and waits to hear it echo ("ping") back from a submerged object, the network user can ping another node on the network and wait to see if it responds.

pleisochronous   Nearly synchronous, except that clocking comes from an outside source instead of being embedded within the signal as in synchronous transmissions.

PLP   Packet Level Protocol: Occasionally called X.25 Level 3 or X.25 Protocol, a Network-layer protocol that is part of the X.25 stack.

PNNI   Private Network-Network Interface: An ATM Forum specification for offering topology data used for the calculation of paths through the network, among switches and groups of switches. It is based on well-known link-state routing procedures and allows for automatic configuration in networks whose addressing scheme is determined by the topology.

point-to-multipoint connection   In ATM, a communication path going only one way, connecting a single system at the starting point, called the "root node," to systems at multiple points of destination, called "leaves." *See also: point-to-point connection.*

point-to-point connection   In ATM, a channel of communication that can be directed either one way or two ways between two ATM end systems. *See also: point-to-multipoint connection.*

poison reverse updates   These update messages are transmitted by a router back to the originator (thus ignoring the split-horizon rule) after route poisoning has occurred. Typically used with DV routing protocols in order to overcome large routing loops and offer explicit information when a subnet or network is not accessible (instead of merely suggesting that the network is unreachable by not including it in updates). *See also: route poisoning.*

polling   The procedure of orderly inquiry, used by a primary network mechanism, to determine if secondary devices have data to transmit. A message is sent to each secondary, granting the secondary the right to transmit.

POP   (1) Point Of Presence: The physical location where an interexchange carrier has placed equipment to interconnect with a local exchange carrier. (2) Post Office Protocol (currently at version 3): A protocol used by client e-mail applications for recovery of mail from a mail server.

port security   Used with Layer-2 switches to provide some security. Not typically used in production because it is difficult to manage. Allows only certain frames to traverse administrator-assigned segments.

PDU   Protocol Data Unit: Is the name of the processes at each layer of the OSI model. PDUs at the Transport layer are called segments; PDUs at the Network layer are called packets or datagrams; and PDUs at the Data-Link layer are called frames. The Physical layer uses bits.

PPP   Point-to-Point Protocol: The protocol most commonly used for dial-up Internet access, superseding the earlier SLIP. Its features include address notification, authentication via CHAP or PAP, support for multiple protocols, and link monitoring. PPP has two layers: the Link Control Protocol (LCP) establishes, configures, and tests a link; and then any of various Network Control Programs (NCPs) transport traffic for a specific protocol suite, such as IPX. *See also: CHAP, PAP, and SLIP.*

Presentation layer   Layer 6 of the OSI reference model, it defines how data is formatted, presented, encoded, and converted for use by software at the Application layer. *See also: Application layer, Data-Link layer, Network layer, Physical layer, Session layer, and Transport layer.*

PRI   Primary Rate Interface: A type of ISDN connection between a PBX and a long-distance carrier, which is made up of a single 64Kbps D channel in addition to 23 (T1) or 30 (E1) B channels. *See also: ISDN.*

primary nodes   SDLC protocol nodes that are responsible for the control of secondary stations and for link management, such as link setup and teardown.

priority 1   Production network down situation. This is the highest priority when opening a ticket with the Cisco TAC.

priority 2 Production network performance seriously degraded. This is the second highest priority when opening a ticket with the Cisco TAC.

priority 3 Network performance degraded. This is the third highest priority when opening a ticket with the Cisco TAC.

priority 4 Information needed on Cisco products. This priority is associated with cases that do not require immediate troubleshooting support.

priority queueing A routing function in which frames temporarily placed in an interface output queue are assigned priorities based on traits such as packet size or type of interface.

problem definition The step in the troubleshooting model where details are used to define the most likely cause of a problem. This should be a concise yet accurate description of the problem at hand.kh 1

process switching As a packet arrives on a router to be forwarded, it's copied to the router's process buffer, and the router performs a lookup on the Layer 3 address. Using the route table, an exit interface is associated with the destination address. The processor forwards the packet with the added new information to the exit interface, while the router initializes the fast-switching cache. Subsequent packets bound for the same destination address follow the same path as the first packet.

PROM programmable read-only memory: ROM that is programmable only once, using special equipment. *Compare with: EPROM.*

propagation delay The time it takes data to traverse a network from its source to its destination.

protocol In networking, the specification of a set of rules for a particular type of communication. The term is also used to refer to the software that implements a protocol.

protocol analyzer Also known as network analyzers. A device that collects and analyzes data on a connected broadcast domain. The information provided is a packet decode of data transiting the network. This also includes a protocol analysis of the traffic that is captured from the network. This data is used to troubleshoot network problems.

protocol parameters The options that are passed with connection setup within many connection-oriented protocols. An example would be the TCP window size.

protocol stack A collection of related protocols.

PSE Packet Switch Exchange: The X.25 term for a switch.

PSN packet-switched network: Any network that uses packet-switching technology. Also known as packet-switched data network (PSDN). *See also: packet switching.*

PSTN Public Switched Telephone Network: Colloquially referred to as "plain old telephone service" (POTS). A term that describes the assortment of telephone networks and services available globally.

PVC permanent virtual circuit: In a Frame-Relay network, a logical connection, defined in software, that is maintained permanently. *Compare with: SVC. See also: virtual circuit.*

PVP permanent virtual path: A virtual path made up of PVCs. *See also: PVC.*

PVP tunneling permanent virtual path tunneling: A technique that links two private ATM networks across a public network using a virtual path; wherein the public network transparently trunks the complete collection of virtual channels in the virtual path between the two private networks.

q.921 The q.921 is the Layer 2 protocol used by ISDN, on the D channel. It establishes a connection between the central office switch and the router.

q.931 The third layer of ISDN is addressed in the ITU-T I.451 specification, which is also called *q.931.* This protocol includes several message commands, which are viewed with the debug isdn q931 command. These commands include call setup, connect, release, cancel, status, disconnect, and user information.

QoS Quality of Service: A set of metrics used to measure the quality of transmission and service availability of any given transmission system.

queue   Broadly, any list of elements arranged in an orderly fashion and ready for processing, such as a line of people waiting to enter a movie theater. In routing, it refers to a backlog of information packets waiting in line to be transmitted over a router interface.

R reference point   Used with ISDN networks to identify the connection between an NT1 and an S/T device. The S/T device converts the 4-wire network to the two-wire ISDN standard network.

RAM   random access memory: Used by all computers to store information. Cisco routers use RAM to store packet buffers and routing tables, along with the hardware addresses cache.

RARP   Reverse Address Resolution Protocol: The protocol within the TCP/IP stack that maps MAC addresses to IP addresses. *See also: ARP.*

rate queue   A value, assigned to one or more virtual circuits, that specifies the speed at which an individual virtual circuit will transmit data to the remote end. Every rate queue identifies a segment of the total bandwidth available on an ATM link. The sum of all rate queues should not exceed the total available bandwidth.

RCP   Remote Copy Protocol: A protocol for copying files to or from a file system that resides on a remote server on a network, using TCP to guarantee reliable data delivery.

redistribution   Command used in Cisco routers to inject the paths found from one type of routing protocol into another type of routing protocol. For example, networks found by RIP can be inserted into an IGRP network.

redundancy   In internetworking, the duplication of connections, devices, or services that can be used as a backup in the event that the primary connections, devices, or services fail.

RJ connector   registered jack connector: Is used with twisted-pair wiring to connect the copper wire to network interface cards, switches, and hubs.

reload   An event or command that causes Cisco routers to reboot.

RIF   Routing Information Field: In source-route bridging, a header field that defines the path direction of the frame or token. If the Route Information Indicator (RII) bit is not set, the RIF is read from source to destination (left to right). If the RII bit is set, the RIF is read from the destination back to the source, so the RIF is read right to left. It is defined as part of the Token Ring frame header for source-routed frames, which contains path information.

ring   Two or more stations connected in a logical circular topology. In this topology, which is the basis for Token Ring, FDDI, and CDDI, information is transferred from station to station in sequence.

ring topology   A network logical topology comprising a series of repeaters that form one closed loop by connecting unidirectional transmission links. Individual stations on the network are connected to the network at a repeater. Physically, ring topologies are generally organized in a closed-loop star. *Compare with: bus topology* and *star topology.*

RIP   Routing Information Protocol: The most commonly used interior gateway protocol in the Internet. RIP employs hop count as a routing metric. *See also: Enhanced IGRP, IGP, OSPF,* and *hop count.*

RMON   Remote Monitoring: RMON is another method for obtaining environmental and statistical information from devices. Much of the RMON technology implementation is based on the deployment of RMON probes that gather the information from the circuit (physical media) because the router or switch may not support all levels of RMON information.

ROM   read-only memory: Chip used in computers to help boot the device. Cisco routers use a ROM chip to load the bootstrap, which runs a power-on self test, and then find and load the IOS in flash memory by default.

root bridge   Used with the Spanning-Tree Protocol to stop network loops from occurring. The root bridge is elected by having the lowest bridge ID. The bridge ID is determined by the priority (32,768 by default on all bridges and switches) and the main hardware address of the device. The root bridge determines which of the neighboring Layer-2 devices' interfaces become the designated and nondesignated ports.

routed protocol Routed protocols (such as IP and IPX) are used to transmit user data through an internetwork. By contrast, routing protocols (such as RIP, IGRP, and OSPF) are used to update routing tables between routers.

route maps Small scripts used to manipulate routing that can contain multiple instances and multiple conditions for each instance. Route maps are somewhat like access lists if you specify that the packet must match an access list. In addition to having the capability of permitting or denying the packet, you can define what is done before the packet is forwarded. Route maps can be used to set metrics for route updates, set a command to its default value, and so on.

route poisoning Used by various DV routing protocols in order to overcome large routing loops and offer explicit information about when a subnet or network is not accessible (instead of merely suggesting that the network is unreachable by not including it in updates). Typically, this is accomplished by setting the hop count to one more than maximum. *See also: poison reverse updates.*

route summarization In various routing protocols, such as OSPF, EIGRP, and IS-IS, the consolidation of publicized subnetwork addresses so that a single summary route is advertised to other areas by an area border router.

router A Network-layer mechanism, either software or hardware, using one or more metrics to decide on the best path to use for transmission of network traffic. Sending packets between networks by routers is based on the information provided on Network layers. Historically, this device has sometimes been called a gateway.

routing The process of forwarding logically addressed packets from their local subnetwork toward their ultimate destination. In large networks, the numerous intermediary destinations a packet might travel before reaching its destination can make routing very complex.

routing domain Any collection of end systems and intermediate systems that operate under an identical set of administrative rules. Every routing domain contains one or several areas, all individually given a certain area address.

routing metric Any value that is used by routing algorithms to determine whether one route is superior to another. Metrics include such information as bandwidth, delay, hop count, path cost, load, MTU, reliability, and communication cost. Only the best possible routes are stored in the routing table, while all other information may be stored in link-state or topological databases. *See also: cost.*

routing protocol Any protocol that defines algorithms to be used for updating routing tables between routers. Examples include IGRP, RIP, and OSPF.

routing table A table kept in a router or other internetworking mechanism that maintains a record of only the best possible routes to certain network destinations and the metrics associated with those routes.

RP Route Processor: Also known as a supervisory processor, a module on Cisco 7000 series routers that holds the CPU, system software, and most of the memory components used in the router.

RSP Route/Switch Processor: A processor module combining the functions of RP and SP used in Cisco 7500 series routers. *See also: RP and SP.*

RTMP Routing Table Maintenance Protocol. This protocol is responsible for AppleTalk routing tables and their information. This is AppleTalk's proprietary method of maintaining route tables on AppleTalk-enabled machines.

RTS Request To Send: An EIA/TIA-232 control signal requesting permission to transmit data on a communication line.

S reference point ISDN reference point that works with a T reference point to convert a 4-wire ISDN network to the 2-wire ISDN network needed to communicate with the ISDN switches at the network provider.

SAGE Synergy Advanced Gate-Array Engine: This chip is used for non-Ethernet applications—including FDDI, ATM LANE, Token Ring, and the Network Management Processor on the Supervisor engine.

SAINT Synergy Advanced Interface and Network Termination: The SAINT handles Ethernet switching on the Catalyst 5000 platform, and it also handles ISL encapsulation.

SAMBA ASIC ASIC located on line modules and the Supervisor modules. On the line cards, this chip is responsible for broadcast suppression, based on thresholds established by the administrator. This ASIC also maintains statistics on packets.

sampling rate The rate at which samples of a specific waveform amplitude are collected within a specified period of time.

SAP (1) Service Access Point: A field specified by IEEE 802.2 that is part of an address specification. (2) Service Advertising Protocol: The Novell NetWare protocol that supplies a way to inform network clients of resources and services availability on network, using routers and servers. *See also: IPX.*

SCR Sustainable Cell Rate: An ATM Forum parameter used for traffic management, it is the long-term average cell rate for VBR connections that can be transmitted.

SDLC Synchronous Data Link Control: A protocol used in SNA Data-Link layer communications. SDLC is a bit-oriented, full-duplex serial protocol that is the basis for several similar protocols, including HDLC and LAPB. *See also: HDLC and LAPB.*

secondary nodes Nodes as designated by the SDLC protocol. Secondary nodes talk only to the primary node when they fulfill two requirements. First, they have permission from the primary node; second, they have data to transmit.

seed device A root device specified in a NMS configuration. From this device the network discovery begins. The seed device's neighbors are discovered and the continuing process spreads out starting at the seed device.

seed router In an AppleTalk network, the router that is equipped with the network number or cable range in its port descriptor. The seed router specifies the network number or cable range for other routers in that network section and answers to configuration requests from nonseed routers on its connected AppleTalk network, permitting those routers to affirm or modify their configurations accordingly. Every AppleTalk network needs at least one seed router physically connected to each network segment.

sequenced data transfer This is the process of assigning sequence numbers to every PDU that leaves a host so that it may be resequenced once all of the PDUs in a transmission reach the destination host.

server Hardware and software that provide network services to clients.

set-based Set-based routers and switches use the set command to configure devices. Cisco is moving away from set-based commands and is using the Command-Line Interface (CLI) on all new devices.

Session layer Layer 5 of the OSI reference model, responsible for creating, managing, and terminating sessions between applications and overseeing data exchange between Presentation layer entities. *See also: Application layer, Data-Link layer, Network layer, Physical layer, Presentation layer, and Transport layer.*

setup mode Mode that a router will enter if no configuration is found in nonvolatile RAM when the router boots. Allows the administrator to configure a router step-by-step. Not as robust or flexible as the Command-Line Interface.

SF super frame: A super frame (also called a D4 frame) consists of 12 frames with 192 bits each, and the 193rd bit providing other functions including error checking. SF is frequently used on T1 circuits. A newer version of the technology is Extended Super Frame (ESF), which uses 24 frames. *See also: ESF.*

signaling packet An informational packet created by an ATM-connected mechanism that wants to establish connection with another such mechanism. The packet contains the QoS parameters needed for connection and the ATM NSAP address of the endpoint. The endpoint responds with a message of acceptance if it is able to support the desired QoS, and the connection is established. *See also: QoS.*

silicon switching A type of high-speed switching used in Cisco 7000 series routers, based on the use of a separate processor (the Silicon Switch Processor, or SSP). *See also: SSE.*

simplex The mode at which data or a digital signal is transmitted. Simplex is a way of transmitting in only one direction. Half duplex transmits in two directions but only one direction at a time. Full duplex transmits both directions simultaneously.

sliding window The method of flow control used by TCP, as well as several Data-Link layer protocols. This method places a buffer between the receiving application and the network data flow. The "window" available for accepting data is the size of the buffer minus the amount of data already there. This window increases in size as the application reads data from it and decreases as new data is sent. The receiver sends the transmitter announcements of the current window size, and it may stop accepting data until the window increases above a certain threshold.

SLIP Serial Line Internet Protocol: An industry standard serial encapsulation for point-to-point connections that supports only a single routed protocol, TCP/IP. SLIP is the predecessor to PPP. *See also: PPP.*

SMDS Switched Multimegabit Data Service: A packet-switched, datagram-based WAN networking technology offered by telephone companies that provides high speed.

SMTP Simple Mail Transfer Protocol: A protocol used on the Internet to provide electronic mail services.

SNA System Network Architecture: A complex, feature-rich, network architecture similar to the OSI reference model but with several variations; created by IBM in the 1970s and essentially composed of seven layers.

SNAP Subnetwork Access Protocol: SNAP is a frame used in Ethernet, Token Ring, and FDDI LANs. Data transfer, connection management, and QoS selection are three primary functions executed by the SNAP frame.

SNMP Simple Network Management Protocol: This protocol polls SNMP agents or devices for statistical and environmental data. This data can include device temperature, name, performance statistics and much more. SNMP works with MIB objects that are present on the SNMP agent. This information is queried then sent to the SNMP server.

socket (1) A software structure that operates within a network device as a destination point for communications. (2) In AppleTalk networks, an entity at a specific location within a node; AppleTalk sockets are conceptually similar to TCP/IP ports.

software test equipment *See: Network Monitor.*

SONET Synchronous Optical Network: The ANSI standard for synchronous transmission on fiber-optic media, developed at Bell Labs. It specifies a base signal rate of 51.84Mbps and a set of multiples of that rate, known as Optical Carrier levels, up to 2.5Gbps.

SP Switch Processor: Also known as a ciscoBus controller, it is a Cisco 7000 series processor module acting as governing agent for all CxBus activities.

span A full-duplex digital transmission line connecting two facilities.

SPAN Switched Port Analyzer: A feature of the Catalyst 5000 switch, offering freedom to manipulate within a switched Ethernet environment by extending the monitoring ability of the existing network analyzers into the environment. At one switched segment, the SPAN mirrors traffic onto a predetermined SPAN port, while a network analyzer connected to the SPAN port is able to monitor traffic from any other Catalyst switched port.

spanning explorer packet Sometimes called limited-route or single-route explorer packet, it pursues a statically configured spanning tree when searching for paths in a source-route bridging network. *See also: all-routes explorer packet, explorer packet,* and *local explorer packet.*

spanning tree A subset of a network topology, within which no loops exist. When bridges are interconnected into a loop, the bridge, or switch, cannot identify a frame that has been forwarded previously, so there is no mechanism for removing a frame as it passes the interface numerous times. Without a method of removing these frames, the bridges continuously forward them—consuming bandwidth and adding overhead to the network. Spanning trees prune the network to provide only one path for any packet. *See also: Spanning-Tree Protocol* and *spanning tree algorithm.*

spanning-tree algorithm (STA) An algorithm that creates a spanning tree using the Spanning-Tree Protocol (STP). *See also: spanning tree and Spanning-Tree Protocol.*

Spanning-Tree Protocol (STP) The bridge protocol (IEEE 802.1d) that enables a learning bridge to dynamically avoid loops in the network topology by creating a spanning tree using the spanning-tree algorithm. Spanning-tree frames called bridge protocol data units (BPDUs) are sent and received by all switches in the network at regular intervals. The switches participating in the spanning tree don't forward the frames; instead, they're processed to determine the spanning-tree topology itself. Cisco Catalyst series switches use STP 802.1d to perform this function. *See also: BPDU, learning bridge, MAC address, spanning tree,* and *spanning-tree algorithm.*

SPF Shortest Path First algorithm: A routing algorithm used to decide on the shortest-path spanning tree. Sometimes called Dijkstra's algorithm and frequently used in link-state routing algorithms. *See also: link-state routing algorithm.*

SPID Service Profile Identifier: A number assigned by service providers or local telephone companies and assigned by administrators to a BRI port. SPIDs are used to determine subscription services of a device connected via ISDN. ISDN devices use SPID when accessing the telephone company switch that initializes the link to a service provider.

split horizon Useful for preventing routing loops, a type of distance-vector routing rule where information about routes is prevented from leaving the router interface through which that information was received.

spoofing (1) In dial-on-demand routing (DDR), where a circuit-switched link is taken down to save toll charges when there is no traffic to be sent, spoofing is a scheme used by routers that causes a host to treat an interface as if it were functioning and supporting a session. The router pretends to send "spoof" replies to keepalive messages from the host in an effort to convince the host that the session is up and running. *See also: DDR.* (2) The illegal act of sending a packet labeled with a false address, in order to deceive network security mechanisms such as filters and access lists.

spooler A management application that processes requests submitted to it for execution in a sequential fashion from a queue. A good example is a print spooler.

SPX Sequenced Packet Exchange: A Novell NetWare transport protocol that augments the datagram service provided by Network layer (Layer 3) protocols, it was derived from the Switch-to-Switch Protocol of the XNS protocol suite.

SQE Signal Quality Error: In an Ethernet network, a message sent from a transceiver to an attached machine that the collision-detection circuitry is working.

SRB Source-Route Bridging: Created by IBM, the bridging method used in Token-Ring networks. The source determines the entire route to a destination before sending the data and includes that information in route information fields (RIF) within each packet. *Contrast with: transparent bridging.*

SRT Source-route Transparent bridging.: A bridging scheme developed by IBM, merging source-route and transparent bridging. SRT takes advantage of both technologies in one device, fulfilling the needs of all end nodes. Translation between bridging protocols is not necessary. *Compare with: SR/TLB.*

SR/TLB source-route translational bridging: A bridging method that allows source-route stations to communicate with transparent bridge stations aided by an intermediate bridge that translates between the two bridge protocols. Used for bridging between Token Ring and Ethernet. *Compare with: SRT.*

SSAP Source Service Access Point: The SAP of the network node identified in the Source field of the packet. *See also: DSAP and SAP.*

SSE Silicon Switching Engine: The software component of Cisco's silicon switching technology, hardcoded into the Silicon Switch Processor (SSP). Silicon switching is available only on the Cisco 7000 with an SSP. Silicon-switched packets are compared to the silicon-switching cache on the SSE. The SSP is a dedicated switch processor that offloads the switching process from the route processor, providing a fast-switching solution, but packets must still traverse the backplane of the router to get to the SSP and then back to the exit interface.

standard IP access list   IP access list that uses only the source IP addresses to filter a network.

standard IPX access list   IPX access list that uses only the source and destination IPX address to filter a network.

star topology   A LAN physical topology with endpoints on the network converging at a common central switch (known as a hub) using point-to-point links. A logical ring topology can be configured as a physical star topology using a unidirectional closed-loop star rather than point-to-point links. That is, connections within the hub are arranged in an internal ring. *See also: bus topology* and *ring topology.*

startup range   If an AppleTalk node does not have a number saved from the last time it was booted, then the node selects from the range of values from 65280 to 65534.

state transitions   Digital signaling scheme that reads the "state" of the digital signal in the middle of the bit cell. If it is five volts, the cell is read as a one. If the state of the digital signal is zero volts, the bit cell is read as a zero.

static route   A route whose information is purposefully entered into the routing table and takes priority over those chosen by dynamic routing protocols.

static VLANs   Static VLANs are manually configured port-by-port. This is the method typically used in production networks.

statistical multiplexing   Multiplexing in general is a technique that allows data from multiple logical channels to be sent across a single physical channel. Statistical multiplexing dynamically assigns bandwidth only to input channels that are active, optimizing available bandwidth so that more devices can be connected than with other multiplexing techniques. Also known as statistical time-division multiplexing or stat mux.

STM-1   Synchronous Transport Module Level 1. In the European SDH standard, one of many formats identifying the frame structure for the 155.52Mbps lines that are used to carry ATM cells.

store-and-forward packet switching   A technique in which the switch first copies each packet into its buffer and performs a cyclical redundancy check (CRC). If the packet is error-free, the switch then looks up the destination address in its filter table, determines the appropriate exit port, and sends the packet.

STP   (1) Shielded Twisted Pair: A two-pair wiring scheme, used in many network implementations, that has a layer of shielded insulation to reduce EMI. (2) Spanning-Tree Protocol.

stub area   An OSPF area carrying a default route, intra-area routes, and interarea routes, but no external routes. Configuration of virtual links cannot be achieved across a stub area, and stub areas are not allowed to contain an ASBR. *See also: non-stub area, ASBR,* and *OSPF.*

stub network   A network having only one connection to a router.

STUN   Serial Tunnel: A technology used to connect an HDLC link to an SDLC link over a serial link.

subarea   A portion of an SNA network made up of a subarea node and its attached links and peripheral nodes.

subarea node   An SNA communications host or controller that handles entire network addresses.

subchannel   A frequency-based subdivision that creates a separate broadband communications channel.

subinterface   One of many virtual interfaces available on a single physical interface.

subnet   *See: subnetwork.*

subnet address   The portion of an IP address that is specifically identified by the subnet mask as the subnetwork. *See also: IP address, subnetwork,* and *subnet mask.*

subnet mask   Also simply known as mask, a 32-bit address mask used in IP to identify the bits of an IP address that are used for the subnet address. Using a mask, the router does not need to examine all 32 bits, only those selected by the mask. *See also: address mask* and *IP address.*

subnetwork (1) Any network that is part of a larger IP network and is identified by a subnet address. A network administrator segments a network into subnetworks in order to provide a hierarchical, multilevel routing structure, and at the same time protect the subnetwork from the addressing complexity of networks that are attached. Also known as a subnet. *See also: IP address, subnet mask,* and *subnet address. (2)* In OSI networks, the term specifically refers to a collection of ESs and ISs controlled by only one administrative domain, using a solitary network connection protocol.

SVC switched virtual circuit: A dynamically established virtual circuit, created on demand and dissolved as soon as transmission is over and the circuit is no longer needed. In ATM terminology, it is referred to as a switched virtual connection. *See also: PVC.*

switch (1) In networking, a device responsible for multiple functions such as filtering, flooding, and sending frames. It works using the destination address of individual frames. Switches operate at the Data-Link layer of the OSI model. (2) Broadly, any electronic/mechanical device allowing connections to be established as needed and terminated if no longer necessary.

switch fabric Term used to identify a Layer-2 switched internetwork with many switches.

switched LAN Any LAN implemented using LAN switches. *See also: LAN switch.*

switching path The logical path that a packet follows when it's switched through a router. Some examples are process swithcing, fast switching, optimum, CEF, dCEF, and distributed switching.

synchronous transmission Signals transmitted digitally with precision clocking. These signals have identical frequencies and contain individual characters encapsulated in control bits (called start/stop bits) that designate the beginning and ending of each character. *See also: asynchronous transmission* and *isochronous transmission.*

T reference point Used with an S reference point to change a 4-wire ISDN network to a 2-wire ISDN network.

T1 Digital WAN that uses 24 DS0s at 64K each to create a bandwidth of 1.536Mbps, minus clocking overhead, providing 1.544Mbps of usable bandwidth.

T3 Digital WAN that can provide bandwidth of 44.763Mbps.

tag switching Based on the concept of label swapping, where packets or cells are designated to defined-length labels that control the manner in which data is to be sent, tag switching is a high-performance technology used for forwarding packets. It incorporates Data-Link layer (Layer 2) switching and Network layer (Layer 3) routing and supplies scalable, high-speed switching in the network core.

tagged traffic ATM cells with their cell loss priority (CLP) bit set to 1. Also referred to as discard-eligible (DE) traffic. Tagged traffic can be eliminated in order to ensure trouble-free delivery of higher priority traffic, if the network is congested. *See also: CLP.*

TCP Transmission Control Protocol: A connection-oriented protocol that is defined at the Transport layer of the OSI reference model. Provides reliable delivery of data.

TCP/IP Transmission Control Protocol/Internet Protocol. The suite of protocols underlying the Internet. TCP and IP are the most widely known protocols in that suite. *See also: IP* and *TCP.*

TDM time division multiplexing: A technique for assigning bandwidth on a single wire, based on preassigned time slots, to data from several channels. Bandwidth is allotted to each channel regardless of a station's ability to send data. *See also: ATDM, FDM,* and *multiplexing.*

TDR Time domain reflectors: these are complex cable testers. They are used to locate physical problems in a cable. They can detect where an open circuit, short circuit, crimped wire, or other abnormality is located in a cable.

TE terminal equipment: Any peripheral device that is ISDN-compatible and attached to a network, such as a telephone or computer. TE1s are devices that are ISDN-ready and understand ISDN signaling techniques. TE2s are devices that are not ISDN-ready and do not understand ISDN signaling techniques. A terminal adapter must be used with a TE2.

TE1 A device with a four-wire, twisted-pair digital interface is referred to as terminal equipment type 1. Most modern ISDN devices are of this type.

TE2 Devices known as terminal equipment type 2 do not understand ISDN signaling techniques, and a terminal adapter must be used to convert the signaling.

telco A common abbreviation for the telephone company.

Telnet The standard terminal emulation protocol within the TCP/IP protocol stack. Method of remote terminal connection, enabling users to log in on remote networks and use those resources as if they were locally connected. Telnet is defined in RFC 854.

terminal adapter A hardware interface between a computer without a native ISDN interface and an ISDN line. In effect, a device to connect a standard async interface to a non-native ISDN device, emulating a modem.

terminal emulation The use of software, installed on a PC or LAN server, that allows the PC to function as if it were a "dumb" terminal directly attached to a particular type of mainframe.

TFTP Conceptually a stripped-down version of FTP, it's the protocol of choice if you know exactly what you want and where it's to be found. TFTP doesn't provide the abundance of functions that FTP does. In particular, it has no directory-browsing abilities; it can do nothing but send and receive files.

Thicknet Also called 10Base5. Bus network that uses a thick cable and runs Ethernet up to 500 meters.

Thinnet Also called 10Base2. Bus network that uses a thin coax cable and runs Ethernet media access up to 185 meters.

token A frame containing only control information. Possessing this control information gives a network device permission to transmit data onto the network. *See also: token passing.*

token bus LAN architecture that is the basis for the IEEE 802.4 LAN specification and employs token passing access over a bus topology. *See also: IEEE.*

token passing A method used by network devices to access the physical medium in a systematic way

based on possession of a small frame called a token. *See also: token.*

Token Ring IBM's token-passing LAN technology. It runs at 4Mbps or 16Mbps over a ring topology. Defined formally by IEEE 802.5. *See also: ring topology* and *token passing.*

toll network WAN network that uses the Public Switched Telephone Network (PSTN) to send packets.

trace IP command used to trace the path a packet takes through an internetwork.

transparent bridging The bridging scheme used in Ethernet and IEEE 802.3 networks, it passes frames along one hop at a time, using bridging information stored in tables that associate end-node MAC addresses within bridge ports. This type of bridging is considered transparent because the source node does not know it has been bridged, because the destination frames are sent directly to the end node. *Contrast with: SRB.*

Transport layer Layer 4 of the OSI reference model, used for reliable communication between end nodes over the network. The Transport layer provides mechanisms used for establishing, maintaining, and terminating virtual circuits, transport fault detection and recovery, and controlling the flow of information. *See also: Application layer, Data-Link layer, Network layer, Physical layer, Presentation layer,* and *Session layer.*

TRIP Token Ring Interface Processor: A high-speed interface processor used on Cisco 7000 series routers. The TRIP provides two or four ports for interconnection with IEEE 802.5 and IBM media with ports set to speeds of either 4Mbps or 16Mbps set independently of each other.

troubleshooting engine Part of the Online Technical Support menu. This tool can be used to help isolate and diagnose many networking problems, based on user input and the Cisco database.

troubleshooting model A series of steps or procedures that can be executed or followed to methodically and effectively troubleshoot and resolve network failures or outages.

trunk link   Link used between switches and from some servers to the switches. Trunk links carry information about many VLANs. Access links are used to connect host devices to a switch and carry only VLAN information that the device is a member of.

TTL   Time To Live: A field in an IP header, indicating the length of time a packet is valid.

TUD   Trunk Up-Down: A protocol used in ATM networks for the monitoring of trunks. Should a trunk miss a given number of test messages being sent by ATM switches to ensure trunk line quality, TUD declares the trunk down. When a trunk reverses direction and comes back up, TUD recognizes that the trunk is up and returns the trunk to service.

tunneling   A method of avoiding protocol restrictions by wrapping packets from one protocol in another protocol's packet and transmitting this encapsulated packet over a network that supports the wrapper protocol. *See also: encapsulation.*

U reference point   Reference point between a TE1 and an ISDN network. The U reference point understands ISDN signaling techniques and uses a 2-wire connection.

UDP   User Datagram Protocol: A connectionless Transport layer protocol in the TCP/IP protocol stack that simply allows datagrams to be exchanged without acknowledgments or delivery guarantees, requiring other protocols to handle error processing and retransmission. UDP is defined in RFC 768.

underrun   Occurs when the transmitter runs at a higher rate than the packets sent from the hardware buffer.

unnumbered frames   HDLC frames used for control-management purposes, such as link start-up and shutdown or mode specification.

UTP   unshielded twisted-pair: Copper wiring used in small-to-large networks to connect host devices to hubs and switches. Also used to connect switch to switch or hub to hub.

VBR   Variable Bit Rate: A QoS class, as defined by the ATM Forum, for use in ATM networks that is subdivided into real time (RT) class and non-real time (NRT) class. RT is employed when connections have a fixed-time relationship between samples. Conversely, NRT is employed when connections do not have a fixed-time relationship between samples, but still need an assured QoS.

VCC   Virtual Channel Connection: A logical circuit that is created by VCLs. VCCs carry data between two endpoints in an ATM network. Sometimes called a virtual circuit connection.

VIP   (1) Versatile Interface Processor: An interface card for Cisco 7000 and 7500 series routers, providing multilayer switching and running the Cisco IOS software. The most recent version of VIP is VIP2. (2) Virtual IP: A function making it possible for logically separated switched IP workgroups to run Virtual Networking Services across the switch ports of a Catalyst 5000.

virtual circuit   Abbreviated VC, a logical circuit devised to assure reliable communication between two devices on a network. Defined by a virtual path connection (VPC)/virtual path identifier (VCI) pair, a virtual circuit can be permanent (PVC) or switched (SVC). Virtual circuits are used in Frame Relay and X.25. Known as virtual channel in ATM. *See also: PVC and SVC.*

virtual ring   In an SRB network, a logical connection between physical rings, either local or remote.

VLAN   Virtual LAN: A group of devices on one or more logically segmented LANs (configured by use of management software), enabling devices to communicate as if attached to the same physical medium, when they are actually located on numerous different LAN segments. VLANs are based on logical instead of physical connections and thus are tremendously flexible.

VLSM   variable-length subnet mask: Helps optimize available address space and specify a different subnet mask for the same network number on various subnets. Also commonly referred to as "subnetting a subnet."

VTP VLAN Trunk Protocol: Used to update switches in a switch fabric about VLANs configured on a VTP server. VTP devices can be a VTP server, client, or transparent device. Servers update clients. Transparent devices are only local devices and do not share information with VTP clients. VTPs send VLAN information down trunked links only.

WAN wide area network: Is a designation used to connect LANs together across a DCE (data communications equipment) network. Typically, a WAN is a leased line or dial-up connection across a PSTN network. Examples of WAN protocols include Frame Relay, PPP, ISDN, and HDLC.

wildcard Used with access-list, supernetting, and OSPF configurations. Wildcards are designations used to identify a range of subnets.

window size The amount of data that a station can transmit before needing an acknowledgment from the destination system. The acknowledgment confirms that all the data was received without error, or that errors existed and part of the data will need to be retransmitted.

windowing Flow-control method used with TCP at the Transport layer of the OSI model.

WinSock Windows Socket Interface: A software interface that makes it possible for an assortment of applications to use and share an Internet connection.

The WinSock software consists of a Dynamic Link Library (DLL) with supporting programs such as a dialer program that initiates the connection.

workgroup switching A switching method that supplies high-speed (100Mbps) transparent bridging between Ethernet networks as well as high-speed translational bridging between Ethernet and CDDI or FDDI.

X.25 An ITU-T packet-relay standard that defines communication between DTE and DCE network devices. X.25 uses a reliable Data-Link layer protocol called LAPB. X.25 also uses PLP at the Network layer. X.25 has mostly been replaced by Frame Relay.

ZIP Zone Information Protocol: A Session-layer protocol used by AppleTalk to map network numbers to zone names. NBP uses ZIP in the determination of networks containing nodes that belong to a zone. *See also: ZIP storm and zone.*

ZIP storm A broadcast storm occurring when a router running AppleTalk reproduces or transmits a route for which there is no corresponding zone name at the time of execution. The route is then forwarded by other routers downstream, thus causing a ZIP storm. *See also: broadcast storm and ZIP.*

zone A logical grouping of network devices in AppleTalk. *See also: ZIP.*

Index

Note to the Reader: Throughout this index **boldfaced** page numbers indicate primary discussions of a topic. *Italicized* page numbers indicate illustrations.

B

C

G

H

O

S

U

X

X.25 protocol, **99**, *99*, 734
    frame structure in, **100**, *100*
    troubleshooting, **399**
        debug commands in, **401**
        problems and action plans summary, **402**
        show interface serial command in, **399–400**
        symptoms and problems summary, **401–402**

Z

ZIP (Zone Information Protocol), 523, 734
ZIP packets, 543
ZIP storms
    in AppleTalk, **544–545**
    defined, 734
Zone Information Protocol (ZIP), 523, 734
zones in AppleTalk protocols, 78, 734
    names and networks for, 528–529
    updates, 543

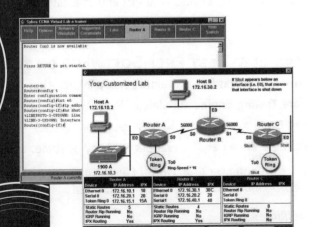

GET CISCO CERTIFIED WITH THE EXPERTS!

CCNA™: Cisco®
Certified Network Associate®
Study Guide, 2nd Edition
0-7821-2647-2

CCDP™: Cisco® Internetwork
Design Study Guide
0-7821-2639-1

CCDA™: Cisco® Certified Design
Associate Study Guide
0-7821-2534-4

CISCO STUDY GUIDES FROM SYBEX

- ◆ Written by renowned author Todd Lammle and his team of expert authors
- ◆ Up-to-date, comprehensive coverage of the revised Cisco exam
- ◆ Hands-on and written labs, plus hundreds of sample question
- ◆ Assessment tests and practice exams
- ◆ Two technical edits ensure accuracy and relevance of informati
- ◆ 700-800 pp; 7.5x9; Hardcover; $49.99

CUTTING-EDGE TEST PREP SOFTWARE ON THE CD

Electronic Flashcards help reinforce key information

Custom Testing Engine simulates Cisco's test format

Bonus Exam assesses knowledge retention

Searchable Ebook allows readers to study anytime, anywhere

Bonus CD Content: *CCNA Virtual Lab e-trainer* demo, *Dictionar of Networking* Ebook, and software utilities!

Also available:

CCNP™: Support Study Guide • 0-7821-2713-4 • Summer 2000
CCNP: Remote Access Study Guide • 0-7821-2710-x • Summer 2000
CCNP: Switching Study Guide • 0-7821-2711-8 • Fall 2000
CCNP: Routing Study Guide • 0-7821-2712-6 • Fall 2000
CCIE™: Cisco® Certified Internetwork Expert Study Guide
0-7821-2657-X Summer 2000

www.sybex.com   SYBE

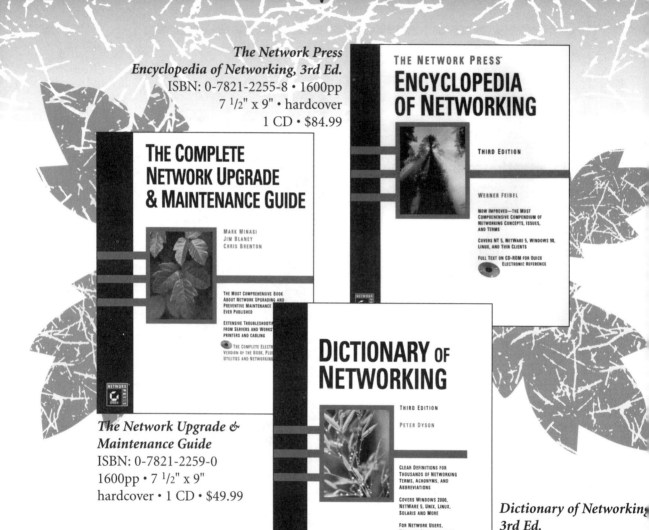

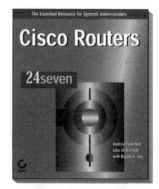

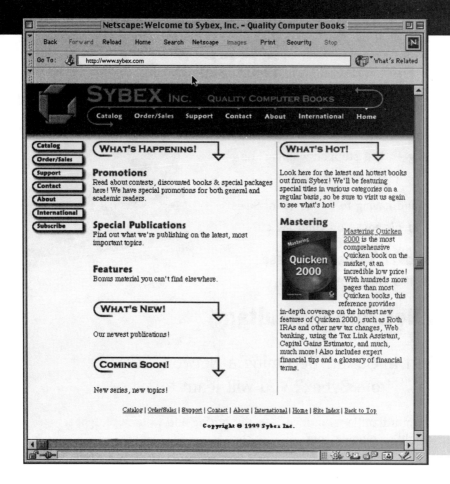

Get ready for Cisco's CCNP: Support exam with the most comprehensive and challenging sample tests anywhere!

The Sybex EdgeTests feature:

- Chapter-by-chapter exam coverage of all the review questions from the book

- Random tests that simulate the exam format from Cisco

- A bonus exam available only on the CD

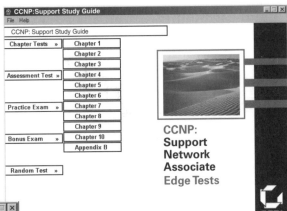

CCNP:
Support
Network
Associate
Edge Tests

©2000 Sybex, Inc. Produced by Matt Sheltz and the Edge Group

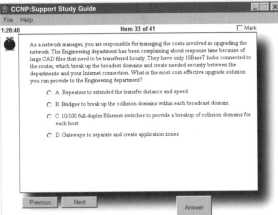

Use the Electronic Flashcards to jog your memory and prep last-minute for the exam!

- Reinforce your understanding of key CCNP: Support exam concepts with 150 hardcore flashcard-style questions.

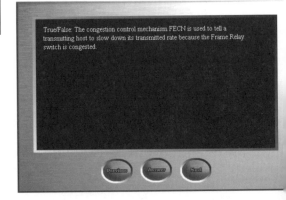

Electronic Flashcards now available for your Palm device as well!

- Download the Flashcards to your Palm device and go on the road. Now you can study for the CCNP exam anywhere, any time.